The Economic Value of Education:
Studies in the Economics of Education

The International Library of Critical Writings in Economics

Series Editor: Mark Blaug

Professor Emeritus, University of London
Consultant Professor, University of Buckingham
Visiting Professor, University of Exeter

This series is an essential reference source for students, researchers and lecturers in economics. It presents by theme an authoritative selection of the most important articles across the entire spectrum of economics. Each volume has been prepared by a leading specialist who has written an authoritative introduction to the literature included.

A full list of published and future titles in this series is printed at the end of this volume.

The Economic Value of Education:
Studies in the Economics of Education

Edited by

Mark Blaug

Professor Emeritus
University of London

An Elgar Reference Collection

Published by
Edward Elgar Publishing Limited
Gower House
Croft Road
Aldershot
Hants GU11 3HR
England

Edward Elgar Publishing Limited
Distributed in the United States by
Ashgate Publishing Company
Old Post Road
Brookfield
Vermont 05036
USA

CIP catalogue records for this book are available from
the British Library and the US Library of Congress.

ISBN 1 85278 542 X

Printed in Great Britain at the University Press, Cambridge

Contents

Acknowledgements

The editor and publishers wish to thank the following who have kindly given permission for the use of copyright material.

American Economic Association for articles: H. Gintis (1971), 'Education, Technology and the Characteristics of Worker Productivity', *American Economic Review*, **61** (2), May, 266–79; E. Lazear (1977), 'Academic Achievement and Job Performance: Note', *American Economic Review*, **67** (2), March, 252–4; E. Lazear (1981), 'Agency, Earnings Profiles, Productivity, and Hours Restrictions', *American Economic Review*, **71** (4), September, 606–20; M. Boissiere, J.B. Knight and R.H. Sabot (1985), 'Earnings, Schooling, Ability, and Cognitive Skills', *American Economic Review*, **75** (5), December, 1016–30; M. Blaug (1976), 'The Empirical Status of Human Capital Theory: A Slightly Jaundiced Survey', *Journal of Economic Literature*, **14** (3), September, 827–55, E.A. Hanushek (1986), 'The Economics of Schooling: Production and Efficiency in Public Schools', *Journal of Economic Literature*, **XXIV** (3), 1141–77.

American Educational Research Association for article and excerpt: J. Mincer (1989), 'Human Capital and the Labor Market: A Review of Current Research', *Educational Researcher*, **18** (5), May, 27–34; M.J. Bowman (1974), 'Learning and Earning in the Postschool Years', *Review of Research in Education, 2*, F.N. Kerlinger and J.B. Carroll (eds), 202–44.

Basil Blackwell Ltd for article: E.G. West (1964), 'The Role of Education in Nineteenth-Century Doctrines of Political Economy', *British Journal of Educational Studies*, **12** (2), May, 161–72.

British Review of Economic Issues for article: A.K. Whitehead (1981), 'Screening and Education: A Theoretical and Empirical Survey', *British Review of Economic Issues*, **3** (8), Spring, 44–62.

Cambridge University Press for article: R.A. Easterlin (1981), 'Why Isn't the Whole World Developed?', *Journal of Economic History*, **XLI** (1), March, 1–19.

Carfax Publishing Company for article: G. Psacharopoulos (1981), 'Returns to Education: An Updated International Comparison', *Comparative Education*, **17** (3), 321–41.

Cato Journal for article: J.R. Lott, Jr (1987), 'Why is Education Publicly Provided?: A Critical Survey', *Cato Journal*, **7** (2), Fall, 475–501.

Generalitat Valenciana, Spain for excerpt: D. Mitch (1990), 'Education and Economic Growth: Another Axiom of Indispensability? From Human Capital to Human Capabilities', *Education and Economic Development Since the Industrial Revolution*, G. Tortella (ed.), 29–45.

Kluwer Academic Publishers for articles: G. Williams and A. Gordon (1981), 'Perceived Earnings Functions and Ex Ante Rates of Return to Post Compulsory Education in England', *Higher Education*, **10**, 199–227; A. Mingat and J.-P. Tan (1986), 'Financing Public Higher Education in Developing Countries', *Higher Education*, **15**, 283–97.

Oxford University Press for article: G.S. Fields (1975), 'Higher Education and Income Distribution in a Less Developed Country', *Oxford Economic Papers*, NS, **27** (2), July, 245–59.

Pergamon Press plc for articles: K.-H. Lee and G. Psacharopoulos (1979), 'International Comparisons of Educational and Economic Indicators, Revisited', *World Development*, **7** (11/12), November/December, 995–1004; C. Colclough (1982), 'The Impact of Primary Schooling on Economic Development: A Review of the Evidence', *World Development*, **10** (3), March, 167–85.

Review of Economic Studies Ltd for article: G. Psacharopoulos and R. Layard (1979), 'Human Capital and Earnings: British Evidence and a Critique', *Review of Economic Studies*, **XLVI** (3), 485–503.

Sage Publications, Inc. for article: H.M. Levin (1974), 'Measuring Efficiency in Educational Production', *Public Finance Quarterly*, **2** (1), January, 3–24.

University of Chicago Press for article: M. Carnoy (1977), 'Education and Economic Development: The First Generation', *Economic Development and Cultural Change*, Supplement, **25**, 428–48.

University of Wisconsin Press for articles: M. Carnoy and D. Marenbach (1975), 'The Return to Schooling in the United States, 1939–69', *Journal of Human Resources*, **X** (3), Summer, 312–31; G. Psacharopoulos (1985), 'Returns to Education: A Further International Update and Implications', *Journal of Human Resources*, **XX** (4), Fall, 583–604.

Every effort has been made to trace all the copyright holders but if any have been inadvertently overlooked the publishers will be pleased to make the necessary arrangement at the first opportunity.

In addition the publishers wish to thank the library of The London School of Economics and Political Science and The Alfred Marshall Library, Cambridge University, for their assistance in obtaining these articles.

Introduction

It was almost thirty years ago that three American scholars, Jacob Mincer, Gary Becker and Theodore Schultz, revived the age-old idea that education is a process whereby individuals accumulate 'human capital'. They do so on principles identical to the ways in which they accumulate physical capital, that is they sacrifice time and/or money in the present for the sake of a larger return in the future. This notion of education as investment rather than consumption was previously regarded as little more than a striking metaphor. What Mincer, Becker and Schultz now demonstrated was that education is indeed a way in which individuals invest in themselves in the simple sense of incurring financial costs today in order to enhance potential earnings tomorrow. Of course, no individual student can be certain that more schooling will raise his or her lifetime earnings but he or she can rely on the following remarkable fact of life: between any two groups of individuals of the same age and sex, the one with more formal education will have higher average earnings than the one with less, even if the two groups are employed in the same occupational category in the same industry. The universality of this positive association between education and earnings is one of the most striking findings that one can make about labour markets in all countries, whether capitalist or communist, and it is this generalization that forms the bedrock of the doctrine of education as human capital.

The fact that education and personal earnings are highly correlated does not by itself *prove* that the cause of higher earnings is extra schooling but, nevertheless, the simplest explanation for the observation that employers offer higher pay to more highly educated workers is that education imparts vocationally useful skills that are in scarce supply. This simple explanation has been questioned in more recent years – an issue to which we return below – but suffice it to say that the first generation of human capital theorists more or less took it for granted that schooling makes people more productive.

The assertion that education renders people more productive is liable to be misunderstood. It seems to imply that labour makes a definitive contribution to output which can be distinguished without much difficulty from the contribution of other factors of production, such as management and capital equipment. But of course all factors of production participate jointly in the productive process and the separate contributions of each to final output can only be assessed at the margin by holding constant the quantity and quality of all the other factors. It was precisely the practical difficulty of this hypothetical operation that led to the categorical identification in the 1960s and early 1970s of higher productivity with higher earnings.

If only we knew the precise characteristics of existing techniques of production and could safely assume that all labour markets are perfectly competitive, we could, indeed, infer the productivity of labour from the earnings of labour. This is the gist of Edward Denison's work on growth accounting, which did so much to promote the human investment revolution in economic thought in the 1960s and 1970s. By assuming a particular type of 'production function' as representative of American industry, Denison was able to trace American economic growth to its sources in individual factors of production culminating in the famous assertion that the expansion of education in the United States during the period 1930–60 accounted for as much as 23 per cent of the annual growth rate, more in fact than any other single source of growth except the increase in the number of workers themselves. The spurious precision of Denison's statement is due to a number of critical assumptions, including the one shared by all human capital theorists, namely that the bulk of the earnings differentials associated with differences in educational attainments are attributable to the effect of education alone.

If education is a type of investment, it ought to be possible to measure its rate of return in a manner analogous to the measurement of rates of return to physical capital. And indeed the calculation of both private and social rates of return to educational investment for all stages of post-compulsory education in both developed and developing countries was part and parcel of the human investment revolution that swept through economic thought after 1960. The first seven papers in this collection will introduce the reader to both the technical difficulties of such calculation and to their implications for educational policy.

We begin with a survey article of the entire field which I published fifteen years ago (Chapter 1). It is remarkable that any survey published fifteen years ago should have dated as little as this one – but that conclusion may of course be part and parcel of my 'jaundiced' assessment of this field of enquiry. It seemed to me then and now that human capital theory was degenerating in the sense of endlessly repeating itself without shedding new light on issues of education and training and in fact without facing up to the increasing empirical anomalies that had been generated by the development of the human capital research programme in the 1970s. Now this is clearly a controversial view and one of the functions of this anthology is to acquaint readers with the nature of this controversy. I have therefore included a 1989 paper by Jacob Mincer (Chapter 8), which demonstrates the continued faith in the vitality of the human capital research programme by one of its original and some would say *the* original, founders. In addition, there are two papers by another true believer, George Psacharopoulos, Mr Rate-of-Return himself, which update his earlier compendium volume *Returns to Education: An International Comparison* (1973).

The essay by Carnoy and Marenbach (Chapter 2) shows how even radical economists have been unable to resist the conceptual appeal of rate-of-return calculations, particularly when they are available on a time-series basis. The case for calculating the *private* rate of return on educational investment by way of casting light on the private demand for education has always been stronger than the case for calculating *social* rates of return to serve as decision criteria for public investment policies in education. The paper by Williams and Gordon (Chapter 3) – a classic of its kind – is designed to show that students do indeed perform something resembling a crude calculation of an expected private rate of return on their own educational investment; in short, private rate-of-return calculations cannot be faulted on grounds of lack of realism.

In this first part of the collection, the paper by Mary Jean Bowman (Chapter 6), is neither for nor against human capital theory: rather it explores the connections between the economics of education and the sociology of education and continues the age-old debate on nature versus nurture in respect of the impact of schooling on subsequent earnings from employment. The problem of separating the effects of native endowment, pre-school learning, home and peer influences during the period of school attendance from the formal schooling process itself raises horrible statistical difficulties, which are touched upon in my paper (Chapter 1) but which are more thoroughly explored in this essay by Bowman. The paper by Psacharopoulos and Layard on Mincer's 'schooling model' (Chapter 7) touches on many of the same issues as discussed by Bowman.

We turn now to six papers on the profoundly subversive 'screening hypothesis', which argues that education is indeed associated with increased earnings, and perhaps even with increased productivity, but that it does not cause them. Employers seek high-ability workers but are unable, prior to employing them, to distinguish them from those with low ability. Faced with little information about the personal attributes of job applicants, employers are forced to make use of 'screens' to separate high-ability from low-ability workers, such as evidence of previous work experience, personal references and, of course, educational qualifications. Moreover, knowing that employers are making use of screens for hiring purposes, job applicants have an incentive to make themselves distinct by some sort of 'signal'. According to the screening hypothesis, post-compulsory schooling fills exactly this function. By and large, it is high-ability individuals who perform well in the educational system. Educational achievement is therefore correlated with higher productivity but does not cause it, and hence is no more than a screening or signalling device to prospective employers which it is in the individual's, although not necessarily in society's, interest to acquire. Just as an individual's good health may be due more to a naturally strong constitution than to medical care, so according to this view is productivity the result of natural ability rather than post-primary education.

The screening hypothesis, in its strongest version, argues that secondary and higher education do nothing to increase individual productivity and hence have no economic value at all. There are at least three counter-arguments to this contention. The educational system may select students according to their natural aptitudes but in the process it may also improve these aptitudes; thus, the educational system is perhaps more than just a screening device. Second, the screening hypothesis may explain the association between education and earnings at the point of hiring workers but, surely once at work, employers will soon be able to sort out the more from the less able without resort to paper qualifications? In other words, employers no doubt use education as a screen but experience is constantly testing the accuracy of that screen. Third, an information problem is inherent in the process of hiring workers and if we somehow eliminated the use of educational qualifications as proxies of ability, it is not at all clear that we could replace it by some superior social selection mechanism, as for example a National Aptitude Testing Centre; in short, the educational system may well be the most efficient social screen we can devise.

Whether there is any validity in the screening hypothesis, and to what extent, is an empirical matter. Despite a good deal of research the verdict is undecided and given the almost intractable problem of testing the hypothesis, is likely to remain so. 'Credentialism' or the use of educational qualifications as proxy measures of ability, so contaminates all features of labour markets around the world that it would require a long-sustained taboo on the issue of diplomas and certificates to discover the precise impact of education on individual productivity. The screening hypothesis at its strongest cannot be true but it is not yet possible to show whether it is partially or wholly false. Nevertheless, to the extent that it is a half-truth or even a quarter-truth, it throws decisive doubt on the use of social rates of return as criteria for public investment in education.

As I remarked earlier, the first generation of human capital theorists took it more or less for granted that schooling makes people more productive, meaning that an increase in cognitive knowledge enhances a worker's productivity. But the screening hypothesis plants the suspicion that the economic value of education may reside much more in the realm of effective behaviour than in the realm of cognitive knowledge. This profound idea, which ramifies in all directions, was first forcibly brought home to me by the 1971 essay by Herbert Gintis (Chapter 9). What I made of it is evidenced by my 1985 lecture (Chapter 10), which, for better or for worse, must serve as a kind of appendix to my 1976 'jaundiced survey' of human capital theory (Chapter 1).

There follow two papers by Edward Lazear (Chapters 11 and 12), which suggest that screening induces employers to steepen the age-earnings profiles of employees, such that they earn less than their spot marginal product in the early years of employment only to earn more than their future marginal product in the later phases of their careers; in consequence, they *never* earn their marginal products at any moment in time. If so, the very foundations of human capital theory, which are grounded in observed age-earnings-by-education profiles, are brought into question. Finally, there is a survey paper by Whitehead (Chapter 13) which will bring the reader up to date on the inconclusive attempts over the last ten years to test the validity of the screening hypothesis. As they say in the USA, the jury is still out on that one!

The famous battle between academic and vocational education is one of the issues that might be resolved by a conclusive vindication of the screening hypothesis – a point I argue in my paper (Chapter 10). As a matter of fact, vocational education has long been on the defensive against the repeated demonstration on the part of economists of education that employers simply do not value vocationally qualified job applicants. But new and better evidence may be altering that viewpoint as exemplified by a much-discussed paper by John Bishop (Chapter 14).

As a glance at the *Economics of Education Review* will show, there is more to the economics of education than human capital theory: hence the twelve papers of Parts III, IV and V of this collection. We begin with a superb survey article by Eric Hanushek (Chapter 15) of the literature on educational production functions. Much has been learned about the effects of classroom instruction and yet all the evidence that figures in the literature on educational production functions has been highly ambiguous. The problem is that schools pursue a multiplicity of objectives and yet do not necessarily maximize anything. In consequence, the variation among schools in cognitive achievement scores – the standard measure of educational output in these studies – may not have any definite meaning in terms of the effectiveness of different inputs. This is the basic argument of Henry Levin (Chapter 16) against this entire approach to the study of efficiency of schooling.

The papers of Part IV take us into new territory relating to the age-old question of the relationship between education and economic growth, particularly in the Third World. Martin Carnoy (Chapter 17) sets the stage and Boissiere, Knight and Sabot (Chapter 18) take us right back to human capital theory in the Third World setting of Africa. However, apart from rate-of-return calculations, economists have also correlated almost every conceivable measure of educational attainment with almost every possible indicator of economic performance in the effort to demonstrate that the observed association between education and economic growth around the world is causal and not just casual. Lee and Psacharopoulos (Chapters 19 and 25) review this literature and David Mitch (Chapter 20) and Richard Easterlin (Chapter 21) look at the same question from the standpoint of the industrial revolution in the eighteenth and nineteenth centuries. Winding up this set of papers is Colclough's superb review (Chapter 22) of the evidence on the recent impact of primary education in Asia, Africa and Latin America.

Turning now however briefly to the important question of the finance of education in developing countries, Mingat and Tan (Chapter 23) and Gary Fields (Chapter 24) examine the issue from the viewpoint of both efficiency and equity considerations. The final papers in Part V of the collection continue the theme of educational finance. Edward West (Chapter 26) reminds us of a time when all the financial shibboleths of today had not yet settled into dogmas, while John Lott (Chapter 27) asks again why education should everywhere have come to be publicly provided irrespective of how it was or is financed. If this paper does not make the reader think again about issues he or she thought were settled long ago, this entire set of readings has missed its mark.

Part I
Human Capital Theory

[1]

The Empirical Status of Human Capital Theory: A Slightly Jaundiced Survey

By Mark Blaug

*University of London Institute of Education
and London School of Economics*

I owe thanks to F. Bosch-Font, M. J. Bowman, R. Layard, G. Psach-aropoulos, the participants of the 1975 Conference of the International Institute of Public Finance, and several anonymous referees of this journal for helpful comments on an earlier version of this paper. However, being obdurate by nature, I have not taken account of all their comments. They are therefore in no way responsible for what follows.

THE BIRTH OF human-capital theory was announced in 1960 by Theodore Schultz. The birth itself may be said to have taken place two years later when the *Journal of Political Economy* published its October 1962 supplement volume on "Investment in Human Beings." This volume included, among several other path-breaking papers, the preliminary chapters of Gary Becker's 1964 monograph *Human Capital,* which has ever since served as the *locus classicus* of the subject.[1] Thus, the theory of human capital has been with us for more than a decade, during which time the flood of literature in the field has

never abated and seems, if anything, to be increasing lately at an increasing rate.[2] The first textbook exclusively devoted to the subject appeared in 1963 [87, Schultz, 1963].[3] After a lull in the mid-sixties, the textbook industry started in earnest: between 1970 and 1973 as many as eight authors tried their hand at the task, not to

---

[1] Earlier papers by John R. Walsh [98, 1935] and Jacob Mincer [64, 1958], and particularly the Milton Friedman–Simon Kuznets book on *Income from Independent Professional Practice* [37, 1945], provided some of the key elements of the new theory. Hints and suggestions of the theme of human-capital formation occur all through the eighteenth and nineteenth centuries but these *obiter dicta* were never tied together before Schultz and Becker; a reading of Bernard F. Kiker [52, 1968], the standard history of human-capital doctrines since Petty, leaves no doubt on that score; see also Blaug [10, 1976].

[2] A fairly comprehensive annotated bibliography by Blaug [11, 1976], published in 1966, contained 800 items; the second edition of this bibliography, published in 1970, contained 1,350 items, and the third 1976 edition contains almost 2,000 items. In an analysis of all articles in 114 major economic journals, published between 1970 and 1974, Naomi W. Perlman and Mark Perlman [73, 1976] show that articles on "human capital" rose from 1.34 to 1.75 percent of all classified articles, which they characterize as an extremely rapid rate of growth. During the same period, articles in the "economics of education (consumption side)" rose from 1.31 to 1.69 percent, an almost identical level and rate of growth to health economics. To put these figures into perspective, compare the corresponding figures for urban economics, 3.26 to 2.73, regional economics, 3.80 to 4.15, and trade unions, 2.54 to 3.73.

[3] Earlier textbooks on the economics of education by Charles S. Benson [6, 1961] and John E. Vaizey [97, 1962] paint a wider canvass and deal only parenthetically with human-capital theory.

mention the appearance of seven anthologies of classic articles on human-capital-and-all-that.[4] It may be time therefore to ask what all this adds up to. Has the theory lived up to the high expectations of its founders? Has it progressed, in the sense of grappling ever more deeply and profoundly with the problems to which it was addressed, or are there signs of stagnation and malaise?

I adopt the Popperian methodological position that all theories must be judged ultimately in terms of their falsifiable predictions, a position to which almost all modern economists subscribe—and which some even take seriously. What I hope to do in this paper is to assess what Sir Karl Popper calls the "degree of corroboration" of human-capital theory. "By the degree of corroboration of a theory," Popper explains, "I mean a concise report evaluating the state (at a certain time t) of the critical discussion of a theory, with respect to the way it solves its problems; its degree of testability; the severity of the tests it has undergone; and the way it has stood up to these tests. Corroboration (or degree of corroboration) is thus an evaluating report of past performance" [76, Popper, 1972, p. 18].

Such an "evaluating report of past performance" can never be absolute: a theory can only be judged in relation to its rivals, purporting to explain a similar range of phenomena. Even such a relative comparison is never final because we cannot accurately predict the future evolution of a theory. Moreover, it is inappropriate to appraise individual theories in isolation of the general framework in which such theories are typically embedded. What ought to be appraised are clusters of interconnected theories, or what Imre Lakatos has called "scientific research programs." In the process of testing the predictions of a particular research program, some fal-

sifications are invariably encountered, and all scientific research programs tend to be continuously reformulated to avoid refutation. Borrowing from the post-Popperian methodological writings of Lakatos, we may distinguish between the "hard core" and "the protective belt" of a scientific research program: the "hard core" consists of the set of purely metaphysical beliefs that inspire and define the research strategy of the program; it is in "the protective belt," however, that this "hard core" is combined with auxiliary assumptions to form the specific testable theories with which the research program earns its scientific reputation.[5] We may further distinguish "progressive" and "degenerating" research programs: the former consists of programs whose successive reformulations contain "excess empirical content" in the sense of predicting novel, hitherto unexpected facts; the latter, on the other hand, accommodate whatever new facts become available by endless additions of *ad hoc* "epicycles."

Armed with these methodological distinctions, we may now reformulate the aims of the paper. What is the "hard core" of a human-capital research program, whose abandonment is tantamount to abandoning the program itself? What refutations have been encountered in the "protective belt" of the program, and how have the advocates of the program responded to these refutations? Lastly, is the human-capital research program a "progressive" or a "degenerating" research program, which is virtually like asking, has the empirical content of the program increased or decreased over time?

I. *Hard Core Versus Protective Belt*

The so-called "theory" of human capital is of course a perfect example of a research program: it cannot be reduced to one, sin-

---

[4] For a complete list, see Blaug [11, 1976].

[5] For references and further discussion of Lakatos' philosophy of science in relation to economics, see Blaug [12, 1976].

gle theory, being in fact an application of standard capital theory to certain economic phenomena. The concept of human capital, or "hard core" of the human-capital research program, is the idea that people spend on themselves in diverse ways, not for the sake of present enjoyments, but for the sake of future pecuniary and nonpecuniary returns. They may purchase health care; they may voluntarily acquire additional education; they may spend time searching for a job with the highest possible rate of pay, instead of accepting the first offer that comes along; they may purchase information about job opportunities; they may migrate to take advantage of better employment opportunities; and they may choose jobs with low pay but high learning potential in preference to dead-end jobs with high pay. All these phenomena—health, education, job search, information retrieval, migration, and in-service training—may be viewed as investment rather than consumption, whether undertaken by individuals on their own behalf or undertaken by society on behalf of its members. What knits these phenomena together is not the question of who undertakes what, but rather the fact that the decision-maker, whoever he is, looks forward to the future for the justification of his present actions.

Having said this much, it takes only an additional assumption, namely, that the decision-maker is a household rather than an individual, to extend the analogy to family planning and even to the decision to marry.[6] We are not surprised to see life-cycle considerations applied to the theory of saving, but prior to what Mary Jean Bowman has aptly called "the human

[6] We will omit discussion in this paper of the recent extension of the human-capital research program by Becker and others to the "economics of the family." For a highly critical review of the population aspects of this extension, see Harvey Leibenstein [57, 1974] and the instructive reply by Michael C. Keely [51, 1975].

investment revolution in economic thought," it was not common to treat expenditures on such social services as health and education as analogous to investment in physical capital, and certainly no one dreamed in those days of finding common analytical grounds between labor economics and the economics of the social services.

There is hardly any doubt therefore of the genuine novelty of the "hard core" of the human-capital research program. Nor is there any doubt of the rich research possibilities created by a commitment to this "hard core." The "protective belt" of the human-capital research program is replete with human-capital "theories," properly so labeled, and indeed the list is so large that we can hardly hope to give an exhaustive account of them. But few human-capital theorists would, I think, quarrel with those we have selected for emphasis.

In the field of education, the principal theoretical implication of the human-capital research program is that the demand for upper secondary and higher education is responsive both to variations in the direct and indirect private costs of schooling and to variations in the earnings differentials associated with additional years of schooling. The traditional pre-1960 view among economists was that the demand for post-compulsory education was a demand for a consumption good, and as such depended on given "tastes," family incomes, and the "price" of schooling in the form of tuition costs. There was the complication that this consumption demand also involved an "ability" to consume the good in question, but most economists were satisfied to leave it to sociologists and social psychologists to show that both "tastes" and "abilities" depended in turn on the social class background of students, and particularly on the levels of education achieved by their parents. Since this pre-1960 theory of the consumption demand for education was never used to explain real-world attendance rates in high schools and colleges, it makes little difference what particular formulation of it we adopt. The point is that the notion that earnings forgone constitute an important element in the private costs of schooling and that students take a systematic, forward-looking view of earnings prospects in the labor market would have been dismissed in the pre-1960 days as implausible, on the grounds that students lack the necessary information and that the available information is known to be unreliable. The human-capital research program, on the other hand, while also taking "tastes" and "abilities" as given, emphasizes the role of present and future earnings, arguing in addition that these are much more likely to exhibit variations in the short term than the distribution of family background characteristics between successive cohorts of students.

The difference between the old and the new view is therefore fundamental and the auxiliary assumptions that convert the "hard core" of the human-capital research program into a testable theory of the demand for upper secondary and higher education are almost too obvious to require elaboration: students cannot easily finance the present costs of additional schooling out of future earnings; they are aware of the earnings they forgo while studying and hence demand more schooling when there is a rise in youth unemployment rates; current salary differentials by years of schooling provide them with fairly accurate estimates of the salary differentials that will prevail when they enter the labor market several years later; *et cetera, et cetera.* Furthermore, the theory comes in two versions: it claims modestly to predict total enrollments in post-compulsory schooling, and, more ambitiously, to predict enrollments in specific fields of study in higher education, and even enrollments in different types of institutions at the tertiary level.

As originally formulated by Schultz, Becker, and Mincer, the human-capital research program was characterized by "methodological individualism," that is, the view that all social phenomena should be traced back to their foundation in individual behavior. For Schultz, Becker, and Mincer, human-capital formation is typically conceived as being carried out by individuals acting in their own interests. This is the natural view to take in respect of job search and migration, but health care, education, information retrieval, and labor training are either wholly or in part carried out by governments in many countries. However, familiarity with private medicine and private education, and the almost total absence of government-sponsored training schemes in the American context (at least before 1968), gave support to an emphasis on the private calculus. But when health and education are largely in the public sector, as is the case in most of Europe and in most of the Third World, it is tempting to ask the question of whether the human-capital research program is also capable of providing new normative criteria for public action. In education at any rate, the human-capital research program did indeed furnish a new social investment criterion: resources are to be allocated to levels of education and to years of schooling so as to equalize the marginal, "social" rate of return on educational investment, and, going one step further, this equalized yield on educational investment should not fall below the yield on alternative private investments. However, this normative criterion was not advocated with the same degree of conviction by all adherents of the human-capital research program. Furthermore, the so-called "social" rate of return on educational investment is necessarily calculated exclusively on the basis of observable pecuniary values; the nonpecuniary returns to education, as well as the externalities associated with schooling, are invariably accommodated by qualitative judgments, and these differ from author to author [8, Blaug, 1972, pp. 202–05]. Thus, the same observed "social" rates of return to investment in education frequently produced quite different conclusions about the optimal educational strategy.

Being normative, the cry to equalize the "social" rate of return to education raises no questions of empirical testing. In the mood of positive economics, it may be interesting to ask whether governments do indeed allocate resources to the educational system so as to equalize the social yield to all levels and types of education, but few human-capital theorists would commit themselves to a definite prediction about the outcome of such a calculation.[7] In the absence of any generally accepted theory of government behavior, the advocates of the human-capital research program may be forgiven for slighting the normative implications of their doctrines.[8] Unfortunately, it seems difficult to test any positive prediction about the demand for post-compulsory schooling without taking a view of the norms that underlie government action in the field of education. The world provides few examples of countries in which the

demand for post-compulsory education is not constrained by the supply of places that governments decide to make available. In testing predictions about private demand, we therefore end up testing predictions about the supply function as well as the demand function. To give the human-capital research program a run for its money, therefore, we must go to such open-door systems of higher education as exist only in the United States, Japan, India, and the Philippines.

These comments no doubt help to explain why almost all empirical work about the demand for education has been confined to the United States. But even with respect to the United States, it is surprising how little attention has actually been devoted to an explanation of the private demand for schooling. As we shall see, almost nothing with any cutting edge was accomplished before 1970 or thereabouts, and even now the demand for education remains a curiously neglected subject in the vast empirical literature exemplifying the human-capital approach.

We turn now from formal schooling to labor training. Almost from the outset, the human-capital research program was as much preoccupied with the phenomenon of training as with that of education. Becker's fundamental distinction between "general" and "specific" training produced the startling prediction that workers themselves pay for "general" training via reduced earnings during the training period, thus contradicting the older Marshallian view that a competitive market mechanism fails to provide employers with adequate incentives to offer optimum levels of in-service training. Predictions about the demand for training fitted neatly with predictions about the demand for education because formal schooling is an almost perfect example of "general" training; indeed, Becker's model has the virtue of correctly predicting that employers will rarely pay directly for the schooling acquired by their em-

---

[7] Similarly, it is interesting to ask what impact education has on economic growth, irrespective of the motives that lie behind the provision of formal schooling. The attempt to answer this question was at the center of the burgeoning literature on growth accounting in the early 1960's, but recent doubts about the concept of aggregate production functions have virtually dried up all further interest in the question: *e.g.*, see Richard R. Nelson [69, 1973] but also Edward F. Denison [26, 1974]. In retrospect, it seems doubtful in any case whether growth accounting of the Denison-type has much to do with the crucial issues in human-capital theory [8, Blaug, 1972, pp. 99–100].

[8] Besides, what needs to be explained about formal schooling is not so much why governments subsidize it as they do, but why they insist on owning so much of it in every country around the world. On this crucial question we get no help, and cannot expect to get help, from the human-capital research program, even when it is supplemented by the theory of externalities and public goods of modern welfare economics. The answer, surely, lies elsewhere, perhaps in voting behavior and the internal logic of public bureaucracies?

ployees, a generally observed real-world phenomenon unexplained by any alternative research program (except perhaps that of Marx).

The distinction between two kinds of post-school learning soon led to fruitful discussion about the extent to which training is or is not fully vested in individual workers, but it largely failed to inspire new empirical work on labor training in industry [7, Blaug, 1972, pp. 191–99]. In part, this was due to the inherent difficulty of distinguishing costless on-the-job learning from both informal on-the-job and formal off-the-job-but-in-plant training. (I say nothing about formal off-the-job-out-of-plant training, the so-called manpower retraining programs, whose evaluation raises different problems not especially related to Becker's distinction). For the rest, Becker's emphasis on training as the outcome of an occupational choice by workers seemed to ignore complex questions about the supply of training by firms with well-developed "internal labor markets." All in all, it can hardly be said that the human-capital approach to labor training has yet been put to a decisive empirical test (on which more anon).

The subject of migration gives rise to similar difficulties in assessing degrees of success or failure. There is a rich economic and sociological literature on geographical migration going back to the nineteenth and even eighteenth century, to which the human-capital approach adds little except a pronounced emphasis on the role of geographical disparities in real incomes. There is little doubt that recent empirical work on migration has been deeply influenced by human-capital considerations, but an appraisal of the empirical status of the human-capital research program in the field of migration is by no means straightforward. We shall simply ignore this area because it has been surveyed again and again by others: *e.g.*, see Michael Greenwood [39, 1975].

This leaves us with health, job search, and labor market information networks. We shall say little about the human-capital approach to health because the virtual explosion of health economics in recent years would require a paper by itself to do justice to the theme: but, *e.g.*, see Herbert E. Klarman [53, 1965] and Michael H. Cooper and Anthony Culyer [25, 1973]. Likewise, George J. Stigler's pioneering article on "Information in the Labor Market" in the 1962 supplement volume of the *Journal of Political Economy* [93, 1962], in conjunction with work on the Phillips curve, sparked off a long line of papers on what has come to be known as the "new theory of voluntary unemployment," or the "microeconomic foundations of employment theory." To survey this area would take us far afield—but, *e.g.*, see Edmund Phelps *et al.* [75, 1970] and David Whipple [102, 1973]—and the precise relationship between these developments in labor economics and the human-capital research program is in any case somewhat tenuous.

Taking all these together, the program adds up to an almost total explanation of the determinants of earnings from employment, predicting declining investments in human-capital formation with increasing age, and hence lifetime earnings profiles that are concave from below. No wonder the bulk of empirical work inspired by the human-capital framework has taken the form of regressing the earnings of individuals on such variables as native ability, family background, place of residence, years of schooling, years of work experience, occupational status, and the like—the so-called "earnings function." It is sometimes difficult in all this research to see precisely what hypothesis is being tested, other than that schooling and work experience are important and that native ability and family background are not. Apart from earnings functions, some effort has also been devoted to explaining the size distribution of personal earnings, culminating in the somewhat surprising conclusion that the joint effect of years of schooling and years of work experience alone accounts for as much as half of the observed variance in the distribution of earnings. If true, this is perhaps the most powerful test of the human-capital research program that it would be possible to find. There is reason to believe, however, that this result depends on the assumption that labor markets are sufficiently competitive to equalize the private yields on all types of education and training. Alas, the empirical evidence leaves little doubt that these yields are not in fact equalized at the margin.

In summary, it may be said that the human-capital research program has displayed a simply amazing fecundity, spawning new research projects in almost every branch of economics. Nevertheless, we hope to show in the pages that follow that the program is actually not very well corroborated. That is of course no reason for abandoning the human-capital research program. To believe that scientific research programs are given up the moment a refutation is encountered is to fall victim to "naive falsificationism." What is required to eliminate a scientific research program is, first of all, repeated refutations, secondly, an embarrassing proliferation of *ad hoc* adjustments designed to avoid these refutations, and thirdly, and most importantly, a rival program that purports to account for the same evidence by a different but equally powerful theoretical framework. Such a rival to the human-capital research program may now have made its appearance: it travels under the name of the "screening hypothesis" or "credentialism," and it is linked up in some of its versions to the new theory of "dual labor markets," or labor market "segmentation." Its origins lie in the theory of decision-making under uncertainty and its impact derives from the discovery

that the process of hiring workers is merely a species of a larger genus, namely, the problem of selecting buyers or sellers in the presence of inadequate information about their characteristics. The issue, however, is whether this "screening hypothesis" is truly a rival framework, or instead a complement to the human-capital research program, which may in the end subsume rather than displace it. At any rate, the appearance of the screening hypothesis has at long last presented the human-capital research program with a challenge on its own grounds, making it necessary to ask: what precisely is the empirical status of human-capital theory?

II. *Demand for Schooling*

We begin our review of the evidence by considering the demand function for formal schooling. Becker's *Human Capital* noted that observed changes in American school and college attendance rates over the last thirty years can be satisfactorily explained by the persistently high yield of educational investment to individuals [3, Becker, 1975, pp. 169–73, 179–81]. No doubt, if his calculations had yielded negative or absurdly low private rates of return, the human-capital research program would have died there and then. On the other hand, it can hardly be said that his test was a severe one: an almost infinite number of alternative theories can easily account for the enrollment changes in question.

Robert Campbell and Barry N. Siegel [18, 1967] were the first to attempt to estimate the demand function for higher education in the United States: they regressed the fraction of the age group enrolled in institutions of higher education over the period 1919 to 1964 on time-series data of real tuition costs and real disposable incomes per household. Apart from their rather unconvincing attempt to "identify" a demand rather than a supply function, they failed to include either forgone earnings or any measure of expected future earnings as independent variables in their regression, and hence ended up testing, not the human-capital explanation of the demand for higher education, but rather the standard consumption explanation. The fact that they obtained a good fit with an $R^2 = 0.93$ suggests immediately that the concept of "education as investment" may be less promising than was imagined at first.

Two years later, Harvey Galper and Robert M. Dunn [38, 1969] improved this estimate by introducing distributed lags in their regressions. Their only independent variables were high school enrollments, household incomes, and the size of the armed forces. Even without tuition costs, they obtained an excellent fit on 1929–65 data. Once again, therefore, their results refute the human-capital model, at least by implication.[9] Oddly enough, when enrollment data are taken state by state on a cross-section basis, good results are obtained using such independent variables as parental education, test scores, tuition fees, and current earnings by levels of education [32, Feldman and Hoenack, 1969], thus confirming a weak version of the human-capital explanation of the demand for higher education.[10] On the other hand, Leonard S. Miller [63, 1971], using a similar approach, found significant differences between low and high achievers, with high achievers displaying few of the cost-conscious characteristics of students in the human-capital image of the world;

in other words, the human-capital research program may be said to apply to the lower half of the American ability range.

With Freeman [34, 1971] attention shifted away from the explanation of the total demand for higher education to the demand for specialized fields of study and, in particular, to the career choices of engineers and scientists. Freeman introduced five new elements into the analysis: firstly, he allowed for the fact that earnings today can only influence the supply of graduates four years later; secondly, he intended to discount expected lifetime incomes, thus treating the present value of earnings as the relevant explanatory variable; thirdly, he found empirical counterparts for certain nonpecuniary factors affecting occupational choice; fourthly, he took account of expected lifetime incomes in alternative occupations; and fifthly, he allowed for the effects of employers' demand in the labor market by including the output of industries hiring scientists and engineers. His entire model formed a recursive structure that first explained the number of first-year enrollments in, say, B.Sc. engineering courses, then the number of engineers graduating with a B.Sc. degree four years later, and, finally, the starting salaries of graduate engineers.[11] Furthermore, the distributed lag structure of his equations made it possible to estimate the speed at which the model attained an equilibrium solution.

Freeman's results for engineers, accountants, chemists, and mathematicians constitute a striking confirmation of human-capital theory: all the coefficients have the expected signs and the wage elas-

---

[9] See, likewise, the latest attempt in this area by Sandra Christensen, John Melder, and Burton A. Weisbrod [23, 1975]; see also Michael L. Handa and Michael L. Skolnik [42, 1972] for a review of similar Canadian studies, and George Psacharopoulos [77, 1973] for a study of Hawaii.

[10] For stronger evidence, see Handa and Skolnik [43, 1975] for Canada and Richard B. Freeman [35, 1975] on the recent downturn in American college enrollment rates. But Handa and Skolnik's results are marred by poor earnings data and Freeman concedes that recent changes in the draft law may be responsible for some of his findings.

[11] This summary of his procedure is too terse. Actually, he estimated three models: a recursive cobweb model; a recursive but "incomplete adjustment model"; and a simultaneous equation model. The manner in which he moves back and forth between these models, substituting estimated variables from one model into the equations of another model, create difficulties in interpreting his results.

ticity is well above unity; the entire model is stable and yields a rapid adjustment to equilibrium. Furthermore, he produced additional findings from a survey of students in the Boston area to show that the typical student is indeed attentive and responsive to variations in occupational earnings. Nevertheless, the usual gap between the hypothesis to be tested and the variables employed in empirical estimation do raise doubts about his findings. In the absence of lifetime earnings profiles for all his professional categories, Freeman treated starting salaries as a proxy for lifetime earnings and thus failed in fact to test the hypothesis that students take a lifecycle view of career opportunities. Even the dynamic structure of his model is purely mechanical, reflecting the four-year production period of engineers, and not the tendency of students and employers to form a particular set of adaptive expectations about the future course of prices and quantities. To be sure, the use of arbitrarily distributed lags in the estimation of economic relationships is well established in the econometric literature. But the absence of a truly dynamic theory of the formation of expectations is particularly damaging here: what is at issue in the theory of human capital is precisely whether students take *any* forward view of economic variables. As a matter of fact, Alan N. Freiden and Robert J. Staaf [36, 1973] manage to successfully predict the pattern of subject changes by students in a particular American college, not by invoking the theory of human capital, but by applying the standard theory of consumer behavior.[12]

Let us pause for a moment to note that there is a world of difference, at least for the United States, between an explanation of the entry demand for a specialized field of study and an explanation of the num-

bers actually graduating in that field of study. About 40 percent of freshman students in American colleges switch their major subjects somewhere between the freshman and the senior year: over the four-year period, such subjects as engineering and natural science are net losers, while education and social science subjects are net gainers, which is to say that the net flow is from subjects with higher to subjects with lower income expectations. The explanation for this phenomenon has clearly much to do with the lower probability of surviving a course in engineering and natural science, owing to the fact that these subjects have higher grading norms than education and social science. In so far as Freeman explains such switches of majors by relative wages and salaries, he must be assuming that relative nonpecuniary benefits (including the chances of surviving a course) do not change across majors over the period of observation. But Freiden and Staaf [36, 1973], followed at book-length by McKenzie and Staaf [62, 1974], argue that the distribution of grades across majors changes much more frequently than do relative salaries, and they therefore explain the switches between majors by the economic logic of consumer behavior theory applied to the student's choice between university subjects. This line of argument may not refute the human-capital explanation of the supply of professional manpower but it certainly complicates it.

Indeed, when John F. O'Connell [70, 1972] carried Freeman's analysis one stage further, many of Freeman's sharp results evaporated. O'Connell concentrated attention on the supply of graduate engineers, irrespective of the point at which students have decided to study engineering; he also provided something like a fully specified demand function for engineers; and he estimated a simultaneous equation model rather than a recursive model. He found that the supply of engi-

---

[12] See also the damaging evidence of low elasticities in reference to costs and earnings in Walter Fogel and Daniel J. B. Mitchell [33, 1974].

neers was indeed responsive to absolute although not to relative earnings differences, duplicating one of Freeman's results, but also that the demand for engineers was fairly insensitive to relative wage differences. However, his results are extremely unstable: the signs and the magnitudes of the coefficients, as well as the levels of statistical significance, change from one specification of his model to the next and, in particular, from one engineering field to another. All this is to say that despite Freeman's impressive early results, the problem of developing a satisfactory model of the American labor market for engineers, not to mention the demand for engineering as a field of study, remains unresolved.

In European countries, the effective rationing of higher education by the State makes it virtually impossible to test the hypothesis that subject choice in higher education is sensitive to earnings.[13] Worse than that, there is actually no convincing data outside the United States to show that students are informed of the pattern of earnings in the labor market, much less that they take them into account in reaching educational decisions, even when the earnings in question are currently forgone rather than expected in the future. There are of course innumerable European surveys to indicate that students and parents are principally motivated by "vocational factors" or "financial considerations" [8, Blaug, 1972, pp. 181, 187–88], but such vague replies to questionnaires should provide little comfort to human-capital theorists. After all, sociologists do not deny that people are generally aware of the fact that additional education opens the door to high-paying occupations; it is

[13] See Ruth Klinov-Malul's [54, 1971] totally negative results for Britain and Frank A. Sloan's [89, 1971] finding that applications to American medical schools are positively related to the supply of places, medical education being the one clear case where the supply of American higher education is rationed in terms of quantity rather than quality.

simply that they consider this to be a minor factor in the demand for post-compulsory schooling.[14] Even in the United States, this type of direct survey evidence leaves much to be desired.

As for actual behavior apart from knowledge and information, we have seen that the empirical evidence for the human-capital explanation of the demand for schooling is far from unambiguous: it is true that it has never been decisively refuted on its own grounds, but on the other hand it has only been corroborated in its weaker versions. Moreover, alternative economic models have yielded equally good and even better results. When we consider that the private demand for formal schooling is, as it were, at the center of the human-capital research program, the results to date begin to raise doubts as to whether the program is indeed "progressing."

III. *Labor Training*

From the earliest formulations of the human-capital model by Schultz, Becker, and Mincer, it was on-the-job training and not formal schooling that was taken to be the paradigm case of self-investment. In the absence of post-school investment, lifecycle earnings profiles were assumed to show neither appreciation as a result of learning-by-doing, nor depreciation as a result of biological aging and obsolescence of knowledge; in graphical terms, the picture was that of a series of perfectly horizontal profiles, each higher profile being associated with an additional year of schooling. It was argued, however, that individuals tend to invest in themselves after completing schooling by choosing occupations that promise "general training"; in so doing, they lower their starting salaries below alternative opportunities in

[14] The major factor, much neglected by human-capital theorists, may well be demographic forces: e.g., see Douglas L. Adkins [1, 1974] and Stephen P. Dresch [27, 1975].

exchange for higher future salaries as the training begins to pay off. Provided a sufficient number of workers with a given level of education behave in this fashion, the model predicts that the age-earnings profiles of different educational cohorts that we actually observe will be concave from below, a prediction that was immediately confirmed by American census evidence and that has since been confirmed again and again by evidence for some forty countries around the world.

Unfortunately, any psychological theory of "learning curves," in which appreciation over time is partly but only partly offset by depreciation and obsolescence, will likewise account for concave age-earnings profiles. Furthermore, it is not easy even in principle to separate off-the-job-in-plant "general" and "specific" training, which clearly implies a direct cost that must be borne by either workers or employers, from either on-the-job-learning-by-doing or on-the-job-doing-under-supervision. Both learning-by-doing and doing-under-supervision are costly in terms of output forgone, but the former is unavoidable and hence is not subject to individual choice. In short, it is difficult to see how individuals can choose more or less learning-by-doing, although no doubt business firms will want to minimize the number of inexperienced workers, everything else being the same. Of course, entry into certain professions, such as medicine, law, and accountancy, do entail long periods of learning-by-doing at low rates of pay. But this kind of post-school investment is artificial, in the sense of being the result of the restrictive practices of professional associations. The difficulty is that of believing that occupational choice is generally characterized under competitive conditions by the choice of low-paying occupations whose learning potential (apart from formal training) will subsequently raise earnings to more than justify the period of low pay. On this absolutely fun-

damental question, Mincer's new book, *Schooling, Experience and Earnings,* has little to add to Becker's earlier arguments in *Human Capital:* "The assumption of costless opportunities for augmenting productivity, which is sometimes implied in the notion of 'learning by doing,' cannot be descriptive of labor markets where labor mobility is the norm rather than the exception" [67, Mincer, 1974, p. 65; also p. 132]. Granting the point about labor mobility as the norm rather than the exception, it is nevertheless doubtful that all interoccupational, and even more intraoccupational, movements of labor can be reduced to the action of sowing and reaping the advantages of labor training, widely defined so as to include not just formal in-plant training and learning under supervision, but also learning by experience.[15] The use of such portmanteau terms as "on-the-job-training" or "work experience" to cover what is in fact a number of quite distinct phenomena merely adds to our doubts.

The question is further complicated by the introduction of Mincer's new concept of "overtaking." According to human-capital theory, all individuals with a given level of schooling choose occupations, so

[15] If alternative techniques for producing a given product involve more or less learning-by-doing, and if firms can predict these learning characteristics of alternative techniques (a big if), learning-by-doing would indeed become a decision variable for firms. Workers, on the other hand, would have to be able to predict the learning characteristics of different techniques ruling in different industries, so as to make it possible by choice of employment to invest in more or less learning-by-doing. I know of no evidence to suggest that this is a realistic picture of the elements that enter into occupational choice. As George Psacharopoulos and Richard Layard [81, 1976] put it: "Is costless learning impossible? For this to be the case there must always exist a job at which no learning occurs and at which we could currently produce more (net) than in any job where we can learn anything. There need not actually be anybody doing this job, though in a perfect market it would be surprising if someone were not doing it . . . We have spent some years trying to think what this job is . . . But we have found it impossible to think of any such job."

as to equalize the present value of lifetime earnings (this conveniently ignores the nonpecuniary attractions of different occupations); since individuals have different time preferences, the effect of these post-school investment decisions is to produce an initial dispersion of earnings by levels of education. It follows from the logic of the equalization of present values that the dispersion must decline subsequently, only to increase again in the later stages of working life; in other words, the different profiles must cross each other at some point. The time at which the dispersion of earnings is minimized is called the point of "overtaking" and Mincer shows that, in the United States at any rate, the cross-over years are bunched together at about 7–9 years after entry into the labor force, that is, at ages 23 to 33, depending on what level of education we are talking about. The point of "overtaking," by the way, is also the point at which the effects of formal schooling on earnings are maximized: at this point the returns on post-school investments just about equal their current costs to individuals in terms of earnings forgone. In other words, if we concentrate attention on a cohort of men with 7–9 years of work experience, Mincer argues, we can in fact explain about one-third of the inequality in earnings solely by differences in formal schooling [67, Mincer, 1974, pp. 133–34].

The problem with the concept of "overtaking" is similar to that of distinguishing costly on-the-job training from costless learning-by-doing, namely, the failure to observe the lifetime earnings profiles of individuals who have neither invested in nor received any post-school training. Mincer assumes that these base-line earnings profiles would remain perfectly horizontal throughout working life, but no such profiles have ever been observed for any category of individuals. He further assumes that rates of return to investment in formal schooling are identical to rates

of return to post-school investment, and it is particularly the latter assumption that allows him to separate the costs from the returns to post-school investment [8, Blaug, 1972, pp. 197–98]. The finding that the "overtaking point" occurs about 7–9 years after completion of schooling is therefore dependent both on the assumption of a once-and-for-all effect of schooling on earnings (no net appreciation of human capital from costless work experience) and on the assumption that general equilibrium is actually attained in human-capital markets. Alas, there is simply overwhelming evidence, both for the United States and for other countries, that private rates of return to successive years of formal schooling are not equalized at the margin; indeed, they decline with successively higher levels of schooling [80, Psacharopoulos and Hinchliffe, 1973]. Mincer's attempt to reinterpret this evidence is not entirely convincing[16] and without the assumption of equality in all private rates of return to formal schooling, there would seem to be no way of disentangling the effects of investment in schooling from the effects of post-school

[16] He argues that differences in the amount of time worked per year account for almost all of the observed differences in rates of return to levels of schooling: rates of return calculated from hourly or weekly rather than annual earnings do not differ significantly by levels of schooling [67, Mincer, 1974, pp. 54–55]. This result is actually rather paradoxical. It is a fact that average weeks worked per year increase with levels of schooling [67, 1974, p. 121]. Hence, if we standardize for the numbers of weeks worked per year by calculating rates of return to schooling from weekly rather than annual earnings, the decline in rates of return to successively higher levels of schooling should increase, not decrease, the more so as there is some evidence that weekly earnings tend to be positively correlated with weeks worked per year [67, 1974, p. 94]. Mincer's own conclusion seems to be based on what happens to the negative squared coefficient of schooling in his earnings function when he adds in the effect of weeks worked [67, 1974, pp. 54, 93]. For the reasons given above, however, I am inclined to argue that this result is due to a misspecification of the model. On the general question of standardizing rates of return for time worked per year, see also Richard S. Eckaus [29, 1973] and Cotton M. Lindsay [58, 1973].

investment. Furthermore, his earlier attempt to compare estimates of the returns to formal schooling with some independent estimates of the returns to training, so as to show that they are indeed roughly equalized [65, Mincer, 1962, pp. 63–66], is vitiated by the fact that the training studies in question refer to apprenticeship programs, an amalgam of learning-by-doing and doing-under-supervision, sometimes but not always involving off-the-job-in-plant courses.

Enough has now been said to suggest that the human-capital explanation of labor training founders on the failure to provide a testable theory of occupational choice. Nothing is said about the non-pecuniary attractions of alternative occupations, the costs of gaining adequate information, and the imperfections of the capital markets, which inhibit some individuals from financing their desirable occupational choices. Moreover, the model concentrates all its attention on the supply of human capital, while virtually ignoring the nature of demand in labor markets. But the earnings function, from which all the basic results are derived, is itself a "reduced-form" equation, the outcome, that is, of an interaction of the forces of demand and supply.

In distinguishing between "general" and "specific" training, Becker conceded that employers can vary the turnover of labor in a plant by a variety of devices: the lower the turnover, the greater the willingness of firms to pay for training and, hence, the more "specific" the training, whatever its content.[17] Thus, the nearer we approach the monopsony model of firm behavior, the less likely the relevance of a worker self-investment approach to the question of labor training. Sherwin Rosen [84, 1972; 85, 1972] has indeed generalized the Becker-Mincer approach by recasting the problem in terms of an implicit market for learning opportunities, overlapping the explicit market for jobs: in effect, employers attempt to sell training services as a way of inducing people to work for them and, of course, the price of such services is a lower wage than workers could have obtained in alternative employments. Given the market price for learning on-the-job, however, employers can frequently redesign jobs so as to maximize the net returns from a given work force.[18] What emerges from this extension of the Becker-Mincer thesis is a more general conception of the training process, giving due scope both to the recruitment and hiring practices of firms and to the sequential job choices of workers over their working lives, a process in which the trade-off between learning and earning is gradually altered in favor of the latter.

We are left, therefore, with two unsolved riddles. The first is how to separate appreciation of human capital over time due to costless learning-by-doing from appreciation due to costly self-investment by workers, both of which tend to be offset as time passes by the natural deterioration or obsolescence of human capital. The second is how to square the picture of workers choosing between jobs with different earning-learning ratios with the notion of firms jointly producing goods and services for their customers and learning opportunities for their employees. These unsolved riddles have so far spoiled all efforts to solve the problem of human-capital formation at a still higher level of abstraction than that adopted by Becker and Mincer. The process of investment in schooling followed by investment in job search and post-school training is in effect a sequential process of individual decisions, subject at each stage to the constraints of past decisions and the stock of human capital

---

[17] Donald O. Parsons [72, 1972] and Masatoshi Kuratani [55, 1973] have attempted to develop these ideas into a testable theory of quit and lay-off rates.

[18] The work of James Scoville [88, 1972] has laid particular emphasis on the much-neglected variable of job design.

accumulated to date. Expressed in this way, the natural technique to apply to the problem is optimal control theory. In Yoram Ben-Porath's [4, 1967] pioneering application of optimal control theory to human-capital formation, every individual begins with an initial endowment of human capital, capable of generating earnings at a declining rate through time, subject to an exogenously determined rate of deterioration; this endowment can be invested throughout the lifecycle either in learning or in earning but, unfortunately, not in both. The empirical implications of this model are not very rich. It predicts the typical concave shape of age-earnings profiles, and it implies that investment in learning will be concentrated in the early years of the lifecycle. Subsequent attempts by Ben-Porath [5, 1970] to test the model on earnings data proved to be unsuccessful: apart from the failure to isolate the depreciation-obsolescence parameter, he found it impossible to allow for the possible jointness of earning and learning in the post-school investment process.[19]

All in all, the question of labor training continues to haunt the human-capital research program. It is ironic to realize that the program was first developed in its most general form with reference to training, of which formal schooling is only a special case. Nevertheless, the bulk of the work in the human-capital research program has been devoted to investment in education; to this day we have had to make do with rates of return to educational investment that are actually averages of rates of return to schooling and rates of return to training, in the fond belief that the yields on all types of human-capital formation are more or less equalized in the labor market. As we have seen, there is little empirical evidence to support this belief, and there is a great deal of evidence that flatly contradicts it.

[19] For a more detailed discussion of this and other optimal control models, see Bowman [16, 1974, pp. 214-19, 225-29].

IV. *Private and Social Rates of Return*

Calculations of the rates of return to investment in formal schooling have proved to be the bread-and-butter of the human-capital research program: literally hundreds of such studies have now been carried out around the world in both developed and developing countries and even the recent comprehensive survey by George Psacharopoulos and Keith Hinchliffe [80, 1973] is already badly out of date: *e.g.*, see Richard S. Eckaus, Ahmad El Safty, and Victor D. Norman [30, 1974] and Carnegie Commission [19, 1974]. Nevertheless, despite considerable refinements in recent calculations, certain anomalies in the reported rates have largely escaped notice.

The vast majority of calculated rates have fallen within the range of 5–15 percent, although private rates as high as 80 percent for primary education in certain developing countries and as low as minus 2–3 percent for certain types of graduate education in the United States have been reported: *e.g.*, see Psacharopoulos and Hinchliffe [80, 1973] and John M. Campbell and Thomas D. Curtis [17, 1975]. The modal figure of 5–15 percent has been generally interpreted as reflecting a certain underlying rationality in both private and public decisions about schooling. This picture of social harmony is somewhat marred by the persistent observation of unequal private rates of return to successive years of schooling and, in particular, by the "sheepskin" effect of higher rates of return to the last years of schooling in a given educational cycle compared to the earlier years.[20] In general, private rates of return tend to decline monotonically with additional years of schooling, thus implying a chronic tendency on the part of individuals to over-invest in their education as a function of the acquisition of previous schooling. There are, of course, no dearth

[20] For new American evidence, see Richard Raymond and Michael Sesnowitz [83, 1975].

of *ad hoc* explanations of this phenomenon, most of which involve imperfections in the human-capital market, that is, the absence of banking institutions that will furnish students with unlimited funds to finance their education at a constant rate of interest. But there is no general theory which can predict how self-financed students will behave in the face of a given pattern of the private returns to schooling. Moreover, there is the suspicion that family finance is highly intercorrelated with academic ability and achievement drive, thus opening the door to another rich source of *ad hocery,* easily derivable from the voluminous writings of sociologists of education.

Furthermore, the variance of rates of return by years of schooling between individuals is more significant for the private calculus than the average rates for educational cohorts highlighted in rates-of-return studies. The fact that rates of return by levels of education display considerable variance has, of course, been known ever since Becker drew attention to it [3, 1975, pp. 181–90]. But the problems this creates for interpreting private rates of return have been generally ignored. The rates that motivate students are expected rates of return, and there is no reason to think that risk aversion is uniformly distributed among the members of a particular educational cohort. Thus, even when we know both the mean and variance of *ex post* returns and, in addition, assume that students will treat these *ex post* returns as best estimates of *ex ante* returns, we still cannot predict how they will behave in choosing schooling without taking a view of their attitudes toward risk. Recent attempts to show that risk differentials among individuals in respect to educational and occupational choices are not very important [100, Weiss, 1972], have begged as many questions as they have answered [45, Hause, 1974] and, on balance, it must be concluded that the human-capital research program has so far

evaded the problem of portfolio selection in human-capital formation.

If all this were not enough, there is evidence that the relative constancy of private rates of return in the United States between 1939 and 1971 was associated with significant shifts in age-earnings profiles by levels of education in certain years during that 30-year period [49, Johnson and Hebein, 1974; 20, Carnoy and Marenbach, 1975]. If there were perfect capital markets for educational loans, this would make little difference to our interpretations of the private calculus. In the absence of perfect capital markets, however, we cannot treat direct costs and forgone earnings on the same footing as expected earnings. In abandoning this principle, however, we virtually abandon the human-capital interpretation of private rate-of-return calculations.

Lastly, there is the unresolved problem that students choose, not just schooling, but schooling of a certain type and quality, and few rate-of-return calculations have succeeded in successfully standardizing the calculated yields for quality of educational institution. Most of the American work in this area has been confined to interstate differences in the quality of elementary and secondary education, quality being measured by average per pupil state expenditures on education, with only an occasional glance in higher education at two-year junior colleges and particular graduate programs, employing measures of quality that are frequently indistinguishable from measures of the average ability of the relevant student body.[21] So far, very little has been done to calculate private rates of return for particular colleges or groups of colleges in a contiguous area. A recent calculation for the Philippines, however, estimated the private rate of return to college education, not only by field of study but even by individual insti-

[21] For a useful survey of these findings, see Psacharopoulos [79, 1975, ch. 4] and Paul Wachtel [99, 1975].

tution attended [47, International Labor Office, 1974, pp. 317–18, 632–44]. Although the estimates are crude, being based only on the first 4–6 years of employment suitably projected over the lifecycle, they reveal that an over-all, average private rate of return of 9 percent to university education is perfectly compatible with negative rates of return to certain fields of study at certain low-quality institutions. If it is going to be argued that students are quite rational to demand college education because the private rate of return is 9 percent as against an interest rate of 8–10 percent in the organized money market, it will have to be conceded that some students are quite irrational in demanding a college education whose yield is negative, unless, of course, they are poorly informed, or risk lovers, or well endowed with family finance, or. . . .

The hallmark of a "degenerating" research program is the capacity to account for all the facts, whatever they are. The endless rate-of-return calculations of human-capital theorists have turned up plenty of anomalous facts crying out for explanation, such as the low or even negative private rates of return to graduate education in the United States. The steadfast refusal to exploit these anomalies in a further burst of fruitful theorizing is perhaps the best indication we have that the human-capital research program may indeed have started to "degenerate."

V. *The Earnings Function*

This brings us quite naturally to a famous question so far neglected, namely, the influence of native ability and family background on earnings. It is sometimes argued [40, Griliches, 1970, pp. 100–3] that we can safely ignore these factors in calculating social rates of return to educational investment, at least if our motive in making such calculations is to induce marginal policy changes in the allocation of resources between different educational

sectors. Even if that argument is accepted, it is perfectly clear that we cannot ignore all of nature and so much of nurture for other purposes, in particular for the measurement of the contribution of schooling to earnings differentials. Only a few years ago, most investigators were content to follow Edward F. Denison by making the so-called "two-thirds assumption," that is, to attribute two-thirds of the earnings differentials associated with different amounts of education to the pure effect of schooling, ascribing the rest to some amalgam of genetic endowment and social origins: *e.g.*, see Blaug [8, 1972, pp. 51–52]. But the present view is either that Denison underestimated the pure effect of education, as Zvi Griliches has argued, or that the interaction effect between native ability and family background on the one hand, and schooling on the other, exceeds the separate effect of each.

The bewildering flood of literature in recent years on earnings functions defies anything less than a book-length summary.[22] Our aim here, however, is merely to suggest that the battle lines are now clearly drawn, and to venture the prediction that the eventual outcome of this ongoing debate may be as surprising to advocates of the human-capital research program as to most of its critics.

The classic stance of the human-capital research program is to play down the influence of preschool factors on lifetime earnings, be it native ability or preschool investment of family time, or at any rate to claim that the combined effect of preschool factors and the subsequent influence of these on academic achievement is greatly exceeded by the separate effect of sheer duration of formal schooling and training. Needless to say, the human-capi-

[22] For literature surveys and commentaries largely confined to the United States and a few European countries, see Lewis C. Solmon [90, 1973], F. Thomas Juster [50, 1975], and Psacharopoulos [79, 1975]. There are, in addition, some half-dozen studies of earnings functions in less developed countries.

tal model in no way denies the interaction of all of these factors, but it does claim that whatever interaction there is still leaves considerable room for the purely additive effects of the various explanatory variables. This classic position continues to be upheld by many—*e.g.*, see John Conlisk [24, 1971] and Zvi Griliches and William M. Mason [41, 1972]—and it is more or less endorsed by the authoritative work of Peter M. Blau and Otis D. Duncan [7, 1967] on occupational mobility in the United States (see sequel by O. D. Duncan, D. L. Featherman and B. Duncan [28, 1972]). However, most empirical work in this area lacks measures of native ability at an early age, much less measures taken in the preschool years, and the measures of family background that are invoked rarely go beyond father's occupation, father's or mother's education, and place of residence; what is conspicuously lacking are reliable measures of family income and wealth. It is difficult, therefore, to be entirely confident about the many findings that confirm the classic position.

Within the ranks of the human-capital research program, however, there are some who continue to emphasize the quantitative importance of the interaction between inborn ability and schooling [44, Hause, 1972; 46, Hause, 1975; 95, Taubman and Wales, 1974] and outside these ranks, there are others equally insistent that genetic endowment as measured by I.Q.'s counts for little because family background counts for so much [13, Bowles, 1972; 14, Bowles, 1973]. That says nothing about Christopher Jencks [48, 1972] who purports to demonstrate that nothing counts except luck, a finding that is almost entirely due to the fact that he explains, not the distribution of age-specific earnings from employment, but rather the distribution of total income averaged over people in four ten-year age groups, switching on unspecified occasions to all people aged 25 to 65.

The major shortcomings of all these investigations may perhaps be summarized under three headings: the identification problem; the problem of proxy-variables; and the problem of data sources. Take first the identification problem, of which we have already had occasion to speak. An earnings function is a reduced-form equation and in the absence of estimated structural parameters of the underlying simultaneous-equation model, we have every reason to suspect that the coefficients of the single equation are biased. This suspicion is borne out by Robert D. Morgenstern [68, 1973], who estimates both a nonrecursive, single-equation earnings function for the United States and a recursive model to explain the distribution of years of schooling in the labor force, as well as the distribution of earnings from employment. He shows that schooling certainly exerts a strong independent influence on earnings but, on the other hand, home background exerts weak direct as well as strong indirect effects on earnings, and this produces a bias in the schooling coefficient of single-equation earnings function.

The next heading is the problem of proxy-variables. First, there are the difficulties already referred to of measuring family background as an index of the environment in which children are brought up. Whether measured in terms of income, occupation, or education, we can never be sure whether the reported measures of family background refer to preschool investment, to later investments complementary with schooling, to postschool influences, or simply to certain attitudinal changes that provide children in certain homes with a set of self-fulfilling aspirations. Native ability is an even better example of a variable we cannot measure satisfactorily because there is simply no agreement about what we are supposed to be measuring. Is I.Q. really relevant, or instead should we be measuring "achievement motivation"? [61, McClelland, 1961]. To date, most of the work on earnings functions has been satisfied with measuring variables one way and one way only, as if any proxy will do. If we hope to make any progress in this area, the time has surely come to fit earnings functions with alternative proxies of the crucial variables.

The last heading is that of data sources. Virtually all fitted earnings functions have made use of either cross-section or time-series data, aggregated over cohorts. Only two or three studies have employed longitudinal or genuinely individualized data, although the temporal order of such variables as native ability, family background, formal schooling, occupational status, and personal earnings points to longitudinal data as the natural empirical framework for the analysis. The latest example of a longitudinal study of the economic benefits of education amply conveys the power of this type of data [31, Fägerlind, 1975]. Fifteen thousand individuals from Malmö, Sweden, were followed up from the age of 10 in 1938 to the age of 43 in 1971; I.Q. was measured at ages 10 and 20, and information on scholastic achievements was obtained throughout their period of schooling; occupational careers were monitored year by year, and information about earnings before tax were gathered from the tax records. The data were analyzed by means of path analysis, which is basically linear regression with standardized variables, but interaction terms were added in an effort to go some way towards a multiplicative model. The basic findings of the study directly contradict the conclusion of Jencks that "neither family background, cognitive skill, educational attainment, nor occupational status explains much of the variance in men's incomes" [48, 1972, p. 226]. Jencks explained only 22 percent of the variance in income among males

aged 25 to 65.[23] The Fägerlind study, using almost the same explanatory variables as Jencks, explains only 2 percent of the variance in earnings of males aged 25; there is a steep rise in variance explained, however, after the age of 30, reaching 30 percent at age 35, and more than 50 percent at age 43, thus confirming Mincer's view that the correlation between schooling and earnings is maximized at the "overtaking point."[24]

The direct effect of years of schooling on earnings is insignificant, except for earnings at age 43 when the effect is nevertheless very weak. But type of schooling does exert a strong and increasing effect on earnings, both directly and indirectly as a mediator of family background and early cognitive ability. Family background, on the other hand, exerts only a minor influence on earnings independently of education, and the same thing is true of early cognitive ability, which seems to interact with type rather than quantity of schooling. Fägerlind's summary of his results is nothing but judicious [31, 1975, p. 78]:

> It is not possible to endorse conclusions that formal education is nearly insignificant in determining adult success in occupational status and earnings. On the other hand, the view advanced that amount of formal education is the main explanatory factor in status attainment and earnings cannot find full support from this investigation either, since other factors such as family background and cognitive ability play important indirect roles. The overall conception of the relationship between earnings and the various predictors included here is the following: The resources the individual has access to in early childhood, mainly family resources and personality assets, are converted into "marketable assets" mainly through the formal educational system. The present study reveals that although the direct effects of early cognitive

[23] As calculated from Jencks [48, 1972, Fig. B-7, p. 346].

[24] Fägerlind's overtaking point, however, occurs almost 10 years after Mincer's. A longer overtaking point than 7–9 years also emerges in the British data [81, Psacharopoulos and Layard, 1976].

ability on earnings are either small or insignificant, their indirect effects are relatively strong. Later assets, such as the quality of education, have both strong direct and indirect effects on earnings. . . . The school system alone is [therefore] not an adequate instrument for equalizing opportunities. This is because educational benefits are best used by those who come from advantaged backgrounds. Without some kind of equalization of home and child-care resources the educational system will function as a stratifier, wherein successful performances in one socializing setting are used to justify different and more advantageous treatments in the next.

The picture that emerges from studies such as these does not marry well with the so-called "schooling model" explanation of income distribution in the writings of Becker, Mincer, and Chiswick, which, it must be emphasized, is one and only one human-capital interpretation of the income distribution problem: *e.g.*, see Mincer [66, 1970] and Chiswick [22, 1974, ch. 3]. The schooling model necessarily implies the paradoxical conclusion that an increase in the average level of schooling of the population, given a constant distribution of schooling and a constant private rate of return to investment in education, causes the distribution of income to become more unequal. This conclusion depends critically, however, on the assumption of an equal rate of return to all types of human investment, an assumption which, as we have seen, is denied by the evidence [59, Marin and Psacharopoulos, 1976].[25]

[25] It is ironic to observe that a recent Marxist critique of human-capital theory, after berating the human-capital research program for its superficial approach to labor market phenomena, commits itself to two and only two predictions: "there is no reason at all to expect equality in rates of return, either among different types of schooling or between schooling and other forms of investment"; and "reduction in inequalities in the distribution of schooling might lead to changes in income inequality in any particular direction" [15, Bowles and Gintis, 1975, pp. 80, 81]. It is, however, difficult to find any connection between these predictions and the Marxist research program adopted by the authors.

Moreover, the schooling model explains the distribution of earnings by the distribution of accumulated human capital, and it explains the latter in turn by the exogenously determined distribution of "abilities" and "opportunities." But the "distribution of abilities and opportunities" is merely shorthand for the effects of early cognitive ability and parental background on the demand for formal schooling, both of which are endogenously determined variables in any intergenerational view of the process of human-capital formation [71, Oulton, 1974]. Thus, at best, the schooling model is incomplete and, at worst, it is misleading.

After ten years of work on earnings functions, all we have is a dim light at the end of a tunnel: everyone has been wrong and everyone has been right because the problem has proved to be more complicated than was originally imagined. This has proved to be a "progressive" research program in the sense that the basic model has come to be better specified, the variables better measured, and the range of statistical techniques gradually widened beyond classical least squares regression of a single equation. Nevertheless, the fact remains that no one has so far succeeded in specifying and testing the simultaneous demand and supply equations that generate the earnings function, without which empirical work on earnings function amounts to little more than trying to walk on one leg.

VI. *The Screening Hypothesis*

We come, at long last, to the screening hypothesis as a possible substitute or complement to the human-capital research program. According to human-capital theory, the labor market is capable of continually absorbing workers with ever higher levels of education, provided that education-specific earnings are flexible downwards. Since the educational hiring standards for an occupation is itself a decision variable, it matters little whether better educated workers are absorbed into lower-paying occupations, while holding average earnings per occupation constant, or into the same occupations as before, while reducing earnings by occupation. In any case, there is sufficient variance of earnings within 2-digit and even 3-digit occupations [60, Mayhew, 1971] to suggest that both of these effects occur simultaneously; in addition, occupations can be redesigned so as to destroy any basis of comparison between old and new occupations. In short, nothing is more alien to the human-capital research program than the manpower forecaster's notion of technically-determined educational requirements for jobs.

These self-regulating labor markets may or may not work smoothly, in the sense of keeping the demand for educated manpower continuously in line with its supply, but they will not work at all unless employers prefer more to less educated workers, everything else being the same. The human-capital research program is silent on why there should be such a persistent bias in the preferences of employers: it may be because educated workers possess scarce cognitive skills, it may be because they possess desirable personality traits, such as self-reliance and achievement-drive, and it may be because they display compliance with organizational rules. But whatever the reason for the preference, the fact remains that all of these desirable attributes cannot be known with certainty at the time of hiring. The employer is therefore faced with a selection problem: given the difficulties of accurately predicting the future performance of job applicants, he is tempted to treat educational qualifications as a screening device to distinguish new workers in terms of ability, achievement motivation, and possibly family origins, that is, in terms of personality traits rather than

cognitive skills; cognitive skills are largely acquired by on-the-job training, and employers are therefore fundamentally concerned with selecting job applicants in terms of their trainability. This may not be the whole story but it is, surely, a good deal of the story. If so, the observed correlation between earnings and length of schooling, which figures so prominently in the writings of human-capital theorists, disguises a more fundamental correlation between schooling and the attributes that characterize trainability. The contribution of education to economic growth, therefore, is simply that of providing a selection device for employers, and the way is now open to consider the question of whether formal schooling is indeed the most efficient selection mechanism that we could design for the purpose. This is the so-called "screening hypothesis" or "theory of credentialism," which, in one form or another, has now been expounded by a large number of writers [74, Phelps, 1972; 2, Arrow, 1973; 86, Rothschild, 1973; 95, Taubman and Wales, 1974; 96, Thurow, 1974; 91, Spence, 1973; 92, Spence, 1974; 103, Wiles, 1974; 94, Stiglitz, 1975].

This thesis runs into the serious objection that it accounts at best for starting salaries and not for the earnings of long-time employees in different firms. Earnings are not only highly correlated with length of schooling but also with years of work experience. An employer has ample opportunity with long-time employees to acquire independent evidence of job performance without continuing to rely on educational qualifications. Besides, the evidence suggests that the correlation between earnings and length of schooling actually increases in the first 10–15 years of work experience, a fact difficult to explain by this weak version of the screening hypothesis [9, Blaug, 1972, pp. 73–75; 21, Chiswick, 1973; 56, Layard and Psacharopoulos, 1974; 78, Psacharopoulos, 1974].

A stronger version of credentialism,

however, surmounts these difficulties by adding the consideration that job performance is typically judged within firms on a departmental basis [82, Rawlins and Ulman, 1974]. Each hierarchically-organized department operates its own Doeringer-Piore "internal labor market," whose principal function is to maintain output in the face of unpredictable variations in demand, while minimizing the costs of labor turnover to the firm as a whole. In consequence, departments operate with enough manpower slack to ensure every new recruit a well-defined sequence of promotions throughout his working life. In this way, the kind of statistical discrimination based on paper qualifications that operates to determine starting salaries in the weak version of credentialism is hereby extended to lifetime earnings. The argument is strengthened by the introduction of various "institutional" factors such as (1) the tendency of monopsonistic employers to share the costs of specific training with workers, (2) the lagged response of firms to cyclical contractions, (3) the effects of collective bargaining in promoting substitution of more for less educated workers, and (4) the phenomenon of "seller's credentialism," whereby professional associations press for increased educational requirements under state licensing laws [82, Rawlins and Ulman, 1974, pp. 224–32].

The theory of credentialism, especially in its stronger version, appears to have radical implications for educational policy. It suggests, for example, that educational expansion is unlikely to have much impact on earnings differentials because an increased flow of college graduates will simply promote upgrading of hiring standards: college graduates will be worse off in absolute terms but so will high school graduates, and hence earnings differentials by education will remain more or less the same. However, there is nothing about this argument that is incompatible with

human-capital theory. The question at issue is whether upgrading can be carried on indefinitely, implying that college graduates are perfect substitutes for high school graduates, and high school graduates for elementary school leavers, and therefore that the educational system is merely an arbitrary sorting mechanism. Even in this extreme version of credentialism, we are still left with an explanation of the demand for schooling that is the same as that of human-capital theory: screening by employers in terms of educational credentials creates an incentive on the part of employees to produce the "signal" that maximizes the probability of being selected, namely, the possession of an educational qualification, and this signaling incentive is in fact conveyed by the private rate of return to educational investment.

If college graduates are not perfect substitutes for high school graduates, and so on down the line, it may well be that the true "social" rate of return to educational investment is positive. In that case, what the theory of credentialism amounts to is the charge that human-capital theorists have been measuring the wrong thing: the social rate of return to educational investment is a rate of return to a particular occupational selection mechanism, and not the yield on resources invested in improving the quality of the labor force. However, no advocate of credentialism has so far succeeded in quantifying the social rate of return understood in this sense.

The screening hypothesis is clearly much less ambitious than the human-capital research program: it is silent on questions of health care and geographical migration. It is also obvious that the screening hypothesis concentrates its fire on the demand side in the labor market, whereas the human-capital research program is strong, where it is strong, on the supply side. Thus, it may well be true that the two research programs are complements, not substitutes. Indeed, Finis Welch has observed: "the fundamental notion of human capital, of foregoing current income for the prospect of increased future earnings, assumes only that the schooling-income association is not spurious. As such, it is fully consistent with the screening view that schools primarily identify pre-existent skills and with the view that market skills are produced in school" [101, 1975, p. 65]. If the difference between the two explanations is indeed that of discovering whether schools produce or merely identify those attributes that employers value, the empirical evidence that would be capable of distinguishing between them is presumably evidence about what actually happens in classrooms. However, both sides have instead looked to labor market data with which to assail their opponents. For example, Paul J. Taubman and Terence Wales attempt to vindicate the screening hypothesis by comparing the distribution of education within occupations with what the distribution would have been if employers had selected workers solely on the basis of measures of general ability (such as I.Q. scores and scores on tests of mathematical competence) [95, 1974]. But what if employers actually select workers on the basis of occupation-specific abilities? Why assume that employers screen all workers for the same attributes? If individuals have different comparative advantages in carrying out different tasks involved in different occupations, and if education is an efficient sorter of these comparative advantages, screening by educational qualifications may in fact be highly productive. Indeed, so far not a single convincing piece of evidence has been produced to show that the educational system is not an efficient sorter of students according to their manifest aptitudes and abilities.

Mincer on the other hand, throws cold water on credentialism by citing American survey data that show that seniority is a relatively minor factor in the promotion of white-collar workers and that educational qualifications are rarely mentioned as a factor in promotion in most major collective bargaining agreements [67, 1974, pp. 80–82]. But if credentialism creates self-fulfilling expectations in both employers and employees, evidence relating to seniority provisions in employment practices may prove little one way or the other. As Layard and Psacharopoulos point out, no simple market test is likely to discriminate between human capital and screening explanations because the question is not whether schooling explains earnings, but rather why it does [56, 1974].

One is left with the uneasy feeling that the advocates of credentialism are largely content to verify their theory by pointing to "educational inflation" without committing themselves to a decisive prediction that might falsify it. The point of a testable theory is to define states of the world that cannot occur if the theory is true. It is sometimes difficult to see what states of the world are excluded by credentialism, particularly as credentialists have so far studiously avoided any investigation of "educational production functions." But this is not to say that the debate is merely a tempest-in-a-teapot. What is at issue is whether the labor market generates private signals to individuals that are totally at variance with social signals. The debate is about the meaning of the social rather than the private rate of return on investment in human capital. In this sense, the argument is about normative values: do we want to select individuals for the world of work by means of educational credentials because, surely, it is not beyond the wit of men to concoct other devices for sorting workers for purposes of assigning them to particular occupations?

But as is so often the case with normative problems, there is an underlying positive issue to be settled first: how efficient *is* the educational system in assigning people to jobs? Before joining Illitch in "deschooling society," we ought to try to answer that question.

VII. *Conclusion*

We began by asking: is the human-capital research program "progressing" or "degenerating"? Having reviewed the development of the program over the last decade, are we any nearer to an answer?

A research program, as we said, can only be adequately appraised in relation to its rivals of roughly equal scope. The human-capital research program, however, has no genuine rival of equal breadth and rigor. The standard, timeless theories of the behavior of consumers and firms provide some explanation of such phenomena as school enrollments and on-the-job training, but they are powerless to account for the sharing of training costs between employers and workers. Classic sociology certainly furnishes alternative explanations of the correlation between education and earnings, and quasi-sociological theories of dual or segmented labor markets undoubtedly poach in the territory staked out by human-capital theorists. The difficulty here is one of lack of precision in formulating hypotheses and, in particular, of commitment to new, falsifiable hypotheses outside the range of the human-capital research program. The screening hypothesis presents similar difficulties because its advocates seem largely satisfied with providing different causal explanations for facts discovered by the human-capital research program. The Marxist research program, on the other hand, has hardly begun to attack the question of earnings differentials and thus in effect fails to compete in the same terrain with human-capital theory.

We are thus condemned to judge the human-capital research program largely in its own terms, which is strictly speaking impossible—even the flat-earth research program, judged in its own terms, is not faring too badly! There are certainly grounds for thinking that the human-capital research program is now in something of a "crisis": its explanation of the private demand for education seems increasingly unconvincing; it offers advice on the supply of education, but it does not begin to explain either the patterns of educational finance or the public ownership of schools and colleges that we actually observe; its account of post-school training continues to underemphasize the role of costless learning-by-doing as a simple function of time, not to mention the organizational imperatives of "internal labor markets"; its rate-of-return calculations repeatedly turn up significant, unexplained differences in the yields of investment in different types of human capital, but its schooling-model explanation of the distribution of earnings nevertheless goes on blithely assuming that all rates of return to human-capital formation are equalized at the margin. Worse still, is the persistent resort to *ad hoc* auxiliary assumptions to account for every perverse result, culminating in a certain tendency to mindlessly grind out the same calculation with a new set of data, which are typical signs of degeneration in a scientific research program.

At the same time, we must give credit where credit is due. The human-capital research program has moved steadily away from some of its early naive formulations, and it has boldly attacked certain traditionally neglected topics in economics, such as the distribution of personal income. Moreover, it has never entirely lost sight of its original goal of demonstrating that a wide range of apparently disconnected phenomena in the world are the outcome of a definite pattern of individual decisions, having in common the features of forgoing present gains for the prospect of future ones.[26] In so doing, it discovered novel facts, such as the correlation between education and age-specific earnings, which have opened up entirely new areas of research in economics. Whether this momentum can be maintained in the future is, of course, anybody's guess, but it is noteworthy that the screening hypothesis first emerged in the writings of adherents to the human-capital research program, and to this day the most fruitful empirical work in the testing of credentialist hypotheses continues to emerge from the friends rather than the enemies of human-capital theory.

Nothing is easier than predicting the future course of scientific development —and nothing is more likely to be wrong. Nevertheless, let me rush in where angels fear to tread. In all likelihood, the human-capital research program will never die, but it will gradually fade away to be swallowed up by the new theory of signaling, the theory of how teachers and students, employers and employees, and indeed all buyers and sellers select each other when their attributes matter but when information about these attributes is subject to uncertainty. In time, the screening hypothesis will be seen to have marked a turning point in the "human investment revolution in economic thought," a turning point to a richer, still more comprehensive view of the sequential lifecycle choices of individuals.

---

[26] The emphasis on individual choice is the *differentia specifica* of the human-capital research program. It has been argued that education improves allocative efficiency in production and in consumption; it accelerates technical progress; it raises the saving rate; it reduces the birth rate; and it affects the level as well as the nature of crime: *e.g.*, see Juster [50, 1975, chs. 9–14]. But unless these effects motivate individuals to demand education, they have nothing whatever to do with the human-capital research program.

REFERENCES

1. ADKINS, DOUGLAS L. "The American Educated Labor Force: An Empirical Look at Theories of its Formation and Composition," in *Higher education in the labor market*. Edited by MARGARET S. GORDON. New York: McGraw-Hill, 1974, pp. 111–46.

2. ARROW, KENNETH J. "Higher Education as a Filter," *J. Publ. Econ.*, July 1973, *2*(3), pp. 193–216.

3. BECKER, GARY S. *Human capital.* Second edition. New York: Columbia University Press, [1964] 1975.

4. BEN-PORATH, YORAM. "The Production of Human Capital and the Life Cycle of Earnings," *J. Polit. Econ.*, Part I, August 1967, *75*(4), pp. 352–65.

5. _____. "The Production of Human Capital Over Time," in *Education, income, and human capital.* Edited by W. LEE HANSEN. New York: National Bureau of Economic Research; distributed by Columbia University Press, 1970, pp. 129–47.

6. BENSON, CHARLES S. *The economics of public education.* Boston: Houghton Mifflin, 1961.

7. BLAU, PETER M. AND DUNCAN, OTIS DUDLEY, *The American occupational structure.* New York and London: Wiley, 1967.

8. BLAUG, MARK. *An introduction to the economics of education.* Baltimore and Middlesex, England: Penguin Books, 1972.

9. _____. "The Correlation Between Education and Earnings: What Does it Signify?" *Higher Education*, Feb. 1972, *1*(1), pp. 53–76.

10. _____. "The Economics of Education in English Classical Political Economy: A Re-Examination," in *Essays on Adam Smith.* Edited by ANDREW S. SKINNER AND THOMAS WIL-

SON. London: Oxford University Press, 1976.

11. ———. *The economics of education: An annotated bibliography.* Third edition. Oxford: Pergamon Press, 1976.

12. ———. "Kuhn versus Lakatos, or Paradigms versus Research Programmes in the History of Economics," *Hist. Polit. Econ.,* Jan. 1976, *8*(1), pp. 399–433.

13. BOWLES, SAMUEL. "Schooling and Inequality From Generation to Generation," in *Investment in education: The equity-efficiency quandary.* Edited by THEODORE W. SCHULTZ. Chicago: Chicago University Press, 1972.

14. ———. "Understanding Unequal Economic Opportunity," *Amer. Econ. Rev.,* May 1973, *63*(2), pp. 346–56.

15. ——— AND GINTIS, HERBERT. "The Problem with Human Capital Theory—A Marxian Critique," *Amer. Econ. Rev.,* May 1975, *65*(2), pp. 74–82.

16. BOWMAN, MARY JEAN. "Learning and Earning in the Postschool Years," in *Review of research in education.* Edited by FRANK N. KERLINGER, JOHN B. CARROLL. Itasca, Illinois: Peacock, 1974, pp. 202–44.

17. CAMPBELL, JOHN M., JR. AND CURTIS, THOMAS D. "Graduate Education and Private Rates of Return: A Review of Theory and Empiricism," *Econ. Inquiry,* March 1975, *13*(1), pp. 99–118.

18. CAMPBELL, ROBERT AND SIEGEL, BARRY N. "The Demand for Higher Education in the United States, 1919–1964," *Amer. Econ. Rev.,* June 1967, *57*(3), pp. 482–94.

19. CARNEGIE COMMISSION ON HIGHER EDUCATION. *Higher education: Who pays? Who benefits? Who should pay? A report and recommendations.* New York: McGraw-Hill, 1973.

20. CARNOY, MARTIN AND MARENBACH, DIETER. "The Return to Schooling in the United States, 1939–69," *J. Human Res.,* Summer 1975, *10*(3), pp. 312–31.

21. CHISWICK, BARRY R. "Schooling, Screening, and Income," in *Does college matter?* Edited by LEWIS C. SOLMON AND PAUL J. TAUBMAN. New York: Academic Press, 1973, pp. 151–58.

22. ———. *Income inequality: Regional analysis within a human capital framework.* New York: National Bureau of Economic Research; distributed by Columbia University Press, 1974.

23. CHRISTENSEN, SANDRA; MELDER, JOHN AND WEISBROD, BURTON A. "Factors Affecting College Attendance," *J. Human Res.,* Spring 1975, *10*(2), pp. 174–88.

24. CONLISK, JOHN. "A Bit of Evidence on the Income-Education-Ability Interrelation," *J. Human Res.,* Summer 1971, *6*(3), pp. 358–62.

25. COOPER, MICHAEL H. AND CULYER, ANTHONY H. *Health economics.* Penguin Modern Economics Readings. London: Penguin Books, 1973.

26. DENISON, EDWARD F. *Accounting for U.S. growth, 1929–1969.* Washington: The Brookings Institution, 1974.

27. DRESCH, STEPHEN P. "Demography, Technology, and Higher Education: Toward a Formal Model of Educational Adaptation," *J. Polit. Econ.,* June 1975, *83*(3), pp. 535–69.

28. DUNCAN, OTIS DUDLEY; FEATHERMAN, DAVID L. AND DUNCAN, BEVERLY. *Socioeconomic background and achievement.* New York: Seminar Press, 1972.

29. ECKAUS, RICHARD S. "Estimation of

the Returns to Education with Hourly Standardized Incomes," *Quart. J. Econ.*, Feb. 1973, *87*(1), pp. 121–31.

30. ———; SAFTY, AHMAD EL AND NORMAN, VICTOR D. "An Appraisal of the Calculations of Rates of Return to Higher Education," in *Higher education and the labor market.* Edited by M. S. GORDON. New York: McGraw-Hill, 1974, pp. 333–72.

31. FÄGERLIND, INGMAR. *Formal education and adult earnings.* Stockholm: Almqvist & Wicksell International, 1975.

32. FELDMAN, PAUL AND HOENACK, STEPHEN A. "Private Demand for Higher Education in the United States," in *The economics and financing of higher education in the United States.* U.S. Joint Economic Committee, 91st Congress, 1st session. Washington: U.S.G.P.O., 1969, pp. 375–95.

33. FOGEL, WALTER AND MITCHELL, DANIEL J. B. "Higher Education Decision Making and the Labor Market," in *Higher education and the labor market.* Edited by M. S. GORDON. New York: McGraw-Hill, 1974, pp. 453–502.

34. FREEMAN, RICHARD B. *The market for college-trained manpower.* Cambridge: Harvard University Press, 1971.

35. ———. "Overinvestment in College Training," *J. Human Res.*, Summer 1975, *10*(3), pp. 287–311.

36. FREIDEN, ALAN N. AND STAAF, ROBERT J. "Scholastic Choice: An Economic Model of Student Behavior," *J. Human Res.*, Summer 1973, *8*(3), pp. 396–404.

37. FRIEDMAN, MILTON AND KUZNETS, SIMON. *Income from independent professional practice.* New York: National Bureau of Economic Research, 1945.

38. GALPER, HARVEY AND DUNN, ROBERT M., JR. "A Short-Run Demand Function for Higher Education in the United States," *J. Polit. Econ.*, Sept./Oct. 1969, *77*(5), pp. 765–77.

39. GREENWOOD, MICHAEL J. "Research on Internal Migration in the United States: A Survey," *J. Econ. Lit.*, June 1975, *13*(2), pp. 397–433.

40. GRILICHES, ZVI. "Notes on the Role of Education in Production Functions and Growth Accounting," in *Education, income, and human capital.* Edited by W. LEE HANSEN. New York: National Bureau of Economic Research; distributed by Columbia University Press, 1970, pp. 71–115.

41. ——— AND MASON, WILLIAM M. "Education, Income and Ability," in *Investment in education: The equity-efficiency quandary.* Edited by T. W. SCHULTZ. Chicago: Chicago University Press, 1972, pp. 74–103.

42. HANDA, MICHAEL L. AND SKOLNIK, MICHAEL L. "Empirical Analysis of the Demand for Education in Canada," in *Canadian higher education in the seventies.* Edited by SYLVIA OSTREY. Ottawa: Economic Council of Canada, 1972, pp. 5–44.

43. ——— AND SKOLNIK, MICHAEL L. "Unemployment, Expected Returns, and the Demand for University Education in Ontario: Some Empirical Results," *Higher Education*, Feb. 1975, *4*(1), pp. 27–44.

44. HAUSE, JOHN C. "Earnings Profile: Ability and Schooling," in *Investment in education: The equity-efficiency quandary.* Edited by T. W. SCHULTZ. Chicago: Chicago University Press, 1972, pp. 108–38.

45. ———. "The Risk Element in Occupational and Educational Choices: Comment," *J. Polit. Econ.*, July/August 1974, *82*(4), pp. 803–08.

46. ———. "Ability and Schooling as Determinants of Lifetime Earnings,

or If You're So Smart, Why Aren't You Rich?" in *Education, income and human behavior.* Edited by F. THOMAS JUSTER. New York: McGraw-Hill, 1975, pp. 123–49.

47. INTERNATIONAL LABOUR OFFICE. *Sharing in development: A programme of employment, equity, and growth for the Philippines.* Geneva: ILO, 1974.

48. JENCKS, CHRISTOPHER, ET AL. *Inequality: A reassessment of the effect of family and schooling in America.* New York: Basic Books, 1972.

49. JOHNSON, THOMAS AND HEBEIN, FREDERICK J. "Investments in Human Capital and Growth in Personal Income 1956–1966," *Amer. Econ. Rev.,* Sept. 1974, *64*(4), pp. 604–15.

50. JUSTER, F. THOMAS. "Introduction and Summary," in *Education, income and human behavior.* Edited by F. T. JUSTER. New York: McGraw-Hill, 1975, pp. 1–43.

51. KEELY, MICHAEL C. "A Comment on Leibenstein's 'An Interpretation of the Economic Theory of Fertility'," *J. Econ. Lit.,* June 1975, *13*(2), 461–68.

52. KIKER, BERNARD F. *Human capital: In retrospect.* Columbia: University of South Carolina, Bureau of Business and Economic Research, 1968.

53. KLARMAN, HERBERT E. *The economics of health.* New York: Columbia University Press, 1965.

54. KLINOV-MALUL, RUTH. "Enrolments in Higher Education as Related to Earnings," *Brit. J. Ind. Relat.,* March 1971, *9*(1), pp. 82–91.

55. KURATANI, MASATOSHI. "A Theory of Training, Earnings, and Employment: An Application to Japan," unpublished Ph.D. thesis, Columbia University, 1973.

56. LAYARD, RICHARD AND PSACHAROPOULOS, GEORGE. "The Screening Hypothesis and the Returns to

Education," *J. Polit. Econ.,* Sept./ Oct. 1974, *82*(5), pp. 985–98.

57. LEIBENSTEIN, HARVEY. "An Interpretation of the Economic Theory of Fertility: Promising Path or Blind Alley?" *J. Econ. Lit.,* June 1974, *12*(2), pp. 457–79.

58. LINDSAY, COTTON M. "Real Returns to Medical Education," *J. Human Res.,* Summer 1973, *8*(3), pp. 331–48.

59. MARIN, ALAN AND PSACHAROPOULOS, GEORGE. "Schooling and Income Distribution," *Rev. Econ. Statist.,* forthcoming 1976.

60. MAYHEW, ANNE. "Education, Occupation and Earnings," *Ind. Lab. Relat. Rev.,* Jan. 1971, *24*(2), pp. 216–25.

61. MCCLELLAND, DAVID C. *The achieving society.* Princeton, N. J.: Van Nostrand, 1961.

62. MCKENZIE, RICHARD B. AND STAAF, ROBERT J. *An economic theory of learning.* Blacksburg, Virginia: University Publications, 1974.

63. MILLER, LEONARD S. *Demand for higher education in the United States.* Stony Brook, New York: Economic Research Bureau, State University of New York, 1971.

64. MINCER, JACOB. "Investment in Human Capital and Personal Income Distribution," *J. Polit. Econ.,* August 1958, *66*, pp. 281–302.

65. ———. "On-the-Job Training: Costs, Returns, and Some Implications," *J. Polit. Econ.,* Supplement, Part 2, Oct. 1962, *70*(5), pp. 50–79.

66. ———. "The Distribution of Labor Incomes: A Survey with Special Reference to the Human Capital Approach," *J. Econ. Lit.,* March 1970, *8* (1), pp. 1–26.

67. ———. *Schooling, experience and earnings.* New York: National Bureau of Economic Research; distributed by Columbia University Press, 1974.

854   *Journal of Economic Literature*

68. MORGENSTERN, ROBERT D. "Direct and Indirect Effects on Earnings of Schooling and Socio-Economic Background," *Rev. Econ. Statist.*, May 1973, *55*(2), pp. 225–33.

69. NELSON, RICHARD R. "Recent Exercises in Growth Accounting: New Understanding or Dead End?" *Amer. Econ. Rev.*, June 1973, *63*(3), pp. 462–68.

70. O'CONNELL, JOHN F. "The Labor Market for Engineers: An Alternative Methodology," *J. Human Res.*, Winter 1972, *7*(1), pp. 71–86.

71. OULTON, NICHOLAS. "The Distribution of Education and the Distribution of Income," *Economica*, Nov. 1974, *41*(164), pp. 387–402.

72. PARSONS, DONALD O. "Specific Human Capital: An Application to Quit Rates and Layoff Rates," *J. Polit. Econ.*, Nov./Dec. 1972, *80*(6), pp. 1120–43.

73. PERLMAN, NAOMI W. AND PERLMAN, MARK. "The Changing Modes of Data in Recent Research," in *The organization and retrieval of economic information.* International Economics Association Symposium. Edited by MARK PERLMAN. New York: Macmillan, 1976.

74. PHELPS, EDMUND S. "The Statistical Theory of Racism and Sexism," *Amer. Econ. Rev.*, Sept. 1972, *62*(4), pp. 659–61.

75. _____, ET AL. *Microeconomic foundations of employment and inflation theory.* New York: Norton; London: Macmillan, 1970.

76. POPPER, [SIR] KARL. *Objective knowledge: An evolutionary approach.* Oxford: Clarendon Press, 1972.

77. PSACHAROPOULOS, GEORGE. "A Note on the Demand for Enrollment in Higher Education," *De Economist*, 1973, *121*(5), pp. 521–25.

78. _____. "College Quality as a Screening Device?" *J. Human Res.*, Fall 1974, *9*(4), pp. 556–58.

79. _____. *Earnings and education in OECD countries.* Paris: OECD, 1975.

80. _____ AND HINCHLIFFE, KEITH. *Returns to education: An international comparison.* Amsterdam: Elsevier Scientific; San Francisco: Jossey-Bass, 1973.

81. _____ AND LAYARD, RICHARD. "Human Capital and Earnings: British Evidence and a Critique," London School of Economics, Department of Economics, mimeo., 1976.

82. RAWLINS, V. LANE AND ULMAN, LLOYD. "The Utilization of College-Trained Manpower in the United States," in *Higher education and the labor market.* Edited by M. S. Gordon. New York: McGraw-Hill, 1974, pp. 195–236.

83. RAYMOND, RICHARD and SESNOWITZ, MICHAEL. "The Returns to Investments in Higher Education: Some New Evidence," *J. Human Res.*, Spring 1975, *10*(2), pp. 139–54.

84. ROSEN, SHERWIN. "Learning and Experience in the Labor Market," *J. Human Res.*, Summer 1972, *7*(3), pp. 326–42.

85. _____. "Learning by Experience as Joint Production," *Quart. J. Econ.*, August 1972, *86*(3), pp. 366–82.

86. ROTHSCHILD, MICHAEL. "Models of Market Organization With Imperfect Information: A Survey," *J. Polit. Econ.*, Nov./Dec. 1973, *81*(6), pp. 1283–1308.

87. SCHULTZ, THEODORE W. *The economic value of education.* New York: Columbia University Press, 1963.

88. SCOVILLE, JAMES. *Manpower and occupational analysis: Concepts and measurements.* Lexington, Mass.: Heath, Lexington Books, 1972.

89. SLOAN, FRANK A. "The Demand for Higher Education: The Case of Medical School Applicants," *J. Hu-*

man Res., Fall 1971, *6*(4), pp. 466–89.

90. SOLOMON, LEWIS C. "Schooling and Subsequent Success," in *Does college matter?* Edited by LEWIS C. SOLMON AND PAUL J. TAUBMAN. New York: Academic Press, 1973, pp. 13–34.

91. SPENCE, MICHAEL. "Job Market Signaling," *Quart. J. Econ.*, August 1973, *87*(3), pp. 355–74.

92. ———. *Market signaling*. Cambridge: Harvard University Press, 1974.

93. STIGLER, GEORGE J. "Information in the Labor Market," *J. Polit. Econ.*, Part 2, Oct. 1962, *70*(5), pp. 94–105.

94. STIGLITZ, JOSEPH E. "The Theory of 'Screening', Education and the Distribution of Income," *Amer. Econ. Rev.*, June 1975, *65*(3), pp. 283–300.

95. TAUBMAN, PAUL J. AND WALES, TERENCE. *Higher education and earnings: College as an investment and a screening device*. New York: McGraw-Hill, 1974.

96. THUROW, LESTER C. "Measuring the Economic Benefits of Education," in *Higher education and the labor market*. Edited by M. S. GORDON. New York: McGraw-Hill, 1974, pp. 373–418.

97. VAIZEY, JOHN E. *The economics of education*. New York: Free Press of Glencoe; London: Faber & Faber, 1962.

98. WALSH, JOHN RAYMOND. "Capital Concept Applied to Man," *Quart. J. Econ.*, Feb. 1935, *49*, pp. 255–85.

99. WACHTEL, PAUL. "The Returns to Investment in Higher Education: Another View," in *Education, income and human behavior*. Edited by F. THOMAS JUSTER. New York: McGraw-Hill, 1975, pp. 151–70.

100. WEISS, YORAM. "The Risk Element in Occupational and Educational Choices," *J. Polit. Econ.*, Nov./Dec. 1972, *80*(6), pp. 1203–13.

101. WELCH, FINIS. "Human Capital Theory: Education, Discrimination, and Life Cycles," *Amer. Econ. Rev.*, May 1975, *75*(2), pp. 63–73.

102. WHIPPLE, DAVID. "A Generalized Theory of Job Search," *J. Polit. Econ.*, Sept./Oct. 1973, *81*(5), pp. 1170–88.

103. WILES, PETER. "The Correlation Between Education and Earnings: The External-Test-Not-Content-Hypothesis (ETNC)," *Higher Education*, Feb. 1974, *3*(1), pp. 43–58.

[2]

THE RETURN TO SCHOOLING
IN THE UNITED STATES, 1939–69*

MARTIN CARNOY
DIETER MARENBACH

ABSTRACT

Rates of return to investment in schooling unadjusted for nonschooling factors are estimated in four Census years by sex and race. In general, social rates to whites' high school investment declined in the 30-year period, while the payoff to college remained stable and the payoff for graduate training rose sharply in 1959–69. This pattern of rate change apparently is not the result of differences in overall unemployment in Census years. Rather, in some sense the aggregate demand for the college-educated probably increased more rapidly than for those with secondary and primary schooling. Differences in ability and social class between primary and high school graduates also may have declined.

Empirical analyses of the economic value of investment in schooling have been undertaken since the first decade of this century,[1] and were systematized into human capital theory in the 1950s and 1960s [1, 8, 13, 16]. Despite some important contributions to the understanding of economic behavior, however, the theory had little to say about secular movements in the return to schooling. In a static equilibrium, the notion of diminishing returns argues for decreasing rates of return to progressively higher schooling levels.[2] Thus, if investment in

---

Carnoy is Associate Professor in the Stanford International Development Committee (SIDEC), School of Education, Stanford University. Marenbach was formerly with the Syntex Corporation.

* The authors would like to thank the Spencer Foundation for the grant which made this research possible. We would also like to thank Richard Meredith and Luis Reyes Valencia for their invaluable assistance in preparing the 1969 data used in the paper. Henry Levin made helpful comments on an earlier draft. [Manuscript received November 1973; accepted January 1975.]

1 For examples of early work, see Smith [17] and Walsh [22].

2 More recently Psacharopoulos [14, p. 8] has used this argument in comparing average rates of return to schooling in different countries: "Using an aggregate production function with human capital as a separate input, we see that the reason for the declining rates is simply a reflection of the law of diminishing returns to investment in this form of capital. That is, the more one country invests in education, keeping all other factors of production constant, the less will be the payoff to that investment at the margin."

education increased more rapidly than investment in physical capital, the average rate of return to schooling would decline; moreover, the rate of return to primary schooling should be higher than to secondary schooling which, in turn, should be higher than the payoff to university schooling. However, it was recognized that, empirically, the rates of return would depend largely on the demand for educated labor (which depended, in turn, on changes in technology and the demand for final goods) and on changes in the relative number of educated persons.[3]

Welch [23] observed that the private rates of return to high school and college did not fall between 1939 and 1959, and he identified several important sources of growth in demand for education which could keep rates stable or increasing in the face of a rapidly increasing supply of graduates: (1) changes in the composition of output such that the most rapidly expanding industries are the most skill intensive; (2) increase in productivity of more skilled relative to less skilled labor because of a possible complementarity between physical capital and skills; (3) nonneutrality of technology—technological change favors higher skilled labor productivity; and (4) an increase in the quality of schooling (as represented by resource cost) that may raise returns relative to cost.

While Welch's analysis is useful, much more attention is needed on the supply side. Furthermore, we would suggest that changes in the supply of schooled people are only in part a function of the payoff to the investment in schooling; there are, in addition, public sector responses to political pressure for more education.[4]

In this paper, we estimate rates of return for the United States for Census years during the period 1939–69. In each of the four Census years, we estimate rates to investment in schooling for four groups of individuals: white males, nonwhite males, white females, and nonwhite females. Although in 1969 the Census estimates incomes for Negroes rather than for nonwhites, the nonwhite category of previous Census years was essentially a Negro category, since both male and female "nonwhite" groups average more than 90 percent black.[5]

---

3 Becker [1, pp. 129–31]. In addition, Becker mentions the decline in mortality rates as increasing the rate of return to schooling.

4 For models which incorporate political forces on the supply side, see Bowles [3] and Carnoy [4]. For historical evidence on the political struggles over the nature and amount of schooling in the U.S., see Katz [11] and Spring [18].

5 The use of "nonwhite" instead of Negro incomes in years other than 1969 does create some problems at higher levels of schooling. The percentage of nonwhites who were Negroes in 1959, for example, ranged from 84 to 96 for all eight schooling categories among women and for the six lowest school categories for men. In the categories 13–14 and 16+ years of schooling completed, however, the male percentage Negro was 83 and 72, respectively [19]. However, 1969 estimated incomes for blacks are represented by actual incomes of blacks. Hence, 1959 rates of return to college education for blacks (and probably 1939 and 1949 rates as well) may be overestimated relative to 1969 rates.

After a short discussion of the way in which our cross-sectional estimates are made, we analyze the time trends in the cross-sectional rates to primary school, high school, and college. We follow this with estimates of rates from longitudinal "cohort" data also taken from the Censuses. The paper ends with some speculation on the movement of rates of return in the future.

ESTIMATES OF THE RATES OF RETURN

We estimate rates of return from income data taken directly from the four decennial United States Censuses for 1940, 1950, 1960, and 1970. The rates for 1949, 1959, and 1969 are based on income means estimated from the 1950, 1960, and 1970 Censuses. The means by sex, race, years of schooling, and age were calculated identically for each of the three Census years, using comparable data on incomes for all those who reported income in the Census year and who were also in the labor force.[6] The 1939 rates are estimated from earnings data for native-born Americans in the labor force. We also estimate rates of return based on both income *and* earnings data from the 1970 Census, to focus on possible differences in results stemming from different data bases. The methods of estimation are discussed in an appendix to the paper.

The rates of return are estimated using the standard discount formula:

$$0 = \Sigma_{i=1}^{n} \frac{Y_i - C_i}{(1 + r)^i}$$

where Y_i = the difference in average earnings or income in period i between those with one level of schooling and those with the next highest level; C_i = the cost of schooling in period i, where private cost equals income forgone (taken at 75 percent of the annual income of those with the lower level of schooling) and social cost equals income forgone plus average institutional cost; r = the marginal internal rate of return to schooling; and n = the number of periods from the beginning of the level of school being analyzed to the end of working life.

To allow comparisons with previous studies, we will use cross-sectional data to represent income streams over time. In other words, the average income of, say, white males 40 years old in 1959 is taken as the single best estimate of the real income 20 years hence of a white male 20 years old in 1959.

Some studies have attempted to adjust cross-section age-income profiles for some average rate of growth of the economy. A uniform rate of growth applied to all incomes would tend to increase the rate of return to schooling, since *absolute* differences in income would increase with age. The problem with

---

6 Besides those difficulties in getting comparable results discussed in the appendix, it is hard to get comparable relations between income and education because of changes in Census undercount, changes in errors in reporting education, changes in the degree to which earnings are underreported, and changes in Census questions.

applying a uniform rate of economic growth to all incomes is that we would not expect the incomes at all levels of schooling to grow uniformly as the economy grows. Since we have data for four Census years, we are able to make direct estimates of longitudinal age-income profiles for those who, for example, were 20 years old in 1939 and those who were 20 years old in 1949. For the most part, the relative rates of return calculated from the longitudinal profiles are similar to those estimated from 1939 and 1949 cross-section data.

We estimate both private rates of return to schooling (costs = income forgone; benefits = income differences between those with different amounts of schooling) and a limited social rate (costs = private costs plus institutional costs; benefits = private benefits). We make no attempt to measure other, broader social costs and returns of going to school.[7]

Generally, previous studies have adjusted private rates of return for taxes and social rates for mortality.[8] Along with others who have made the mortality adjustment to U.S. income streams, we find that such an adjustment has a negligible effect on rates of return. The effect of adjusting private rates for taxes is more controversial. Although Becker [1] and Hansen [8] adjust incomes used in the estimate of private rates for tax rates, it is unclear whether they also adjust income forgone. As Hines and others [10] point out, although federal income taxes are highly progressive, other federal taxes as well as state and local taxes are regressive, resulting in quite constant incidence of total taxation over income groups. We report the effect of adjusting private rates of return for *federal income taxes only,* applying the tax schedule to both benefits and income forgone. The effect is generally small, even though such an adjustment *overcorrects* for the effect of total taxation, since federal income taxes are much more progressive than other taxes.[9]

It is important to note that we assume that private costs are zero at the primary level (in other words, that children younger than age 14 do not work), and that private costs other than income forgone equal zero at the high school and college levels. Private net tuition payments probably averaged about $140 in

---

7 For a summary discussion of schooling's social value, see Blaug [2].

8 Private rates are usually not adjusted for mortality because people do not take into account the probability of their dying at a certain age when calculating the payoff to an investment. Individuals assume that they will complete their working lives. On the other hand, when the society looks at the payoff to a public good, it must include mortality rates of those in whom the investment is being made. Individuals do take account of taxes on income when estimating net returns, but the society should not net out taxes, since taxes paid by an individual are transferred back to that individual in the form of public services or are transferred to others in the society.

9 Eckaus [5, p. 4] also argues, "[T]rial calculations indicated a reasonably close correspondence of the results using unadjusted reported income and income adjusted only for expected mortality, unemployment and taxes." In addition, he shows that, at least for white males in 1959, the relative rates of return at all levels of schooling are almost unaffected by a rate of growth adjustment (Table 1, p. 5).

TABLE 1

UNADJUSTED MARGINAL PRIVATE RATES OF RETURN TO INVESTMENT
IN HIGH SCHOOL AND COLLEGE, BASED ON INCOMES
OF THOSE IN LABOR FORCE (UNEMPLOYED INCLUDED),
BY SEX AND RACE, 1939–69, U.S. (PERCENT)

				1969	
	1939	1949	1959	Income	Earnings
White Males					
High school 12/8	49.1 (20.3)[a]	22.7	14.6	18.8	14.0
College 16/12	21.4 (16.3)[a]	13.2[b]	17.6	15.4	16.2
Black Males					
High school 12/8	27.1 (30.0)[a]	14.7	13.1	16.1	19.9
College 16/12	14.6 (5.9)[a]	7.7	13.9	14.3	13.6
White Females					
High school 12/8	25.2 (13.7)[a]	20.0	14.8	19.2	15.1
College 16/12	18.4 (14.8)[a]	11.0	12.2	17.0	14.9
Black Females					
High school 12/8	10.0 (11.6)[a]	15.2	12.9	11.6 (13.8)[c]	19.1
College 16/12	30.0 (21.2)[a]	17.0	19.1	19.6	19.4

Source: See text. Income and earnings taken from U.S. Censuses for 1940, 1950, 1960, and 1970.
Note: We also corrected the male private rates for federal income taxes. We assumed that incomes were taxed at the single taxpayer rate (one exemption, standard deduction) up to age 22; the married taxpayer rate from age 23 to 26 (two deductions, standard exemption); three exemptions, standard deduction from age 27 to 30; four exemptions from age 31 to

TABLE 1 (*Continued*)

50; and two exemptions from age 50 to 60. Although this set of assumptions probably overestimates the tax adjustment, we found significant reductions in the private rates only in the case of college over high school. Even here, the adjusted rates were reduced by from 0 to 0.8 percentage point for the groups. (Details are available from the authors.)

We did not adjust rates for women because of the difficulty of determining the tax rates paid on women's incomes. Nevertheless, the effect of taxes on women's rates should not be very large, partly because their incomes are lower than men's and partly because of the same reason that the effect is small for males: The taxes applied to income forgone lowers the cost of going to school and offsets much of the decrease in income differentials due to federal income taxes.

[a]Marenbach rates for the sample with zero incomes omitted.

[b]If it is assumed that the 16+ category in the 1949 Census represents 16.5 years completed rather than 16 years, the rate of return to college education for white males is 12.8 percent. Adjusted for taxes, the rate is 12.4 percent.

[c]Rate adjusted for possible overestimate of income forgone.

1939, $150 in 1949, $350 in 1959, and $400–$500 in 1969 out of a total college current direct social cost of $500, $800, $1800, and $2500 per student, respectively.[10] Leaving out private tuition would therefore bias upward our private rate of return estimates to college education by approximately one to two percentage points. Furthermore, unlike Hines and others' estimates of 1959 rates [10], we do not assign different institutional costs of primary and secondary schooling to different races; undoubtedly this makes our rates underestimates of the "true" rates to black schooling and overestimates of the "true" rates to white schooling at all schooling levels.

We also assume that earnings forgone for those 14 or older equal 75 percent of a full year's salary of a person of the same race, sex, and age with the level of schooling completed below that being taken by the observed individual. The 75 percent figure assumes that even someone full-time in school can find work at average salary for 25 percent of the year (the summer months plus vacations). Some authors, such as Hines and others [10], assume that the income forgone by students equals a full year's income of those in the labor force, with money earned by students working part time used to cover miscellaneous expenses such as school supplies, tuition, etc. However, at the high school level, these expenses are minimal, so that income earned would offset income forgone. At the college level Hines and others' figures on average earnings of college students indicate that such earnings for males are substantially larger than costs of tuition and

10 We add capital costs to graduate schooling but not to undergraduate schooling. This makes the latter equal to $2482 and the former, $3058. However, college rates of return are not very sensitive to the inclusion or exclusion of capital costs. The direct social costs of schooling were derived from [15, Tables 3 and 6] for 1939 and 1949, and from [21] for 1959 and 1969. Details are available from the authors.

TABLE 2

UNADJUSTED MARGINAL SOCIAL RATES OF RETURN TO INVESTMENT
IN PRIMARY SCHOOL, HIGH SCHOOL, AND COLLEGE,
BASED ON INCOMES OF THOSE IN THE LABOR FORCE
(UNEMPLOYED INCLUDED), BY SEX AND RACE, 1939–69, U.S.
(PERCENT)

	1939	1949	1959	1969 Income	1969 Earnings
White Males					
Primary 8/0	11.6 (12.6)[a]	12.7	13.2	7.2	–
High school 12/8	18.2 (11.3)[a]	14.2	10.1	10.7	9.0
College 16/12	10.7 (9.0)[a]	10.6[b]	11.3	10.9	11.0
Black Males					
Primary 8/0	10.5 (14.7)[a]	13.9	10.6	6.3	–
High school 12/8	10.4 (14.2)[a]	9.1	8.3	9.0	11.2
College 16/12	6.5 (2.7)[a]	4.6	7.2	8.0	7.7
White Females					
Primary 8/0	4.7 (10.9)[a]	7.8	3.9	neg.	–
High school 12/8	12.7 (9.6)[a]	11.5	9.3	8.3	7.4
College 16/12	9.8 (8.6)[a]	7.0	6.6	9.4	7.9
Black Females					
Primary 8/0	6.8 (8.1)[a]	9.8	4.8	4.2	–
High school 12/8	4.8 (6.3)[a]	8.7	8.2	6.9 (7.6)[c]	10.3
College 16/12	11.1 (10.0)[a]	9.2	8.8	10.5	10.6

TABLE 2 (*continued*)

Source: See Table 1.
[a]Marenbach rates for the sample with zero incomes omitted.
[b]If it is assumed that the 16+ category in the 1949 Census represents 16.5 years completed rather than 16 years, the rate of return to college education for white males is 9.9 percent.
[c]Rate adjusted for possible overestimate of income forgone.

books. This all implies that income forgone is *less than* a full year's income of someone in the labor force and lends at least some support to our assumption of 75 percent.[11]

THE TRENDS IN THE RATES OVER TIME

Tables 1 and 2 present unadjusted private and social rates of return to primary, secondary, and university schooling over three decades. The 1939, 1949, and 1959 rates are based largely on Marenbach's earlier work.[12]

Although there are a number of studies which have calculated rates of return to schooling for the years covered, we will focus our comparison on three: Becker [1], Hansen [8], and Hines and others [10]. Becker's estimates for 1939—a 14.5 percent private rate of return to white male college education and a 16 percent rate to high school—were based on M. Zeman's analysis, derived from 1940 Census earnings data which covered earnings of native white and nonwhite males living in *urban* areas and who were employed [1, Table 1 and p. 128].

Our results, based on Marenbach's estimates, are for both urban and rural native-born persons and include zero incomes (unemployment). As shown in column (1) of Table 1, this different sample produces a 49 percent private rate of return to white male high school education and a 21 percent return to college investment. Marenbach also estimated rates of return *omitting* zero incomes. These are shown in parentheses in column (1) and are much closer to the Becker

---

11 In order to make a comparison of our assumption vs. full-year income forgone, we estimated a number of college rates for males using the full-year assumption. Private rates obviously are more sensitive to the change in assumption than are social rates, which include institutional costs. The full-year assumption tended to reduce private rates almost two percentage points at the college level, and reduced social rates about 0.5–1.0 percentage point. Detailed calculations are available from the authors.

12 Marenbach [12]. The principal change is that Marenbach's estimates omitted the highest income category in 1949 and 1959, an omission which was intended to focus on earnings. However, we have concluded that *including* the highest income category gives a better estimate of mean earnings than excluding it did. This is borne out by comparing the 1969 estimated rates using earnings and incomes (which include the highest income category). The return to college (16/12) would be most affected by any bias caused by income-earnings differentials; yet, the two sets of rates to college investment are very similar.

rates—20.3 percent for high school and 16.3 percent to college. For black males the corresponding rates for the sample without zero incomes are 30.1 and 5.9 percent. Marenbach also assumed that the 16+ education category in the Census represents four years of college; this assumption probably biases his estimate slightly upward.[13] However, both sets of rates are probably biased downward, at least for whites, since they are based on earnings of the native-born.[14]

Becker estimates private rates to white males in 1949 of 20 percent for high school graduates and 13+ percent to college over high school. Our rates to both high school and college are very close to Becker's estimates. Unlike in 1939, including or not including zero incomes of the unemployed has little effect on the rates, as Marenbach shows. The high school rate, for example, falls from 22.7 to 20.5 percent.

Hansen estimated rates from 1949 Census income data, but for *all* males together rather than for white and black separately. His results show a 15.3 percent private rate to high school investment and an 11.6 percent rate to college over high school. Both of these rates are lower than either Becker's or our estimates, but they do fall in the ranges bracketed by the estimates for the two color groups separately, shown in Table 1. In addition, Hansen adjusted for taxes without applying taxes to income forgone. This would tend to lower his estimates relative to ours and to Becker's.

Comparisons with the Hines and others' results are more difficult since the data base used was not the aggregative means published in Census tabulations, but means derived from earnings data in a 1/1,000 sample from the 1960 Census of persons 14 years of age and older not enrolled in school. Zero earnings were included. The authors point out that the reliability of the elementary schooling profiles is weak for all race-sex groups because of the numerically small sample in the lower age bracket [10, p. 322].

The secondary (12/8) private rate for white males estimated by Hines and

---

13 The extra one-half year of costs lowers private rates about 0.5–0.8 percentage point. Becker also includes tuition fees (about $140 in 1939–40) paid in his private rate estimates for college. We did not, which would explain another percentage point difference in the two rates.

14 Native-born Americans probably earned more than foreign-born with the same amount of schooling. There also is probably a higher percentage of white foreign-born at lower than at higher levels of schooling, although this would be more likely to be true for older than for younger workers. (Younger workers in 1939, even if foreign-born, are likely to have received their schooling in the U.S. because they would have had to immigrate before restrictions to immigration in the early 1920s.) Assuming that these two assumptions are true, average incomes including foreign-born would be lower at all levels, but average incomes at lower levels of schooling would decline more because the percentage of foreign-born would be greater at those levels. Thus, differences in income would increase if the foreign-born were included, and income forgone would decrease. Both effects would increase the rate of return to schooling for white males based on the incomes of everyone in the labor force, compared to rates based on incomes of the native-born.

others is 19.5 percent, compared to our figure of 14.6 percent. For the same group, they show a 13.6 percent rate to college (16/12); our estimate is 17.6 percent. Their rates to high school for white females and black males and females are generally more than double our rates shown in Table 1, and their rates for college are usually considerably smaller, except for a larger rate for black females. We suggest that poor data at lower ages for these groups in the Hines and others sample may be responsible for the difference.

In addition, the higher secondary rates in the Hines and others estimate may result from an underestimate of earnings forgone. As Hanoch noted in an earlier work based on the same data, mean incomes of those under 18 years of age in the sample are approximate, since they are estimated from few observations.[15] The lower college rates may be explained by Hines's use of earnings rather than income and in part by their assumption of a full year's forgone income.

We have gone through all of these comparisons because possible biases in the rates are important to our understanding of the movements of the rates over time. In analyzing the trend from 1939 onward, our base year (1939) is not a "normal" one because of the high rate of unemployment at the end of the depression. For example, the social rates based on mean incomes (excluding zero incomes) for native white males in that year were 12.6 percent to primary school, 11.3 percent to high school, and 9.0 percent to college. Black males had rates of 14.7, 14.2, and 2.7 percent to the same investment. The rates to white females were 10.9, 9.6, and 8.6 percent, and to black females they were 8.1, 6.3, and 10.0 percent. Based on these results, the analysis here will assume that the rate of return to secondary school and college under "normal" unemployment conditions would have been below the measured rate of return for the labor force as a whole. (See below for a further discussion of the unemployment correction.)

Now let us discuss the social rates of return, shown in Table 2. We argue that the social rate of return to primary schooling has fallen between 1939 and 1969 for all groups. There was a rise in the primary rate for all groups between 1939 and 1949, but it appears that this rise, at least for whites, was due to the reduction in unemployment. For blacks, the rise may have gone beyond the unemployment adjustment. After 1949, the rates fell to all groups except white males in 1959. At the same time, of course, the private rates of return to primary schooling were and are extremely high because the forgone earnings are so low, approaching zero in recent years.

The decline in the social rates occurred in the face of a rapid decrease in the number of people in the labor force with only primary schooling.[16] The

---

15 [7, p. 323]. As Hanoch noted in an earlier work based on the same data, mean incomes of those under 18 years old in the sample are approximate, since they are estimated from few observations.

16 The number of males 25 years old or older in the labor force with 1–8 years of

unadjusted social rate of return to primary schooling is now below the rates to secondary and higher education.

The trend in secondary social rates is less clear, but it appears that the payoff to investment in secondary education fell for whites, particularly between 1949 and 1959, but stayed rather constant for blacks and possibly rose in the 1959–69 decade. Private rates of return to secondary education fell for all groups between 1949 and 1959 and rose between 1959 and 1969.

The social rates to white male college education appear to have stayed fairly constant in the 30-year period covered. The private rates have had wider fluctuation than the social rates, and they show a decline—matched to some extent by the social rates—between 1939 and 1949 and then a rise in the next decade. Both social and private rates may have declined slightly for white males in the 1959–69 period. The rates to black males' college education, on the other hand, have risen significantly since the thirties and forties, and the rates to females fell and then rose after 1959. There is a discrepancy between social and private rates for black females as to when the increase began.

Thus, we find a constant social payoff to investment in college education for white males between 1939 and 1969, while the payoff to primary and high school education fell. The social rate of return to college is now higher than to primary and to high school education. The social and private rates of return to investment in high school for black males appear to have risen in the last decade, after a long decline, so that they are about equal to the white male rates for the first time. The rates to black male college education also have risen, but are still substantially below the white rates. Similar comparisons can be made for females.

THE ADJUSTMENT OF THE RATES OF RETURN FOR OTHER FACTORS AND THE EFFECT ON THE RATES OVER TIME

The rates of return in Tables 1 and 2 are based on calculations which assume that the entire observed increase in income or earnings associated with different amounts of schooling is due to schooling itself. A number of studies have attempted to adjust the returns to schooling by accounting for "ability" differentials between those with different amounts of schooling.[17] In general, a

---

schooling declined from 15.9 million in 1950 to 9.1 million in 1970. The number of black males in the same schooling category declined from about 2.2 million to 1.4 million, and the number of females from 4.4 million to 3.8 million. The number of women with primary schooling increased between 1950 and 1960 to 5.0 million and then declined rapidly.

17 See Becker [1] for a summary of earlier work. Hines and others [10], using Morgan and David's study, reduce the rates by about 30–40 percent for secondary schooling and about 17 percent for college, for white males. More recent studies include work by Hansen, Weisbrod, and Scanlon [9] and Griliches and Mason [6].

person who graduates from college comes from a higher income family and has a higher IQ than a person with a lesser amount of schooling. Thus, part of the income differential associated with more schooling should be attributed to these nonschooling, income-generating differentials.[18]

Furthermore, Eckaus argues that a large percentage of income differentials between those with different levels of schooling is due to the greater number of hours worked by people with more schooling.[19] Thus, he says, people with less schooling consume the extra hours in leisure valued at their wage rates, and he concludes that the income differences between those with different amounts of schooling—if they include the extra hours worked by the more schooled workers—*overestimate* the returns to schooling.

On the other hand, it could be argued that access to high income jobs, even though they require more hours of work, is part of the payoff to schooling. Perhaps the less schooled would work more hours for more income if they could, in which case their leisure would have a lower value than Eckaus assumed. The income associated with more schooling would then be linked more closely to schooling investment itself.

A related issue is that the chances of *finding* work apparently are enhanced by taking more schooling. Income means estimated for the entire labor force are lower for those in lower schooling groups in part because there is a higher percentage of nonworkers with zero incomes among those with less schooling.

The relevance of these adjustments to our analysis is in the way they affect the rates of return over time. Our thesis is that the rates of return to high school and primary schooling fell relative to university schooling, especially for white males. Did the rates fall because of secular effects or because of a combination of cyclical effects? Changes in overall unemployment rates from Census year to Census year reflect such cyclical effects. We want to correct rates to schooling so

---

18 The question of *how much* of the income differentials should be attributed to schooling and to nonschooling variables, however, is very much in question. On the one hand, Morgan and David's results on nonschooling differences argue for a rather high adjustment of secondary rates; Hansen and others' regression estimates for low achievers with an average schooling of 9+ years also point to a large (50 percent) adjustment for differences in ability among those with some high school education. But Griliches and Mason argue that the maximum adjustment for social class/ability should be about 20 percent. Their sample covers those in high school and college (the average schooling in the sample is about 12 years), so the 20 percent adjustment may be an average of ability differentials among high school and college trained males.

19 For 1959 data (the same used by Hines and others), Eckaus shows that correcting for hours worked has its most important effects between those who graduate from high school and those who either take some high school and do not graduate or those who graduate from primary school only. This reduces the under-rated high school private rate from 22 percent (approximately the Hines rate, but higher than our estimate) to 4 percent. The private rate to primary schooling (8 years over 0–7 years) appears to rise with the adjustment for hours worked (from 14 to 32 percent). On the other hand, the rates to college and graduate school (similar to ours) are scarcely affected by the adjustment.

that they are based on some "average" or "normal" rate of unemployment in the economy. On the other hand, we contend that changes in the proportion of income differences due to factors such as "ability" and social class result from trends that are intimately connected with the function and expansion of schooling.

In different historical time periods, different levels of schooling serve different functions. When college graduation was relatively rare and associated with the well-to-do, one could argue that the ability differences between college graduates and those who only finished high school may not have been as great as they became when college attendance greatly expanded. On the other hand, since the high school level was an important academic differentiator between white collar and blue collar jobs in the 1940s and 1950s, we would expect that a large part of the income gain associated with going to high school was due to social class/ability differences. When high school graduation became almost universal, the screening function, and hence the large correction for social class/ability, shifted to college. Therefore we would expect that the ratio of adjusted to unadjusted incomes rose over time for high school compared to primary school graduates, and that the ratio of adjusted to unadjusted incomes fell for college compared to high school graduates.

Similarly, we would expect differences in hours worked between high school and elementary school graduates to disappear over time, and differences between college and high school graduates to fall, primarily because the kinds of jobs graduates of these different levels could get in 1939 and in 1969.

Does correcting for cyclical unemployment change our conclusions about the behavior of rates of return? The unemployment rate did change significantly between 1939 and 1969. It fell from 17 percent in 1939 to about 6 percent in 1949 and 1959 and down to 3 percent in 1969. It is useful to correct mean incomes for the probability of being unemployed during a period of "normal" unemployment. Since 1947, during peacetime years, this "normal" level was about 5–5.5 percent unemployment overall, and it differed among the sex, race, age, and schooling groups.

Correcting incomes in this way would leave the 1949 and 1959 rates of return essentially unchanged, would lower both high school and college rates to white males in 1939 (as we have shown by eliminating zero incomes from our estimates of 1939 means), and would tend to raise rates of return somewhat in 1969 because the unemployment rate was particularly low that year. Differential unemployment rates thus also account for much of the fall in the white male high school rates between 1939 and 1949, and correcting for differential unemployment may produce a rise in the rates between 1959 and 1969. However, adjusting for cyclical unemployment rate differences does not offset the secular fall in rates of return to investment in high school between 1939/49 and 1959/69. Neither is the pattern of white male college rates of return affected significantly by cyclical differences in unemployment.

Why did the fall in the social rates of return to white male high school investment occur? Why did college rates apparently remain at their 1939/49 level? We suggest two possible reasons:

1. There was a rapid increase in white male high school graduates during this period, from 6.8 million in the 25+ labor force in 1950 to 12.1 million in 1970, an 84 percent rise, while the total male labor force increased by only 28 percent. However, the rate of increase of male college graduates was even more rapid. Thus, the high school rates have fallen relative to college rates even though the number of white males with a college education rose relatively. If technological change were "neutral" and the composition of output remained the same, the college rate would have declined relative to the high school rate.

2. It is possible, however, that the social class/ability difference between high school and primary school graduates declined in these years, thereby lowering the unadjusted rates to a high school education. No direct evidence is available, but Becker points out:

> One might well believe that the differential ability of high school graduates rose over time because now only the physically handicapped, dullards, or least-motivated persons fail to go to high school.... [N]ote that Morgan and David actually find a larger ratio of adjusted to unadjusted earnings differentials between high school and elementary school graduates at younger than at older ages. The ratios between college and high school graduates, on the other hand, are smaller at younger ages. [1, p. 139]

Rates to college graduates probably remained constant in part because of the preference of employers for college graduates over high school graduates. Average income of white male college graduates 35–44 years old rose relative to white high school graduates between 1959 and 1969; the ratio of mean income of white male college graduates to the mean income of white male high school graduates 35–44 in 1959 was 1.54, while in 1969 it was 1.60.

These points can also be examined for other groups besides white males. In contrast, black male college graduates have increased less rapidly in the black labor force than have high school graduates. Despite the rapid increase in black males with a high school education, the rate of return to that level apparently has risen for blacks.

The growth of the female labor force is similar to its male counterpart at the high school level, and the same sort of statements can be made for white females as for white males. The primary difference is that the rates of return to investment in high school fell for white females in the face of a rapid increase (much more rapid than for white males) of female high school graduates in the labor force, and the rate to white female college graduates rose in the face of an increase similar to the increase in white male college graduates. Thus, parallel to black males, white and black female secondary school graduates were absorbed into the labor force with a smaller fall in rates of return than occurred for white males with the same education, even though the latter increased less rapidly than the former. White and black female college graduates had an increase in the rates of return to their investment in college education despite an increase in their relative number in the labor force which was as rapid as that of white male college graduates, although only black women improved their income position relative to white males.[20]

RATES OF RETURN ESTIMATED FROM COHORT (LONGITUDINAL) DATA

For two of the Census years, 1939 and 1949, it is possible to estimate rates of return based on Census mean incomes for a "cohort" growing 10 years older with each succeeding Census sample.[21] In effect, the age-income profiles produced by such a calculation (all incomes expressed in 1969 dollars) reflect the conditions which actually prevailed in each of four Census years for those with different levels of schooling.

For purposes of simplicity, we assumed that the costs of going to school—both income forgone and institutional costs—were equal in real terms to income forgone and institutional costs per student at a corresponding age in 1939 or 1949.

The estimates for white and black males are presented in Table 3. They tend to be higher than the cross-sectional rates, which is to be expected since multiplying two incomes by the same growth rate increases the absolute difference between them. In general, the rates to higher levels of schooling show a greater increase compared to the cross-sectional estimates than those to primary school, especially for those who were 20 years old in 1949. Again, this is the expected result. The greatest apparent error in using cross-sectional data occurs for black male high school graduates 20 years old in 1939, white male high school graduates in 1949, and black male college graduates in 1949. It seems that these three groups did considerably better as they grew older than they could have predicted from income differentials between older workers at the time these cohorts were investing in high school.

---

20 We also estimated rates of return to graduate education in 1959 and 1969 (the only two Censuses which separate out incomes for those with more than a college education). Graduate education is a very heterogeneous level of schooling, and rates differ widely among various professions. We are not even sure from the Census data as to the average length of time represented by the Census category 5+ or 6+ years of college. The results show that the rates of return to investment in graduate schooling were low for white men and women in 1959, but that these rates rose sharply in the next 10 years. In general, the rates for all four sex-race groups are not very different in 1969 from the rates for four years of college except among black males, for whom the rates to graduate education are around 15 percent. Detailed data are available from the authors.

21 The "cohort" is not the same individuals at each point in time; however, if the Census sample is random, we would expect that it would be representative of 20-year-olds in 1939, of the 20-year-olds who had become 30-year-olds in 1949, etc.

TABLE 3

UNADJUSTED MARGINAL SOCIAL RATES OF RETURN TO INVESTMENT
IN PRIMARY SCHOOL, HIGH SCHOOL, AND COLLEGE,
BASED ON "COHORT" INCOMES OF THOSE IN THE LABOR FORCE
(UNEMPLOYED INCLUDED), MALES, BY RACE, 1939 AND
1949 COHORTS, U.S. (PERCENT)

	1939[a]	1949[b]
White Males		
Primary 8/0	13.4 (11.6)[c]	13.6 (12.7)
High school 12/8	19.6 (18.2)	18.3 (14.2)
College 16/12[d]	12.3 (10.7)	12.5 (10.6)
Black Males		
Primary 8/0	12.2 (10.5)	13.9 (13.9)
High school 12/8	16.7 (10.4)	11.4 (9.1)
College 16/12	7.0 (6.5)	5.8 (4.6)

Source: See Table 1.

[a]Cohort of white or black males, 20 years old in 1939 (23 years old in 1939 in the case of college vs. high school educated), 30 (33) years old in 1949, 40 (43) years old in 1959, 50 (53) years old in 1969. Income forgone and institutional costs (in 1969 dollars) assumed to be equal to 1939 cross-section income forgone and 1939 institutional costs. All incomes adjusted to 1969 prices. Income differences from age 50 (53) to 65 taken equal to difference at 50 (53) years old.

[b]Cohort of white or black males, 20 years old in 1949 (23 years old in the case of college vs. high school educated), 30 (33) years old in 1959, 40 (43) years old in 1969. Income forgone and institutional costs (in 1969 dollars) assumed to be equal to 1949 cross-section income forgone and 1949 institutional costs. All incomes adjusted to 1969 prices. Income differences from age 40 (43) to 50 (53) are assumed to increase at the same rate as for the same ages in the 1939 cohort. Income differences from age 50 (53) to 65 are taken equal to difference at 50 (53) years old.

[c]Figures in parentheses are rates of return based on cross-section incomes (see Table 2).

[d]We also estimated college rates assuming that the 16+ category represents 16.5 years of college rather than 16 years. The rates are the following: For white males—1939, 11.8; 1949, 12.1. For black males—1939, 6.5; 1949, 5.4.

The longitudinal estimates do not change the ordering of the social rates among levels of schooling indicated by cross-sectional estimates. In fact, they tend to confirm that the estimated rates using 1939 cross-sectional data which *include* those with zero incomes are a better reflection of future income differences under more normal employment conditions than cross-sectional rates which exclude the zero income group. However, the longitudinal rates raise some questions about the time trend of payoffs to different levels of schooling. Since the social rates based on cohort data change little for white males between 1939 and 1949 at any level, will high school rates fall for the 1959 and 1969 cohort as the cross-sectional data indicate? Unless there is reason to believe that the growth of the economy affected (and will affect) high school graduates particularly favorably in the 1960s and 1970s (as it apparently did black graduates in the 1940s and 1950s), we should expect that the 1959 and 1969 cohort estimates for the white male secondary social rate of return would be considerably lower than those for 1939 and 1949.

SOME SPECULATIONS

What do these results tell us about the movements of rates of return to schooling in the next decade or so? The average social rate of return to schooling has declined from about 13–14 percent in 1939 to about 9 percent in 1969, and we speculate, first, that it will continue to decline gradually, both because of the continued increase in schooling relative to physical capital and because of the greater participation of women (who have lower average rates of return to schooling than white men) in the labor force.

As far as the white labor force is concerned, we would argue that the social rates to investment in high school will continue to fall gradually while the private rates may rise. Income forgone to those attending high school should continue to fall relative to benefits. The social rate of return to college will either stay constant or begin to fall in the next decade, while the private rates to white males could rise. (They already are rising for white females.) We would expect that the relative increase of college graduates will continue and that employers will prefer those with graduate training over college graduates, putting downward pressure on college rates but keeping graduate rates as high as they are now and perhaps even higher.[22]

With the social rates of return to college probably falling and the private rates probably rising (as earnings forgone relative to benefits fall), we should also

---

22   The slowdown now taking place in the population growth rate will have two effects: On the one hand, it will reduce the number of young people entering the labor force relative to earlier years. This will tend to reduce the decline in rates of return to both secondary and college rates. However, more women will want to enter the labor force if there are less children to care for (especially if the women's liberation movement has a significant effect on family roles). This will continue a trend which we observe since at least 1950 of a higher and higher fraction of women age 25 and older in the total labor force (26 percent in 1950, 31 percent in 1960, and 37 percent in 1970), and could lead to an increase in the rates of return for women since they will earn returns to the educational investment over a longer working life. The slowdown in population growth also will slow down the rate of public school expansion, which implies a reduction in the growth of jobs, particularly for women with college and graduate education.

observe a shift in undergraduate enrollment from private universities charging ever higher tuition to subsidized public universities. We should also see a continued expansion of junior colleges, state colleges, and other forms of post-high school public schooling—all this in the face of possibly *declining* social rates of return to college education.

These movements in rates may also have important implications for the distribution of income. Since in this model the last social class groups to get a particular level of schooling generally receive lower rates of return to the total investment made in them than the groups which came before, the same social investment will yield them a lower payoff than the returns to those who received their schooling 10 or 20 years ago.

APPENDIX: METHODS OF ESTIMATION

1939: The 1939 Census data are in the form of *earnings* (compensation for work or services performed as employees) of *native-born* Americans 14 years old and older in the labor force. We estimated the means of these earnings, which were reported as zero earnings for those who were unemployed.

1949, 1959, and 1969: The Census data are in the form of income of all those in the population 14 years old or older. In younger age groups and among women, the number reporting income is much larger than the labor force. In many age and education categories, there also are significantly large numbers who report· that they received income but did not specify *how much* income they received.

Since we are primarily interested in the mean income of those in the labor force, we attempted to eliminate systematically from the income data those who reported income but were not in the labor force. First, we assumed that those who did not specify income ("income not reported") earned the mean income of the category, so that their exclusion would not bias the results.[23]

Second, we "corrected" the data on mean incomes reported by subtracting the *assumed* income of those reporting income who were not in the labor force. We assumed that those who were not in the labor force but reported income were in the *lowest* income category. We subtracted the difference between the number who reported income and the number in the labor force in the same race/sex/education/age category from the $1–499 and $1–999 income category. Our "corrected" income is therefore higher than the estimated mean shown in the Census for a particular age/education category.[24]

---

23 This assumption was supported by the fact that average schooling in the "income not reported" groups was close to the average schooling for the category as a whole.

24 For example, we took the number of white males 25–34 years old with 12 years of schooling (N_{12}) who were in the labor force, including those unemployed, and subtracted it from the number of white males in the same category who reported income (Y_{12}). We assumed that those who reported income but were not in the labor

330 | THE JOURNAL OF HUMAN RESOURCES

1969 Earnings Data: In order to make comparisons with the 1969 rate of return estimates based on income, we also calculated rates based on mean *earnings* from a different set of Census data. Earnings data are reported for all those 18 years old or older in the experienced civilian labor force.[25] The advantage of earnings data is that they do not include income from investments. The rate of return estimated from earnings thus better represents the economic value of investment in human capital. But the earnings forgone in high school investment is based on extrapolation to younger ages of earnings of those older than 18. Thus, the rates of return we get from earnings data may have serious biases in earnings forgone and, hence, in rates of return even though they may reflect more accurately than do income data the return in higher age groups to investment in schooling.[26]

REFERENCES

1. Gary Becker. *Human Capital.* New York: National Bureau of Economic Research, 1964.
2. Mark Blaug. *Introduction to the Economics of Education.* Baltimore: Penguin Books, 1970.
3. Samuel Bowles. "Class Power and Mass Education." Cambridge, Mass.: Harvard University, 1971. Mimeographed.
4. Martin Carnoy. "Class Analysis and Investment in Human Resources: A

---

force received very low incomes. Thus we multiplied $(Y_{12} - N_{12})$ times the mean of the lowest income class, $500 (in some cases the difference exceeded the number reporting $1–999, so we took the excess and multiplied by the mean of the next highest category, $1500), and subtracted $(Y_{12} - N_{12}) \times 500 from the total income of all white males 25–34 with 12 years of schooling (TY_{12}). We then recalculated a new mean based on the number in the labor force: new mean income = $[TY_{12} - (Y_{12} - N_{12})500]/N_{12}$. We repeated this for each race/sex/age education category.

25 The experienced civilian labor force is somewhat smaller than the total civilian labor force. There are probably a number of people looking for their first jobs and some unemployed who are not included in the former category. The omission of the unemployed would tend to lower rates of return to schooling. We have made two "adjustments" on average earnings data as reported in the Census [20, Tables 1, 2, 5, 7, 8, 11]. The first of these adjustments was made to approximate earnings of 35–44-year-olds compared to 45–54-year-olds, since the earnings tables in the Census show means only for 35–54-year-olds. Income data were used to make this approximation, on the assumption that the earnings curves are shaped like the income curves. Second, we had to estimate from income data the earnings of those with 8 years of schooling, since the earnings tables in the Census showed mean earnings only for those with 0–8 years of schooling. The ratio of incomes of those with 8 years to those with 0–8 years of schooling in each age category was applied to the mean earnings data.

26 We do not present the actual income data by age, level of schooling, race, and sex in tabular form in order to save space. They are available from the authors for 1969 and for earlier years.

Dynamic Model." *Review of Radical Political Economics* (Fall-Winter 1971).

5. Richard Eckaus. *Estimating the Returns to Education: A Disaggregated Approach.* Berkeley, Calif.: The Carnegie Corporation, 1973.

6. Zvi Griliches and William M. Mason. "Education, Income, and Ability." *Journal of Political Economy* 80 (May/June 1972): Pt. 2, S74–103.

7. Giora Hanoch. "An Economic Analysis of Earnings and Schooling." *Journal of Human Resources* 2 (Summer 1967): 310–29.

8. W. Lee Hansen. "Total and Private Returns to Investment in Schooling." *Journal of Political Economy* 71 (April 1963): 128–40.

9. W. Lee Hansen, Burton A. Weisbrod, and William J. Scanlon. "Schooling and Earnings of Low Achievers." *American Economic Review* 60 (June 1970): 409–18.

10. Fred Hines, Luther Tweeten, and Martin Redfern. "Social and Private Rates of Return to Investment in Schooling, by Race-Sex Groups and Regions." *Journal of Human Resources* 5 (Summer 1970): 318–40.

11. Michael Katz. *The Irony of Early School Reform.* Boston: Beacon Press, 1970.

12. Dieter Marenbach. "The Rates of Return to Education in the U.S. from 1939–1959." Ph.D. dissertation, Stanford University, 1973.

13. Herman Miller. "Annual and Life-Time Income in Relation to Education: 1949–1959." *American Economic Review* 50 (December 1960): 962–86.

14. George Psacharopoulos. *Returns to Education.* San Francisco: Jossey-Bass, 1973.

15. T. W. Schultz. "Capital Formation by Education." *Journal of Political Economy* 68 (December 1960): 571–83.

16. _____. "Investment in Human Capital." *American Economic Review* 51 (March 1961): 1–17.

17. Henry Louis Smith. "Working One's Way Through College (For the Guidance and Encouragement of Young Men Who Are Richer in Brains, Energy, and Character Than in Available Cash)." *Washington and Lee University Bulletin* 17 (December 15, 1918).

18. Joel Spring. *Schooling and the Rise of the Corporate State.* Boston: Beacon Press, 1973.

19. U.S. Department of Commerce, Bureau of the Census. *Census of Population, 1960–Special Reports on Educational Attainment and Non-white Population.* Washington: U.S. Government Printing Office, 1963.

20. _____. *United States Census, 1970, Special Report, Occupation and Earnings.* Washington: U.S. Government Printing Office.

21. U.S. Department of Health, Education, and Welfare. *Digest of Educational Statistics, 1971.* Washington: U.S. Government Printing Office, 1972.

22. J. R. Walsh. "Capital Concept Applied to Man." *Quarterly Journal of Economics* (February 1935).

23. Finis Welch. "Education in Production." *Journal of Political Economy* 78 (January/February 1970): 35–59.

[3]

Higher Education 10 (1981) 199–227
Elsevier Scientific Publishing Company, Amsterdam – Printed in the Netherlands

PERCEIVED EARNINGS FUNCTIONS AND EX ANTE RATES OF RETURN TO POST COMPULSORY EDUCATION IN ENGLAND*

GARETH WILLIAMS
University of Lancaster, Lancaster, U.K.

ALAN GORDON
University of Bristol, Bristol, U.K.

ABSTRACT

This article offers a direct empirical test of one of the main tenets of the human capital model. It shows that by the end of their compulsory education English pupils in general are aware of the relationship between educational qualifications and average earnings. For the first time in Britain direct calculations are made of *ex ante* perceived rates of return to upper secondary and higher education. The perceived rates correspond closely to the actual rates estimated by earlier studies. The article also provides useful evidence of differences between social classes and ability groups. In particular it shows that the human capital model offers a much less satisfactory explanation of the behaviour of low ability and working class pupils than it does of high ability and middle class pupils.

A sample of just under 3,000 16-years-old students in England were tested on their reasoning ability and asked about their family backgrounds, self concepts, educational intentions and anticipated earning capacity at various stages of their working lives.

Introduction

Studies of rates of return to investment in education are commonplace. The reasoning behind these calculations is that a substantial part of the average earnings differentials in favour of the highly educated can be attributed to their higher levels of education [1]. However, doubts about the causes of the positive association between education and income have also led to a burgeoning of earnings functions studies which explore the nature of

* The research project on which the results in this article are based is funded by the Social Science Research Council.

200

the relationships between educational qualifications and earnings, taking into account the effects of intervening and complementary variables such as ability and social class [2]. Such studies can help in the formulation of educational policy in two ways. The *social* rate of return (see, for example, Morris and Ziderman, 1971; Morris, 1973) can be used to compare the cost-benefit relationships in education with those in other social investments, and to compare the returns from different categories of educational expenditure. The *private* rate of return helps to explain and hence to predict the private demand for voluntary education and for its different subject specialisms and institutional provisions (see, for example, Freeman, 1971 and Freeman 1976).

An essential step in any model which links private rates of return with the demand for post-compulsory education is that students and potential students are aware of these returns and act upon them. A high rate of return will not influence student decision-making if this return is not perceived. Similarly, individual students may believe that high returns can be achieved through continued education but consider that their lack of ability or their disadvantaged family background make it unlikely that they will be able to take personal advantage of these high returns. Others may simply have a fatalistic view of how life's rewards are shared out.

It is, therefore, surprising that there have been very few studies of the perceived (ex ante) returns to continued education [3], and no economic analyses at all of earnings functions as perceived by young people who are taking decisions about whether or not to stay on in full-time education.

In the first part of the article we examine the earnings expectations of a sample of English students in their last year of compulsory education in the context of various personal characteristics, their family backgrounds and their intentions regarding post-compulsory education. Subsequently we use the information obtained from these earnings functions to compute perceived rates of return to upper secondary and higher education by different groups of school leavers.

The Data

The data were obtained in Spring 1977 from a sample of 2944 students in their final year of compulsory education attending 110 secondary schools in England.

Each student completed a questionnaire containing information on his family background, his educational performance to date, his educational and career intentions, his earnings expectations at the start of his working life and at age 26 and 46, and his perceptions of the financial and other characteristics of a variety of occupations. Students planning to go on to higher education were asked to estimate the prevailing level of the full value student maintenance grant. Finally each student completed a short standardised verbal reasoning test. Respondents who showed hesitation in providing details of their own earnings expectations or those of the various occupations selected were asked to make a reasoned guess. This was legitimate in that the aim of the study was to obtain an impression of their general picture of the world they would be entering, not to try to force them to make what would have been very artificial calculations. In estimating their own prospects they were told to disregard the effects of inflation by saying what they thought they would earn if they were that age now with the qualifications they expected to get. In the event very few respondents were unwilling or unable to answer such questions; and clearly, for many, the questions, although artificial, were not considered at all irrelevant.

Earnings Functions

All respondents were asked to give an estimate of expected earnings when they started work, at the age of 26 and at the age of 46. They were also asked when they intended to leave full-time education and the highest qualification they expected to obtain. This information enables a crude expected age-earnings profile for each individual to be constructed (Table I). It was assumed that expected earnings at 46 correspond to anticipated peak annual earnings [4]. Figures 1 and 2 show the median perceptions of earnings by age for boys and girls and compares these with actually observed age-earnings profiles in the 1975/76 General Household Survey (OPCS, 1978). There is considerable similarity between the actual and perceived lifetime earnings schedules suggesting that, overall, young people do have a fairly accurate perception of the earnings prospects associated with the different educational paths they might follow. (Appendix A contains details of education, age and earnings data from the 1975/76 General Household Survey.)

It is, however, well established that not all of the higher earnings of the more highly schooled can be attributed to their education alone. Those who proceed to higher education have, on average, higher levels of academic ability and a more favourable social background than young people who do not continue their studies. In Table II the anticipated age-earnings profiles of each of 24 groups of boys and girls have been aggregated into a single estimate of total expected lifetime earnings. Inspection of this table shows that anticipated lifetime earnings are strongly associated with educational intention and positively associated with ability (as measured by a verbal reasoning test [5]). There is, however, little association between social class (measured by father's occupation) and anticipated future earnings. This suggests that young people of 16 see their future earning capacity as being particularly

202

TABLE I

Median Expected Earnings of 16 year-old Boys and Girls by Educational Intention (£ per annum)

		Age 17	19	22	26	46
Educational intention						
Higher	Boys	–	–	2100	3371	5199
education	Girls	–	–	1835	2587	3391
Upper secondary	Boys	–	1556	–	2598	3893
education	Girls	–	1317	–	2075	2822
Work and part time	Boys	1052	–	–	2337	3485
education	Girls	1032	–	–	1812	2584
Work, no education	Boys	1051	–	–	2093	3126
	Girls	1036	–	–	1709	2346

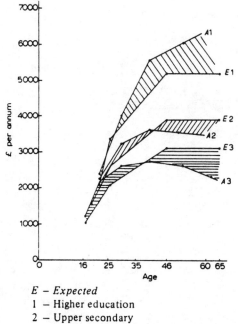

Medians

A – Actual	*E – Expected*
1 – Degree	1 – Higher education
2 – GCE 'A' levels	2 – Upper secondary
3 – No qualifications	3 – Work

Source: "Actual" profiles for males derived from OPCS (1978) Table 7.9. Full details are given in Appendix A.

Fig. 1. Actual and expected relative age earnings profiles of males.

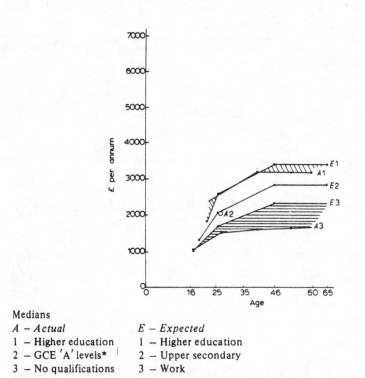

Medians

A – Actual	E – Expected
1 – Higher education	1 – Higher education
2 – GCE 'A' levels*	2 – Upper secondary
3 – No qualifications	3 – Work

*Only one observation of actual earnings, · A 2, is available for women with GCE 'A' levels.

Source: "Actual" profiles for females derived from SED 4A GHS 1975/76. Kindly made available by OPCS. Full details are given in Appendix A.

Fig. 2. Actual and expected relative age-earnings profiles of females.

associated with the amount of post-compulsory education undertaken and with their own ability, but do not in general see their family background as directly enhancing or inhibiting their propensity to earn high incomes. Of course, social background may well affect earning capacity via its effect on their educational decisions. This possibility is explored later.

Table II suggests the interaction of five variables – educational intention, social class, ability, sex and earnings. In order to specify these relationships more precisely and to include other variables that may possibly influence expected earnings, various versions of a multivariate earnings function were computed. The general form of the function was:–

$$ELE = f(HE, SL, A, S, F, X, BR, RISK, DG)$$

The variables are defined as follows:

204

TABLE II

Estimated Expected Average Lifetime Earnings of Boys and Girls by Ability and Social Class Group and by Educational Intention

	Higher Education	Leave at 18	Part-time Education 16–18	Leave at
Girls				
White collar: top ability	140,401	115,941	94,603	107,680
White collar: middle ability	126,851	108,933	103,867	94,084
White collar: low ability	111,786	119,418	105,972	86,577
Manual: top ability	125,849	107,490	100,037	98,687
Manual: middle ability	111,777	104,512	99,194	96,656
Manual: low ability	114,240	102,253	98,943	98,445
Boys				
White collar: top ability	199,625	175,065	133,188	126,719
White collar: middle ability	184,615	131,065	140,582	124,181
White collar: low ability	183,185	149,582	138,201	125,433
Manual: top ability	204,890	157,702	139,481	136,892
Manual: middle ability	204,895	145,259	133,311	128,062
Manual: low ability	114,384	127,773	136,630	117,756

Method of calculation

Expected Lifetime Earnings = 0.5 (26-Age of starting work) (Expected starting earnings + expected earnings at 26) + 10 (Expected earnings at 26) + 29 (Expected earnings at 46). (For those who intend going on to higher education, an amount equal to three times their perceived value of the student grant has also been added.)

ELE = Expected Lifetime Earnings

These were computed for each respondent on the basis of his expected earnings in the first year of full-time work and at ages 26 and 46. It was assumed that earnings rise linearly between these points, that peak earnings occur at 46 and that these are maintained until retirement at 65. The shape of the age-earnings profiles thus specified correspond to those given in Figs. 1 and 2. More complex functions were examined but performed no better than the simple linear form. In the case of respondents expecting to enter higher education their perceptions of the maximum value of student grants were treated as earnings for three years between the ages of 19 and 22.

HE, SL = Educational Intention

After various experiments in which educational expectations were treated as both continuous and dichotomous variables, the specification that both performed best and appeared most logical was to treat this as two separate dichotomous variables as follows:

	HE	SL
Intention to continue study to degree level	1	0
Intention to undertake full-time study to A level or equivalent	0	0
Intention to leave full-time education at 16	0	1

HE (the intention to undertake higher education) is thus expected to be positive, showing the average anticipated increase in earnings associated with entering higher education; while *SL* (the intention to leave school at 16) is expected to be negative, showing the expected loss of earnings associated with leaving at minimum school-leaving age.

A = Verbal Reasoning Test Score

Each respondent was given a short verbal reasoning test [6]. Each pupil had a score between 0 and 65 and this score was treated as a continuous variable. The distribution of scores on the test was normal with a mean score of 36.4 and a standard deviation of 10.8.

S = Sex

In the preliminary analysis this was treated as an independent dichotomous variable where male = 1, female = 0. Subsequently the data for males and females were analysed separately.

F = Family Background

Stated father's occupation was classified into the Registrar General's six social class categories [7] and subsequently treated as a dichotomous variable where those with fathers (or guardians) in non-manual occupations scored 1, the remainder 0.

X = General Perceptions of Earnings

This variable was intended to provide a means of standardising different individuals' estimates of their own future earning capacity by taking into account their views of what people actually earn in a wide range of jobs. It is described in the subsequent text, therefore, as a *standardising* variable. The rationale for such a variable is that different individuals have different views

206

about earnings in the labour market generally. Thus, any particular student may expect to get high (money) earnings in the future either because he thinks that on average earnings are high (in relation to what other respondents think) or he may believe that he personally will obtain earnings that are higher than average. Since the aim was to see how individuals' perceptions of their *relative* earnings were associated with their educational intentions, it was necessary to have an indication of each individual's perceptions of *average* earnings in addition to his expectations about his own. This was obtained by asking the respondents to estimate average earnings at age 26, 36 and 46 in 12 occupations requiring differing educational qualifications. A straightforward arithmetic average of these estimates was used as an indicator of views of average earnings in the labour market generally.

BR = Subjective Estimate of Intellectual Ability

One of the problems with using a test score as an indication of ability in this kind of analysis is that what is presumably important in determining the "ability effect" on pupils' earnings expectations is not how able they actually are, but how able they believe themselves to be. An index of subjective perception of ability was constructed on the basis of the extent of agreement with the sentence, "I have enough brains for this kind of job", for six widely differing occupations. There was a positive but far from perfect correlation between score on the verbal reasoning test and this index ($R^2 = 0.49$). In many instances both BR and A have an independent effect in explaining the variance of perceived lifetime earnings.

RISK = Attitude to Risk in Employment

An index was constructed with scores 0–8 depending on the claimed attraction of jobs with the following characteristics:
  (i)   "a job where you can earn large amounts of money but which is insecure";
  (ii) "a job where pay is about average but where there is little risk of being unemployed".
The coefficient of this variable gives an indication of the extent to which individuals preferred to trade off job security against high income. In general, as will be seen, the variable performed rather well, suggesting that there is such a trade-off in the minds of many young people.

DG = Deferment of Gratification Index

This was an index on which each respondent was assigned a score between 0 and 16 depending on the extent to which he agreed with each of the following statements:
  (i)   "I would like a job with good pay to start off but without much chance of promotion."

(ii) "I would like a job with good prospects for pay after 10 years, but with low starting pay."

(iii) "I don't mind going without things now if I can have a better life later on."

(iv) "It is more important to enjoy yourself when you can than to worry about the future."

High scores on this index were obtained by respondents willing to defer gratification, i.e. with a low subjective rate of discount. It was also anticipated, of course, that there would be a positive correlation between this variable and the intention to continue to higher levels of education. But it was hypothesised, in addition, that those with high scores would, other things being equal, expect higher total *lifetime* earnings than other respondents since they would be more likely to be prepared to invest in their training after leaving formal education.

The Regression Analyses

Earnings functions were estimated by means of ordinary least squares regression using the SPSS package. From these regression equations we can extract five types of relevant information.

(1) From the B coefficients the average amount of extra lifetime income expected as a result of undertaking upper secondary and higher education.

(2) From the β (beta) coefficients the relative importance of the different variables described above in explaining the expected lifetime earnings of young people in their last year of compulsory education.

(3) From a comparison of the B or β coefficients of the education variables (with and without the other variables included) an estimate of the a priori α (alpha) coefficient. This shows the proportion of expected extra income associated with higher education or upper secondary education that can actually be attributed directly to the extra intended education.

(4) From a comparison of the B or β coefficients an indication of differences between social class and ability groups in the impact of each of the variables considered on expected lifetime earnings.

(5) From the correlation coefficients (R^2) an estimate of the success of the postulated earnings function in explaining anticipated lifetime earning differences; in particular, from comparisons of the R^2 between different ability and social class groups an indication of the extent to which the meritocratic human capital model implied in the formulation accurately reflects the perceptions of young people from different social backgrounds.

208

TABLE III

Regressions of Expected Lifetime Earnings on Educational Intentions and Other Variables

	B £'000				β (Beta)									R^2	α	
	HE	SL	S	F	HE	SL	S	F	A	BR	DG	RISK	X			
Whole (1)	50	-20	-	-	0.26	-0.09	-	-	-	-	-	-	-	0.25	HE/18	0.70
sample (2)	35	-12	24	(-1)	0.18	-0.05	0.15	(-0.02)	0.09	0.09	0.09	-0.17	0.32	0.31	18/16	0.60
Boys (3)	67	-19	-	-	0.31	-0.07	-	-	-	-	-	-	-	0.25	HE/18	0.74
(4)	50	-12	-	(1.9)	0.23	-0.05	-	(0.01)	0.08	0.08	0.06	-0.14	0.33	0.28	18/16	0.64
Girls (5)	36	-17	-	-	0.23	-0.10	-	-	-	-	-	-	-	0.19	HE/18	0.63
(6)	23	-10	-	9.6	0.14	-0.06	-	0.06	0.08	0.09	0.12	-0.20	0.30	0.23	18/16	0.63

Figures in brackets are *not* significantly different from zero at the 5% level.

Equation $ELE = K + \beta_1(HE) + \beta_2(SL) + \beta_3(S) + \beta_4(F) + \beta_5(A) + \beta_6(BR) + \beta_7(DG) + \beta_8(RISK) + \beta_9(X)$

Key to variables
HE = intention to enter higher education
SL = intention to leave school at 16
S = sex
F = family background
A = "ability" score
BR = self-perceptions of ability
DG = propensity to defer gratification
RISK = attitude to risk in employment
X = perception of general average earnings

Table III gives the results of the regressions for the whole sample population and for boys and girls separately. Boys anticipate higher earnings than girls, expecting, on average, £24,000 more over their lifetime after taking education and other differences into account. This is shown by the *SEX* variable in Equation (2). Equation (1) shows that, for the whole sample, those who intend to go on to higher education expect to earn £50,000 more than those who leave at 18, and those in turn expect £20,000 more than those who leave at 16. However, when we take other variables into account (which are themselves often associated with a propensity to undertake post-compulsory education) the additional expected earnings that can be attributed to higher education falls to £35,000, with a rather greater relative fall in the case of those expecting to continue only until age 18 and not go on to higher education (Equation (2)). This corresponds to an overall alpha coefficient (α) of 0.70 for higher education and 0.60 for post-compulsory education to age 18.

The alpha coefficients are rather higher for boys than for girls, especially for those groups planning to go on to higher education. Psacharopoulos (1975) has shown in his review of 16 case studies in the United States estimates of the actual or implied "α" coefficient for higher education varied from 0.65 to 0.97, while for secondary education they varied from 0.40 to 0.88. Although such calculations have not been made for Britain because of an absence of suitable data, our estimate of the perceived "α" must, in the light of the U.S. data, be considered suggestive of an instinctive awareness by school students of the operations of the labour market for qualified manpower.

All the variables in the multiple regression appear to exert an independent effect on expected lifetime earnings that is significantly different from zero, with the exception of family background. The influence of this social class variable is small and non-significant for boys and just significant for girls. Measured ability (A) and subjective perception of ability (BR) exert independent positive and approximately equal significant effects on anticipated earnings. In other words, both measured ability and students' beliefs about how able they are, seem to exert independent effects on expected earnings. There is clear evidence that a willingness to defer gratification (DG) (having a low subjective rate of discount) is positively associated with expected total earnings, significantly more so in the case of girls than for boys. The evidence of a trade-off between willingness to take risks ($RISK$) and expected earnings is also strong and significant. Those who express a preference for risky jobs expect on average to have higher earnings: this effect also is more marked for girls than for boys.

210

Social Class and Ability Interactions

Table III has shown that both "objective" and "subjective" measures of ability have an independent direct effect on earnings expectations, while family background has little effect.

The aim of this section is to examine social class and ability in rather more detail in an attempt to detect evidence of systematic interaction between "actual" ability, family background, educational intention and expected earnings. In the absence of any prior knowledge of the form such interactions might take, the first step, in Tables IV and V, was to estimate regression equations separately for each of three ability and two social class groups.

For all ten groups the intention to enter higher education is associated with expectations of substantially higher earnings. For both boys and girls the biggest earnings advantage resulting from higher education is seen by those from manual home backgrounds and those in the middle of the ability range.

The "social class" effect suggests that in order to be persuaded of the desirability of entering higher education, boys and girls from manual homes need the expectation of a higher potential earnings advantage than their non-manual counterparts.

Somewhat similar reasoning may apply to those in the middle of the ability range. The most able pupils are likely to have been progressively socialised towards education and would anticipate leaving the escalator only if they had very promising prospects elsewhere. Pupils in the middle of the ability range are far less likely to see the issue as an open and shut case and will require higher average earnings prospects before they are convinced that higher education is worthwhile. Those at the lower levels of ability intending to go on to higher education are very largely from middle class home backgrounds. Seventeen per cent of low ability non-manual students and only 7 per cent of low ability manual students expected to proceed to higher education. It is probable that the former group's intention to proceed to higher education results from long-held family expectations, but by the age of 16 the individuals concerned have little confidence in their own ability to benefit substantially from higher education (at least in financial terms).

It is also worth noting in this context that amongst boys, only those in the low ability group are significantly affected by social class in their earnings expectations. "Low ability" boys from non-manual home backgrounds expect to do better than their manual working class counterparts independently of their educational intentions. For all other groups of boys and girls the effect of social class on earnings expectations appears to be very largely mediated through their intended post-compulsory education.

However, possibly the most noteworthy result from this part of the

TABLE IV

Social Class and Ability Interactions Influencing Expected Lifetime Earnings and Educational Intentions – Boys

| | | B (£'000) | | | β (Beta) | | | | | | | | R^2 |
	HE	SL	F	HE	SL	F	A	BR	DG	RISK	X	
"White collar" (7)	39	(−29)	—	0.17	(−0.07)	—	(0.01)	0.19	(0.05)	−0.21	0.44	0.37
"Other" (8)	58	(−13)	—	0.26	(−0.06)	—	0.13	(−0.02)	(0.07)	(−0.06)	0.23	0.19
High ability (9)	49	(1)	(−2.4)	0.22	0	(−0.01)	—	0.10	(0.08)	−0.22	0.39	0.32
Middle ability (10)	57	−28	(−4.6)	0.25	−0.10	(−0.02)	—	(0.04)	(0.02)	(0.06)	0.36	0.24
Low ability (11)	24	(−10)	17.4	0.13	(−0.09)	0.15	—	(0.09)	(0.04)	(−0.07)	0.14	0.10

Figures in brackets are *not* significantly different from zero at the 5% level.
For explanation of symbols see Table III.

212

TABLE V

Social Class and Ability Interactions Influencing Expected Lifetime Earnings and Educational Intentions – Girls

		B (£'000)			β (Beta)								R^2
		HE	SL	F	HE	SL	F	A	BR	DG	RISK	X	
"White collar"	(12)	20	−24	—	0.14	−0.11	—	(0.08)	(0.08)	(0.04)	−0.22	0.35	0.28
"Other"	(13)	26	(−7)	—	0.14	(−0.04)	—	(0.07)	0.10	0.16	−0.18	0.29	0.17
High ability	(14)	16	(−12)	13.1	0.11	(−0.05)	(0.09)	—	(0.07)	(0.05)	−0.25	0.37	0.30
Middle ability	(15)	27	(−7)	(2.5)	0.14	(−0.04)	(0.01)	—	0.10	0.13	−0.18	0.37	0.24
Low ability	(16)	17	−13	12.6	0.15	−0.17	0.14	—	(0.07)	0.16	−0.13	0.20	0.19

Figures in brackets are *not* significantly different from zero at the 5% level.
For explanation of symbols see Table III.

analysis is the marked differences between social class and ability groups in the explanatory power of the model. The correlation coefficient (R^2) for non-manual boys is nearly double that for manual boys, while for girls it is 65 per cent higher. Similarly, the R^2 for high ability boys is three times that of low ability boys, and for girls the difference is 60 per cent. One possible explanation for this result is that young people in the lower social class and ability groups are likely to be "fatalistic" rather than "meritocratic" in their interpretations of the way life's rewards and chances are distributed. Some evidence for this hypothesis is given in Table VI. For this table a variable was constructed in which each respondent could score 0–4 depending on the degree of agreement with the proposition: "Success in life is largely a matter of luck." High scores indicate disagreement with the proposition. The average score was compiled for each of twelve social class and ability groups. As Table VI shows, there is a good correlation between these scores and the correlation coefficients on the earnings functions [8]. Table VI also summarises

TABLE VI

Expected Financial Benefits from Sixth Form and Higher Education by Social and Ability Groups; and Correlation Belief in Luck and Explained Variance in Perceived Earnings*

	HE £'000	*SL*	Other significant variables	R^2	*LUCK*
	(1)	(2)	(3)	(4)	(5)
M F 1 A1	52.4	(+17.9)	*RISK*	0.372	4.02
M F 1 A2	59.7	(−54.3)	*RISK, BR*	0.421	3.84
M F 1 A3	57.2	(−24.5)	*RISK, BR*	0.176	3.32
M F 2 A1	71.3	(−9.3)	*RISK*	0.246	3.82
M F 2 A2	55.5	−25.9	–	0.122	3.69
M F 2 A3	(1.4)	−10.4	–	0.078	3.31
F F 1 A1	23.1	(−22.9)	*RISK*	0.291	3.97
F F 1 A2	28.9	−21.3	*RISK, BR*	0.428	3.96
F F 1 A3	20.8	−42.6	–	0.248	3.73
F F 2 A1	28.5	(−4.4)	–	0.308	3.97
F F 2 A2	42.2	(−8.8)	*RISK, DG*	0.211	3.82
F F 2 A3	21.4	−10.7	*RISK, BR, DG*	0.159	3.08

Correlation Coefficient between Columns (4) and (5): $r^2 = 0.55$

Key: *LUCK* = Measure of Extent of agreement with proposition that "success in life is largely a matter of luck". M = Male, F = Female.

Other Variables as in previous Tables and in Notes [5] and [7].

* Figures in parentheses are *not* significantly different from zero at 5% level.

214

the significant variables in the regression equations for each of these twelve groups. In all cases except low ability working class males, higher education is expected to be associated with significantly higher lifetime earnings. Conversely, staying on to age 18 has a tendency to be associated with higher earnings but the level of significance is not high, indicating a considerable variability of expectations in relation to this variable. Of the other variables, attitude to *RISK* exerts a significant effect in the majority of cases, the perceived ability (*BR*) variable in a few cases and the attitude to deferment of gratification variable (*DG*) in the case of medium and low ability working class girls.

Path Analysis

It is possible to carry the study of perceived earnings functions a stage further. So far the analysis has been concerned with estimating the direct effects of factors such as social class, sex, ability and educational intentions on expected lifetime earnings. However, there is little doubt that the effects of some of these variables, especially ability and social class, are mediated through intended education rather than having a direct effect on the dependent variable.

In order to explore these relationships a path model was constructed based on the correlation matrix using the simplified procedures suggested by Blau (1973) [9]. The aim of the model was to explore the extent to which the antecedent variables of sex, social class and ability affect expected lifetime earnings, first *directly* and second *indirectly*. The basic form of the model was thus shown in Fig. 3.

Of course, path analysis is only as reliable as the regression equations on which it is based, and regression equations say nothing about directions of causation. In order to establish causal links it is necessary to have some prior model of the system that the regression equations describe. In the present case the basic direction of causation is clear. Each of the antecedent variables may affect expected lifetime earnings directly or it may affect them via atti-

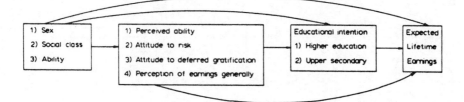

Fig. 3. Direct and indirect effects on lifetime earnings.

tudes and via educational intentions. It should be emphasised that the present study is concerned not with *actual* causal relationships but the causal relationships *as perceived by* fifth formers. This presents no additional statistical problems; but in interpreting the results we should remember that we are trying to obtain an indication of what are, in effect, maps of the minds of young people that explicitly or implicitly help them plot their route through the various educational options open to them from the age of 16 onwards. The self-concept variables we have described as "Br", "Risk" and "Deferred Gratification" require special care in interpretation since they probably reflect to some extent characteristics with which individuals are born and to some extent characteristics they acquire as they interact with their social, economic and educational environments. We have treated them as intervening variables through which the effects of sex, social class and ability are mediated.

Table VII distinguishes the direct effects of sex, social class and measured ability on expected lifetime earnings from their indirect effects as mediated by students' attitudes to risk, the deferment of gratification and their educational intentions. Figure 4 shows the same information in the form of a path diagram [10].

It is apparent that girls expect to earn less than boys largely simply

TABLE VII

Direct and Indirect Effects of Social Class and Ability on Anticipated Lifetime Earnings

		Direct	Via higher education	Via sixth form education	Via perceptions of general earnings	Via self-concept variables*	r
All sample	Sex	0.15	0	0	0.07	0.04	0.26
	Social class	(0.03)	0.05	(0.01)	0.04	0.05	0.18
	Ability	0.08	0.07	(0.01)	(0.02)	0.05	0.23
	Overall $R^2 = 0.31$						
Boys	Social class	(0.01)	0.09	(0.01)	0.06	0.03	0.20
	Ability	0.08	0.10	(0.01)	0.04	0.04	0.27
	Overall $R^2 = 0.28$						
Girls	Social class	0.06	0.04	0	0.03	0.06	0.19
	Ability	0.08	0.05	0.02	(0.01)	0.05	0.19
	Overall $R^2 = 0.23$						

Note:
The coefficients in the first column are the βs from the relevant equations. In the remaining columns the figures are obtained by computing $r_{ix} \beta^*_{yi}$ where r_{ix} is the simple correlation between the relevant row and column variables and β^*_{yi} is the direct effect of the mediating variables (i.e., the columns of the table) on expected lifetime earnings.
*In Fig. 3 these are separated into separate effects of "risk", "deferment of gratification" and "perceived ability".
Figures in brackets are *not* significantly different from zero at the 5% level.

216

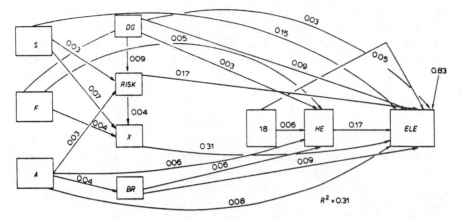

Key: *S* = Sex, *F* = social class, *A* = ability, *DG* = deferred gratification, *RISK* = attitude to risk, *X* = standardising variable(earnings), *BR* = perception of ability, *ELE* = estimated lifetime earnings.

Fig. 4. Path diagram showing effects of antecedent variables on educational intention and expected lifetime earnings. (All path coefficients with a value <0.02 or which are not significantly different from zero at 5% level have been omitted.)

because they are girls, and partly because their view of earnings in general is consistently below that of their male contemporaries. The only other intervening variable is attitude to risk, which shows that girls are more likely to be risk-averters than boys, and this is associated with their lower expected earnings. However, different post-compulsory education intentions make no contribution at all to the lower earnings expectations of girls.

The pattern of social class effects is very different. The direct effect is small and is considerably less than the effect of higher education as an intervening variable. In other words, young people from non-manual home backgrounds expect to achieve higher earnings than their manual counterparts largely as a result of the higher education they expect to undertake. The effect is particularly marked for boys. It is also worth noting that young people from non-manual home backgrounds perceive earnings in general as being higher than do their working class contemporaries.

The effect of measured ability is rather more complex. Its direct effect on expected earnings is considerably greater than social class and so is its effect via the intervention of higher education. However, "ability" seems also to interact strongly with attitudes to risk, deferred gratification and, of course, self-perceptions of ability. It is also the case that there are substantial differences between boys and girls in particular with the intervening effects of higher education.

In summary, the effect of sex on expected earnings is direct (girls

expect to earn less than boys); the effect of social class is very largely mediated by educational intention (with the effect being greater for boys than
for girls); while the effect of ability is shared almost equally between its
direct effect, the mediation of higher education and, to a slightly smaller
extent, the different attitudes of pupils with different levels of ability.

Perceived Private Rates of Return

The perceived age-earnings profiles shown in Figs. 1 and 2 were "well-
behaved" (Blaug, 1970); they rise with age, and the profiles of those young
people intending to continue their full-time studies beyond the age of 16
both rise more sharply and reach higher income levels than those of the
school leavers. In fact, the hierarchy of perceived age-earnings profiles related
to educational intention correspond remarkably well to established *ex post*
profiles. Implicit in such profiles of perceived earnings, therefore, is an
ex ante private rate of return to upper secondary and higher education,
exactly analogous to the *ex post* rates of return usually computed.

In the earlier estimation of perceived earnings functions, expected lifetime earnings were computed from anticipated earnings at the start of work
and at ages 26 and 46 from the following formula:—

$$ELE = 0.5(26 - A)(E_1 + E_2) + 10(E_2) + 29(E_3) + 3G$$

where:—

    ELE = Estimated expected lifetime earnings
    A = Assumed age of starting full-time work
    E_1 = Expected earnings when starting full-time work
    E_2 = Expected earnings at age 26
    E_3 = Expected earnings at age 46
    G = Estimated value of student grant by those respondents who
           intend to enter higher education.

The estimated expected lifetime earnings were replaced by estimated *discounted* life-time earnings as follows:—

$$DLE_r = 3G(1\text{-}r)^3 + (0.5)(26 - A)(E_1 + E_2(1\text{-}r)^{26\text{-}A}) + 10\,E_2(1\text{-}r)^{10} + 10\,E_3(1\text{-}r)^{30} + 19(1\text{-}r)^{49}$$

where G = expected student grant
and r = rate of discount.

A diagrammatic explanation of the steps in the computation of DLE_r is
given in Fig. 5.

218

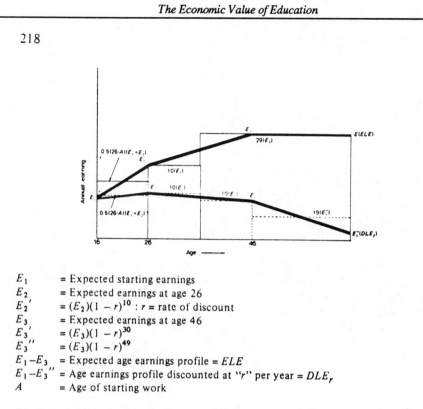

E_1 = Expected starting earnings
E_2 = Expected earnings at age 26
E_2' = $(E_2)(1 - r)^{10}$: r = rate of discount
E_3 = Expected earnings at age 46
E_3' = $(E_3)(1 - r)^{30}$
E_3'' = $(E_3)(1 - r)^{49}$
E_1-E_3 = Expected age earnings profile = ELE
E_1-E_3'' = Age earnings profile discounted at "r" per year = DLE_r
A = Age of starting work

Fig. 5. Derivation of discounted expected lifetime earnings.

The earnings functions were now of the form:—

$$DLE_r = K + \beta_1 HE + \beta_2 SL + (\text{etc.} \ldots)$$

Obviously, in cases where $r = 0$ the results are exactly the same as the case where ELE is the dependent variable.

When there is a positive rate of discount (i.e., $0 < r < 1$) the effect is to reduce the explanatory power of HE and SL on the dependent variable since most of the anticipated higher earnings associated with education occur later in life. Thus, the higher is r, the lower is the value of β_1 and β_2. Where $\beta_1 = 0$, the intention to enter higher education has no net effect on discounted expected lifetime earnings. Thus, the value of r where $\beta_1 = 0$ corresponds to the rate of discount at which the average expected net benefit from higher education rather than leaving school at 18 is zero. This corresponds to the perceived internal rate of return. Similarly, the value of r at which $\beta_2 = 0$ gives the perceived rate of return to leaving at 18 as opposed to leaving at 16.

The values of r for which β_1 and β_2 are equal to zero are given for boys and girls separately in Table VIII. For boys the "unadjusted" marginal rate of return to higher education is 13 per cent, and for girls it is just under 10

TABLE VIII

Ex Ante Private Rates of Return to Post-Compulsory Education in England

Educational level	Unadjusted marginal rate of return		Tax-adjusted marginal rate of return	
	Boys	Girls	Boys	Girls
Higher education/18	13.0	9.9	10.1	7.7
18/16	21.6	11.7	16.8	9.1

per cent. The perceived returns to upper secondary education are higher, nearly 22 per cent for boys and nearly 12 per cent for girls. These estimates are, however, based on estimates of gross income. These figures are, therefore, in Table VIII also corrected to allow for the effect of a 22 per cent average proportion of income paid in tax (Stephenson, 1978) [11]. It would have been theoretically possible to make more sophisticated adjustments to allow for tax thresholds and higher marginal rates of tax at higher levels, but this refinement did not seem to be justified in the type of data being used. We are left with the conclusion that in 1977 16-year-old boys perceived the private rate of return from staying on to age 18 as 17 per cent, with a further 10 per cent from continuing further to take a degree. For girls the expected returns were lower: 9 per cent for upper secondary and 8 per cent for higher education. Variables corresponding to ability, social class and other attitude variables were included in the estimating equation, so no further adjustment was needed for these factors.

The only other estimate we know of perceived rates of return in Britain was made by Pissarides (1979) who, using an entirely different computational procedure (based on time series analysis of entry rates to higher education and graduate starting salaries), arrived at an estimate of 13.5 per cent as the perceived private rate of return for boys of 18 staying on to higher education. His paper seems to make no allowance for taxes on income and so should be compared with our unadjusted figure of 13 per cent. The similarity of the two figures based on entirely different procedures and data is extremely satisfactory.

The most recent calculation of *actual* private rates of return to A level courses and first degree courses are contained in Psacharopoulos and Layard (1979). Their estimates of a marginal rate of return of 12 per cent for A level and 10 per cent for a first degree (tax adjusted) in 1972 are also gratifyingly close to our figures. Comparisons with this and earlier studies are given in Table IX.

Finally, in Table X we examine the hypothesis that perceived rates of

220

TABLE IX

Actual and Perceived [12] Marginal Rates of Return

Results	Year	Marginal education level			
		HE/18		18/16	
Perceived:		Boys	Girls	Boys	Girls
Present study	1977	10.1	7.7	16.8	9.1
Pissarides (1979)		13.5	–	–	–
Actual:					
Psacharopoulos and Layard					
(1979) [13]	1972	9.6	–	11.7	–
Ziderman (1973) [14]	1966–67	20.0	–	8.5	–
Blaug et al. (1967) [15]	1965	11.0	–	8.0	–
Blaug (1965) [16]	1963	14.0	–	13.0	–

return differ between social class and ability groups and that this may help to account for differences in the propensity to stay on at school by young people from different family backgrounds. Even ignoring the tax adjustment (which has the effect of compressing differentials), it is evident that there is no clear pattern of "ability" or "social class" effects. However, there are a few interesting points to note in Table X. A hypothesis was offered earlier that it could be the case that young people from "working class" home backgrounds might well require a better return on their investment in higher education as an incentive to continue their studies. While the difference is

TABLE X

Ex Ante Private Rates of Return by Social Class and Ability

Group	Unadjusted return				Tax-adjusted return			
	Boys		Girls		Boys		Girls	
	HE/18	18/16	*HE*/18	18/16	*HE*/18	18/16	*HE*/18	18/16
All	13.0	21.6	9.9	11.7	10.1	16.8	7.7	9.1
Non-manual	12.3	21.8	9.3	17.4	9.6	17.0	7.3	13.6
Manual	13.4	25.4	10.3	10.3	10.5	19.8	8.0	8.0
High ability	12.9	0.0	9.1	10.8	10.1	0	7.1	8.4
Middle ability	13.8	22.0	9.9	11.6	10.8	17.2	7.7	9.0
Low ability	9.4	28.0	8.5	13.5	7.3	21.8	6.6	10.5

not great, it would appear that manual working class boys might well "require" a higher rate of return than their non-manual peers to persuade them to stay on after compulsory schooling and to go on to higher education two years later. For girls the evidence is ambiguous, since non-manual girls seem to find it particularly worthwhile staying at school to 18. High ability boys, while perceiving a good return on higher education, seem to feel that sixth form education without going on to higher education offers no prospect of pecuniary return. And, once again, with the exception of this last group, girls in every other instance have lower perceived rates of return than the boys from the corresponding social class or ability category.

Concluding Remarks

This paper provides direct evidence to support some of the assumptions of the human capital model. At the end of their compulsory education English pupils in general have fairly accurate perceptions of the labour market opportunities that confront them and how these opportunities are related to educational qualifications. Boys expect to earn more than girls regardless of their education, and young people of high intellectual ability tend to expect to earn more than those of lower ability independently of their education. However, social background exerts very little independent influence. Pupils from white collar homes expect to earn more than others; but as a *result* of their continued education, not independently of it.

These earnings functions produce average *ex ante* perceived rates of return similar to the *ex post* actual rates of return estimated in previous studies.

The implications of these findings for an understanding of changes in the demand for higher education during the 1960s and 1970s are considerable. They lend support to claims that one of the prime motives for the rapid expansion of the 1960s and much slower growth of the 1970s was economic. The results do not demonstrate unequivocally that young people *are* influenced by perceived rates of return in taking educational decisions. They *do* suggest that pupils are *aware* of the rates of return, which is an essential first step.

The suggestion that somewhat higher perceived rates of return are necessary to encourage working class children to stay on at school and into higher education than is necessary for their middle class counterparts leads to the prediction that when actual rates of return are high, as in the 1960s, we should expect rising working class participation; when the actual rates fall, as in the 1970s, we should expect working class participation to fall. C.U.A. (1978) suggests that such movements did in fact occur amongst university entrants.

222

As far as policy is concerned, these results aid in the prediction of the demand for higher education in that they help to demonstrate that the demand is not autonomous but influenced by changes in the private economic costs and benefits of a degree level qualification. However, they suffer from the weakness of all rate of return calculations in that they offer no guide as to how actual rates of return will move in the future. Nor, of course, do they contribute to the debate about the social rate of return which many economists would consider a more valid concept in determining appropriate national expenditures on post-compulsory education.

Notes

1 A useful summary of these studies is contained in Psacharopoulos (1973) and (1975), and an examination of the issues involved are discussed by Blaug (1970) and (1972).
2 Psacharopoulos (1975) and Juster (1975) examine and review this evidence.
3 One exception is McMahon and Greske (1981).
4 This may well have resulted in a slight under-statement of the true expected lifetime earnings for those expecting to follow career paths in which earnings continue to rise with age and/or experience beyond their mid-40s.
5 The verbal reasoning test used was Part I of the NFER test AH4, designed for use with secondary school students of this age. For the Table, and in subsequent discussion, "high ability" refers to those respondents scoring in the top 30 per cent by ability, "middle ability" refers to the next 40 per cent and "low" to the bottom 30 per cent by alility. In Table VI these are referred to as A1, A2, A3.
6 It should be noted that although described as a verbal reasoning test, AH4 Part I also includes numerical manipulations.
7 Professional, Intermediate, Skilled non-manual, Skilled manual, Semi-skilled manual and Unskilled manual. In Table VI, F1 = non-manual, F2 = manual.
8 This kind of result is fairly common in the sociological and social-psychological literature. See, for example, Gouldner (1955), Katz (1964) and Banks (1976).
9 "The direct effect of an independent on the dependent variable is indicated by its beta weight or standardized regression coefficient, as already noted. The indirect connections between any independent and the dependent variable, which account for the difference between their simple correlation (r) and beta weight (b^*), are necessarily due to the other independent variables in the regression problem. Each indirect connection between an independent variable, x, and the dependent variable, y, resulting from a single other independent variable, i, is produced by the correlation between the independent variable under consideration and the other variable (r_{ix}) and the other's direct effect on the dependent variable (b^*_{yi}). The product of these two values $(r_{ix}b^*_{yi})$ indicates the strength of the indirect connection. The sum of all indirect connections between x and y, so computed, and the direct effect of x on y represented by the beta weight, equals their zero-order correlation. The assumptions about causal order among independent variables are required to decide which indirect connections are spurious and which are indirect effects. The part of the correlation between x and y produced by i's assumed to precede x is spurious, whereas the part mediated by i's assumed to follow x in the causal sequence is indicative of indirect effects." Blau (1973).

10 Appendix B contains the correlation matrix and the vectors of β coefficients on which path coefficients are based.
11 This includes income tax, surtax and employees' National Insurance contributions.
12 Tax-adjusted.
13 The rate of return figures quoted here are derived from a general earnings function and relate to annual earnings. The range of rate of return values found by Psacharopoulos and Layard vary depending on the form of earnings function considered and on the income time period considered. Details are given below:
    Rate of return to A-level and degree (percentage)

| | Using general earnings function | | Using specific earnings function | |
	Annual earnings	Weekly earnings	Annual earnings	Weekly earnings
	(1)	(2)	(3)	(4)
A-level	11.7	9.2	17.3	12.2
First degree	9.6	7.7	9.2	7.4

    Source: Psacharopoulos and Layard (1979)

14 The figures given refer to marginal private rates of return, crudely adjusted to take account of ability and other factors. For details, see Ziderman (1973). Ziderman makes the point that education to 18 carries a high option value to continue the post-compulsory education to degree level, and that his recorded returns will thus be underestimates.
15 The study by Blaug et al. (1967) computed a private marginal rate of return to a pass degree of 8.5 per cent. The figure given is for an honours degree. However, no adjustment was made for non-educational variables, although a tax adjustment was undertaken.
16 Blaug (1965) allows for 40 per cent of earnings differentials being due to non-educational factors for the 18-year-olds ($\alpha = 0.6$), and for 34 per cent for those with higher education ($\alpha = 0.66$).

References

Banks, O. (1976). *The Sociology of Education*. London: Batsford. (Ch. 4).

Blau, P. M. (1973). *The Organization of Academic Work*. New York: Wiley.

Blaug, M. (1965). "The money rate of return on education in the UK," *Manchester School*. 33(3): 205–251.

Blaug, M. (1970). *An Introduction to the Economics of Education*. London: Allen Lane.

Blaug, M. (1972). "The correlation between education and earnings: what does it signify?" *Higher Education* 1(1): 53–76.

Blaug, M., Peston, M. and Ziderman, A. (1967). *The Utilization of Educated Manpower in Industry*. Edinburgh: Oliver and Boyd.

Conference of University Administrators (C.U.A.) (1978) Group on Forecasting and University Expansion: Final Report.

Freeman, R. (1971). *The Market for College-Trained Manpower*. Cambridge, Mass.: Harvard University Press.

224

Freeman, R. (1976). *The Over-Educated American.* New York: Academic Press.

Gouldner, A. W. (1955). *Patterns of Industrial Bureaucracy.* London: Routledge and Kegan Paul.

Juster, F. T. (ed.) (1975). *Education, Income and Human Behaviour.* New York: McGraw-Hill.

Katz, F. M. (1964). "The meaning of success: some differences in the value systems of social classes," *Journal of Social Psychology.* Vol. LXII.

McMahon, W. W. and Geske, J. (1981). "Financing education: efficiency and equity," (ch. 5), in W. W. McMahon (ed.) *Educational Finance.* New York: Allyn and Bacon.

Morris, V. (1973). "Investment in higher education in England and Wales: the human capital approach to educational planning," in Fowler, G., Morris, V. and Ozga, J. (eds.). *Decision Making in British Education.* London: Heinemann.

Morris, V. and Ziderman, A. (1971). "The economic returns on investment in higher education in England and Wales," *Economic Trends.* No. 211: xx-xxxi.

Office of Population Censuses and Surveys (O.P.C.S.) (1978). *The General Household Survey 1976.* London: HMSO.

Pissarides, C. A. (1979). *Staying on at School in England and Wales and Why Nine Per Cent of the Age Group Did Not.* Centre for Labour Economics, London School of Economics, Discussion Paper No. 63 (mimeo).

Psacharopoulos, G. (1973). *Returns to Education: An International Comparison.* Amsterdam: Elsevier.

Psacharopoulos, G. (1975). *Earnings and Education in OECD Countries.* Paris: OECD.

Psacharopoulos, G. and Layard, R. (1979). "Human capital and earnings: British evidence and a critique," *Review of Economic Studies* XLVI: 485–503.

Stephenson, G. A. (1978). "The effects of taxes and benefits on household income 1976," *Economic Trends* 292: 78–91.

Williams, G. L. (1974). "The events of 1973–74 in a long term planning perspective," *Higher Education Bulletin* 3(1): 17–52.

Ziderman, A. (1973). "Does it pay to take a degree? The profitability of private investment in university education in Britain," *Oxford Economic Papers* XXV: 262–274.

Appendix A

MEDIAN ANNUAL EARNINGS OF MALES BY HIGHEST QUALIFICATION LEVEL ATTAINED BY AGE

Males aged 16–64 in full-time employment (excluding full-time students)[1]   Great Britain 1975–76 combined

| | Highest qualification level attained[2] | | | | | | |
	Degree or equivalent	Below degree higher education	GCE "A" level or equivalent	GCE "O" level or equivalent/ CSE Grade 1	CSE other grades/commercial apprenticeships	No qualifications[3]	Total
Median Annual Earnings:[4]							
Age:							
16–19	*	*	*	£1172	£1032	£1256	£1172
20–24	£2399	*	£2260	£2344	£2372	£2232	£2288
25–34	£4018	£3376	£3236	£3097	£2902	£2623	£2985
35–44	£5580	£4185	£3627	£3348	£2930	£2762	£3097
45–59	£6054	£4325	£3571	£3460	£2818	£2623	£2874
60–64	*	*	*	*	£2567	£2344	£2427
All 16–64	£4687	£3655	£2985	£2790	£2706	£2539	£2790
Bases:	No.	No.	No.	No.	No.	No.	No.
Age:							
16–19	Nil	Nil	70	398	167	364	1006
20–24	170		301	369	135	443	1435
25–34	357	337	392	688	377	1424	3730
35–44	232	204	193	386	470	1459	3100
45–59	246	240	137	302	661	2703	4500
60–64	28	30	16	52	180	732	1096
All 16–64	937	907	1109	2195	1990	7125	14867

Appendix A (continued)

MEDIAN ANNUAL EARNINGS OF FEMALES BY HIGHEST QUALIFICATION LEVEL ATTAINED BY AGE

Females aged 16–64 in full-time employment (excluding full-time students)[1]   Great Britain 1975–76 combined

| | Highest qualification level attained[2] | | | | | | |
Age	Degree or equivalent	Below degree higher education	GCE "A" level or equivalent	GCE "O" level or equivalent/ CSE Grade 1	CSE other grades/commercial apprenticeships	No qualifications[3]	Total
Median Annual Earnings:[4]							
16–19	*	*	*	£1032	£948	£1064	£1023
20–34	£2894	£2323	£2048	£1851	£1675	£1525	£1787
35–44	£3196		*	£1979	£1922	£1597	£1766
45–59	£3193		*	£2129	£2047	£1637	£1781
All 16–64	£3121	£2638	£1886	£1639	£1613	£1541	£1699
Bases:	No.	No.	No.	No.	No.	No.	No.
16–19	Nil	1	32	342	180	292	856
20–34	129	223	136	517	264	709	2053
35–44	137		13	108	113	598	1008
45–59	163		13	113	143	1164	1666
All 16–64	189	474	199	1084	715	2881	5743

[1] Full-time employment = 31 hours or more per week (26 hours for teachers and lecturers) excluding paid overtime
[2] For details of qualification levels see Appendix A GHS Report 1976
[3] Including foreign and "other" qualifications
[4] Annual earnings will be understated for people who entered or left the labour force in the course of the previous 12 months, in particular those aged under 25 with higher qualifications and for those aged 16–19 with lower or no qualifications
* Too few observations for reliable estimates
Source: SED4A GHS 1975/76

Appendix B

CORRELATION MATRIX AND *B* COEFFICIENTS (WHOLE SAMPLE)

	SEX	F	A	DG	RISK	BR	X	SL	HE	ELE
SEX	0	0.03	0.06	−0.09	0.06	0.22	−0.07	0.01	0.26	
F		0.26	0.12	0.03	0.19	0.13	−0.20	0.31	0.18	
A			0.25	0.15	0.43	0.06	−0.28	0.38	0.23	
DG				0.55	0.40	0.05	−0.17	0.19	0.12	
RISK					0.23	−0.04	−0.01	−0.03	−0.12	
BR						0.19	−0.20	0.36	0.23	
X							−0.07	0.11	0.40	
SL								−0.34	−0.21	
HE									0.33	

(ELE)	0.15	0.03	0.08	0.09	−0.17	0.09	0.31	−0.05	0.17
(F)(Statistic)	(73.8)	(3.4)	(16.9)	(16.0)	(62.0)	(18.9)	(311.2)	(7.6)	(73.0)

Adjusted R^2 = 0.304

Key to variables

SEX:	Boys = 1, Girls = 0
F:	White collar families = 1, others = 0
A:	Verbal reasoning score
DG:	+ = Willingness to defer gratification
RISK:	+ = Risk averters
BR:	Self perception of ability
X:	Perception of earnings in general
SL:	Intention to leave school at 16 = 1, others = 0
HE:	Intention to enter Higher Education = 1, others = 0
ELE:	Expected lifetime earnings

Returns to Education: an updated international comparison

GEORGE PSACHAROPOULOS

One of the first questions that was asked following on from what Mary Jean Bowman (1966) described as the human capital revolution in economic thought, was: what is the profitability of investing in the new form of capital? Hesitantly, at first, but more eagerly thereafter, researchers around the world started estimating the social or private returns associated with educational and other human-capital-related expenditures for diverse population subgroups, from special samples, using a variety of assumptions and methodologies ranging from back of envelope calculations to extremely sophisticated econometric techniques.

The year 1973 was a landmark in the 'rate of return' literature—as it came to be known thereafter—because of the publication of the first systematic comparative study in this respect, (Psacharopoulos, 1973). A total of 53 rate of return case-studies were reviewed covering 32 countries.

This paper is an attempt to update the earlier rate of return evidence by considering studies that have been conducted in the seventies. The result of this update is the addition of 13 new country cases and a revision of most of the figures in the old country set.

However, I go beyond the compilation of comparable figures and discuss a series of controversial arguments that have been associated with the rate of return literature of the 1970s. Also, I try to give an interpretation of the summary findings following the expanded data set.

Trends in the Rate of Return Literature

Putting aside what is claimed to be the first empirical cost-benefit analysis of education by a Soviet economist (Strumilin, 1929) the real rate of return estimation activity started in the late fifties (see, e.g. Becker, 1960), T. W. Schultz's (1961) presidential address to the American Economic Association and the publication of Becker's (1964) NBER book gave a further boost to the subject, especially as a topic of PhD dissertations in US universities. The estimation procedure used during this first wave of rate of return literature was of the 'elaborate type', as described in the next section.

The second wave of the 'rate of return' literature starts somewhere in the early 1970s and is established with the publication of Mincer's (1974) NBER book. The estimation technique now becomes increasingly of the 'earnings function' type, as described in the next section. This technique is still going strong today and tends to be the dominant rate of return estimation procedure.

It is also interesting to note that the alternative to the rate of return cost-benefit measure, the

322   Comparative Education   *Volume 17 No. 3 1981*

'net present value', has lost ground in the recent literature, mainly because it does not have a readily intelligible interpretation.

RATE OF RETURN ESTIMATION PROCEDURES

For the purpose of this paper it is sufficient to distinguish three main methods for estimating the rate of return to investment in education: the elaborate method, the earnings function method and the short-cut method.

(a) *The Elaborate Method*

This follows from the exact algebraic definition of the rate of return, which is the discount rate that equates a stream of benefits to a stream of costs at a given point in time. For example, consider the estimation of the private rate of return to investment in higher education in Fig. 1. If Y stands for labour earnings, and h and s subscripts for higher and secondary education, respectively, the rate of return (r) in this case is found by solving the following equation for r:

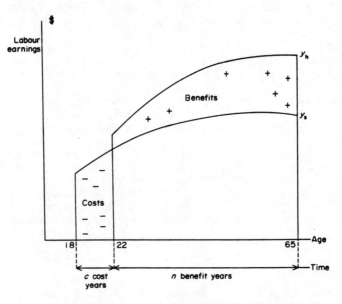

FIG. 1. A rate of return estimation according to the elaborate method.

discounted benefits to age 22 = cumulated costs at age 22.

(+ + + area) = (− − − area)

$$\sum_{t=1}^{n}(Y_h - Y_s)_t(1+r)^{-t} = \sum_{t=1}^{c}(Y_s)_t(1+r)^t. \qquad (1)$$

This high power equation is usually solved by an iterative computer programme that starts

Comparative Education *Volume 17 No. 3 1981* 323

from an arbitrary value of r and keeps modifying it by small increments in the right direction until the left-hand side is equal to the right-hand side.

Note that in the above *private* rate of return calculation the only cost of the 'education project' under evaluation is the opportunity cost of staying on in school beyond the age of 18 instead of working in the labour market. This opportunity cost is measured by the earnings of labour with secondary school qualifications.

Should the estimation of a *social* rate of return be desired, one can simply add the resource cost of an university place in the right-hand side of equation (1) and repeat the calculation. Of course earnings in this case should be before tax, whereas in the private rate of return calculation earnings should be after tax. But contrary to popular belief, the post- versus pre-tax treatment of earnings does *not* make a big difference in a rate of return calculation. It is the addition of the *direct cost* of schooling that mainly accounts for the fact that a social rate of return is lower relative to a private rate of return.

This way of estimating the profitability of investment in education requires in the first place detailed data on age-earnings profiles by educational level. This information is rare in most countries. Even if this information were available, the problem of small number cells arises. Namely, the plotted actual age-earnings profiles exhibit a saw-tooth patten making the rate of return estimation very sensitive, especially regarding the initial years after graduation which carry a high weight in the discounting.

It is for this reason smoothing-out procedures have been used, the rate of return being estimated in three steps: in step one a regression of the type:

$$Y_i = a + b \cdot AGE_i + c \cdot AGE_i^2 \qquad (2)$$

is fitted within subgroups of workers with the same educational level for the purpose of summarising the data.

In step 2 an idealised age-earnings profile is constructed by predicting the value of $\hat{Y}$ for given ages and educational levels, using the estimated function (2).

In step 3, the predicted values of earnings are inserted in formula (1), in order to compute the rate of return.

(b) *The Earnings Function Method*

Equation (2) in the above smoothing out procedure should not be confused with what is known as the earnings function method of estimating the rate of return. This is a regression of the basic form

$$\ln Y_i = a + b \cdot S_i + c \cdot EX_i + d \cdot EX_i^2 \qquad (3)$$

where S is the number of years of schooling of the individual (i) and EX his years of labour market experience. Equation (2) is an *ad hoc* fitting regression. Equation (3) is based on human capital theory where $b = r$, i.e. the estimated regression coefficient (b) is interpreted as the *average private* rate of return to one extra year of schooling.

An illustrative proof of this proposition (that is essentially due to Mincer, 1974) is that

$$b = \frac{\partial \ln Y}{\partial S} = r, \qquad (4)$$

i.e. the rate of return is nothing else than the relative change in earnings ($\partial \ln Y$) following a given change in schooling (∂S).

There exist two ways one can add an educational level dimension to this 'average' rate of return concept. The first way is to add an $e \cdot S^2$ term in equation (3), where e is the estimated coefficient on years-of-schooling-squared. In this case, differentiation with respect to S yields

$$r = b + 2eS. \qquad (5)$$

By substituting different values of S in the right-hand side of equation (5), one can arrive at a regression-derived rate of return structure corresponding, say, to primary education ($S = 6$), secondary education ($S = 12$) and higher education ($S = 16$).

The second way is to specify different educational levels in the earnings function by means of a series of dummy variables, say PRIM, SEC and HIGH, having a value of 1 if the individual belongs to the particular educational level and 0 otherwise:

$$\ln Y = a + b \cdot \text{PRIM} + c \cdot \text{SEC} + d \cdot \text{HIGH} + e \cdot \text{EX} + f \cdot \text{EX}^2. \qquad (6)$$

In this case, the rates of return to the different levels of education are derived from the estimated coefficients b, c and d in the above function as follows:

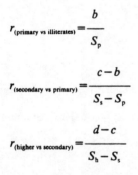

$$r_{\text{(primary vs illiterates)}} = \frac{b}{S_p}$$

$$r_{\text{(secondary vs primary)}} = \frac{c - b}{S_s - S_p}$$

$$r_{\text{(higher vs secondary)}} = \frac{d - c}{S_h - S_s}$$

where S stands for the number of years of schooling of the subscripted educational level (p = primary, s = secondary and h = higher).

The rationale of this procedure is that effectively one computes the rate of return by means of the following formula that is educational-level-specific

$$r_k = \frac{\ln Y_k - \ln Y_{k - \Delta S}}{\Delta S}. \qquad (7)$$

Here k is the higher educational level in the comparison and ΔS the difference in years of schooling between k and the control group.

The advantage of estimating the rate of return by the dummy variable method rather than the years-of-schooling-squared method is that a great deal of sensitivity is added: i.e. the actual rate of return structure might not be as smooth as that suggested by formula (5).

However, the problem with the earnings function approach in general is that the rates of

Comparative Education   *Volume 17 No. 3 1981*   325

return are estimated on the basis of the following implicit assumptions:

  (i) the age-earnings profiles are either flat or equidistant between adjacent educational
      levels throughout their range;
 (ii) the age-earnings profiles last for ever (to infinity); and
(iii) the only cost of schooling is the foregone earnings of the individual (see Fig. 2).

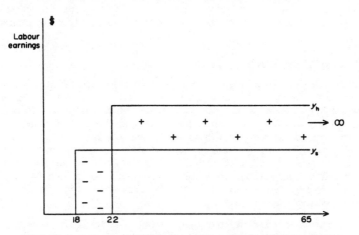

FIG. 2. The rate of return estimation procedure implicit in the short-cut method.

These assumptions are not as damaging or unrealistic as they seem and they have been
sufficiently defended (and debated) in the earnings function literature (see, e.g. Blinder, 1976).
For example, the fact that age-earnings profiles are assumed to last for ever makes little
difference to the discounted present value and hence the estimated rate of return.

The main problems with this method, however, are first, one cannot readily incorporate cost
data in order to estimate social rates of return, and secondly, this method understates the
returns to primary education. The reason for the downward bias on the return to primary
education is that *the estimation formula automatically assigns foregone earnings to primary
school children.* This is just not true in most country settings and one should have this
understatement in mind when interpreting the results.

(c) *The Short-Cut Method*

This amounts to doing in an explicit way what the earnings function method is doing
implicitly, i.e. the returns to education are estimated on the basis of the simple formula

$$r_k = \frac{\bar{Y}_k - Y_{k-\Delta s}}{S \cdot (\bar{Y}_{k-\Delta S})} \qquad (8)$$

where $\bar{Y}$ refers to mean earnings of employees with the subscripted educational level.
Formulae (7) and (8) are very similar, the difference lying in the mathematical approximation
$\ln(1+x) \approx x$ which is good for values of x of the order of the rate of return to education. The
great advantage of this formula is that one can use already tabulated information on the

earnings of workers by educational level in order to estimate the private rate of return. Also, it is rather easy to add the resource cost of schooling in the denominator in order to estimate the social returns. Hence, it is of great value in cases where information on individual earnings is not available.

Of course the main problem with this formula is that the age (or experience) standardisation is absent. However, this can be rectified in case the mean earnings by educational level are available for large age groups. Then choice of, say, the 35–45 age group for computation of the rate of return somehow prevents biases associated with the early experience profiles.

AN UPDATED RATE OF RETURN SET

Table I presents private and social rates of return by educational level in 44 countries. This is an update of table 4.1 in my 1973 book. Estimates based on old surveys were replaced by newer ones when available, as in the case of Kenya, India, Philippines, Brazil, Colombia, Greece, Belgium, Japan, Malaysia, United Kingdom and the United States. New country observations were added referring to Ethiopia, Malawi, Morocco, Sierra Leone, Indonesia, Taiwan, Cyprus, Spain, Yugoslavia, Iran, France and Italy. And, faute de mieux, the previous set of rates of return was retained in countries where no newer estimates were available.

As in the previous compilation, an attempt was made to include rates of return as comparable as possible between countries. Thus, where the relevant information was available in the original study, the reported rates are:

Marginal, in the sense that they refer to investment at the margin between the educational levels considered (e.g. primary graduation vs illiterates, secondary general vs primary and higher education vs secondary general).
Unadjusted, for economic growth, ability differences and unemployment. (The rationale for this choice is explained in a later section of this paper.)
Elaborate-method derived in most cases (except in the cases of Colombia, Cyprus, and the United Kingdom where the regression method was used, and Malawi, Indonesia and Italy where the short-cut method was used).

Rate of Return Patterns

Nobody can claim that the combination of diverse assumptions, estimation procedures, sample data and years of reference would have ever resulted to an absolutely comparable rate of return set to the last decimal point. But Table I contains some strong features that cannot be due to comparability biases. The rate of return patterns in this table are fully compatible, validate and reinforce the conclusions reached on the basis of the 1973 international comparison. It is easier to discover the underlying patterns by averaging within country groups, as shown in Table II.
Pattern No. 1 The returns to primary education (whether social or private) are the highest among all educational levels.
Pattern No. 2 The private returns are in excess of social returns, especially at the university level.
Pattern No. 3 All rates of return to investment in education are well above the 10% common yardstick of the opportunity cost of capital.
Pattern No. 4 The returns to education in developing countries are higher relative to the corresponding returns in more advanced countries.

The above four propositions not only make economic sense, but also have important policy implications to be elaborated in the last section of this paper.

Comparative Education   Volume 17 No. 3 1981   327

TABLE I
Returns to education by level and country type (%)

Country	Survey year	Private			Social		
		Prim.	Sec.	Higher	Prim.	Sec.	Higher
Africa							
Ethiopia	1972	35·0	22·8	27·4	20·3	18·7	9·7
Ghana	1967	24·5	17·0	37·0	18·0	13·0	16·5
Kenya*	1971	28·0	33·0	31·0	21·7	19·2	8·8
Malawi	1978				15·1		
Morocco	1970				50·5	10·0	13·0
Nigeria	1966	30·0	14·0	34·0	23·0	12·8	17·0
Rhodesia	1960				12·4		
Sierra Leone	1971				20·0	22·0	9·5
Uganda	1965				66·0	28·6	12·0
Asia							
India	1965	17·3	18·8	16·2	13·4	15·5	10·3
Indonesia	1977	25·5	15·6				
South Korea	1967				12·0	9·0	5·0
Malaysia	1978		32·6	34·5			
Philippines	1971	9·0	6·5	9·5	7·0	6·5	8·5
Singapore	1966		20·0	25·4	6·6	17·6	14·1
Taiwan	1972	50·0	12·7	15·8	27·0	12·3	17·7
Thailand	1970	56·0	14·5	14·0	30·5	13·0	11·0
Latin America							
Brazil	1970		24·7	13·9		23·5	13·1
Chile	1959				24·0	16·9	12·2
Colombia	1973	15·1	15·4	20·7			
Mexico	1963	32·0	23·0	29·0	25·0	17·0	23·0
Venezuela	1957		18·0	27·0	82·0	17·0	23·0
Intermediate							
Cyprus	1975	15·0	11·2	14·8			
Greece	1977	20·0	6·0	5·5	16·5	5·5	4·5
Spain	1971	31·6	10·2	15·5	17·2	8·6	12·8
Turkey	1968		24·0	26·0			8·5
Yugoslavia	1969	7·6	15·3	2·6	9·3	15·4	2·8
Israel	1958	27·0	6·9	8·0	16·5	6·9	6·6
Iran	1976		21·2	18·5	15·2	17·6	13·6
Puerto Rico	1959		38·6	41·1	21·9	27·3	21·9
Advanced							
Australia	1969		14·0	13·9			
Belgium	1960		21·2	8·7		17·1	6·7
Canada	1961		16·3	19·7		11·7	14·0
Denmark	1964			10·0			7·8
France	1970		13·8	16·7		10·1	10·9
Germany	1964			4·6			
Italy	1969		17·3	18·3			
Japan	1973		5·9	8·1		4·6	6·4

TABLE I *(continued)*

Country	Survey year	Private			Social		
		Prim.	Sec.	Higher	Prim.	Sec.	Higher
Netherlands	1965		8·5	10·4		5·2	5·5
New Zealand	1966		20·0	14·7		19·4	13·2
Norway	1966		7·4	7·7		7·2˙	7·5
Sweden	1967			10·3		10·5	9·2
United Kingdom†	1972		11·7	9·6		3·6	8·2
United States	1969		18·8	15·4		10·9	10·9

Source:

Ethiopia	from Hoerr (1974, table 3).
Kenya	private rates, from Fields (1975, table II).
Malawi	preliminary estimate based on Heyneman (1980a).
Morocco	from Psacharopoulos (1976, p. 136).
Sierra Leone	from Ketkar (1974, table 5).
India	from Pandit (1976) as reported by Heyneman (1980b, p. 146).
Indonesia	from Hallak & Psacharopoulos (1979, p. 13).
Malaysia	from Lee (1980).
Philippines	from ILO (1974, p. 635).
Singapore	from Clark & Fong (1970).
Taiwan	from Gannicott (1972)
Brazil	from Jallade (1977, table 4).
Colombia	regression-derived from Fields & Schultz (1977, table 8A, col.(4)).
Cyprus	from Demetriades & Psacharopoulos (1979, table 9).
Greece	from Psacharopoulos & Kazamias (1978, table 19.1).
Spain	from Quintas & Sanmartin (1978, table 1).
Turkey	from Krueger (1972, table 4).
Yugoslavia	from Thomas (1976, table 3).
Iran	from Pourhosseini (1979). ·
Puerto Rico	from Carnoy (1972).
Australia	from Blandy & Goldsworthy (1973, p. 9).
Belgium	from Meulders (1974, table II).
France	from Eicher & Lévy-Garboua (1979, chapter 5).
Italy	based on income data from Bank of Italy (1972, table 10).
Japan	from Umetani (1977, pp. 113–114).
United Kingdom	private rates from Psacharopoulos & Layard (1979, table IX).
USA	from Carnoy & Marenbach (1975).

Ghana, Nigeria, Uganda, South Korea, Thailand, Chile, Mexico, Venezuela, Israel, Canada, Denmark, Germany, Netherlands, New Zealand, Norway, Sweden and the United Kingdom (social returns only) from Psacharopoulos (1973, p. 62).

Notes
* Social rates refer to 1968.   † Social rates refer to 1966.

TABLE II
The returns to education by region and country type (%)

Region or country type	N	Private			Social		
		Prim.	Sec.	High.	Prim.	Sec.	High
Africa	(9)	29	22	32	29	17	12
Asia	(8)	32	17	19	16	12	11
Latin America	(5)	24	20	23	44	17	18
LDC average	(22)	29	19	24	27	16	13
Intermediate	(8)	20	17	17	16	14	10
Advanced	(14)	(a)	14	12	(a)	10	9

Source: Table I.
(a) Not computable because of lack of a control group of illiterates.
N   = Number of countries in each group.
Prim. = primary educational level.
Sec. = secondary educational level.
High. = higher educational level.

Evidence from Earnings Functions

Table III presents another compilation of rates of return, this time derived exclusively from earnings functions. In most cases, the reported coefficient is the partial derivative of the logarithm of earnings with respect to years of schooling, years of labour market experience or age, being held constant. As noted earlier, the resulting rate of return is private and does not refer to any particular educational level. In poor countries, however, it must refer to the typical year of primary education as the mode of years of schooling distribution corresponds to this level. It is in this sense that the rates of return reported in Table III are underestimates of the true profitability of education at the lower educational level as they incorporate the implicit assumption of foregone earnings at an early age.

Table IV provides a summary of earnings-functions derived rates of return by country type. Again, the same overall pattern is observed, namely the returns decline with the level of economic development.

ON QUALIFICATIONS AND CONTROVERSIES

The 'rate of return' subject is still highly controversial in the literature, although it is now more widely accepted than, say, 15 years ago. Let us give a brief summary of the major objections raised against the usefulness of rates of return as a tool for the formulation of educational policy, along with the answer of the proponents of this concept.

Data Quality

This is a problem common in all empirical work and the rate of return estimation makes no exception to it. In the above international comparison I would put greatest faith in the estimates referring to the United States and the United Kingdom, since I known these numbers come from official census statistics using rigorous sampling techniques covering the population as a whole. At the same time I would put least faith in the rate of return estimates for Yugoslavia, the information coming from a short article where the reporting of the exact sampling procedures, response errors etc. cannot be described in detail. This does not mean,

TABLE III

The percent increment in earnings associated with one extra year of schooling

Country	Year	$\dfrac{\partial \ln Y}{\partial S}$	Source
Africa			
Ethiopia	1972	8·0	Hoerr (1974)
Kenya	1970	16·4	Johnson (1972)
Morocco	1970	15·8	Psacharopoulos (1977a)
Asia			
Malaysia	1978	22·8	Lee (1980)
Singapore	1974	8·0	Fong (1976)
S. Vietnam	1964	16·8	Stroup & Hargrove (1969)
Thailand	1971	10·4	Chiswick (1976)
Taiwan	1972	6·0	Cannicott (1972)
Latin America			
Brazil	1970	19·2	Psacharopoulos (1980a)
Colombia	1973	20·5	Fields & Schultz (1977)
Mexico	1963	15·0	Carnoy (1967)
Intermediate			
Cyprus	1975	12·5	Demetriades & Psacharopoulos (1979)
Greece	1977	5·9	Psacharopoulos & Kazamias (1978)
Iran	1976	10·7	Scully (1979)
Advanced			
Canada	1971	5·2	Gunderson (1979)
France	1964	10·9	Riboud (1975)
Japan	1970	7·3	Kuratani (1973)
Sweden	1974	6·7	Gustafsson (1977)
United Kingdom	1975	7·8	Psacharopoulos (1980b)
United States	1973	8·2	Young & Jamison (1975)

TABLE IV

The returns to education irrespective of educational level, country group averages

Region or country type	N	Rate of return (%)
Africa	(3)	13·4
Asia	(5)	12·8
Latin America	(3)	18·2
LDC average	(11)	14·4
Intermediate	(3)	9·7
Advanced	(6)	7·7

Source: Table III.
Note: rate of return is private, estimated by an earnings function and refers to the average year of schooling.

Comparative Education   *Volume 17 No. 3 1981*   331

however, that one has to dismiss such estimates as unreliable. The criterion here is that the particular author and/or journal referee/or PhD thesis committee felt the quality of the work was suitable for 'publication' (in the wider sense of the term).

In some country cases I had a choice between alternative estimates from several authors using different estimation procedures or sample bases. The rates of return I retained in such case were from the study that in my opinion was the best in terms of comparability to the rest.

The Social Productivity of Education

This is the most often cited objection to rate of return estimations; namely, one cannot approximate the true social productivity of education by working with the earnings of employees by level of educational attainment. This common-sense objection has recently been weakened because of an accumulation of studies on the effect of education on farmers' productivity (see, e.g. Jamison & Lau, 1978). If more education (mostly at the basic level) contributes (other things being equal) to extra rice production, this extra rice is an ultimate demonstration of the social productivity of education.

At the higher levels of education where the production of, say, university graduates, cannot be measured in such tangible terms, objections here have been raised to the use of earnings as a proxy for productivity. These objections take specific labels and the major ones are known in the literature as 'screening or certification', 'bumping or job competition' and 'labour market segmentation'. All these are very sensible, common-sense hypotheses and have appealed to many analysts and politicians alike. However, these hypotheses are found wanting when put to the test.

Screening or Certification [1]

What this theory says is that schools produce just diplomas or sheepskins helping the holder to get a *privately* well paid job, although the *social* payoff of the human investment he has undertaken might be minimal [2]. However, there exists one major objection to this view: when one makes the distinction between 'initial' and 'persistent' screening, it is very hard to find evidence corroborating the latter, namely that employers keep paying wages above the worker's productivity *after* they have the employee under their observation for some time [3]. Initial screening certainly exists, i.e. employers may hire someone on the basis of his expected productivity given his educational qualifications. But there is nothing wrong with it as, after all, it has an informational social value (see Psacharopoulos, 1980c).

Differential Ability

Embedded in the screening argument is the ability factor: because those who have more education than others allegedly also have a higher level of ability, wage differentials are not solely due to learning, a great part of them being due to differential ability. This highly intuitive argument combined with some aggregate, cross-tabulation evidence by Becker (1964) and Denison (1967) resulted in the enthronement of this myth. However, micro-data plus scrutinisation of what 'ability' really means resulted in the highly counter-intuitive finding that ability differentials do not account for much of the variation in earnings (see Psacharopoulos, 1975 and Griliches, 1979).

The Job Competition or Bumping Model

This is another highly intuitive notion, i.e. workers compete for jobs rather than wages, and those with more educational qualifications bump out from the labour queue the less qualified

332   Comparative Education   *Volume 17 No. 3 1981*

and get the job [1]. That is certainly true, but this view fails to show why such bumping should be socially wrong. If the more qualified perform better in the job they are in, this is socially healthy. There exists plenty of micro-evidence that the latter is likely to be the case as the more qualified earn more relatively to the less qualified even after one standardises for occupation.

Is there a Dual Labour Market?

Another attack comes from the so-called dual or segmented labour market hypothesis (Gordon, 1972). According to it, education helps workers belonging to the 'primary segment' of the market (i.e. those in good jobs), but not those in the 'secondary segment' (i.e. those with inferior jobs). For several reasons the dual labour market fashion that started in the early 1970s has already faded away, although it is still echoed in some quarters (for a critique see Cain, 1976). In the first place, testing it is extremely difficult because the hypothesis has never been stated in a rigorous manner. Secondly, the separation of the upper from the lower segment is a major problem on its own. Where should one draw the dividing line between the two allegedly separate labour markets? Also, empirical attempts to test whatever bits and pieces of the theory are testable have failed to reject the orthodox functioning of labour markets (see Psacharopoulos, 1978 and McNabb & Psacharopoulos, 1981).

On Social Class

Another commonly held belief is that education serves the maintenance of the *status quo* from generation to generation (Bowles, 1972). Although this might be true to a large extent, it does not constitute a challenge to the use of earnings as a proxy for productivity. For two interesting recent results show that, first, family background (or social class) has only an indirect effect on earnings and this is via education. The direct effect of social background on earnings is rather weak. Also, it is those who acquire more education that are socially more upwardly mobile (Psacharopoulos, 1977b and Psacharopoulos & Tinbergen, 1978).

The Role of the Public Sector

In some instances, rates of return have been estimated on the basis of public sector earnings. Since the public sector is the major employer of educated labour in developing countries, its non-profit maximising behaviour has been used as an argument against the use of earnings in rate of return computations. However, recent evidence from Brazil and Malaysia on public-private sector comparisons indicates that the contrary is likely to be the case. Namely, public sector based rate of return calculations are likely to *under*estimate the true returns to education, as judged from private sector employment (see Psacharopoulos, 1980d).

Graduate Unemployment

One widespread view is that education produces unemployed graduates. This is a more serious challenge relative to the ones mentioned above, as it denies even the private benefits accruing to the individual investor. However, this argument is put in the right perspective when a distinction is made between the *incidence* and the *duration* of unemployment. Unemployment is high among young people; but in the majority of cases it lasts for a few months at the most. (For detailed evidence on the incidence and duration of unemployment as related to education in developing countries, see Psacharopoulos, 1980d.) Hence, one might consider the lack of employment immediately after graduation to be the reflection of a 'job search' process. And certainly it would be a mistake to reduce a whole age-earnings profile by the average rate of unemployment that mainly refers to young people.

Comparative Education   *Volume 17 No. 3 1981* 333

SOME POLICY IMPLICATIONS

To the extent that the figures presented above, represent valid indicators of the true relative rate of return structure by level of education and country type, they have at least the following specific policy implications:

Policy Implication No. 1

A look at Fig. 3 leaves no doubt that top priority should be given to primary education as a form of human resource investment.

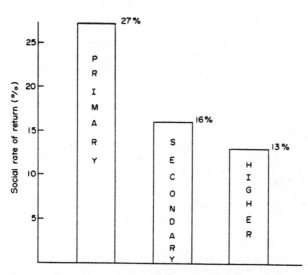

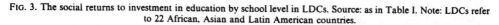

FIG. 3. The social returns to investment in education by school level in LDCs. Source: as in Table I. Note: LDCs refer to 22 African, Asian and Latin American countries.

Policy Implication No. 2

Secondary and higher education are also socially profitable investments and therefore should be pursued alongside with primary education in a programme of balanced human resource development.

Policy Implication No. 3

The large discrepancy between the private and social returns to investment in higher education (24 vs 13%, respectively) suggests there exists room for private finance at the university level. A shift of part of the cost burden from the state to the individual and his family is not likely to lead to a disincentive of investing in higher education given the present high private profitability margin.

Policy Implication No. 4

As a country develops and/or the capacity of its educational system expands, the returns to education are definitely falling, although not to a large extent. Therefore, the fear of a drastic fall of the returns to education following educational expansion is unfounded.

Since this fear is a commonly held belief among educational planning practitioners, the following sub-section elaborates this point.

Educational Expansion and Rates of Return

The evidence needed to investigate this topic is time-series rates of return, a luxury available in only a couple of countries. But even if one had a complete historical time trend of rates of return, this is no guarantee that their structure will be valid in the future beyond the available range of observations. Therefore, in making predictions in this respect one must also rely on a theory of some sort.

The international comparison presented earlier provides the basis for a cross-sectional reconstruction of time series by comparing the returns to education at different levels of economic development. From Table II one gets the following world-wide picture:

Country type	Social returns to investment in education (%)		
	Primary	Secondary	Higher
LDC	27	16	13
Intermediate	16	14	10
Advanced	na	10	9

Namely, the returns do fall as a country passes from one stage of development to the next, which occurs *pari passu* with educational expansion. However, the decline of the returns is minimal when one considers the big educational expansion steps implied between rows in the above tabulation.

Also, the international comparison of earnings functions yields the following picture regarding the returns to the typical year of schooling by country type:

Country type	Rate of return
LDC	14
Intermediate	10
Advanced	8

Namely, the same conclusion is supported regarding the gradual fall óf the overall rate of return associated with economic development (read, educational expansion).

Moving beyond these extremely aggregate figures, we can concentrate on what has happened within single countries where time-series evidence is available on the returns to

Comparative Education   *Volume 17 No. 3 1981* 335

education. One cannot be very choosey in this respect, so here is the picture of what has happened in one DC and one LDC.

The United States

Rate of return estimates for this country exist for every census year since 1939 and for every single year since 1970. Table V gives a summary picture of the evolution of the rate of return over nearly 40 years. The returns to education have been falling, although to a limited extent. The rate of return to secondary education fluctuates since 1959 at above the 10% level. The rate of return to higher education has been virtually constant at the 11% level between 1939 and 1969, in spite of the tremendous college expansion that occurred during the 1960's. Thereafter, it seems to be dropping, although there exists great controversy in the literature on the validity and interpretation of this decline [5].

TABLE V
Time series returns to education in the United States (%)

Year	Secondary	Higher
1939	18·2	10·7
1949	14·2	10·6
1959	10·1	11·3
1969	10·7	10·9
1970	11·3	8·8
1971	12·5	8·0
1972	11·3	7·8
1973	12·0	5·5
1974	14·8	4·8
1975	12·8	5·3
1976	11·0	5·3

Source: 1939–69 social rates from Carnoy & Marenbach (1975, table 2).
1970–76 private rates from Psacharopoulos, (1980e, table 4).

The apparent 'puzzle' of the stability of the returns to education in the presence of educational expansion has been explained in terms of supply and demand terms, namely the demand for educated labour keeps pace with a rapidly increasing supply, the end result being a near constant rate of return (see, e.g. Welch, 1970). Or, to put it in Tinbergen's (1975) terms, this phenomenon can be explained in terms of a 'race' between education (supply curve shifting to the right) and technology (demand curve shifting to the right), as shown in Fig. 4.

Colombia

As shown in Table VI the structure of the Colombian labour force has shown a dramatic improvement within a decade, the proportion of university graduates doubling between 1964 and 1974. The question is what happened to the rate of return during this period?

As expected, the rates of return have in fact fallen (Table VII) although investment in education at all levels remains a highly profitable activity.

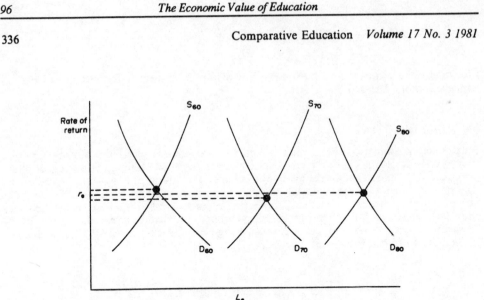

Fig. 4. A hypothetical 'race' between education and technology resulting in a more or less constant rate of return to education over time. S=supply curve; D=demand curve; L=labour; r=rate of return. Subscripts: e=educated; n=non-educate; 60, 70, 80=year.

TABLE VI
The changing educational structure of the Colombian labour force (%)

Educational level	1964	1974
Illiterates	5·0	3·5
Primary school	57·3	45·4
Secondary school	29·5	34·8
Higher eduction	8·2	16·3

Source: Bourgignon (1980, table 1).

TABLE VII
The returns to education in Colombia by educational level

Educational level	1963–66	1974
Primary	53·1	36·0
Secondary	31·7	21·9
Higher	29·2	18·5

Source: based on Bourgignon (1980, table 5). Rates are private calculated by the short-cut method.

337

Additional evidence from earnings functions analysis corroborates this result:

Year	Rate of return
1963–66	19·8
1965	17·3
1971	16·7
1974	15·1

Source: Bourgignon (1980, table 4).

An earlier analysis by Dougherty (1971) using 1963–66 data has actually simulated the behaviour of the rate of return as a function of educational expansion in Colombia. Fig. 5 shows the expected path of the rate of return to secondary education if enrolments followed the historical growth rate of 10% per year (path A) or a hypothetical 15% rate (path B). As expected, the returns to education fall but not so drastically that this type of investment becomes socially unprofitable in a 16-year interval.

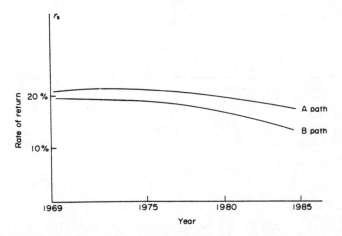

FIG. 5. An actual simulation of the social rate of return to secondary education in Colombia as a function of enrolments. Note: figure is approximate. r_s = rate of return to secondary education; A path = based on the assumption of a 10% per year historical expansion of enrolments; B path = based on a hypothetical 15% per year growth of enrolments.

This earlier analysis has also demonstrated using Colombian data the importance of the 'elasticity of substitution' between different types of educated labour in affecting the future structure of rates of return [6]. This concept measures the degree of easiness or flexibility that exists in a given economy to accommodate different labour skill mixes in production without affecting the relative labour rewards. The higher the value of the elasticity of substitution, the longer a present rate of return measure will remain valid in the future following educational expansion.

There exists an immense literature on empirical estimates of elasticities of substitution between different types of labour in a variety of country settings. As shown in Table VIII this elasticity is on high side, i.e. well above the value of unity. This evidence supports a theory on the basis of which one can confidently plan for educational expansion without affecting the rate of return to the point of such investment becoming socially unprofitable. At least this is

TABLE VIII

Estimates of the elasticity of substitution between highly trained and other labour (absolute values)

Nature of study	Elasticity estimate	Author
Cross-section, 22 countries	1	OECD (1971)
Cross-section, 22 US States	3·3–9·0	Dougherty (1972)
Cross-section, 12 countries	4·8	Bowles (1969)
Cross-section, 18 countries	2·2	Psacharopoulos & Hinchliffe (1972)
Time series, USA 1956–68	3·8	Dresch (1976)
Cross-section, 22 countries	0·6–3·5	Fallon & Layard (1975)
Time series, USA 1929–68	4·9–6·1	Bernt & Christensen (1974)
Time series, USA	2·3	Freeman (1971)
Time series, USA 1900–63	1·5	Ullman (1972)

Source: As compiled from original sources by Tinbergen & Psacharopoulos (1980).

what might be expected in the medium term in LDCs where the returns to the lower levels of schooling are of such magnitude that the possibility of over-investing in education is extremely remote.

ACKNOWLEDGEMENT

This paper is based on part II of a background document prepared for the 1980 World Development Report. (See T. King, Ed., *Education and Income*, World Bank Staff Working Paper No. 402, July 1980). The views expressed here are those of the author and should not be attributed to the World Bank.

NOTES

[1] This sub-section partly draws from Psacharopoulos (1980b) to which the reader is referred to for further elaboration of points.
[2] For a formal analysis of the screening hypothesis see Arrow (1973). For empirical tests see Layard & Psacharopoulos (1974).
[3] For a theoretical distinction and an empirical test between the 'weak' versus the 'strong' version of the screening hypothesis, see Psacharopoulos (1979).
[4] For the main variant of this model see Thurow & Lucas (1972).
[5] See Freeman (1976), Smith & Welch (1978) and the exchange in the Winter 1980 issue of the *Journal of Human Resources.*
[6] See also Dougherty (1972).

REFERENCES

ARROW, K. (1973) Higher education as a filter, *Journal of Public Economics*, July.

BANK OF ITALY (1972) *Quindicinale di Note e Commenti*, Anno VIII. N.162–63, 15 May.

BECKER, G. (1960) Underinvestment in college education?, *American Economic Review*, May.

BECKER, G. (1964) *Human Capital*, 1st edn (NBER).

BERNT, E.R. & CHRISTENSEN, L.R. (1974) Testing for the existence of a consistent aggregate index of labour inputs, *American Economic Review*, p. 391.

BLANDY, R. & GOLDSWORTHY, T. (1973) Private returns to education in South Australia, *Working Paper No. 3* (Institute of Labour Studies, The Flinders University of South Australia).

BLINDER, A. S. (1976) On dogmatism in human capital theory, *Journal of Human Resources*, Winter.

BOWLES, S. (1969) *Planning Educational Systems for Economic Growth* (Harvard University Press).

BOWLES, S. (1972) Schooling and inequality from generation to generation, *Journal of Political Economy*, May–June. Supplement.

BOWMAN, M. J. (1966) The human investment revolution in economic thought, *Sociology of Education*, Vol. 39, No. 2.

BOURGIGNON, F. (1980) The role of education in the urban labour market during the process of development: the case of Colombia, paper presented at the *6th World Congress of the International Economic Association*, Mexico City. August.

CAIN, G. (1976) The challenge of segmented labour market theories to orthodox theory: a survey, *Journal of Economic Literature*, December.

CARNOY, M. (1967) Earnings and schooling in Mexico, *Economic Development and Cultural Change*, July.

CARNOY, M. (1972) The rate of return to schooling and the increase in human resources in Puerto Rico, *Comparative Education Review*, February.

CARNOY, M. & MARENBACH, D. (1975) The return to schooling in the United States, 1939–69, *Journal of Human Resources*, Summer.

CHISWICK, C. (1976) On estimating earnings functions for LDC's, *Journal of Development Economics*. pp. 67–78.

CLARK, D. H. & FONG, P. E. (1970) Returns to schooling and training in Singapore, *Malayan Economic Review*, October.

DEMETRIADES, E. & PSACHAROPOULOS, G. (1979) Education and pay structure in Cyprus, *International Labour Review*. January–February.

DENISON, E. F. (1967) *Why Growth Rates Differ?* (The Brookings Institution).

DOUGHERTY, C. R. S. (1971) Optimal allocation of investment in education, in: CHENERY, H. B. (Ed.) *Studies in Development Planning* (Harvard University Press).

DOUGHERTY, C. R. S. (1972) Estimates of Labour Aggregation Functions, *Journal of Political Economy*, November.

DRESCH, S. P. (1976) Demography, Technology and higher education, *Journal of Political Economy*.

EICHER, J.-C. & LÉVY-GARBOUA, L. (1979) *Economique de l'Education* (Paris, Economica).

FALLON, P. & LAYARD, R. (1975) Capital-skill complementarity, income distribution and output accounting, *Journal of Political Economy*.

FIELDS, G. S. (1975) Higher education and income distribution in a less developed country, *Oxford Economic Papers*, July.

FIELDS, G. S. & SCHULTZ, T. P. (1977) Sources of income variation in Colombia: Personal and regional effects. *Paper No. 272* (Economic Growth Center, Yale University).

FONG, P. E. (1976) Education, earnings and occupational mobility in Singapore, (ILO, World Employment Programme). *Paper WEP 2-18/WP 13*.

FREEMAN, R. (1971) *The Market for College Trained Manpower* (Harvard University Press).

FREEMAN, R. (1976) *The Overeducated American* (London, Academic Press).

GANNICOTT, K. (1972) *Rates of return to education in Taiwan, Republic of China* (Planning Unit, Ministry of Education, mimeo).

GORDON, D. (1972) *Theories of Poverty and Unemployment* (Lexington).

GRILICHES, Z. (1979) Sibling models and data in economics: beginnings of survey, *Journal of Political Economy*. October. Supplement.

GUNDERSON, M. (1979) Earnings differentials between the public and private sectors, *Canadian Journal of Economics*. May.

GUSTAFSSON, S. (1977) Rates of depreciation of human capital due to nonuse, *Working Paper No. 14*, (The Industrial Institute for Economic and Social Research).

HALLAK, J. & PSACHAROPOULOS, G. (1979) The role of education in labour recruitment and promotion practices in Indonesia, *IIEP Working Paper*.

HEYNEMAN, S. (1980a) *The Status of Human Capital in Malawi*, March draft (World Bank, Education Department).

HEYNEMAN, S. (1980b) Investment in Indian education: uneconomic? *World Development*. pp. 145–163.

HOERR, D. (1974) Educational returns and educational reform in Ethiopia, *Eastern Africa Economic Review*. December.

ILO (1974) *Sharing in Development: a Programme of Employment, Equity and Growth for the Philippines*.

JALLADE, J. P. (1977) Basic education and income inequality in Brazil: the long term view, *Staff Working Paper No. 268* (World Bank).

JAMISON, D. & LAU, L. (1978) *Farmer education and farm efficiency*, (World Bank, mimeo).

JOHNSON, G. E. (1972) The determination of individual hourly earnings in urban Kenya, *Paper No. 22* (Center for Research on Economic Development, University of Michigan).

KETKAR, S. L. (1974) Benefit-cost analysis, manpower training and the Sierra Leone educational system, no affiliation.

KRUEGER, A. O. (1972) Rates of return to Turkish higher education, *Journal of Human Resources*, Fall.

KURATANI, M. (1973) A theory of training, earnings and employment: an application to Japan, *unpublished PhD dissertation*, Columbia University.

LAYARD, R. & PSACHAROPOULOS, G. (1974) The screening hypothesis and the returns to education, *Journal of Political Economy*.

LEE, K. H. (1980) Education, earnings and occupational status in Malaysia, 1978, *unpublished PhD dissertation*, London School of Economics.

MCNABB, R. & PSACHAROPOULOS, G. (1981) Further evidence on the relevance of the labour market hypothesis for the U.K., *Journal of Human Resources, Summer*.

MEULDERS, D. (1974) Coûts et avantages sociaux des dépenses d'enseignement: Un example belge, *Cahiers Economiques de Bruxelles*, No. 2.

MINCER, J. (1974) *Schooling, Experience and Earnings* (NBER).

OECD (1971) *Occupational and Educational Structures of the Labour Force and Economic Development* (Paris, OECD).

PANDIT, H. N. (1976) Investment in Indian education: size, sources and effectiveness, *IIEP Occasional Paper No. 43*.

POURHOSSEINI, M. (1979) The social and private rates of return to investment in education in Iran, *NEP Research Paper No. 89* (University of Birmingham).

PSACHAROPOULOS, G. (1973) *Returns to Education: an International Comparison* (Jossey-Bass, Elsevier).

PSACHAROPOULOS, G. (1976) Earnings determinants in a mixed labour market, in VAN RIJCKEGHEM, W. (Ed.), *Employment Problems and Policies in Developing Countries: the case of Morocco* (Rotterdam University Press).

PSACHAROPOULOS, G. (1975) *Earnings and Education in OECD Countries*, (Paris, OECD).

PSACHAROPOULOS, G. (1977a) Schooling, experience and earnings: the case of an LDC, *Journal of Development Economics*, pp. 39–48.

PSACHAROPOULOS, G. (1977b) Family background, education and achievement, *British Journal of Sociology*, September.

PSACHAROPOULOS, G. (1978) Labour market duality and income distribution: the case of the U.K., in KRELLE, W. & SHORROCKS, A. (Eds), *Personal Income Distribution* (Amsterdam, North-Holland).

PSACHAROPOULOS, G. (1979) On the weak versus the strong version of the screening hypothesis, *Economic Letters*.

PSACHAROPOULOS, G. (1980a) *Unpublished Estimates using the 1970 Brazilian 1 percent Census Tape* (London School of Economics).

PSACHAROPOULOS, G. (1980b) Educational planning and the labour market, *European Journal of Education*, 15, pp. 201–220.

PSACHAROPOULOS, G. (1980c) Qualifications and employment at IDS, Sussex, *IDS Bulletin*.

PSACHAROPOULOS, G. (1980d) *Higher Education in Developing Countries: a Cost-Benefit Analysis* (World Bank, Education Department).

PSACHAROPOULOS, G. (1980e) Spending on education in an era of economic stress, *Journal of Educational Finance*.

PSACHAROPOULOS, G. & HINCHLIFFE, K. (1972) Further evidence on the elasticity of substitution among different types of educated labour, *Journal of Political Economy*.

PSACHAROPOULOS, G. & KAZAMIAS, A. (1978) *Report of the Post-Secondary Education Study Team*, (Greek Ministry of Education, in Greek).

PSACHAROPOULOS, G. & LAYARD, R. (1979) Human capital and earnings: British evidence and a critique, *Review of Economic Studies*, July.

PSACHAROPOULOS, G. & TINBERGEN, J. (1978) On the explanation of schooling occupation and earnings: some alternative path analyses, *De Economist*, Vol. 126, No. 4.

QUINTAS, J. R. & SANMARTIN, J. (1978) Aspectos economicos de la education, *Informaçion Comercial Española*, May.

RIBOUD, M. (1975) An analysis of the income distribution in France, paper presented at the *Workshop on the Economics of Education*, London School of Economics.

SCHULTZ, T. W. (1961) Investment in human capital, *American Economic Review*, March.

SCULLY, G. W. (1979) *Economic development, income and wealth inequality*, Southern Methodist University (mimeo).

SMITH, J. P. & WELCH, F. (1978) The overeducated American? A review article, *Paper P-6253*, The Rand Corporation.

STROUP, R. H. & HARGROVE, M. M. (1969) Earnings and education in rural South Vietnam, *Journal of Human Resources*, Spring.

STRUMILIN, S. G. (1929) The economic significance of national education, *The Planned Economy*, reprinted in UNESCO, *Readings in the Economics of Education*, 1968.

THUROW, L. & LUCAS, R. (1972) *The American Distribution of Income: a Structural Problem* (Joint Economic Committee, U.S. Congress).

Comparative Education   *Volume 17 No. 3 1981*   341

TINBERGEN, J. (1975) *Income Distribution: Analysis and Policies* (Amsterdam, North-Holland).

TINBERGEN, J. & PSACHAROPOULOS, G. (1980) *Long Range Educational Perspectives in OECD Countries,* mimeo (Paris, OECD).

THOMAS, H. (1976) Labour markets and educational planning in Yugoslavia. *Economic Analysis and Workers' Management,* Vol. 10, No. 1–2.

ULLMAN, C. (1972) The growth of professional occupations in the American labour force, 1900–1963, *unpublished PhD dissertation.* Columbia University.

UMETANI, S. (1977) The college labour market and the rate of return to higher education in Postwar Japan, 1954–1973, *unpublished PhD dissertation,* University of Wisconsin-Madison.

WELCH, F. (1970) Education in production. *Journal of Political Economy.*

YOUNG, K. H. & JAMISON, D. (1975) The effects of schooling and literacy on earnings, paper presented at the *3rd World Congress of the Econometric Society,* Toronto.

[5]

RETURNS TO EDUCATION: A FURTHER INTERNATIONAL UPDATE AND IMPLICATIONS*

GEORGE PSACHAROPOULOS

ABSTRACT

This paper updates evidence on the returns to investment in education by adding estimates for new countries and refining existing estimates to bring the total number of country cases to over 60. The new cross-country evidence confirms and reinforces earlier patterns, namely, that returns are highest for primary education, the general curricula, the education of women, and countries with the lowest per capita income. The findings have important implications for directing future investment in education which, for efficiency and equity purposes, should concentrate on these priority areas.

Estimates of the profitability of investment in human capital have proliferated since the field was established in the early 1960s. Such estimates have been used to illuminate a number of key developmental issues, like the explanation of past economic growth rates (Schultz [74]), the optimality of resource allocation within education and between education and other sectors (Dougherty and Psacharopoulos [17]), the determinants of income distribution (Chiswick and Mincer [13]), and the behavior of students and their families as investors and consumers of education (Freeman [21]).

One of the earliest questions following the human capital revolution in economic thought was: If education is a form of capital, what is the rate of return to it? This led to a related question: How does the prof-

The author is an Economist in the Education and Training Department of the World Bank.
* I am grateful to all those who over the years have kept me informed on their work, and especially those who by correspondence provided clarifications so that the figures appearing here are more comparable. The views expressed are those of the author and should not be attributed to the World Bank. [Manuscript received February 1985, accepted April 1985.]

The Journal of Human Resources • *XX* • *4*
0022-166X/85/0004-0583 $01.50/0

itability of investment in education compare to investment in physical capital? Such comparisons, it was thought, would serve as ex ante signals to guide resource allocation between two forms of capital in developmental planning. They have also been used ex post to explain a great part of the "residual" that puzzled scholars examining economic growth in the 1950s.

Other questions follow. What priority should be given to primary versus university education? Allocative decisions have to be made within education, and rates of return have been used as guides to such decisions. Furthermore, a given level of education can offer various types of curricula—for example, secondary general versus secondary technical—and estimates of the profitability of investment by type of schooling can illuminate decisions on where the relative emphasis should lie.

If human capital investment is like any other type of investment, diminishing returns should apply to it. Hence, another major issue in the early days was whether and by how much the yield on human capital investment would decline following the expansion of education. When the human investment revolution began, there were no time-series estimates of the rate of return.

The contrast between the social and private rate of return could highlight the extent of public subsidization of education. The size of the private returns could also explain the individual demand for certain types of schooling. And since the private rate of return is the price one receives on his or her human resource endowments, it could further explain personal income distribution.

For all the above reasons researchers in the United States, and later around the world, began estimating the returns to investment in education. The first rate of return to education collection appeared in the Summer 1967 issue of the *Journal of Human Resources* and covered only four countries—Mexico, Italy, the United States, and Great Britain. Three years later Hansen [28] produced another review covering 14 countries as background for an OECD conference on education. My 1973 book [56] attempted to derive rate-of-return patterns based on evidence from 32 countries. Seven years later I updated and expanded the rate-of-return estimates, covering 45 countries, as a background to the World Bank's *World Development Report* that dealt with human resources (Psacharopoulos [57]). Since that collection, further estimates have been published for additional countries or for more recent years in countries for which evidence on the returns to education already existed. As a result of the literature growth in this field, my "Rate of Return—New Estimates" file has become overly thick and unmanageable. Perhaps the time has come for another stock-taking exercise to determine if the earlier documented rate-of-return patterns have been maintained, or whether new ones are emerging. The enlarged and updated data set on which this paper is based covers 61 countries.

THE EVIDENCE

The rate-of-return evidence has been organized into a set of master tables that appear in the Appendix. The tables correspond roughly to issues to be discussed in this paper. When several rate-of-return estimates were available for a given country, year, or level of education, I have selected for inclusion in the master tables the one that in my judgment would be most comparable to the rest. This was not an easy task since many authors of the original studies do not always state explicitly the nature of the sample used (for example, urban, rural, national) or the methodology according to which the estimates are made (especially what adjustments have been made on the benefits side). Although correspondence with several authors has resulted in a more comparable set of figures, methodological and sample-reference differences remain. Hence, the reader should be cautious in attaching importance to one (or even two) percentage point differences in the returns across countries and years. Of course, greater reliance should be placed on within-country estimates (for example, by level of education or by gender) that are based on a common sample and methodology.

Most of the lengthy reference list is "marginal" in the sense that the reader can refer to Psacharopoulos [56, 58] to trace the original source of previously reviewed estimates. The reader is also referred to these earlier publications for details on the theoretical and methodological aspects of rate-of-return estimations.

Table 1 is a summary of the master table that provides estimates of average private and social returns by level of education for countries grouped by their level of economic development.[1]

The table confirms the earlier well-documented declining rate of return pattern by level of education. Primary education is the most profitable educational investment opportunity, followed by secondary education. This decline is the result of the interaction between the low cost of primary education (relative to other levels) and the substantial productivity differential between primary school graduates and those who are illiterate. The productivity of primary school graduates is not only proxied by their earnings, but has also been confirmed by studies using differences in physical output as an educational outcome.[2]

---

1   All figures in the text tables are simple arithmetic averages of the corresponding rates in the master tables.
2   See D. Jamison and L. Lau, *Farmer Education and Farm Efficiency* (Baltimore: Johns Hopkins University Press, 1982).

TABLE 1
AVERAGE RETURNS TO EDUCATION BY COUNTRY TYPE AND LEVEL
(percent)

Region/	Social			Private		
Country Type	Primary	Secondary	Higher	Primary	Secondary	Higher
Africa	26	17	13	45	26	32
Asia	27	15	13	31	15	18
Latin America	26	18	16	32	23	23
Intermediate	13	10	8	17	13	13
Advanced	NA	11	9	NA	12	12

Source: Based on Appendix Table A-1, latest year available.
Note: NA = not available because of lack of a control group of illiterates.

TABLE 2
INDEX OF PUBLIC SUBSIDIZATION OF EDUCATION
BY LEVEL AND REGION

Region/Country Type	Educational Level		
	Primary	Secondary	Higher
Africa	92	51	157
Asia	58	13	9
Latin America	104	47	50
Intermediate	51	6	7
Advanced	NA	21	44

Source: Based on Appendix Table A-1, strictly comparable rates.
Notes: The subsidization index for a given level of education is defined as the percent by which the private rate of return exceeds the social rate. NA = not available.

The declining rate-of-return pattern is also observed across levels of per capita income. For example, the returns to any level of education are highest in Africa and lowest in the advanced industrial countries. This is explained by the relative scarcity of human-to-physical capital within each group of countries.

In all countries and levels of schooling, private returns exceed social returns because education is publicly subsidized. However, the private-public distortions are greatest in the poorest group of countries and in the higher levels of education (Table 2). Figure 1 illustrates this phenomenon for Africa. Whereas the social rates of return follow a declining

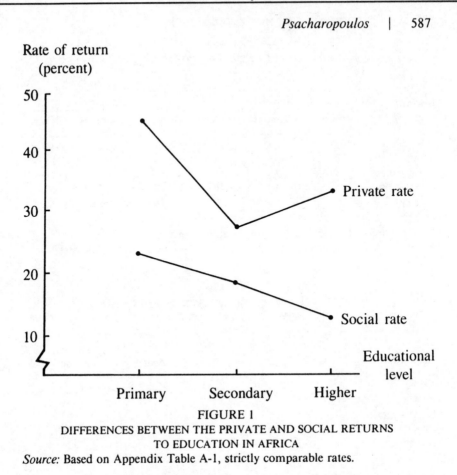

FIGURE 1
DIFFERENCES BETWEEN THE PRIVATE AND SOCIAL RETURNS
TO EDUCATION IN AFRICA
Source: Based on Appendix Table A-1, strictly comparable rates.

pattern by ascending level of education, the private rates are not only higher than social rates, but they increase after the secondary level.

Table 3 gives means of the regression coefficient on years of schooling in a semi-log (Mincer-type) earnings function in which log earnings is a function of years of schooling, years of experience, and years of experience squared. The figures are interpreted as private returns to the typical year of education (that is, undifferentiated by level). Again, the declining pattern of the returns across country type is largely maintained.

Rate-of-return estimates in recent years have been refined in the sense that they are increasingly based on the earnings of those employed in the competitive sector of the economy where the benefits of education better reflect the worker's productivity. Table 4 shows that in studies where the returns have been differentiated by economic sector, the returns in the competitive setting exceed those in the noncompetitive sector by

588 | THE JOURNAL OF HUMAN RESOURCES

TABLE 3

MINCER-TYPE RETURNS TO EDUCATION BY COUNTRY TYPE

Region/Country Type	Coefficient on Years of Schooling (percent)
Africa	13
Asia	11
Latin America	14
Intermediate	8
Advanced	9

Source: Master table listing the individual country rates is available from the author on request.

Note: The following countries are included in each region: Africa: Ethiopia, Kenya, Morocco, Tanzania; Asia: Hong Kong, Malaysia, Pakistan, Singapore, South Korea, South Vietnam, Sri Lanka, Taiwan, Thailand; Latin America: Brazil, Chile, Colombia, Costa Rica, El Salvador, Guatemala, Mexico, Venezuela; Intermediate: Cyprus, Greece, Iran, Portugal; Advanced: Australia, Canada, France, Germany, Japan, Sweden, United Kingdom, United States.

TABLE 4

AVERAGE RETURNS TO EDUCATION BY ECONOMIC SECTOR

Sector Specification	Rate of Return (percent)
Competitive, private	13
Noncompetitive, public	10

Source: Master table listing individual countries is available from the author on request.

Note: The countries included in this table are Brazil, Colombia, Greece, Guatemala, Japan, Malaysia, Pakistan, Portugal, United Kingdom, Tanzania, and Venezuela.

three percentage points. This means that previous estimates based on the earnings of workers in all sectors have in fact *under*estimated the returns to education. The inclusion of public-sector earnings in particular, because of the equalization policy of pay scales, flattens mean earnings differentials and, hence, depresses the returns to education.

For a variety of reasons, women in all countries earn on average substantially less than men. Because the rate of return is a relative concept, it should not be surprising if the profitability of investment in women's education is greater than that of men. This is, indeed, the case, as shown in Table 5, where in developing countries the Mincer-type average rate of return for women exceeds that for men by four percentage points. This rate-of-return differential in favor of women may be an underestimate because the rate of return to investment in women's education, as commonly calculated, does not take into account the increased probability of more educated women participating in the labor force. For example, Mohan [47] reports that in Colombia in 1984 the labor force participation rate of working-age women aged over 15 ranged from 31 percent for those who had no schooling to 53 percent for those with a university education.

It is commonly thought that introducing a vocational element in the secondary school curriculum, especially in developing countries, is conducive to economic development. But, as shown in Table 6, the returns to investment in traditional academic (general) curricula are greater on average than the returns to investment in specialized subjects. Again, this is due to the higher unit cost of producing technical graduates and the fact that graduates from both streams are absorbed equally well by the labor market.

TABLE 5
AVERAGE RETURNS TO EDUCATION BY GENDER
(percent)

Country Group	Educational Level	Men	Women
All countries	Primary	19	17
	Secondary	16	21
	Higher	15	14
Developing countries	Overall	11	15

Source: Based on Appendix Table A-2.

TABLE 6
AVERAGE RETURNS TO ALTERNATIVE SECONDARY SCHOOL CURRICULA

Curriculum Type	Rate of Return (percent)
General, academic	16
Vocational, technical	12

Source: Master table listing individual countries is available from the author on request.
Note: Countries included in this table are Colombia, Cyprus, France, Indonesia, Liberia, Taiwan, and Tanzania.

The same pattern observed regarding the type of secondary school curriculum also applies to higher education programs. The high-cost specialties like agronomy exhibit low returns, whereas humanities and the social sciences exhibit high returns (Table 7).

Rate-of-return estimates over time within countries are rare. What is even rarer are estimates based on the same sampling frame and methodology from year to year. In the country where the highest quality time series data exist, the United States, the returns have shown a remarkable stability over a 30-year period. For example, the social returns to higher education fluctuated around the 10–11 percent mark between 1939 and 1969 (Appendix Table A-1). In Japan, the corresponding returns fell from 6.4 to 5.7 percent in a seven-year period. In Great Britain, the returns remained virtually constant between 1971 and 1978. In Colombia, the returns to education (Mincer-type estimation) declined from 17.6 to 14.4 percent between 1973 and 1978, while in the same five-year period the percentage with higher education in the labor force has more than doubled (from 6 percent in 1973 to 13 percent in 1978, based on Mohan [48], pp. 40, 43).

This relative stability of average returns over time has been explained by the fact that the demand for educated manpower has kept increasing along with the supply of education (a phenomenon Jan Tinbergen has lucidly described as the race between technology and education [80]).

Table 8 presents comparisons of average returns to physical and human capital in two time periods. Given the roughness of the data, the evidence suggests that in advanced countries the gap has narrowed somewhat between the returns to physical and human investment, and the convergence indicates that a 10 percent return may be indicative of some equilibrium. In developing countries, however, there is a clear advantage of human versus physical capital investments. Of course this advantage

TABLE 7
AVERAGE RETURNS FOR SELECTED UNIVERSITY PROGRAMS

Program	Rate of Return (percent)
Economics	13
Law	12
Social sciences	11
Medicine	12
Engineering	12
Sciences, math, physics	8
Agriculture	8

Source: Based on Appendix Table A-3.

TABLE 8

RETURNS TO HUMAN AND PHYSICAL CAPITAL BY TYPE OF COUNTRY

(percent)

Type of country	1960s		1970s	
	Human	Physical	Human	Physical
Developing	20	> 15	15	> 13
Advanced	8	< 10	9	< 11

Source: 1960s from Psacharopoulos [56], Table 5.3; 1970s from
Psacharopoulos [64], Table 8.

Note: Developing countries included in the table are Mexico, Colombia,
Venezuela, Chile, Brazil, India, Philippines, Ghana, Kenya, Uganda, and
Nigeria. Advanced countries are United States, United Kingdom, Canada,
Netherlands, and Belgium.

diminished from the 1960s to the 1970s, following the relatively greater
investment in developing countries.

IMPLICATIONS

These rate-of-return patterns have several implications for the shaping
of educational policy, especially in developing countries.

Underinvestment exists at all levels of education, especially in Africa.
This proposition is supported by evidence that the social returns to education in the region are well above any plausible social discount rate
used in project evaluation.

Primary schooling remains the number-one priority for investment.
This is evidenced by the fact that the social rate of return to primary
education exceeds by several percentage points the returns to secondary
and higher education.

The degree of public subsidization of higher education is such that
there is considerable margin for reducing subsidy levels. This stems from
the calculations that a reduction of public subsidies to higher education
would drive down the private rate closer to the social rate, still leaving
an attractive return to private investment. The savings from the reduction
of university subsidies could be used to expand primary education.

Reducing public subsidies to higher education and reallocating them
to primary education would have additional benefits that can be viewed
as equitable. To a great extent, universities are attended by those who
can afford to pay, whereas the less well-off portion of the population would
now find educational opportunities more open and accessible.

592 | THE JOURNAL OF HUMAN RESOURCES

Expanding the provision of school places to cover women is not only equitable but socially efficient as well. Although counter-intuitive, this proposition is based on the evidence that the rate of return to women's education is at least as attractive as the rate of return on investment for men.

Within the secondary or university level, the general curricula or programs offer as good investment opportunities as the more vocational pursuits. This is because the higher unit costs of vocational/technical education depress the social rate of return to this type of schooling.

Judging from past trends and the degree of underinvestment in education in developing countries, the fears that further educational expansion would lead to unemployed graduates or would lower social rates of return are unfounded. This proposition is based on time series evidence which shows that rates of return have not changed much as educational investment increases.

The traditionally estimated returns on the basis of observed earnings may underestimate the true social profitability of education. The flatness of civil service pay scales depresses the size of earnings differentials on which early rate-of-return estimates were based.

Finally, it should be mentioned that the conclusions presented here are based on estimates of the returns to education that follow the accepted methodology over the past 25 years. But when one adds the series of qualifications (such as externalities and nonmarket effects) recently enumerated by Haveman and Wolfe [29], then all of the above implications are strengthened.

REFERENCES*

1. A. D. Adamson and J. M. Reid. "The Rate of Return to Post-Compulsory Education During the 1970's: An Empirical Study for Great Britain." United Kingdom, Department of Education and Science, 1980. Mimeo.
2. Lascelles Anderson. "Rates of Return to Human Capital: A Test Using El Salvador Data." *American Economic Review* 70 (May 1980): 138–41.
3. A. Armand. "The Rate of Return to Education in Iran." Ph.D. dissertation, University of Maryland, 1976.
4. J. Armitage and R. Sabot. "Efficiency and Equity Implications of Subsidies of Secondary Education in Kenya." In *Modern Tax Theory for Developing Countries*, eds. D. Newbery and N. Stern. Washington: Development Research Department, The World Bank, 1984. Mimeo.
5. Moo-Ki Bai. *Education, Workers' Behavior and Earnings: A Case Study of Manufacturing Workers in Korea.* Seoul: Institute of Economic Research,

---

* Many of these citations are not referenced in the text but are included for the benefit of other researchers.

Seoul National University, August 1977. (Also in *Seoul National University Economic Review* (December 1977): 1–69.)

6. M. Baldares-Carazo. "The Distribution of Income and Wages in Costa Rica." Ph.D. thesis, University of Birmingham, 1980.

7. A. Berhanu. "Modeling Manpower in Development Planning: Methodological and Empirical Problems with Sudanese Illustrations." Ph.D. dissertation, University of Pennsylvania, 1982.

8. M. Boissiere, J. B. Knight, and R. Sabot. "Earnings, Ability and Cognitive Skills." Washington: Development Research Department, The World Bank, April 1984. Mimeo.

9. Botswana Ministry of Finance and Development Planning. "Botswana: Education and Human Resource Sector Assessment." USAID, June 1984. Mimeo.

10. F. Bourgignon. "The Role of Education in the Urban Labor-Market During the Process of Development: The Case of Colombia." Paper presented at the 6th World Congress, International Economic Association, Mexico City, August 1980.

11. Martin Carnoy. "The Rate of Return to Schooling and the Increase in Human Resources in Puerto Rico." *Comparative Education Review* 16 (February 1972): 68–86.

12. Barry R. Chiswick and P. W. Miller. "Immigrant Generation and Income in Australia." Department of Economics, University of Western Ontario, 1984. Mimeo.

13. Barry R. Chiswick and Jacob Mincer. "Time Series Changes in Personal Income Inequality in the United States from 1939, with Projections to 1985." *Journal of Political Economy* 80 (May-June 1972): S34–71.

14. Carmel U. Chiswick. "On Estimating Earnings Functions for LDCs." *Journal of Development Economics* 4 (March 1977): 67–78.

15. W. Clement. *Kinkimmenverteilung und Qualifikation: Empirische Ergebnisse aus dem osterreichischen Mikrozensus 1981.* Signum-Verlag, 1984.

16. W. Clement, M. Tessaring, and C. Weisshuhn. *Ausbildung und Einkommen in der Bundesrepublik Deutschland.* Beitrab 80. Nurnberg: Institut fur Arbeitsmarkt- und Berufsforschung der Bundesanstalt, 1983.

17. Christopher Dougherty and George Psacharopoulos. "Measuring the Cost of Misallocation of Investment in Education." *Journal of Human Resources* 12 (Fall 1977): 446–59.

18. J. Ducci and K. Terrell. "Earnings and Occupational Attainment in a Developing Country." Department of Economics, Cornell University. Paper presented at the Econometric Society Meetings, September 1980.

19. A. Dumlao and A. Arcelo. "Financing Private Education." *FAPE Review* 16 (July-October 1979).

20. A. C. Edwards. "Wage Indexation, Real Wages and Unemployment." Washington: Development Research Department, The World Bank, 1983. Mimeo.

21. Richard B. Freeman. *The Overeducated American.* New York: Academic Press, 1976.

22. A. Gabregiorgis. "Rate of Return on Secondary Education in the Bahamas."

594 | THE JOURNAL OF HUMAN RESOURCES

Ph.D. thesis, Department of Educational Administration, University of Alberta, 1979.

23. K. Gannicott. "Male and Female Earnings in a Developing Economy: The Case of Taiwan." Department of Economics, University of New South Wales, 1984. Mimeo.

24. N. Gebre-ab. "Cost-Benefit Analysis of Education in Lesotho." Lesotho Ministry of Education, November 1983.

25. S. E. Guisinger, J. W. Henderson, and G. W. Scully. "Earnings, Rates of Return to Education and the Earnings Distribution in Pakistan." *Economics of Education Review* (December 1984).

26. E. Gutkind. "Earnings Functions and Returns to Education in Sri Lanka." Geneva: International Labor Office, 1984. Mimeo.

27. K. A. Hamdani. "Education and the Income Differentials: An Estimation for Rawalpindi City." *Pakistan Development Review* 16 (Summer 1977): 144–64.

28. W. Lee Hansen. "Patterns of Rates of Return in Education: Some International Comparisons." In *Conference on Policies for Educational Growth.* Paris: OECD, 1970. Mimeo, DAS/EID/70.3.

29. Robert H. Haveman and Barbara L. Wolfe. "Schooling and Economic Well-Being: The Role of Nonmarket Effects." *Journal of Human Resources* 19 (Summer 1984): 377–407.

30. J. W. Henderson. "Earnings Functions for the Self-Employed." *Journal of Development Economics* 13 (August-October 1983): 97–102.

31. J. W. Henderson and G. W. Scully. "The Impact of the Elasticity of Substitution on Rates of Return to Education." Waco, TX: Baylor University, 1984. Mimeo.

32. W. J. House and O. Stylianou. "Population, Employment Planning and Labor Force Mobility in Cyprus: An Interim Report." Nicosia: Department of Statistics and Research, Ministry of Finance, 1981.

33. Fan-Sing Hung. "Private and Social Rates of Return on Investment in Education in Hong Kong." Master's thesis, School of Education, Chinese University of Hong Kong, 1982.

34. J-P. Jarousse. "La Rentabilite des Etudes en France entre 1970 et 1977." Paris: CREDOC, 1984. Mimeo.

35. Chang Yong Jeong. "Rates of Return on Investment in Education: The Case of Korea." KDI Working Paper No. 7048, September 1974.

36. Hwai-I Juang. "Rates of Return to Investment in Education in Taiwan and Their Policy Implications: A Cost-Benefit Analysis of the Academic High School and the Vocational High School." D. Ed. thesis, Teachers College, Columbia University, 1972.

37. J. B. Knight and R. Sabot. "The Returns to Education: Increasing with Experience or Decreasing with Expansion." *Oxford Bulletin of Economics and Statistics* 43 (February 1981): 51–71.

38. Kwok-Chuen Kwok. "An Analysis of the Earnings Structure in Hong Kong." M. Phil. thesis, Graduate School, Chinese University of Hong Kong, 19??.

39. Yong Woo Lee. "Human Capital and Wage Determination in South Korea." Kyungbook National University, 1984.

40. L. Levy-Garboua and A. Mingat. "Les Taux de Rendement de l'Education." Ch. 5 in *Economique de l'Education*, eds. J-C. Eicher and L. Levy-Garboua. Paris: Economica, 1979.

41. Liberia Ministry of Planning and Economic Affairs. "Liberia: Education and Training Sector Assessment." Joint Committee for the Government of Liberia/USAID Education, Training and Human Resources Assessment, December 1983. Mimeo.

42. Pak-Wai Liu and Yeu-Chim Wong. "Human Capital, Occupation and Earnings." Department of Economics, Chinese University of Hong Kong, 1984.

43. D. Mazumdar. *The Urban Labor Market and Income Distribution: A Study of Malaysia.* Oxford: Oxford University Press, 1981.

44. P. W. Miller. "The Rate of Return to Education: The Evidence from the 1976 Census." *Australian Economic Review* (3rd quarter 1982).

45. A. Mingat and J-P Jarousse. "Analyse Economique et Fondements Sociaux des Disparites de Salaires en France." Paris: CREDOC, 1985. Mimeo.

46. A. Mingat, J-P. Tan, and M. Hoque. "Recovering the Cost of Public Higher Education in LDCs: To What Extent Are Loan Schemes an Efficient Instrument?" Washington: Education Department, The World Bank, 1984. Mimeo.

47. R. Mohan. "Labor Force Participation in a Developing Metropolis, Does Sex Matter?" Paper presented at the Latin American Econometric Society Meeting, Bogota. Washington: Development Research Department, The World Bank, July 1984. Mimeo.

48. ———. *The Determinants of Labor Earnings in Developing Metropoli: Estimates from Bogota and Cali, Colombia.* Staff Working Paper No. 498. Washington: The World Bank, 1981.

49. R. M. Morgan, ed. *System Analysis for Educational Change: The Republic of Korea.* Tallahassee: Florida State University, 1971.

50. K. Okachi. "An Analysis of Economic Returns to Educational Investment: Its Role in Determining the Significance of Educational Planning in Japan." Ph.D. dissertation, Florida State University, 1980.

51. ———. "An Analysis of Economic Returns to Japan's Higher Education and Its Application to Educational Finance." *Journal of Education Finance* 9 (Fall 1983).

52. Funkoo Park. "Return to Education in Korea." *Journal of Economic Development* 1, No. 1 (1976).

53. Funkoo Park and Seil Park. *Wage Structure in Korea*, Korea Development Institute, 1984.

54. Seil Park. "Wages in Korea: Determination of the Wage Levels and the Wage Structure in a Dualistic Labor Market." Ph.D. dissertation, Cornell University, 1980.

55. M. Pourhosseini. "Investment in Human Capital and Educational Planning in Iran." Ph.D. thesis, Department of Economics, University of Birmingham, 1980.

56. George Psacharopoulos. *Returns to Education: An International Comparison.* San Francisco: Elsevier-Jossey Bass, 1973.

596 | THE JOURNAL OF HUMAN RESOURCES

57. ————. *Higher Education in Developing Countries: A Cost-Benefit Analysis.* Staff Working Paper No. 440. Washington: The World Bank, 1980.

58. ————. "Returns to Education: An Updated International Comparison." In *Education and Income,* ed. T. King. Staff Working Paper No. 402. Washington: The World Bank, 1980. Reprinted in *Comparative Education* 17 (1981a): 321–41.

59. ————. "Education and the Structure of Earnings in Portugal." *De Economist* 129 (1981b): 532–45.

60. ————. "Indonesia: Manpower Considerations in the Energy Sector." Washington: Education Department, The World Bank, May 1982a. Mimeo.

61. ————. "Peru: Assessing Priorities for Investment in Education and Training." Washington: Education Department, The World Bank, 1982b. Mimeo.

62. ————. "Upper Volta: Is It Worth Spending on Education in a 'High-Cost' Country?" Washington: Education Department, The World Bank, 1982c. Mimeo.

63. ————. "Earnings and Education in Greece, 1960–1977." *European Economic Review* 17 (1982d): 333–47.

64. ————. "The Economics of Higher Education in Developing Countries." *Comparative Education Review* 26 (June 1982e): 139–59.

65. ————. "Sex Discrimination in the Greek Labor Market." *Modern Greek Studies* 1 (October 1983a): 339–58.

66. ————. "Education and Private Versus Public Sector Pay." *Labour and Society* 8 (April–June 1983b): 123–34.

67. George Psacharopoulos and W. Loxley. *Diversified Secondary Education and Development: Evidence from Colombia and Tanzania.* Baltimore: Johns Hopkins University Press, 1985.

68. George Psacharopoulos and A. Zabalza. "The Effect of Diversified Schools on Employment Status and Earnings in Colombia." *Economics of Education Review* 3, No. 3 (1984).

69. J. R. Quintas. *Economia y Educacion.* Piramide, 1983.

70. M. Riboud. *Accumulation du Capital Humain.* Paris: Economica, 1978.

71. E. Rodriguez. *Rentabilidad y crecimiento de la Educacion Superior en Colombia.* Facultad de Estudios Interdisciplinarios, Pontificia Universidad Javeriana, 1981.

72. P. N. Savvides. "Work Experience and Earnings Differentials: The Case of Cyprus." M. A. thesis, Department of Economics, Southern Illinois University, 19??.

73. T. P. Schultz. "Conventional Income Equations for Rural and Urban Workers by Current Residence and Birthplace: Colombia 1973." Yale University, April 1979. Mimeo.

74. T. W. Schultz. "Education and Economic Growth." In *Social Forces Influencing American Education.* Chicago: National Society for the Study of Education, 1961.

75. K. Sethasathien. "Thailand: Using Cost-Benefit Analysis to Derive the Rates of Return in Different Levels of Education. Ph.D. dissertation, College of Education, Florida State University, 1977.

76. Somalia Ministry of National Planning. "Somalia: Education and Human Resources Sector Assessment." USAID, January 1984. Mimeo.

77. F. Steier. "Educational Policies in Venezuela: An Appraisal." Ph.D. dissertation, Columbia University, in progress 1985.

78. D. A. Sumner. "Wage Functions and Occupational Selection in a Rural Less Developed Country Setting." *Review of Economics and Statistics* 63 (November 1981): 513–19.

79. J. B. C. Tilak. "Inequality in Returns to Education." Ph.D. dissertation, Delhi School of Economics, 1980.

80. J. Tinbergen, *Income Distribution: Analysis and Policies.* Amsterdam: North-Holland, 1975.

81. G. Weisshuhn and W. Clement. "Analyse der qualifikations spezifischen Verdienstrelationen in der Bundesrepublik Deutschland auf der Basis der Bescheftigtenstatistik 1974/1977." *Mitteilungen aus der Arbeitmarkt und Berufsforschung* 1 (1982): 36–49.

APPENDIX TABLE A-1
RETURNS TO INVESTMENT IN EDUCATION BY LEVEL (percent)

Country	Year	Social			Private		
		Prim.	Sec.	Higher	Prim.	Sec.	Higher
Africa							
Botswana	1983	42.0	41.0.	15.0	99.0	76.0	38.0
Ethiopia	1972	20.3	18.7	9.7	35.0	22.8	27.4
Ghana	1967	18.0	13.0	16.5	24.5	17.0	37.0
Kenya	1971	21.7	19.2	8.8	28.0	33.0	31.0
	1980		13.0			14.5	
Lesotho	1980	10.7	18.6	10.2	15.5	26.7	36.5
Liberia	1983	41.0	17.0	8.0	99.0	30.5	17.0
Malawi	1978		15.1				
	1982	14.7	15.2	11.5	15.7	16.8	46.6
Morocco	1970	50.5	10.0	13.0			
Nigeria	1966	23.0	12.8	17.0	30.0	14.0	34.0
Rhodesia	1960	12.4					
Sierra Leone	1971	20.0	22.0	9.5			
Somalia	1983	20.6	10.4	19.9	59.9	13.0	33.2
Sudan	1974		8.0	4.0		13.0	15.0
Tanzania	1982		5.0				
Uganda	1965	66.0	28.6	12.0			
Upper Volta	1970	25.9	60.6				
	1975	27.7	30.1	22.0			
	1982	20.1	14.9	21.3			
Asia							
Hong Kong	1976		15.0	12.4		18.5	25.2
India	1965	13.4	15.5	10.3	17.3	18.8	16.2
	1978	29.3	13.7	10.8	33.4	19.8	13.2
Indonesia	1977				25.5	15.6	
	1978	21.9	16.2	14.8			
Malaysia	1978					32.6	34.5
Pakistan	1975	13.0	9.0	8.0	20.0	11.0	27.0
	1979				14.6	6.7	9.4
Philippines	1971	7.0	6.5	8.5	9.0	6.5	9.5
	1977			8.5			16.0
Singapore	1966	6.6	17.6	14.1		20.0	25.4
South Korea	1967		9.0	5.0			
	1969		11.0	9.5			
	1971		14.6	9.3		16.1	16.2
	1973		12.2	8.8			
	1980		8.1	11.7			
Taiwan	1970		26.5	15.0		17.6	18.4
	1972	27.0	12.3	17.7	50.0	12.7	15.8

APPENDIX TABLE A-1 (Continued)

Country	Year	Social			Private		
		Prim.	Sec.	Higher	Prim.	Sec.	Higher
Thailand	1970	30.5	13.0	11.0	56.0	14.5	14.0
	1972	63.2	30.9	18.4			
Latin America							
Bahamas	1970		20.6			26.1	
Brazil	1970		23.5	13.1		24.7	13.9
Chile	1959	24.0	16.9	12.2			
Colombia	1973				15.1	15.4	20.7
	1976			18.4			24.9
	1981		9.6				
Costa Rica	1974				13.1	8.7	25.7
Mexico	1963	25.0	17.0	23.0	32.0	23.0	29.0
Paraguay	1982	14.0	11.0	13.0			
Peru	1972	46.9	19.8	16.3			
	1974	34.3	9.0	15.0			
	1980	41.4	3.3	16.1			
Puerto Rico	1959	24.0	34.1	15.5	68.2	52.1	29.0
Venezuela	1957	82.0	17.0	23.0		18.0	27.0
	1984				32.5	11.7	20.6
Intermediate							
Cyprus-1	1975				15.0	11.2	14.8
	1979				8.6	8.1	14.1
Cyprus-2	1975		10.5	9.7		11.6	8.6
	1979	7.7	6.8	7.6	15.4	7.0	5.6
Greece	1962		6.3	13.7		7.2	14.0
	1977	16.5	5.5	4.5	20.0	6.0	5.5
Iran	1972	34.0	11.5	15.0			
	1976	15.2	17.6	13.6		21.2	18.5
Iran-2	1975				10.6	15.3	19.3
Israel	1958	16.5	6.9	6.6	27.0	6.9	8.0
Spain	1971	17.2	8.6	12.8	31.6	10.2	15.5
Turkey	1968			8.5		24.0	26.0
Yugoslavia	1969	9.3	15.4	2.8	7.6	15.3	2.6
Advanced							
Australia	1969					14.0	13.9
	1976			16.3		8.1	21.1
Austria	1981					11.3	4.2
Belgium	1960		17.1	6.7		21.2	8.7
Canada	1961		11.7	14.0		16.3	19.7
Denmark	1964			7.8			10.0

APPENDIX TABLE A-1 (Continued)

Country	Year	Social Prim.	Sec.	Higher	Private Prim.	Sec.	Higher
France	1962				14.3	11.5	9.3
	1969		10.1	10.9	16.2	12.0	9.6
	1976				13.5	10.8	9.3
Germany	1964						4.6
	1978					6.5	10.5
Great Britain	1971		11.0	7.0		14.0	27.0
	1972		3.6	8.2		11.7	9.6
	1973		8.0	8.0		6.0	16.0
	1975		7.0	7.0		9.0	22.0
	1977		8.0	6.0		9.0	17.0
	1978		9.0	7.0		11.0	23.0
Italy	1969					17.3	18.3
Japan	1967						10.5
	1973		4.6	6.4		5.9	8.1
	1976	9.6	8.6	6.9	13.4	10.4	8.8
	1980			5.7			8.3
Netherlands	1965		5.2	5.5		8.5	10.4
New Zealand	1966		19.4	13.2		20.0	14.7
Norway	1966		7.2	7.5		7.4	7.7
Sweden	1967		10.5	9.2			10.3
United States	1939		18.2	10.7			
	1949		14.2	10.6			
	1959		10.1	11.3			
	1969		10.7	10.9		18.8	15.4
	1970					11.3	8.8
	1971					12.5	8.0
	1972					11.3	7.8
	1973					12.0	5.5
	1974					14.8	4.8
	1975					12.8	5.3
	1976					11.0	5.3

Sources: Australia: 1976, Miller [44], Tables 1 and 2; Austria: Clement [15]; Bahamas: Gabregiorgis [22]. Table 33; Botswana: Botswana Ministry of Finance [9], Table 2-50; Colombia: 1976, Higher, Rodriguez [71], Table 6, 1981, Psacharopoulos and Zabalza [68], average of all secondary school subjects; Costa Rica: based on Baldares-Carazo [6], Table 7.19; Cyprus-1: regression derived rates (1979), private rates, House and Stylianou [32], Table VI-4, 1975, private rates, Psacharopoulos [58], Table 1; Cyprus-2: rates refer to males, House and Stylianou [32], Table VI-3; France: 1962, Riboud [70], 1969 and 1976, Mingat and Jarousse [45], social and private rates not comparable for 1969 as estimation in each year based on different methodologies, see

APPENDIX TABLE A-1 (Sources, continued)

Jarousse [34]; Germany: 1978, Clement, Tessaring, and Weisshuhn [16]; Great Britian: Adamson and Reid [1], Table 5; Greece: Psacharopoulos [63], Table 8; Hong Kong: Hung [33], Table 6; India: 1978, Tilak [79], Table 6.3; Indonesia; Psacharopoulos [60], Table 7.1; Iran: Armand [3], Table 5.7; Iran-2: Henderson and Scully [31], Table 1; Iran: Pourhosseini [55], Table 9.2; Japan: higher education from Okachi [51], Table 12, other levels from Okachi [50], Tables 17 and 10; Kenya: 1980, Armitage and Sabot [4], Table 3, government schools; South Korea: 1969, Morgan [49], 1971, social, Jeong [35], 1971, private, Lee [39], Table 4, both sexes, col. B, 1973, Park [52], 1980, Park and Park [53]; Lesotho: Gebre-ab [24], Table 12; Liberia: Liberia Ministry of Planning/USAID [41], Table 2-26; Malawi: Mingat, Tan, and Hoque [46], Table 5; Pakistan: 1975, Hamdani [27], Table 3, 1979 based on mean earnings in urban areas, Population and Labour Migration Survey, kindly supplied by Shahrukh Rafi Khan; Paraguay: based on income and cost data supplied by Ernesto Schiefelbein; Peru: Psacharopoulos [61], Table 3.4; Philippines: 1977, University of Philippines, Dumlao and Arcelo [19], p. 161; Puerto Rico-2: Carnoy [11], Tables 2 and 4, average of males and females in urban areas; Somalia: Somalia Ministry of National Planning [76], Table 2-36; Spain: Quintas [69], Table 2.3; Sudan: Berhanu [7], Table 4.12; Taiwan: Juang [36], Tables 6-U-36 and 6-44; Tanzania: Psacharopoulos [67], average of all secondary school subjects; Thailand: Sethasathien [75], Table 9; Upper Volta: Psacharopoulos [62], Table 2.6; Venezuela: 1984, Steier [77], short-cut method, average for males and females.

For the original source of all other countries and survey years not explicitly mentioned above, see Psacharopoulos [58], Table 1.

Note: Private rates to primary education in excess of 100 percent have been set to 99.0.

APPENDIX TABLE A-2
RETURNS TO EDUCATION BY GENDER (percent)

Country	Year	Educational Level	Men	Women
Australia	1976	University	21.1	21.2
Austria	1981	All	10.3	13.5
Colombia	1973	All—urban	18.1	20.8
		—rural	10.3	20.1
Costa Rica	1974	All	14.7	14.7
France	1969	Secondary	13.9	15.9
		University	22.5	13.8
	1976	Secondary	14.8	16.2
		University	20.0	12.7
Germany	1974	All	13.1	11.2
	1977	All	13.6	11.7
Great Britain	1971	Secondary	10.0	8.0
		University	8.0	12.0
Greece	1977	All	4.7	4.5
Japan	1976	University	6.9	6.9
	1980	University	5.7	5.8
South Korea	1971	Secondary	13.7	16.9
		University	15.7	22.9
	1976	All	10.3	1.7
	1980	All	17.2	5.0
Sri Lanka	1981	All	6.9	7.9
Portugal	1977	All	7.5	8.4
Puerto Rico	1959	Primary	29.5	18.4
		Secondary	27.3	40.8
		University	21.9	9.0
Taiwan	1982	Primary	8.4	16.1
Thailand	1971	All	9.1	13.0
Venezuela	1984	All	9.9	13.5

Sources: Australia: Miller [44], Table 1; Austria: Clement [15], Table III, 5; Colombia: Schultz [73], Table 4; Costa Rica: Baldares-Carazo [6], Table 7-18; Germany: Weisshuhn and Clement [81], Table 3; Greece: Psacharopoulos [65], Table 7; Great Britain: Adamson and Reid [1], Table 2, social rates; Japan: Okachi [51], Table 12-13, social rates; South Korea: 1971, Lee [39], Table 4, col. B, 1976, Bai [5], Tables IX.3 and 4, col. 3, 1980, Park and Park [53], Table 2-3; Portugal: Psacharopoulos [59], Table 2; Puerto Rico: Carnoy [11], Table 4, social rates in urban areas; Taiwan: Gannicott [23], Table 1, log earnings coefficient on primary schooling vs. illiterates; Thailand: Chiswick [14]; France: Jarousse [34]; Sri Lanka: Gutkind [26], Table 5; Venezuela: Steier [77].

APPENDIX TABLE A-3
RETURNS TO HIGHER EDUCATION BY SUBJECT (percent)

Country	Year	Subject	Social	Private
Belgium	1967	Economics	9.5	
		Law	6.0	
		Sciences	8.0	
		Medicine	11.5	
Brazil	1962	Economics	16.1	
		Law	17.4	
		Medicine	11 .9	
		Engineering	17.3	
		Agriculture	5.2	
Canada	1967	Economics	9.0	16.3
		Engineering	2.0	4.5
Colombia	1976	Economics	26.2	32.7
		Engineering	24.8	33.7
		Medicine	23. 7	35.6
		Law	22.7	28.3
		Agronomy	16.4	22.3
Denmark	1964	Economics	9.0	
		Law	10.0	
		Engineering	8.0	
		Medicine	5.0	
France	1970	Law and Economics		16.7
		Sciences		12.3
Greece	1977	Physics and Mathematics	1.8	2.1
		Agronomy	2.7	3.1
		Law	12.0	13.8
		Engineering	8.2	12.2
		Economics and Politics	4.4	5.4
Great Britain	1967	Arts	13.5	
		Social Sciences	13.0	
		Engineering	11.4	
		Sciences	11.0	
	1971	Arts	7.0	26.0
		Sciences	7.0	38.0
		Engineering and Technology	6.0	32.0
		Social Sciences	11.0	48.0
India	1961	Humanities	12.7	14.3
		Engineering	16.6	21.2
Iran	1964	Economics	18.5	23.9
		Humanities	15.3	20.0
		Engineering	18.2	30.7
		Agriculture	13.8	27.4

604 | THE JOURNAL OF HUMAN RESOURCES

APPENDIX TABLE A-3 (Continued)

Country	Year	Subject	Social	Private
Malaysia	1968	Engineering		13.4
		Medicine		12.4
		Agriculture		9.8
Norway	1966	Economics	8.9	
		Law	10.6	
		Arts	4.3	
		Engineering	8.7	
		Sciences	6.2	
		Medicine	3.1	
		Agriculture	2.2	
Philippines	1969	Economics	10.5	14.0
		Law	15.0	18.0
		Engineering	8.0	15.0
		Agriculture	5.0	5.0
Sweden	1967	Economics	9.0	
		Law	9.5	
		Medicine	13.0	
		Engineering	7.5	

Sources: Colombia: Rodriguez [71], Table 6; Greece: Psacharopoulos [63], Table 8; Great Britain: Adamson and Reid [1], Table 3. All other countries from Psacharopoulos [57], Appendix G, and Psacharopoulos [56], Table 4.9.

[6]

Excerpt from *Review of Research in Education*, 2, 202–44

6

Learning and Earning in the Postschool Years

MARY JEAN BOWMAN *
University of Chicago

This chapter is concerned with basic research in positive economics: identification and explanation of the economic aspects of learning after entry into employment and of the remuneration paid for acquired skills. Broad societal concerns such as optimality or waste in the allocation of resources, and the distribution of earnings and of access to learning options —problems to which many engaged in basic research direct their attention —are included. However, work directed primarily to narrower policy questions or to narrowly delimited project assessments such as the benefit-cost assessments of programs under the Manpower Development and Training Act is excluded. (For a systematic summarization of the extensive work on cost-benefit analysis and manpower programs, including an up-to-date bibliography, see Barsby, 1972.) Also excluded are studies focusing on particular occupations or career lines. Even with such exclusions, the task of this chapter is enormous. Economic analyses of postschool learning and earning have multiplied in recent years and even in recent months.

I. RECENT RESEARCH DEVELOPMENTS

Shift in Emphasis: From Schooling to the Postschool Years

Recently there has been a marked shift in the work of economists from emphasis primarily or solely on schooling toward emphasis also on postschool earning and learning. It is not just that one fad has been

---

FINIS WELCH, University of California at Los Angeles and The Rand Corporation, was the editorial consultant for this chapter.

*I am indebted for helpful comments to William Brock, Thomas Johnson, Jacob Mincer, T. W. Schultz, and Finis Welch. None of them can be held responsible for the result, however.

replaced by another.[1] The change has deep roots in seminal theoretical developments in human capital theory, and it also reflects persisting societal issues.

At the start of the 1960s, increased schooling was acclaimed as a worldwide panacea. Most immediately, for the less developed countries it was a symbol of international status, and schooling of national leadership was an obvious necessity for effective participation in world affairs. Furthermore, the notion of central planning for development was pervasive, and increasing numbers of economists came to view manpower planning as essential in planning for economic growth. Estimates of increases in qualified manpower "required" to attain growth targets were matched against estimated flows of trained men coming out of the schools. With notable exceptions, manpower forecasters viewed their count of manpower supplies as tidily finished units ready for delivery. Learning from postschool experience and training was accepted only as an inferior alternative, a patch job necessitated by inadequacies or errors in prior educational planning. Creative man was entirely exogenous, existing only by implication (and repressed) in "technical progress."

However, attempts to identify manpower requirements empirically proved frustrating, even when the counting was by jobs or occupations. There was a severe breakdown in attempts to specify relationships between schooling and manpower requirements. These very frustrations have brought clearer thinking about skill formation and adaptation in more flexible life cycle perspectives. Although the present vogue of "career education" has little novelty, the realities behind this basic idea are indisputably important for the understanding of a dynamic society. Also apparent is the principal danger—of concluding that because "nonformal education" and learning by experience are important, central planners must "do something about them" in a managerial way.

While manpower planners and forecasters were pursuing their regressions in quantitative style, another group of economists was using neoclassical instruments to analyze postschool learning and earning. As with the manpower planners, the direction their efforts would take them was not immediately evident. In the late 1950s, national income accountants and econometricians from several nations demonstrated what Jan Tinbergen (1959) had shown in 1942: conventional models left unexplained a major proportion of the growth in national incomes over the previous quarter of a century. These findings, along with less dramatic empirical work on economic growth, lent support to the thesis pressed by T. W. Schultz (1959,

---

[1]The rapid succession from schooling, to antischooling, to nonformal education is irrelevant here. It is, of course, a commentary on the superficiality of much intellectualism.

1961, 1962) that human capital, heretofore neglected in growth accounting, was an important contributor to economic growth. The notion of investment in human beings was by no means new,[2] but Schultz imparted a fresh and powerful thrust to the development of a more penetrating and pervasive theory of investment in human beings.[3]

Even though Schultz's conception was wide in scope, the first applications of his thesis were to schooling only. Returns to college education, for example, were seen as the difference between the life earnings stream of a man with college and one with high school education only. But it was also clear that gains in earnings attributable to experience were higher for the college graduate than for the high school graduate. Indeed, the interaction between schooling and experience confounds measures of the contribution of schooling to economic growth. And that is not all. As Becker (1962) was to point out, estimated rates of return to schooling are in fact averages of rates of return to schooling and to subsequent investments of individuals in postschool learning and training. Furthermore, firms as well as individuals invest in the formation of skills, but returns on their investments show up in national accounts as returns to capital, not to labor. In Japan, where there is a pervasive system of life commitment to the firm among employees in big modern enterprises, this probably leads to a gross understatement of the role of human resources in economic product and growth (Bowman, 1972, in press). Few implications of these insights in the analysis of economic growth have yet been explored.

The analysis of postschool formation of human resources has not been confined to analysis of economic growth, however. Much of the recent work is focused on explaining the shapes of earning streams as a puzzle to be solved in its own right, with whatever spillover effects this may generate for analysis of broader societal questions. Some of the societal questions, though perennial, have taken on more salience in the mood of our times. In particular, we have seen renewed concern about the distribution of opportunity. That concern goes way beyond the "war on poverty," an increasingly vacuous slogan, into opportunities for blacks and other ethnic minorities and for women. In this setting, the inadequacy of analyses that

---

[2]The concept of "human capital" and its application in a growth context can be traced back as far as William Petty, circa 1665 (Petty, 1889), and it has appeared off and on over the centuries since that time. In 1906, Irving Fisher established the theoretical groundwork for an all-inclusive concept of capital, explicitly including human capital: his theoretical formulation provides the base for Schultz's work and, most notably, for that of Gary Becker (1962, 1964, 1965).

[3]Modern applications of the concept of investment in human capital have not been confined to economists. In the academic year 1948-49, C. Arnold Anderson conducted a sociology seminar course under the title "Investment in Human Resources," and he launched some of these ideas in discussions at Iowa State College in 1941-42. He in turn was started in this direction by reading a dissertation by Ray Walsh on human capital, completed in the early 1930s.

disregard career paths, promotion prospects, and opportunities for postschool training or learning by doing has become obvious. Over the past decade new tools have been forged for analysis of these problems, and the problems have become more visible and more sharply defined.

A Guide to Current Research

Three dichotomies can serve as a preliminary guide to mapping out characteristics of recent research on postschool learning and earning. These are: (1) full vesting of human capital in the individual versus partial vesting in the firm, (2) sequential opportunity-cost investments versus pure human capital appreciation, and (3) assumptions of full knowledge versus uncertainty, sorting, and search.

1. The first of these dichotomies is at the heart of the distinction between what Becker terms "general" and "specific" training. Becker-general training is fully vested in the individual; he can go elsewhere and reap the returns to such training. Becker-specific training, on the other hand, will yield him a return only in the firm or agency in which the skills are acquired. The training of carpenters, however vocationally specialized, is nevertheless Becker-general; it is fully vested in the individual. However, there will always be elements of "specific" training in the skills of an experienced secretary who has come to know the affairs of the office in which she works, the habits of her boss, and the people with whom he is most often in communication. She cannot take that part of her knowledge elsewhere and retain its value, nor can the employer replace her competence simply by hiring an equally able new secretary. In practice most people possess a mixture of general and specific skills in the Becker sense.

It must be emphasized that Becker-specific skills are not the same as what is usually meant by "specialized" or by "vocational" skills. In fact, constraining institutions that prevent interfirm mobility regardless of the technical transferability of a man's skill can have the same effect on investment behavior as firm specificity of the skill itself; in either case, costs and returns to investments in human capital will be shared between the individual and the firm. It is inability of the individual to take his skill elsewhere, for whatever reason, that makes the human capital embodied in him Becker-specific. Some implications for postschool learning and earning are discussed in Part V.

2. The standard models of sequential choice in formation of human capital (whether with vesting in the individual or the firm) posit situations in which investment decisions are made explicitly or implicitly in each successive (short) time period over the life cycle of the individual. Moreover, the effects of these decisions are sequentially interdependent, which is the foundation of their analysis using optimal control theory. In the perspective of the individual, the sequential choice models are the pure opportunity-cost models of investment in human beings. Costs may be incurred by

taking time from work (earnings foregone) for learning, or the individual may forego the extra pay available on a high-wage, dead-end job to take lower pay now on a job with a high learning component. The pure human capital appreciation model, by contrast, treats increases in productivity as a delayed spinoff from prior schooling, released as the individual gains work experience. Closely related is the predetermined life cycle of learning by doing inherent in entry upon some occupations. Costs and returns in these cases refer to choices among entire life earnings streams, fully determined by the initial decision. There are no subsequent points at which the individual will be making decisions to forego some earning for the sake of learning. A theoretical statement of the pure case of delayed maturation of effects of schooling is compared and contrasted with the Becker-Mincer sequential individual investment model in Bowman (1966). The simple appreciation model is applied empirically with very interesting results in Castro's (1972) study of types of schooling and career paths in Brazil. The main thrust of recent human capital research, however, has been to develop the full implications of the sequential decision models at more general levels of analysis, rather than to pursue studies that emphasize diversities in schooling and career options. The latter have been largely descriptive and, for the most part, have not been well integrated into modern human resource economics.

3. Most of the theoretical and empirical work relating to paths of life earnings and investments by individuals in themselves has assumed either full information or random errors that introduce no bias into either expectations or decisions. However, as attention is focused on job markets or Becker-specific training, the costs of acquiring information command attention. Indeed, the general concept of investment in human beings as investment in the acquisition of future earning power includes more than training and learning—among other things, it includes also investments in health, migration, and job search.[4] Meanwhile, entirely independent of what has amounted to a "human investment revolution in economic thought" has been a new emphasis on the economics of information more generally.[5] Here again there are, of course, forerunners, including studies of business

---

[4]The broad scope of the idea of investment in human beings is illustrated by the range of papers included in *Investment in Human Beings*, a supplement to the *Journal of Political Economy* (October 1962), edited by T. W. Schultz. Included is Stigler's "Information in the Labor Market" (1962).

[5]This work is not to be confused with mathematical communication or information theory, with the communication theories most familiar to sociologists, or with Hägerstrand's (1965, 1967) seminal work in human geography. The communication process as such and the nature and formation of "information fields" is not a part of the economics of information proper, and, with the exception of work at the Comparative Education Center in Chicago, there have been few systematic attempts to join economic decision models with communication theory from other disciplines.

decision making under various kinds and degrees of uncertainty that go back to Frank Knight's classic work, *Risk, Uncertainty and Profit* (1921), but the contemporary thrust is Bayesian. This approach has lent itself to analysis of "certification bias" in terms of the sorting and sifting of information about individuals not only through the schools but also on the job (Arrow, 1972; Berg, 1970; Spence, 1972; Stiglitz, 1972; and Taubman, 1972). However, the debates on this subject at the moment are a quagmire, confounded by ambiguities in interpretations of associations between ability and the pace of advance in earnings. With one or two notable exceptions, to the present time most of the research relating the economics of information to career choice and postschool learning and earning paths remains either informal or, if formal, mathematically abstract.

In sum, the theory of investment in human capital has been a wellspring of proliferating studies of economic learning (with or without earning) in the postschool years. The "learning by doing" of Arrow's (1962) formal dynamic growth theory barely touches any of this because it is not vested in anyone; neither individuals nor firms can claim returns for themselves on investments in such learning, which affects society as a whole. Studies building in various ways on concepts in the economics of information have appeared, both in accord with the theory of human capital and in confrontation with it. There have been other confrontations as well. Most notable, perhaps, is the Thurow (1972) and Thurow and Lucas (1972) theory of job competition and queuing, which displaces wage competition in the determination of access to job ladders and opportunities for subsequent learning at work, although the conflict in this case is less important than it seems. A few studies that bear upon postschool learning and earning are neutral with respect to human capital or directly attack one or another facet of that theoretical structure. Others bear evidence of the infiltration of human capital thinking, but without making such thinking central to their analysis.

II. INVESTMENTS OF INDIVIDUALS IN THEMSELVES: DOLLAR EQUIVALENTS

The Basic Opportunity-Cost Model of Postschool Learning

Estimates of net present values and internal rates of return to investments of an individual (or his family) in his schooling were a relatively obvious step once economists who used modern capital theory came to focus attention on human capital. What made Becker's theoretical formulation of "general" training so important was the fact that he applied it to successive decisions over the entire span of life, not just to investments during the school years. Further, it could be used to explain the concave shapes of observed age-earnings curves. In the most general terms, as stated above, the amount an individual invests in himself is measured by the income he foregoes in order to have higher earning power in the future. If we let C_i stand for the amount invested in the year $t = i$ and simplify for the moment by assuming no depreciation or appreciation, we can write the definitional equation:

$$C_i = (Y_i^* - Y_i) + D_i, \qquad (1.1)$$

where Y_i^* is potential earnings in the year i, Y_i is observed earnings in that year, and D_i is direct monetary outlays on schooling or training by the individual. The amount that the individual could potentially earn is defined recursively by the equation:

$$Y_i^* = Y_o^* + \sum_{t=o}^{i-1} a_t r_t C_t, \qquad (1.2)$$

where Y_o^* is the individual's potential earnings without schooling or training on the job, C_t is the amount invested in each year t, and $a_t r_t$ is the amount added to future annual earning power per dollar invested in the year t. The coefficient a_t is an adjustment for finite life:

$$a_t = \frac{1}{1 - [1/(1+r_t)]^{T-t}},$$

where T is the time limit of working life.

In principle, it is easy enough to split the components of potential earnings between those attributable to initial earning power, to investments during the school years, and to investments in the postschool years, as in Equation 1.3.

$$Y_i^* = [Y_o^* + \sum_{t=o}^{s-1} a_t r_t C_t] + \sum_{t=s}^{i-1} a_t r_t C_t \qquad (1.3)$$

$$Y_i^* = Y_o^* + Y_s^* + \sum_{t=s}^{i-1} a_t r_t C_t$$

If the internal rate of return, r, is allowed to vary among individuals and from year to year in both the schooling and postschooling sequence, and no other constraints are imposed on this model, it is almost completely general,[6] but also completely tautological. The general formulation becomes a behavioral theory when it is stipulated that choices between earning and investment will be made to optimize the present value of the stream of future earnings at each successive decision point, t. The behavioral theory can be

---

[6]It cannot accommodate costless increments to earnings. As the cost of any given increment to earnings approaches zero, the rate of return approaches infinity.

made empirically operational if we make constraining assumptions about the behavior of r_t and the depreciation of skills for specified groups of people.

Mincer's 1962 Estimates of On-the-Job Training

Jacob Mincer (1962) provided the first empirical breakthrough in estimation of the extent of postschool investments made by individuals in themselves. The basic information he used was census data (for 1939, 1949, and 1950) on earnings by age and schooling for the male population of the United States. He also made estimates of direct schooling costs and part-time earnings while in school, which he netted out to get the earnings figures for each age-schooling cell. These data sufficed to provide estimates of the rates of return to each increment of schooling on the assumption that the same rates of return applied to schooling and to the marginal on-the-job investments associated with each increment of schooling. In essentials, his 1962 procedure was as follows:

1. Earnings of the lowest education group were treated as the base line, with the identification assumption of no on-the-job learning in this group. He avoids this assumption in later work (Mincer 1970, 1973), discussed below.
2. For the next level of education (elementary 5–8), the path of postschool investments was estimated by a recursive procedure. Taking r_1 as the estimated average internal rate of return to elementary education, Y_{io} as earnings in the year i of men with education 0–4, and Y_{i1} and D_{i1} as earnings and as direct costs, respectively, in the year i of men with education 8, for $i = 1$:

$$C_i = (Y_{io} - Y_{i1}) + D_{i1}.$$

For $i = 2$:

$$C_i = [(Y_{io} + r_1 C_1) - Y_{i1}] + D_{i1}.$$

Generalizing for all i gives the recursive equation:

$$C_i = [(Y_{io} + r_1 \sum_{t=o}^{i-1} C_t) - Y_{i1}] + D_{i1}. \tag{2}$$

3. This process was repeated for the next schooling increment, and so on.

Total investments up to any year are, of course, the summation of the estimated investments for each year, and splitting this total between the school and postschool years is a simple matter.

Mincer's results were startling in the estimated amount of total on-the-job investments expressed in cost terms, even ignoring the unmeasured costs of training paid for by firms. Expressed in 1954 dollars, the estimated school and postschool (on-the-job) investments by individuals were as shown in Table 1. For all schooling levels in all years the total estimated investments in on-the-job training exceeded those for schooling. Equally important, estimates of on-the-job investments by college men exceeded by far those of high school graduates, which were in turn substantially larger than the estimates for elementary-school youth. This is especially marked in the 1958 data. Although by his estimates real schooling costs rose at all levels of schooling over the 20-year span covered in Table 1, the big increases in dollar estimates of on-the-job training occurred primarily among college men.

TABLE 1

Mincer's 1962 Estimates of per Capita Lifetime Investment in Training at School and on the Job; U.S. Males, 1939, 1949, 1958, by level of schooling (thousands of 1954 dollars)

Educational Level	Marginal Cost			Total Cost		
	School	On the Job	Sum	School	On the Job	Sum
1939						
College	9.4	6.7	16.2	14.7	15.2	29.9
High school	3.9	4.6	8.5	5.2	8.5	13.7
Elementary school	1.3	3.9	5.2	1.3	3.9	5.2
1949						
College	11.5	17.7	29.3	18.0	27.4	45.4
High school	4.6	5.3	9.9	6.4	9.7	16.0
Elementary school	1.8	4.4	6.2	1.8	4.4	6.2
1958						
College	15.3	21.2	36.5	24.1	28.8	52.9
High school	6.6	2.7	9.3	8.8	7.6	16.4
Elementary school	2.2	4.9	7.1	2.2	4.9	7.1

Source: J. Mincer, "On-the-Job Training: Costs, Returns and Some Implications," *Journal of Political Economy*, October 1962, *70*, 55. Reprinted by permission of the University of Chicago Press.

To be sure, interpretations of these findings can easily be debated. As Mincer has emphasized (1962), the results are highly sensitive to the assumption that marginal rates of return to schooling and to postschool learning are the same for individuals within each schooling category. In addition, the 1962 estimates of total on-the-job training were biased downward by the assumption that there was no such training in the lowest (0–4) schooling group, and this was most serious, relatively, for estimates in the lower schooling range. Accepting Mincer's assumption concerning the internal rate of return, the method he used in 1962 also gave some downward bias to estimates of marginal schooling costs and a corresponding upward bias to estimates of on-the-job training for better educated men. This latter problem is easily illustrated. The difference between observed and potential earnings of high school graduates in their first year in the labor market counts as an on-the-job investment of the college man. The foregone earnings associated with the first year of college education are correspondingly underestimated. In his more recent work (1970, in press), Mincer avoids some of these biases, but to do this he has to make other constraining assumptions. (See below, pages 222–23.)

There is, of course, the general run of problems associated with interpretations of observed earnings differentials by schooling, any special assumptions of Mincer's analysis aside. One set of problems is due to changes in the situation from one cohort to the next; cross-sectional data generally are flatter than true cohort experiences, imparting a downward bias to both rates of return and estimated total on-the-job training. There is also the often-mentioned problem that better educated men may have the advantage in other ways as well. Adjustments to take this into account have not brought substantial changes in estimated rates of return overall. However, effects of ability differences on the paths of earnings through time may be another matter.

Finally, and most fundamentally, there is the further problem in Mincer's model that he can identify investment costs only under the restrictive assumption that in each period average equals marginal learning cost. But this assumption is inconsistent with optimal decision behavior.

Schooling and On-the-Job Components of Lifetime Earnings

Whatever the range of estimates of investments in schooling and on-the-job learning, and whatever the debates over their interpretation, there can be no doubt that postschool learning and training are substantial. It is useful for some purposes to turn Mincer's analysis around to ask what part of observed earnings cumulated over the course of a man's life may be attributed to learning in the postschool years.

Figure 1 denotes as Y_m the path of the observed differential earnings of a man who has completed schooling level m over a man who had no schooling, where T marks termination of his working life. The area under this curve measures the total incremental rental values (earnings) associated with the schooling, plus the subsequent extra on-the-job training received by schooled as compared with unschooled individuals. We can get some idea of what part of this area is legitimately attributable at a maximum to schooling and what part at a minimum to postschool learning of the schooled over the unschooled man if we make use of Mincer's assumptions to estimate the cumulative cost of the investment in schooling, C_m, and the

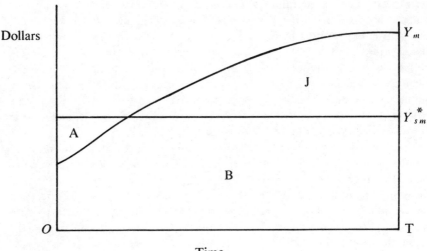

Figure 1. Relation of incremental postschool learning to observed incremental lifetime earnings of men with the schooling m.

rate of return on that investment, r_m. Since this is at an early stage in the life sequence, the adjustment for finite life can be ignored and the product, $r_m C_m$, is the horizontal earning stream, Y^*_{sm}, attributable to schooling, from the date of completion of schooling, at $t = 0$. At first Y^*_{sm} lies above the stream of observed earnings, because part of these incremental potential earnings are used for postschool investments. We can nevertheless specify $(A + B)$, the rectangular area under Y^*_{sm} from the origin (O) to the termination (T) of working life, as the gross rental values attributable to education over that life span. The difference $(J - A)$ between that area and the total area under Y_m is the net rental value attributable to on-the-job training (ignoring direct outlays).[7]

If we maintain Mincer's assumptions, the ratio of the area of residual net returns $(J - A)$ to on-the-job learning to the total area under the Y_m curve constitutes a downward-biased index of the proportion of total productivity and of observed postschool earnings attributable to postschool investment. Even if Mincer's assumptions are considered unacceptable in first approxi-

---

[7]The *net* contribution of schooling (undiscounted) would be area $(A + B)$ *minus* costs of schooling incurred before $t = 0$: call these costs C. Then the undiscounted net total becomes $(B + J - C)$, and the postschool share in this is $(J - A)/(B + J - C)$ instead of $(J - A)/(B + J)$.

mation, the index is nevertheless descriptive of relationships observable in the data.

I estimated such indexes for males at several education levels in the United States in 1939, 1949, and 1958, for Japan in 1961, and for white and nonwhite males in the South and in the rest of the United States in 1959 (Bowman, 1968, 1970). Three findings are particularly relevant.

First, among black males of 1959 these indexes were approximately zero, except at the elementary school level, where the southern index was .40 and the northern an impressive 1.66. Above the elementary level, it is apparent in the cross sections for 1959 that growth in individual earnings after entry to jobs was much too small to counteract any dampening effects that might be attributed to changes across cohorts in favor of the younger men. There is ample evidence that this situation has changed recently, although how far the changes in what we observe may be attributed to improvements in the relative quality of education of the younger black men (argued especially by Welch, 1972), and how far to changes in the range of options open to blacks for postschool training and promotion (which I am more inclined to emphasize, especially at the higher levels of schooling) is still subject to debate.

Second, among white males of 1959 the pattern was the reverse of that among blacks. Among white males who had graduated from high school or completed college, the northern indexes were .82 to .85 and the southern, .99 to 1.10. Roughly, there was an even balance in these estimates of contributions of schooling and on-the-job learning (or of more arbitrary seniority effects?) to earnings. Cohort adjustments would tip the balance toward on-the-job learning. For the least educated white males, however, the indexes were zero or negative; this is a striking illustration of the shift in composition of the least educated men from the cohorts of oldsters to those more recently entering the labor market. It provides a dramatic lesson in the dangers of disregarding shifts in the composition of nominally homogeneous categories of schooling from one cohort to another.

Third, the indexes are much higher in Japan than they are for comparable groups in the United States. Moreover, the "overtake point,"[8] at which the horizontal curve of potential returns to schooling, Y^*_{sm} , cuts the observed net earnings curve, comes at a later age in Japan. This is in spite of the fact that interfirm mobility of labor is less in Japan and the Becker-

---

[8]The term "overtake point" was not used in my articles. Here I have taken it from Mincer (1970, in press). While we used the same concept, our purposes were different. Mincer was interested in analysis of the distribution of income at any given time, rather than of human resource components in national income or income growth. In this connection he dropped the distinction of rates of return by levels of education and dollar estimates of costs, to treat simply years of schooling as an independent variable in a human capital model. This brings us to the "time equivalent" models in analysis of life earnings paths.

specific component of on-the-job training (not included theoretically in the Mincer model) is almost certainly of relatively great importance there. This points up some important questions concerning treatment of seniority, for example, that have been generally neglected in the human capital literature.

III. INVESTMENTS BY INDIVIDUALS IN THEMSELVES: TIME EQUIVALENTS

Optimal Control Models and the Allocation of Time

In Becker's theory of general training there was nothing to specify the sequential path that foregoing of earnings would take. It could be that time was divided between working and learning, and opportunity costs of postschool learning primarily took the form of the earnings that would have been possible had hours not been given up to specialized learning activities. But it could equally be the case that the decisions were between dead-end jobs with high immediate pay but no built-in opportunities to learn or to advance one's career, and jobs that might pay less initially but entailed learning and corresponding chances for later promotion. In some years of teaching these ideas to students in education, I have found that this second interpretation was much more quickly assimilated as referring to the real world within their purview. In most of the literature, however, there has been a branching off in one or the other of two directions. The first has been the development of models that focus on the allocation of time, whether literally or as "time equivalence." The second features analysis of job choice, with joint production of goods or services for customers of the firm and of learning opportunities for employees.

The time allocation approach was a natural and convenient route to pursue initially, for several reasons. First, it followed directly from the treatment of foregone earnings as costs of schooling, which was prominent in T. W. Schultz's work. Second, analysis of the allocation of time facilitated examination of economics of the household, participation in the labor market, and the distribution of consumption over time (independently of the path of earnings) that had been emphasized by Irving Fisher in 1906. Third, it had the advantage of allowing work with years of schooling alone, thereby bypassing complications of cost estimation in dollars. Becker and Mincer both contributed again in seminal works to shaping this direction of research, but the first application for analysis of paths of life earnings was a simplified optimal control model by Ben-Porath (1967, 1970).

Though developed by mathematicians, from the point of view of the economist optimal control theory is identical in general form with capital theory, which has often been defined as "the economics of time." A theory of behavior that specifies the sequence of choices that will maximize the present value of expected future income streams is essentially an example of optimal control theory. In Dorfman's (1969) words, optimal control theory "deduces both normative and descriptive conclusions about the time path of the accumulation of capital by economic units and entire economies" [p. 817]. Optimal control theory in its more technical forms is based on the new calculas of variations. The modern classic is by Pontryagin, Bol'tyanskii, Gamkrelidze, and Mischenko (1964).

Optimal control theory accounts for the affinity between some of the work in mathematical dynamic growth theory and the analysis of accumulation of human capital by individuals (and also, as we will see, by firms). Specifically, the problem to which this theory is directed in applications to accumulation of human capital is the determination at each point in time, t, of the decision variable that will maximize the present-value streams of future earnings, subject to the constraints of present human capital stock and available decision options—which, in turn, depend upon initial human capital stock and decisions made in periods prior to t. Application of optimal control theory requires a capital production function (in this case a human capital one) and selection of sequential choices consistent with maximizing the net present value of current and future benefits.

Neither Becker nor Mincer specified characteristics of the human capital production function. In this respect there was an important gap in the theory of human capital accumulation, which Ben-Porath (1967) set out to fill by application of optimal control theory. The first crucial point in his analysis is that formation of human capital requires the participation of the individual. He described his purpose in these words: "I shall show how the production function . . . enters into the determination of the optimal path of investment, and demonstrate how the life cycle of earnings can be affected by various properties of the production function [1967, p. 352]."

In Ben-Porath's model (1967, 1970) the stock of human capital is implicitly defined in terms of the annual potential earnings it can engender:

$$Y^*_t = a_o K_t, \tag{3.1}$$

where Y^*_t is maximum annual earnings, K_t is the stock of human capital, and a_o is the rental value per unit of human capital.[9] Every individual has an initial endowment of K, which (in his 1967 model) is subject to an exogenously given rate of deterioration, δ. Ben-Porath also assumes perfect capital markets, with unlimited borrowing and lending taking place at a constant rate of interest, r. (This is quite different, it must be emphasized, from Mincer's assumptions of constant internal rates of return for sequential schooling and postschool investments associated with given marginal

---

[9]Ben-Porath uses simply Y_t instead of Y^*_t. I have retained Y^*_t to keep notation as consistent as possible, though some differences cannot be avoided.

increments to schooling.) He simplifies a complex problem by assuming that there is no joint production of learning and earning, so that the fraction of time allocated to learning identifies the proportion of human capital so allocated. That fraction at date t is denoted as s_t, purchased inputs at t as D_t, and the human capital produced at t as Q_t. (All time is divided between work and learning; there is no substitution between these and leisure.) Ben-Porath's production function is then written:

$$Q_t = \beta_o (s_t K_t)^{\beta_1} D_t^{\beta_2}, \qquad (3.2)$$

where $\beta_1, \beta_2 > 0$ and $\beta_1 + \beta_2 < 1$. The term $s_t K_t$ is the amount of human capital used in the formation of human capital at t, and the fraction s_t is constrained by the condition $0 \leq s_t \leq 1$. Given the deterioration rate δ, the rate of change of the capital stock is:

$$\dot{K}_t = Q_t - \delta K_t. \qquad (3.3)$$

Investment costs, I_t, have two components, opportunity costs of time and purchased inputs:

$$I_t = a_o s_t K_t + P_t D_t, \qquad (3.4)$$

where P_t is the price of the inputs, D_t, purchased at t. The objective of the individual is to maximize the present value of his disposable earnings:

$$W_t = \int_t^T e^{-rv} [a_o K(v) - I(v)] \, dv. \qquad (3.5)$$

The demand price for K declines over time because of the shortening period in which the annual returns to an increase in K can be realized. This would suggest concentration of all production of human capital at the earliest possible stage, with s equal to 1, and no investment thereafter. This is where the characteristics of the production function come in. In both of his articles Ben-Porath assumes that within any short period, t, there are decreasing returns to scale in the production of human capital; as already specified, the sum of $\beta_1 + \beta_2 < 1$. He specifies a rising marginal cost (MC) curve as a function of Q, starting from the origin and unchanging through time, and a perfectly elastic demand curve that slides down with time. These forms of the demand and cost functions are illustrated geometrically in Figure 2. The gross additions to K at date t are determined by the intersection of the unchanging marginal cost curve and the demand price line at t. Net additions to K depend not only on Q but also on δ.

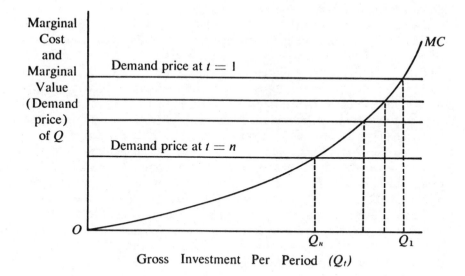

Figure 2. Determination of quantity of investment per period (Q_t).

Ben-Porath defines three earnings variables:

$Y_t^* =$ Maximum potential earnings at t.

$E_t =$ Disposable income at t, which is $(Y_t^* - I_t)$.

$\hat{E}_t =$ Observed earnings at t. These are higher than E_t by the direct outlay component of I_t. In other words,

$$\hat{E}_t = Y_t^* - a_o s_t K_t.$$

His 1967 model generates a life cycle of earnings with the typical observed characteristics of an initial period of no earnings followed by a period in which earnings rise at a declining rate and, eventually, decline absolutely. Attainable maximum earnings, Y_t^*, peak first, followed by observed earnings, E_t, and then by disposable earnings, E_t. This model "thus specifies the nature of the bias that may exist when earnings are used, as they often have been, to infer changes in productive capacity with age [Ben-Porath, 1967, p. 353]."

Although this mathematical model is highly relevant to real-world situations, it was not empirically testable in the form in which it was first developed. Ben-Porath's second contribution to the subject (1970) was the specification of a similar model, but without the deterioration factor, δ, or the purchased inputs. Using Mincer's estimates of cumulative investments in human capital, Ben-Porath (1970) tested the fit of his simplified model, which predicted continuing investments in formation of human capital damped only by the effects of the fact that working life is finite. The important question was the validity of a "neutrality" hypothesis that the efficiency of K with respect to learning and to earning is the same at each stage in the life cycle. Ben-Porath (1970) found that estimated investments were too truncated in time and the neutrality hypothesis was not supported. Unfortunately, however, as Sherwin Rosen (1972a) has pointed out, Mincer's procedures are inconsistent with Ben-Porath's model and cannot be used to test it; the biases generally are toward underestimation of investment, but most strongly so for the later years. In addition, Ben-Porath's results could have reflected a substantial impact of deterioration or obsolescence, which he included in his initial theoretical model but was unable to specify in adapting it for an empirical check. The question of the "neutrality" of K with respect to ability to learn (to increase future earning power) and ability more directly and immediately to earn has yet to be tested. This is a crucial issue for much of the work that applies human-capital theory to analysis of the time shapes of earning streams. In my judgment the strongest a priori justification for continuing to make use of the neutrality assumption is one that has rarely been mentioned in this connection: in a dynamic economy the ability to learn and to adapt quickly is itself a valuable attribute for which employers (and the market more generally) are willing to pay.

Several economists have been concerned with analysis of the transition from full-time investment in human capital to the labor market, with or without part-time investments. Do optimal decisions entail a sharp break, involving a corner solution when the amount of K becomes large enough to allow optimization with $s < 1$, or is there a smoother transition? Johnson (1970), fitted a continuous form of Equation 1.3 to observed earnings streams, using an assumed form of the investment fraction s, which allowed a corner solution in accord with the data he was using. (Johnson also showed (1969) that his formulation reduced to Ben-Porath's result when it is required that $r(t) = r$ and $\delta(t) = \delta$.)

Haley (1971, 1972) has challenged Johnson's findings as a misreading of the empirical evidence, and there can be no doubt that the data used most often have understated or totally ignored the work for pay and increasing hours spent on such work among youth still in school. Haley's own study is entirely abstract, however, with an optimal control model that closely resembles Ben-Porath's in most of its key features. Haley excludes purchased inputs, so that the only choice variable is allocation of time; he includes a scale coefficient and an exogenously determined coefficient of depreciation of capital, δ. An interesting feature of Haley's model is his distinction between original capital endowment of the individual and an "ability" parameter that measures the individual's ability to produce further capital from any given stock of capital.[10] The higher the ability coefficient, the lower the individual's marginal cost curve; this implies that the higher the ability parameter the longer the period of specialization and also the greater the amount of human capital that will be invested at each later date. On the other hand, with ability held constant the higher the initial capital endowment, the sooner will the individual reach a point at which K is large enough that the optimal solution is no longer with $s = 1$. Speculations about the empirical relevance of this model are interesting but difficult because of both the conceptual and empirical problem in identifying just what is meant, in Haley's analysis, by initial capital endowment.

Human Capital Accumulation and the
Explanation of Variance in Earnings

It is a well-known fact that schooling alone accounts for only a very small fraction of variance in earned incomes. However, human capital theory properly applied may explain a very substantial part of that variance. The most intensive research on this topic has been the work of Mincer (in press). Before turning to that work, however, it is well worthwhile to take note of recent research by Lillard (1972a, 1972b).

Lillard starts out with an optimal control model that modifies Haley's treatment in two respects: he removes the assumption of constancy over the life cycle in the effect of ability, and he eliminates the initial human capital by making it redundant. He does this by a formulation in which net earnings functions are determined simultaneously with age at termination of full-time specialization on learning; the age-earnings profiles are determined by effects of ability, schooling, *and their interaction*. Lillard tested his model empirically by using linear Taylor series approximations for exponential functions of age and schooling on data for a national cohort of 1955 male high school sophomores who were given achievement tests in 1955 and answered a follow-up survey in 1970. Use of this approximation was necessary in his model to separate r and δ from the age variable. He justified use of the linear form on the grounds that his data covered the earlier part of the life cycle only.

The postschool human investment and earnings paths generated by this experiment were then used in an analysis of determinants of the distribution of earned incomes within various subcategories of the population. The interaction between ability and schooling built into the model admits nega-

---

[10]Becker (1967), used a similar definition of ability in his Woytinsky lecture.

tive partial effects of schooling on earnings at younger ages, when more schooling implies less time in the labor force, associated in turn with a more intensive incidence of post school investment in human capital. (Mincer handles experience in the labor force more directly and ignores effects of ability.) Lillard is currently extending this analysis to include also the effects of differential access to funds (imperfect capital markets).

Although both Mincer and Lillard base their research on a Becker-general model of investment in human capital, their procedures are very different. To understand Mincer (in press), it is necessary first to look at the "schooling model" in its simplest form, as first introduced by Mincer (1958) and as used by Becker and Chiswick (1966) and by Chiswick and Mincer (1972). This model disregards any purchased inputs, or assumes that they are cancelled out by unmeasured earnings during the school years. Thus all investments can be thought of in time-equivalent units. Critical also is the assumption that the internal rate of return is a constant from one level of schooling to another. In the schooling model:

n = Length of working life plus schooling for all persons.
Y_s = Annual earnings of individuals with s years of schooling.
V_s = Present value of their life earnings at start of schooling.
r = Rate of return on investments in schooling.
Δ = Difference in amount of training, in years.

Thus,

$$V_s = Y_s \sum_{t=s+1}^{n} \left(\frac{1}{1+r}\right)^t.$$

Treating the process as continuous, with e as the base of natural logarithms, this becomes:

$$V_s = Y_s \cdot \int_s^n e^{-rt}\, dt = \frac{Y_s(e^{-rs} - e^{-rn})}{r}. \qquad (4.1)$$

Similarly, the present value of life earnings of individuals with $(s - \Delta)$ years of schooling is:

$$V_{s-\Delta} = \frac{Y_{s-\Delta}(e^{-r(s-\Delta)} - e^{-rn})}{r}. \qquad (4.2)$$

The ratio $k_{s, s-\Delta}$ of annual earnings of persons differing by Δ years of training is found by equating $V_s = V_{s-\Delta}$. This assumes equilibrium adjustments consistent with optimizing decisions. Then:

$$k_{s,\,s-\Delta} = \frac{Y_s}{Y_{s-\Delta}} = \frac{e^{\,r(n+\Delta-s)} - 1}{e^{\,r(n-s)} - 1}. \tag{4.3}$$

The ratio is, of course, larger than unity; it is a positive function of r, and it is larger the shorter the span of working life, n. It is also, less obviously, a positive function of s for any given Δ. However, change in $k_{s,\,s-\Delta}$ with a change in s and in n is negligible when n is large. For all practical purposes those effects can be ignored, and therefore:

$$k_{s,\,s-\Delta} = \frac{Y_s}{Y_{s-\Delta}} = \frac{e^{\,-r(s-\Delta)}}{e^{\,-rs}} = e^{\,r\Delta}. \tag{4.4}$$

This says that the earnings ratio k of individuals differing by Δ years of schooling does not depend on the level of schooling or on the length of earning life. Therefore, $k_{s,o} = \dfrac{Y_s}{Y_o} = k_s$. Then, by Equation 4.4, $k_s = e^{\,rs}$. In logarithms, the formula becomes the approximating equation cited by Welch in Chapter 5.

$$\ln Y_s = \ln Y_o + rs. \tag{4.5}$$

Thus if we ignore postschool investments in formation of human capital, percentage differentials in earnings are strictly proportional to absolute differentials in time spent at school, with the rate of return as the coefficient of proportionality.

It is not surprising that regressions using this equation on average earnings of men with various amounts of schooling, regardless of age, gave estimates of the coefficient r that were much smaller than direct estimates of rates of return, as well as yielding very low coefficients of determination. The prediction was improved somewhat and the coefficient raised by introducing controls for age, but estimates are still substantially biased, and such controls do not build the full human capital model into the analysis.

Mincer (in press) took advantage of the conversion of investment costs into time-equivalent values suggested by the schooling model. Extending this idea to the full life span of human capital investments, he arrived, through a process I shall not reproduce here, at the equation:

$$\ln Y^*_j = \ln Y^*_s + r_j K_j, \qquad (4.6)$$

where Y^*_j is the maximum potential earnings (gross earnings in his terminology) in year j, Y^*_s is the gross earnings of men with schooling s but no on-the-job training, K_j is the cumulative postschool investment in human capital prior to the year j, and r_j is the rate of return on all postschool investments.

(Expressing investment in the year j as a ratio to gross earnings, and denoting that ratio as

$$k_j = \frac{C_j}{Y^*_j},$$

the logarithm of observed earnings in the year j is:

$$\ln Y_j = \ln Y^*_j - k_j = \ln Y^*_s + r_j K_j - k_j .)$$

By assuming that the rate of return to postschool and to school investments is the same, Mincer could arrive, as indicated above, at an estimate of Y^*_s, and he could then identify the overtake point. From this he went on to an empirical study of the determinants of variance in earnings within "experience" and within age groups, defining experience as years in the labor market. Years of schooling explained much more of the earnings variance within experience groups than within age categories; the highest coefficient of determination in the within-experience samples was .33, in the overtake range, dropping off sharply thereafter. The highest coefficient of determination for the within-age regressions was only half that much, for men in their forties. Both theoretically, drawing upon the logic of optimal investment decisions and Ben-Porath's work, and empirically in these regressions, Mincer (in press) has demonstrated the importance of distinguishing between age profiles and experience profiles of earned incomes. (It has been noted that Lillard's findings also are consistent with this argument, although his empirical formulation is quite different.)

Using his theoretical formulation together with observed experience-earnings profiles for each school completion category, Mincer found that:

1. Total dollar value of postschool investments rises with schooling.
2. *Actual* time spent probably diminishes with schooling.
3. The proportion of earnings foregone (time-equivalent investments) has no clear relation with schooling.

He also found marked stability in estimated "overtaking years" from one schooling level to another. Taking advantage of this and using the lower bound, at seven years, as the overtaking year for the lowest schooling group, Mincer made new estimates of investments in on-the-job training. These were substantially higher than his earlier estimates, especially for men in the lower schooling categories.

A critical problem that must be considered in empirical application of human capital theory to the explanation of earnings is the treatment of weeks worked during the year, or other indicators of the proportion of time employed among men who are out of school. If unemployment is involuntary and its incidence is associated with amount of schooling, presumably the appropriate measure is annual earnings. However, if much of the part-time or part-year employment is voluntary, there is the presumption that the value of time in other uses is at least as high as it is in the labor market. A number of economists—including Lindsay (1971), T. P. Schultz (1971), and Mincer (1970, in press) and Chiswick and Mincer (1972)—have grappled with one or another aspect of this problem in relation to applications of human capital theory. Whatever the interpretation, the empirical evidence that weeks worked adds substantially to schooling and years of experience in the statistical explanation of variance in earnings is irrefutable. Mincer's strong defense of the power of human capital theory to explain variance in earnings has sometimes been attacked on these grounds. Nevertheless, in the last part of the very important book (Mincer, in press) to which I have been referring repeatedly in these pages, Mincer has shown that he could explain statistically at least 35 percent of the variance in earnings using a Gompertz function of the net earning stream that incorporates plausible assumptions concerning human capital depreciation, without consideration of weeks worked. (Schooling alone explained only 7 percent of the variance.) With an experience term in the Gompertz function, he also removed the bias in estimated rates of return. Alternative specifications of the experience variables made very little difference. By an ingenious procedure, he estimated how much larger the coefficients of determination would be if information had been available on postschool investments of each individual and on variation in the quality of education received by individuals at each school completion level (as indexed by variations in school expenditures). This maneuver resulted in an estimated R^2 of .63. Calculations of net effects of variations in weeks worked (treating part of such variation as transitory) brought Mincer to an upper limit of 75 percent of the nontransitory variance explainable by a human capital model.

The Special Case of Women

Empirical research such as Mincer has done has been remarkably successful in analyzing earnings of men. Without further elaboration, it does not get very far with women. Some of the reasons are obvious. Women are in and out of the labor market, they have different expectations and different opportunity sets. Different patterns of behavior with respect to investments should be expected. One of the many areas of research into which the modern theory of investment in human beings and of allocation of time has been penetrating is indeed the explanation of rates of labor-force participation among women (along with fertility rates, consumption behavior, and so on). Two unpublished papers are of special interest.

The main thrust of studies by Polachek (1972a, 1972b) is to test the hypothesis that depreciation of human capital proceeds at a more rapid rate during years at home than during years in the labor market. Taking data from a longitudinal study of women aged 30 to 44, he regressed the logarithm of earnings on years of schooling, using a segmented experience model. For married women he found that the period of time at home was associated with a significant depreciation of human capital stock. This work is being extended.

Willis' (1971) paper is an insightful analytical essay, written in the fall of 1971 for a report to the planning office for the National Institute of Education. His argument is consistent with Polachek's findings, but it distinguishes between learning that increases productive competence in the market and in the home. The general theme, which he develops with great skill, could be applied in many other contexts, and not just for women or for home versus labor-market activities. It is interesting also for the way in which the two main approaches to the analysis of human capital formation are linked: investments that are associated directly with allocation of time, and those that are associated with choices between jobs that inherently entail more learning or less.

IV. OBSOLESCENCE, VINTAGE, AND EXOGENOUS GROWTH

An Empirical Approach to the Vintage-Growth-Obsolescence Problem

Johnson (1969) presented a model that was built in part on Ben-Porath's work but designed to test statistical fit to observed paths of rental values of human capital over the life cycle. He assumed that the exogenous (exogenous to the model of individual postschool human capital investment decisions) rate of growth, $g(t)$, plus the rate of depreciation of human capital stock, $\delta(t)$, summed to a constant value, D. That is, $g(t) + \delta(t) = D$. The fraction of earning capacity invested in human capital at "age" t, denoted as $k(t)$, was assumed to take the form:

$$k(t) = \alpha - \alpha(t - s) / (T - s),$$

where $s = $ years of school and $T = $ "age" at retirement (assumed to be the 65th birthday). One of the parameters estimated was $\delta(t)$, which came out to have values Johnson regarded as implausibly high.

Hebein (1972) and Johnson and Hebein (1972) developed a statistical model of life cycle earnings that combined time-series and cross-sectional data. Again the basic equation was built up from human capital equations. They specified that:

1. Observed earnings in the year t equal potential earnings minus investment in human capital in that year.
2. The rental rate, $R(t)$, on an investment at t remains constant on the undepreciated portion until retirement. (Also $R(t) = R$.).
3. Exogenous growth, $g(t)$, accrues equally to the value of all human capital at t, but the model allows for a changing growth rate to cohorts.
4. $\delta(t)$, the rate of depreciation of the total stock, and the exogenous rate of growth, $g(t)$, are independent of each other and of all other parameters in the model. (Also $\delta(t) = \delta$.)
5. $k(t)$, the proportion of gross earnings invested at (t), follows the time path:

$$k(t) = \begin{cases} 1.0 & t \leqslant s \\[2em] \alpha - \dfrac{\alpha(t-s)}{T-s} & t > s \end{cases}$$

There were also specifications concerning error terms. The cohorts θ are defined by their t "age" in 1960, so that $\theta = t - (C - 1960)$, where C is the calendar year. Like Mincer, Johnson and Hebein specified a statistical model in which the dependent variable was expressed in logarithmic form, in this case as $\ln Y(\tau, \theta)$, where τ is $(t - s)$ and $s \leqslant t \leqslant T$.

Estimates of the parameter δ were consistently smaller and more plausible than in Johnson's earlier work (1969, 1970); it was greatest for high school graduates and those who had some college but had not completed four years. Schooling and on-the-job training accounted for larger proportions of the variance in earnings as schooling level rose. Tests for differential impacts of autonomous growth by levels of schooling completed indicated that there had been a substantial differential impact between the high school and college groups, with the former experiencing a significantly higher upward shift; the null hypothesis was accepted for differences in autonomous growth between eighth-grade completers and high school graduates. The authors raise questions as to how far these differences may be vintage effects rather than autonomous growth, noting also objections to such an interpretation.

Optimum Control Theory in a Job-Market Model

Some of the models discussed to this point are linked directly with the idea of allocation of time between earning and learning activities. Ben-

Porath set his analysis up in that way. Others have left this question open, though expressing relationships in time-equivalent units; this was implicit in using the logarithmic models which permit expression of relationships in ratio terms, disregarding absolute values. Rosen (1972a, in press) has taken a different direction, though still within the same general human capital model and using the concept of opportunity cost. In the two papers discussed here, his concern is with the formation of capital that is vested in the individual. Rosen opens his first paper (1972a) with the statement that it "models the role of the labor market in the transmission and acquisition of skills and knowledge, based on the hypothesis that individuals learn from their working experiences. The problem is cast in terms of an implicit market for learning opportunities that is dual to the market for jobs [p. 326]." In ordinary language, this is to say that some jobs have large learning components in them, while others may entail little learning; when people choose between such alternatives they are choosing whether or not to invest in further training. It is also saying that employers can offer training services as a way of inducing people to work for them and that the costs of such training to the employer can be passed on to the worker in lower wages. For an early statement on this point, see my paper for the 1963 meeting of the International Economics Association on the economics of education (Bowman, 1966).

The idea of learning as a joint product is modeled by linking the theory of optimal accumulation of capital by the individual to analysis of market adjustments and "equalizing wage differences." As in all the models discussed thus far, the difference between the worker's potential immediate earning power and his actual wage at date t is what he pays for learning. Also as in those models, the learning at t affects not only potential future earnings (or rental values) but also potential future learning power. (This heads into Ben-Porath's neutrality question, though Rosen does not deal with it.) At the same time, the symmetry in the situation and in its labor market implications is pointed up by the proposition that the training or learning provided with the job is part of the gross revenue of the firm; the learning opportunity is implicitly sold to the worker, who buys it when he accepts lower wages. Rosen puts a great deal of stress on costs to the employer, who is seen as in the "education business," whatever his other business. In providing greater learning opportunities he incurs costs in many ways, including reduced physical output. There is presumably a rising supply price of learning opportunities. Here again, Rosen brings optimization into play: "Given market prices for learning, employers choose the optimum combination of work-learning activities offered by *designing* jobs in the appropriate manner [Rosen, in press, p. 11]."

Rosen's emphasis on the rising supply price of work-learning activities disregards consideration of a type of situation that may nevertheless be approximated very closely in many cases—situations in which the most efficient mode of production automatically also provides learning for those participating in it. He leaves the impression that he is discarding this, as an empty box. But if opportunity for automatic learning is provided, this does not mean it will be costless. There will be an opportunity cost of learning to the individual because market adjustments to allow for these indirect costs will bring wages down, just as they do in situations in which the employer incurs direct costs. Furthermore, given competitive conditions, this situation will attract more firms into the sort of production that yields automatic learning by-products, reducing the prices of their market products. It may be worth emphasizing that there is no implication that the worker is being exploited in this process. It is not true, as some people suggest, that when workers accept lower pay on jobs with higher learning content the employer "pockets the difference." In fact, that is not true even when the employer incurs no voluntary costs in providing the training.

Rosen stresses the implications of his way of looking at things for interoccupational mobility over the life cycle, as men move through a hierarchy of jobs with progressively less opportunity-cost learning and more earning, whether they move within the firm or to jobs in other firms. I wonder whether, in pointing this out, he in fact strengthens or weakens the arguments for a human-investment interpretation of the *sequential details* in career patterns. This brings into greater visibility the assumption that underlies much of the work discussed thus far—that choices are in fact open in a sequence of short intervals leading from one period to the next (one job to the next), rather than being made in longer commitments to entire courses of earning paths associated with choice of one occupation or another. Surely both of these things in fact happen.

Rosen (1972a) also takes note of how differences among individuals in various respects will affect differences in the choices they make between jobs with large and small learning components. Further, he points out that minimum wages put a ceiling on learning opportunities of workers, since workers cannot buy such opportunities from employers by taking pay below the legal minimum. This may especially affect the learning opportunities of young, relatively unqualified workers. Pursuit of thoughts such as these lead to comments on discrimination and the efficiency of wage-subsidy training programs.

A more formal and elaborate analysis is presented in Rosen (in press), which builds upon the 1972 article discussed above but gives special attention to questions of obsolescence and vintage. He constructed an optimal control model that incorporates the following assumptions about the learning and the cost functions. First, he took $z = \alpha f(I,h)$, where

z = Gross learning.

α = A generalized ability parameter (differing from person to person).

I = Job learning potentials.

h = Knowledge (which in turn affects learning capacity).

He assumed that jobs with greater learning content increase real learning, that the possession of additional knowledge does likewise, and that in both cases the increases are at diminishing rates.

$$f_I > 0 \qquad f_{II} < 0$$

$$f_h > 0 \qquad f_{hh} > 0$$

Rosen also specified some characteristics of the costs of learning. The marginal cost of learning is positive and increasing: $(F_1 > 0, F_{11} > 0)$. Greater knowledge decreases the cost of learning but at a diminishing rate $(F_2 < 0, F_{22} > 0)$. Greater knowledge can decrease marginal costs of learning, but to a limited extent $(F_{12} \leq 0)$. Total cost is a strictly convex function of learning and knowledge $(F_{11}F_{22} - F_{12}^2 > 0)$. With these stipulations, Rosen sets up an earnings generation function over the individual's working life, with optimal gross learning positive to some date $t < T$, and zero thereafter. The problem, subject to these constraints, is then to maximize:

$$\sum_{t=0}^{N} [R_t h_t - F(h_{t+1} - (1-\delta)h_t, h_t)] / (1+r)^t. \qquad (5.1)$$

Assuming that vintage changes in knowledge are negligible and can be ignored, Rosen used a nonlinear maximum-likelihood method of estimation within education groups to estimate the key parameters of the learning model from data on the 1/1000 sample from the 1960 census. Among other results, he estimated rates of return to postschool investments in learning as 23 percent for high school graduates and 8 percent for college graduates. The depreciation-obsolescence parameter in his model could not be identified because the sample was inadequate at the older ages. However, by assuming that the learning function can be approximated by a Cobb Douglass form ($z = \alpha I^{1-\beta} h^\beta$) and that equalizing wage differences are quadratic, he could identify a function relating β (the marginal production of knowledge) and δ (depreciation and obsolescence): $G(\delta, \beta) = 0$. Then G (δ, β) is a locus of pairs (δ, β) implying the same realized age-earnings pattern for the phase $t < T$. β can be interpreted as an index of the efficiency of embodied knowledge in creating new knowledge relative to other requisites for learning. Rosen's estimates suggested that values of β at every possible depreciation-obsolescence rate were larger for college than for high school graduates. He points out that the higher earnings of college graduates can reflect higher initial knowledge, greater all-round ability, higher learning capacity, and lower real rates of interest. As Rosen is fully aware, his model (like others) provides no basis for distinguishing between the effects of college education as a selection process and its effects on productive capabilities.

V. LABOR MARKETS AND INVESTMENTS IN HUMAN CAPITAL BY THE FIRM

The Concept of "Specific Training" and Some Implications

"Specific training" has been defined here as training (learning) designed to increase a man's productivity only in the firm in which it takes place, whether because of the nature of what is learned or because of institutional constraints on the mobility of workers. Most of the discussions of specific training have proceeded with an assumption (tacit or explicit) that the only impediments to mobility of workers to "better" job situations are costs of job search or migration. In this context, specific training inheres entirely in the nature of what is learned and its degree of specificity to the particular enterprise. It is recognized, of course, that there will be at least some small "specific" component in the skills of almost anyone who has been with a particular enterprise for more than a very short term and in other than a completely routine job that can be replicated elsewhere. Equally or more important, there will always be some "general" components in the learning that takes place, formally or informally, on the job. In reality, people have various mixes of general and specific skills attained before and since coming to their present employment. If we assume that there are no major institutionally supported constraints on interfirm mobility (whether by law or binding customs), we could define the rental value of the specific human capital embodied in an individual at date t simply as the difference between his marginal value product in the firm in which he is employed and the gross earnings that he could claim elsewhere. Thus:

$$R_{ist} = MP_{ijt} - Y^*_{izt} , \qquad (6.1)$$

where R_{ist} is the rental value of the specific human capital embodied in individual i at date t, MP_{ijt} is the marginal value product of services of i in the firm j in which he is employed at the date t, and Y^*_{izt} is the maximum earning potential of individual i at date t in other firms. However, there are costs to the individual of moving, even in the absence of institutional constraints. From the point of view of the firm, the relevant margin for maneuver with respect to wages while still retaining an employee exceeds R_{ist} by what it would cost the individual to move. Thus:

$$G_{ijt} = (M_{ijt} - Y^*_{izt}) + C_{ijz}$$
$$= R_{ist} + C_{ijz} \qquad\qquad (6.2)$$

Here G_{ijt} is the gap for maneuver by the firm in realizing returns on the specific training embodied in individual i, and C_{ijz} is what it would cost i in job search and other moving costs to leave firm j for a job elsewhere.

What employer j actually obtains in economic rent on the specific human capital embodied in individual i at date t is the difference between the marginal value product of services of individual i in firm j (M_{ijt}) and the wages he is paid there (W_{ijt}). Oi (1961, 1962) has called this the "periodic rent":

$$R_{ijt} = M_{ijt} - W_{ijt} . \qquad\qquad (6.3)$$

Dropping the i subscript to view these adjustments in a more general context, it becomes clear that R_{jt} is a policy variable; its value normally will fall somewhere between G_{jt} and zero. By keeping wages, W_{jt}, for the moment close to the limiting short-term value $(Y^*_{zt} - C_{jz})$, the worker's wage opportunity elsewhere minus his cost of moving, the firm's rental return, R_{jt}, could be pushed to its upper limit of G_{jt}. However, no firm would pursue this policy, since it would soon begin to lose workers. Even without any substantial specific training component in its employees, the firm would have hiring costs, just as the workers have moving costs. Moreover, employees with experience and training (formal or informal) in the firm will have gained skills that cannot be reproduced immediately by newly hired workers. The firm will want to pursue a policy that discourages quits and encourages attachment to the firm among those with large components of specific human capital. For such people, wages will be determined at some level above Y^*_{zt}, so that R_{jt} will be significantly below the short-run maximum gap, G_{jt}.

This has implications in the longer view for the sharing between individuals and the firm in the costs of specific training. Looking ahead, the firm will anticipate a "periodic rent" from employees with substantial amounts of specific human capital: the present value of that anticipated rental stream is a human capital asset of the firm. But there is a tension between maximization of that value per man for those staying with the firm and the retention of staff. Expressing this in more technical language, maximization of the present value of the firm's expected rental stream requires optimization of the wage policy, taking into account effects on the average duration of employment, which is one of the dimensions over which the expectation is taken. A wage policy that raises the periodic rent to the firm from any given amount of specific human capital embodied in its employees will have the effect at the same time of increasing the proportions of specifically trained persons who leave the enterprise for jobs elsewhere. A wage policy that lowers the periodic rent reduces the gross returns to the firm on the specific human capital embodied in its employees. The result is a sharing of the investment costs between employer and employee.

We are dealing here, as in all longer term decisions, with probability distributions of expectations. What distinguishes this from the decisions discussed on an "as if certain" basis in preceding sections is that the probability element has to be made explicit before we can go any further. The firm is betting both on expected future periodic rentals of those who will stay with the firm and on the quit rates to be anticipated, and these two variables are interdependent. The individual is betting on the likelihood of realizing returns to his share in the specific training costs if he continues employment in the enterprise. As in the case of general training, the worker pays by accepting wages during the training period that are less than his potential earnings at that date. This sharing of investments in specific on-the-job training implies an earning curve that rises less steeply with age, and to a lower peak, than would occur with the same time path of investment in the formation of general human capital. It is fully consistent, nevertheless, with an individual optimizing model that equates the present values of earning streams of the individual with primarily general training and the individual who receives proportionately more specific than general training. These two alternatives from the point of view of the individual are illustrated in Figure 3.

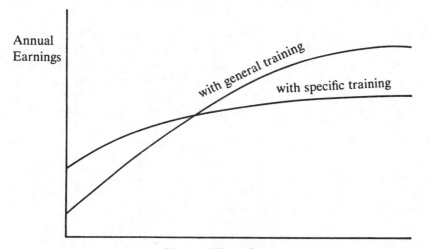

Figure 3. Typical earning curves for general and specific training.

Quits, Layoffs, and Specific Training

The relationships discussed above have important implications for the functioning of labor markets, especially with respect to short-term adjustment processes. The greater the specific human capital component in the marginal value products of workers, the greater is the firm's incentive to retain these workers and to avoid loss through temporary layoffs from which some may not return. From the worker's point of view, also, the greater the specific relative to the general training component in present and expected future earning potentials, the greater the inducement to stay with the enterprise. For one reason or the other, or both together, we should expect lower turnover of workers where the specific component in human capital is relatively high.

Many labor economists have studied the patterns of labor turnover and noted some of the seeming puzzles in them. I will refer only to a few that impinge clearly upon the question of specific investments in human capital. Miller (1968) observed that productivity often *dropped* when aggregate production declined, contrary to what economic theory had normally predicted; the weeding out of less efficient workers and the inverse effects of diminishing marginal returns to labor seemed not to be operative. He attributed this to what he termed the "reserve labor" phenomenon. Although his analysis is concerned primarily with hiring and related turnover costs, it is highly relevant to the specific human capital hypothesis—and also to some of the recent work in economics of information. In a seminal study, Oi (1961, 1962) attacked the specific training question and its short-term labor market implications more directly, as did Mincer (1962) and, most recently, Parsons (1970, 1972) and Telser (1972). Telser's focus is quite different, however. His interest is in identifying the accumulation of human capital as an asset of the firm and the biases in reported profit rates due to neglect of cumulated human capital investments in the firm's capital accounts. His work lacks the linkage with education and the concern for individual earning and learning paths that receives primary attention in much of the work on Becker-specific human capital and the functioning of labor markets.

One of the most critical problems in most of these studies has been the empirical identification of extent of specific training and of the claims of individuals and employers on returns to that training, which is related to, but by no means the same as, statistical predictions of turnover or of quit and layoff rates. Particularly awkward is the interpretation of the wage coefficients in these regressions. The assumption that higher wages go along with more *specific* on-the-job training is a strange one, in view of the sorts of earning paths that the theoretical model predicts when the comparison is between equal accumulations of human capital along a specific versus general route. There is clearly confusion here between comparisons that would relate specific capital to no postschool training at all and those that would separate the specific from the general in postschool investments. Parsons' treatment of specific human capital is tidier than the others if we interpret it as distinguishing between the share of investment in specific human capital that is made by the firm (and hence the share of returns that accrue to it), as compared to that made by the individual. But even the empirical evidence is confounded in several ways, including the inadequacy of simple controls for age. Awkward but challenging problems persist.

Equilibrium in Human Investment Decisions of the Firm and Worker

The roots of an analysis of shared investments in human capital formation and the relationships between these decisions and labor market behavior are in the decision making of firms and individuals. Recently two economists have developed optimal control models relating human investment decisions of the firm and the worker: Millar (1971) and Kuratani (1973). Millar's model combines an individual human capital accumulation model in the tradition of Ben-Porath, an optimizing model for the firm, and market equilibrium. However, it refers to training that is Becker-general, and though it is ingenious I shall not take space to discuss it here.

Kuratani's work is focused on decisions where there is a mix of Becker-general and Becker-specific human capital formation. He combines human capital theory and search theory in a symmetrical treatment of the worker and the firm in the human investment decision. His analysis incorporates (1) a production function of human capital, (2) the worker's quit function, and (3) the firm's layoff function. He assumes complementarity between learning and working in the production of human capital on the job; pure learning without practical experience is seen as inefficient. (On this point, see Bowman, 1965 and 1971.) The quit and layoff functions are specified in terms of probability distributions of expected options in the firm and elsewhere, together with costs of search. Workers face probability distributions of potential earnings elsewhere relative to those in the present firm. Firms face distributions of workers whose potential marginal products if hired would exceed their current wages elsewhere; they can choose to recruit trained workers from other firms or to train untrained workers. Both workers and firms search, but search is costly. When the firm faces fluctuations in product demand, the marginal products of its workers change. For simplicity, Kuratani assumes that the firm and the workers anticipate random fluctuations of marginal products in each decision period, and the wage level in the firm is assumed to be rigid. He shows formally that the value of the sharing ratio between workers and firm in returns to investments in training will affect the value of expected profits for the worker and the firm, not only in the directly obvious division of increased productivity but also indirectly through anticipated quit rates (in the perspective of the firm) and layoff rates (in the perspective of the worker).

Kuratani goes on to identify the optimal investment as a joint decision by a worker and a firm, analyzing "how they share the returns and costs and how they determine the scale of investments [1973, p. 13]." He shows how age and differences in access to investment funds will affect the results. In a modification of his model, Kuratani relaxes initial assumptions of homogeneity to allow sorting in the initial selection by firms of workers to be trained and by individuals among firms in which to accept employment. This treatment of sorting is based on concepts of interactive effects of characteristics of individuals and firms on their combined expected returns. In empirical application to Japan, he assumes that "ability" of firms is a function of size and that there is a positive cross-derivative between the ability of the individual and the firm—hence the steeper earning curves and greater investment in human capital in the big enterprises. Several questions are addressed in the empirical part of this study, but the main empirical focus is on job separation rates in Japan. The results of his analysis of these rates confirm Kuratani's key hypotheses, even as they raise further questions. This is the best specified theoretical and empirical analysis of investment in specific human capital that I have seen. It is of interest also in that it leads into analysis of relationships between investments in training on the job and the pace of economic growth, although on this subject it is no more than suggestive.

Optimal Control Theory and Knowledge as a Firm-Specific Capital Good

Rosen (1972b) has developed a model in which, "knowledge affects the technology of production and new knowledge is acquired through production experience. Knowledge is treated as a firm-specific capital good, entering the production function along with conventional outputs [p. 366]." This model is closely related to his other papers, but the firm is now the investor and the recipient of future income (profit) streams. By hypothesis, production knowledge must be gained through "experience" and cannot be hired from outside. Rosen distinguishes two possibilities in the content of these ownership rights: they may be completely vested in the owners (or managers) of the firm, or they may be vested in the "firm" as an entity. In the former case the operative life of the asset will be limited to the working life of owner or manager, and it will be an asset of the "firm" only as there is a tie-in contract. In the latter case the value of the acquired knowledge becomes an asset of the firm, transferable by selling of the firm. It is the market value of the firm's specific knowledge capital. Although by this definition Rosen can include specific capital embodied in employees attached to the firm, his emphasis is on entrepreneurial, organizational competence. Rosen's model resembles the various treatments of "learning by doing" in Alchian (1963), Arrow (1962), Fellner (1969), Sheshinski (1967) and Uzawa (1969) in that all are oriented primarily to entrepreneurship. However, among the important differences in these papers is the treatment of vesting. At one extreme, Arrow (who followed Alchian, but whose work has stimulated much of the subsequent treatment of "learning by doing" in growth theory) assumed that all such learning was openly available to all, and hence unmarketable. This implies discrepancy between social and private returns. In Rosen's model, by contrast, there are no spillover effects; all the additional knowledge is fully vested.

Rosen (1972b) specified knowledge production functions in two main variants. One of these makes learning a function of output; the other makes it a function of inputs. In both models:

Z_t = Accumulated knowledge related to production at the beginning of period t.

X_t = Output of the firm in period t, at price p.

L_t = A composite market input, at price w.

Output is a function of L and Z:

$$X_t = F(L_t, Z_t). \tag{7.1}$$

In both versions Rosen assumes that F is concave (diminishing returns to both factors) and that L and Z are complements, $F_{L,Z} > 0$. In the first, "joint product" version, Rosen specifies

$$\Delta Z_t = Z_{t+1} - Z_t = \beta X_t, \tag{7.2}$$

where β is a constant. This asserts that learning is proportional to current production. The other version is:

$$\Delta Z_t = \alpha L_t, \tag{7.3}$$

which makes learning independent of output but directly proportional to input. Rosen states more explicitly that Equation 7.3 "asserts that learning is proportional to 'experience' relating to the supervision and direction of inputs, rather than output."

Given these specifications, Rosen's analysis is a relatively straightforward application of optimal control theory to a problem with a specified time horizon. He goes on (essentially in the style of much modern dynamic growth theory) to specify the model for an infinite horizon, identifying conditions for existence of a steady-state solution. In conclusion, Rosen points first to the neglect of Z in studies of growth. He goes on to remarks about "infant industries" that are better taken up in the next section.

Joint Production, Learning, and the Dynamics of Growth

The dynamics of growth to be discussed in this section is not the aggregative dynamics of mathematical growth theory but the much more down-to-earth dynamics of adaptive behavior of firms with respect to formation of skills. Included, however, are some comments concerning debates over economic "dualism" and what I termed a decade ago "infant training industries" in the less developed countries (Bowman, 1965). Before coming to those debates, however, it will be worth while to take a brief look at a study for the United States that is more in the tradition of institutional economics than of human capital theory.

Piore's paper (1968) and a questionnaire and interview investigation for the U.S. Department of Labor on internal labor markets by Doeringer and Piore (1966) complement the more formal models of learning at work, although in method and conception they are very different. Doeringer and Piore were concerned mainly with the problem of balance or imbalance in labor markets in the United States, and the debates over structural interpretations of unemployment and how adjustments are made to labor scarcities—especially skills in growing demand because of technological innovations. Their question is how economic institutions operate to provide education and training for adults in the skills demanded by a dynamic economy.

Piore distinguishes between minor and major innovations. For ordinary situations in which there is only minor technical change, he stresses the significance of informal learning of a job; continuity of job activity is achieved through direct transmission, orally and by example. Piore (1968) argues that

the training process yields one explanation for the rigidity of internal wage structure and the use of seniority to govern promotion and lay-off. Without the protection which these provide, experienced workers would be reluctant to cooperate in training, for fear that the competition of newly trained workers would undermine income and job security [p. 439].

He attempted to identify a rationale for on-the-job training by the firm as against training in school, but he had no analytical framework for thinking the problem through systematically. (See Bowman, 1971.)

Major innovations, in contrast to minor ones, create discontinuities in the transfer of job skills, redistributing employment opportunities among existing jobs and creating new types of jobs. Piore reports that firms rely heavily on flexibility in adjustments of on-the-job training procedures, which are associated with patterns of adjustment to plant expansion, to exogenous increases in labor turnover, or to a tightening labor market. Firms engage in experimentation in the design and construction of equipment and in methods for installation, start-up, and debugging. These activities involve shifts of R & D people between the laboratory and the workshop and draw some of the operating people into the R & D activities. The latter then become teachers of others on the job. Also important in some cases is the provision by vendors of craftsmen to help with installation and instruction in the use of new equipment.

In sum, Doeringer and Piore's work stands at the opposite extreme from the abstract optimal control models. It is a good descriptive analysis of some of the options in adjustment to and furtherance of innovative change. Without such insights the theoretical models are nothing but games of chess. Because they lack tools of analytical theory (though not necessarily mathematical theory), studies such as this are less productive than they could be, however. What is most interesting, perhaps, is how easily, nevertheless, some of the theoretical constructs discussed earlier can be merged with findings such as Piore's, despite the tendency to assume that they are incompatible.

Concern with economic growth was one of the main stimulants to the incorporation of the human investment concept in many branches of recent economic research. However, there has been hardly a word about less developed nations in this chapter, aside from the opening pages, primarily for two reasons. First, empirical work thrives on data, and data for this sort of research have been meager in the less developed nations, whereas the United States has provided rich sources. Second, the more abstract theoretical formulations, and related empirical applications of optimal control theory, rest largely on simplified behavioral assumptions and assumptions about market situations that are reasonable approximations to the realities of most industrialized nations, but those assumptions are much further removed from the realities of most less developed nations. It is easier to apply the simplified theories (however mathematically complex) to understanding the former than the latter. These two facts are not entirely unrelated; there has been a tendency to join model building with empirical studies in the United States, each contributing to the other in a progressive sequence. Such possibilities are remote for the less developed nations.

I have made no attempt, therefore, to bring within the bounds of this chapter the scattered work on postschool learning and earning in less developed countries. A few points that impinge in particularly relevant ways upon work already discussed are nevertheless worth noting.

First, if we take the concept of specific capital in an analytical sense and apply it to earlier stages in economic development, it becomes apparent that this concept can have high explanatory value—not only for quits and layoffs but for the evolution of agencies of education and training. Anderson and I (Anderson & Bowman, 1968) have used the distinction between general and specific training in this way, as I did implicitly in an opportunity-cost analysis of the evolution of apprenticeship institutions in England and colonial United States (Bowman, 1965). Moreover, a priori, we should expect the specific components in postschool human resource formation in less developed nations to be relatively high, not because of more extensive learning on the job (such learning is probably less) but because of a much narrower market in which men who have acquired skills can sell their services. Where there is only one textile mill, spinners and weavers have "specific" training.

Illustrations could be multiplied ad infinitum, and they have important implications for the development process and the costs sustained in that process. Difficulties become more obvious when we look at the "raw group problem" (Bowman, 1965), by which I refer to the costs incurred in setting up a new operation where there is no ongoing activity into which new workers can find their way and be helped to learn. Piore's (1968) observations concerning the ordinary situation, or one with only minor technical change, illustrate this problem in reverse: the presence of experienced workers is critical in the informal training process. Rosen (1972b, in press) comes to the edge of the problem, and Millar (1971) has "modeled it" quite explicitly in some respects. But none has turned the situation around to point directly to the difficulties that may face a firm, or a nation, when experience is not at hand. Even Piore's discussion of adaptations to major innovations does not confront the problems faced in other countries that are far behind instead of out in front.

In discussing infant training industries, I (Bowman, 1965) examined modes of transfer of know-how and the acquisition of modern production skills in developing nations, as well as impediments to such transfers. My thesis was that the key to persisting dualism in the economies of less developed nations was to be found in the lack of the kinds of human capital that are accumulated through experience on the job. The dilemma posed by this problem is obvious, and it suggests that subsidy to infant training industries may be one strategy for furthering economic advance.

Rosen (1972b) broached a related question, but in the context of the industrialized nations, noting that "If learning by experience is an important source of productivity advance, there is a real sense in which all industries are 'infants' [p. 376]." But he then argued that

. . . subsidizing new firms in an industry on account of losses then would amount to reducing social rates of return on investment in industry below the social opportunity cost of capital, resulting in inefficiency. Therefore, if dynamic internal economies describe the infant industry case, it is not necessarily true that protection is required to establish a competitive position . . . qualifications stem from the possibility of capital market imperfections, which might work against the establishment of new firms in any event [p. 376].

This position is unassailable so long as the learning is entirely firm-specific, without societal spillovers. But what about the assumptions of perfect capital markets and full vesting in the firm? What sort of biases in these respects exist in fact, and can we dismiss the problem of an imperfect capital market, if it exists, as a general one, with no special relevance to learning and training at work? If the spillover effects are substantial—the extreme case would be Arrow's (1962) model—social efficiency would dictate subsidization of training for growth. If the imperfections in capital markets are biased, as they normally are, against outlays for on-the-job training in the private sector, then again the policy inference is altered. These are large questions, and their implications can be very different in application to a small, relatively backward nation from the conclusions we might draw with reference to the United States.

VI. CHALLENGE AND SPECULATION

Harris (1949) warned that the market for college graduates would not absorb the large and growing numbers coming through the higher institutions, and that we were in for social, economic, and political trouble if we didn't take heed of this. Over two decades later, some have begun to wonder if perhaps Harris was right, but just a bit off on his dates. Until recently, students, new Ph.D's, and professors were riding a long wave, and economists shared richly in this bonanza. We have now gone over the crest, and things look bleak by comparison. This experience has lent support to those who challenge the faith of the 1960s in what schooling contributes to economic productivity. However, this is not in itself a negation of the thrust of the analytical work that has been discussed in this chapter. It says only that the exogenous growth factor that affects both cross-sectional and cohort life earnings data is not constant over time, nor can we make intelligent decisions on the assumption that growth will be neutral in its effects on all. But this has been recognized by economic researchers all along. If this were all there is to today's challenge, everyone could agree and we could just get on with pursuit of human-capital theory and its applications. But this is not the whole story.

A much more serious challenge is carried by the assaults on credentialism and associated assertions that schooling acts mainly as a filter to sort people out, without doing much of anything to make them more productive. This debate impinges on the analysis of postschool learning for two reasons. First, as argued by some (but by no means all), it constitutes an attack not only on economic faith in schooling but on the foundation of neoclassical economics itself. There is nothing peculiarly related to the human investment theme in this challenge. Second, the charge with respect to schooling could be particularly serious, if it were valid, in those empirical applications that incorporate returns to schooling as part of the method by which they arrive at assessments of postschool learning. Two dogmatic statements may be justified at this point. As all economists who have been analyzing the problem will agree, schooling does in fact contribute to productive capability; the question is how much of what schools do has this effect, how much of what we observe in earnings differentials is attributable to the use of schools as selection agencies or filters through which people pass (that is, as information agencies). It is agreed, also, that even if the primary effect of schooling were merely as a selection device, it has social as well as private benefits; the trouble is that the former may be much less than the latter. What this is leading to (and this is undoubtedly important) is a reexamination of just how schools do function in the career development process, including both direct training and learning effects and selection into opportunities for greater or lesser training and learning at work.

The other prong of the credentialism attack is the job competition thesis. The argument in this case is that the wage competition assumed in most of the neoclassical discussions is a false picture of the way the labor market works; instead, wages are very rigid and people queue up for jobs, which fall to them in rank order. Thurow (1972) has been a main protagonist of this point of view. He puts it this way: "Thus the labor market is primarily a market, not for matching the demands for and supplies of different job skills, but for matching trainable individuals with training ladders. *Because most skills are acquired on the job, it is the demand for job skills which creates the supply of job skills* [italics his]." The affinity of this statement with Piore (1968) is evident, and indeed Thurow was influenced by Piore's work. Thurow develops the argument about the importance of seniority and other protections if workers are to be willing to pass their skills on to others. Postschool learning clearly is in vogue. Of education, Thurow says, " . . . although education can affect the shape of the labor queue, this does not necessarily mean that it can change the actual distribution of income [p. 74]." People are just rearranged by education in their ranking on the queue. How these rigidities can be sustained in the longer run is not made clear. Perhaps the lesson that is to be learned from these attacks is the rather obvious one, that facts are always somewhere in between the polemical extremes. The question is, of course, where?

What are the begging questions, the opportunities, and the likely directions of research and analysis relating to postschool learning and earning in the decade ahead? There will no doubt be more mathematical models of individual human capital accumulation, and more attempts to test them. I suspect, however, that the greater payoffs lie mainly in other directions, and methodologies will not always be so elegant. First steps have barely been taken toward economic analysis of proprietary schools and other agencies of adult education. In-house training in firms has been explored only to a limited degree and in piecemeal fashion. The economics of information has yet to be joined with other parts of the information and communication process in an analysis of career paths. Theoretical and empirical research into decision making under uncertainty and its implications for career choices and their sequencing has barely begun. The list is easily extended by any able young person with a glint in his eye.

REFERENCES

Alchian, A. A. Reliability of progress curves in airframe production. *Econometrica*, 1963, *31*, 679-693.

Anderson, C. A., & Bowman, M. J. Human capital and economic modernization in historical perspective. Paper presented at the meeting of the International Economic History Association, Bloomington, Ind., September 1968.

Arrow, K. J. The economic implications of learning by doing. *Review of Economic Studies*, 1962, *29*, 155-173.

Arrow, K. J. Higher education as a filter. Technical Report No. 71, September 1972, Institute for Mathematical Studies in the Social Sciences, Stanford University.

Barsby, S. L. *Cost-benefit analysis and manpower programs*. Lexington, Mass.: D. C. Heath, 1972.

Becker, G. S. Investment in human capital: A theoretical analysis. *Journal of Political Economy*, 1962, *70* (5, Part 2), S9-S49.

Becker, G. S. *Human capital*. New York: National Bureau of Economic Research, 1964.

Becker, G. S. A theory of the allocation of time. *Economic Journal*, 1965, *75*, 493-517.

Becker, G. S. *Human capital and the personal distribution of income: An analytical approach*. (Woytinsky Lecture No. 1) Ann Arbor: Institute of Public Administration and Department of Economics, University of Michigan, 1967.

Becker, G. S., & Chiswick, B. R. Education and the distribution of earnings. *American Economic Review*, 1966, *56*, 358-369.

Ben-Porath, Y. The production of human capital and the life cycle of earnings. *Journal of Political Economy*, 1967, *75*, 352-365.

Ben-Porath, Y. The production of human capital over time. In W. L. Hansen (Ed.), *Education, income and human capital*. Vol. 35. *Studies in income and wealth*. New York: National Bureau of Economic Research, 1970. Pp. 129-147.

Berg, I. *Education and jobs: The great training robbery*. New York: Frederick A. Praeger, 1970.

Bowman, M. J. From guilds to infant training industries. In C. A. Anderson & M. J. Bowman (Eds.), *Education and economic development*. Chicago: Aldine, 1965. Pp. 98-129.

Bowman, M. J. The costing of human resource development. In E. A. G. Robinson & J. E. Vaizey (Eds.), *The economics of education*. New York: St. Martin's Press, 1966. Pp. 421-450.

Bowman, M. J. The assessment of human investments as growth strategy. In *Federal programs for the development of human resources*. (Joint Economic Committee, 90th session) Washington, D.C.: U.S. Government Printing Office, 1968. Pp. 84-99.

Bowman, M. J. Education and economic growth. In R. L. Johns, I. J. Goffman, K. Alexander, & H. Stollar (Eds.), *Economic factors affecting the financing of education.* Gainesville, Florida: National Educational Finance Project, 1970. Pp. 83-120.

Bowman, M. J. Decisions for vocational education: An economist's view. In C. J. Schaefer & J. J. Kaufman (Eds.), *Vocational education: Social and behavioral perspectives.* Lexington, Mass.: D. C. Heath, 1971. Pp. 81-101.

Bowman, M. J. Dynamic disequilibria and the role of learning in economic growth. Paper presented at the meeting of the Southern Economic Association, Washington, D.C., November 1972.

Bowman, M. J. Postschool learning and human resource accounting. *Review of Income and Wealth*, in press.

Castro, C. de M. Educação, ensino técnico e perfis de idade-renda. In *Ensaios economicos.* (Essays in honor of Gouvea de Bulhoes.) Rio de Janeiro, Brazil: APEC Editôra S.A., 1972.

Chiswick, B. R., & Mincer, J. Time-series changes in personal income inequality in the United States from 1939, with projections to 1985. *Journal of Political Economy*, 1972, *80* (3, Part 2), S34-S66.

Doeringer, P. B., & Piore, M. J. *Internal labor markets, technological change and labor force adjustment.* Report submitted to the Office of Manpower Policy, Evaluation, and Research, U.S. Department of Labor, October 1966.

Dorfman, R. An economic interpretation of optimal control theory. *American Economic Review*, 1969, *59*, 817-831.

Fellner, W. Specific interpretations of learning by doing. *Journal of Economic Theory*, 1969, *1*, 199-240.

Hägerstrand, T. Quantitative techniques for analysis of the spread of information and technology. In C. A. Anderson & M. J. Bowman (Eds.), *Education and economic development.* Chicago: Aldine, 1965. Pp. 244-280.

Hägerstrand, T. *Innovation diffusion as a spatial process.* Chicago: University of Chicago Press, 1967.

Haley, W. J. Human capital accumulation over the life cycle. Unpublished doctoral dissertation, North Carolina State University, Raleigh, 1971.

Haley, W. J. Human capital: The choice between earning and investment. Unpublished paper, Michigan State University, 1972.

Harris, S. *The market for college graduates.* Cambridge, Mass.: Harvard University Press, 1949.

Hause, J. C. Earnings profile: Ability and schooling. *Journal of Political Economy*, 1972, *80* (3, Part 2), S108-S138.

Hebein, F. J. Investment in human capital: Growth of earnings and rate of return. Unpublished doctoral dissertation, Southern Methodist University, Dallas, 1972.

Johnson, T. Returns from investment in schooling and on-the-job training. Unpublished doctoral dissertation, North Carolina State University, Raleigh, 1969.

Johnson, T. Returns from investment in human capital. *American Economic Review*, 1970, *60*, 546-560.

Johnson, T., & Hebein, F. J. Investment in human capital and growth in personal income, 1956-66. Unpublished paper, Southern Methodist University, Dallas, 1972.

Knight, F. H. *Risk, uncertainty and profit.* New York: Hart, Schaffner & Marx, 1921.

Kuratani, M. Investment in human capital and economic growth: A theoretical study. Unpublished paper, University of Chicago, February 1973.

Lillard, L. A. An explicit solution to the human capital life cycle of earnings model and its application to earnings distributions. Unpublished doctoral dissertation, North Carolina State University, Raleigh, 1972. (a)

Lillard, L. A. The implications of the life cycle of earnings model for personal income distribution. Paper presented at the meeting of the Econometric Society, Toronto, Ont., Canada, December 1972. (b)

Lindsay, C. M. Measuring human capital returns. *Journal of Political Economy*, 1971, *79*, 1195-1215.

Millar, J. R. On-the-job training and wage determination. Unpublished doctoral dissertation, Carnegie-Mellon University, Pittsburgh, 1971.

Miller, R. L. The reserve labor hypothesis: A study in short-run decision making. Unpublished doctoral dissertation, University of Chicago, 1968.

Mincer, J. Investment in human capital and personal income distribution, *Journal of Political Economy*, 1958, *66*, 281-302.

Mincer, J. On the job training: Costs, returns and some implications. *Journal of Political Economy*, 1962, *70* (5, Part 2), S50-S80.

Mincer, J. The distribution of labor incomes: A survey with special reference to the human capital approach. *Journal of Economic Literature*, 1970, *8*, 1-26.

Mincer, J. *Schooling, experience and earnings.* New York: National Bureau of Economic Research, in press.

Oi, W. Y. Labor as a quasi-fixed factor of production. Unpublished doctoral dissertation, University of Chicago, 1961.

Oi, W. Y. Labor as a quasi-fixed factor. *Journal of Political Economy*, 1962, *70*, 538-555.

Parsons, D. O. Specific human capital: Layoffs and quits. Unpublished doctoral dissertation, University of Chicago, 1970.

Parsons, D. O. Specific human capital: An application to quit rates and lay-off rates. *Journal of Political Economy*, 1972, *80*, 1120-1143.

Petty, Sir W. *Verbum sapienti.* (c. 1665) Republished in C. H. Hull (Ed.), *The economic writings of Sir William Petty.* 2 Vols. Cambridge, England: Cambridge University Press, 1899.

Piore, M. J. On-the-job training and adjustment to technological change. *Journal of Human Resources*, 1968, *3*, 435-449.

Polachek, S. W. An analysis of male-female wage differentials in terms of differing post-school investment behavior. Unpublished doctoral dissertation, Columbia University, 1972. (a)

Polachek, S. W. A comparison of male and female post-school investment behavior and earnings using the 1967 longitudinal survey of work experience of women 30-40 years of age. Unpublished paper, University of Chicago, October 1972. (b)

Pontryagin, L. S., Bol'tyanskii, V. G., Gamkrelidze, R. W., & Mischenko, E. F. *The mathematical theory of optimal processes.* New York: Macmillan, 1964.

Rosen, S. Learning and experience in the labor market. *Journal of Human Resources*, 1972, *7*, 326-342. (a)

Rosen, S. Learning by experience as joint production. *Quarterly Journal of Economics*, 1972, *86*(3), 366-382. (b)

Rosen, S. Some externalities in program evaluation. In M. Borus (Ed.), *Evaluating the impact of manpower programs.* Lexington, Mass.: D. C. Heath, 1972. Pp. 215-229. (c)

Rosen, S. Measuring the obsolescence of knowledge. In T. Juster (Ed.), *Education, income and human behavior*. New York: National Bureau of Economic Research, in press.

Schultz, T. P. Long term change in personal income distribution: Theoretical approaches, evidence and explanations. Paper delivered at meetings of the American Economic Association, New Orleans, December 1971.

Schultz, T. W. Investment in man: An economist's view. *Social Service Review*, 1959, *33*, 109-117.

Schultz, T. W. Investment in human capital. *American Economic Review*, 1961, *51*, 1-17.

Schultz, T. W. Reflections on investment in man. *Journal of Political Economy*, 1962, *70* (5, Part 2), S1-S8.

Sheshinski, E. Tests of the learning by doing hypothesis. *Review of Economics and Statistics*, 1967, *49*, 568-578.

Spence, A. M. Market signalling. Unpublished doctoral dissertation, Harvard University, 1972.

Stigler, G. J. Information in the labor market. *Journal of Political Economy*, 1962, *70* (5, Part 2), S94-S105.

Stiglitz, J. Education as a screening device and the distribution of income. Unpublished paper, Yale University, 1972.

Taubman, P. Annual and lifetime earnings distributions: Information and tests of some theories. University of Pennsylvania, Philadelphia, 1972.

Telser, L. G. An analysis of turnover in selected manufacturing industries. In L. G. Telser (Ed.), *Competition, collusion and game theory*. Chicago: Aldine, 1972. Pp. 339-352.

Thurow, L. Education and economic equality. *The Public Interest*, 1972, *28*, 66-81.

Thurow, L., & Lucas, R. E. B. *The American distribution of income: A structural problem*. (Joint Economic Committee, 92nd Cong., 2d sess.) Washington, D.C.: Government Printing Office, 1972.

Tinbergen, J. On the theory of trend movements. In L. H. Klaassen, L. M. Koyck, & H. J. Witteveen (Eds.), *Jan Tinbergen: Selected papers*. Amsterdam, Netherlands: North Holland Publishing, 1959. Pp. 182-221.

Uzawa, H. Time preference and the Penrose effect in a two-class model of economic growth. *Journal of Political Economy*, 1969, *77* (4, Part 2), 628-652.

Welch, F. Black-white differences in returns to schooling. Unpublished paper, 1972.

Willis, R. *Fertility, consumption and education: An economic approach*. (Appendix to Bowman, M. J., *Educational outcomes, processes and decisions*.) Report to the Planning Officer for the National Institute of Education, December 1971.

[7]

Human Capital and Earnings: British Evidence and a Critique

GEORGE PSACHAROPOULOS and RICHARD LAYARD

London School of Economics

INTRODUCTION AND SUMMARY

What is the private rate of return to schooling and to on-the-job training? and how far does human capital explain the inequality of earnings? We try to answer these questions for Britain for a random sample of about 7,000 employed males. Basically, we use the framework of Mincer (1974), but at some important points we find this unsatisfactory, and offer our own critique.[1] In Mincer's regression approach log earnings are regressed on schooling, work experience and experience squared. (The effects of experience are held to reflect the influence of costly investment in on-the-job training.) But this method only yields valid estimates of the direct effects of schooling on earnings if there is no relationship between schooling and the amount of post-school investment and its profitability. A necessary (though not sufficient) condition for this to be true is that the profiles of log-earnings, as experience varies, are vertically parallel for all schooling groups. Casual inspection is not sufficient to verify whether this is so. So the obvious approach is to specify a model in which the pattern of post-school investment and its profitability are allowed to depend on schooling. Such a model also allows one to estimate the rate of return to on-the-job training.

When we estimate the model, we do indeed find a strong relation between schooling and post-school training. The rate of return to training grows with schooling and is much higher than the rate of return to schooling. As in the United States, the estimated direct rate of return to schooling is around 10 per cent. The fraction of the variance of log annual earnings of men under 65 that is explained by the simple regression model is about a third, as in the US—though there is much more inequality to be explained in the US.

However, this approach does not capture all the effect of human capital on earnings, since there are unmeasured differences between people in human capital investment. If there are periods of life when people vary less in the net effect of post-school investment than they do at other times, then we can learn something by confining our measure of the unexplained variation in earnings to its level in those periods of life. But when are those periods? According to Mincer they are likely to occur at the "overtaking year", when individuals are actually just earning as much as they could have earned when they left full-time education, had they taken the highest-paying job available (and consequently the job with the lowest learning opportunities). But according to our estimates this overtaking year comes quite quickly, rather than 7–9 years after leaving full-time education as Mincer argues. More importantly, there is no reason why those people on steep earnings profiles and those on flatter profiles should have their profiles cross in the same year that they are "overtaking". So we think it is quite reasonable that "cross-over" should occur 9–11 years after the end of education, as British evidence tends to suggest. Taking the unexplained variance in that year as the true measure of unexplained variance, we estimate that human capital (meaning schooling and on-the-job training) explains about a half the variance of earnings—again as in the US. However we think this is an overestimate, since it assumes that all the increased variance of log earnings in later life is due to human capital, that costless learning from work experience is impossible and that schooling is uncorrelated with ability, opportunity and other determinants of earnings. Despite Mincer's claim that human capital (as defined) explains " close to two-thirds " of annual earnings inequality (p. 96), we should be surprised if it really explained more than a third. This does not mean that human capital is unimportant, but only that the more complex models of human capital need to be applied (Becker, 1975, pp. 94ff).

After indicating the fallacy in Mincer's so-called " short-cut " approach to the rate of return to schooling, we estimate a model of weekly earnings and weeks worked. One extra year of schooling raises weekly earnings by about 8·5 per cent. If we assume (rather extremely) that all the unexplained variance in weeks is transitory, we can then obtain an estimate of the share of permanent income explained by human capital.

We end by examining special features of the British educational system—in particular the importance of part-time education, which is not measured by our years of full-time schooling variable. This leads to more detailed rates of return. Earnings are rather better explained by educational qualifications than by years of full-time education, but this is not evidence in favour of the screening hypothesis. Rather it reflects the importance of part-time qualifications.

1. THEORY

We can start with Mincer's model. A man with no schooling and no training is assumed to earn E_0 in each year of his life. If a man receives one year's education this raises these earnings by a fraction r, the rate of return to schooling. Let us use E_S to denote the level of the flat earnings profile of an untrained man with S years of schooling. So[2]

$$E_S = E_0 e^{rS}.$$

For each person, there is thus assumed to be some job in which he would not acquire any new marketable skill. He receives training if he takes a job where he produces less net output now than his current maximum, in order to raise his maximum in the next period. If the training is general, the trainee bears the cost in reduced earnings and reaps the returns in increased future potential earnings. Thus the potential earnings of the ith person with t years of work experience are given by

$$\ln E_{it} = \ln E_0 + rS_i + \sum_{j=0}^{t-1} q_i k_{ij}.$$

where q_i is the rate of return to training for this individual and k_{ij} is the fraction of his potential earnings which he has foregone in his jth year of experience. It follows that observed earnings are given by

$$\ln Y_{it} = \ln E_0 + rS_i + \sum_{j=0}^{t-1} (q_i k_{ij}) - k_{it}.$$

For simplicity we shall confine ourselves to the case where the investment ratio k_{it} falls linearly with years of experience (t_i) so that

$$k_{it} = k_{i0} - b_i \cdot t_i$$

where k_{i0} and b_i are parameters.[3] So, integrating and adding an error term,

$$\ln Y_{it} = \ln E_0 - k_{i0} + rS_i + (q_i k_{i0} + b_i + \tfrac{1}{2}q_i b_i)t_i - \tfrac{1}{2}q_i b_i t_i^2 + u_{1it}. \qquad \ldots(1)$$

This is Mincer's quadratic earnings function. Alternatively we can rewrite the function as if everyone had the same values of k_0, b, and q—in which case we are pushing the effects of any individual variation in these parameters into the error term u_{2it}

$$\ln Y_{it} = \ln E_0 - k_0 + rS_i + (qk_0 + b + \tfrac{1}{2}qb)t_i - \tfrac{1}{2}qb t_i^2 + u_{2it} \qquad \ldots(2)$$

It follows that var (u_2) exceeds var (u_1).

1.1. Can the returns to schooling be identified?

We are now ready to ask: Can the rate of return to schooling in this model be identified? Mincer offers three approaches. What we shall call Method 1 is a regression of the form of Equation 2. But is it true that in such a regression the coefficient on S_i is an unbiased estimator of the rate of return to schooling (r)? Clearly it must be if in (1) k_{0i}, b_i and q_i are independent of schooling (and experience). But there is no reason why they should be independent of schooling. If they were independent, then the profile of log earnings against experience would, of course, look the same for each schooling group except for a vertical shift. It is sometimes suggested that this independence can be inferred from the alleged fact that the profiles of log earnings against experience, when drawn for different schooling groups, are roughly parallel. But casual inspection is not really enough. The obvious procedure is to set up the model explicitly in a way that does not assume independence. In this context the simplest assumption is that, for all individuals in the S_ith schooling group,[4]

$$q_i = q_1 + q_2 S_i$$
$$k_{0i} = k_1 + k_2 S_i$$
$$b_i = b_1 + b_2 S_i.$$

Substituting in, we get an expression which looks unwieldy, but, when estimated for Britain, yields extremely sensible results:

$$\ln Y_{it} = \ln E_0 - k_1 + (r - k_2)S_i + (k_1 q_1 + b_1 + \tfrac{1}{2}q_1 b_1)t_i - \tfrac{1}{2}q_1 b_1 t_1^2$$
$$+ (k_1 q_2 + q_1 k_2 + b_2 + \tfrac{1}{2}q_1 b_2 + \tfrac{1}{2}q_2 b_1)S_i t_i + (k_2 q_2 + \tfrac{1}{2}b_2 q_2)S_i^2 t_i - \tfrac{1}{2}(q_1 b_2 + q_2 b_1)S_i t_i^2$$
$$- \tfrac{1}{2}q_2 b_2 S_i^2 t_i^2 + u_{3it}. \quad \ldots(3)$$

This is our basic estimating equation and its results do not support the hypothesis that k_0, q or b are independent of schooling. Nor do they support the notion that the rate of return to training is the same as that to schooling—a point to which we return later.

We turn next to Mincer's Method 2. This is designed to cut through the difficulties connected with the shape of age-earnings profiles, by using data only for one year of experience. It tries to get at E_S directly by only looking at earnings in that year $\jmath_S$ when actual current earnings $(Y_{S\jmath_S})$ equal potential earnings with no training (E_S). Thus, if we knew the "overtaking" year $\jmath$ for each schooling group, we could readily compute the rate of return to any particular level of schooling S by simply taking $\ln Y_{S\jmath_S} - \ln Y_{S-1, \jmath_{s-1}}$. However, unless we know the rate of return to training we cannot compute the overtaking year for each group.

We might of course assume the overtaking years were the same $(\jmath)$ for each individual. In this case, from (1),

$$-k_{i0} + (q_i k_{i0} + b_i + \tfrac{1}{2}q_i b_i)\jmath - \tfrac{1}{2}q_i b_i \jmath^2 = 0 \quad \text{(all } i)$$

So we have

$$\ln Y_{i\jmath} = \ln E_0 + rS_i + u_{1i\jmath} \qquad \ldots(1')$$

This would enable us to identify r by multiple regression, using only data for the year $\jmath$.

But the assumption of uniform $\jmath$ is very stringent. Suppose it were not true. In the early years of life, earnings grow rapidly with experience—often by up to 10 per cent per annum. Suppose those with S years of schooling "overtake" one-half year later than those with $S-1$ years of schooling. The rate of return to schooling will be underestimated by up to 5 percentage points, and vice versa. How likely is it that $\jmath$ will be identical for all schooling groups? If all groups have parallel profiles, and q is the same for each group, then $\jmath$ must be the same for each group.[5] But there is no reason why these assumptions should hold.

However, suppose $\jmath$ is the same for all groups. How can it be identified? If one knew the rate of return to training there would of course be no problem, but we do not, using this method, have any method of computing it. Instead Mincer offers an approach which involves an essentially independent idea, which we shall call the "cross-over"

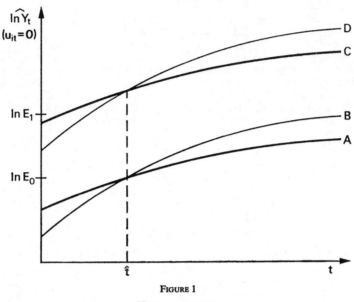

FIGURE 1

The cross-over year.

year. As Equation (1) indicates, two individuals A and B in any particular schooling group (say with no schooling) may have different earnings streams. But ignoring non-pecuniary factors, information problems and capital market imperfections, the present value of the two expected streams must be the same. So the two streams must cross over. We shall call the cross-over year $\hat{t}$ (see Figure 1). There is no logical reason why crossing over should occur at the overtaking year. So in Figure 1 we have assumed that cross-over in fact occurs before the overtaking year of either A or B. Now suppose that the profiles of C and D, each with one year of education, cross over at the same number of years of experience as the profiles of A and B. We now estimate for year of experience ($\hat{t}$)

$$\ln Y_{it} = a_0 + a_1 S_i + u_{1it} \qquad \qquad ...(1'')$$

Is a_1 an unbiased estimator of r? Not necessarily, for as we have drawn it, the overtaking year for C and D comes before $\hat{t}$ and that for A and B after $\hat{t}$. So

$$\ln \hat{Y}_{Ct} - \ln \hat{Y}_{At} > \ln \hat{E}_1 - \ln \hat{E}_0.$$

However, if the average profiles of both groups are parallel and q is the same for both groups, then for *any* experience group the difference in log earnings is a good measure of the rate of return to schooling. $\hat{t}$ is a good age at which to run regressions because at that level of experience the residual variance due to differences in individual profiles is much less. This also makes the cross-over year regressions especially relevant to the question of the explanatory power of human capital, to which we shall shortly return.

However first we must refer to Mincer's Method 3. This " short-cut method "[6] involves using the conventionally-calculated rate of return to compute estimates of E_S for each level of schooling (S). The rate of return to the Sth year of schooling is then $(\hat{E}_S/\hat{E}_{S-1}) - 1$, where $\hat{E}_S$ is the estimate of E_S. The method is only correct if the rate of return to training equals the rate of return to schooling. Mincer claims that the method can be used to check that this is so. However, as Note 2 demonstrates, this claim is incorrect and the method, which is now being used in many countries, ought to be discarded.[7]

1.2. *How much does human capital explain?*

Instead we can concentrate on Methods 1 and 2 and ask: How much of the variance in log earnings is due to human capital?[8] The most obvious approach is to examine the residual variance in Equation (2)—or better still (3). Concentrating for the moment on (2), if var (ln Y) is the variance of log earnings for the whole population (including people with all years of experience), the fraction of it explained by human capital is

$$1 - \frac{\text{var}(u_2)}{\text{var}(\ln Y)}$$

Using this approach Mincer explains 0·31 of earnings inequality. However a glance at Figure 1 shows that there is far less inequality at $\hat{t}$ years of experience than there is before or after this. This is because the difference in earnings due to differences in k_0, b and q are not present at that stage of working life. So the only unexplained variance is that due to the variation of u_1, whereas if the whole working population is analysed the unexplained variance will also include that part of u_2 due to the assumption that all individuals with a given schooling have the same k_0, b and q. So Mincer argues that a better measure of the overall unexplained variance is the unexplained variance in the cross-over year. Indeed if all cross-overs were at exactly the same year, and this were the overtake year, the unexplained variance in that year would correspond exactly to var (u_1) in Equation (1), which is the true measure of variance not explained by human capital. So, if we now ran Equation (1″) and computed var (u_{1t}), the fraction of overall variance among people with all years of experience that is explained by human capital would be

$$1 - \frac{\text{var}(u_{1t})}{\text{var}(\ln Y)}$$

To find the cross-over year, Mincer runs equation (1″) for different years of experience and picks that year ($\hat{t}$) when the R^2 is highest. R^2 rises (though rather slightly) up to 7–9 years of experience, and then falls (his Table 3.4). It also turns out that overtaking, as he calculates it, occurs within this range of years.[9] On the assumption that the model is correct, human capital now explains 0·50 of earnings inequality in the US.[10]

But apart from doubts about the assumptions, there are some major arguments against accepting so high a figure.

(i) It involves attributing the growth in residual variance in later life entirely to unrecorded differences in earlier human capital investments. But this growth must in part reflect the growing ability of employers to discriminate between more and less productive workers and hence to pay them a more individually-tailored wage.

(ii) Human capital is earning power acquired at a cost. It is true that every time earning power increases with work experience, this is because a cost has been incurred? Is costless learning impossible? For this to be the case there must always exist a job at which no learning occurs and at which we could currently produce more (net) than in any job where we can learn anything. There need not actually be anybody doing this job, though in a perfect market it would be surprising if someone were not doing it, since the present values of all jobs are equalized. We have spent some years trying to think what this job is for us, since it would be much easier to persuade students to accept the theory if one could illustrate it. But we have found it impossible to think of any such job for us or for most professional people one can imagine. It seems that costless learning may be possible. But of course the crucial question is how fast earnings rise with experience in the job where the least learning occurs. For any *additional* growth of earnings with experience could then be attributed to human capital. Perhaps most of the growth of earnings with experience is due to human capital, but not, we think, all of it.

(iii) A person's productivity is affected by dimensions of ability, acquired without cost. Most studies have been relatively unsuccessful at isolating the effects of this, but this does not mean it is not there. Since this is correlated with schooling, we continue to believe that the coefficients on schooling are biased upwards.

We therefore conclude that a half is an over-estimate of the fraction of annual earnings variance due to human capital.

1.3. *Treatment of weeks worked*

This completes what in our view can be sensibly said about the variation of annual earnings. Those of Mincer's findings that we have reported so far are recorded in the first row of Table I. But these all ignore the variation of weeks worked. These are of interest from two points of view. In the first place a good part of the variance of annual earnings is associated with variation in weeks worked, and a part of the variation of weeks worked is transitory. For this reason the variance of " permanent " annual earnings is less than the variance of annual earnings in any one year. The following model seems to capture the essence of the system. If R_{it} is weekly earnings and Z_{it} is the vector (S_i, t_i, t_i^2) and W_{it} is weeks worked,

$$\ln R_{it} = b_0 + b_1 Z_{it} + u_{4it} \qquad \qquad ...(4)$$

$$\ln W_{it} = c_0 + c_1 Z_{it} + c_2 \ln R_{it} + u_{5it} \qquad \qquad ...(5)$$

$$\ln Y_{it} \equiv \ln W_{it} + \ln R_{it}. \qquad \qquad ...(6)$$

Equation (2) is the reduced form of this system.[11] Clearly Equation (5) is also a reduced form of some other system. There are many demand and supply influences that could make weeks vary positively with weekly earnings. On the demand side, employers vary their demand for skilled manpower less than for unskilled when product demand varies— hence higher unemployment of the unskilled. On the supply side, workers may concentrate their lifetime labour supply towards periods when their earnings are high (Ghez and Becker, 1975).

If we now want a measure of permanent earnings (Y_p) we might assume that u_{5it} measures the transitory component of log annual income.[12] Thus

$$\ln Y_{ip} = \ln Y - u_{5it}.$$

TABLE I

Proportion of variance of log annual earnings explained by schooling and experience
(earnings of full-time male employees who worked at least 1 week)

	USA 1959	Britain 1972
Using residual variance from regressions for:		
All years of experience	0·31	0·32
Cross-over year	0·50	0·48

Sources:

For USA (all from Mincer (1974))   For UK
  0·31: Table 5·1 eq. P(2);   0·32: Table 3;
  0·50: Table 3.3 Top Row, var ln Y = 0·668.   0·48: 0·206/0·436 (see Table 6).

So the fraction of the variance of permanent income explained by the model is

$$\frac{\text{var}(\ln \hat{Y})}{\text{var}(\ln Y) - \text{var}(u_s)}. \qquad \qquad ...(7)$$

The preceding model is also interesting from a second point of view: it shows the role of human capital in explaining weekly earnings. Of course, once variation in weeks is taken into account, the ordinary human capital model ought in principle to be expanded, assuming that weeks worked in the past affect present earnings potential. This applies equally to the explanation of annual and weekly earnings. But in any case weekly earnings is a more accurate measure than annual earnings of current productivity and thus it is of interest.

2. BRITISH EVIDENCE

The study is based on the General Household Survey, using data for 1972 (see OPCAS, 1973 and 1975).[13] The survey covers over 10,000 different households, interviews being spread evenly over the year. Our analysis is for 6,873 men aged 15–64 who in their main occupation were " employees " and had worked at least 1 week in the 52 weeks before the interview, people with Scottish educational qualifications being excluded.

We use the following variables:

Y Annual real earnings[14] in the previous year
S Years of full-time education[15]
t Years of work experience (= Age − Years of full-time education − 5)
W Weeks worked in the previous year.

Table IIA shows the relevant variances and Table IIB the correlation coefficients. As Table IIA shows, the inequality of schooling is much less in Britain than in the USA. Figure 2 shows the mean annual earnings for some key levels of education, measured for groups with different numbers of years of experience (1–10 years, 11–20 years, and so on).

TABLE IIA

Variances of key variables in Britain (and the USA)

Variable	Definition	Britain	(USA)
ln Y	Annual earnings	0·436	(0·668)
S	Year of schooling	4·805	(12·250)
t	Years of experience	207	
ln W	Weeks	0·128	(0·106)
ln Y/W	Weekly earnings	0·235	

Source: USA—Mincer (1974, pp. 60, 96).

TABLE IIB

Correlation coefficients, Britain

	ln Y	S	t	ln W	ln (Y/W)
ln Y	1·000	0·176	0·216	0·697	0·849
S	0·176	1·000	−0·404	0·001	0·239
t	0·216	−0·404	1·000	0·140	0·191
ln W	0·697	0·001	0·140	1·000	0·212
ln (Y/W)	0·849	0·239	0·191	0·212	1·000

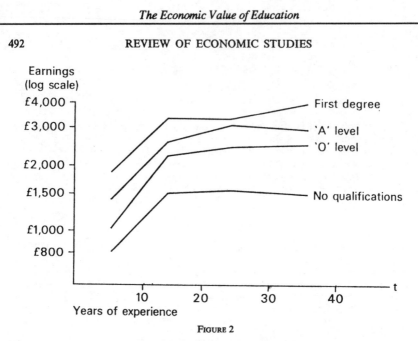

FIGURE 2

Experience profiles of annual earnings.

Notes: " A " level is normally taken at the end of secondary schooling (after 13 years of schooling).
        " O " level is normally taken 2 years earlier.

2.1. *Annual earnings: the basic analysis*

Moving to the regression analysis, we begin with annual earnings (see Table III). We can start with simpler functions, before looking at our general form. In Regression (3.1), log earnings are simply regressed on schooling. The coefficient on schooling is quite low and the explanatory power negligible. In Regression (3.2), however, experience (and its square) is added. The coefficient on education nearly doubles—in Regression (3.1) it was held down due to the negative correlation of schooling and experience. The private rate of return to an additional year's schooling is now estimated at about 10 per cent. The explanatory power of schooling and experience taken together is 32 per cent (31 per cent for the comparable analysis for the US). According to this regression, maximum earnings are reached after about 30 years' experience and are equal to about four times initial earnings.

Before proceeding further, we need to allow for the possibility that the marginal rate of return may differ according to the level of schooling. This is done in Regression (3.3) by introducing separate dummies for each number of years of education. As regards explanatory power there is little increase over the previous equation. But we can now see more clearly the pattern of incremental returns from one year to the next. The return is very high for the first few years and then fluctuates sharply. However in the British educational system there is a sharp distinction between those who leave at the minimum school leaving age and those who go on: until recently the only children who had more than 10 years of schooling were drawn from those who at 11 were judged to be above the top quartile of ability. For this reason one should not focus too sharply on the distinction between the earlier rates of return and the later ones, as we think the earlier ones are more biased upwards by ability factors.[16]

In Regression (3.4) we allow the level of schooling to influence the slope of the log earnings profile (but not its rate of change). As in the US schooling appears to reduce the

PSACHAROPOULOS & LAYARD   HUMAN CAPITAL   493

TABLE III

Regression of log annual earnings on schooling (S) and experience (t)

	(3·1)	(3·2)	(3·3)	(3·4)	(3·5)	(3·6)	(3·7)
Constant term	6·604	5·199	5·917	5·790	5·824	6·010	5·143
S	0·053	0·097					0·094
	(0·004)	(0·003)					(0·008)
t		0·091	0·093	0·113	0·065	−0·212	−0·166
		(0·002)	(0·002)	(0·004)	(0·009)	(0·030)	(0·019)
t^2		−0·0015	−0·0015	−0·0016	−0·00041	0·0053	0·0047
		(0·00004)	(0·00004)	(0·00004)	(0·00020)	(0·0007)	(0·0005)
St				−0·0018	0·0033	0·0476	0·041
				(0·0003)	(0·0008)	(0·0047)	(0·003)
St^2					−0·00012	−0·0011	−0·00098
					(0·00002)	(0·0001)	(0·00009)
S^2t						−0·0017	−0·0014
						(0·0002)	(0·0001)
S^2t^2						0·00004	0·000033
						(0·000004)	(0·000004)
S = 10			0·225	0·303	0·277	0·100	
11			0·333	0·438	0·391	0·144	
12			0·539	0·666	0·590	0·289	
13			0·501	0·647	0·541	0·215	
14			0·642	0·808	0·684	0·363	
15			0·726	0·909	0·752	0·446	
16			0·770	0·987	0·801	0·527	
17			0·878	1·09	0·873	0·676	
18+			1·003	1·29	0·980	1·144	
R^2	0·031	0·316	0·324	0·327	0·331	0·339	0·337
vâr (u)	0·422	0·298	0·295	0·294	0·293	0·288	0·289

Notes: 1. Standard errors are in brackets.
  2. The omitted schooling dummy is 9 years or less. All the schooling dummies have highly significant coefficients. The standard errors rise from 0·03 for $S = 10$ to 0·09 for $S = 18+$.

slope but the effect is one-third of its value in the US (0·0018 compared with 0·0043).[17] In Regression (3.5) we also allow the rate of change of the slope to be affected by schooling.

But neither of these specifications is consistent with our basic model, which is estimated in Regression (3.6). Here the coefficients on all the various interaction terms are highly significant. From them we can compute the values of the underlying parameters in the functions determining k_0, b and q.[18] These are

$$q = -0·313 + 0·0491 \, S$$
$$k_0 = 0·767 - 0·0330 \, S$$
$$b = 0·0337 - 0·00145 \, S$$

The most interesting result of course concerns the rate of return to training. For someone with 10 years of education this is 18 per cent and for someone with 16 years' education nearly 50 per cent. This is much higher than the rate of return to schooling. The rest of the results make good sense. The investment ratio in the first year of work is 44 per cent for people with 10 year's education and rather less for more educated people (in Britain apprenticed manual workers receive very low relative pay). The investment ratio falls each year for someone with 10 years of education by 1·9 per cent and more slowly for more educated people. The peak of earnings is reached after 29 years for people with 10 years education and rather earlier for the more educated groups. But the overall rise from starting salary to peak earnings is slightly higher for the more educated. The ratio of peak to starting salary is about 4·2 for those who left school after 10 years and 4·9 for those who had 16 years education. Since the overtaking year is approximately $1/q$, overtaking occurs a good deal earlier than the 7–9 years normally assumed; the shorter period is more consistent with what many of us suppose about ourselves.[19]

2.2. *Weekly earnings and weeks*

We can now repeat the basic analysis for weekly earnings (see Table IV). If we use the simple model of Regression (4.2) the rate of return to schooling compared with that in Regression (3.2) is now reduced by just over 1 percentage point, to 8·5 per cent. This is to be expected, for people with higher weekly earnings work for more weeks.[20] If variations in weeks reflect private choice, then 8·5 per cent would be the relevant private rate of return, but if not the more relevant figure comes from the annual earnings function.[21]

Regression (4.6) shows our basic model but applying it to weekly earnings. The results are quite similar to those for annual earnings. The implicit equations for q, k_0 and b are

$$q = -0.217 + 0.0389\,S$$

$$k_0 = 0.592 - 0.0247\,S$$

$$b = 0.0266 - 0.00113\,S$$

Again the rate of return to training is much higher than the rate of return to schooling. The profiles for weekly earnings are less steep than for annual earnings, since over much of the range weeks rise with experience. So the ratio of peak to initial earnings is 3 for people with 10 years schooling and 3·4 for people with 16 years schooling.

As regards explanatory power, human capital is slightly better at explaining weekly than annual earnings. There is no logical necessity for this. It depends on the size of the

TABLE IV

Regression of log weekly earnings on schooling (S) and experience (t)

	(4·1)	(4·2)	(4·3)	(4·4)	(4·5)	(4·6)	(4·7)
Constant term	2·751	1·692	2·337	2·251	2·271	2·373	1·627
S	0·053	0·085					0·086
	(0·003)	(0·002)					(0·005)
t		0·070	0·072	0·085	0·058	−0·105	−0·115
		(0·001)	(0·001)	(0·003)	(0·006)	(0·021)	(0·014)
t^2		−0·0012	−0·0012	−0·0012	−0·0006	0·0029	0·0034
		(0·00002)	(0·00003)	(0·00002)	(0·0001)	(0·0005)	(0·0004)
St				−0·0010	0·0018	0·0279	0·030
				(0·0002)	(0·0006)	(0·0033)	(0·002)
St^2					−0·00007	−0·0006	−0·00073
					(0·00001)	(0·00008)	(0·00006)
S^2t						−0·0010	−0·0011
						(0·0001)	(0·0001)
S^2t^2						0·00002	0·000026
						(0·000003)	(0·000003)
$S = 10$			0·183	0·234	0·220	0·121	
11			0·279	0·348	0·322	0·184	
12			0·456	0·541	0·497	0·329	
13			0·460	0·558	0·496	0·319	
14			0·567	0·678	0·607	0·427	
15			0·679	0·800	0·710	0·540	
16			0·695	0·839	0·732	0·580	
17			0·726	0·869	0·743	0·637	
18+			0·873	1·066	0·886	0·989	
R^2	0·057	0·366	0·377	0·379	0·382	0·387	0·385
vâr (u)	0·222	0·149	0·147	0·146	0·146	0·144	0·145

Notes: See notes to Table III.

TABLE V

Regression of log weeks worked on schooling (S), experience (t) and log weekly earnings (Y/W)

	(5·1)	(5·2)	(5·3)
Constant	3·331	3·272	4·107
S	−0·00081	0·048	−0·112
	(0·00222)	(0·015)	(0·041)
S^2		−0·0014	0·0042
		(0·0006)	(0·0015)
t	0·0025	0·0211	−0·095
	(0·0003)	(0·0012)	(0·023)
t^2		−0·00034	0·0019
		(0·00002)	(0·0005)
St			0·017
			(0·004)
St^2			−0·00032
			(0·00008)
S^2t			−0·00059
			(0·00014)
S^2t^2			0·000011
			(0·000000)
$\ln(Y/W)$	0·143		0·085
	(0·009)		(0·011)
R^2	0·055	0·056	0·071
vâr (u)	0·121	0·121	0·119

coefficients in Equations (4) and (5) and on the relative size of the variances of u_4 and u_5. Equation (5) is estimated in Table V. As can be seen the power of human capital to explain weeks is not large, which helps to explain the limited power of human capital to explain annual earnings, given the fact that the variance of log weeks is over a quarter the total variance of log annual earnings.

We can now use Table V to provide an estimate of the fraction of the variance of permanent income explained by human capital. If we assume that var (u_5) reflects only transitory income variation (which must be an exaggeration) we find that the share of permanent income explained by human capital is 0·46.[22]

2.3. *The cross-over year of experience*
We turn now to Mincer's method 2, based on the cross-over year. As Mincer explains, regressions using all years of experience will tend to understate the explanatory power of human capital because they wrongly assume that all individuals have the same investment profile. According to the cross-over theory, if we estimate

$$\ln Y_i = a + a_1 S_i + u_{1i} \qquad \qquad ...(1'')$$

within groups which differ by years of experience, we should find that var (u_1) falls as we approach the cross-over year from either side. As Table VI shows, var (u_1) does indeed fall monotonically with experience up to 12–17 years of experience and then fluctuates about a somewhat higher level.[23] By the same token var $(\ln Y)$ falls up to those years of experience and then fluctuates around a somewhat higher level. One would expect that R^2 would follow the same pattern—indeed Mincer only presents the data on R^2 and var $(\ln Y)$. But in fact R^2 fluctuates completely erratically and never reaches the high level of 0·33 which Mincer finds for 7–9 years of experience (his Table 3.4). This is partly because var (S) varies unsystematically, while a_1 also varies substantially. If we had concentrated on Mincer's R^2 approach, we should have been led to completely reject the cross-over hypothesis for Britain. However the movements of var (u_1) do lend some support to it, and we shall therefore pursue its implications. One cannot, as we have

TABLE VI

Regression of annual earnings on schooling: within experience groups

t	a_1	R^2	var (u_1)	var S	var $(\ln Y)$	N
0– 2	0·166	0·161	0·946	6·60	1·127	448
3– 5	0·114	0·236	0·273	6·50	0·357	455
6– 8	0·064	0·068	0·263	4·67	0·282	475
9–11	0·068	0·105	0·206	5·24	0·230	518
12–14	0·078	0·151	0·138	4·04	0·162	476
15–17	0·079	0·182	0·135	4·75	0·165	444
18–20	0·069	0·092	0·224	4·80	0·247	428
21–23	0·084	0·158	0·194	5·20	0·230	396
24–26	0·103	0·254	0·206	6·50	0·276	306
27–29	0·104	0·150	0·191	3·20	0·225	366
30–32	0·108	0·103	0·274	2·72	0·306	421
33–35	0·093	0·137	0·185	3·39	0·214	442
36–38	0·093	0·110	0·182	2·62	0·204	445
39–41	0·117	0·120	0·278	2·79	0·316	331

Note: The data relate to the equation $\ln Y = a_0 + a_1 S + u_1$

argued earlier, have confidence that it yields unbiased estimates of the rate of return to schooling. But it may still give us a reasonable feel for the variance in log earnings that cannot be explained by human capital. A crucial issue here is where we take the cross-over year to occur. Var (u) is at its lowest from 12–17 years after beginning work, but this seems implausibly late for crossing-over. (It is clearly too late for the overtake year, but as we have explained, there is no logical connection between " overtaking " and " crossing-over ".) So we shall take the variance unexplained by human capital to equal var (u) at 9–11 years of experience. Thus we would compute that human capital explains just under a half the variance of annual income. But, for the general reasons we have already given, we believe this is an overestimate.

2.4. *The rate of return to educational qualifications*

Finally to learn more about the effects of schooling we turn to an altogether different line of thought. The British education system is in many ways more varied than the American. In particular, part-time education is much more highly developed,[24] and many of those who reach degree-level qualifications as engineers, accountants or the like have had only 10 years of full-time schooling. An analysis based entirely on years of full-time schooling therefore fails to capture a good part of reality. In Table VII we show the main quali-fications in what is generally considered to be ascending order.[25] Individuals are classified according to their single highest qualification (be it part-time or full-time). There are two columns according to whether the qualification is mainly obtained by full-time or part-time study. As can be seen, *within* each column the average years of full-time schooling rise with level but there are many part-time qualifications with lower years of schooling than a full-time qualification to which they are superior (e.g. Higher National Certificate compared with " A-level " of the General Certificate of Education).

The interesting questions are: How much of earnings inequality does this battery of qualifications explain, and does the pecking order of qualifications correspond to an order of earnings? Table VIII shows regressions comparable to Regressions (3.2) and (4.2) but with years of education replaced by qualifications. The comparable R^2s are as follows

	Annual earnings	Weekly earnings
Years of schooling (dummies)	0·339	0·387
Qualifications	0·365	0·420

TABLE VII

Average years of schooling by highest educational qualification

Full-time qualification	Part-time qualification	S		N	
		FT	PT	FT	PT
None	None	9·7		4872	
1–4 " O " levels		11·3		317	
	C and G craft/ordinary		10·5		359
5+ " O " levels		11·9		283	
	C and G advanced/final		10·8		134
	Ordinary Nat. Cert./Dip.		11·3		117
1+ " A " levels		13·4		132	
	C and G tech. and prof. Level C		12·5		142
	Higher Nat. Cert./Dip.		12·5		139
	Prof. Level B		14·0		140
Non-graduate teaching cert.		15·8		66	
First degree		17·7		145	
Higher degree		18·7		27	

Notes: " O " level is the Ordinary Level of the General Certificate of Education and " A " level is the
   Advanced Level.
   C and G qualifications are issued by the City and Guilds of London Institute and are mainly in
   technical subjects or skills, as are the Ordinary and Higher National Certificates.
   Professional qualifications shown separately are mainly in engineering or commercial fields, level B
   being treated as of degree-equivalent status for purposes of schoolteachers' pay.

The difference of about 3 per cent may not appear large in relation to the original figure
(of over 30 per cent). But it is more relevant to relate it to a figure such as $0·097^2$.
Var $(S)(= 4·5$ per cent), which measures the contribution of schooling, holding experience
constant, in Equation (3.2). Even so, it is small in relation to the overall R^2, which is why
our earlier discussion of the *share* of earnings inequality explained by human capital
remains valid.

But to understand the *effect* of education on earnings it is clearly better to look at
qualifications than years of schooling. As Table VIII shows, the established pecking order
seems to correspond remarkably to the order of earnings. The one exception is non-
graduate school-teaching qualifications. Holders of these take a 3-year course (2 years
till 1960) and about half of them have " A " level and half " O " level qualifications. They
end up earning barely more than those with " A " level only—partly presumably due to
the length of their paid holidays. But, this case apart, the rise of earnings with educational
" level " is remarkably smooth.

We can look first at the full-time qualifications, using annual earnings data. To
compute the rate of return to each course we need to know the entry qualification to it:
roughly speaking, " A " level requires five or more " O " levels, and a first degree requires
" A " level. We also need to know the corresponding period of study (ΔS). We take
this from Table VII.[26] The resulting rates of return are shown in Table IX, Columns (1)
and (2). In Columns (3) and (4) we do the same thing, but estimating an earnings function
confined to people with the two qualifications being compared. Thus in comparing degree
graduates with " A " level holders we run the equation

$$\ln Y_i = a_0 + a_1 D_i + a_2 t_i + a_3 t_i^2$$

for these two groups where D is a dummy variable (= 1 for degree graduates and = 0
for " A " level holders). We then report the coefficient a_1 divided by the relevant number
of years. Given the roughness of the data on which they are based, we would only conclude
that the rates of return to " A " level and degrees are broadly similar—and similar to the

TABLE VIII

Annual earnings: using highest educational qualification

Variable	Annual earnings		Weekly earnings	
	FT	PT	FT	PT
Constant	6·144		2·536	
t	0·087		0·067	
t^2	−0·0015		−0·0012	
No qualification*	0·000		0·000	
1–4 " O " levels	0·180		0·138	
C and G craft/ordinary		0·298		0·193
5+ " O " levels	0·286		0·298	
C and G advanced/final		0·362		0·234
Ordinary Nat. Cert./Dip.		0·369		0·272
1+ " A " levels	0·462		0·436	
C and G tech. and prof. Level C		0·546		0·461
Higher Nat. Cert./Dip.		0·555		0·454
Prof. Level B		0·763		0·676
Non-graduate teaching cert.	0·506		0·421	
First degree	0·876	0·76	0·769	
Higher degree	1·097		0·990	
R^2	0·339		0·393	

Notes: All coefficients are significantly different from zero at 1 per cent level.
    *" No qualification " is the omitted category in the regression.

TABLE IX

Rate of return to " A " level and degree (percentage)

	Using general earnings function		Using specific earnings function	
	Annual earnings	Weekly earnings	Annual earnings	Weekly earnings
	(1)	(2)	(3)	(4)
" A " level	11·7	9·2	17·3	12·2
First degree	9·6	7·7	9·2	7·4

average rate of return to schooling. (The rates to " A " level appear to be higher but the relative number of years taken to obtain the qualification may be underestimated.)

As part-time qualifications increase, earnings also increase sharply. For example, people with Higher National Certificate earn nearly 20 per cent more than those with Ordinary National Certificate. They only have one extra year of full-time schooling but in addition a good deal of part-time schooling, which would need to be taken into account before a valid rate of return could be calculated.

NOTE 1

Parallel experience–earnings profiles do not prove q, k and b independent of S

In the following example experience-log-earnings profiles are parallel even though q and k vary with S. As a result any regression estimate of r would be biased.

In Figure 3 we draw two profiles—one for people with no schooling (ln Y_0) and one for people with one year of schooling (ln Y_1). For simplicity, the profiles have been

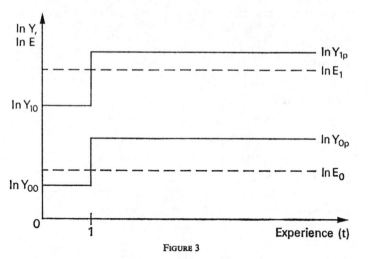

FIGURE 3

The logic of parallel profiles.

drawn with only one step in them: training occurs in one period only. The profiles are parallel: $(\ln Y_{1t} - \ln Y_{0t})$ is the same (Δ) for all years of experience (t). Thus if $\ln Y$ is regressed on schooling and experience the coefficient on schooling will equal Δ. Δ is also approximately the conventionally-calculated rate of return.[27] But we cannot infer that Δ is the true rate of return $(\ln E_1 - \ln E_0)$. It might or it might not be. For example suppose that people with 1 year of schooling invest more than people with no schooling but get a proportionately lower rate of return to training. Then, as the diagram shows, $(\ln E_1 - \ln E_0)$ exceeds $(\ln Y_{1t} - \ln Y_{0t})$. Yet the profiles are parallel. This happens because for each educational group i

$$\ln Y_{ip} = \ln E_i + k_{0i} \cdot q_i$$

and

$$\ln Y_{i0} = \ln E_i - k_{0i}$$

so that

$$\ln Y_{ip} - \ln Y_{i0} = k_{0i}(q_i + 1)$$

and in our particular case $k_{0i}(q_i+1)$ is the same for both educational groups. But the investment rate (k_0) is higher for the more educated group and the rate of return (q) is lower.

So, even if profiles are parallel, nothing can be inferred about rates of return to schooling from vertical differences between earnings profiles.

NOTE 2

Mincer's short-cut method[28]

Description

Let Y_{Sx} be the average earnings of people with S years of schooling at age x. The short-cut method then proceeds as follows:

    (i) *Estimate* the internal rate of return to education (conventionally-calculated), by solving for ρ_S in

$$\sum_{x=p+s+1}^{T} Y_{Sx}(1+\rho_S)^{-x} = \sum_{x=p+s}^{T} Y_{S-1,x}(1+\rho_S)^{-x} \qquad \ldots(A.1)$$

where p is the number of pre-school years and T the age of retirement.

(ii) *Assume* initially that the rate of return to training (q) is the same as the true rate of return to schooling (r_S). This implies that each of the two is equal to the conventionally-calculated rate of return to education (ρ_S), since the latter is a weighted average of the first two. Now, from the definition of the rate of return to training (q)

$$E_S \sum_{x = p+S+1}^{T} (1+q)^{-x} = \sum_{x = p+S+1}^{T} Y_{Sx}(1+q)^{-x}.$$

So, approximately

$$E_S = q(1+q)^{p+S} \sum_{x = p+S+1}^{T} Y_{Sx}(1+q)^{-x}.$$

If we assume $q = \rho_S$ we obtain an estimate of E_S from

$$\hat{E}_S = \rho_S(1+\rho_S)^{p+S} \sum_{x = p+S+1}^{T} Y_{Sx}(1+\rho_S)^{-x} \qquad \qquad ...(A.2)$$

and of E_{S-1} from

$$\hat{E}_{S-1} = \rho_{S-1}(1+\rho_{S-1})^{p+S-1} \sum_{x = p+S}^{T} Y_{S-1,x}(1+\rho_{S-1})^{-x}. \qquad ...(A.3)$$

The estimate of the true rate of return to schooling is now

$$\hat{r}_S = \frac{\hat{E}_S}{\hat{E}_{S-1}} - 1$$

(iii) However, this estimate is only correct if $q = \rho_S$. Therefore, says Mincer, now *check whether the assumption was correct* by checking whether

$$\hat{r}_S = \rho_S.$$

If the true rate of return to schooling ($\hat{r}_S$), computed on the assumption that the rate of return to training (q) equalled itself ($\hat{r}_S$), turns out to be equal to a weighted average of the two represented by ρ_S, then the assumption has, he claims, been verified.

Critique

This is not, however, the case. In fact, subject to one minor assumption, $\hat{r}_S$ must always equal ρ_S, as a tautology. For, from (A.1), (A.2) and (A.3),

$$\hat{r}_S = \frac{\hat{E}_S}{\hat{E}_{S-1}} - 1 = \frac{\rho_S(1+\rho_S)^{p+S}}{\rho_{S-1}(1+\rho_{S-1})^{p+S-1}} \frac{\sum_{x = p+S}^{T} Y_{S-1,x}(1+\rho_S)^{-x}}{\sum_{x = p+S}^{T} Y_{S-1,x}(1+\rho_{S-1})^{-x}} - 1$$

Now suppose that $\rho_S = \rho_{S-1}$. This is certainly logically possible (and in equilibrium to be expected from human capital theory). In that case

$$\hat{r}_S = (1+\rho_S)-1 = \rho_S.$$

But ρ_S is definitely an average of the rate of return to schooling and training and so therefore is $\hat{r}_S$. So the computation cannot in general tell us anything about the rate of return to training. Moreover even if $\rho_S \neq \rho_{S-1}$, it is not obvious which discount rate should be used to convert the profile $Y_{S-1,x}$ into an equivalent annuity. One could equally well argue in favour of using ρ_{S-1} and ρ_S—the one is the rate of return to additional education ending at age $S-1$ and the other is the rate to additional education beginning at age $S-1$. If ρ_S were used to discount $Y_{S-1,x}$ and also to discount Y_{Sx}, we are back with $\hat{r}_S = \rho_S$. So the ratio of annuities method cannot check whether the rates of return to schooling and training are the same. For this reason neither ρ_S nor $\hat{r}_S$ can be used as estimates of the true rate of return to education. And the computation of $\hat{r}_S$ adds nothing to knowledge, once ρ_S has been computed.

Finally it may be useful to use the preceding framework to demonstrate in what sense the calculated rate ρ_S is a weighted average of the true rate of return to schooling (r_S) and the rate of return to training (q), assuming the latter is the same for people with S and

$S-1$ years of schooling. From the definition of the rate of return to training, the true E_S is

$$E_S = q(1+q)^{p+S} \sum_{x=p+S+1}^{T} Y_{Sx}(1+q)^{-x}$$

and

$$E_{S-1} = q(1+q)^{p+S-1} \sum_{x=p+S}^{T} Y_{S-1,x}(1+q)^{-x}.$$

Now

$$r_S = \frac{E_S}{E_{S-1}} - 1 = (1+q)\frac{\Sigma Y_{Sx}(1+q)^{-x}}{\Sigma Y_{S-1,x}(1+q)^{-x}} - 1$$

$$\therefore \frac{1+r_S}{1+q} = \frac{\Sigma Y_{Sx}(1+q)^{-x}}{\Sigma Y_{S-1,x}(1+q)^{-x}} \qquad \text{...(A.4)}$$

But by the definition of the conventionally-calculated rate of return (ρ_S), the right-hand side of this equation equals unity if $q = \rho_S$ and exceeds unity if $q < \rho_S$. Therefore if $q < r_S$, $q < \rho_S$. This is not the same as saying that, if $q < r_S$, then $q < \rho_S < r_S$, which is the normal definition of a weighted average.

In fact one can imagine some curious situations. For example suppose that the profiles are parallel, so that

$$Y_{S,x} = Y_{S-1,x-1}(1+d) \quad \text{all } S, x.$$

Then

$$\rho_S = d.$$

And, if q is the same for both groups,

$$r_S = \frac{E_S}{E_{S-1}} - 1 = d.$$

So $r_S = \rho_S$ whatever the value of q. One can only loosely say that ρ_S is a weighted average of r_S and q.

First version received October 1976; final version accepted June 1978 (Eds.).

We are most grateful to Louise Hamshere for intelligent and efficient programming, to Stephen Nickell for suggesting the model of equation (3), to the journal's reviewers for helpful comments, to Mark Stewart for helpful discussions, to the Office of Population Censuses and Surveys for making the data available and to the Esmee Fairbairn Charitable Trust for making the money available.

NOTES

1. For other recent evaluations of the Mincer model see Blinder (1976) and Klevmarken and Quigley (1976). These are chiefly concerned with the relative roles of experience and age, not discussed in the present paper. See also Hanushek and Quigley (1978a and b).

2. The true private rate of return to one year's education is

$$(E_S - E_{S-1})(1-t)/(E_{S-1}(1-f)+T-G)$$

where t is the marginal tax rate, f the average tax rate, T tuition fees and G scholarship. Only if the relevant items balance each other is the private rate of return equal to $(E_S - E_{S-1})/E_{S-1}$ as is assumed in this paper. In Britain $f < t$, but $T - G < 0$, since nearly all students have no fees or have fees paid out of scholarships.

3. What follows is based on Mincer (1974, pp. 85–86, 90 and 97–98).

4. Note that even if the profiles were parallel, this would not rule out the possibility that q, k and b depend on S. An example is given in Note 1. However there is no way in which the data normally available could be used to investigate such occurrences. Our approach (below) uses functional forms that could hope to pick up some but not all cases where q, k and b depend on S.

5. For any group S, f is given by the following relations. From the definition of q

$$E_S = q\Sigma_{t=0}^{L} Y_{St}(1+q)^{-t}$$

where L is the length of working life; and from the definition of f

$$Y_{Sf} = E_S$$

If for another group M, $Y_{Mt} = \lambda Y_{St}$ (all t), f for that group must be the same as for group S.

6. Mincer, pp. 49–50.

7. Mincer offers one other approach which we have not so far mentioned. If the investment ratio is assumed to decay exponentially (so that $k = k_0 e^{-\beta t}$) then, if β can be identified, so can q. Mincer gives

only a partial reporting on his estimates here (pp. 93–94). For Britain we have found it impossible to obtain sensible estimates using this form of function, and so has Riboud (1975) for France.

8. See Mincer (1974, pp. 85–86, 90 and 97–98).

9. The evidence for the cross-over model, as presented by Mincer, is not in fact overwhelming. For example on p. 105 he shows the pattern of variance of weekly earnings in relation to experience. One would expect this to fall up to $\hat{t}$ and then rise. But for people with 16 years of schooling it tends to rise continuously, while for people with 8 years of schooling it falls up to $\hat{t} = 8$ and is then level. Only for people with 12 years' schooling is the predicted U-shape found.

10. Table 3.3 (top row) gives var $(u) = 0.333$; $0.50 = 0.333/0.668$.

11. By contrast Mincer runs the equation

$$\ln Y_{tt} = d_0 + d_1 Z_{tt} + d_2 \ln^* W + u$$

and finds (as we do) that the coefficient on d_2 exceeds unity. However this is probably due to misspecification (Hall (1975)). If the correct specification is as in the text, the estimate of d_2 in Mincer's equation is biased upwards, i.e. it is biased to exceed unity.

12. Mincer makes two assumptions. (i) All variation in weeks worked is transitory. But if this is so, weeks worked would not be partially related to human capital in the way we find them to be. (ii) There is no transitory variation in weeks worked and all the (permanent) variation in weeks worked is due to human capital. This is equally extreme in the opposite direction. Using residuals for the cross-over year, Mincer finds the functions of variance explained by human capital to be 0.62 (Assumption (i)) and 0.70 (Assumption (ii)) (his p. 96). This is the basis of his claim that human capital explains " close to two-thirds of the inequality of adult, white urban men in the US in 1959 ".

13. For previous annual earnings functions using these data see Layard (1977), Psacharopoulos (1977) and Stewart (1977). An hourly earnings function appears in Layard, Metcalf and Nickell (1978), and in Layard, Piachaud and Stewart (1978).

14. Earnings in the year preceding the interview divided by the monthly index of earnings in the month of interview (C.S.O. (1973, Table 16)) to reduce the effects of inflation. Self-employment earnings are included where they occur (the average value is £6 for the year).

15. This is computed as the age on completing full-time education minus 5, subject to one proviso. For each qualification we constructed a maximum such age that was possible if the individual had had no gap in his full-time education. If the reported age exceeded this age we replaced it by this maximum age. About 3.5 per cent of the sample were affected by this adjustment. The mean years of schooling are 10.5 years compared with 10.9 in the US. (Mincer (1974, p. 60)): compulsory schooling in Britain begins on the 5th birthday.

16. The numbers in each schooling group are:

9 or less	2464
10	2322
11	963
12	336
13	249
14	65
15	86
16	119
17	135
18+	134

17. If St is added to Regression 3.2 it only attracts a coefficient of -0.00046.

18. There are two algebraic solutions of which only one makes sense. The same exercise was also repeated treating S as a continuous variable rather than using a set of dummies (Regression 3.7). The resulting values were

$$q = -0.23 + 0.039\ S; \quad k_0 = 0.86 - 0.035\ S; \quad b = 0.040 - 0.0011\ S.$$

Interestingly the coefficient on schooling was 0.094—almost the same as in Regression 3.2.

19. However this highlights the fact that the rate of return to training may be overestimated if not all the upwards slope in earnings profiles is due to human capital.

20. Note that weekly earnings vary less than annual earnings.

$$\text{var}(\ln Y) = \text{var}\ln(Y/W) + \text{var}(\ln W) + 2\ \text{cov}(\ln Y/W, \ln W).$$

In our case the corresponding figures are

$$0.436 = 0.235 + 0.128 + 0.073$$

21. If work is preferred *per se* to non-employment, one ought even to reduce the measured earnings of those who work shorter weeks to allow for the disvalue of non-work. This would raise the rate of return to education above 10 per cent. If we were concerned with the *social* returns to education we should use weekly earnings. For it is not very plausible to suppose that for males the average level of schooling affects

PSACHAROPOULOS & LAYARD   HUMAN CAPITAL   503

the average level of weeks worked very much, even though individual schooling affects who works which number of weeks.

22. $0·46 = 0·436(0·339)/(0·436−0·119)$. The relevant figures are taken from Regressions (3.6) and (5.3).

23. The size of the sample does not permit an analysis of the pattern of experience-specific earnings variation *within* schooling groups, comparable with Mincer's (pp. 104–105).

24. Successful part-time students most commonly attend college one full weekday and 1–3 evenings a week.

25. See Robbins Committee (1963) Appendix Two B and Appendix One, pp. 192–196.

26. This gives 1·5 years for " A " level and 4·3 years for a first degree, as compared with the conventional stereotype of 2 and 3 years respectively. However, one needs to remember that " A " level can be taken in one year, whereas some first degrees involve four-year courses. The essential point is that earnings differences must be related to the actual schooling differences which generate them.

27. ρ_1 is defined by

$$(0 - Y_{00}) + \frac{(Y_{10} - Y_{0P})}{1 + \rho_1} + \frac{(Y_{1P} - Y_{0P})}{\rho_1(1 + \rho_1)} = 0$$

But $Y_{10} = Y_{00}(1+d)$ and $Y_{1P} = Y_{0P}(1+d)$. If these expressions are substituted in and ρ_1 is set equal to d, the equation still holds. $\Delta \simeq d$.

28. See his pp. 49–50.

REFERENCES

BECKER, G. S. (1975) *Human Capital*, 2nd edition (National Bureau of Economic Research).

BLINDER, A. S. (1976), " On dogmatism in human capital theory ", *Journal of Human Resources*, Winter.

CENTRAL STATISTICAL OFFICE (1973) *Annual Abstract of Statistics* (H.M.S.O.).

GHEZ, G. R. and BECKER, G. S. (1975) *The Allocation of Time and Goods over the Life Cycle* (National Bureau of Economic Research).

HALL, R. E. (1975), Review of Mincer (1974), in *Journal of Political Economy*, April.

HANUSHEK, E. and QUIGLEY, J. M. (1978a), " Implicit investment profiles and Intertemporal Adjustments of Relative Wages ", *American Economic Review*, March.

HANUSHEK, E. and QUIGLEY, J. M. (1978b), " More Exacting Tests of the OJT Investment Model ", Paper presented at the UK/US Conference on Human Capital and Income Distribution, held at Cambridge, March 1978.

KLEVMARKEN, A. and QUIGLEY, J. M. (1976), " Age, experience, earnings and investments in human capital ", *Journal of Political Economy*, February.

LAYARD, P. R. G. (1977), " On measuring the redistribution of lifetime income ", in Feldstein, M. S. and Inman, R. P. (eds.) *The Economics of Public Services* (Macmillan).

LAYARD, P. R. G., METCALF, D. and NICKELL, S. (1978), " The Effects of Collective Bargaining on Relative Wages ", in Krelle, W. and Shorrocks, A. F. (eds.) *Personal Income Distribution* (North-Holland).

LAYARD, P. R. G., PIACHAUD, D. and STEWART, M. (1978) *The Causes of Poverty*, Royal Commission on the Distribution of Income and Wealth, Background Paper No. 5 (H.M.S.O.).

MINCER, J. (1974) *Schooling, Experience and Earnings* (National Bureau of Economic Research). (For a useful summary see Mincer, J., " Progress in Human Capital Analyses of the Distribution of Earnings ", in Atkinson, A. B. (ed.) *The Personal Distribution of Incomes*, 1976.) (All our references are to the main book.)

OFFICE OF POPULATION CENSUSES AND SURVEYS (1973) *The General Household Survey. An Introductory Report* (H.M.S.O.).

OFFICE OF POPULATION CENSUSES AND SURVEYS (1975) *The General Household Survey: 1972* (H.M.S.O.).

PSACHAROPOULOS, G. (1977), " Family Background, Education and Achievement: A Path Model of Earnings Determinants in the U.K. and Some Alternatives ", *British Journal of Sociology*, September.

RIBOUD, M. (1975), " An analysis of the earnings distribution in France ", paper presented to the Workshop in the Economics of Education, L.S.E.

ROBBINS COMMITTEE ON HIGHER EDUCATION (1963) *Higher Education*, Appendix One: The Demand for Places in Higher Education, and Appendix Two B: Students and Their Education (H.M.S.O., Cmnd. 2154 and II–I).

STEWART, M. (1977), " The determinants of earnings in Britain: An occupation-specific approach ", Centre for Labour Economics, L.S.E., Discussion Paper No. 4.

[8]

Human Capital and the Labor Market
A Review of Current Research

JACOB MINCER

This is a review of some recent developments in analyses of (a) effects of human capital on the wage structure and on labor turnover and of (b) human capital responses to technological change and consequent wage, turnover, and unemployment effects. These developments represent an extension of the scope of empirical investigations of the role of human capital in the labor market, as well as a new attempt to observe, at the micro-level, some of the ways in which human capital adjusts to technology and thereby promotes economic growth.

Human capital theory is the economist's approach to the analysis of skills, or labor "quality."[1] The central idea is that human capacities are in large part acquired and developed through informal and formal education at home and at school, and through training, experience, and mobility in the labor market. These activities are costly; they involve both direct expenses and earnings or consumption foregone by families, students, trainees, and by workers in the process of labor mobility. Because benefits derived from these activities accrue mainly in the future, the costly acquisition of learned capacities can be viewed as an investment. It follows that the standard tools of economic analysis can be applied to the analyses of the determinants and consequences of investments in human capital. In particular, these analyses have contributed to the understanding of patterns of individual economic growth and individual differences in that growth and of sectoral (industrial) or national economic growth, the twin topics of this review.

An individual's economic growth is described by his earnings or his *wage*

Several studies have investigated survey data on the prevalence of on-the-job training. These studies have sought to discover who receives training and the effects of this labor market experience on workers' wages, wage growth, turnover, and employment. What is the magnitude of workers' and employers' investments in job training? How profitable are such investments? The first part of the article considers these questions. The second reviews studies that provide recent measures of technological change by industry, such as productivity growth indexes or research and development expenditures. The studies explore effects of technological changes on demands for educated and trained workers and on consequent changes in wage structures, labor turnover, and unemployment.

profile, a curve describing the progress of wages over the working life. The typical wage profile is concave: It grows rapidly during the first decade of working life, decelerates subsequently, and levels off or declines ultimately. This pattern of growth reflects returns on the accumulated personal investments. The payoff on them is greater, the longer the payoff period; hence, larger investments take place early and so does steeper wage growth. As investments decline, the rate of wage growth declines. Differences across individuals in levels and shapes of wage profiles produce the *wage structure* in the labor market.

In analyzing the wage structure, it is important to distinguish *levels* of lifetime earnings achieved by individuals from *shapes* of wage profiles, that is, of individual wage growth over the working life. Educational attainment at school that precedes full-time entry into the labor market affects levels of lifetime earnings but not shapes or slopes of the wage profiles. These are affected by time-patterns of human capital investments in training, learning, and job mobility during the working life, generally after completion of schooling. A vast literature, accumulated over the past 30 years, contains a wealth of findings on the effects of school education

on wage levels and on profitability rates of investments in education at various levels of aggregation. Corresponding estimates of effects of job-training were not available until recently. Instead, growth of earnings with working age, known as the "experience-wage profile," was assumed to reflect returns on workers' investments in the labor market, especially in job-training. Indeed, a first comprehensive estimate of the volume of on-the-job training costs (Mincer, 1962) was obtained using this interpretation.

The validity of such indirect estimates does, of course, depend on the validity of the theory. Although the theory has proven quite robust in a number of applications, it cannot be claimed as an exclusive factor in validating any particular application. Not surprisingly, therefore, the absence of direct data on job-training spawned a proliferation of alternative theories that attempt to explain upward slopes of wage profiles either as devices to economize on costs of supervision (Becker & Stigler, 1974; Lazear, 1979) on costs of turnover (Salop & Salop, 1976), or as consequences of job sorting or matching in labor mobility (Jovanovic, 1979). These theories and the human capital job-training theory are not mutually exclusive, nor have they been subjected to much empirical testing. Recently, direct data on job-training has become available from several sources. Clearly, better informed empirical research on the incidence and effects of job-training is not only desirable, but now also possible. I describe the early findings of this research in the first part of this article.

JACOB MINCER *is at Columbia University, New York, New York 10027.*

A second development in empirical economics is the construction of multi-factor productivity growth indexes, at aggregate and at sectoral levels, in the U.S. and in some other economies. The availability of these indexes provides means for observing human capital responses or adjustments to technological change. The approach does not treat human capital as the major source of technical progress, nor does it deny it that role, but looks at human capital behavior more narrowly, as an adjustment of labor quality to facilitate economic growth. Findings of this newly developing research are described in the second part.

Effects of Job-Training and Learning in the Labor Market

Direct information on the incidence, timing, and duration of job-training is available in several data sets. The information represents responses, mainly in household surveys, to questions about formal or informal job-training or learning in the firm or outside during the preceding year. The questions are phrased differently in the various surveys, both in detail and in subjectivity. Nevertheless, the elicited information makes possible qualitative and quantitative estimates, from which a degree of consensus begins to emerge.

The University of Michigan's Panel Study of Income Dynamics (PSID), an annual survey of about 5,000 households, provided usable information on job-training for about 1,200 male heads of households in 1976, 1978, and 1985. Only the first two surveys have been available to researchers thus far. The information covers the length of time of training required during the current job, as well as its learning contents in 1976.[2] Information on *intensity* (hours per week) of training is available in a supplementary time study of PSID workers by Duncan and Stafford (1980). The PSID data were analyzed by Duncan and Hoffman (1978), Brown (1983, 1988), Gronau (1988), and Mincer (1988a, 1988c, 1988d).

The National Longitudinal Samples (NLS) surveys covering several thousand households, conducted at Ohio State University, contain annual or biannual information on job training for two cohorts of young men, those aged 14 to 24 in 1968, and the same age group in 1979, and for one cohort of mature men, those aged 45 to 59 in 1968. The data on the new (1979) cohort

of young men contains information on the duration of a spell of training. In-house training reported for the 1968 cohorts of men and women were studied by Lillard and Tan (1986). The new cohort has been analyzed by Parsons (1986) and Lynch (1988).

The Current Population Survey (CPS) of the U.S. Census, the largest periodic sample of U.S. households, contains the incidence of training in its March 1983 survey. The data were analyzed by Lillard and Tan (1986).

Finally, the 1982 Equal Opportunity Pilot Project (EOPP) is the only survey of employers (about 2,000, in 31 areas). It provides information on hours of training of new hires during the first three months on the job. These data were described and analyzed by Lillard and Tan (1986) and Barron, Black, and Loewenstein (1989).

Incidence of job training and effects on labor turnover.

The various studies differ in focus, but one question explored in each of them was: Who is more likely to get job training? The answers obtained in (regression) analyses where various characteristics of workers were held constant concur that: The likelihood of respondents' receiving training in the survey year (a) increases with education; (b) declines with age and with length of seniority; (c) is greater for married than for single men; (d) is smaller for women, especially married women, than for men; and (e) in the EOPP, is greater in large firms and where machinery is more costly.

These findings are not surprising and are consistent with standard human capital analysis. Reasons for the positive correlation between education and training have been spelled out by Becker (1975): Persons who have greater learning ability and better opportunities to finance the costs of human capital investments do invest more in all forms of human capital, including schooling and job-training. Although this proposition is sufficient, some analysts claim in addition that school education is a complementary factor to job-training in producing human capital. In other words, education enhances the productivity of job-training at work. It is clear, however, that schooling can also be a substitute for job training: The decline of apprenticeships has been attributed to growth, over the long run, in educational levels.

Training is more prevalent among ca-

reer women who work continually and full-time than among more sporadic workers. In the NLS, close to half of the women were not continuously employed (Lillard & Tan, 1986). Their incentives to invest in training were weaker because of the much shorter and uncertain payoff period (remaining time in employment). Employer investments in their training are discouraged for the same reason; employer selection of women into training is likely to be affected by expectations of prospective worker turnover.

The decline of training as workers age and as their seniority (tenure) in the job advances is also explainable by the declining payoff period. The remaining working life is the payoff period, if the investment in training is transferable to other firms; remaining tenure in the firm is the payoff period, if the training is used in the firm in which it was received, but not in others.

The theoretical implications of firm-specificity in training were spelled out in the original contributions of Becker (1962) and in a 1962 article by Oi. According to the argument, worker separations from the firm represent a capital loss, if training is firm specific (more useful in the firm in which it was obtained). Potential layoffs discourage workers from such investments, while potential quits discourage employers from investing in their workers. The solution is a sharing of costs of investment in specific training by employers and workers that produces mutual deterrence: Quits and layoffs are expected to be less frequent where specific training is important.

If training is fully transferable, neither quits nor layoffs matter to the workers' gains from training, and their mobility is not affected. Employers' investments would be at risk in this case, however, so that they have no incentives to finance such training. Note that the information on the incidence and volumes of training tells us neither what part of it is specific, nor what parts of the costs employees bear and employers bear. One may argue, however, that very little, if any, on-the-job training is devoid of elements of firm specificity. Indeed, the greatest opportunities for training are likely to exist where training processes are closely related to and integrated with production activities. Consequently, one may assume that workers who get more training get more of both the general and specific components of training and so expect that all training affects turnover negatively.

Effects of training on turnover have been explored in the PSID data (Mincer, 1988c). Attachment to the firm was more durable, the more training workers received in the firm. This was evident both in terms of their completing longer tenures in the firm as well as in their being less likely to leave the firm after 1976, given incomplete tenure in 1976. Two other findings in that study are noteworthy: First, both quits and layoffs appeared to be reduced by training. Second, turnover of workers from firm to firm who reported more training in 1976 appears to be lower over longer periods, even beyond the period of stay in the 1976 firm. The former indicates a sharing of training costs by workers and employers. The latter is to be expected, if workers tend to engage in training or learning repeatedly over their careers in more than one firm. Indeed, a positive correlation between training in the 1976 firm, the previous, and the subsequent firm was observed in the PSID data.

Although the persistence of mobility behavior is likely to be a consequence of the persistence of training, it may also antedate it: Stable workers are more likely to be selected for training by firms that invest in training. The evidence indicates that trainees are, on average, less mobile prior to the observed training than other workers, but that their mobility is reduced further by that training.

Effects of skill training on unemployment. On average, nearly half of the workers who separate from a job experience unemployment in transition to another job. Because job training reduces separations, it is likely also to reduce the probability of experiencing unemployment, $P(u)$, among trained workers. By definition, $P(u) = P(s) \cdot P(u/s)$, where $P(s)$ is the probability of separating from a firm, and $P(u/s)$ the probability of unemployment when separated. Unless the latter is increased by training, the conclusion follows. There is no obvious reason for $P(u/s)$ to increase as a result of training and several reasons, elaborated in Mincer (1988a), for its decline, as is observed in the PSID data.

These effects of training on unemployment underlie the ubiquitous negative relation between education

and unemployment. This relation is due, in large measure, to the fact that more educated workers continue to train and to learn on the job, to a greater extent, than less educated workers, as was shown in a number of studies listed earlier.

Table 1 shows unemployment rates, by education level, and their components, all of which are lower, the higher the level of education.[3] The relations visible in Table 1, which are summarized in the ratio column, are not standardized for other worker characteristics, but they are not much affected when such standardization is performed by means of regression analysis. However, to some extent, educated workers appear to experience less unemployment even without (observed) training. (Reasons and some evidence have been analyzed in the Mincer study, 1988a.)

Job training and wage growth. All of the studies listed at the outset have investigated effects of job-training on wage growth. An early study of the PSID by Brown (1983) showed significant positive effects of training on wages during the 1976 to 1981 period, both in the cross-section and over time. In a replication (Mincer, 1988c), I compared year-by-year wage growth of

workers in the PSID in the 1976 firm, in periods with training, with the wage growth of workers in periods without training[4] between 1968 and 1982. The effect of a year with training so estimated was 4.4%. When restricted to the 1975-76 survey year, the effect was 6.7%, and, when a learning variable[5] was used, the effect was 6.4%. No other variables had much of an effect on wage growth (except for a small negative ef-

---

TABLE 1

Education and Unemployment Components
(Some gross [unadjusted] facts)

Education	Ed	<12	12	13-15	16+	Ratio (col. 1 to col. 4) <12 16+
unemployment rate	u^a	7.0	4.1	3.3	1.9	3.7
Prob. (incidence) of unemployment	$P(u)$	9.5	6.4	4.7	3.5	2.7
Prob. of separation	$P(s)$	17.9	13.4	12.8	10.5	1.7
Prob. of unemployment of job separators	$P(u/s)$	53.2	48.6	37.8	33.2	1.6
Duration of unemployment (in weeks)	Du	13.8	12.1	11.6	11.0	1.26
Labor force participation	LFP^b	92.1	97.0	96.4	98.2	.94

[a]Bureau of Labor Statistics (BLS) data, White Men, age 25-54 in 1979.
[b]BLS data, same, age 35-44 in 1979 (Special Labor Force Report).
All other rows: PSID, White Men, years 1976-81, 11-25 years of work experience.

---

fect of prior experience), which may be attributed to aging.

The effect of training on wage growth was greater (9.5%) at younger ages (working age 12 years or less) than the effect (3.6%) was at older ages. The difference reflects greater intensity of training among young workers, as was shown in the Duncan and Stafford (1980) time study.

The findings that wage growth decelerates with age because training does and that no other variable appears to affect individual wage growth significantly (apart from economy- or industry-wide productivity growth, to be discussed in the next section) go a long way in confirming the importance of job training or learning in producing the typical upward sloping and decelerating wage profiles over working lives.

In a recent thorough revision of his

earlier study, Brown (1988) has found larger effects of training on contemporaneous wage growth in the PSID data covering the years 1976 to 1984. To avoid possible misclassification, he narrowed the sample to workers who did not require prior training to enter the 1976 firm and who were in their first job position in that firm. For these workers, training-related wage growth was close to 9% per year.

Although the average training period in his sample is a little over one year, the first year wage growth, which some researchers attributed to considerations other than training, appeared to be substantial only if skill acquisition (training or learning) took place.

Turning from wage growth in the firm to wage growth over the longer periods that transcend tenure in one firm, I found, in the PSID, that growth of wages over the whole period 1968 to 1983 was positively related to training in the 1976 job. Given some persistence and transferability of training, the result is not surprising. A more interesting finding is that the slope of the long-run wage trajectory is flatter for the more

frequent movers: The flatness reflects lesser investments in job-training which, in turn, permits greater mobility. The lesser wage growth of frequent movers holds, despite gains obtained in moving.[6] These are, on average, positive and add up to about 15% of long-term wage growth.

With the exception of Lillard and Tan's (1986), the studies based on other data sets reported on effects of job-training over the period of training. Bar-

ron et al. (using EOPP data) reported that new hires who spent 151 hours in training during the first three months of employment had wages that were 15% higher after two years compared to entry wages. In the new youth cohort of the NLS, Lynch (1988) found that wages of young workers with job training rose 11% per year, whereas an additional year of tenure without training increased wages by 4%. In the 1968 youth cohort, Lillard and Tan found that company training raised wages about 12% over the year with training, but this gain declined afterward. Less plausibly, they found a similar effect of a year with training in the CPS.

Profitability and volumes of training. Table 2 shows the magnitudes of effects of a year with training on wage growth ($\dot{w}$), estimated from the various data sets (col. 1). The numbers are comparable in magnitude to a range of familiar estimates of the effect of an additional year of schooling on wages. They could be interpreted, similarly, as rates of return on training, if all (100%) hours of employment during the year were spent in training. If the actual fraction of time spent in training is k, and $k = 20\%$, then the numbers in column 1 would have to be multiplied by 5 to yield estimates of rates of return. Information on k is available in some of the data sets, and column 2 shows estimates of rates of return r, calculated in this fashion ($r = \dot{w}/k$). A further correction is required if skills acquired in training depreciate without retraining, because of technical obsolescence or because of job separations, in the case of firm specific skills. The only available estimate, by Lillard and Tan (1986, Table 4.3), suggests that the wage gain due to training depreciates at the rate of about 15-20% per year. Estimates of corrected rates of return (r) based on wage growth, duration of training, and depreciation[7] are shown in columns 3 and 4.

Interestingly, fragmentary estimates of rates of return on apprenticeship training in a 1962 study (Mincer) ranged from 9 to 18% in 1949, a range not outside those in columns 3 and 4 here. The study also estimated total volumes of investment in job-training of men in three census years (1939, 1949, and 1958, the last based on CPS) using earnings growth observed in wage profiles.

The assumption in the 1962 procedure was that growth of wages in the profile was due exclusively to worker investment in the labor market. This assumption can be dropped now, as the opportunity costs of job training are calculated directly from the available information: If the proportion of workers engaged in training during a year is p, and the fraction of their working time spent in training is k, a rough estimate of the fraction of total wages and salaries invested in training is kp. Obtained in this fashion, estimates of male worker opportunity costs of training in 1985 dollars are shown in column 5 of Table 2 for PSID, and CPS, which are the only data that cover the whole male workforce. Expressing these costs as ratios to costs of school expenditures

TABLE 2
Estimates of Profitability and Volumes of Job Training
(U.S., 1985)

Data set	$\dot{w}$(%)	r	Corrected[1] (%) at depreciation 20%	Corrected[1] (%) at depreciation 15%	Training ($ bils.) Males	Ratio of training to ed costs Males	All training[7] ratio $ bils.	All training[7] ratio to GNP
	(1)	(2)	(3)	(4)	(5)	(6)	(7)	(8)
EOPP[2] New hires	7.5	32.0	4.0	10.5				
NLSY[3] New entrants	7.0	32.0	5.6	12.2				
NLSY[4] Youth cohort	12.0	48.0	18.4	25.6				
PSID[5] '76 trainees	6.7	33.0	6.4	13.0	84.0	.42	210.0	5.2%
CPS[6] '82 trainees	12.0	48.0	18.4	25.6	70.0	.35	175.0	4.4%

[1]Corrected $r = \dot{w}/k\ (1-d) - d$, where d is the depreciation rate per year.
[2]Based on Barron et al. (1989).
[3]Based on Lynch (1988).
[4]Based on Lillard and Tan (1986) with k assumed as in Lynch.
[5]Based on Mincer (1988d).
[6]k assumed the same as in Mincer (1988d).
[7]Includes women's and employers' costs, estimated in Mincer (1988d).

(including estimates of opportunity costs of schooling) yields a 35-42% range. The NLS data suggest that training incidence of women is half or less that of men. When estimates of women's training costs and employer training costs are included, the dollar figures more than double (col. 7) and the fraction of GNP devoted to training is 4.4% to 5.2% (col. 8).[8]

Estimation of employer costs represents a problem, because firm accounting data are, at best, restricted to formal training programs, a tip of the iceberg. Even if the accounting data were to cover all training, the costs shown would not necessarily be costs *borne* by firms. Firms are providing training for which workers pay, fully or partly, by (initial) reductions in wages. In principle, the best way to assess how much firms invest in addition to workers is to compare increases in wages resulting from training with increases in productivity of the same workers. The excess, if any, of the latter over the former represents employers' return on the *costs they bear*. The estimates shown in Table 2 are based on the assumption that employer investments in training are as profitable as worker investments and on information in two studies in which the increase in productivity were just about double the increase in wages (Barron et al., 1988; Blakemore & Hoffman, 1988).

Returning to column 6 in Table 2, the ratio of male job-training investments to educational costs (35 to 42%) is much lower in the 1980s than it was in 1958 according to my 1962 study. The 67% ratio there was based on the assumption that *all* of observed wage growth was attributable to training. It is reduced to 57%, if mobility gains are excluded, according to current estimates of the latter. If the current more directly estimated ratio, 38% on average, were correct also for 1958, it would mean that two-thirds, rather than all, of wage growth in individual wage profiles is attributable to training. It is possible and, indeed, likely that the true ratio declined over time as the growth of public expenditures on education in the 1960s and 1970s exceeded the growth of wages by over 50%, probably inducing a substitution of schooling for job-training.

The estimates of the profitability rates of job training shown in columns 3 and 4 are of interest from a policy perspective: If they exceed rates of return on

other investments, the economy would benefit from increasing training. Although the lower figures do not suggest underinvestment, the higher figures might.[9] The safe and perhaps not surprising conclusion is that overinvestment in job-training appears to be unlikely. However, the same conclusion seemed warranted in 1962 (on shakier grounds). If valid, a remaining research question is why training volumes did not expand since that time.

Human Capital Responses to Technological Change and Their Effects in the Labor Market

Human capital plays a dual role in the process of economic growth. As a stock of knowledge, it is a source of technological change. At the same time, the formation of adaptable skills in the work force is, in part, induced by changes in technology. A process of adjustment or of "embodiment" of technology in the skills of the work force can be observed in micro-data, thanks to the availability of the new statistics described as well as of new indexes of technological change at the sectoral (industry) level.

The indexes of technological change include statistics on newest vintages of capital goods and their research and development (R&D) intensity in a number of industries, as well as measures of multi-factor productivity growth by industrial sector. These are now available for several decades in the U.S. and in some other countries. Multi-factor productivity is the ratio of output to inputs (capital and labor), each weighted by its share in production costs. In constructing such ratios and tracing their growth over time, analysts differ in whether they adjust labor and/or capital for quality and in how they measure output (gross or value added).

Productivity growth is, of course, a consequence of technological change, not a measure of it. It may serve as a measure, if other factors affecting productivity growth, such as business cycles and economies (or diseconomies) of scale do not obscure the developments. The problem of business cycles is mitigated by the use of averages over longer periods cutting across the cycles. The observed effects of productivity growth on labor market phenomena tend to be attenuated if sizable measurement errors, to which such data are prone, remain in the averages.

The studies reviewed here used productivity growth indexes constructed by Gollop and Jorgenson (1980) and Conrad and Jorgenson (1985), because their measures contain detailed adjustments of labor inputs for education, age, and sex. The productivity growth indexes are thus largely purged of human capital components, so that empirical relations between net productivity growth and human capital can be properly interpreted.

Pace of productivity growth and the utilization of human capital. Does more rapid technical change resulting in more rapid productivity growth bring about greater utilization of human capital? The proposition that more educated labor can deal more effectively with a rapidly changing environment brought about by technological change has been forcefully stated and empirically documented, mainly in an agricultural context, by Schultz (1975) and Welch (1970). More recently, the effects of technical change on the educational composition of employment in industrial sectors extending to manufacturing and to the whole economy have been studied by Bartel and Lichtenberg (1987), and the effects on the incidence of job training have been explored by Lillard and Tan (1986).

Using census data on the education composition of the labor force in 61 manufacturing industries in each of the years 1960, 1970, and 1980, Bartel and Lichtenberg (1987) related the proportion of employees with more than a high school education to the mean age of capital equipment in the industry, as well as to the R&D intensity (ratio of expenditures on R&D to the value of output). The R&D variable was interacted with age of capital on the assumption that new capital is most likely to embody new technology in R&D intensive industries. They found that the relation is significant. More educated workers were utilized, the younger the age of equipment, and this effect of new equipment was magnified in R&D intensive industries. The results held for workers with relatively recent vintages of education; they were not significant for workers above age 45.

Gill (1988) relates proportions of full time workers with specified education levels in annual pooled CPS data to Jorgenson's measures of multifactor productivity growth in 28 industries covering the whole economy over the periods 1960-1979 and 1970-1979. Correlations were positive for workers with more than high school, negative for high school dropouts, and zero for high school graduates. Gill also found that the proportion of more educated workers was greater in technologically progressive industries within each of eight broad occupation groups.

Lillard and Tan (1986) found a greater prevalence of job-training in sectors in which (Gollop & Jorgenson, 1980) measures of long-term productivity growth were high using CPS, NLS, and EOPP micro-data samples for between the late 1960s and early 1980s. In an unpublished paper, Tan (1987) focused on the relations between job-training and technical change in 1983-1984 CPS data, using Gollop-Jorgenson indexes for (1947-1973) and (1973-1979) periods. He found that the lagged, long-term productivity growth (1947-1973) had a positive effect on in-house training, reported in 1983-1984 jobs, and a negative effect on outside (classroom) training. The shorter run (1973-1979), productivity growth had the opposite effect: Classroom training increased, whereas on-the-job training was either unaffected or declined. It is not clear whether this effect represents "short-term" as distinguished from "long-run" trends or whether it was due to the specific historical period in which productivity stagnated.

My own study (1988d) utilized the Conrad-Jorgenson (1985) indexes[10] for an 18-industry coverage in the PSID. Each of the workers in the sample was classified by industry in which he worked in each of the years from 1968 to 1982. Proportions of workers whose education exceeded high school were larger in industries in which productivity growth was more rapid. This effect was observed without standardization as well as with standardization for the person's working age and the industry's rate of employment growth (or decline). The results of using contemporaneous (1970-1979) and lagged (1968-1969) productivity growth indexes in 1968-1982 PSID data suggest that an acceleration of productivity growth within one decade results in a much greater increase in utilization of more educated workers than the same rate sustained over two decades. The findings also suggest that, as productivity growth stops and so, presumably, technology ages, fewer educated workers are needed to handle it. Evidently,

worker training substitutes for the use of more educated workers in handling technologies that had been new in the initial decade.

The proportion of workers receiving training or learning on the job in 1976 was not clearly related to productivity growth in the 1970s but was strongly positively related to their industry's productivity growth earlier, in the 1960s. In sum, the findings in the PSID suggest that acceleration of technological change in a sector raises the share of educated workers in it, although initial effects on training are small. In the longer run, the use of training increases, both when technology ages and when it grows at a steady pace. The incidence of training effects is more pronounced for younger than for older workers.

Wage effects of industry demands. If the increased utilization of human capital reflects increases in industry demand, conditioned by the needs of technology, we should observe increases in relative wage differentials by education in industries with rapid productivity growth, at least in the short-run: The profitability of training should increase in such sectors. Strictly speaking, this is true if technological change is biased toward human capital, that is, if it increases the marginal productivity of more educated (trained) workers more than the marginal productivity of less educated (trained) workers. The relative increase in wages of more educated workers in progressive sectors was observed in the NLS by Lillard and Tan and in the CPS by them and by Gill (1988). The PSID data show similar results. The relative wage effects are smaller in the longer run than in the concurrent decade, but remain positive. We also observe steeper tenure-wage growth in industries with higher long-run productivity growth, an implication of longer-run increases in training that follow the initial acceleration of more educated hires. The effect for younger workers is larger than for older workers, as might be expected.

Wage growth with tenure in the firm is ascribable to training, whether or not the latter is firm specific, that is, whether or not it is usable in other firms. If the training is largely general, wage growth should also be steeper over total work experience in the more progressive industries, not only within the current firm. But industry experi-

ience is not well defined, because it is unlikely that a person observed working in an industry at a particular survey has been employed in it all along, although all of tenure is clearly spent in the indicated industry.

Still, using CPS data, Gill (1988) finds that long-run productivity growth raises the level and steepness of the putative experience-wage profiles of more educated workers, but it lowers and flattens the experience profiles of less educated workers. In sum, the evidence from various sources agrees that relative demands for education and training are increased by technological progress.

Turnover and unemployment. We have good evidence that the response to concurrent productivity growth is an increase in the proportion of educated workers, and the longer run response is an increase in training. Turnover rates behave correspondingly in the PSID. They are lower in the sectors with long-run high rates of productivity growth, and they are weakly or not at all affected in the sectors with concurrently accelerating productivity growth.

The negligible effect of concurrent productivity growth (1970-1979) on separation rates conceals some interesting differences. In the short run, separations actually increased for more educated workers (16 years and older). This increase was due to quits, not to layoffs. Quits increased among young workers, whereas layoffs declined more strongly (Mincer, 1988b). An interpretation of these findings is that, in the short run, rapid technological changes increase hiring of more educated workers. Some of the new hires come from other firms within the sector, which shows up in increased quits of the more educated, especially younger, workers in the sector. Other new hires of the better educated young workers come from inflows into sectors with higher rates of productivity growth from other sectors (Mincer, 1988b). In the longer run, when training activities increase in high productivity growth sectors, separation rates in them decrease. Even then, layoffs are reduced more than quits. This asymmetry in effects on quits and layoffs was not observed in the effects of training not linked to technological change reported in the first part of this article. The likely reason is that firms compelled by competition to technological innovations tend to finance much of the training of workers who may be more reluctant to invest in such training in view of looming obsolescence.[11]

The reduction in turnover, and especially in layoffs, implies that the incidence of unemployment also declines among experienced workers, at least in the longer run. Reported turnover declines in the longer run among all workers, but only slightly in the shorter-run among older workers. Conditional unemployment, that is, unemployment of movers, also declines among older workers whereas younger movers are not affected. Consequently, unemployment incidence declines in sectors with rapidly growing productivity in the long run among all workers, but less so in the short run.

The probability or incidence of unemployment $P(u)$ is not the same thing as the unemployment rate (u). The unemployment rate is the product of incidence $P(u)$ and of duration of unemployment $d(u)$. Evidence in the PSID shows that productivity growth in a sector tends to reduce the duration of unemployment slightly, if at all, in the short run, but clearly in the longer run (Mincer, 1988b). The main reason is the larger reduction in layoffs than in quit unemployment, as layoff unemployment is characterized by longer duration than quit unemployment.

The finding that technological change *tends to reduce* unemployment in "high-tech" sectors runs counter to the widely held fear of the "specter of technological unemployment." Economic theorists from Ricardo to Hicks held technological unemployment to be a likely possibility in the short-run, but less likely in the longer run. And workers' fear of technological displacement is not uncommon. The recent finding that, *on average*, unemployment is reduced in the longer run and *not increased* in the short run seems rather surprising (Mincer, 1988b). Yet, what the old and still standard analyses miss is the insight that two processes are set-off by technological changes: A waning series of displacements and a waxing process of worker adaptation that makes attachment to the firm more durable. The data suggests that in the aggregate the two forces practically cancel in the short run and that the second, which is due to human capital responses, dominates in the long run.[12]

Several considerations are worth not-

ing in connection with the findings: (a) The short run is a decade, which may conceal even shorter run effects. On the other hand, in the very short run, it is difficult to disentangle effects of productivity shocks from effects of business cycle phases. (b) Growth of the "open" economy, that is, of world trade, in recent times may have placed the specter of technological unemployment in sectors with lagging rather than leading productivity. This is entirely consistent with the findings and with the apparent

paradox that Japan, which has experienced the most rapid productivity growth in recent decades, also had the lowest unemployment rates. (c) The analyses did not distinguish explicitly between technological changes resulting in cost-cutting in producing old products and the introduction of new products. The latter are more likely to have positive employment effects, even in the short run, and may create new industries at a more detailed level of aggregation. (d) Indexes of labor productivity growth, that is, of growth of output per hour of labor were also used as alternatives to total (multifactor) productivity growth in our equations, but are not shown here. They were no less significant than the productivity growth indexes, suggesting that human capital complementarity or "bias" applies both to technical change and to physical capital, though vintages of the latter clearly matter.

Some Applications

The remarkably low labor turnover rate (and related unemployment rate) in Japan has attracted a great deal of attention. Often exaggerated as "life-time employment," it is seen as a reflection of a culture that puts great emphasis on loyalty. Yet, in the same culture, turnover rates were a great deal higher prior to World War II. Their decline is attributable to remarkably rapid technological progress in Japan since 1950. The technological catch-up required

sizable investments in human capital in schools and in enterprises. The phenomenal growth of educational attainment in Japan in the recent decades is well known. The even more intense effort to adapt, train, and retrain workers for continuous rapid technological change is not visible in national data, given the accounting difficulties described in the first section. However, effects of training on wage growth and turnover are visible in a negative relation within industrial sectors observed in Japan and in the U.S. (Mincer & Higuchi, 1988). Moreover, industries with more rapid productivity growth had both steeper individual wage profiles and lesser turnover rates in both countries. Indeed, given estimates of productivity effects in that study, a four-fold rate of productivity growth in Japan compared to the U.S. in the 1960-1979 period, predicted rather well the over three-fold steeper wage pro-

---

TABLE 3
Annual Productivity Growth, Tenure-Wage Growth, Separation Rates (%) per month in Japan and in the U.S. (1960-1979)

A. Comparisons of Productivity Effects	Japan	U.S.	B. Training Costs in Comparable Plants	Japan	U.S.
Productivity growth	1.12	.26	Proportion of workers receiving training	24.4%	13.5%
Tenure-wage growth	4.7	1.5	Cost per worker	$134	$59
Separation rate	.9	3.5	Cost per new hire	$1000	$215

Rows 2 and 3 in panel A of Table 3 show the differences between the U.S. and Japan, which can be explained as effects of differential rates of productivity growth (row 1). Differences in training which produce the effects are shown in panel B, based on a sample survey of comparable U.S. and Japanese manufacturing plants.

files and the less than one-third frequency of firm separations in Japan (Table 3, panel A). Differences in training costs in a sample survey of comparable U.S. and Japanese plants are shown in panel B of Table 3. These represent the link between the rates of productivity growth and the wage growth and turnover effects.

Current research suggests that technological change produces increased market demands for human capital. The reviewed evidence is stronger on the effects of *acceleration* of productivity growth than on long-term trends in rates of growth. More research across sectors, periods, and countries is needed. Even at this stage, the evidence suggests the resolution of the longstanding puzzle of the long-run relative stability of rates of return to education in the face of continuous expansion of education. Without growing demands by industry for educated and skilled workers, increasing supplies of such workers would depress educational differentials in wages to the point where rates of return to educational investments would fall to zero or below. But, because growing demands by industry, conditioned by technological change and capital accumulation, are a major factor in inducing increasing supplies of educated labor, the profitability of education can be maintained, in the long-run, at levels roughly comparable to that of other investments. □

---

[1]Two expositions accessible to noneconomists are in Mincer (1979, 1984).

[2]One question asked was: "On a job like yours, how long would it take the average new person to become fully trained and qualified?" This question followed another about training prior to the current job, thereby indicating an estimate of training attached to the current job. Another question asked whether the current job provided "learning that could help in promotion or in getting a better job."

[3]It can be shown that the unemployment rate $u = P(u) \times d(u)/1-d(o)$, where $d(u)$ is the duration (weeks) of unemployment, and $d(o)$ is the time out of the labor force during the year. The negative relation between education and duration of unemployment is not pronounced. A study by Topel (1984), based on other data sources (CPS) and methodology, finds a weak positive relation.

[4]Or with unreported training. Training was not reported in jobs preceding the 1976 firm nor in jobs which started after 1978. Consequently, the effects cited in the text are understated.

[5]See note 2 above.

[6]Gains in moving were measured as the percentage change in wages over the year during which the worker changed employers.

[7]The formula shown in Table 2, footnote 1, is derived in Mincer (1988d).

[8]Details of these calculations are presented in Mincer, 1988d.

[9]Reasons for underinvestment in training may involve workers' low income, minimum wages, and fears of capital loss in the case of specific training.

[10]The Conrad-Jorgenson indexes are an aggregation of Gollop-Jorgenson indexes to a broader industry level, matching more closely the industrial detail of the PSID. Also, the time period covered in Conrad-Jorgenson (1960-1979) is more congruent with the period covered in the PSID.

[11]Moreover, it appears (according to calculations in Mincer, 1988d) that, despite the high rate of obsolescence, 75% of the potential returns on the investment in training are captured within four to five years.

[12]Training and retraining responses appear to be quicker in Japan, where productivity growth has been much more rapid than in the U.S. in the recent (post-1950) decades. In Japan all the "longer run" effects show up in the concurrent decade (Mincer & Higuchi, 1988).

Acknowledgement: Research summarized here was partially supported by the Spencer Foundation, National Science Foundation, and the U.S. Department of Education. Helpful comments were received from the editors and from Robert Topel.

Barron, J., Black, D., & Lowenstein, M. (1989). Job matching and on the job training. *Journal of Labor Economics, 7*, 1–19.

Bartel, A., & Lichtenberg, F. (1987). The comparative advantage of educated workers in implementing new technology. *The Review of Economics and Statistics, 69*, 1–11.

Becker, G. (1975). *Human capital* (2nd ed.). Chicago, IL: University of Chicago Press.

Becker, G., & Stigler, J. (1974). Law enforcement, malfeasance, and compensation of enforcers. *Journal of Legal Studies, 3*, 1–18.

Blakemore, A., & Hoffman, D. (1988). *Seniority rules and productivity*. Unpublished manuscript, Arizona State University, Tempe, AZ.

Brown, J. (1983). *Are those paid more really no more productive?* Unpublished manuscript, State University of New York, Stony Brook, NY.

Brown, J. (1988). *Why do wages increase with tenure?* Unpublished manuscript, State University of New York, Stony Brook, NY.

Conrad, K., & Jorgenson, D. (1985). *Sectoral Productivity Gaps, 1960–1979*. Cambridge, MA: Harvard University, Economics Department.

Duncan, G., & Hoffman, S. (1978). Training and earnings. In G. Duncan & J. Morgan (Eds.), *Five thousand American families*. Ann Arbor, MI: University of Michigan, Institute for Social Research.

Duncan, G., & Stafford, F. (1980). The use of time and technology by households in the United States. *Research in Labor Economics, 3*, 335–374.

Gill, I. (1988). *Technological change, education, and obsolescence of human capital*. Unpublished manuscript, University of Chicago, Chicago, IL.

Gollop, F., & Jorgenson, D. (1980). U.S. productivity growth by industry. In J. Kendrick & B. Vaccaro (Eds.), *New developments in productivity measurement*. Chicago, IL: University of Chicago Press. NBER Studies in Income and Wealth.

Gronau, R. (1988). Sex related wage differentials. *Journal of Labor Economics, 6*, 277–301.

Jovanovic, B. (1979). Job matching and the theory of turnover. *Journal of Political Economy, 87*, 972–990.

Lazear, E. (1979). Why is there mandatory retirement? *Journal of Political Economy, 87*, 1261–1284.

Lillard, L., & Tan, H. (1986). *Private sector training* (Report No. 3331-DOL). Santa Monica, CA: Rand Corporation.

Lynch, L. (1988). *Private sector training and its impact*. Unpublished manuscript, Massachusetts Institute of Technology, Cambridge, MA.

Mincer, J. (1962). On the job training: Cost, returns, and implications. *Journal of Political Economy, 70*(2), 50–79.

Mincer, J. (1979). Human capital and earnings. In D.M. Windham (Ed.), *Economics dimensions of education*. Washington, DC: National Academy of Education:

Mincer, J. (1984). Human capital and economic growth. *Economics of Education Review, 3*, 195–205.

Mincer, J. (1988a). *Education and unemployment*. Unpublished manuscript, National Center for Education and Employment, Teachers' College, Columbia University, New York.

Mincer, J. (1988b). *Human capital effects of technological change*. Unpublished manuscript, National Center for Education and Employment, Teachers' College, Columbia University, New York.

Mincer, J. (1988c). *Job training, wage growth, and labor turnover*. Unpublished manuscript.

Mincer, J. (1988d). *Labor market effects of human capital*. Paper presented at the NAVE Conference, Washington, DC.

Mincer, J., & Higuchi, Y. (1988). Wage structures and labor turnover in the U.S. and in Japan. *Journal of the Japanese and International Economies, 2*, 97–133.

Oi, W. (1962). Labor as a quasi-fixed factor of production. *Journal of Political Economy, 70*, 538–555.

Parsons, D. (1986). *Job-training in the postschooling period*. Unpublished manuscript, Ohio State University, Columbus, OH.

Salop, J., & Salop, S. (1976). Self-selection and turnover in the labor market. *Quarterly Journal of Economics, 90*, 619–628.

Schultz, T. W. (1975). The value of the ability to deal with disequilibria. *Journal of Economic Literature, 13*, 827–846.

Tan, H. (1987). *Technical change and its consequences for training and earnings*. Unpublished manuscript, Rand Corporation, Santa Monica, CA.

Topel, R. (1984). Equilibrium earnings, turnover, and unemployment. *Journal of Labor Economics, 2*, 500–522.

Welch, F. (1970). Education in production. *Journal of Political Economy, 78*, 35–59.

Part II
Screening, Signalling and All That!

EDUCATIONAL PRODUCTION RELATIONSHIPS

Education, Technology, and the Characteristics of Worker Productivity*

By HERBERT GINTIS
Harvard University

Economists have long noted the relationship between the level of schooling in workers and their earnings. The relationship has been formalized in numerous recent studies of the rate of return to schooling and the contribution of education to worker productivity. Almost no attempt has been made, however, to determine the mechanism by which education affects earnings or productivity. In the absence of any direct evidence, it is commonly assumed that the main effect of schooling is to raise the level of cognitive development of students and that it is this increase which explains the relationship between schooling and earnings. This view of the schooling-earnings linkage has provided the conceptual framework for studies which seek to "control" for the quality of schooling through the use of variables such as scores on achievement tests and IQ. [26, 46]

* This research was supported by a grant from the Carnegie Foundation of New York to the Center for Educational Policy Research, Harvard Graduate School of Education, and a separate grant from the Social and Rehabilitation Service, U. S. Dept. of Health, Education, and Welfare. Special thanks are due to Stephan Michelson, Christopher Jencks and Samuel Bowles, who aided the research through its various stages, and the Union for Radical Political Economics collective at Harvard, whose members helped broaden its scope. This work is part of a larger project in process jointly with Samuel Bowles, on the political economy of education. The arguments presented herein have been significantly abridged, in conformance with stringent space limitations. Requests for amplification of the material should be addressed to the author.

The objective of this paper is to demonstrate that this interpretation is fundamentally incorrect. It will be seen that rejection of the putative central role of cognitive development in the schooling-earnings relationship requires a reformulation of much of the extant economic research on education, as well as a radical rethinking of the normative bases of the economics of education in particular, and neo-classical welfare economics in general. In Section I, I will present data to suggest that the contribution of schooling to worker earnings or occupational status cannot be explained by the relationship between schooling and the level of cognitive achievement. Indeed, the data there introduced strongly suggest the importance of noncognitive personality characteristics which have direct bearing on worker earnings and productivity. In Section II, I will give substantive content to the relevant personality variables operative in the relationship between education and earnings. With the theoretical literature on the personality requisites of adequate role-performance in a bureaucratic and hierarchical work-enrivonment as a frame of reference, I will sketch some mechanisms through which schools affect earnings. This involves scrutinizing the social relations of education and the pattern of rewards and penalties revealed in grading practices. I will argue that the authority, motivational, and interpersonal relations codified in the "social structure" of schools are closely similar to those of the factory and office. Thus a path of individual personality development conducive to performance in the student's future work roles is facilitated. Further, I will show that the grading structure in the classroom reflects far more than student's cognitive attainment, by affording independent reward to the development of traits necessary to adequate job performance.

If my basic thesis is correct, much of the existing body of economic literature on schooling must be reconsidered. First, we must redefine the concept of "quality" in education, particularly in studies of the determinants of earnings which have thus far relied on measures of cognitive development as the sole measure of educational quality (e.g., [9]). Second, the extensive body of research on "educational production functions" is seen to lack economic relevance, since the dependent variables in most of these studies have been restricted to measures of cognitive achievement [4, 9, 28]. Third, the extensive body of literature on resource allocation in schooling—extending from planning model to rate of return studies—requires reformulation. The normative base of these studies requires that the mechanism by which schooling contributes to earnings operates independently from the character structures of the individual students. That is, they assume that the process of schooling does not affect the tastes and personalities of the future workers being processed for higher productivity. Yet the data below strongly suggest that the economic productivity of schooling is due primarily to the inculcation of personality characteristics which may be generally agreed to be inhibiting of personal development. The "economic productivity" of schooling must be measured against an "opportunity cost" reflected in the development of an alienated and repressed labor force. Fourth, the

above point is simply a special case of a more general problem in neoclassical welfare economics. Our analysis shows that taste and personalities are not determined outside the economic system, but are rather developed as part of the economic activities about which social policy is to be made. Thus the main theorems of welfare economics, being based on the independence of individual preferences from the structure of economic institutions [19], fail.

While our evidence suggests the reformulation of much of the existing work in the economics of education and welfare theory, it may also provide resolutions to some of the outstanding anomalies that have arisen in recent years. For example, a number of studies have shown very low monetary returns to the education of lower class people and blacks in the U. S., even with the level of cognitive development taken into account [51]. These results are readily explained by our model, where they likely result from the failure of schooling to inculcate the required noncognitive personality traits in the observed groups. Moreover, it is often found, both in the U. S. and in underdeveloped countries, that the economic return to vocational schooling is quite low [45]. This is especially surprising in that vocational education dwells exclusively on the supposedly "economically relevant" content of schooling. Our interpretation renders the finding of low economic returns of vocational schooling understandable, in view of its misplaced emphasis on the "skill content" of schooling, and a corresponding underemphasis on the broader socialization function involving the generation of a disciplined, obedient, and well-motivated workforce. Lastly, recent years have seen the revival of so-called "genetic" theories to explain the pattern of racial and social class inequalities [15, 32]. Neither proponents nor opponents of this view seem seriously to have questioned the importance of cognitive ability in occupational status and earnings, but have restricted their considerations to the narrow question of "heritability" of intelligence, in the naive view that IQ lies at the heart of economic success. Our results would indicate that this debate is close to irrelevant, save at the very extremes of the "ability" distribution.

The Cognitive Element in Schooling's Contribution to Worker Earnings

The "market value" of a worker depends on a certain array of personal characteristics—cognitive, affective, and ascriptive.[1] The bulk of modern sociological theory affirms the minor importance of ascriptive traits in the general allocation of social roles and status positions, at least among white, male Americans. Thus we may take the individual traits generated or selected through schooling, insofar as they relate to the augmentation of worker earnings, as predominantly cognitive and affective. Hence we propose to test the adequacy of two polar "ideal type" models—the Cognitive and the Affective. According to the Cognitive Model of education's contribution to worker earnings and occupational status (Y), the variable E (years of education, corrected for differences in "quality" in the form of physical, teacher, peer-group, and content resources) is a proxy for a set of cognitive achievement variables A (e.g., reading speed, comprehension, reasoning ability, mathematical or scientific achievement). According to the Affective Model, on the

[1] By 'cognitive characteristics' we mean individual capacities to logically combine, analyze, interpret, and apply informational symbols. By 'affective characteristics' we mean propensities, codified in the individual's personality structure, to respond in stable emotional and motivational patterns, to demands made upon him in concrete social situations; and by 'ascriptive characteristics', we mean such non-operational attributes as the individual's race, sex, caste, religion, social class, eye color, geographical region, etc.

other hand, E is a proxy for a set of relevant personality variables P. Using a linear regression model to capture the income- and occupational-status-generating process, a test of the Cognitive Model is particularly immediate. If Y is a measure of income and/or occupational status, then the "contribution of education" can be interpreted as the beta coefficient in the regression

$$(1) \qquad Y = a + b_{YE}E + u.$$

If the Cognitive Model is correct, then in the extended regression

$$(2) \qquad Y = a + b_{YA \cdot E}A + b_{YE \cdot A}E + u,$$

we expect $b_{YE \cdot A} = 0$. That is, introducing achievement variables into the restricted regression (1) reduces the contribution of E by 100%. If, on the other hand, the Affective Model is correct, and if A and P are related only through their common dependence on E, then $b_{YE} = b_{YE \cdot A}$, and the reduction in the contribution of E is 0%.

Clearly we have divergent implications, empirically testable by available data. Appendix I exhibits the results of many studies, including measures of Y, A, and E, comprising all investigations the author has come upon.[2] These studies, despite their divergent measures of relevant variables and use of distinct sample populations, show two broad uniformities: (a) The reduction in the coefficient of E due to the introduction of achievement variables is much closer to zero than to 100%—the actual range is 4% to 35%; and (b) the increase in explained variance is negligible—i.e., less than 5% of explained variance. At first glance, these studies provide strong support for the Affective Model, and indi-

[2] These are restricted to U. S. samples, predominantly white, male, average mean intelligence. Also, I have indiscriminantly mixed "achievement" and "intelligence" measures of A. The results of these investigations are strikingly similar for both measures, so their synthesis presents no problems for the purposes of our investigation.

EDUCATIONAL PRODUCTION RELATIONSHIPS 269

cate that cognitive development is not the central means by which education enhances worker success.

Two possible objections to this analysis, however, induce us to expand the model. On the one hand, there may be relations between P and A beyond their common dependence on E. This might occur either through a direct relation between P and A (i.e., income-relevant personality traits facilitate the acquisition of cognitive achievement—see below) or because both A and P depend on variables not included in our simple equations, such as genes and social class. In either case, the reduction in b_{YE} through the inclusion of A would exceed that of a properly specified model, and the outcome would be even more in favor of the Affective Model, in that this model becomes compatible with the observed small but significant reduction (see below). On the other hand, one might hold that while theoretically the introduction of A into the income-education regression should reduce the coefficient of E to zero, in fact, both A and E are so subject to errors in measurement that the results are significantly altered in practice.[3] In particular, if E is really a "proxy" for A, but A is measured with significantly greater error than E, the latter becomes a more reliable indicator of achievement than A itself.

We shall take these objections seriously and introduce a more extensive model, including important background measures of abilities (I) and social class (S). Moreover, we shall allow for the "observed" measures of E and A, which we denote by

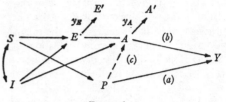

FIGURE 1

E' and A', to include an element of random error, so that $r_{EE'} = y_E$ and $r_{AA'} = y_A$. It will be assumed that all errors are uncorrelated, so that recursive regression analysis may be applied.[4] The recursive schema is shown in Figure 1, where the elimination of path (a) corresponds to the Cognitive Model, and the elimination of path (b) to the Affective Model (the dotted arrow (c) will be discussed later).[5] Here P is treated as a "hypothetical variable" [29], in that we shall not specify its content in this Section. As part of the Affective Model, however, we shall assume that education (E) and social class (S) are *important* elements in the determination of P, and that education has at least as great a direct importance as social class.

We must now recalculate the "expected" fall in b_{YE} due to the introduction of cognitive variables, based on this larger model, and with y_A and y_E as parameters. It will be shown that for all reasonable values of these parameters—and for many unreasonable as well—the Affective Model predicts far more accurately than the Cognitive. The Affective Model in its crude form tends to *underpredict* (predicted reduction=0%, while actual re-

---

[3] By "errors of variables" we include more than simple test reliabilities and validities in reportage, but the larger errors arising from an incomplete or a partially misdirected measuring instrument. Thus to measure E by "years of educational attainment" introduces errors because this measure abstracts from the *quality* of schooling. Similarly, a measure of "achievement" may inherently capture only a portion of the "theoretical" variable.

[4] The statistical techniques of recursive regression, or "path analysis", are described in [14].

[5] It might be asked why certain paths have been *a priori* excluded from Figure 1. That Y depends directly only on A and P follows from our exclusion of the influence of ascriptive traits and further from the very definition of A and P themselves; insofar as Y depends on I, I should be included among the variables A, and insofar as Y depends on traits involved in S, S must be included directly in P. Studies show moreover, that the direct path from S to A is negligible [29, 40].

duction $= 4\% - 35\%$). Hence in reestimating its predictions, we shall remain conservative by always underestimating the Affective Model's predicted reduction in b_{YE} when A is introduced. Manipulation of the normal equations in two-variable regression ([33], p. 61) gives

$$\frac{b_{YE \cdot A}}{b_{YE}} = 1 - \frac{r_{EA}}{1 - r_{EA}^2}(z - r_{EA})$$

where $z = r_{AP}/r_{EP}$. In terms of the imperfectly measured variables E' and A', this clearly becomes

$$(4) \quad \frac{b_{YE' \cdot A'}}{b_{YE'}} = 1 - y_A^2 \frac{r_{EA}}{1 - y_A^2 y_E^2 r_{EA}^2}$$
$$\cdot [z - r_{EA}] + [1 - y_E^2]r_{EA}.$$

To estimate this equation, taking y_E and y_A as parameters, we require estimates of r_{EA} and $[z - r_{EA}]$. A conservative assessment of the Affective Model requires that we choose a small value for r_{EA}, since the larger is r_{EA} (holding $z - r_{EA}$ constant), the larger the predicted reduction in $b_{YE'}$. Empirical measures [11, 13, 26] show $r_{E'A'} \approx .6$ to .7. Since $r_{EA} = r_{E'A'}/y_A y_E$, the assumption of significant errors in variables pushes r_{EA} quite high (in terms of the assumptions of Table 1, even above unity).

TABLE 1

y_A^2	y_E^2	Reduction in $b_{YE'}$, percentage		
		Model A $p_{AP}=0$	Model A $P_{AP}=.12$	Cognitive Model
1.00	1.00	00%	24%	100%
0.75	0.85	08%	19%	73%
0.60	0.70	11%	18%	49%
0.50	0.70	09%	15%	40%
0.80	0.80	12%	22%	72%
0.80	0.70	16%	27%	71%
0.70	0.60	17%	26%	62%

However, there is reason to believe the error in measuring A is *not* independent of E (e.g., through the conceptual variable

"test-taking ability," which might increase with level of education) so our underestimate of r_{EA} will take the form of *not* correcting for measurement error; that is, we assume E accounts for about 50% of the variance in achievement.

Similarly, we shall settle for an underestimate of $[z - r_{EA}]$. Abstracting from p_{AP}, and using the fundamental theorem of path analysis [14], we have

$$(5) \quad r_{AP} - r_{AE}r_{PE}$$
$$= p_{AI}p_{PS}\{r_{EA}[1 - p_{EI}^2 - p_{EA}^2$$
$$- r_{EA}p_{EI}p_{ES}] - p_{EI}p_{ES}\}.$$

Thus in general we have

$$(6) \quad [z - r_{EA}]$$
$$= r_{PE}^{-1}\{p_{AP} + p_{AI}p_{PS}$$
$$\cdot [r_{EA}(1 - R_E^2)p_{EI}p_{ES}(1 - r_{EA}^2)]\}.$$

Using figures from [11, 40], we find the highest estimate of the second term on the left-hand side of (6) to be $p_{PS}(.05)/r_{PE}$. Since

$$(7) \quad r_{PE} = p_{PE} + r_{ES}p_{PS},$$

we have

$$(8) \quad 1 = (p_{PE}/r_{PE}) + r_{ES}(p_{PS}/r_{PE}).$$

Since $r_{ES} \geq 0.6$ [15], we have (p_{PS}/r_{PE}) < 1.7. But assuming the direct link between E and P to be strong (an assumption of the Affective Model), this estimate is seen to be significantly inflated. Indeed, if S and E are roughly equal in their direct linkage with P, (p_{PS}/r_{PE}) is significantly *less* than unity. At any rate, the elimination of the second term in (6) will not bias our results greatly against the Affective Model.

In treating r_{PE}, we shall again settle for an underestimate of $[z - r_{EA}]$. We have

$$(9) \quad P = p_{PE} \cdot E + p_{PS} \cdot S + p_u U_p$$

where U_p is the contribution to P outside the model. If we then write $p_{PS} = p_{PE/e}$, we find that

(10) $r_{BP} = R_p/\sqrt{[(1-r_{ES}^2)/(a+r_{ES})^2]+1}$.

where R_P is the "proportion" of the variance of P explained within the model. Moreover, taking $r_{ES} = .6$ [1, 13], the denominator on the right side of (10) declines from 1.24 to 1.00 as "a" passes from $\frac{1}{2}$ to infinity. Thus we can safely take

(11) $R_P^{-1} < r_{BP}^{-1} < (1.2)R_P^{-1}$.

Returning to (6) and (4), we find that the Affective Model implies a reduction in $b_{YE'}$ with the following upper bound:

(12) $\dfrac{b_{YE' \cdot A'}}{b_{YE'}} < 1 - y_A^2 \cdot \dfrac{r_{BA}}{1 - y_A^2 y_E^2 r_{BA}^2}$
$\cdot \{ p_{AP} R_P^{-1} + [1 - y_E^2] r_{BA} \}$.

Moreover, this upper bound is probably a good approximation as well, so (12) can be treated as the "prediction" of the reduction in $b_{YE'}$ by the Affective Model.

We shall test equation (12) using two estimates of p_{AP}. First, we shall assume there is no direct relation between A and P, so $p_{AP} = 0$. Second, we shall assume a small direct relation, taking (arbitrarily) $p_{AP} = .12$.[6]

The corresponding analysis for the Cognitive Model's prediction of the reduction in $b_{YE'}$ follows from a similar but simpler derivation. We find

(13) $\dfrac{b_{YE' \cdot A'}}{b_{YE'}} = 1 - \dfrac{y_A^2}{1 - y_A^2 y_E^2 r_{BA}^2}$
$\cdot [1 - y_E^2 r_{BA}^2]$.

Table 1 illustrates our predictions for alternative hypotheses as to the validities of A and E, and with our alternative

[6] Theoretical evidence of such a direct relationship can be found in [44]. In addition, I shall suggest below that a central trait developed through schooling and relevant to job adequacy is "motivation according to external reward," which is clearly conducive to higher levels of cognitive achievement.

assumptions concerning p_{AP}.[7] If the empirically derived reductions shown in Appendix I are correct, the Cognitive Model must be fairly decisively rejected. Moreover, the Affective Model "predicts" with the proper order of magnitude. Of course, the latter's validity can only be ascertained when a correct specification of the variables P are obtained. A preliminary attempt in this direction will be presented in the following Section. Roughly, if education does contribute to earnings, and if this contribution cannot be accounted for in terms of cognitive variables, it is reasonable to expect the noncognitive traits rewarded through grading and promotion, hence presumably integrated into the student's personality, to do the job.[8]

The Structure of Social Relations and the Pattern of Rewards in Schooling

The cogency of the Affective Model depends in the last instance on the quantative specification of the personality variables P. Ideally, this would involve isolating a fixed set of measurable traits, exhibiting their concordance with level of occupational status or income, showing their correlation with years of school, and describing the mechanisms by which schools generate them. In this section, our

[7] As previously noted, Table 1 is based on the assumption that $r_{BA}^2 = .5$. The reader can verify that these results are quite insensitive to alternative specifications of r_{BA}^2.

[8] Approaches to the sources of worker productivity other than that followed in this Section are available. For instance, noting that the demand and supply of educated labor have increased in step in recent years, in that relative wages have not significantly changed [2, 22], we may ask if the rise in demand can be accounted for in terms of cognitive variables. The cognitive requirements for jobs included in [47] exhibit high reliabilities [16], and even tend to overestimate these requirements [38]. An analysis of this body of data [48, 39] shows cognitive demands requiring a total increase of 0.44 years of education per worker, between 1940 and 1960, whereas the actual increase in level of education is several times this value. Thus the demand for "educated labor" must include significant noncognitive components.

aim will be considerably less ambitious. We shall outline a set of traits held by long sociological tradition [37, 49, 50] as requisite for adequate job functioning in production characterized by bureaucratic order and hierarchical control. We then show that schooling is conducive to the development of these traits in students.[9]

We shall focus on two aspects of schooling central to the patterning of personality development. First, the *structure of social relations* in education—including sources of motivation, authority and control, and types of sanctioned interpersonal relations—by requiring the student to function routinely and over long periods of time in role situations comprising specific expectations on the part of the teacher, other students, and administrators, tends to elicit uniformities of response codified in individual personality [5, 12]. Second, the system of grading, by rewarding certain classroom behavior patterns and penalizing others, tends to reinforce certain modes of individual response to social situations. According to any of the variants of behaviorist psychology, this *pattern of reward* will educe the corresponding pattern of personality traits in the students. Part of the myth of liberal education is that, however important the teacher's expectation may be in eliciting student performance, his actual *assessment* and *grading* of this performance depends only on concrete, observed cognitive attainments. Yet

[9] In this paper we shall treat only those required traits which are *common* to all levels in the hierarchy of production, and are inculcated in most schools on all levels. Actually the personality requisites of job adequacy no doubt vary from level to level within the hierarchy of production, and different levels of schooling (e.g., grade school, high school, junior college, college) likely reflect these differential needs. Moreover, within a particular educational level, we would expect different types of schooling to subsist side by side (e.g., ghetto, working-class, and middle-class-suburban high schools), reflecting the differential positions in the production hierarchy that its students are destined to fill. These complications, however important, cannot be treated here.

studies show that cognitive variables never account for more than 30% of the variance in grade point average (37). In addition, many studies illustrate the importance of specific personality measure in prediction grades [17, 25, 30], although these by and large correct inadequately for actual achievement levels.

Before attempting a systematic assessment of the body of empirical information on the effect of social structure and pattern of reward in schooling on personality development, I should like to present two studies [19] illustrating the breadth and counter-intuitive nature of the process of grading, in which explicit measures of cognitive achievement are available. First, an analysis based on data collected on 649 upper-ability senior-high school males [31] (National Merit Scholarship Finalists) shows no value of any combination of five achievement variables (College Entrance Examination Board: SAT-Math, SAT-Verbal, Scientific Performance, Humanities Comprehension, Scientific Comprehension), despite significant variance in these achievement measures and in grades within the sample. Of some 65 additional personality variables, two-"Citizenship-Teacher's Rating" (CitT) and "Drive to Achieve-Student Self Rating" (DrA)— have greatest power to predict GPA, with $p < .001$. This example illustrates (a) since these traits are not rewarded *through* their contribution to achievement, that teachers grade *independently* on the basis of personality; (b) since DrA is rewarded, that subjective motivation is taken into consideration in grading; (c) since CitT is positively rewarded and can be interpreted as "conforming to the dominant role-structure" of the school, that grading reinforces the student's personality development through participation in the particular structure of social relations in schools, and; (d) while grades depend on achievement in general, when 'ability' is controlled, little additional effect of achievement can be detected, so the *subjective experience* of an individual student (who of course cannot control his intelligence) is that grades depend primarily on affective behavior. In this study, the pattern of reward is no less reflected in the remaining personality traits (Tables 2–4). Thus Table 2 shows that students are uniformly penalized for creativity, autonomy, initiative,

TABLE 2—PERSONALITY VARIABLES CORRELATED WITH GPA CORRECTED FOR ACHIEVEMENT, CITT, AND DRA (SIGNIFICANCE LEVELS IN PARENTHESIS)

Positively Rewarded:	SAT-Math (15%)
Perseverance (1%)	Scientific Comprehension (15%)
Good Student (1%)	*Negatively Rewarded (Penalized):*
Self-Evaluation (5%)	Independence-Self-Reliance (1%)
Popular (5%)	Initiative (5%)
Acceleration of Development (5%)	Complexity of Thought (5%)
Mastery (5%)	Originality (Barron) (6%)
Control (6%)	Originality (11%)
Status (11%)	Independence of Judgment (13%)
Popularity (TR) (13%)	Creative Activities (13%)
Suppression of Aggression (14%)	Curious (14%)

TABLE 3—CORRELATIONS OF VARIOUS PERSONALITY TRAITS WITH CITT

Positively Rewarded:	Mastery (15%)
Deferred Gratification (1%)	Initiative (15%)
Perseverance (1%)	*Negatively Rewarded (Penalized):*
Control (1%)	Cognitive Flexibility (1%)
Popularity (1%)	Complexity of Thought (1%)
Social Leadership (1%)	Originality (Barron) (1%)
Good Student (Parent value) (1%)	Sense of Destiny (1%)
Self-Evaluation (1%)	DRS-Creativity (1%)
Scientific Comprehension (1%)	Independence of Judgment (5%)
Intellectuality (1%)	Independence-Self-Reliance (10%)
Esthetic Sensitivity (5%)	Curious (15%)
Suppression of Aggression (5%)	Self-Confidence (15%)
Comradeship-Sharing (5%)	Verbal Activity (15%)
SAT-Math (10%)	
Artistic Performance (10%)	

TABLE 4—CORRELATIONS OF VARIOUS PERSONALITY TRAITS WITH DRA

Positively Rewarded:	Initiative (1%)
Self-Evaluation (1%)	Status (1%)
Perseverance (1%)	Breadth of Interest (5%)
Deferred Gratification (1%)	SAT-Math (5%)
Originality (1%)	Scientific Performance (5%)
Independence (1%)	Verbal Activity (5%)
Responsibility (1%)	Conformity (10%)
Control (1%)	*Negatively Rewarded (Penalized):*
Artistic Performance (1%)	Cognitive Flexibility (1%)
Creative Activities (1%)	Complexity of Thought (1%)
Sense of Destiny (1%)	Originality (1%)
Popularity (1%)	Independence of Judgment (1%)
Social Leadership (1%)	SAT-Verbal (5%)
Good Student (1%)	
Mastery (1%)	

tolerance for ambiguity, and independence, even after correcting for achievement, CitT, and DrA, and rewarded for perseverance, good student values, and other traits indicative of docility, industry, and ego-control. Moreover, the content of CitT is exhibited in Table 3, showing a similar pattern of evaluative behavior on the part of the teacher, especially in the penalized traits (no doubt as a result of the objective needs of 'classroom control' in the typically-structured school, rather than his personal value-preferences). Lastly, Table 4 shows that DrA is associated with the same pattern of penalized traits, while the rewarded traits exhibit two separate dimensions: on the one hand, high DrA may involve conformity with classroom norms, and on the other, to their rejection in favor of autonomous personal development—hence the appearance of Artistic Performance, Creative Activities, Self-Confidence, Initiative, Self-Assurance, Breadth of Interest as associated with DrA.[10]

The National Merit Scholarship study is weak in two respects. First, it deals with only one ability grouping, and second, it aggregates over diverse study-areas—natural science, social science, humanities, language, etc. A similar result can be derived, however, from a path analysis the author has fit to data supplied by Cline [7], covering 114 high school seniors of varying ability, in the specific area of natural science performance. This data-source includes a measure of intelligence, three creativity measures, achievement level in science, a teacher rating of the student's "science potential," and average science grades over the three years of high school. Path analysis [19] indicates that

over the broader ability spectrum of students: (a) teacher attitudes are the major determinants of grades; (b) "achievement" is only one determinant of teacher attitudes, and hence of grades received; (c) intelligence is directly rewarded in terms of grades, beyond its contribution to actual achievement, whereas many other equally important determinants of achievement (e.g., "creativity") are in no way rewarded; (d) the direct effect of actual achievement on teacher attitudes is statistically insignificant.

The bulk of existing studies are compatible with these results, and hence tend to lend credence to the Affective Model. Moreover, these studies show that both structure and pattern of reward in schooling conform to the requisites of adequate job-performance in bureaucratically structured and hierarchically organized enterprise [37, 49, 50]. We can organize this discussion around four types of personality requisites—"Subordinancy," "Discipline," "Supremacy of Cognitive over Affective Modes of Response," and "Motivation according to External Reward."

Subordinacy. "The principle of hierarchical authority . . . is found in all bureaucratic structures . . . (in a) firmly ordered system of super- and sub-ordination." [49]. Subordinacy and proper orientation to authority are induced through the strict hierarchical lines—administration-teacher-student—of the school. As the worker relinquishes control over his activities on the job, so the student is first forced to accept, and later comes personally to terms with, his loss of autonomy and initiative to a teacher who acts as a superior authority, dispensing rewards and penalties. That proper subordinacy is a factor in grading as well is dramatized in our National Merit Scholarship study. It is supported by Gough [24], where "overachievers" (students whose grades exceed

[10] This divergence replicates [18]. Here, as throughout this Section, space limitation forbids adequate explanation of the content of these personality measures. Their precise coutent can be found in the corresponding sources, or in [19].

that predicted by their IQ) are marked by their teachers as "appreciative," "cooperative," and "reasonable," while "underachievers" are deemed "dissatisfied," "preoccupied," "rebellious," and "rigid." Striking additional support is found in [6] (see [19]).

Discipline. Weber emphasizes, "organizational discipline in the factory is founded upon a completely rational basis ... the optimum profitability of the individual worker is calculated like that of any material means of production. On the basis of this calculation, the American system of 'Scientific Management' enjoys the greatest triumphs in the rational conditioning and training of work-performance ... the psycho-physical apparatus of man is completely adjusted to the demands of the outer world . . . ." The extension from production on simple factory lines to bureaucratic organization both conserves and expands this need. In Merton's words [37], "bureaucratic structure exerts a constant pressure ... to be 'methodical, prudent, disciplined.' ... The bureaucracy ... must attain a high degree of reliability of behavior, and unusual degree of conformity with prescribed patterns of actions. Hence the fundamental importance of discipline. ... " Discipline is reflected in the educational system where regularity, punctuality, and quiescence assume proportions almost absurd in relation to the ostensible goals of "learning." Thus Gough [24] finds overachievers consistently rewarded for being "dependable," "reliable," "honest," and "responsible," (teacher ratings), and Gebhart and Hoyt [17] find them rewarded for "Consistency" (Edwards Personal Preference Inventory); our National Merit Scholarship study shows deferred gratification, perseverance, and control as central elements in the teacher's assessment of "citizenship," a highly rewarded trait. Dramatic conforma-

tion of discipline as independently rewarded through grades is supplied by a brilliant series of studies by Smith [42, 43, 44]. Noting that personality inventories suffer from low validities due to their abstraction from real-life environments, and low reliabilities due to the use of a single evaluative instrument, Smith turned to student peer-ratings of 42 common personality traits, based on each student's observation of the actual classroom behavior of his classmates. Factor analysis allowed the extraction of five general traits, stable across different samples and national cultures. One of these, a discipline factor which Smith calls "Strength of Character"—including such traits as "not a quitter," "conscientious," "responsible," "insistently orderly," "not prone to daydream," "determined-persevering,"—exhibits three times the contribution of R^2 in predicting post-high-school performance than any combination of thirteen cognitive variables.

Cognitive vs. affective modes of response. Occupational roles have been characterized as requiring an upgrading of cognitive demands. Yet the contribution of schooling to job-adequacy may be more accurately described as evincing a *cognitive mode,* and suppressing an affective mode, of reacting to bureaucratic situations. That bureaucratic order requires the dominance of cognitive modes of response has been emphasized by Weber [49]: "bureaucratization ... very strongly furthers the development of 'rational matter-of-factness' ... Its specific nature, which is welcomed by capitalism, develops the more perfectly the more the bureaucracy is 'dehumanized,' the more completely it succeeds in eliminating from official business love, hatred, and all purely personal, irrational, and emotional elements which escape calculation." More recently, Keniston [35] notes, "The preferred technique of technology involves two related principles: that we give priority to cognition, and we subordinate feeling. . . . Thus feeling as a force of independent value—all of the passions, impulses, needs, drives, and idealisms which in some societies are the central rationales of existence—are increasingly minimized, suppressed, harnessed, controlled, and dominated by the more cognitive parts of the psyche." The structure of social relations in education speak to industrial needs. In Dreeben's [12] words, "Although affection is not proscribed in schools, it is expressed less intensely and under more limited circumstances (than in family or peer-group relations). In the long run, matter-of-factness in the accomplishment of tasks governs the relationship between teachers and pupils. . . . " This pattern is repeated in the pattern of rewards in schools. Thus Gebhart and Hoyt [17] find overachievers in high school higher on "Order," and underachievers higher on "Nurturance," and "Affiliation." (Edwards Personal Preference Inventory) Our analysis of the National Merit Scholarship data shows "Originality," "Complexity of Thought," and "Creative Activities" penalized, and similar measures of affective dominance are negatively related to the two main predictors of high grades—CitT and DrA. A similar tension between norms of education and affective, creative development is dramatically illustrated in [18]. Lastly, the Cline study reported above again illustrates that teachers tend to reward the development of cognitive modes but not affective modes, even when these affective modes are conducive to higher levels of cognitive achievement.

Cathection of External Reward. In a situation where the attributes of work and technology are determined essentially independent of human needs and worker control, by criteria of profit and "efficiency"

in the narrow sense, the process of work—as an activity which ideally might provide immediate satisfaction and contribute to individual psychic development as an outlet for creativity, initiative and worker solidarity—naturally acquires little intrinsic subjective value. Moreover, in the absence of a solidary and cohesive social community, and in a situation where workers have essentially no control over the attributes of the product of their work the internal *goal* of work—the contribution to social dividend—provides no source of gratification and personal reward [20, 22, 23]. The lack of subjective reward of work either in terms of process or goal is the key to what in Marxist terms is called "alienation from process and product" [23], and requires workers to be motivated to conscientious and efficient activity through rewards external to work as such —money or hierarchical status [41].

The development of this motivational capacity is entrusted to socialization mechanisms, among which educational institutions are the most prominent and socially flexible. Indeed, in important respects the system of universal education arose during the Industrial Revolution in response to this need [8, 34]. The structure of social relations in schools reproduce rather faithfully the capitalist work-environment. Learning (the activity) is not undertaken through the student's intrinsic interest in the *process* of learning, nor is he motivated by the *goal* of the educational process (possession of knowledge). Thus the student learns to operate efficiently in an educational environment, unmotivated by either the process or product of his activities—in short, in an alienated educational environment in which rewards are in all cases external: grades, class standing, and the threat of failure. The cathection of such forms of "external reward" is a prime outcome of educational socialization

The Economic Value of Education

EDUCATIONAL PRODUCTION RELATIONSHIPS

[12], and doubtless an important contribution to "productive" worker characteristics.

APPENDIX

1. Study: Hansen and Weisbrod (mimeo)
   Sample: 2284 predominantly white, non-southern, above-average IQ veterans
   Y: Earnings
   A: American Air Force Qualification Test
   Other Variables: Age, Race
   Reduction: 19%
2. Study: Conlisk [10]
   Sample: 75 males over a thirty year observation period
   Y: Occupational status, scaled by census-average income for the occupation
   A: IQ, taken at various ages between ages one and 18.
   Other Variables: Parental Income
   Reduction: Less than 10%
3. Study: Duncan [13]
   Sample: CPS-NORC, Oct. 1964; white men 25–34 years of age CPS-OCG (Oct. Changes in a Generation), March 1962: Non-black, non-farm
   Y: 1964 earnings; 1964 Occupational Status
   A: early IQ, later IQ
   Reduction: between 10% and 25%, depending on the particular Y and A used.
4. Study: Cutwright [11]
   Sample: 1% random sample of men registered with Selective Service on April 30, 1953.
   Y: Earnings
   A: AFQT
   Reduction: Between 22% and 35%
5. Study: Duncan, Featherman, and Duncan [15]
   Sample: OCG study, all men 20–64 years old; for details see [18] pp. 103 ff.
   Y: Status of first job
   A: IQ, Army General Classification Test
   Reduction: 20%
6. Study: Bajema [1]
   Sample: 437 males

Y: Occupational Status, NORC prestige index, age 45
A: Early IQ Terman Group Intelligence, sixth grade
Reduction: 13%
7. Griliches and Mason [26]
   Sample: 1964 CPS-NORC veterans file, males, 25–34 years, who have been in army
   Y: log actual income
   A: AFQT
   Other Variables: age, race, sex, SES regional location
   Reduction: 12% to 15%, depending on which of the 'other variables' are entered in.
8. Study: Sewell, Haller and Ohlendorf [40]
   Sample: a one-third random sample of Wisconsin high school seniors of 1957, follow-up in 1968.
   Y: Occupational attainment, using Duncan's (1961) socioeconomic index of occupational status, using data obtained in 1964–65.
   A: IQ, Henman-Nelson Test of Mental Ability
   E: high school = 1; vocational school = 1; some college = 2; college grad = 3
   Reduction: 7%
9. Taubman and Wales [46]
   Sample: All Minnesota high school graduates of 1936
   Y: income in 1953
   A: IQ
   Reduction: 4%

REFERENCES

1. C. J. Bajema, "Interrelations Among Intellectual Ability, Educational Attainment and Occupational Achievement," *Soc. of Educ.*, 1969.
2. Victoria Bonnell and Michael Reich, *Workers in the American Economy*, New England Free Press, 1969.
3. John Bowers, "Interactive Effects of Creativity and IQ on Ninth Grade Achievement," *Jour. Educ. Meas.*, Fall, 1969.
4. Samuel Bowles, "Towards an Educational Production Function," in *Education In-*

come, and Human Capital, Studies in Income and Wealth, Vol. 35, National Bureau of Economic Research, 1970.

5. P. F. Breer and E. Locke, *Task Experience as a Source of Attitudes,* Homewood, Ill., 1965.

6. Frank M. Chambers, "Empathy and Scholastic Success," *Personnel and Guidance Jour.,* Dec., 1957.

7. Victor B. Cline, *et. al.,* "Creativity Tests and Achievement in High School Science," *Jour. Appl. Psych.,* 1963.

8. D. K. Cohen and Marvin Lazerson, "Education and the Industrial Order," paper presented at the AERA meetings, March, 1970.

9. James Coleman et. al., *Equality of Educational Opportunity,* U.S. Dept. of Health, Education and Welfare, Government Printing Office, Washington, D.C., 1966.

10. John Conlisk, "Evidence on the Income-Ability-Education Interrelation," University of California at San Diego, mimeo, 1968.

11. Phillips Cutwright, *Achievement, Military Service, and Earnings,* Social Security Administration, Contract No. SSA 67-2031, May 20, 1969.

12. Robert Dreeben, *On What Is Learned in School,* Reading, Mass., 1968.

13. Otis Dudley Duncan, "Achievement and Ability," *Eugenics Quarterly,* 1968.

14. Otis Dudley Duncan, "Path Analysis: Some Sociological Examples," *American Jour. of Sociology,* July, 1966.

15. Otis Dudley Duncan, David L. Featherman, and Beverly Duncan, "Socioeconomic Background and Occupational Achievement," U.S. Department of Health, Education, and Welfare, Project No. S-0074 (EO-191), May 1968.

16. Sidney A. Fine and Carl A. Heintz, "The Estimate of Worker Trait Characteristics for 4,000 Jobs as Defined in the Dictionary of Occupational Titles," *Personnel and Guidance Jour.,* 1957.

17. G. Gary Gebhart and Donald P. Hoyt, "Personality Needs of Under- and Over-Achieving Freshmen," *Jour. Appl. Psych.,* 1958.

18. J. W. Getzels and P. W. Jackson, "Occupational Choice and Cognitive Functioning," *Jour. of Abnormal and Social Psych.,* 1960.

19. Herbert Gintis, *Alienation and Power: Towards a Radical Welfare Economics,* unpublished Ph.D. dissertation, Harvard University, May, 1969.

20. Herbert Gintis, "Neo-Classical Welfare Economics and Individual Development," Union for Radical Political Economics *Occasional Paper #3,* August, 1970.

21. Herbert Gintis, "Commodity Fetishism and Irrational Production," *Harvard Inst. for Economic Research,* May 1970.

22. Herbert Gintis, "New Working Class and Revolutionary Youth," *Review of Radical Political Economics,* Summer, 1970.

23. Herbert Gintis, "The Structure of Alienation," in Michael Reich et. al. (eds.) *American Society: Conflict and Power,* Prentice-Hall, forthcoming.

24. G. H. Gough, "The Construction of a Personality Scale to Predict Scholastic Achievement," *Jour. Appl. Psych.,* 1953.

25. G. H. Gough and Wallace B. Hall, "Prediction of Performance in Medical School through the CPI," *Jour. Appl. Psych.,* 1964.

26. Zvi Griliches and B. Mason, unpublished data based on on-going research, Harvard University, 1970.

27. J. P. Guilford, "Factors that Aid and Hinder Creativity," *Teachers College Record,* 1962.

28. Eric Hanushek, *The Education of Negroes and Whites,* unpublished Ph.D. dissertation, MIT, August, 1968.

29. Arnold Hauser, "Schools and the Stratification Process," *Am. Jour. of Sociology,* May, 1969.

30. Alfred B. Heilbrun, Jr., "Personality Factors in College Drop-out," *Jour. Appl. Psych.,* 1965.

31. John L. Holland, "Creative and Academic Performance Among Talented Adolescents," in Robert E. Grinder (ed.), *Studies in Adolescence,* New York, 1963.

32. Arthur Jensen, "How Much Can We Boost IQ and Achievement?" *Harvard Educational Review,* Winter, 1969.

33. J. Johnston, *Econometric Methods*, Mc-Graw-Hill, 1963.

34. Michael Katz, *The Irony of Early School Reform*, Harvard University Press, 1968.

35. Kenneth Keniston, *The Uncommitted*, New York, 1960.

36. Cathleen M. Kubiniec, "The Relative Efficiency of Various Dimensions of the Self-Concept in Predicting Academic Achievement," *American Educ. Res. Jour.*, May, 1970.

37. Robert K. Merton, "Bureaucratic Structure and Personality," *Social Forces*, 1940.

38. Joseph L. Norton, "A Study of Worker Traits Requirements for 4,000 Jobs," *Personnel and Guidance Jour.*, 1957.

39. James Scoville, "Education and Training Requirements for Occupations," *Review of Economics and Statistics*, 1966.

40. William H. Sewell, Archibald P. Haller, and George W. Ohlendorf, "The Education and Early Occupational Status Attainment Process," report to the American Sociological Assn., mimeo, San Francisco, Sept., 1969.

41. Herbert Simon, *Administrative Behavior*, New York, 1945.

42. Gene M. Smith, "Usefulness of Peer Ratings of Personality in Educ. Research," *Educ. and Psych. Meas.*, 1967.

43. Gene M. Smith, "Personality Correlates of Academic Performance in Three Dissimilar Populations," *Proceedings of the 77th Annual Convention*, American Psych. Assn., 1967.

44. Gene M. Smith, "Non-intellective Correlates of Academic Performance," mimeo, 1970.

45. Donald E. Super and John O. Crites, *Appraising Vocational Fitness*, Harper, 1962.

46. Paul Taubman and T. Wales, "Effect of Educational and Mental Ability on Income," Mimeo., University of Penna., Nov. 1969.

47. U.S. Dept. of Labor, Div. of Occ. Analysis, *Dictionary of Occupational Titles*, 2nd. ed., Wash. D.C., GPO, 1949.

48. U.S. Dept. of Labor, Div. of Occ. Analysis, *Estimates of Worker Trait Requirements for 4,000 Jobs*, Wash., D.C., GPO, 1956.

49. Max Weber, "On Bureaucracy," in Hans Gerth and C. Wright Mills, *From Max Weber: Essays in Sociology*, New York, 1958.

50. Max Weber, "The Meaning of Discipline," op. cit.

51. Randall Weiss, "The Effects of Scholastic Achievement on the Earnings of Blacks and Whites," Harvard University honors thesis, March, 1968.

[10]

Where Are We Now in the Economics of Education?

MARK BLAUG

Netherlands Institute for Advanced Study and University of London Institute of Education,
56 Gordon Square, London WC1H 0NT, U.K.

Abstract — This essay offers a bird's eye view of new directions in the economics of education. An increasing awareness of the socialization function of education, of the screening hypothesis, of the 'incomplete' employment contract and of labour market segmentation is leading, it is argued, to a picture of the economic value of schooling which is simply miles removed from the old-fashioned belief that education enhances cognitive knowledge and that employers pay educated people more because they know more. The new way of looking at the economic value of schooling is illustrated by the example of youth training and work experience programmes.

INTRODUCTION

THE ECONOMICS of education, conceived either as a specialized branch of economics or as a separate area of educational studies, was born somewhere around 1960. Its heyday was the decade of the 1960s, reaching a peak at, say, 1970 or thereabouts: those were the days when Denison's sources-of-growth accounting was generally believed to have demonstrated the precise quantitative contribution of education to economic growth, when Becker's *Human Capital* (1964) was widely acclaimed as opening up new vistas in labour economics, when every discussion of educational planning revolved around the respective merits of the 'social-demand approach', the 'manpower-requirements approach' and 'rate-of-return analysis'.[1] Those were, in short, the 'golden years' of the economics of education when no self-respecting Minister of Education would have dreamed of making educational decisions without an economist sitting at his right hand.

The early 1970s witnessed a profound change in the dominant role of economists in educational policy making. The enrolment explosion that had marked the history of educational systems all over the world since 1945 began to slow down. The earlier optimism that the expansion of education would effectively equalize life chances in industrialized societies gave way to a new pessimism about the possibilities of altering the distribution of incomes by educational means. Best-sellers like Jencks *et al.*'s *Inequality* (1972) were harbingers of the new scepticism about education that now swept through the First and Third Worlds. Influential studies like the Fauré Report, *Learning to Be* (Fauré *et al.* 1972), assumed without question that the prevailing system of education was largely dysfunctional and then went on to pin their faith on new educational structures which would alternate schooling and work throughout the lifetime of individuals. But the movement towards what has come to be called 'recurrent education' failed to catch on. Worried about inflation, youth unemployment and the actual or impending glut of highly educated people, most governments in the 1970s cut back on educational expenditure and hence were reluctant to venture forth to any significant extent into the unchartered territory of recurrent education (Blaug and Mace, 1977). What enthusiasm survived for educational reform now came to be increasingly devoted to qualitative reform rather than quantitative expansion. In promoting qualitative improvements in education, however, economists were found to be

Editor's note: This is the second paper in our series of invited papers. [Manuscript received and accepted 19 July 1984.]

17

less useful than psychologists and psychometricians. No wonder then that economists were less prominent on the educational scene in the 1970s than in previous years.

Nevertheless, the economics of education did not die out in the 1970s as a field of academic study. On the contrary, the decade saw a vigorous development of the subject into new directions, such that we can now distinguish a well-defined second, as contrasted with a first, generation of economists of education.[2] The second generation no longer believes that the projection of private demand — the so-called 'social demand approach' — provides a sufficient basis for quantitative educational planning. Such projections almost always take for granted the existing patterns of finance for education and the second generation is keen to re-examine the prevailing patterns of educational finance. The second generation has likewise abandoned manpower forecasting as a planning tool if only because it begs too many questions about the relationship between the structure of occupations in an economy and the educational requirements for jobs, not to mention the notorious inaccuracy of such forecasts for any period in the future that is longer than 1 or 2 years. As for rate-of-return analysis, even first-generation economists of education were reluctant to employ it wholeheartedly for purposes of public policy making, a reluctance which is now enforced by the general endorsement of some version of the 'screening hypothesis' among second-generation economists of education. Gone, too, is the facile notion of the earlier generation that more education would steadily erode the income advantages of the highly educated, so that educational expansion would inevitably entail greater equality. The effect of education on income distribution is now understood to rest as much on the distribution as on the level of schooling in the population and, depending on how education is financed, it is now appreciated that more schooling can actually increase observed inequalities in income.

But perhaps the most far-reaching changes in the economics of education have come from the work of institutional and radical economists in the United States, emphasizing the 'socialization' function of schooling in contrast to its vocational function in teaching cognitive skills, the 'segmentation' of labour markets which generates different economic values of schooling to identical individuals and,

more generally, the 'invisible handshake' between employers and workers, which governs the personal rewards of education and training. Adding all these elements together, the 'new' economics of education is hardly recognizable as the same subject which ruled the roost in the 1960s. Of course, elements of the 'old' economics of education survive and even the recent pages of this journal can be employed to demonstrate that human capital theory and earnings regressions still serve many as suitable paradigms for studying the economic effects of education. Nevertheless, I claim that the vital parts of the subject lie elsewhere, linking up with similar developments in labour economics.

What follows, therefore, is not a review of the state of the arts in the economics of education but a deliberately provocative bird's-eye view of new directions in thinking among economists concerned with educational issues.

THE SOCIALIZATION FUNCTION OF SCHOOLING

The year 1976 saw the publication of a book by Samuel Bowles and Herbert Gintis entitled *Schooling in Capitalist America* (1976), which immediately became something of a minor educational classic among radical economists and sociologists. The centrepiece of the Bowles–Gintis book is the argument that the economic value of education in a capitalist economy has been grossly misunderstood by orthodox economists of education. The widely observed association between personal earnings and schooling is usually attributed to the influence of education on the levels of cognitive knowledge in the working population. But effective performance in most jobs, argue Bowles and Gintis, depends very little on directly usable cognitive skills and much more on certain non-cognitive personality traits. Moreover, these personality traits are also rewarded in the classroom and hence are systematically encouraged by the educational system.

What are these non-cognitive, affective outcomes of schools? At the risk of oversimplification, we can divide them into two broad categories. In the wide spectrum of lower level occupations to which unqualified school leavers are largely condemned they are the behavioural traits of punctuality, persistence, concentration, docility, compliance and the ability to work with others. However, the top of the occupational pyramid, accessible largely to university graduates, calls for a different set of personality traits, namely, self-esteem, self-reliance, versatility and the capacity to assume leadership roles. In a nutshell, we may say that elementary and secondary education breed the foot-soldiers, while higher education trains the lieutenants and captains of the economy.

Indeed, schools under capitalism are mini-factories and promote the same values which are prized in the labour market. Capitalist factories are hierarchically organized, and so are capitalist schools; capitalist factories require obedience and subservience to a central authority, and so do capitalist schools; capitalist factories 'alienate' workers from the products of their labour, and capitalist schools 'alienate' students from the products of their learning; workers are motivated, not by the intrinsic value of work, but by the promise of pay, and students are likewise motivated by the extrinsic reward of examination grades; and competition rather than co-operation, self-interest rather than comradeliness, governs the relations among workers as it governs the relations among students. In short, according to this view there is a nearly perfect correspondence between the educational system and the capitalist economic system: the educational system lacks any administrative and intellectual autonomy of its own, shining as it were only by reflected light emanating from the labour market. As Bowles and Gintis express it in their favourite Althusserian jargon: "the social relations of schools reproduce the social division of labour under capitalism".

Unfortunately, this entire line of argument, even if it were valid as it stands, is not very original. Ever since Emile Durkheim, mainstream sociologists have underlined the fact that 'socialization', that is, the inculcation of definite values and attitudes in children, is one of the principal functions of the educational system in any society. Bowles and Gintis complain that the school system has played an important role in preserving the capitalist order, but surely this is an obvious and even trivial proposition? Does the school system in a socialist society not play a similar role in preserving the socialist order? The viability of any economic system depends on citizens respecting 'the rules of the game', whatever they are, and clearly schools play a major part in legitimizing these rules.

Nevertheless, Bowles and Gintis are perfectly correct to reject cognitive development and, in-

cidentally, the development of psychomotor skills as the central economic function of schools. The notion that most jobs in a modern economy require high levels of literacy and numeracy, and increasingly so as industry becomes more sophisticated, has been productive of a whole series of misdirected educational reforms. It lies behind the frequent tendency to 'vocationalize' secondary education in the fond belief that this will increase the employability of school leavers. The familiar finding of the low economic returns to vocational schooling, vocational school graduates being frequently less employable than academic school graduates (Psacharopoulos, 1980), is easily explained when it is remembered that most employers, whether public or private, care less about what potential workers know than about how they will behave. The very distinction between 'academic' and 'vocational' education, in which only the latter is supposed to be geared to the needs of the labour market, falsely suggests that much, if not most, education is economically irrelevant. But the 'hidden curriculum' of teacher–pupil relations in academic-style education has as much to do with the world of work as the explicit curriculum of mental and manipulative skills in vocational education. The frequently repeated research finding that few workers ever make specific use of the cognitive knowledge acquired in schools (Gintis, 1971) thus indicates, not some sort of monstrous mismatch between education and work, but the pivotal role of affective behavioural traits in job performance. The truth of the matter is that most jobs in a modern economy require about as much cognitive knowledge and psychomotor skills as are used to drive an automobile!

I am, of course, exaggerating. It is not to be denied that many professional qualifications do involve an indispensable element of cognitive knowledge and that, say, an oil company employing a chemist is looking for a minimum level of competence in the science of chemistry. But even at the level of professional studies, the cognitive knowledge which is said to be indispensable frequently consists of perfectly general communication skills and problem-solving abilities rather than occupation-specific competences; and to that extent implies a combination of particular personality traits and certain cognitive achievements. If this were not so, it would be difficult to explain the widespread employment of sociology and history graduates in public and private sector jobs. There are occupations, like that of the aeroplane pilot or the brain surgeon, where, indeed, nothing matters except cognitive judgement and psychomotor skills. Additional examples where cognitive knowledge looms large are accountants, lawyers, computer scientists — and perhaps even university teachers. Even here, however, success has frequently more to do with achievement-motivation — the motivation to excel in whatever one does for its own sake — than with factual or conceptual knowledge; and, surely, achievement-motivation is a personality trait? At any rate, all that we are claiming in endorsing Bowles and Gintis is that none of the occupations just mentioned are typical modes of employment in a modern economy. The vast bulk of jobs in an industrial economy involve competences that are acquired on the job in a few weeks and require, not a given stock of knowledge of facts and concepts, but the capacity to learn by doing.

Bowles and Gintis are also correct in asserting that first-generation economists of education, and particularly those advocating the theory of human capital, frequently implied in so many words that the economic value of education is due entirely to the effects of cognitive learning in schools. That is not to say, however, that mainstream economists of education committed themselves explicitly to this view. To a surprising extent they viewed schooling as a 'black box': without pretending or even caring to know what went on in classrooms, they simply insisted that passing through schools increased the earning power of people independently of differences in both family origins and inborn or acquired mental abilities (see Blaug, 1976, pp. 847–848). Nevertheless, their writings lent themselves naturally to the cognitive-knowledge interpretation. Furthermore, human capital theory with its rates of return to educational investment flourished alongside an extensive body of research on 'educational production functions', all or almost all of which related the inputs into schools to an 'output' consisting solely of scores of students on tests of cognitive achievement.[3] At the same time, another line of work attempted to forecast the educational requirements of particular patterns of economic growth. While these forecasts rarely asked the question of the sense in which the growth of certain jobs depended rigidly on the growth of educational qualifications, the implicit notion was always that each job entailed a definite complement of cognitive skills which could only be acquired via formal

schooling. The moment we argue that the chief contribution of education to economic growth is to complement the socialization function of families in instilling values and attitudes requisite to adequate job functioning in an industrial society, we necessarily jettison the concepts of any precise quantitative relationship between the growth of the economy and the growth of the educational system. The question is no longer whether manpower forecasts are accurate or not, which is typically how the issue was posed in the 1960s, but whether the entire exercise is not perhaps misconceived in its very foundations.

No doubt there remains the problem of assessing the future supply of accountants, lawyers, doctors, computer scientists, etc., that is, professions which necessarily involve training in specific cognitive skills. This type of training typically requires long-cycle education, lasting 5–7 years. But manpower forecasts over periods of such length are hopelessly inaccurate and little better than guesswork (see Ahamad and Blaug, 1973). In the circumstances, what scope is there for educational planning? One general answer to the inherent imperfection of manpower forecasting is to shorten educational cycles so as to make it unnecessary to forecast 5 or 7 years into the future. But the professions in question are dominated by professional associations who have steadily lengthened the training period required to reach entry standards and who see any move to lower the training period as a threat to their monopoly power. That leaves us with the possibility of using the short-term signals of labour markets — unemployment rates, vacancy rates, wages rates, etc. — to register trends in the pattern of employment. This is not an entirely satisfactory solution to the problem of educated manpower but it is the best available. Fortunately, private demand for professional qualifications is sensitive to short-term indicators of labour market prospects and, indeed, has proved better at forecasting future trends than most public authorities. The best guide to policy in this case would actually seem to be *laissez-faire, laissez-passer*, and certainly doing nothing is preferable to engaging in meaningless forecasts of the demands for educated manpower 5–10 years hence.

THE SCREENING HYPOTHESIS

To return to Bowles and Gintis: the emphasis in our schools on affective behaviour rather than mental attainments is not, they argue, the unintended consequence of schooling carried out for other purposes. So long as production is hierarchically organized along capitalist lines, what is required at the bottom of the job pyramid is the ability to take orders, while at the top of the pyramid what is required is the ability to give orders. Teachers are perfectly aware of this spectrum of vocational demands and hence reward students in classrooms accordingly. Employers, on the other hand, have learned from past experience that there is a general concordance between the attributes required at various levels of the educational pyramid and educational attainments. In that sense, educational credentials act as surrogates for qualities which employers regard as important, predicting a certain level of job performance without, however, making any direct contribution to it. This 'screening hypothesis' neatly accounts for the fact that earnings rise with additional education; it even explains why so many educational qualifications appear to be unrelated to the type of work that students eventually take up; and it certainly helps to explain why the educational explosion of the last 35 years has had so little effect on equalizing the distribution of income.

If education acts merely as a filter to separate the chaff from the wheat, the steady expansion of higher education dilutes the significance of a degree and induces employers to upgrade the hiring standards of jobs previously filled by university and college graduates; graduates will then be worse off in absolute terms. But if secondary schooling is expanding at the same time, so that high school leavers are likewise being squeezed into lower-level jobs, earnings differentials between the two cohorts may nevertheless remain more or less the same. What is true of these two categories of labour is true of every category — the expansion of post-compulsory education is simply passed down the line and ends up in a chronic core of unemployed school leavers without, however, much visible effect on the distribution of earned income from employment.

The 'screening hypothesis' clearly has dramatic implications for educational policy. The difficulty with the hypothesis is that it comes in two versions, a strong version and a weak one. In its strong version it is virtually untenable, whereas in its weak version it is difficult to pin down with any precision. The strong version of the screening hypothesis asserts that education merely identifies students with particular attributes, acquired either at birth or by virtue of family background, but does not itself produce or in any way improve those attributes. It is difficult to conceive how this strong version of the hypothesis could be true. After all, schools screen twice, once when they select students for admission and a second time when they pass or fail students at the end of an educational cycle. If there is screening in the strong sense, only the first screen serves any useful economic function, the second being a piece of window-dressing designed purely to create employment for teachers. But as every teacher knows, the correlation for any individual student between predicted and actual education success is by no means perfect: selection for admission to courses is wrong almost as often as it is right. In other words, 'good' students have to be discovered and it takes a protracted sequence of hurdles, such as any educational cycle provides, to identify the traits and attributes that lead to success. The notion that they are present, only waiting to be sifted out by some ingenious filter, and that any filter will do, schooling being simply one, is a naïve psychological fallacy.

Moreover, the strong version of the screening hypothesis implies that there is little reward to an incompleted degree or certificate, or at any rate that the extra rewards of, say, 2 years of university education are much less than two-thirds of the rewards of a university degree completed in 3 years. In other words, educational credentials act like a 'sheepskin' that disguises the true difference between dropouts and graduates. Similarly, strong screening implies that, whatever differences in starting salaries between university graduates and secondary school leavers, the gap in the two salary streams gradually disappears with additional years of work experience: employers may use educational qualifications as a screen at the time of hiring when they are ignorant of the true abilities of potential workers, but as time passes they can actually observe their job performance and reward them in accordance with their true personal abilities. Finally, strong screening makes it difficult to understand why employers have not sought to replace the educational system by a cheaper screening mechanism. Surely, it is cheaper to incur the personal costs of independently testing the abilities of individual workers, say, by a battery of psychological aptitude tests, than to pay all university graduates more simply because they are university graduates.

Thus the strong version of the screening hypothesis carried with it at least three definite empirical implications. All of these three implications, however, are firmly refuted by the evidence (Layard and Psacharopoulos, 1974). Firstly, the private rate of return to education for university dropouts sometimes actually exceeds the yield of a completed university degree. Secondly, the effect of years of education on personal earnings generally rises rather than falls with additional years of work experience. Thirdly, business firms and government departments do sometimes test individual workers at the point of recruitment; nevertheless, in no country in the world have such independent testing services effectively replaced the role of educational credentials in screening out job applicants. Furthermore, strong screening additionally implies that education has no effect on personal earnings when it comes to the self-employed since there is little point in self-screening. However, the impact of years of education on earnings is as great for self-employed accountants, doctors and lawyers as it is for wage and salary earners. Of course, that may be due to screening by the customers of self-employed professionals, which in turn leads professional associations of accountants, doctors and lawyers to press for increased educational qualifications under state occupational licensing laws. Nevertheless, the evidence on the association between education and earnings for the self-employed does cast some doubt on screening in its stronger versions (see Lazear, 1977; Whitehead, 1981).

All these refutations, however, fall to the ground if we give the screening hypothesis a weaker interpretation. After all, employers face considerable information costs in recruiting suitable workers and assigning them appropriately to different tasks. Every new worker takes days or weeks to reach an adequate level of performance and thus mistakes in hiring are costly in terms of output forgone, not to mention the administrative costs of posting vacancies, sorting applicants and inducting successful recruits. No wonder, then, that employers resort to stereotypes like sex, colour, ethnic background, educational credentials, marital status, age and previous work experience, indicators which experience has shown to be good predictors of job performance, at least on average. Obviously, for crucial jobs like those of supervisors, junior managers and executives, it may pay to engage in expensive search procedures, including the use of aptitude tests, to select a particular candidate from among a group of job applicants with similar characteristics. But for most jobs it is cheaper to rely

on group characteristics and to run the risk of occasional errors. Thus 'educational credentialism' or the use of educational qualifications as a hiring screen is a species of a larger genus of 'statistical discrimination' in the hiring of labour: the costs of truly identifying the talents of potential workers forces employers to discriminate against atypical members of social groups. The fact that educational qualifications stand out among all the other stereotypes as being legally permitted and generally approved — most people nowadays regard educational meritocracy as being perfectly fair and legitimate — only encourages screening by education on the part of the employers.

So interpreted, the 'screening hypothesis' is a label for a classic information problem in a labour market. So far, however, we have only dealt with hiring at the point of recruitment and we have said nothing to explain the association between education and earnings right through the entire working life of individuals. Granted that employers will pay more to better educated workers when they know nothing about their individual aptitudes, why should they almost invariably continue to do so when they have had ample opportunity to monitor their performance over long periods of time?

One explanation may be the existence of what is called 'internal labour markets' in many business firms and government departments. It does not pay any large organization with a complex occupational structure to recruit every vacancy from an external labour market. Instead, most vacancies are filled by internal promotion and external recruitment is confined to a few 'ports of entry' at the bottom and the top of the occupational pyramid (Doeringer and Piore, 1971). This confers a double advantage: it promotes the morale of the workforce by providing a number of lifetime careers within the organization and it enhances the efficiency of recruitment because hiring is always confined to the same categories of jobs. However, once such an 'internal labour market' takes a firm foothold in an enterprise, it creates claims to eventual promotion among all workers in the firm at the time of hiring. In short, workers tend to be recruited in such enterprises not to a job but to a career path, and this means that any advantages at the point of recruitment tend to be converted into persistent advantages throughout a working life with the company. In this way the use of educational qualifications as a screen at the point of hiring becomes an effective screen throughout the period of association with a particular enterprise. Even if he or she leaves the company to work elsewhere, the next employer is likely to give credit both for previous experience and for previous earnings, which perpetuates the earlier link between schooling and earnings. To sum up: the notion of 'statistical discrimination' in hiring and the presence of 'internal labour markets' taken together are perfectly capable of explaining why highly educated people *on average* earn more than less educated people even though they may not be inherently more productive.

I say 'on average' advisedly. Clearly, employers do make mistakes in hiring and do discover in due course that, say, some university graduates are worse than others; these they will not promote or will only promote more slowly; alternatively, they may rotate them to a different job from the one for which they were recruited; contrariwise, the jobs of 'high flyers' may be enriched as time passes or combined with other jobs into a new job title. Therefore, when we study the structure of personal earnings by education and occupation in any modern economy, we observe: (i) a strong positive association between earnings and education when expressed in terms of averages; (ii) considerable variance in the association between education and earnings, such that the worst paid university graduates actually earn less than the best paid secondary school leavers, and so on for all other educational cohorts; and (iii) a considerable variance for every occupational category, however finely defined, in the years of schooling of incumbents of that occupation — such evidence is accountable by an element of 'statistical discrimination' at the hiring stage and the presence of 'internal labour markets' of various degrees of strength in many private companies and government departments.

THE INCOMPLETE EMPLOYMENT CONTRACT

We now take the argument a step further. Just as educators have always objected to the phrase 'human capital' to describe personal investment in education because it appears to demean education, so trade union leaders have long objected to the economist's habit of writing about labour problems as if labour was a commodity like any other to be bought and sold in the market place. But labour under capitalism is not in fact a commodity like any

other because its hiring contract is typically 'incomplete'. A contract of employment typically specifies the duration of work and the rate of pay for that work in terms of hours per day and days per week. What is most important in the hiring decision, however, is not written into the contract, namely, the intensity and quality of the effort to be expended, if only because there appears to be no dimension in which to express this effort. Obviously, if it is possible to isolate what each worker produces, workers are paid by the piece and the employment contract is complete. But in most production processes it is impossible to attribute every portion of final output to the contribution of some individual worker; production is carried out jointly by teams of workers, in which case the rate of pay must be expressed in terms of time. The famous slogan 'a fair day's pay for a fair day's work' highlights this double dimension of the employment contract of production systems in which output cannot be unambiguously traced to individual workers.

Thus for the bulk of manufacturing and service industries, not to mention the civil service and local government, the hire of labour implies the conscious willingness to work at a minimum level of intensity which simply cannot be fully spelled out in a contractual agreement. To secure the co-operation of workers in the production process, employers must prevent shirking by constant monitoring and policing, backed up by the promise of promotion and the threat of summary dismissal. Nevertheless, in the final analysis employers are forced to rely on what has been aptly named 'the invisible handshake' of trust and loyalty to replace 'the invisible hand' of competition that secures the effective provision of most other goods and services.

Experts in industrial relations will hardly be surprised by this concept of the incomplete employment contract. Economists, however, have, so to speak, forgotten it, or perhaps have never learned it until recently. Economists have, of course, long recognized that the business firm as a whole is a particular non-market institution in which authoritarian allocation replaces allocation by the price system, but they have neglected to analyse the principles which govern this internal allocation system (see Williamson, 1975). Thus, when certain labour economists developed the concept of 'internal labour markets' in the early 1970s, the very term 'internal labour *markets*' was misleading in suggesting a market mechanism rather than an administrative and organizational procedure for minimizing the potential sources of conflict in the employment relation. Similarly, economists have largely tended to treat trade unions as extra-economic forces having no reason for being in a competitive economy. But the incomplete labour contract makes it all too easy to account for the rise of trade unions as an attempt on the part of workers to choose collective rather than individual labour contracts in order to countervail the employer's control over the production process.

It is obvious that employers are at a disadvantage in completing the labour contract if workers act in concert. It will be to the interest of employers, therefore, to 'divide and rule'. One way of doing so is to buy individual loyalty by the promise of eventual promotion and treat all promotions as a race between a number of competitors. Another is to capitalize on the socially legitimate or illegitimate indicators that are employed in the hiring process and to assign men and women, married men and single men, whites and blacks, youths and adults, school leavers and university graduates, etc. to different lifetime career paths in the enterprise. This brings us squarely to the last element in our story, the concept of 'labour market segmentation'.

LABOUR MARKET SEGMENTATION

The theory of segmented labour markets (SLM) started out as a contrast between two *sectors* of the modern economy, the so-called 'primary' labour markets of large corporations, trade unions, job security and steady career prospects, and the 'secondary' labour markets of small businesses, no unions and dead-end jobs. It was designed to explain the fact of significant earnings differences between males and females and between whites and blacks even when age, schooling and years of work experience are held constant, and the persistent failure of education and training programmes specifically directed at low-paid workers to erode these differences. However, theories of SLM have since been radicalized and in such books as the *Contested Terrain* (1979) by Richard Edwards, segmentation of labour is not so much a matter of two or three contrasting *sectors* of economic activity as of many contrasting *categories* of workers within each and every capitalist enterprise in every sector of the economy.

As with the screening hypothesis, theories of SLM seem to imply certain definite predictions. Firstly, they imply that if we select some index of the quality of jobs, made up, for example, of starting wages, turnover rates, bouts of unemployment, increments of pay with the same employers and so forth, it will prove to be bimodally or multimodally distributed across different but well-defined categories of workers; in other words, 'good' jobs are not randomly assigned to workers whatever their personal characteristics. Secondly, and more importantly, SLM theories imply that there will be very little mobility over time between these well-defined job clusters. The last of these two implications has been pretty well refuted, at least for the American economy. The first implication, however, has been generally corroborated, although the dust has by no means settled in this controversial area.[4]

Internal labour markets and segmentation of labour markets destroy much of the elegant simplicity of Becker's famous distinction between 'general training' and 'specific training'. *General* training was said to raise the trainee's productivity, not just in the firm providing the training but in any firm whatsoever; private firms have no incentive to pay the costs of such training because they cannot guarantee that they will be able to retain workers who have received such training; in consequence, general training will only be provided if trainees pay for it themselves in the form of reduced earnings during the training period. The classic example of such general training is, of course, apprenticeship training, not just in industry but also in the professions. *Specific* training, on the other hand, raises the productivity of trainees only in the firm providing the training, so that firms do have an incentive to finance such training. Leading examples of this universal class of training are induction programmes for newly hired workers coupled with probationary periods of supervision. The question now is: is training, whether on or off the job, largely general rather than specific? This is like asking: who actually pays for most training, firms or workers? The difficulty with the question is that business firms may well pay for some portion of general training if they can thereby retain labour and reduce turnover costs. Once a firm is committed to sharing even general training costs with its workers, labour training may become a fringe benefit in an 'internal labour market', another method of bidding away labour from rivals. We are left at the end of the story with no general guidance on the financing of training, whether general or specific: in some firms it is paid for by the company and in others it is paid for by workers; it all depends on the strength of internal labour markets in certain lines of economic activity and on the degree to which the work force in an enterprise is segmented or not.

SOME IMPLICATIONS

If we now add together the vital 'socialization' function of schools, the 'screening hypothesis' in the sense of statistical discrimination, the concept of the 'incomplete' employment contract, the phenomenon of 'internal labour markets' and the notion of labour market 'segmentation', we arrive at a picture of the economic value of schooling that is simply miles removed from the old-fashioned belief that education makes workers more productive and that employers pay them more because they are more productive. The basic problem in hiring workers is to induce them to co-operate in carrying out the tasks to which the enterprise is committed. At the same time, there is the information problem of discovering the potential aptitudes of individual workers so as to combine them together into a loyal team. The need for artificial filters or screens arises not just because genuine hiring search procedures are costly but also because they are socially divisive. The beauty of such filters as age, sex, race, marital status, years of work experience and, above all, educational qualifications is that at least some of them are generally regarded as socially legitimate, 'just', 'fair' and so on. Educational credentials, in particular, are widely held to be the product of individual effort and to that extent their use in recruitment and promotion meets with the approval of workers, employers and customers alike — a perfect social consensus!

It may be that schooling increases the productivity of individuals by making them more effective members of a production team or better able to handle machines and materials, but it would matter little if it were not so provided everyone thought it was so — which, of course, they do. What is important is that every worker accepts the principles on which some are paid more and some are paid less. Even if these payments are in reverse order of the true spot marginal products of individual workers, assuming that the marginal product of an individual worker can even be identified, the maximization of the output and minimization of the

costs of the firm depend critically, not on the scale of individual rewards, but on the mutual co-operation of all workers in the enterprise. In short, screening by educational qualifications is economically efficient not because 'good' students are always 'good' workers but because educational credentialism avoids the inherent conflict of interests between workers and employers.

What follows from all this for educational policy? Firstly, we have said enough to show why labour markets tend to react to changes in effective demand by adjusting quantities rather than prices, numbers employed rather than wages: layoffs in a lump threaten the morale of the workforce less than an across-the-board cut in wages, particularly if the layoffs are concentrated among certain 'inferior' groups, like youngsters, women, blacks, etc.; likewise, fresh hiring in a boom generates the expectation of promotion among older workers, which is even more effective in raising morale than an actual promotion. Thus labour markets are inherently capable of continually absorbing workers with ever higher levels of education simply by adjusting the customary educational hiring standards for jobs. However, such adjustments, precisely because they must win, and must be seen to win, general approval, take time. A rapid flooding of a labour market with, say, university graduates may well produce graduate unemployment, whereas the same numbers could have been absorbed if they had been forthcoming at a slower rate. Similarly, a sudden glut of university graduates produces graduate unemployment because employers have misgivings about hiring overqualified applicants who tend to feel underutilized, making them ineffective workers. But declining job opportunities for university graduates forces degree holders to adjust their job aspirations downwards. In time, therefore, BAs will cease to feel themselves to be overqualified for, say, a secretarial post and in that sense the original objection to hiring them for such jobs will lose its force. Once again, it is not an absolute oversupply of university graduates but a rapid increase in that supply that causes graduate unemployment.

Contrariwise, there is no real sense in which a given level of education in the economically active population of a country can be said to be technically 'required' to permit the achieved level of economic growth of that country. That sort of argument grossly exaggerates the contribution of manipulative and cognitive skills in the performance of economic functions, ignores the fact that such skills are largely acquired by on-the-job training, and utterly neglects the vital role of suitable personality traits in securing the 'invisible handshake' on which production critically depends. In short, educational policies may be fitted to literally any level or rate of economic growth and cannot be justified in terms of those patterns of growth. Education does make a contribution to economic growth, not as an indispensable input into the growth process, as first-generation economists of education used to argue, but simply as a framework which willy-nilly accommodates the growth process.

One is tempted at this point to provide numerous illustrations of the powerful policy implications of this new way of looking at the economic value of schooling. A single but telling example, however, must suffice for present purposes. One of the outstanding social problems of recent years has been the rising incidence of youth unemployment which has everywhere accompanied the appearance of slumpflation since the early 1970s. Most governments in industrialized countries have reacted to this problem by expanding training and work-experience programmes for out-of-school youngsters aged 16–19 years (Magnussen, 1977). Indeed, if we add all public expenditure on such schemes to those that directly subsidize the employment of young people, we reach figures for government expenditure on the employment and training of 16- to 19-year-olds that in some European countries equal the levels of expenditure on college and university education.

The motive for these programmes is sometimes taken to be simply that of removing as many people as possible from the unemployment rolls so as to put the best face on deflationary policies. But that is perhaps an unduly cynical interpretation. Governments themselves defend training and work-experience programmes for youngsters as repairing the deficiencies of formal schooling. In other words, their theory of why there is now so much youth unemployment is that secondary schools have failed to inculcate the requisite skills and positive attitudes that render a school leaver employable. From our standpoint, it is highly significant that many youth training programmes include training, not just in the three Rs and in low-level manipulative skills, but also in techniques of interviewing and presentation of biographical information, thus recognizing that employability depends as much on personality traits as on physical competence and cognitive knowledge.

However, the difficulty with this quasi-official theory of youth unemployment is that it fails utterly to account for the emergence of heavy youth unemployment all over the industrialized world in the last half of the 1970s except by the implausible assumption that the quality of secondary education suddenly deteriorated badly in 1973 or thereabouts.

There is nothing new about the fact that in a recession the rates of joblessness for young people exceed those for adults. What is new about youth unemployment in recent years is that the gap which always opens up between the two unemployment rates in a recession has never been as large as it is today in most countries, and this despite a steady upward trend in the proportion of young people staying on in schools beyond the compulsory leaving age. Even when we standardize the figures for demographic changes and for changes in labour force activity rates, the size of the gap seems to be without historical precedent: in almost all capitalist countries unemployment for people under the age of 21 constitutes 40 and sometimes 50% of total unemployment (see Sorentino, 1981). The true causes of this problem still remain somewhat mysterious: it is as if employers all over the industrialized world became strangely reluctant after about 1973 or 1974 to hire young people for regular, full-time jobs; moreover, in some countries, like France, Germany, Sweden, Italy, and the U.K., this reluctance actually manifested itself as early as the late 1960s (Sorentino, 1981).

One can go some way towards explaining this phenomenon by taking account of the world-wide shift in the pattern of demand from the industrial sector to the service industries but this phenomenon still leaves unexplained a considerable proportion of youth unemployment. A more significant factor may be the gradual strengthening of job security provisions for adult workers in most industrialized countries. Traditional management prerogatives in dismissing labour have been substantially curtailed everywhere, and increasingly so in the 1970s — consider, for example, the successive impact in Britain of the Redundancy Payments Act of 1965, the Industrial Relations Act of 1972 and the Employment Protection Act of 1975 — and this has encouraged the substitution of older, experienced workers for younger, inexperienced workers in order to minimize rates of labour turnover. At the same time, a general narrowing of wage differentials between youth and adult workers, frequently as a result of minimum wage legislation and union pressure, has tended to price youngsters out of the labour market. But a final element in the explanation of rising youth unemployment must be the phenomenon referred to earlier, namely, that of educational inflation in which the educational hiring standards of jobs are continually raised to absorb the ever-growing number of educated entrants into the labour force, a process which has no natural halting place other than the legal school leaving age. In other words, the problem of youth unemployment is to a considerable extent the product of the post-war explosion in post-compulsory education.

Be that as it may, current training, work-experience, job-creation and job-subsidization programmes for the age group 16–19 years continue to expand in most countries under the impetus of untested if not implausible hypotheses about the collapse of formal schooling coupled with half-baked ideas about the long-term training requirements of growing economies which private industry is somehow incapable of providing. There is, surely, a world of difference between creating jobs for which labour can be trained when it is recruited (with appropriate assistance from a relevant government department) and training people via special programmes for jobs which do not exist and may never exist. This elementary distinction is almost totally neglected in the recent world-wide upsurge of out-of-school programmes for youngsters aged 16–19 years.

If this much is accepted, we have illustrated a more general thesis, namely, that effective educational planning must be based on a realistic assessment of the operations of labour markets. Such markets are in a continuous state of flux, particularly in terms of employment patterns rather than relative wage differentials, and with the best will in the world it is difficult to avoid a situation in which every educational reform is addressed to curing yesterday's rather than today's ills. Economic growth and technical progress are just as capable of de-skilling existing jobs as of generating new jobs and new skills: consider, for example, the way in which the development of hand-held calculators and word processors has reduced the importance of functional numeracy and literacy in the work force and increased the importance of favourable affective attitudes to computer aids. The expansion of new industries and the contraction of old ones, changes in employment legislation, changes in trade union regulations, etc. are capable of rapidly altering existing patterns of recruitment. No method of educational planning can keep pace with this kaleidoscope and in this sense there is a real economic merit in general, academic education as a hedge against technical dynamism. The old battle cry for vocational job-specific education, which at first glance might seem to be the rallying grounds of economists, is actually the very opposite of what is implied by the 'new' economics of education. Here, as in so many other educational debates, the enemy is a Neanderthal economics of education concocted of a vulgar version of first-generation economics of education and old-fashioned shibboleths about the alleged economic value of schooling.

Acknowledgements — This paper was originally commissioned by the Organization for Economic Co-operation and Development (OECD) Directorate for Social Affairs, Manpower and Education (SME/ET/82.29) and was subsequently published (in a slightly different version) in a series of special public lectures by the University of London Institute of Education (1983).

NOTES

1. My own textbook (Blaug, 1972) reflects those concerns almost perfectly.
2. See Carnoy (1977), the first to suggest that the 1970s saw some sort of watershed in the subject.
3. For some attempt to include non-cognitive outcomes see Bridge *et al.* (1979, pp. 59–67, 205–212) and Cohn (1975). On the general distinction between cognitive and non-cognitive outcomes of schooling, see Bloom *et al.* (1956).
4. See Cain (1976), Carnoy (1980), Gordon *et al.* (1982) and Blaug (1983. pp. 225–227).

REFERENCES

AHAMAD, B. and BLAUG, M. (1973) *The Practice of Manpower Forecasting: a Collection of Case Studies*. Amsterdam: Elsevier.

BECKER, G. S. (1964) *Human Capital*. Princeton, NJ: Princeton University Press.

BLAUG, M. (1972) *Introduction to the Economics of Education.* London: Penguin Books.
BLAUG, M. (1976) The empirical status of human capital theory: a slightly jaundiced survey. *J. econ. Lit.* **14**, 827–855.
BLAUG, M. (1983) A methodological appraisal of radical economics. *Methodological Controversy in Economics. A Historical Perspective* (Edited by COATS, A.W.). Greenwich, CT: JAI Press.
BLAUG, M. and MACE, J. (1977) Recurrent education — the new Jerusalem. *Higher Educ.* **6**, 277–300.
BLOOM, B. S. *et al.* (1956) *Taxonomy of Educational Objectives.* New York: David McKay (2 vols).
BOWLES, S. and GINTIS, H. (1976) *Schooling in Capitalist America.* New York: Basic Books.
BRIDGE, R. G., JUDD, C. M. and MOOCK, P. R. (1979) *The Determinants of Educational Outcomes.* Cambridge, MA: Ballinger.
CAIN, G. C. (1976) The challenge of segmented labor market theories to orthodox theory: a survey. *J. econ. Lit.* **14**, 1215–1257.
CARNOY, M. (1977) Education and economic development: the first generation. *Econ. Dev. cult. Change* **25** (Suppl.), 448–488.
CARNOY, M. (1980) *Education, Work and Employment,* II. *Segmented Labour Markets.* Paris: UNESCO — International Institute of Educational Planning.
COHN, E. (1975) *Input–Output Analysis in Public Education.* Cambridge, MA: Ballinger.
DOERINGER, P. B. and PIORE, M. J. (1971) *Internal Labor Markets and Manpower Analysis.* Lexington, MA: D.C. Heath.
EDWARDS, R. C. (1979) *Contested Terrain: The Transformation of the Working Place in the Twentieth Century.* New York: Basic Books.
FAURÉ, E. *et al.* (1972) *Learning to Be.* Paris: UNESCO.
GINTIS, H. (1971) Education, technology and the characteristics of worker productivity. *Am. econ. Rev.* **61**, 266–279.
GORDON, D. M., EDWARDS, R. C. and REICH, M. (1982) *Segmented Work, Divided Workers: The Historical Transformation of Labor in the United States.* London: Cambridge University Press.
JENCKS, C. *et al.* (1972) *Inequality.* New York: Basic Books.
LAYARD, R. and PSACHAROPOULOS, G. (1974) The screening hypothesis and the returns to education. *J. polit. Econ.* **82**, 985–998.
LAZEAR, E. (1977) Academic achievement and job performance. *Am. econ. Rev.* **67**, 252–254.
MAGNUSSEN, O. (1977) *Education and Employment: the Problem of Early School-leavers.* Paris: Institute of Education of European Cultural Foundation.
PSACHAROPOULOS, G. (1980) *Higher Education in Developing Countries: a Cost–Benefit Analysis.* Washington, DC: World Bank.
SORENTINO, C. (1981) Youth unemployment: an international perspective. *Monthly Labor Rev.* **38** (July), 73–98.
WHITEHEAD, A. K. (1981) Screening and education: a theoretical and empirical survey. *Br. Rev. econ. Issues* **2** (8), 44–62.
WILLIAMSON, O. E. (1975) *Market and Hierarchies: Analysis and Antitrust Implications. A Study in the Economics of Internal Organization.* New York: The Free Press.

[11]

Academic Achievement and Job Performance: Note

By EDWARD LAZEAR*

David Wise's recent paper in this *Review* addresses two questions: First, is there any relationship between the subjective quality of an individual's college institution or his relative position within that college and his eventual job performance? Second, if a relationship exists, what is its causal nature? Specifically, do variations in schooling types affect productivity directly, or are they merely associated with higher productivity through screening channels? Although Wise's analysis yields a convincingly affirmative answer to the first question, it is silent on the second. The "indirect evidence" that Wise offers is quite consistent with the screening as well as the productivity-augmenting hypothesis. His conclusion that college education contributes to productive ability is therefore unwarranted.

The screening hypothesis in its most basic form[1] asserts that schooling acquisition costs differ across individuals according to their ability levels. If high ability individuals face lower marginal cost of schooling schedules than do low ability individuals, the former group will for a given return obtain more education. Employers will pay higher wages to the more educated because they recognize that ability and attained level of education are positively correlated as the result of differential costs.

Screening can be contrasted with the productivity augmentation view of schooling. The latter position holds that schools actually do alter an individual's productivity not simply by producing an optimal sort (although this is not excluded),[2] but primarily by augmenting an individual's *ex post* ability.

What is important here is a fact that has made it virtually impossible to come up with a valid test of the screening hypothesis. That fact is that from an individual's point of view, it is almost always irrelevant whether schooling is a screen or productivity augmenter.[3] Human capital analyses are consistent with both. Since the individual is simply assumed to maximize the present value of his income stream, he is unconcerned with the employer's reason for paying higher wages. As long as the acquisition of schooling is the least expensive way to inform potential employers of his high ability, he will still "invest" in it just as he would if it actually increased his productivity. (In fact, the two hypotheses have different implications for society only when there are lower cost ways to the group of providing information on differential ability. The possibility arises in Spence when individuals know their true abilities and can be more cheaply induced to report them accurately). This brings us back to the Wise paper which, like others,[4] attempts to ascertain the validity of the screening hypothesis.

Wise cites four pieces of evidence which he claims lend support to the productivity-augmenting view of schooling. First, he argues that if grades merely attest to a student's *ex ante* ability rather than to differences in amounts of acquired knowledge (under screening, this is zero for all individuals), grades should have a small effect on compensation for individuals from higher quality colleges. (Students from these schools, he suggests, vary less in innate ability than those from lower quality institutions). The "screening prediction" is not borne out. Nor should it be. Even if differences in ability are finer on the scale of academic per-

*Assistant professor of economics, University of Chicago, and research associate of the National Bureau of Economic Research.
[1] See Michael Spence or Joseph Stiglitz for a clear discussion of the screening hypothesis.
[2] See Finis Welch (1970, 1973) for a variant on this theme.

[3] A possible exception is mentioned below.
[4] See Kenneth Wolpin, for example. This is discussed briefly below.

VOL. 67 NO. 2   *LAZEAR: ACADEMIC ACHIEVEMENT*   253

formance (such as SAT scores), there is no reason to expect that the mapping from school performance or even "innate" ability to worker productivity and compensation is linear.[5] That is, differences in "ability" at high levels may matter more for work-productivity variations than differences in ability at low levels where jobs command less responsibility. Differences in grades at high levels of ability, i.e., where individuals graduate from highly rated institutions, may well be associated with larger wage level and wage growth differences than those at low levels of ability. This result would be quite consistent with screening.

Wise's second argument relates to incremental effects of graduate education. If grades are merely a stamp which certify the individual's underlying attributes, he suggests, there should be no additional impact of graduate school performance on salary once undergraduate records are held constant. His evidence contradicts this prediction. But this can hardly be construed to be inconsistent with screening. All one has to argue is that both pieces of information are useful to an employer's evaluation. Nor does this require that one's imagination be stretched. There is no reason why an individual who obtains an A average as an undergraduate, but a C average in his M.A. program should have the same expected "innate" ability as the student who received A's throughout his education. The fact that an individual is willing to undertake additional schooling may, by itself, say something about inherent skills. His performance in that graduate program merely tells more.

A related piece of evidence deals with high school versus college performance. The prediction of a screening-type explanation, Wise claims, is that the effects of high school grades and undergraduate records should be confounded. Instead, he finds that high school

grades are insignificant and the effect of college grades is virtually unaffected. This does not refute the screening hypothesis. Rather, it says that high school performance as measured by grades does not matter. This finding, if disturbing, is disturbing to the productivity-augmenting hypothesis as well. The insignificance of high school grades probably results from another factor. College quality might say much more about high school performance through selectivity than high school grades themselves. If college quality is included in the (unreported) regression, the insignificance of high school grades would be less than surprising.

The final point relates to the finding that there is little correlation between college quality or rank within the college and initial position within the firm. If we take the evidence at face value, it should suffice to point out that this poses a problem for productivity-augmenting interpretations of schooling as well. This puzzle, along with the corresponding finding that initial salary is unaffected by these factors, can be reconciled. If schooling is merely a screen, then upon entry to the firm, individuals may differ, not in their current productivities, but in their abilities to acquire job-related skills at work. Thus, initial wages would be similar while rates of wage growth would differ.

The point may be generalized. It is often suggested that if schooling acts merely as a screen, it should become relatively less important as one's working life progresses. Thus, differences in wages between schooling groups should be most important upon graduation. However, inferences on screening drawn from this sort of analysis are incorrect. First, even if schooling is not productive per se, the more able, highly schooled individuals may enjoy steeper age-earnings profiles simply because of differential ability growth or depreciation over time. For example, age may have a greater detrimental effect on the productivity of low ability workers who specialize in physical activity than on high ability workers who specialize in mental activity. Second, if innate ability affects the rate of skill acquisition once on the job, more highly schooled workers can anticipate more rapid wage growth as the result of higher returns to

---

[5]Furthermore, there is little reason to even accept the assumption that abilities vary less at high quality schools. As Wise points out, SAT scores are at best ordinal. If ability is distributed normally, the differences between the highest and lowest score in the top and bottom deciles will be larger than the difference between the highest and lowest score in a middle decile.

on-the-job training. This is consistent with the notion of job tracking. If individuals get on job tracks, their perceived initial ability for which schooling may be a signal, can be instrumental in altering the slope of age-earnings relationships.[6]

Additional rationalizations are numerous, but the point is clear. Inferences cannot easily be drawn from wage growth data to either refute or confirm screening explanations of schooling. As already mentioned, the criticism should not be confined to the Wise paper. Attempts to test for the validity of screening have been frustrated elsewhere as well. Therefore, consider two potential tests of screening.

The first is derived from the observation that employers sometimes offer to send employees to school "all expenses paid." If screening were the only motivation for schooling acquisition, one would not observe employers bearing all costs since the screening mechanism works by forcing individuals to bear differential costs of schooling. However, what one observes is that workers in a given job at a given wage receive the same nominal compensation to attend school. Even in the context of screening, those with the highest ability will have the lowest true cost and therefore earn the highest profit on this transaction. Thus, the more able are more likely to accept the employer's schooling offer and the screening hypothesis is saved again.

The second test relies on finding a group of individuals for whom screening is irrelevant. Wolpin uses this approach. He argues that the self-employed will not invest in schooling if it is merely a screen. Thus, under screening, self-employed individuals should have lower at-

tained levels of education. He finds that they do not. This test requires two assumptions: First, it must be the case that individuals determine the probability of self-employment before investing in education. Second, it must be the case that their customers do not use their credentials as a signal in assessing product quality. In the case of physicians, dentists, lawyers, and other professionals, the second assumption is unlikely to be valid.

Valid methods for separating screening from productivity-augmenting views of education on the basis of different implications are hard to come by. The Wise paper, although perhaps misnamed, is interesting and important in providing evidence on differential returns to schooling. It cannot, however, be regarded as a refutation of the screening hypothesis.

---

[6]This is consistent with queue theories of labor markets. Here the most able are most likely to be trained. See (among others) Lester Thurow for a discussion along these lines.

REFERENCES

M. Spence, "Job Market Signalling," *Quart. J. Econ.*, Aug. 1973, *87*, 355–79.

J. Stiglitz, "The Theory of Screening, Education and the Distribution of Income," *Amer. Econ. Rev.*, June 1975, *65*, 283–300.

L. Thurow, "Education and Economic Equality," *Publ. Interest*, Summer 1972, *28*, 66–81.

F. Welch, "Education in Production," *J. Polit Econ.*, Jan./Feb. 1970, *78*, 35–59.

———, "Education, Information, and Efficiency," Nat. Bur. Econ. Res. working pap. no. 1, June 1973.

D. Wise, "Academic Achievement and Job Performance," *Amer. Econ. Rev.*, June 1975, *65*, 350–66.

K. Wolpin, "Education and Screening," Nat. Bur. Econ. Res. working pap. no. 104, Aug. 1975.

[12]

Agency, Earnings Profiles, Productivity, and Hours Restrictions

By EDWARD P. LAZEAR*

Economists have concerned themselves with the relationship between a worker's wage rate and his productivity for many years now. The controversy extends back to the early debates on "marginalism" and attempts to demonstrate that variations in wage rates across workers do not correspond to variations in their productivity. The industrial relations literature is replete with examples of empirical analyses along these lines. Theoretical discussions of the separation between wage rates and productivity are copious as well, suggesting that competition breaks down in the labor market context.

This paper argues that it is optimal to construct age-earnings profiles which pay workers less than the value of marginal products (*VMP*) when they are young and more than the value of marginal products when they are old.

The basic point is that even in the absence of on-the-job training or skill acquisition, upward-sloping age-earnings profiles are prevalent. This payment scheme raises workers' utility at the firm's zero-profit equilibrium above that generated by a profile which pays a worker his spot *VMP* at each point in time. This results because holding out payments until late in the individual's lifetime alters the worker's incentives to reduce his effort on the job. As the result, the wage performs two functions. First, it induces workers to supply hours to the labor market, and second, it determines the productivity of each hour spent working. In order to achieve efficiency on the hours and effort margins, hours restrictions are in-cluded in wage contracts.[1] This yields a number of implications, some of which are identical to earlier models of age-earnings profiles and others of which differ from those models.

The major points are:

First, wages grow with experience, even if productivity does not. Senior workers receive high salaries, not because they are so much more productive than junior workers, but because paying them higher wages produces appropriate work incentives for them and for their more junior coworkers.

Second, as a result of this separation between wages and spot marginal product, the labor supply decision is distorted. Therefore, efficient employment contracts have hours requirements and restrictions.

Third, a temporary separation is an extreme form of apparent deviation between desired and actual number of hours worked. It is argued below that temporary separations bring about an efficient allocation of time. Allowing workers to choose the number of hours worked at each point in time is inferior and results in inefficiencies.

Fourth, piece rate and self-employed workers will have flatter and more variable wage rates over the lifetime than will time-rate workers.

I. A Model

Since workers are agents of the owner of the firm, it is not automatic that the interests of workers and owners coincide. Workers, for example, prefer to exert less effort per

*University of Chicago and National Bureau of Economic Research. I am indebted to Gary Becker, Fischer Black, Dennis Carlton, Merton Miller, Melvin Reder, and Sherwin Rosen for helpful comments on an earlier draft. Financial support from the National Science Foundation is gratefully acknowledged.

[1] The approach is similar to that used in the "agency" literature. A few recent papers on this subject and its relationship to earnings are Armen Alchian and Harold Demsetz, Michael Jensen and William Meckling, Stephen Ross, E. Prescott and R. Townsend, G. Calvo and S. Wellisz, Gary Becker and George Stigler, Robert Barro, Eugene Fama, and W. White.

VOL. 71 NO. 4   LAZEAR: EARNINGS PROFILES AND PRODUCTIVITY   607

unit of time worked if their compensation remains unaltered by this effort reduction. Employers, on the other hand, prefer that workers perform at a higher level of effort in order to increase productivity per dollar of wage payment. Sometimes it is efficient to allow the worker to shirk and to pay him less as the result. This occurs when the gains to the worker exceed the cost to the firm of allowing this type of malfeasant behavior. In other instances, however, both workers and firms prefer that the worker does not shirk. Wages in equilibrium will be sufficiently higher so that workers prefer the high-wage/high-effort package to the low-wage/low-effort package. In such a case, it is necessary to construct a compensation scheme that induces the worker to behave optimally. The worker must be paid in a way which brings his interests as agent into harmony with the employer's interests as principal. In the model presented below, it will be shown that an upward-sloping age-earnings profile performs such a task. Even in the absence of any on-the-job training or investment in human capital, it pays to enter into long-term wage-employment relationships which pay workers wage rates less than their VMP when they are junior, and more than their VMP when they are senior employees.

Let us start by assuming that capital markets are perfect and there is complete information. Under these circumstances, a worker is indifferent between a wage path which offers him his spot wage at each point in time, illustrated by the curve $V(t)$ in Figure 1, and one which pays less than his marginal product initially and more than his marginal product at the end of his working career so long as the present value of the two streams is the same. $W(t)$ in Figure 1 is constructed so that, given the market rate of interest, the present value of the path $W(t)$ from zero to T is equal to the present value of the path $V(t)$ from zero to T. If $\bar{W}(t)$ is the reservation wage profile, then the optimal date of contract termination is T.[2] Note

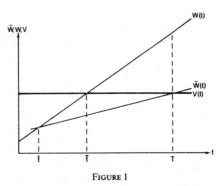

FIGURE 1

that T is the efficient date of retirement; that is, it is the date at which the value of a worker's time used outside this firm exceeds the value of his time used inside the firm. It is therefore the socially efficient point of contract termination.

If other things are equal, workers are indifferent between the two paths. Other things are not equal, however. If receiving one's contracted salary is contingent upon a given performance level at each point in time t, then the costs to the worker associated with shirking are higher given path $W(t)$ than given path $V(t)$. If, at the extreme, shirking results in immediate dismissal, then the larger is the amount of earnings paid at the end of the worklife, the greater would be the cost associated with a given amount of shirking.

Firms may also deviate from the contract. The most obvious form of deviation manifests itself as unanticipated termination of the worker's labor contract before time T. For example, in a world where no information passes from old workers to new workers, it is optimal for the firm to terminate all

---

[2] This result is used in my (1979 b) article in order to generate mandatory retirement. At T, the wage rate is greater than the individual's reservation wage and the

value of his marginal product. Although T is the socially efficient point of retirement, the individual facing a wage path $W(t)$ would not voluntarily retire at that point if given the option. Therefore, the contract must state T as an explicit date of termination. There is no cost to this in an *ex ante* sense because both streams, $W(t)$ and $V(t)$ through T, yield the same present value. Note also that $\bar{W} < W$ for $t < \hat{t}$ in Figure 1 does not imply that the worker chooses leisure. Since $V(t) > \bar{W}(t)$ it is efficient for him to work and since enjoying high wages later in life can be made contingent upon his working now, he will agree to work even though $\bar{W} < W$.

workers at time $\bar{t}$. It is unlikely, however, that contract violations are costless. To the extent that new workers use the firm's history as an indicator of future honesty, a cost is associated with any violation.[3] By altering the shape of the wage profile, the incentives for firm defaults are also altered. Under certain circumstances, a flatter wage profile, that is, one in which a smaller amount of earnings are withheld until late in the worker's life, will result in less dishonesty by firms.

Steeper profiles increase worker effort while flatter profiles will tend to make firms more honest. It seems reasonable, then, to suppose that there will be some optimal profile which minimizes total offenses and therefore maximizes workers' lifetime earnings subject to a zero-profit constraint. Let us proceed more formally.

Let $W(t)$ represent the worker's wage rate at each point in time t. Let $V(t)$ reflect his marginal product at time t if he works at "full" effort. If $\tilde{f}(t)$ is the probability of worker cheating at time t, then $\tilde{f}(t)$ will depend upon the shape of $W(t)$. Suppose that each worker is endowed with a $\theta(t)$, the value of which is known to the worker, but not necessarily known to the firm. Let $\theta(t) \sim f[\theta(t)]$. The term θ is the value (in current dollars) that the worker receives from shirking, reflecting the leisure value of working at a lower effort level. Then $\tilde{f}(t)$ is derived as follows.

Let $\tilde{W}(t)$ be the worker's reservation wage at time t. Let $\tilde{g}(t)$ be the probability that the firm defaults on the contract by terminating the worker at $t < T$. The worker shirks at t if the return $\theta(t)$ exceeds the cost to the worker of shirking. Assume for simplicity that the costs of detection are zero and that the worker is caught and dismissed if he shirks. (This is shown to be an efficient rule below. Replacing this with the assumption that the detection is not certain is trivial. It alters no results, but adds notation.) The cost to the worker of shirking at t is the difference between what he earns at his current firm,

[3] This is the notion that reputation capital is affected by performance. This is analyzed in the context of product quality by Benjamin Klein et al.

$W(t)$, and what he can earn elsewhere (or the value of his leisure if this is higher), $\tilde{W}(t)$. The worker shirks at some point t in his worklife if

$$(1) \quad \theta(t) > \left[e^{rt} \int_t^T \left\{ W(\tau) - W(\tau) \right. \right.$$
$$- \left(\tilde{f}(\tau) + \tilde{g}(\tau) \right)$$
$$\times \left[e^{r\tau} \int_\tau^T \left(W(\delta) - \tilde{W}(\delta) \right) e^{-r\delta} d\delta \right]$$
$$\left. \left. + \tilde{f}(\tau)\theta(\tau) \right\} e^{-r\tau} d\tau \right] \quad \text{for any } t$$

Defining the right-hand side of (1) as $R(t)$, the optimal time of shirking is $\underline{t}$ such that $e^{-r\underline{t}}[\theta(\underline{t}) - R(\underline{t})] > e^{-rt}[\theta(t) - R(t)] \forall t \neq \underline{t}$. Thus $R(t)$ consists of the difference between what the worker can earn at his present firm and what he can earn elsewhere ($e^{rt}\int_t^T [W(t) - \tilde{W}(t)]e^{-r\tau} d\tau$), plus his return to shirking ($e^{rt}\int_t^T (\tilde{f}(t)\theta(t)e^{-r\tau} d\tau$) minus the probability that firm or worker initiated separation occurs in the future times the loss if that occurs

$$e^{rt} \int_t^T \left(\tilde{f}(\tau) + \tilde{g}(\tau) \right) \left[e^{r\tau} \int_\tau^T \left(W(\delta) \right. \right.$$
$$\left. \left. - \tilde{W}(\delta) \right) e^{-r\delta} d\delta \right] e^{-r\tau} d\tau$$

$R(t)$ is the *ex post* rent that the employee receives by staying with the firm. In terms of Figure 2, $R(t^*)$ is roughly the present value of area $AECD$. *Ex post* rent will vary over the contract period, depending upon the difference between the $W(t)$ and $\tilde{W}(t)$ paths, their rates of convergence and the discount rate.

Since $\tilde{W}(t)$, $\theta(t)$, and r are exogenous, specifying the $W(t)$ path defines $R(t)$. Assume for simplicity, that $\underline{t}$, the optimal time of shirking does not vary across workers. (The value of shirking, $e^{-r\underline{t}}[\theta(\underline{t}) - R(\underline{t})]$, does vary across workers since θ varies across workers.) Since $\theta \sim f(\theta)$ across workers the

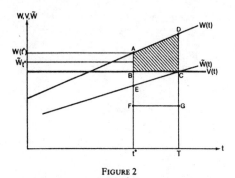

FIGURE 2

probability that a worker shirks at time t is

$$(2) \quad f(t) = \begin{cases} F[R(\underline{t})] & \text{for } t = \underline{t} \\ 0 & \text{otherwise,} \end{cases}$$

where $\quad F[R(\underline{t})] \equiv \int_{R(\underline{t})}^{\infty} f(\theta(\underline{t})) d\theta(\underline{t})$

Therefore the greater is $R(\underline{t})$, the less likely is shirking to occur.

The firm's decision to default on the worker's contract can be modeled similarly. Let $\mu(t) \sim g[\mu(t)]$ be the cost to the firm of early default. This cost may reflect the increased difficulty of attracting workers next period, the cost of strikes which result, or other costs associated with morale problems. The firm defaults if for some t,

$$(3) \quad \mu(t) < e^{rt} \int_t^T \left\{ W(\tau) - V(\tau) - \left(\tilde{f}(\tau) \right. \right.$$

$$+ \tilde{g}(\tau) e^{rt} \int_\tau^T [W(\delta) - V(\delta)] e^{-r\delta} d\delta$$

$$\left. \left. + \tilde{f}(\tau) C(\tau) \right\} e^{-r\tau} d\tau$$

where $C(t)$ is the cost that the firm suffers in loss of output when the worker shirks. Defining the right-hand side of (3) as $D(t)$, the optimal time of firm default is $\bar{t}$ such that $e^{-r\bar{t}}[D(\bar{t}) - \mu(\bar{t})] > e^{-rt}[D(t) - \mu(t)] \forall t \neq \bar{t}$. Thus $D(t)$ consists of the difference between what the worker is paid and what he is

worth, $e^{rt} \int_t^T W(\tau) - V(\tau) e^{-r\tau} d\tau$, minus the probability of separation in the future times what is saved if a separation occurs,

$$e^{rt} \int_t^T \left(\tilde{f}(\tau) + \tilde{g}(\tau) \right) e^{rt} \int_\tau^T (W(\delta)$$

$$- V(\delta)) e^{-r\delta} d\delta$$

plus the probability that the worker shirks times the direct cost imposed on the firm if that happens, $e^{rt} \int_t^T \tilde{f}(\tau) C(\tau) e^{-r\tau} d\tau$. Given (3), a $W(t)$ path defines $D(t)$ so the probability of firm default at time t is

$$(4) \quad g(t) = \begin{cases} G[D(\bar{t})] & \text{for } t = \bar{t} \\ 0 & \text{otherwise} \end{cases}$$

where $\quad G[D(\bar{t})] \equiv \int_{-\infty}^{D(\bar{t})} g[\mu(t)] d\mu(t)$

In terms of Figure 2, $D(t^*)$ is roughly the present value of area $ABCD$. As $D(t)$ increases $R(t)$ tends to increase. This encourages firm default, but discourages worker shirking. (Incidentally, the term "default" is appropriate since the firm essentially is borrowing from the worker by paying him less than VMP when he is young and repaying him by paying more than VMP when old.)

The competitive firm must offer a path $W(t)$ which maximizes the worker's expected wealth subject to the constraint that the expected present value of lifetime marginal product equals the expected value of wages paid out. So the problem is

$$(5) \quad \underset{W(t)}{\text{Max}} \int_0^T \left\{ W(t) - e^{rt} \left(\tilde{f}(t) + \tilde{g}(t) \right) \right.$$

$$\times \int_t^T (W(\tau) - \bar{W}(\tau)) e^{-r\tau} d\tau$$

$$\left. + \tilde{f}(t) \theta_t(t) \right\} e^{-rt} dt$$

where $\theta_t(t)$ is the value of $\theta(t)$ for the marginal worker who shirks at time t and by equation (1), $\theta_t(t) = R(t)$.

The constraints are first, that honest firms pay out a wage stream, the expected value of which equals the expected value of lifetime marginal product:

(6a) $\int_0^T \Big\{ V(t) - e^{rt}\tilde{f}(t) \int_t^T V(\tau)e^{-r\tau}d\tau$

$\qquad - \tilde{f}(t)C(t) \Big\} e^{-rt}dt - \xi = \int_0^T \Big\{ W(t)$

$\qquad - e^{rt}\tilde{f}(t)\int_t^T W(\tau)e^{-r\tau}d\tau \Big\} e^{-rt}dt$

where ξ is hiring cost.[4] Second, the optimal contract length or retirement date T should be chosen efficiently so that at T expected VMP equals the alternative use of time. So select T such that

(6b) $V(T) - \tilde{f}(T)[C(T) - \theta_T(T)] = \tilde{W}(T)$

The problem can now be solved. Substituting (6a) into (5) and rearranging yields

(7) $\underset{W(t)}{Max} \int_0^T \Big\{ V(t) + e^{rt}\tilde{f}(t)\int_t^T [\tilde{W}(\tau)$

$\qquad - V(\tau)]e^{-r\tau}d\tau - \tilde{f}(t)[C(t) - \theta_t(t)]$

$\qquad - e^{rt}(\tilde{g}(t))\int_t^T (W(\tau) - \tilde{W}(\tau))e^{-r\tau}d\tau \Big\}$

$\qquad\qquad\qquad\qquad\qquad \times e^{-rt}dt - \xi$

subject to

$V(T) - \tilde{f}(T)[C(T) - \theta_T(T)] = \tilde{W}(T)$

Since $V(t)$ and ξ are exogenous, maximiza-

---

[4]Dishonest firms are not required to earn zero profits. If they are endowed with a low cost of default, they earn rent as the result. Any firm which offers to pay an amount greater than the left-hand side of (6a) immediately identifies itself as dishonest and therefore draws no workers.

tion of (7) is the same as minimization of

(8)

$\underset{W(t)}{Min} \int_0^T \Big\{ e^{rt}\tilde{g}(t)\int_t^T [W(\tau) - \tilde{W}(\tau)]e^{-r\tau}d\tau$

$\qquad - e^{rt}\tilde{f}(t)\int_t^T [\tilde{W}(\tau) - V(\tau)]e^{-r\tau}d\tau$

$\qquad + \tilde{f}(t)[C(t) - \theta_T(t)] \Big\} e^{-rt}dt,$

subject to (6b).

First, consider the simplest world. Let us suppose that workers have perfect information about a firm's history and know, therefore, whether or not the firm has adopted an honest strategy in the past. If the firm has defaulted in the past, and we assume that $\mu(t)$ does not vary with chronological time, it will do so in the future. As a result, a once dishonest firm is always dishonest. Any contract that it offers is dominated by that of the honest firm. The reason is that in order to induce a worker to accept a long-term contract in the dishonest firm, a flatter $W(t)$ path must be offered (to reduce the firm's incentive to default). But if this is done, the worker's incentive to shirk rises, which causes lower worker productivity.

If we assume that $max[\theta] < C(t) \forall t$ so that $[C(t) - \theta]$ is positive, then shirking associated with the dishonest firm's contract lowers the expected present value of lifetime wealth. (If $C(t) < \theta$, it is efficient to permit the worker to shirk.) The honest firm, on the other hand, can offer a contract which results in less worker shirking. Workers prefer this. Therefore, all dishonest firms vanish. As a result, $\tilde{g}(t) = 0 \forall t$ in equilibrium.

If $\tilde{g}(t) = 0$, however, the solution to (8) becomes obvious. Wealth is maximized when $\tilde{f}(t) = 0 \forall t$ (again, because $C - \theta_t > 0$). The path that sets $\tilde{f}(t) = 0 \forall t$ in general is not unique. Consider a simple case where all workers have $\theta(t) = \bar{\theta} \forall t$. Here, any $W(t)$ path which provides that workers are "owed" more than $\bar{\theta}$ in present value terms at all t induces zero shirking.

Figure 3 illustrates some possible wage paths. One path is ABP. Here the worker receives a constant amount less than his VMP

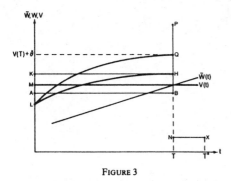

FIGURE 3

over his lifetime, but receives a large lump sum at T to set present values of payment and marginal products equal. There is no worker shirking because $R(t)$ is always greater than $\bar{\theta}$; it never pays to shirk. Another possibility is $LKHQ$. This is the Becker-Stigler solution where the worker posts a "bond" equal to LM, is paid interest on it (KM), and gets back the principal at T ($HQ=LM$). A third possibility is the more conventional $LHNX$. Here the worker is paid less than his VMP initially, more at T, and receives a pension equal to NX. As long as the present value of remaining rent exceeds $\bar{\theta}$ and the present value of lifetime payments equals expected lifetime VMP, this is an optimal path.

The important point is that the optimal paths are upward sloping; $W(T) > W(0)$, even though there is no on-the-job training and no rising VMP schedule. It is optimal to select a profile such that wages are low initially and high later, even in the absence of any experience effect on productivity. Yet, the failure of the spot wage to equal the spot VMP is not a failure of the competitive labor market. On the contrary, it insures higher wealth for the relevant labor force.

In a world which has perfect capital markets, all profiles which yield the same present value are equal. As these assumptions are relaxed below, some changes will result, but the point remains throughout: The link between the spot wage and spot marginal product may be broken even in a fully competitive labor market with risk neutral workers.

II. Determinacy of the Optimum Wage Contract

In the preceding discussion, constraints on the shape of the optimal profile were imposed, but no unique solution could be found. In this section, uniqueness of the optimal path is briefly discussed. The discussion follows three avenues. First, firm default is considered. Second, borrowing constraints are discussed. Third, the effect of taxes is examined.

A. Firm Defaults

The case of perfect information has been analyzed above. The only equilibrium is one with complete honesty by firms. However, if information about the firm's default history is less than perfect, the distribution of default costs, $(g[\mu(t)])$, may well be such that it pays some firms to terminate workers early.[5] Under these circumstances, it is no longer optimal to set the worker shirking probability, $\bar{f}(t)$, equal to zero for all t. The solution in general has $\bar{f}(t)>0$ and $\bar{g}(t)>0$ for some t. Since endweighting the profile tends to increase firm default, the profile will tend to be less endweighted than it will be in the case of perfect information. Additionally, since $\bar{f}(t)>0$ in general, the length of the contract period will tend to be shorter.[6] Finally, since an increase in $R(t)$ can, in general, only be brought about by a decrease in $D(t)$, there is a tradeoff between firm defaults though premature termination and worker shirking which yields a unique solution for the $W(t)$ path. The path has the feature that it is upward sloping and tends to have a pension provision (payment beyond T without work) associated with it.

[5] It is not trivial to generate conditions under which this is so. What is necessary for a stable equilibrium, however, is that $\mu(t)$ is an increasing function of $D(t)$ where $\partial\mu(t)/\partial D(t)<1$ and that $\mu(t)>0$ for some firms even if $D(t)=0$. This says that the larger the gain to the firm from cheating, the larger are the costs borne next period. Without $\mu(t)>0$ and $\partial\mu(t)/\partial D(t)<1$ either all firms will default or raising $D(t)$ will not deter defaults.

[6] Robert Hall uses the notion of optimal contract duration to derive implications for unemployment. This may provide one rationalization for his assumption. Leif Danziger also examines the determination of optimal contract duration.

To see this, consider the general solution to (8). The Euler equation corresponding to (8) is not very useful because neither $\tilde{f}(t)$ nor $\tilde{g}(t)$ is a differential function of $W(t)$. From (1)–(4) it is clear that changes in $W(t)$ change t and $\bar{t}$ which makes the nature of the solution discrete.

It is helpful, therefore, to consider two cases. Consider first the case where $r=0$, and θ is constant over time, but varies across individuals. The optimal path can take one of four basic shapes shown in Figure 4: *ABCD*, *EFG*, *HBCK*, or *LFM* (or can be some hybrid of them). Paths *HBCK* and *LFM* can be ruled out immediately. Any firms for which the distribution of $\mu(t)$ requires the optimal paths to be downward sloping goes out of business. The reason is that paying a wage less than *VMP* at the end of life is only viable if there is slavery. (Otherwise workers quit when $W(t)<\tilde{W}(t)$.) Multiple crossing of V by $W(t)$ is ruled out because arguments which apply to *EFG* below will also apply to these paths. The comparison must then be between *ABCD* and *EFG*.

With *ABCD*, $D(t)$ is the same and equal to segment $\overline{CD}$ for all $0<t<T$ (see equation (3)). So $D(t)=\overline{CD}$ and firms will save hiring costs if they default only at T. The firms defaulting at T are those with $\mu(T)<\overline{CD}$.

$R(t)$, however, varies over time since $\tilde{W}(t)$ varies (see equation (1)). $R(t)$ is maximized at $t=T$. So all workers who shirk do so at T (and forego $\overline{CD}$). The shirking workers are those with $\theta(T)>\overline{CD}$.

Now consider *EFG*. Path $W(t)$ is drawn such that the area of triangle *FGC* equals $\overline{CD}$. Consider $D(t)$: $D(t)$ reaches a maximum at $t=t_1$ and then declines until $D(T)=0$. So all firm defaults occur at t_1. The firms that default are those that have $\mu<\overline{CD}$, so exactly the same firms that defaulted with *ABCD* default with *EFG*, but they will do so at t_1 rather than at T. For workers, $R(t)$ declines throughout and so $R(t)=R(T)$ and $t=T$. But $R(T)$ with *EFG* is in general smaller than $R(T)$ with *ABCD* because the area of *FGH* equals the length of $\overline{CD}$: that is, the worker has already received some of what is owed him before T on *EFG* but not so on *ABCD*. Therefore there is more worker shirking with *EFG* than with *ABCD*. But since the

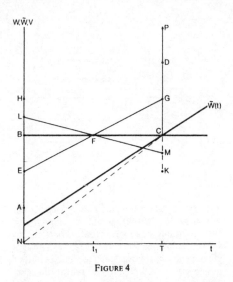

FIGURE 4

amount of firm default is the same in both cases, *ABCD* dominates.

Given that the optimal profile shape is determined, it is a relatively simple matter to solve for the optimal sizes of $R(T)$ and $D(T)$.

Since $\tilde{f}(t)=\tilde{g}(t)=0$ $\forall t\neq T$, $\int_T^T(V(\tau)-\tilde{W}(\tau))e^{-r\tau}d\tau=0$, $R(T)=D(T)=W(T)-\tilde{W}(T)$ (i.e., the worker's potential loss at T is $D(T)=W(T)-V(T)$), and $\theta_T(T)=R(T)$, (8) becomes

(9) $$\underset{R(T)}{Min}\, G[R(T)]R(T)$$
$$+F[R(T)][C(T)-R(T)]$$

Differentiating and setting the first derivative equal to zero yields

(10)
$$G[R(T)]+R(T)G'[R(T)]-F[R(T)]$$
$$+F'[R(T)][C(T)-R(T)]=0$$

or $$G[R(T)]+R(T)g[R(T)]-F[R(T)]$$
$$-f[R(T)][C(T)-R(T)]=0$$

Equation (10) determines the optimal $R(T)$ so that the optimal path is *ABCD* with $\overline{CD}=R(T)$. The spirit of (10) is to select $R(T)$ so as to trade off a dollar loss in worker wealth from worker shirking against a dollar loss in worker wealth through firm default.

Compare this solution to the earlier one with no firm default. There, $\tilde{f}(t)=0\ \forall t$. Here, in general, $\tilde{f}(T)>0$. In addition, $R(T)$ is smaller when there is endogenous firm cheating than when firm cheating is exogenous. So profiles are less endweighted with endogenous firm cheating. Finally, when firm cheating is endogenous, $\tilde{f}(T)>0$, so the optimal length of the contract will be shorter, by equation (6b).

Let us briefly consider another case. If $\mu(t)$ and $\theta(t)$ are not constant over time then the optimal paths have different shapes. Suppose, for example, that $\mu'(t)<0$ and $\theta'(t)<0$. Then the optimal path will have the shape shown by NCP in Figure 4. Since firms face the highest cost of default at low values of t and workers face the highest value of shirking at low values of t, $D(t)$ is relatively high when $\mu(t)$ is high (at low t's). Since $\theta(t)$ is highest for low t's, $R(t)$ is highest for low t's. The profile NCP gives this result. Here the optimal profile is upward sloping throughout.

All the paths discussed have one thing in common: The worker (and firm) is indifferent between a spike at T and a pension from T until death which has the same present expected value. Yet pensions are common and lump sum payments are not. The preference for pensions can be explained in a number of ways. First, if workers' time of death were uncertain and they were risk averse, purchase of a pension annuity would be preferred. The second argument is more compelling. Even if firms and workers can obtain the same before-tax return on their dollars, after-tax returns are larger for firms under many circumstances. Therefore, investing in pension funds rather than taking a lump sum payment may offer higher take-home income.

B. Borrowing Constraints and Taxes

The assumption that borrowing and lending can be undertaken at the market rate of interest is now relaxed. Like endogenous firm defaults, imperfect borrowing also yields a unique solution for the $W(t)$ path which, in general, is smooth and upward sloping. Without providing a great deal of justification, there are conditions under which it may be sensible to relax the assumption.[7] If workers have utility functions which are time separable and concave in income, then the optimal $W(t)$ path will remain upward sloping, even if all borrowing is prohibited, but will tend to be somewhat flatter than they are when no borrowing constraints are imposed. The intuition is straightforward. Steeper profiles reduce shirking and increase the level of wealth. At the same time, however, a steeper profile yields the worker a consumption time path which is less to his liking. Therefore, workers will trade off some wealth for a better time pattern of payments. Additionally, this yields positive worker shirking even if firms never default, a somewhat shorter contract period, and a unique upward-sloping $W(t)$ path.

A progressive income tax has the same effect on the profile as does a borrowing constraint. A borrowing constraint transforms income into utility along a concave schedule whereas a progressive income tax transforms gross income into net income (and then utility) along a concave schedule. Thus, the results are identical to those above. The profile will tend to be flatter (since more endweighting trades off less shirking against higher taxes); there will be positive worker shirking, a shorter contract period, and a unique upward-sloping age-earnings profile.

III. Additional Considerations

A. Unanticipated Events, Contract Rigidity, and Severance Pay

Complete certainty has been assumed so far. This implies that the VMP profile $V(t)$ and the reservation wage profile $\tilde{W}(t)$ are

---

[7]The details are worked out in an earlier draft. To give an example, if the worker has no wealth other than his wage income, the ability of the worker to quit his job to consume leisure (which the bank cannot tax) will affect the willingness of the bank to lend to the worker. This is unrelated to the worker's ability to "shirk" on the firm. Even if output, conditional upon working, were deterministic so that no shirking could occur, the worker has the same option to consume leisure. Therefore, any model which allows for maximization of utility over time is subject to this potentially important criticism.

known and nonstochastic at time zero. We now wish to relax that assumption and to consider the implications of uncertainty for efficiency and determination of the optimal wage profile.

Consider Figure 2. Suppose that at some time t^*, the worker receives an unanticipated wage offer from another firm equal to $\tilde{W}_r$. It is socially efficient for the worker to switch firms at that point since the value of his time in the new firm exceeds the value of his time in the old firm. However, given his wage rate of $W(t^*)$, other things equal he would prefer to remain with his current firm where his labor is less valuable. At time t^*, the firm still owes the worker the present value of trapezoid $ABCD$. If the worker could recoup that value at point t^* as severance pay, then he would choose to leave the firm and to work at the alternative job. Employers break even so the worker and the firm behave efficiently, if severance pay is permitted.

The argument is symmetric. If $V(t)$ were to fall to some unanticipated level below $\tilde{W}(t^*)$, say to $\overline{FG}$ in Figure 2, then there is some scheme which will induce the worker to leave efficiently. Let the firm offer the worker epsilon above the present value of $AECD$ to leave. The worker prefers this since he earns $\int_{t^*}^{T} W(t)e^{-rt}dt = \int_{t^*}^{T} \tilde{W}(t)e^{-rt}dt$ + the present value of $AECD$ if he stays, but he gets a payment of the present value of $AECD$ + epsilon if he leaves and then earns $\int_{t^*}^{T} \tilde{W}(t)e^{-rt}dt$ elsewhere. The latter dominates the former by epsilon. The firm benefits as well. If the worker stays, the *ex post* loss is only the present value of $AECD$ plus epsilon rather than $AFGD$. The advantage that this scheme has over employer initiated termination without severance pay at t^* is that the employer has no incentive to offer severance pay $AECD$ plus epsilon unless $V(t)$ has truly fallen. Employer initiated termination without severance pay creates information problems.

Note also that the efficient contract contains a clause which states that the worker may leave at any t and will be compensated $\int_t^T [W(t) - V(t)]e^{-rt}dt$ as severance pay. In addition, firms have the option to dismiss workers at $t < T$ as long as they pay the worker $\int_t^T [W(t) - \tilde{W}(t)]e^{-rt}dt$. So severance pay is larger when the firm initiates the separation (for reasons other than worker shirking).

This also implies that workers who are older than $\bar{t}$ in Figure 1 will be willing to accept a new job at a wage rate lower than their current wage even if all characteristics of the two jobs are the same and there is no hope of wage increases on the second. If the new wage lies between $V(t)$ and $W(t)$, the worker will leave and accept his severance pay. Public workers often retire from the public sector early to accept another at a lower wage. This "double dipping" phenomenon may well be an efficient arrangement where pension benefits serve as severance pay.[8]

B. *Piece Rates as an Alternative Compensation Scheme*

The contract discussed has the provision that workers who shirk are dismissed. An alternative is to pay the worker a lower salary for that period. This is what Fama refers to as "*ex post* settling up" or what amounts to paying a piece rate, an amount which depends directly upon the individual's output in the preceding time interval.[9] If output were costlessly measurable, *ex post* settling up yields an equally efficient solution. However, if output were costlessly observed, the principal agent distinction loses most of its meaning. Piece-rate workers are, in a relevant sense, self-employed. If it were cheaper to observe that shirking is positive than it was

---

[8]Severance pay may take the form of early pensions which exceed the actuarially fair value of the pension if the worker were to continue through normal retirement. Both R. Burkhauser and Alan Blinder et al. find that workers who retire early enjoy actuarially larger pension benefits.

[9]Piece rates are not easily distinguishable from time rates. To the extent that a worker's hourly wage in the future depends upon his output now, he receives "piece rate" compensation in some sense. The major distinguishing characteristic is that under piece rate compensation, as the term is used in this paper, a worker is compensated at the end of a period for work done during that period. This is not merely a point of semantics since the endgame problem is an essential part of the discussion. See my article with Sherwin Rosen for more on this point.

to determine the precise amount of shirking, the contract which dismissed all shirkers would dominate. The widespread existence of rules which require the dismissal of shirkers is testimony to measurement cost differences. (A worker caught sleeping on the job is usually dismissed rather than docked pay for the hours slept. Embezzlers find themselves without jobs when caught rather than with a smaller paycheck for the month.)

There is, however, a cost to using dismissal over the more continuous piece-rate scheme. Suppose output $V(t)$ were stochastic consisting of an effort component $E(t)$, and a luck component $u(t)$, so $V(t) = E(t) + u(t)$ and that only $V(t)$ could be measured. Under the dismissal scenario, a worker who experiences a bad draw is dismissed, even if his effort level is satisfactory. If there are any costs associated with job changes, this policy results in a loss of wealth to workers. Thus, in occupations where $\sigma_{u(t)}^2$ is large, paying a piece rate may well dominate, even if it is more costly to determine the exact level of shirking than it is to know that it is positive. The prediction is that piece rates will be found not only in occupations where output is measured cheaply, but also in occupations which have a large luck component associated with a given individual's variation in output over time. Salesmen fit this case well.[10]

Once one allows for a choice of compensation schemes, it is natural to consider endogenous monitoring. There is no reason to assume that the probability of detection is one or that detection is not chosen simultaneously with the shape and type of wage path. That much more difficult problem is left unsolved.

IV. Some Implications

A. *The Relationship between the Spot Wage and Marginal Product*

The upward-sloping age-earnings profile is an efficient compensation scheme which does not equalize spot wage rate and spot marginal product. A direct implication of this analysis is that a worker's earnings should rise more steeply than his marginal productivity over the lifetime.[11] This is consistent with often heard complaints that more senior workers earn considerably more than their juniors, but that these salary differences far overstate productivity differences. Senior workers are paid a high wage not because they are productive at that point in time, but rather because paying high wages to older workers induces young workers to perform at the optimal level of effort in hopes of growing old in that firm.

A somewhat trivial extension of this point is that the aggregate income distribution will have positive variance and, in fact, positive skew even if all individuals have the same ability and lifetime marginal product. Young workers are paid less than their marginal products. Old workers receive this amount plus interest which adds variance and skew to the distribution of income.

B. *Hours Constraints and Layoffs*

Consider the age-earnings profile illustrated in Figure 1. Wages are less than VMP when the worker is young and greater than VMP when the worker is old. Consider a time t such that $t < \bar{t}$. The worker's marginal

---

[10]Self-sorting as discussed by Joanne Salop and Steven Salop, and Rosen, insures that individuals who face large job changing costs or the least risk-averse workers who can trade a higher $\sigma_{u(t)}^2$ for a larger $E(t)$ select piece rate firms. This is one way by which the adverse effects of having a risk-averse manager in a risk-neutral firm can be mitigated. This problem, which has been considered by Donald Heckerman, can be solved by fixed "prize" compensation scheme. Here workers are paid W_1 if $V(t) > \bar{V}$ and W_2 if $V(t) < \bar{V}$. Under these circumstances, risk-averse worker do not necessarily avoid variance. My article with Rosen demonstrates that such a scheme is often efficient.

[11]Some evidence on this point is offered by Gene Dalton and Paul Thompson, and more recently, by James Medoff and K. Abraham. By examining data from two major American corporations, Medoff and Abraham find that wage rates grow with experience at a more rapid rate than does productivity when measured by the subjective evaluation of the supervisor. Merton Miller and Myron Scholes also provide evidence on this point. By using data on executive compensation they find that the deferred nature of the compensation package is often tax disadvantageous and argue that the reason for this form of compensation may be incentive related.

product is given by $V(t)$, while his wage rate $W(t)$ is less than that amount. If the worker were permitted to select the number of hours that he wished to work at that point in time, he would select hours consistent with the wage rate $W(t)$ rather than with the social value of time $V(t)$. A positively sloped supply curve of labor implies that the worker would choose to work too few hours at times earlier than t and too many hours at times later than t. (In fact, an extreme case of the desire to work too many hours after t results in mandatory retirement. See my 1979b article.) The steep age-earnings profile $W(t)$ results in an inefficient labor allocation over the lifetime. An efficient contract must constrain the worker to work the efficient number of hours at each point in his worklife. As a result, workers actually prefer to enter into long-term contracts which constrain them to work hours which they know will deviate from their hours choice at the spot wage. The reason is that the lifetime wealth associated with a contract which allows them to choose hours freely is sufficiently low to offset utility gains from flexible hours.[12] The proof of this proposition follows.

Consider a two-period world. Suppose, for simplicity, that the hours supply function is the same in both periods. Let VMP be constant across hours (again for simplicity) so that H^* is the efficient number of hours worked in periods 1 and 2 as shown in Figure 5. Let W_1^* and W_2^* be the wage rates which solve the optimization problem in (8) subject to constraint that total wages paid equal VMP (or that $(W_1^* + W_2^*)H^* = 2VH^*$ if $r=0$). Hours are constrained to be H^* in both periods. The question is, "does there exist another wage vector $[W_1, W_2]$ which allows the worker to choose his hours of work, which yields the worker higher utility and which is viable in that payouts to workers do not exceed VMP?"

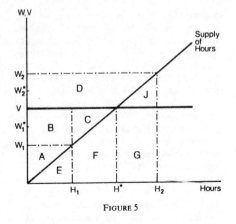

FIGURE 5

Suppose that there were such a wage vector. If it is truly utility increasing then the rent to the worker with $[W_1, W_2]$ and hours $[H_1, H_2]$ must exceed that generated by the constrained hours contract. In order for this to hold, the rent from the flexible hours contract

$$R_f \equiv A + (A + B + C + D)$$

where $A, \ldots, J$ are defined as the areas in Figure 5, must exceed the rent from the constrained hours contract. However, total wages paid under the constrained contract are $2(A + B + C + E + F)$. Total value of leisure foregone is $2(E + F)$. So rent from the constrained contract is

$$R_C = 2(A + B + C + E + F) - 2(E + F)$$
$$= 2(A + B + C)$$

Assume that such a flexible hours contract exists. Then

$$A + (A + B + C + D) > 2(A + B + C)$$

or $D > B + C$. For the flexible hours contract to be viable, it must also be true that wages paid out do not exceed total VMP or

$$(A + E) + (A + B + C + D + E + F + G + J)$$
$$\leqslant (A + E + B) + (A + B + E + C + F + G +)$$

or that $D + J \leqslant B$. This implies that $D < B$ and therefore that $D < B + C$. But this contradicts the assumption that $D > B + C$. This

---

[12] The deviation between desired and actual hours is discussed and analyzed by Orley Ashenfelter and J. Abowd and Ashenfelter. It should be mentioned that a two-part wage could bring about the same allocation of resources as single wage with hours constraint. These schemes imply the same age-earnings profile, however. Hall and Lilien also present a model where the workers give the hours decision over to employers as part of a second best bargaining process.

completes the proof that no flexible hours contract exists which both makes workers better off than the constrained hours contract and does not result in losses for the firm.

An implication is that young workers should complain that they are forced to work too many hours and old workers should similarly complain that they are not permitted to work enough. Complaints about mandatory retirement are extreme manifestations of this phenomenon. A corollary is that old workers are more likely to accept overtime hours than are young workers.

It is straightforward to extend the discussion of hours constraints over the lifetime to temporary separations. Involuntary separations are puzzling because they suggest that the spot wage does not adjust with *VMP*. Once it is recognized, however, that wage rates are not only able to allocate hours efficiently, but may also affect the output per hour, it is no longer surprising that the spot wage is not permitted to reflect spot *VMP* to insure an efficient hours allocation.

Consider the case of anticipated variations in labor demand which, for example, result from seasonal effects. Some workers who are "laid off" might be willing to work at the going wage or at their previous one, but are refused employment. Recall that the wage of employed workers also affect the effort level over the entire year so that bringing wages into line with a low *VMP* results in lower effort and output during the entire contract term.

An efficient contract is illustrated in Figure 6. Consider two workers: A is employed only during peak season and B is employed throughout the year. Suppose that A's and B's reservation wage functions are given by $\tilde{W}_A(t)$ and $\tilde{W}_B(t)$, respectively, in Figure 6. Periods 0 to t_0 and t_1 to t_2 are high seasons, t_0 to t_1 is low season. It is efficient for A to use his time in its alternative use between t_0 and t_1, while B should continue to work at the present firm throughout. The optimal wage path for A will not be the same as that for B, but one point is clear: Although offering $W_A(t) = W_B(t) = V(t)$ will induce efficiency in hours supplied, it will necessarily result in too much shirking. A superior path for A is $W_A(t)$ since it increases effort. But

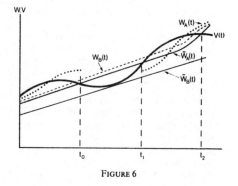

FIGURE 6

this path requires that A is unemployed between t_0 and t_1. Worker B continues to work during this period. There is no real cost to this seasonal layoff. Ex ante, A prefers $W_A(t)$ to path which pays spot *VMP* at each point since the latter induces more shirking and results in lower net *VMP* and lower wealth. Yet if A were asked whether he would like to work at the market wage (either his own wage at t_0 or $W_B(t)$ between t_0 and t_1), he would answer affirmatively, even though $W_A(t)$ with separations is efficient and preferred.[13]

"A" type workers are those with the most elastic labor supply whose alternative use of time is closest to their value at work. This suggests that the young workers (whose alternative may be school) are the first to be laid off in low season. As such, layoff by

---

[13] The notion that long-term contracts which imply layoffs during cyclical downturns dominate spot *VMP* contracts has been analyzed. See, for example, Costas Azariadis, Martin Baily, Herschel Grossman, Dale Mortensen, and James Brown. A major difference between this analysis and those in previous analyses is that risk neutrality is sufficient, whereas in previous analyses, risk aversion is the primary engine of "involuntary separation." In this paper, separations come about because the wage rate is a tool which is reserved to equilibrate the quality-of-hours margin, so that the quantity of hours is necessarily set by explicit means. There is no reason to expect that workers would be paid during layoff periods. If the risk aversion story were correct, one would expect that workers on layoff would receive earnings related to the difference between the wage rate and the value of leisure. This would provide more complete income smoothing. Workers with different values of leisure self-sort across firms which offer different combinations of wages when employed and wages when on layoff, all consistent, of course, with total compensation equal to expected marginal product.

618 THE AMERICAN ECONOMIC REVIEW SEPTEMBER 1981

reverse seniority can be viewed as part of the efficient contract.

This section can be summarized. The wage rate affects two variables. It determines the amount of effort per hour worked and influences the desire to supply hours to the market. Since there is but one degree of freedom, it is superior to allow the wage rate to adjust the effort margin and to use quantity constraints to obtain efficiency on the hours margin. This is because it is cheaper to monitor and directly regulate the quantity of hours worked than it is to monitor and regulate the amount of effort supplied. Note also that piece-rate or self-employed workers, whose wages equal marginal product, do not experience involuntary layoffs even though cyclical variations in their employment may be as pronounced. Since their wages reflect the actual spot value of their output, they will voluntarily slow down or take a vacation during off-peak periods. Also, since piece-rate workers earn what they produce, there will be fewer disciplinary dismissals of piece-rate workers so permanent separation rates should be lower for piece-rate employees.

C. Other Implications

1. *Human Capital*. The upward-sloping age-earnings profiles generated by the model presented in this paper is difficult to distinguish from an upward sloping age-earnings profile generated by the standard human capital theory. Many of the implications are the same.

First, ability constant, both models suggest that steeper age-earnings profiles are coupled with lower starting wages. In a human capital story, this is because workers trade off earnings now in order to purchase human capital which increases their productivity later in life. In the incentives scenario discussed in this paper, workers prefer that firms pay lower wages initially and higher wages later so that incentives to shirk are reduced.

Second, separation of older workers from firms results in a larger decrease in wages than does separation of younger workers from firms in both models. In the human capital model this is the result of specific on-the-job training or specific human capital which the worker has acquired over his

worklife. In the incentives scenario, it is the result of an age-earnings profile which pays workers less than the VMP when they are young and more than the VMP when they are old.

Related to that is the implication that there are fewer worker-firm separations when workers are old than when workers are young. Again, the human capital model yields this as the result of the accumulation of specific on-the-job training. The incentives scheme gives this as an implication when severance pay arrangements are imperfect or taxed. This occurs because the deviation between wages and marginal products increases over the worker's lifetime.

A job switch is often followed by an initial drop in wages with a succeeding increase in the rate of wage growth. Human capital theory can explain this as a reinvestment period during which the individual acquires the new specific capital. The incentives scenario suggests that this is the period during which the worker is putting up collateral.

An important, but overlooked point, is that investment in firm-specific human capital also requires hours constraints and severance pay as part of an optimal contract. Since any sharing of costs and benefits of the firm-specific human capital results in a wage which is below the worker's true marginal product, trained workers voluntarily choose too few hours. The problem is most severe when the firm bears most of the costs and reaps most of the benefits of the specific capital, and hours constraints should be most prevalent under these circumstances.

There are some implications which do differ across models. In the human capital framework, there is no reason to believe that piece-rate workers should have flatter age-earnings profiles than time rate workers. That is, there is no obvious reason why skill acquisition should be less profitable in occupations which pay workers piece rates than in occupations which pay workers time rates. On the other hand, the incentives scheme has the implication that piece rates are used in occupations where the uncontrollable variance in output and therefore income is relatively high. When piece rates are used, the resulting age-earnings profile is flat because piece rates are a substitute for upward-sloping age-earnings profiles. Thus, salesmen should have less steeply rising profiles than should management employees. As a corollary, individuals who work in large firms should have steeper age-earnings profiles than those who work in small owner-operated firms where monitoring costs are low. Self-employed workers should also have flatter profiles.

Of course, the most fundamental difference between the human capital scenario and the incentives scheme is that in the human capital model, earnings and productivity are positively correlated over the life cycle. In the simplest form of the incentives scheme with no skill acquisition or depreciation, the correlation between productivity and wages over the life cycle is zero.

One final point. Some empirical phenomena do not square well with the human capital theory. The discrete nature of the age-earnings profile is difficult to reconcile in terms of standard human capital models. For example, on a given day, all the vice presidents of a corporation may be earning $75,000 per year. The following day, one is promoted to president and earns $250,000 a year. It is difficult to rationalize this jump in earnings as reflecting a jump in human capital. On the other hand, if incentive effects are produced by this wage increase, it can be rationalized easily.

2. *Unions*. The upward-sloping age-earnings profile is the outcome of contract negotiations because of an asymmetry. The worker is finite lived whereas the firm is assumed to operate with a longer time horizon. A labor union is also likely to have a longer relationship with an employer than is an individual worker. If the union can act as an intermediary and, through peer pressure or more direct supervision, can monitor and regulate the work force at a lower cost than can the firm the union may be a substitute for an upward-sloping age-earnings profile. If a worker shirks, the union is taxed in succeeding rounds of negotiations. In turn, the union taxes the actual offender. If this were so, age-earnings profiles would be flatter, but higher, for union workers.[14] Alternatively,

the union may be relatively more efficient at monitoring firms. If this were the case, then union workers would have steeper and higher profiles than their nonunion counterparts.

V. Conclusion

This paper suggests that by using a more steeply rising age-earnings profile, a worker's incentive to shirk is reduced. As the result, workers are better off and their lifetime wealth levels are increased. Age-earnings profiles are upward sloping, even if a worker's productivity does not vary over his life cycle. Setting wages equal to spot marginal product at all points in time is dominated by a contract which selects a steeply rising age-earnings profile and uses quantity restrictions on hours worked to obtain an efficient allocation of time to and effort on the job.

TABLE 1—DEFINITION OF VARIABLES

$W(t)$	observed wage path
$V(t)$	full-effort productivity profile
T	date of retirement
$\bar{W}(t)$	reservation wage profile
$\bar{f}(t)$	probability of worker shirking at t
$\bar{g}(t)$	probability of firm default at t
$\theta, \theta(t)$	utility value of shirking
$f(\theta)$	density of θ across workers
$\mu, \mu(t)$	cost to firm of firm initiated default on worker's contract
$g(\mu)$	density of μ across firms
$C(t)$	cost imposed on firm by worker's shirking
$F(\theta_0)$	$\int_{\theta_0}^{\infty} f(\theta)d\theta$
$G(\mu_0)$	$\int_{-\infty}^{\mu_0} g(\mu)d\mu$
$\underline{t}$	optimal shirking time for worker
$\bar{t}$	optimal default time for firm
$\theta_t(t)$	θ value for marginal worker who shirks
ξ	hiring cost
$R(t)$	present value of difference between earnings at firm and alternative use of time from t to T
$D(t)$	present value of difference between wages paid to worker and his value to the firm from t to T

----

[14]James Heckman and G. Neumann and my 1979a article provide evidence that this is in fact the case.

REFERENCES

J. Abowd and O. Ashenfelter, "Unemployment and Compensating Wage Differentials," unpublished manuscript, Princeton Univ., Nov. 1978.

A. Alchian and H. Demsetz, "Production, Information Costs, and Economic Organization," *Amer. Econ. Rev.*, Dec. 1972, *62*, 777–95.

O. **Ashenfelter**, "Unemployment as Disequilibrium in a Model of Aggregate Labor Supply," working paper no. 104, Ind. Relations Sec., Princeton Univ., Nov. 1977.

C. **Azariadis**, "Implicit Contracts and Underemployment Equilibria," *J. Polit. Econ.*, Dec. 1975, *83*, 1183–1202.

M. N. **Baily**, "Wages and Employment under Uncertain Demand," *Rev. Econ. Stud.*, Jan. 1974, *4*, 37–50.

R. **Barro**, "The Control of Politicians: An Economic Model," *Public Choice*, Spring, 1973, *14*, 19–42.

G. **Becker and G. Stigler**, "Law Enforcement, Malfeasance and Compensation of Enforcers," *J. Legal Stud.*, Jan. 1974, *3*, 1–18.

A. **Blinder, R. Gordon, and D. Wise**, "Market Wages, Reservation Wages and Retirement Decisions," unpublished manuscript, Princeton Univ. 1978.

J. **Brown**, "Employer Risk Aversion, Income Uncertainty and Optimal Labor Contracts," unpublished doctoral dissertation, Univ. Chicago 1979.

R. **Burkhauser**, "Early Pension Decision and Its Effect on Exit from the Labor Market," unpublished doctoral dissertation, Univ. Chicago 1976.

G. **Calvo and S. Wellisz**, "Supervision, Loss of Control, and Optimum Size of the Firm," *J. Polit. Econ.*, Oct. 1978, *86*, 943–52.

G. **Dalton and P. Thompson**, "Accumulating Obsolescence of Older Engineers," *Harvard Bus Rev.*, Sept.-Oct. 1971, *49*, 57–67.

L. **Danziger**, "Risk Aversion and the Duration of Labor Contracts," working paper no. 37-78, Tel Aviv Univ. 1978.

E. **Fama**, "Agency Problems and the Theory of the Firm," unpublished manuscript, Univ. Chicago 1978.

H. **Grossman**, "Risk Shifting, Layoffs and Seniority," working paper no. 76-7, Brown Univ. 1977.

R. **Hall**, "A Theory of the Natural Unemployment Rate and the Duration of Employment," working paper no. 251, Nat. Bur. Econ. Res. 1978.

_____ **and D. Lilien**, "Efficient Wage Bargains Under Uncertain Supply and Demand," working paper no. 306, Nat. Bur. Econ. Res. Dec. 1978.

D. G. **Heckerman**, "Motivating Managers to Make Investment Decisions," *J. Financ. Econ.*, Sept. 1975, *2*, 273–92.

J. **Heckman and G. Neumann**, "Union Wage Differentials and the Propensity to Join Unions," mimeo., Univ. Chicago 1977.

M. **Jensen and W. Meckling**, "Theory of the Firm: Managerial Behavior, Agency Costs and Ownership Structure," *J. Financ. Econ.*, Oct. 1976, *3*, 305–60.

B. **Klein, R. Crawford, and A. Alchian**, "Vertical Integration, Appropriable Rents, and the Competitive Contracting Process," *J. Law Econ.*, Oct. 1978, *12*, 297–326.

E. **Lazear**, (1979a) "The Narrowing of Black-White Wage Differentials is Illusory," *Amer. Econ. Rev.*, Sept. 1979, *69*, 553–64.

_____ , (1979b) "Why Is There Mandatory Retirement?," *J. Polit. Econ.*, Dec. 1979, *87*, 1261–84.

_____ **and S. Rosen**, "Rank-Order Tournaments as Optimum Labor Contracts," *J. Polit. Econ.*, forthcoming.

J. **Medoff and K. Abraham**, "Experience, Performance and Earnings," working paper no. 278, Nat. Bur. Econ. Res. 1978.

M. **Miller and M. Scholes**, "Executive Compensation, Taxes and Incentives," Univ. Chicago, Oct. 1979.

D. **Mortensen**, "On the Theory of Layoffs," disc. paper no. 322, Northwestern Univ. 1978.

E. **Prescott and R. Townsend**, "On the Theory of Value with Private Information," unpublished manuscript, Carnegie-Mellon Univ. 1979.

S. **Rosen**, "Improving the Structure of Labor Markets," unpublished manuscript, Univ. Chicago, Nov. 1977.

S. **Ross**, "The Economic Theory of Agency: The Principal's Problem," *Amer. Econ. Rev. Proc.*, May 1973, *63*, 134–39.

J. **Salop and S. Salop**, "Self-Selection and Turnover in the Labor Market," *Quart. J. Econ.*, Nov. 1976, *90*, 619–27.

W. **White**, "Trust and the Wages of Agents," unpublished manuscript, Univ. Illinois-Chicago Circle 1979.

[13]

British Review of Economic Issues, Vol. 3, No. 8, Spring 1981, pp. 44-62

SCREENING AND EDUCATION:
A THEORETICAL AND EMPIRICAL SURVEY

A. K. WHITEHEAD
Leeds Polytechnic

Few people would doubt that very strong links exist between education and employment. Certainly, educational level correlates highly with employment income and it is broadly true that given types and levels of educational qualifications provide their possessors with access to employments which those without them find difficult to enter. Moreover, there is reason to believe that those who have greater amounts of formal education also receive more training on-the-job.[1] Hence it is clearly important to inquire into the reasons why some people and not others are selected for particular types of occupations and why differential amounts of job training are given to workers with different formal qualifications after entry into the labour market.

At the extremes, there are two schools of thought on the matter. The conventional view is that education is a productivity-augmenting process in the sense that it produces skills and abilities in the individual which previously did not exist, or develops productive characteristics which would otherwise remain largely dormant. It is also argued that educational processes can impart knowledge which is more or less directly usable in productive activities. On this view, the distinction between "education" (as traditionally defined) and "training" (as having a specific vocational bias) becomes blurred and in the limit (which may frequently be reached) the two terms become synonomous.

At the other extreme are those who would argue that education is no more than an elaborate screening device which acts as a filter in directing people with certain characteristics into occupational areas which require them. The screening process merely identifies people with and without particular traits but does not itself produce these attributes.

The development of the screening hypothesis is of quite recent origin, dating from the early 1970s. Hence theoretical embellishments continue to take place with some pace and, as is usually the case, empirical verification or refutation lags behind and as yet does not permit one to come down firmly on either side. One of the problems undoubtedly stems from the fact that there must be at least an element of truth in both points of view. For instance, one can easily give examples of educational courses which have a clear relationship to the individual's future productivity (in engineering, chemistry, business studies, etc.), but it is also probably true that some people could function well in certain occupations, but find them difficult to enter for lack of formal qualifications. Even if employers take the latter to reflect innate rather than produced abilities, why should they accept the additional uncertainty attached to the employment of an uncertificated individual when the probability of occupational failure can evidently be reduced by engaging someone with paper qualifications which, on past experience, appear to be indicative of certain essential qualities? The problem is to determine which view is quantitatively the more important.

Crucial implications follow from acceptance of either theory. If the productivity-augmenting view of the world is accepted, both the structure of the educational system and the content and quality of its courses are important. Clearly, individuals differ in terms of innate characteristics and therefore in the efficiency with which given abilities can be developed, but if certain types of human capital are scarce the educational system performs an important role in alleviating manpower shortages and bottlenecks. It matters, not only how the educational system organises itself, but also how it recruits and examines its students and the relationship of course content to the structure and future development of the economy.

If education is simply a screening device, all that matters is that the pure screening function of the system works efficiently, although educational institutions may act as a double filter: in the first place when they select and admit students; in the second when they fail students or pass them at different levels.[2] If the first filter is sufficient, what goes on inside higher educational establishments is an irrelevant expense from an economic point of view; the second filter is only necessary if it functions in respect of different types or levels of skills. In either case, the post-school education sector would appear to be a needlessly elaborate and expensive method of determining who has what abilities. Moreover, if educational processes do not produce skills, the contents of courses matter only in so far as they facilitate the testing of abilities which was not possible at recruitment.

It is clearly important to investigate the screening theory. The following sections will, therefore, outline the theory and then discuss some of the evidence as it presently exists.

1. The theory of screening

In this section some of the main aspects of the screening theory are considered. It is not the intention to provide an exhaustive account and the reader should be aware that a number of separate models have been developed which are differentiated in various ways while remaining inter-related.

Screening is the identification of relevant characteristics in individuals, and the actual sorting process is accomplished through the use of screening devices such as educational admission or examination procedures. It is, however, sometimes explicitly assumed [e.g. Spence (1973)], that individuals are not expected to invest in acquiring signaling reputations and that they are not frequently in the jobs market. People are in the jobs market only when actively considering alternative occupational opportunities, which makes mere employment an insufficient condition. The economic purpose of the screening or filtering process is to identify people with differential levels of productivity. If people differ in their productive capabilities, total output may be increased if workers can be identified by ability and assigned to appropriate jobs.

Layard and Psacharopoulos (1974) note that the screening hypothesis has received its most rigorous exposition from Arrow [although it should also be mentioned that the work produced by Spence is more comprehensive and provided the springboard for Arrow (1973)] who argues that, although separate from the productivity-augmenting human capital view, the screening approach does not entirely contradict it if, given production techniques, the filtering process allows employers to allocate workers to different jobs according to their different characteristics.

The first set of characteristics may, after Spence (1973) be referred to as "indices". These attributes are given and unalterable. They include age, sex, personal records and race and may be the source of externalities. External effects may occur in the market if an employer treats one individual as representative of the whole group. The indices attaching to that individual will modify the data which an employer obtains from the market and will therefore affect the firm's expectational probabilities at future hiring points. In turn, employer wage-offers are affected and thus the earnings pattern of the next group of workers.

The second set of attributes also give rise to externalities and are referred to as "signals". These are productivity-related characteristics which are capable of being manipulated by the individual and in which he can invest. Within the set are included education and health and, from a screeing viewpoint, a worker is more likely to make investments in such signals the more frequently he is in the jobs market. The term "jobs market" can clearly be taken to refer either to internal or external markets, but the probability of greater activity in one rather than the other may influence the pattern of signals acquired.

A development of the theory may begin with the simplifying assumption that individuals have, for economic purposes, a single characteristic which determines their productivity.[3] While a potential employee may be aware of his own productive ability, the screening theory rests on the assumption that information in the labour market is imperfect and that employers have only statistical information relating to the productivity of workers. When hiring workers, an employer effectively takes a random sample and, without screening, obtains individual employees with different but initially unknown productivities. If the work is such that individual marginal products cannot be measured, or if measurement is too expensive, a worker will receive a wage equal to the average marginal product of all workers thus employed. In this situation, the more productive workers are clearly subsidising the less productive and the former will have an incentive to make their higher value known to employers.

It may be assumed that the cost of making a signal is inversely related to productive capability. If this was not the case there would be an incentive for everyone to invest in signals to the same extent and therefore to be indistinguishable. However, every signal may not be effectively operative for every job and therefore non-negative correlations may occur between signals and jobs. Moreover, while an individual may invest in job market signals he may not be aware that they operate as such. But while the inverse relationship between signaling costs and productivity can be regarded as a necessary condition for effective signalling to take place, it is not a sufficient condition. Suppose that the acquisition of education is not perfectly divisible (or, at least, cannot be signalled as such) and that we have three levels of productivity with three corresponding groups of workers required. Suppose further that Level 2 workers find it profitable to signal for that level but not for Level 3 although they are capable of Level 3 work. The highest level of productive work will not be undertaken because the number of signals is insufficient within the relevant cost range.

The high-productive workers will have an incentive to signal their greater ability to employers providing that this can be done at a cost which is less than the difference between their current and potential wage. However, if that cost is greater than the difference between the value of their higher marginal product, and the average marginal product, it would clearly not be profitable for the more productive workers to pay the cost of screening. Without screening, all workers receive the average; with screening, the more productive receive less than before since the cost of screening is greater than the wage increment received once their higher marginal product is known; the less productive will also be worse off since they now receive a wage which must be less than the average.

However, if the difference between the value of the higher marginal product and the average is greater than the cost of screening, the high-productive workers will be better off after screening even when they have paid for its cost. But the gain made by any such group of workers will be less than the loss sustained by workers with the lower productivity level. The difference between the average and lower level of productivity is greater than the differential wage received by the more productive after screening costs have been paid.

If only one type of work is being undertaken by both groups of workers, screening results in a private gain (to those with higher marginal products). From the individual employer's point of view, output does not increase; workers continue to produce what they did before screening and the wage bill is merely redistributed between them. From society's viewpoint, net total output is less than before because some resources now need to be devoted to screening.

It can, however, be argued that an increase in the cost of screening may make both groups of workers worse off than before. To obtain the higher wage, the more productive workers must signal to employers that they have the necessary ability. Suppose that employers raise the level of educational attainment required for receipt of the higher wage (as frequently happens in conditions of less than full employment). The low-wage group is unaffected, but are worse off than with no screening at all since they receive below the average wage which they would have obtained with a complete absence of screening. But the more productive workers must now either accept the low wage or sustain the additional costs of providing the required signal. Even if the extra cost is worthwhile, in the sense that the total cost is still less than the difference between the high wage and the no-screening average, additional resources must be devoted to acquisition of the signal and correspondingly less can be spent on consumption.

Besides resting on the assertion that education does not raise individual productivity, this rather simplistic view of the world ignores the fact that jobs differ considerably and with complexity in their requirements and that workers vary in respect of a considerable range of types of abilities. If workers of different abilities are inadequately matched to jobs with differing requirements, then a screening process which allows individuals to be identified according to their productive characteristics will facilitate a reallocation of labour resources and a net increase in total output. As Stiglitz (1975) observes, even when a group of workers is employed on the same job, say a production line, members of the group interact in a manner determined by their individual attributes. Hence the less able tend to slow down the rate of production to a greater extent than the more able increase it. Thus total output can be increased by introducing two assembly lines manned respectively by the more and the less productive.

A point of some interest in this connection concerns the effect on labour demand of an increase in manpower heterogeneity and hence in the amount of variation which occurs when an employer hires a sample of workers. Wolpin (1977) argues that while a heterogeneous labour force may be expected to produce a lower output level than one which is homogeneous, it does not follow that the demand for labour will be reduced by an increase in sample variance. In the first place, the rate at which labour is substituted for non-labour inputs may be affected. An increase in the non-labour input may have a proportionately lower effect in reducing the adverse output consequence of variance than a similar increase in the labour input. In this case, labour will be substituted for non-labour inputs. Secondly, there is a "direct production effect" which arises if the firm attempts to regain its initial level of output, whence the demand for all factors will increase. Thirdly, an "induced effect" occurs whereby, when the original level of output has been reached, the increase in factor demand may adversely affect the marginal costs of production so that output and factor demand are reduced. The direct and induced effects will work in opposite directions and their net result cannot be generally predicted. Whether the final demand for labour is higher or lower than before, the increase in variance will depend on whether the substitution effect is greater or less than the net scale effect.

In general, the greater the variation in skill, the lower is expected output and profit. If heterogeneity can be reduced, then expected output and profit can be increased. If, for example, the employing organisation hires two types of worker, and skill level and variance differ as between the two groups, the use of screening devices can increase output and profit by increasing total homogeneity. The use of a screen allows the employer to distinguish between different types of workers and to effectively reduce the heterogeneity of the labour force. The firm can then sample independently from each group. This will tend to increase the demand for both types of worker.

Evidently, even if education plays no productivity-augmenting role, employers can still use records of schooling attainment prior to market entry to increase output and profitability. If it is accepted that academic attainment can be taken as an approximation to productivity on-the-job, if people differ in their productive capabilities and if jobs differ in respect of the manpower characteristics which they demand, then filtering devices can be used to raise output and profit. The validity of the last two conditions cannot be seriously doubted but the first may be somewhat more questionable. Arrow, for example, argues that when estimates of returns to investment in education have been adjusted (downwards) to take account of the possibility that they are inflated because of ability differences which are independent of education, the variable used is typically a measure of intelligence; but intelligence is not the same thing as productive ability.[4] But what employers are using as proxies for productivity are whatever it is that is measured during and on termination of educational processes, and this may be different to intelligence. However, "productive ability" is not a homogeneous commodity since performance in different jobs requires different kinds of attributes. The assumption that is needed here, therefore, is that educational attainment either measures potential productive abilities or reflects the capacity to acquire them, if one wishes to adopt the position that it neither creates nor develops them. In either case, many of the implications of the screening theory are sufficiently different to those of human capital theory to allow independent tests to be made. In some cases, the data available are sufficient to permit such testing. Some of these tests are discussed in the following section, although it should be remembered that the area is of recent development and the evidence consequently limited.

2. Some evidence on the screening theory

An empirical investigation based on the filter theory is that conducted by Taubman and Wales (1973). It had two principal goals: the first was "to obtain good estimates of the rate of return to higher education at various ability and education levels"; the second was "to examine the hypothesis that education adds to income by screening people with low education out of high-paying occupations." In attempting to achieve these goals the authors made use of U.S. Army Air Force volunteer tests made during World War II and follow-up work undertaken by Thorndike and Hagan (1959). The tests were intended to measure a variety of abilities such as reaction to stress, mathematical ability, reasoning, physical co-ordination and spatial perception. In their study, Taubman and Wales also control for education level, biographical history, marital status, father's education, age and, for pre-college teachers, a (dummy) variable to account for non-pecuniary benefits.

In view of the argument that some of the increased earnings which are often attributed to education may in fact be due to innate ability, it is interesting to consider the regression results obtained by Taubman and Wales in this respect. Four abilities were controlled for: spatial perception, physical co-ordination, mathematical and verbal ability. Each ability was identified at five levels. The authors claim to "have extensively analysed the role of ability using the factors mentioned above" and "find that of these ability measures only mathematical ability is a significant determinant of earnings."

Taubman and Wales also consider the relative importance of ability and education over time, using 1955 and 1969 as comparison points, by which time sample members had an average age of 33 and 47 years respectively. (Information was also available on initial wages, though not used in this case because the two later dates provided more reliable data). In 1955, there was a 16 per cent differential between the top and bottom ability groups and this was greater than the differential which was found to be due to education for five out of seven qualification levels. In 1969, the ability differential was in the order of 25 per cent but this was only greater than the education differential in one case, although similar in value to another four. The authors remark that, since the sample was drawn from those in the upper part of the ability distribution, it is safe to conclude that ability is more important than education in determining relative incomes "for those who are at least high school graduates." Taubman and Wales also found little evidence to support the contention that ability and education interact, so that in the main, higher ability groups did not receive more income from ability than those with lower levels of education. Also, with the exception of graduates, mental ability appeared to have no effect on wages paid for initial jobs. The authors argue that, if this finding is related to those on the differentials attributable to ability, it would seem that earnings in the early years of employment are little affected by ability, but that the importance of this factor increases with length of labour force participation.

Taubman and Wales reach two general conclusions from these findings which relate to the character of the labour market. Employers appear to have little idea of the determinants of labour market success or, alternatively, new entrants need so much training initially that marginal products and remuneration are all at a similar level. On the other hand, the differential development of individual productivities is observed over time and used as the basis for promotion so that the more able and highly educated push ahead of the rest. Such a description conforms to human capital theory but, it is argued, may suggest that the behaviour of earnings over the working life-cycle can be explained by the gradual recognition by employers of differences in ability. An extension of this approach would result in a screening model in which firms seek to minimise information costs (presumably by making their initial employee selection from the more highly educated).

The Taubman and Wales findings on the relative roles of ability and education (summarised in Table 1) have considerable interest in relation to the screening vs human capital debate and, as noted, do not contradict the human capital view. However, investments in

52   A. K. WHITEHEAD

TABLE 1

Education and Ability Differentials

Percentage Increase in Extra Earnings from Education for Average High School Graduate			Percentage Earnings Differential between Average High School Graduate and Graduate of Given Ability at Level:		
	1955	1969		1955	1969
College	11	17	1	−7.6	−10.0
Undergrad. Degree	12	31	2	−3.0	−3.9
Graduate	15	26	3	−1.0	−0.4
MA	10	32	4	2.4	2.9
Ph.D	2	27	5	9.2	15.0
MD	72	106			
LLB	19	84	*Source: Taubman & Wales (1973)*		

education and their concomitant effects on earnings are not restricted
to those made prior to labour market entry. The effects of investments
made on- or off-the-job after the commencement of employment are
also important and contribute to increased earnings. While it is
difficult to obtain data on such investments, their omission may
introduce bias into the estimates of other variables. Indeed, post entry
investments in education may well be of equal or greater importance
in explaining differences in earnings.

The bunching of initial salaries is more likely to be due to similar
values in marginal products than employer ignorance of the determinants of success. Hiring is usually done by people who are
themselves successful and who can therefore be presumed to be aware
of the determining factors involved. Moreover, new entrants who are
introduced into an unfamiliar environment, who need to work with
unfamiliar capital and perform unaccustomed functions will tend to
have similar levels of productivity in the initial stages of employment.
Differential productivities will take time to develop. Even if education
is a productivity-augmenting process, formal investments made prior
to market entry do not impart all the skills and abilities necessary for
success and some can only be acquired on-the-job. It is for these
reasons that one might expect increasing earnings differentials over
time, where highly qualified manpower is concerned, and not because
of pre-entry schooling which, in human capital theory, merely
produces a once-for-all upward shift in the age-earnings profile for
each additional increment of investment.

In the later section of their paper, Taubman and Wales report some
direct tests of the screening theory. They postulate that, in order to
demonstrate the use of education as a filtering device which screens

some people out of high-wage employments, it must be shown that some employees "are not in the occupation in which their marginal product and earnings are highest but that highly educated people are allocated properly".[5] In other words, it is presumed that, if education is used as a screening device, employers select the more highly educated and productive workers for high-wage jobs but fail to select some workers with lower educational standards but relatively high marginal products. It is, therefore, being suggested that the screen, if in operation, works imperfectly because factors other than level of education influence an individual's productivity. Although education may contribute to higher earnings these are also the consequence of limitations being placed on supply through the use of education as a screen which reduces initial personnel selection costs for firms who believe that a higher proportion of the more highly educated possess the attributes necessary for success.

Wales and Taubman then use their data to show the actual distribution of educational groups by occupation. This is compared with the distribution that would have been expected if there was "free entry" into occupations in the absence of a screening device, on the assumption that workers enter those occupations which provide the highest income.[6]The results are summarised in Table 2 which shows the actual occupation distributions and those expected assuming free entry and income maximisation.

TABLE 2

Actual and Expected Distribution of Educational Groups by Occupation: 1969			
	Total No.	Percentage in Occupations With	
		Low Pay*	High Pay†
High School:	736		
Actual		38.7	61.2
Expected		4.2	94.9
College:	852		
Actual		16.5	83.6
Expected		2.6	95.5
B.A. Holders:	1026		
Actual		4.0	96.0
Expected		2.2	95.7

*Blue collar, white collar and service occupations.
†Professional, technical, sales and managerial occupations.

Source: Taubman and Wales (1973), Table 5, p. 47.

Taubman and Wales comment that the outstanding feature of this table is the considerable difference between actual and expected distributions in the low-pay occupations for the high school group. The difference for the college group is less marked but still noticeable while very similar for holders of a B.A. While few people in the sample would opt for the low-paying employments, approximately 39 per cent of the high school group, and 16 per cent of the college group, do actually find themselves in such jobs; but only four per cent of those with B.A.'s enter such occupations. On this evidence the authors conclude that education is being used as a screening device and that some workers with relatively low educational levels are being prevented from entering high-pay occupations.

Some of the conclusions reached by Taubman and Wales have received comment from Layard and Psachoropoulos (1974).[7] The latter note the difference between this and other screening models in that employers are here assumed to be able to identify and pay wages equal to marginal products. [However, in some models, such as Spence (1973) it is implied that employers do acquire knowledge of marginal products some time after hiring]. However, their main point is that, if some members of the high school group do enter high-wage occupations while others of the same group do not, the respective distributions cannot be attributed to the use of education as a screen. The reason why some are and some are not selected for high-paying occupations must be that, while they are alike in terms of educational level, they are differentiated in other crucial ways (e.g. by motivation) and employers are aware of the difference.

It may also be noted that by 1969, the average age of workers in the sample was 47, and that they had been members of the labour force for upwards of 20 years. Now, regardless of whether education is a productivity-augmenting process or not, if more members of higher educational groups possess greater productive attributes than those of lower educational levels, employers have had more than sufficient time to discover this and reward accordingly. In any case, distributions at age 47 (or even at 33) can hardly be taken as evidence of screening which must occur on entry to the labour market. Perhaps data at, say, 23 would show a similar distribution, but it is this which is required.

Layard and Psacharopoulos go on to discuss further evidence, provided by Taubman and Wales and others. Some of the points raised can usefully be mentioned here.

The so-called "sheepskin" version of the screening theory implies that what is important for the rate of increase in earnings is not so much completed years of schooling but the certificates obtained. Successful education, evidenced by certification should at least reflect greater dedication and ability than simple attendance for a given period. Layard and Psacharopoulos review the results of five studies[8] which are of relevance. Two of them (including that by Taubman and Wales) estimate rates of return which allow for the differential ability of those who drop out of courses before receiving certificates. In both cases, the rate of return for dropouts exceeds that for completion Layard and Psacharopoulos argue that, unless it is claimed that employers use years of schooling rather than certification, this is a devastating result for the theory. It might also be noted that, if one accepts the diminishing returns hypothesis in respect of investment in education, such differences in rates of return conform to human capital theory.

A second prediction "in the spirit of the screening hypothesis" which is considered by Layard and Psacharopoulos is that "the effect of education on earnings falls with experience." Ignoring the complications which arise from on-the-job training, this prediction is not supported by the Taubman/Wales study. The latter show, with ability held constant, an increase in the education effect between ages 33 and 47 ranging from 6 per cent to 65 per cent. Moreover, the increase tends to become greater as one moves up the hierarchy of qualifications. Although the proportional effect of ability on earnings also increases, this does not occur at the expense of the education effect.

Another aspect of the screening theory relates to the differential wages paid to those with and without higher education. The more highly educated receive a substantial wage premium which, according to human capital theory, is paid because of the greater productivity produced by education. The screening theory, on the other hand, suggests that the differential is paid because employers find it cheaper to pay the higher wage to graduates, more of whom are expected to possess the requisite abilities, than to sustain the costs of selecting those of equal productivity from among non-graduates. If this is the case, the personnel selection costs associated with the hiring of non-graduates must be greater than the (discounted) earnings differential between the two groups.

In refutation of this screening implication, Layard and Psacharopoulos quote Wiles (1974) who argues that a good one-day test would cost only about £20. In this case, it would appear sensible for employers to use it, but Wiles puts forward two reasons why they do not employ such tests. The first reason relates to the public subsidy which is received by higher education, but Layard and Psacharopoulos claim that this is irrelevant since firms still have to pay graduates substantially greater wages.

The second reason advanced by Wiles is that the actual cost to an employer of finding a suitable graduate is considerably below that for discovering a non-graduate of similar capabilities. The difference in cost arises mainly because higher education institutes have already tested the graduate. Layard and Psacharopoulos, however, argue that if this is correct then private enterprise would have found it profitable to set-up a non-graduate testing organisation. The fact that this has not been done tends to refute the hypothesis.

Another investigation stimulated by Taubman and Wales is that produced by Haspel (1978) who also uses the NBER-Thorndike Hagan data. Haspel presents "A New View and Test of 'Screening'" which is actually an interesting application of neoclassical labour supply theory in that he introduces into the screening vs human capital debate an explicit consideration of non-pecuniary factors in the determination of occupational choice. He therefore redefines screening "as occurring when, because of insufficient schooling, a person is excluded from an occupation in which he/she would have received a higher level of satisfaction (not just income)." If one merely considers earnings, an individual may appear to have been excluded from a high-pay occupation when in fact he was attempting to maximise his total (financial-plus-non-financial) income by entering an employment with, for that person, a substantial non-pecuniary element. On this view, screening only occurs if an absence of the required educational qualification prevents entry into a high-pay occupation which a consideration of both financial and psychic benefits would have made preferable.

Having derived occupational supply functions on a basis inclusive of both pecuniary and psychic income, Haspel uses them to determine the probability of entering the range of all occupations, in a methodologically similar manner to that used by Taubman and Wales. Actual and expected proportions are then compared. Screening can be assumed to be present if, at a low educational level, the

TABLE 3

Actual and Expected Occupation Distributions

	Actual		Expected		% Difference between Expected & Actual Percentages
	No.	%	No.	%	
Owners & Managers	2153	49.5	2866	65.8	0.164
Professional	999	22.9	614	14.1	−0.088
Technical etc.	742	17.0	621	14.3	−0.028
Blue Collar	459	10.5	252	5.8	−0.048
TOTAL:	4353	100.0	4353	100.0	0

Source: Haspel (1978) Table I, p. 285.

expected value is greater than the proportion actually entering an occupation.

Occupations were defined in terms of four broad categories: owners and managers; professional; technical, white collar, salesmen and servicemen; and blue collar workers. Individuals were then assumed to enter the job with the highest probability consequent upon both types of income. The actual/expected distributions are given in Table 3 where the only case in which the expected value is greater than the actual value is the highest status category of owners and managers. In order to test the screening theory, the results in Table 3 were distributed over the educational grouping of high school, college and B.A. holders. Table 4 records the result, where a negative sign in the righthand column shows that the expected proportion entering an occupational group was less than the actual proportion entering and vice versa.

TABLE 4

*Individual Actual and Expected Distributions by
Education and Occupation in 1969*

	Actual %	Expected %	Actual Minus Expected
HIGH SCHOOL			
Owners & Managers	43.3 (40.6)	37.6 (42.4)	−5.7 (1.8)
Professional	2.1 (1.5)	17.2 (9.5)	15.1 (8.0)
Technical, etc.	26.8 (29.2)	29.7 (44.9)	2.9 (15.7)
Blue Collar	27.8 (28.6)	15.5 (1.3)	−12.3 (−27.3)
COLLEGE			
Owners & Managers	57.9 (58.5)	61.4 (39.8)	3.5 (−19.0)
Professional	5.4 (5.8)	16.2 (14.8)	10.8 (9.0)
Technical, etc.	24.8 (25.3)	17.7 (42.7)	−7.1 (17.4)
Blue Collar	11.9 (10.2)	4.7 (0.8)	−7.2 (−9.4)
B.A.			
Owners & Managers	59.7 (59.4)	78.2 (38.3)	18.5 (−21.1)
Professional	24.8 (25.0)	13.0 (17.8)	−11.8 (−7.2)
Technical, etc.	13.1ʳ (13.8)	6.6 (40.9)	−6.5 (27.1)
Blue Collar	2.3 (1.8)	2.2 (0.9)	0.1 (−0.9)

Source: Haspel (1978) Tables II (and III), p. 286 (and p. 288).

Ignoring the bracketed values for the moment, more of the high school group were expected to enter the low-status blue collar occupations than actually did enter. Since more became blue collar workers than expected, the screening view is supported. But in the high status owner and manager group there were also actually more than expected, which is contrary to the screening view. Hence it can be argued that screening may be a less important factor than others which also influence occupational entry. On the other hand, the screening theory gains more support from the college educated group since there were fewer than expected in the two top status categories while more than expected went into the two lower status occupational groups. Haspel argues that the college group is the closest to the B.A. credential and therefore a screening effect is more likely here than in the high school group. But, again, support for the existence of screening is reduced by consideration of the B.A. categories. Here, there are considerably fewer in the owner and manager group than expected and more in the next two lower groups than expected, with virtually no difference for the blue collar group. But if education is used for screening purposes, when members of a group have a given educational level, there should be no systematic variation between actual and expected values and a much lower difference between them than is produced by the data. Hence, if a screen does exist, it functions very imperfectly since a large proportion of people in the two lower educational categories do obtain high status jobs. Haspel therefore concludes that there is a clear objective for those suitably qualified to move up the occupational hierarchy but that a "more is better" syndrome exists which is geared, not to income maximisation alone, but to the maximisation of total satisfaction.

A comparison of Haspel's results with those obtained by Taubman and Wales produces some inconsistencies. The latter are included in Table 4 as the bracketed values. Comparing both sets of results, in 50 per cent of cases the actual signs are different. Also, while Taubman and Wales rely largely on the high school group for their conclusions, where the signs in the third column are positive for the three top occupational groups, less were expected in both lowest and highest status jobs and more were expected to enter the middle status occupations, which results do not support the conclusions drawn from the high school observations.

Hence, as Table 4 indicates, Haspel's results, based on the broader concept of income, are largely inconsistent with those of Taubman and Wales. Haspel produces a negative third column value for high school owners and managers, as against a positive Taubman and Wales value; a negative sign for the technical group under college and B.A. categories as against positive signs. Therefore, Haspel concludes that the two models produce conflicting results: an approach based purely on financial motivation tends to give some support for the screening view (although the evidence is somewhat weak), but when non-financial determinants of occupational choice are introduced "many of the actual occupational choices correspond to what was expected."

We may conclude this section by referring again to the work done by Wolpin some of whose theoretical developments were mentioned earlier.

As previously discussed, in a world of imperfect information more able people can benefit by investing in screening signals when it allows employers to identify them as more productive. This is particularly important if firms would otherwise be involved in significant costs in determining productivities before hiring. Wolpin therefore argues that "As long as pre-school productivity is a large component of post-school productivity, individuals who, for whatever reason, need not identify their productivities before employment have less incentive to acquire schooling. Therefore, for given innate productivity, the un-screened worker will acquire less schooling than the screened worker or, conversely, for given schooling, the unscreened worker will be of greater innate productivity, and thus have greater earnings than the screened worker . . . ."[9] As a group to whom this applies, Wolpin chooses the self-employed. To at least partially overcome some of the drawbacks attached to this approach, he selects from the NBER-Thorndike sample (used by Taubman and Wales) only those whose first and last reported jobs over a 20 years period were as self-employed in a non-professional capacity. These were then compared to a selected class of salaried workers.

TABLE 5

Descriptive Statistics for Salaried
and Self-Employed Workers

	Salaried		Self-Employed	
	Mean	Standard Deviation	Mean	Standard Deviation
Schooling	14.55	1.92	13.95	1.81
Ability	−.190	1.72	−.234	1.68
Earnings	8869	6157	12355	10507
Experience	10.98	8.52	11.23	9.31

Source: Wolpin (1977), Table 1, p. 956.

Table 5 gives the descriptive statistics which constitute the comparison made by Wolpin between the two groups. All those in the sample had completed at least high school education and therefore the (0.6) difference in mean years of schooling implies that the self-employed had received approximately 75 per cent of the additional schooling acquired by salary workers. The 17 sections which constituted the ability test are "supposed to approximate an IQ-type test" and would suggest that "the two groups are of similar pre-school productivity with the self-employed slightly less capable on average, and if the self-employed vs salaried comparison approximates an unscreened vs screened comparison, the results suggest that schooling has only a minor screening function." If earnings rather than ability are used to measure innate productivity, there is greater relevance for the screening function since self-employed earnings are the greater despite marginally less schooling. However, as Wolpin observes, the income of the self-employed also contains elements other than wages and is therefore biased upwards.

It may be argued by some that this latter point invalidates the comparison. But, as the result stands, it is at least damaging to the screening case. Notwithstanding this, if the ability tests given to sample members in 1943 are measuring intelligence, then the usual criticisms are in order that such characteristics are not necessarily relevant to productivity and therefore do not measure pre-school productive capabilities. However, the methodology used by Wolpin is an interesting innovation and "with some important qualifications, the fact that self-employed workers in non-professional occupations obtained about the same level of schooling as non-professional salaried workers was taken (by Wolpin) as evidence against a predominant screening interpretation".[12]

On balance, the evidence discussed here would not appear to encourage acceptance of the screening view of education at this time. There are also a number of intuitive points and some casual evidence which throw doubt on its quantitative importance. For example, the distinction between education and training is largley ignored. Large numbers, and perhaps the greater part, of post-secondary school courses have a definite and even substantial vocational bias. It is hardly a tenable view that these are not productivity-augmenting. If, on the other hand, they are to be ruled out as not what is really meant by schooling, then virtually the whole of the U.K. further education sector, most of the work done by polytechnics and a large proportion of University teaching activity are eliminated. Much the same can be said at post-graduate level where many courses are designed to impart vocationally related skills. Moreover, in a human capital context, it is not merely skill but also knowledge which is important; divorcing one from the other is rather like separating a hammer from its shaft, but the significance of knowledge itself is frequently overlooked despite the fact that in many cases its acquisition is maximised by formal learning processes. Also, a number of the theoretical conclusions reached by the screenists depend on the explicit assumption that education does not raise individual productivity. This avoids the whole crux of the argument.

ENDNOTES

1. See Mincer (1962).
2. See Arrow (1973).
3. See, for example, Stiglitz (1975).
4. Arrow (1973) pp. 214-215.
5. Taubman and Wales (1973) p. 43.
6. To obtain estimates of an individual's income in a given occupation the average income value in that occupation is taken for those employed in it who have the same educational and other characteristics. It is then assumed that the residuals in the occupational regression equation would have the same distribution for any given group of workers who are presently employed in other occupations. If is further assumed that there is an independent distribution of earnings about the mean, for any individual, in the various occupations.
7. It should be noted, however, that a slight error occurs in the paper referred to by Layard and Psacharopoulos which may be confusing to the reader interested enough to read this and the one by Taubman and Wales (1973). Layard and Psacharopoulos quote date in their Table 1 for college students, whereas the figures actually relate to holders of B.A.'s in Table 5 of Taubman and Wales.
8. The studies were: Taubman and Wales (1973), Rogers (1969), Hanoch (1967), Hausen (1963), and Becker (1964).
9. Wolpin (1977) p. 955.
10. Wolpin (1977) p. 957.

REFERENCES

Arrow, Kenneth J. (1973), Education as a Filter, *Journal of Public Economics*, Vol. 2.

Becker, Gary S. (1964), *Human Capital: A Theoretical and Empirical Investigation with Special Reference to Education*, NBER.

Hanoch, G. (1967), An Economic Analysis of Earnings and Schooling, *Journal of Human Resources*, Vol. 2, Summer.

Hansen, W. Lee (1963); Rates of Return to Investment in Schooling in the United States, *Journal of Political Economy*, Vol. 81, No. 2.

Haspel, Abraham E. (1978), The Questionable Role of Higher Education As An Occupational Screening Device, *Higher Education*, Vol. 7.

Layard, Richard, and Psacharopoulos, George (1974), The Screening Hypothesis and the Returns to Education, *Journal of Political Economy*, Sept./Oct.

Mincer, Jacob (1962), On-the-job Training: Costs, Returns and some Implications, *Journal of Political Economy*, Supplement, Oct.

Rogers, D. C. (1969), Private Rates of Return to Education in the United States: A Case Study, *Yale Economic Essays*, Vol. 9, Spring.

Spence, Michael (1973), Job Market Signaling *Quarterly Journal of Economics*, Vol. 87.

Spence, Michael (1974), Competitive and Optional Responses to Signals: An Analysis of Efficiency and Distribution, *Journal of Economic Theory*, Vol. 7.

Stiglitz, Joseph E. (1975), The Theory of Screening, Education and the Distribution of Income, *American Economic Review,* Vol. 65, June.

Taubman, Paul J. and Wales, Terence J. (1973), Higher Education, Mental Ability, and Screening, *Journal of Political Economy,* Vol. 81, Jan./Feb.

Thorndike, R. and Hagen, E. (1959), *Ten Thousand Careers,* New York: Wiley.

Wiles, P. (1974), The Correlation Between Education and Earnings: The External-Test-Not-Content Hypothesis (ETNC), *Higher Education,* Vol. 3, No. 1.

Wolpin, Kenneth J. (1977), Education and Screening, *American Economic Review,* Vol. 65, No. 5.

[14]

Economics of Education Review, Vol. 8, No. 1, pp. 1–15, 1989.
Printed in Great Britain.

0272–7757/89 $3.00 + 0.00
Pergamon Press plc

Occupational Training in High School:
When Does It Pay Off?

JOHN BISHOP

New York State School of Industrial and Labor Relations, Cornell University, Ithaca, NY 14851-0925,
U.S.A.

Abstract — Occupationally specific education in high school lowers the dropout rate of at-risk students and, if training related jobs are obtained, it increases the wages and employment after graduation as well. Unfortunately, less than half of vocational graduates work in occupations that match (very broadly defined) their training. High training related placement rates appear to result when well informed career choices precede training, when training is for an occupation in strong demand, when employers are involved in delivery and vocational teachers (not placement directors) take responsibility for the placement of their students. It is recommended that states make local vocational programs more accountable by funding them through a formula that rewards success in serving students, rather than just success in recruiting them, and that offers greater rewards for success with more challenging students.

ABOUT half of all youth either do not complete high school or end their formal education with the high school diploma. Even higher proportions of minority, disadvantaged and handicapped youth do not enter postsecondary education. Should public schools offer these youth occupationally specific education and training? If so, what form should this education take? Should the goal of the occupational component of high school vocational education be occupationally specific skills, career awareness, basic skills or something else? What should be the relationship between programs providing occupationally specific training and the employers who hire their graduates?

In addressing these issues it is important to know how taking occupationally specific courses influences dropout rates, probabilities of employment, wage levels, productivity, access to additional education and training, job satisfaction, basic skills, citizenship, and other positive traits of character. It is also important to understand the relative effectiveness of alternate vocational education programs in achieving these goals. The first part of the paper is a review of what current research tells us about these issues. The review is organized around 7 questions. The questions and the corresponding findings are listed below:

Questions and Answers

(1) How large are the economic benefits of occupationally specific education and what causes them?

(A) Economic benefits are zero if a training related job is not obtained. If a training related job is obtained, monthly earnings are 7–8% greater, unemployment is substantially reduced, labor force participation is more consistent, and productivity on the job is increased.

(2) To what extent are the occupationally specific skills learned in high school being used?

(A) Less than half get training related jobs (rigorously defined).

(3) Why are the occupationally specific skills learned often not used on a job?

(A) Lack of emphasis on placement, insufficient involvement of employers, training for jobs not in demand.

(4) Does vocational education generate non-economic benefits?

(A) There is no evidence that it either increases or decreases non-economic benefits relative to a general curriculum.

(5) Does vocational education lower dropout rates?

(A) Yes. Taking one voc. ed. course each year raises the high school graduation rate by 6 percentage points and this raises expected earnings by about 2%.

(6) Can basic skills substitute for occupational skills?

(A) No, jobs require both.

(7) Have high rates of skill obsolescence drastically lowered the payoff to occupationally specific training?

(A) No. Obsolescence is less important than the risk of not using and forgetting skills.

The research clearly implies that occupationally specific education has a very positive impact on labor market success when training related jobs are obtained. If jobs are not related to training, high school graduates receive no economic or non-economic benefits from their vocational education. The productivity enhancing effects of vocational education also occur only when the job occupied is related to the training. Taking vocational education courses lowers the dropout rate of students at risk of dropping out, but even here its holding power probably derives largely from the student's hope that occupational studies will improve the jobs he/she can get. Unfortunately, less than one-half of the graduates of high school vocational programs who did not go to college, work in occupations that match (very broadly defined) their training. Train-

ing related placement rates vary greatly from program to program and much of the variation can be explained by features of the vocational education program. A very important program feature is vocational teachers (not placement directors) taking responsibility for and devoting time to the placement of their students.

It is also important that a well informed career choice precede entry into intensive occupational training, that training be offered only in occupations with substantial employer demand, and with substantial employer involvement in delivery of the training. Finally it is recommended that state aid for vocational education be allocated by a formula that rewards success in serving students, rather than just success in recruiting them and that offers greater rewards for success with more challenging students.

PART I: REVIEW OF RESEARCH

1. How Large are the Economic Benefits of Vocational Education and What Causes Them?

Students Benefits of High School Vocational Education. The effect of high school vocational education on wage rates and earnings has been extensively studied in the last decade. The consensus of the research is that for women commercial training has substantial positive effects on the earnings, but technical and home economics training

Table 1. The economic effect of vocational education (relative to graduates who pursued a general curriculum)

Groups in comparison to general curriculum	Labor force participation (age 20)	Outcomes Unemployment (age 20)	Monthly earnings (age 20)	Monthly earnings (age 19–26)
Vocational grads				
Training related	20%***	−3*	7%**	8%**
Not training related	2%	1	3%*	−5%
Academic grads	−9%***	1	−5%*	0%

Source: Table 14 and 16 of Campbell *et al.*, *Outcomes of Vocational Education for Minorities, the Handicapped and the Poor*. The classification of students into vocational, academic and general was based on the high school transcript. A graduate was in a training related job when the occupation matched (liberally defined) the field for which he/she trained. Results reported are averages of coefficients on concentrator, limited concentrator and concentrator explorer. For the labor force participation model the values presented in the table are the estimated coefficients divided by the mean labor force participation rate. Coefficients from regressions predicting the log of monthly earnings have been multiplied by 100 to approximate percentage impacts. The regressions included controls for the following: sex, minority status, handicapped, limited English proficient, test scores, grade point average, family background, attitudes, past and present college attendance, employment during high school, aspirations in 8th grade, region, rural–urban. The fourth column reports analyses of NLS data, taken from Table 7 of Campbell *et al.*, 1987b. The first 3 columns are based on HSB data and contain additional controls for presence of a spouse or child, absenteeism and discipline problems in high school. The monthly earnings also contained controls for occupation. The average significance level of the coefficients are indicated by the number of stars. *** is significant at the 0.01 level using a two tail test. ** is significant at the 0.05 level. * is significant at the 0.10 level.

has either zero or negative effects on earnings (Grasso and Shea, 1979; Meyer, 1982; Gustman and Steimeier, 1981). For men the results are less favorable. Campbell *et al.* (1986) summarized the literature by saying "the evidence is mixed as whether male vocationally educated high school graduates (especially white men) earn significantly more/hour or /week than otherwise similar non-vocational graduates" (p. 13). The National Commission for Employment Policy (1981) concluded that "most studies based on nationally representative samples of students could not find convincing evidence of positive labor market effects of secondary vocational education on males, compared to alternative uses of student's time" (p. 15).

Recent research by Campbell *et al.* (1986) and Daymont and Rumberger (1982) have discovered why the overall impact of vocational education is often so small. For graduates who use the training on their job, these two studies demonstrate that vocational education has large positive effects on the earnings of both men and women. The reason overall impacts are so small is that the majority of vocational graduates do not get training related jobs. Table 1 summarizes Campbell *et al.*'s analysis of data on both males and females from two nationally representative longitudinal surveys (High School and Beyond and the National Longitudinal Survey) where participation in vocational education can be defined by reference to high school transcripts rather than student self reports. Vocational graduates who obtain a job in an occupation matching their field of training spend about 20% more time in the labor force than general track graduates.[1] Their rates of unemployment are about 3 percentage points lower. Vocational graduates working outside their field of training are not significantly more likely to be in the labor force or to be employed than general track graduates.

The third and fourth columns of the table present estimates of the effect of vocational education on current monthly earnings controlling for current and past enrollment in college. High school graduates who took a vocational concentration obtain significantly higher monthly earnings (7–8% higher) only when their current job is related to their training. When their current job is not related to their training, they do not receive higher wage rates than students who have pursued a general program of study in high school.[2] Students who pursued an academic curriculum in high school did not do better

than those pursuing a general curriculum; in one data set they were earning 5% less.

If students stay in the occupation for which they train for many years the benefits of the occupational training appear to grow even larger. An analysis of data from the NLS reported in Campbell *et al.* (1987b) found that graduates of vocational programs who spent 100% of their work time since high school in a training related job earned 31% more in 1984 than the vocational graduates who had never had a training related job.

Effects on Productivity and Training Costs. Workers with 12 or fewer years of schooling account for the bulk of the nation's blue collar, sales, clerical and service workers. The training requirements and intellectual demands of many of these jobs are quite considerable. In clerical jobs, for instance, the time and resources devoted to training a new employee during the first 3 months on a job has a value equal to 45% of the output of a worker with 2 years of tenure at the firm. Training costs during the first 3 months are 36% of an experienced worker's potential output for retail sales jobs, 38% for blue collar jobs and 25% for service jobs (Bishop, 1985). Presumably the graduates of vocational programs are more productive workers and require less training. How large are these effects?

Studies of this issue find that vocationally trained workers are somewhat more productive and less costly to train than other workers doing the same job but only when the job is related to their training. The evidence for this statement comes from statistical comparisons of two workers doing the same job.[3] The data are presented in Table 2, which has been summarized from Bishop (1982, 1985). Compared to those without vocational training, new hires who have received secondary or post-secondary vocational training that is not relevant to their job require 6% more training during the first 3 months on the job while those with relevant training from a high school require 9% less. Those with vocational training which is not relevant to their current job were initially less productive and only slightly (1.4%) more productive after a year at the firm. Those with relevant training from a high school were 3% more productive in the first 2 weeks, and 2% more productive during the next 10 weeks and 3% more productive after a year or so at the firm. Not surprisingly, those with relevant

Table 2. Impact of vocational education on training costs and productivity

	Relevant high school training	Relevant public post-secondary training	Non-relevant training
(Percentage difference from workers without vocational training)			
Outcomes			
OJT time	−9	−22**	6.3
Productivity			
in first 2 weeks	3	13**	−3.0
in next 10 weeks	2	4	−0.5
at present or when the employee separated	3	1	1.4

** Significant at the 5% level (two sided).

Source: Columns 1 and 2 estimates for those with relevant training is from Table 3.13 of Bishop *et al.*, 1985. Estimate for those with non-relevant training is from Table 5 of Bishop (1982).

training from post-secondary institutions did even better.

These findings imply that the private and social benefits of vocational education derive from the occupationally specific skills that are developed. Some of the skills taught in vocational classes are transferable — useful in a great variety of occupations — but skills taught in nonvocational classes are transferable as well. Vocational classes are not better at instilling valuable transferable skills than nonvocational classes. In other words, vocational education as now practiced does not do a better job of preparing youth for generic jobs than more academic forms of education. There may be ways of delivering vocational education that do a better job of teaching character or generic skills than an academic education but these programs are not common enough to affect statistics on the aggregate impact of vocational education.

2. To What Extent are the Occupationally Specific Skills Learned in High School Being Used?

During their 4 years in high school, 1982 graduates took an average 2.3 Carnegie units of exploratory vocational courses (industrial arts, home economics, typing I, etc.), 2.1 units of occupational vocational courses and 17.2 units of other courses. The 27% of these graduates who described themselves as specializing in a vocational field, obtained 2.8 units in exploratory vocational courses, 3.7 Carnegie units in occupational vocational and 14.9 units in other areas (Plisko, 1984; Table 3.3). This implies that the 73% of students who report they are not specializing in a vocational field account for 67% of the students in exploratory courses and 52% of the students in occupational courses.

How frequently do students use and therefore benefit from their occupationally specific training? Of the graduates who have taken two or more occupational vocational courses in a specific area (the concentrators, limited concentrators and concentrator explorers of the typology developed in Campbell *et al.*, 1981) 28% enter a 4-year college or university after high school (unpublished tabulation of 1983 NLS youth provided by Paul Campbell). It is not clear how many of these graduates major in subjects which make use of knowledge and skills obtained in vocational courses.

What about the students who seek jobs immediately after graduating from high school? The empirical work reported in the previous section classified a youth as having a training related job when the occupation of the individual's current or most recent job matched his/her field of training. By this definition, 43% of the employed graduates who had been out of school between 1 and 10 years currently had a training related job (broadly defined) in the 1985 National Longitudinal Survey of Youth (Campbell *et al.*, 1987a). Other studies using the same methodology obtain similar results.[4] Felstehausen's (1973) study of 1981 vocational graduates in the State of Illinois found training related placement rates of 27% in business occupations, 17% in trade and industry, 52% in health and 20% in agriculture. Conroy and Diamond's study (1976) of Massachusetts graduates obtained a training related placement rate of 29% for business and 37% for trades and industry. In contrast, 6 months after passing a German apprenticeship examination, 68% of those with civilian jobs were employed in the occupation for which they were trained (much more narrowly defined) (the Federal Institute for Vocational Training, 1986).[5]

3. Why Are The Occupationally Specific Skills Learned So Seldom Used On A Job?

In 1980 the National Center for Research in Vocational Education undertook a massive study of the determinants of training related placement rates (McKinney *et al.*, 1982; Lewis *et al.*, 1982). Controlling for the local unemployment rate and the congruence of school and community racial composition, Lewis *et al.* (1982) found that training related placement rates were higher when vocational teachers accepted responsibility for placement, when they spent considerable time on placement, when admission to the program was restricted and when career exploration was an important part of the program.

Other research suggests that another important cause of the problem is the limited employer involvement in the training. Mangum and Ball (1986) have found in their analyses of NLS data that employer controlled training institutions have much higher training related placement rates. Using a procedure of matching training fields against jobs, they found that the proportion of male graduates who had at least one job in a related field was 85% for company training, 71% for apprenticeship, 52% for vocational-technical institutes, 22% for proprietary business colleges and 47% for military trainees who completed their tour of duty. The rates for females were 82% for company training, 59% for nursing schools, 61% for vocational-technical institutes, 55% for proprietary business colleges and 49% for the military.

The graduates who did not find training related jobs often complained that no such jobs were available. Aggregating the data from three different follow-up studies, Mertens *et al.* (1980) reported that 25% said that no job was available in an area related to training, 11% said their high school training was insufficient and 10% said they could not earn enough money in a related field. These statistics suggest that occupational training needs to be sensitive to the market both in the selection of and design of training programs.

Poor career guidance is apparently contributing to the problem, for 21% said they left the field because they did not like the work, another 2% said they did not know what the job was really like and 5% said that they switched fields when they got training in the military or at a postsecondary institution.

Some of the students apparently take occupational courses without having real plans to pursue a related occupation. Counselors and vocational teachers report that some of the students taking vocational courses are there to avoid more difficult academic subjects or to get permission to take a job during part of the school day. Others apparently changed their career goals. Still others use the courses as a vehicle for career exploration (something for which they are often not really designed).

4. Does Vocational Education Generate Non-economic Benefits?

Some of the leading experts on vocational education argue that occupationally specific training is really intended to achieve a much broader purpose than preparation for a specific cluster of occupations. Silberman (1982), for instance, feels the primary purpose of secondary vocational education is:

> "to promote full human development through exposure of the learner to work experience as part of the education process . . . The purpose of work is to further the education of the student; the work is subordinate to the education process; it is work for education" (p. 299)

If this goal were being achieved, we would expect (a) students to benefit from their vocational education regardless of whether they find a job in the field for which they are trained and (b) vocational students to receive non-economic as well as economic benefits from their education. However, we have seen in Section 1 that, sadly, the students who take occupational courses and the employers who hire them do not benefit economically when students take jobs unrelated to the occupation for which training was received.

What about non-economic outcomes such as participation in organizations, political involvement and job satisfaction? Campbell *et al.* (1982) found that neither taking vocational courses nor finding a training related job appeared to have a significant impact on job satisfaction.[6] Campbell and Basinger (1985) found that vocational students were less likely to participate in most types of school and nonschool youth organizations than students in the general curriculum. After graduating they were also 6 percentage points less likely to register to vote, 9.5 percentage points less likely to have voted in the last 3 years and 2.8 percentage points (10.1 rather than

12.9%) less likely to engage in a political activity such as making a campaign contribution. The lower rates of political participation of vocational graduates appear to be due to their social background, not the vocational program. When controls are entered for years of schooling and social background, high school vocational education appears to have no unique effect on political participation. It also appears to have no significant effects on views regarding whether women should work.

Until new evidence is uncovered which contradicts these findings, the case for vocational education should probably rest on its ability to improve the employability and productivity of its students and to retain them in school.

5. Does Vocational Education Lower the Dropout Rate?

The second way occupationally specific education may be benefiting students is by persuading them to stay in school long enough to graduate. A high school diploma raises earning power by nearly 40%, so students who have been induced to stay in school benefit even if they earn no more than graduates of a general program.

It is very difficult, however, to determine whether vocational education lowers the dropout rate because students who are at higher risk of dropping out and dislike academic subjects tend to be attracted to the program. This means that vocational education's effects on retention cannot be measured without thoroughly controlling for grades, academic ability, alienation from school and a host of other background characteristics.

Using a longitudinal data set which contained controls for many of these variables, Mertens et al. (1982) found that taking and passing a vocational course in 9th grade significantly lowered the dropout rate of dropout prone youngsters during 10th grade (from about 9 to 6%). Taking one vocational course during each of the 3 preceding years lowered the 12th grade dropout rate from about 20 to 14%. The dropout rate during the 11th grade was not affected by taking vocational education in 10th grade. These results imply that consistently taking and passing one vocational course each year from 9th through 11th grade raises the high school completion rate of dropout prone youngsters from about 64–70%. Applying the average effect of obtaining a diploma, this raises expected earnings by approx. 2%. The equations predict that two vocational courses/year

for 4 years would have raised the completion rate to about 76% and expected earnings by 4%.

6. Can Basic Skills Substitute for Occupational Skills?

If choices have to be made, what priority should be given to basic skills and what priority should be given to occupational skills? Basic skills — the ability to read, write, speak, compute and reason — are essential to almost everything a person does. Occupational skills are useful primarily at work and only when there is a correspondence between one's occupational skills and one's job. This suggests that occupationally specific training should occur after a career has been at least tentatively selected. Can one postpone career choice until graduation? Would it be feasible to concentrate solely on basic skills expecting that they would substitute for occupational skills when a career is later selected?

A review of research by industrial psychologists on the relationship between productivity in particular jobs and various predictors of that productivity is helpful in thinking about this issue. This research has found that direct measures of both basic skills (general mental ability tests) and occupational skills (job knowledge tests) have very large associations with reported productivity (Hunter and Hunter, 1984, and Reilly and Chao, 1982).[7] General mental ability (GMA) tests (such as the Armed Forces Qualification Test, the Scholastic Achievement Test and components of the Employment Service's General Aptitude Test Battery) focus on verbal, quantitative, spatial, and reasoning abilities. Thus, they test many of the competencies that are the prime objectives of schooling. School attendance has been shown to improve performance on these tests (Lorge, 1945). Increases in the quality and quantity of education were probably responsible for the increase between World War I and World War II of 0.79 standard deviations in the average test scores of army draftees (the equivalent of 12 points on an IQ test).

The ability of GMA tests to predict job performance is greatest in jobs that are intellectually demanding. Many of the jobs that students enter after completing high school make considerable demands on what has come to be called basic skills, for GMA test validities are quite high for clerical workers (0.54), for service workers (0.48), skilled trades and crafts (0.46), for protective service workers (0.42) and even for semi-skilled factory jobs

(0.37).[8] A validity of 0.54 implies that a one standard deviation difference in true ability is associated with 0.54 of a standard deviation difference in true performance. Since the standard deviation of worker productivity in clerical and semi-skilled blue collar jobs is about 20% of average productivity (Schmidt and Hunter, 1983), we can estimate that the effect of one standard deviation improvement in "basic skills" is associated with an 11% improvement in productivity for clerical jobs, and an 8% improvement for semi-skilled factory jobs.

When, however, job knowledge (occupational skills) tests appropriate for the job compete with GMA (basic skills) tests in predicting job performance measured either by supervisory ratings or actual work samples, the job knowledge tests have the greatest impact (Hunter, 1983). When GMA is held constant, a one standard deviation improvement in job knowledge raises productivity by about 10% (when the standard deviation of output is 20% of the mean). When job knowledge is held constant, a one standard deviation improvement in GMA raises productivity by about 5%. Large improvements in job knowledge are easier to achieve than equivalent (in proportions of a standard deviation) improvements in basic skills. Thus while basic skills are important, there would also seem to be an important role for occupationally specific training. The research suggests that basic skills and GMA have high associations with productivity primarily because they help the worker learn the job and occupation specific skills that are used to do the job.

From this evidence one is forced to conclude that basic skills are not a substitute for skills that are specific to a job or an occupation. Studies that have examined the influence of basic and occupational skills on job performance find that occupational skills have a larger direct impact on productivity than basic skills. Basic skills and occupational skills are both essential. Occupational skills and knowledge are essential because of their large direct effects on productivity. Basic skills are important partly because they also contribute to productivity directly but primarily because they aid the learning of job specific and occupational skills.

7. Have High Rates of Skill Obsolescence Drastically Lowered the Return to Occupationally Specific Training?

It is sometimes argued that high school students should concentrate on basic skills rather than occupational skills because jobs are changing so rapidly that occupational skills learned in school soon become obsolescent. This argument is sometimes preceded by the assertion: "in the future, technological advances will come at an increasingly fast pace" (Levin and Rumberger, 1983, p. 21). In fact, however, the available evidence on changing skill requirements suggests that change is less rapid now than in the past. Rates of job turnover, rates of exit from agriculture and overall technological progress are all lower now than in the first seven decades of the 20th-century. Separation rates in manufacturing were 5% per month during the 1920s and 4.4% during the 1970s. To be sure, the 1982 recession and the overvalued dollar have increased the number of workers being forced to change jobs and occupations. But the changes being experienced by the current generation of working adults pale by comparison to the changes experienced by the generation that lived through the depression, the mobilization for WWII and the rapid demobilization after the War. Workers have always had to learn new occupational skills.

The skill obsolescence argument against locating occupationally specific training in high schools has a number of flaws. First, obsolescence is a pervasive phenomenon. The ability to do square roots and long division by hand or on a slide rule has lost much of its value as the use of calculators has grown. Protons, electrons and neutrons are no longer considered the fundamental particles of nature. Rates of obsolescence are higher in fast changing fields and close to the frontier of knowledge. The labor market responds to high rates of skill obsolescence by paying a higher premium for the skill. The high starting salaries of engineers in part derives from the high rate of obsolescence of their skills. Consequently, there is no reason to expect a negative correlation between rates of skill obsolescence and the rate of return to an investment in a skill.

Occupational knowledge is cumulative and hierarchical in much the same way that mathematics and science is cumulative and hierarchical. Having good basic skills lowers the costs of developing occupational skills but it does not lower these costs to zero. Everyone must start at the bottom of the ladder of occupational knowledge and work their way up. New technology does require that workers learn new skills but the new skills are generally learned as small modifications of old skills. While learning a new skill is easier when the worker has good basic skills, a foundation of job knowledge and occupational skills is even more essential. New skills more often supplement old skills than supplant them. At some point every individual must start building his/her foundation of occupational skills. When the foundation building should begin is primarily a function of when the individual is able to decide which occupation to pursue.

Skills and knowledge deteriorate from nonuse much more rapidly than they become obsolescent. In one set of studies, students tested 2 years after taking a course had forgotten ½ of the college psychology and zoology, ⅓ of the high school chemistry and ¾ of the college botany that had been learned (Pressey and Robinson, 1944). Kohn and Schooler (1978) argue that even the very basic cognitive abilities tend to deteriorate if the worker's job does not call for their use. On the other hand, skills and knowledge that are used are not forgotten. In general, forgetting is a more serious threat to knowledge and skills than obsolescence. Consequently, when deciding what to study, the probability of using a skill or knowledge base is more important than the rate of obsolescence of that knowledge.

Occupational skills become obsolete more rapidly than basic skills and this means that vocational teachers must give high priority to keeping their curriculum and their own skills up-to-date. But differences in rates of obsolescence are not decisive considerations in choosing between an academic and a vocational curriculum. Much more important is whether the knowledge and skills gained will be remembered and used. Basic skills are important to and used in almost all occupations and in most adult roles — parent, citizen and consumer — and, therefore, seldom deteriorate rapidly after leaving school. Basic skills, however, should not be confused with the content of specific academic courses. Much of this content is seldom used and quickly forgotten by those not going to college.

Since occupational skills are useful in a limited cluster of occupations, occupationally specific training needs to be conditioned on a reasonable prospect of soon working in the occupation. The reason for this conclusion is first, that the educational investment pays off only if the skills are used (see Section 1); second, that skills deteriorate with lack of use; and finally that motivation to learn is weak if

there is little prospect of using what is learned. Intensive occupationally specific training should begin after a student has made a reasonably well informed tentative career choice and be for occupations with good job prospects.

PART II: POLICY IMPLICATIONS

High School vocational education has recently been subjected to some severe criticism. The Committee for Economic Development's blueprint for reform of public education, *Investing in Our Children*, made the following statement:

> "Unfortunately, whether measured by future earnings, job placement, or employment success there is today little evidence that vocational education is either meeting the needs of students or of the employeers who are expected to hire them." (p. 30)

Some opinion leaders are arguing that occupationally specific programs should be phased out of high schools and concentrated in post-secondary institutions.

It is sometimes claimed that employers would then provide the training that schools do not, but no evidence for this proposition is provided. In the clerical field, for example, employers expect entry level employees to be able to type and often base their hiring selections on typing speed. If high schools stopped offering clerical training, students who did not want or could not afford to attend college would effectively be denied access to clerical occupations and a shortage of typists would soon result. When jobs requiring a great deal of on-the-job training are being filled, employers prefer recent high school graduates with vocational education in the field to high school graduates with no vocational training in the field (Bishop and Kang, 1988).

Furthermore, post-secondary vocational education is not without its problems: high dropout rates, unimpressive training related placement rates and in the proprietary sector very high default rates on student loans. Many students with serious basic skills deficiencies choose to pursue vocational programs. These deficiencies are not caused by vocational education, for they preexist entry into vocational courses and do not become worse during the final two years of high school (Bishop, 1985).

Who are vocational education students? Often

they find academic learning difficult and their self-esteem has suffered as a result. Often their friends denigrate the goals of schooling and encourage the use of drugs and alcohol. if something does not change, they may drop out. Occupationally specific education offers these students a new forum in which to try their talents; a forum in which success is possible and effort is rewarded. A good vocational program develops both vocational skills and a pride in these skills. Pride comes from succeeding at something that is difficult and that not everyone can do. Vocational clubs are examples of this philosophy in action. If dropout prone students arc to be persuaded to stay in school, they must be offered an opportunity to develop pride and a route to something better than a job in a fast food job restaurant. To a large degree the holding power of vocational education derives from its promise of a better job.

How then can occupationally specific education organize itself so as to better deliver on this promise? The major implications of the research reviewed in Part I of this paper is that the primary outcome of occupationally specific education is occupational knowledge and skills and that the benefits of this knowledge and skills derive from their use.

It is legitimate for vocational educators to focus on imparting occupational skills and knowledge, but they should not disclaim responsibility for whether the skills are used. The character of the programs influence whether students get a job or training opportunity that makes use of the skills and knowledge taught. Implicitly or explicitly, the students have been promised that if they try hard, they will benefit. The research implies that the benefits of occupationally specific education are primarily economic and that they derive from using the skills and knowledge gained. Consequently, programs need to be structured to maximize the probability that students get to use what they have learned either in a job or in further training.

The research discussed above suggests how this may be accomplished: employers need to become more involved in planning and delivering vocational education, teachers and administrators need to give greater priority to the placement function, a well informed career choice needs to precede entry into intensive occupational training and programs need to be up-to-date and for occupations with strong employer demand. Strict new mandates regarding procedures for delivering vocational education are

not desirable, however, for they are nearly impossible to enforce and are potentially counter-productive because there is no single best method of serving students. What is needed most is the systematic collection of data on student outcomes and a funding system that prevents creaming yet rewards programs and teachers for achieving better student outcomes.

State Funding Formulas

State governments pay a major share of the costs of vocational education and thus have a responsibility to see that this money is well spent. The effort to ensure quality by regulating the process by which vocational education is delivered has not been a success (Hoachlander et al., 1985). It is well known that funding formulas have powerful effects on the behavior of local administrators. When devising these formulas it is important to give greater thought to their incentive effects.

The wrong incentives are generated by formulas for state reimbursement of the costs of occupational education that are based upon October enrollments or average daily attendance. The aid received by the district is unrelated to the effectiveness of its programs.[9] Success in recruiting students into the program is rewarded rather than success in serving the student. Since the primary demonstrated benefits of vocational education are economic and derive from using the occupationally specific skills taught in school, it is appropriate for funding formulas to reward programs which do a better job of raising earnings of their graduates, of placing them in jobs or further schooling related to their training and of developing workers who are praised and appreciated by their employers.[10] Since dropout prevention is another important benefit of vocational education, it is also appropriate for the formula to reward programs which lower the dropout rates of high risk students most dramatically.

State reimbursement formulas should be based on outcomes, not inputs, and on students, not programs. The formulas should promote the revamping or discontinuation of programs that do not place a respectable number of graduates in jobs or further education related to the training, raise the earnings of program graduates above those of comparable nonvocational students or achieve some mix of well-defined economic and educational goals.[11]

One of the concerns that has been expressed about performance standards is that it may encourage creaming. This can be avoided, however, by devising a formula that offers larger rewards for success in serving more challenging students: the learning disabled and those at high risk of dropping out. Since teachers quite naturally prefer to teach intelligent, well-behaved, motivated students, there will always be pressure to cream.[12] Only powerful counter-incentives can overcome the natural tendency to cream. State funding formulas can be such a counter-incentive if they offer larger reimbursements for success with more challenging students — the handicapped and those with poor grades in previous grades. If, for example, local districts received $3000 for graduating and placing students scoring in the bottom quartile on standardized tests taken in ninth grade, but only $1000 for graduating and placing students scoring in the top half of the test, a very powerful incentive would exist to seek out and serve the students for whom success is not assured.

The second feature of the proposed performance standards that would counteract existing incentives to cream is that reimbursement would not be based on the rate of the training related placement or on the average earnings gains, but rather on the number of training related placements or the average earnings gain times the number graduated. Teachers and counselors would thus face incentives to recruit/admit into vocational education all students who they feel they can help.

When outcomes such as training related placements are part of the formula, adjustments would also need to be made for the intensity of demand in the local labor market. Since placements are more difficult to arrange when local unemployment rates are high, dollar reimbursements per placement should be higher when local unemployment rates are high. An illustrative formula that does this is given below:

$$R_i = \$1000 - \$250(JHSGPA_i) - \$250(\text{Test } Z \text{ score}_i) + \$100(UnRt - 6)$$

where R_i = state reimbursement for the education of the "i"th student, $JHSGPA_i$ is the "i"th students junior high *GPA Z* score (measured in standard deviations form the mean), Test Z score$_i$ is the Z score on a comprehensive test of aptitude or achievement given in 9th grade and $UnRt$ is the local unemployment rate.[13] Formulas should also be adjusted for fields of study to reflect differences in

goals, costs of instruction, and market conditions (e.g., expected rates of training related placement might be higher for distributive education and for office education).

One potential objection to suggestions that funding allocations be based on success in training related placement is that the figures currently reported to state departments of vocational education are not comparable across districts and programs, are subject to manipulation and suffer from a nonresponse problem. However, there is no reason why a more reliable reporting system cannot be developed. Most states have a computerized wage reporting system for the 99% of all wage and salary workers that are covered by unemployment insurance. Estimates of the earnings impact of vocational rather than a general education can be obtained rather easily by merging wage record data into school files on curriculum and the test scores of students. Since the information system contains the name, address and industry of the student's employer, it can also be the starting point of a follow up system providing a valid count of graduates who have training related jobs.[14]

Rewarding the Teacher

The vocational teacher, not a placement director, should be responsible for placing his/her students. McKinney *et al.* (1982) found that schools with placement officers actually had lower training related placement rates than schools which did not. Leaving the responsibility for placement with the vocational teacher forces more involvement with local employers and helps to foster a mentorship relationship between teacher and student. Teachers should assist their students, current graduates and past graduates to find training related jobs and their success in this area should be evaluated and rewarded.

Rewarding teachers for placing their graduates in a job or further schooling that is training related is appropriate because the necessary outreach work takes time and deserves compensation, and because an incentive to devote time to the task is necessary. Employer satisfaction with graduates, the wage levels of the jobs and the quality of teaching should also be evaluated and rewarded.

Counseling Before Entry into Occupationally Specific Programs

A great deal of counseling and thought should

precede the student's choice of an occupationally specific program. Where possible and appropriate, career exploration courses should be available to 9th and 10th graders considering entry into occupationally specific training. Courses need to be specially designed with this purpose in mind. Skill instruction and hands on experience with the tools and materials of a craft are valuable but this needs to be supplemented by visits to work sites and the opportunity to interview and shadow workers in a variety of jobs in the field. High school laboratories and workshops do not by themselves provide a good preview of what a particular line of work is like.

An individualized employability plan should be developed jointly by school staff and students considering entry into occupational (as distinct from exploratory) vocational courses. For students considering an occupational specialty this process should include the following steps:

— disclosure of the past record of each vocational program in placing graduates in training related jobs or further education and the wages and other characteristics of the jobs obtained;

— student participation in a systematic career selection program;

— student investigation of the occupation through taking a part-time job or interviewing and shadowing people who work in the field. The student should be expected to write an essay about this experience and explain why he/she wants to prepare for this occupation;

— conferences with a guidance counselor on the issue of career choice and curriculum that include both the student and his parents;

— development of an employability plan for/with the student which would result in a "contract" being signed between students, parents, vocational teacher, the school and employer representatives. The student would state an intent to seek employment or further training in the field after graduating and teachers and employer representatives would assure the student of a training related job when the program is completed.

Programs with high placement rates and heavy demand should be expanded but where excess demand exists there is nothing wrong with the common practice of giving preference to students who exhibit a particularly strong commitment to the occupation.[15] Motivation and grades in courses that prepare one for the field might also be considered.

Even where everyone who applied is admitted, it is desirable to project an image of selectivity because it prevents vocational students from being stigmatized and instills pride in the chosen field and a commitment to excel.

Screening students for interest might initially reduce the number of students in occupationally specific educational programs. But if it succeeds in raising the esprit of the students in occupational programs and the payoff to their training, the high standards can be expected to attract additional students into the field just as they have been attracted to the magnet high schools of New York, Chicago and many other cities.

SUMMARY AND CONCLUSIONS

Until new evidence of unique educational effects of vocational education is produced, the primary justification of occupationally specific education must remain an economic one. It must make the students better off economically: either by increasing the probability of graduating or improving employment chances after graduating. Making the vocational students no worse off is not good enough. If the economic effects of taking academic and occupational courses in school were equal, the public would probably want to substitute academic for occupational course work. Their preference for the academic has a rational base.

• Academic courses are less costly to teach (because class sizes are larger and space and equipment needs smaller).

• Employers expect to teach occupational skills to new hires who have not received training in high school but they are unlikely to teach the material covered in academic courses.

• Academic course work is better preparation for college than occupational course work so choosing an occupational curriculum inevitably reduces the ability of the student to choose to attend a 4 year college.

• The public's educational goals are in part cultural and political and nonvocational courses make greater contributions to these goals.

• Occupational skills become obsolescent more rapidly than basic skills.

Raising the proportion of graduates who use the occupational skills taught needs to receive very high priority. Teachers and programs need to be evaluated on the basis of the number of graduates who get a job or continue their education in the field. Employers should become more involved in delivering occupational training. Teachers should no longer be sole instructors for occupation specific skills. Where feasible, co-op employers might become the primary instructors for these skills. The teacher's role would become one of mentor and facilitator of learning and job placement, and the role would not terminate when the student graduates. Much more would be expected of vocational teachers, so it would probably be necessary to increase the teacher–student ratio. New funds would need to be committed to vocational education, but the extra money should be distributed as rewards for results — not as reimbursement for increased expenses. State mandated procedural requirements seldom

work. Local administrators and teachers inevitably have the ultimate responsibility. The resources for implementing reform should come from a generous performance based funding formula.

Acknowledgement — The research that has culminated in this paper was sponsored by the National Center for Research in Vocational Education, Research for Better Schools, Inc. and the National Assessment of Vocational Education all funded in one way or another by the office of Research for Educational Improvement and the Department of Education. I would like to thank William Firestone, Joan Buttram, Ellen Newcombe, Paul Campbell, Larry Hotchkiss, Robert Meyer and Mac MacCaslin for helpful comments on earlier versions of the paper. Points of view and opinions expressed are personal and do not necessarily represent the position of Cornell University, The National Center for Research in Vocational Education or Research for Better Schools.

NOTES

1. The occupation of the current or most recent job is matched against field of training to define training relatedness. One has to be in the labor force at least 1 week during the year to be in a training related job, so the association between the two reflects both directions of causation. Since almost all individuals in the sample had been in at least one job since completing school, this is not likely to be a serious source of bias.
2. All published estimates of the impacts of vocational education (including the estimates of the impact of vocational education that results in a training related job) are potentially subject to selection bias. Even though these estimates are made while controlling for all measurable background characteristics, it is possible that there is some unmeasured personality trait that (a) existed prior to entry into vocational education (b) is stable and (c) has important effects on both the outcomes studied and the probability of participation in vocational education or of finding a training related job. We could, of course, be more confident of our estimates of the impacts of vocational education if they were based on an experimental design, but in the absence of such experiments policy decisions must be based on the high quality nonexperimental longitudinal studies that are available. Selection bias probably exaggerates the effect of training relatedness for unemployment and wage rates. Error in the measurement of training relatedness has the opposite effect. When workers who in fact have a training related job are misclassified as working in an unrelated field, the estimated effect of training relatedness on wages and unemployment will be biased toward zero.
3. The analysis makes use of data on 550 pairs of recently hired workers employed in the same or a very similar job at 550 different firms. The following model was estimated:

$$Y_1 - Y_2 = A (D_1 - D_2) + B (X_1 - X_2)$$

where $Y_1 - Y_2$ = is the difference between the productivity or required training of person 1 and person 2.

D_1, D_2 = A dummy indicating that person 1 or 2 had obtained vocational training from a school that was relevant to the job for which he/she was hired

X_1, X_2 = A vector of control variables for the circumstances of the hire, and the new hires other credentials. When current productivity is Y, tenure squared are included in the X's.

4. When a less rigorous definition of training relatedness is used (e.g. one based on questions like "on your present job, how much do you use the vocational training you received in high school or area vocational center?" Bice and Brown. 1973), more than half of vocational graduates report using their training. This implies that a substantial minority of vocational graduates report making some use of their vocational education even though there is no match between their occupation and their training. The Campbell *et al.* (1986) study implies that the amount of carryover is probably quite small, for these graduates were treated as having an unrelated job and the overall wage impact of vocational education for those with an unrelated job was close to zero.

5. The U.S. rate of training related placement might have been somewhat higher if measured 6 months after high school graduation. However the German definitions of relatedness are more rigorous and applying them to U.S. data would have lowered training related placement rates. High unemployment rates no doubt contribute to the low rates of training related placement in the U.S. However, aggregate differential between the countries in training related placement cannot be attributed to differentials in the general tightness of labor markets.

6. The study derived a four factor representation of job satisfaction from a factor analysis of a battery of the job satisfaction questions in the NLS youth data base and then analyzed the effects of vocational education in high school on these four dimensions of job satisfaction. Neither taking vocational courses nor finding a training related job appeared to have a significant impact on job satisfaction. Two years of data were studied and 3 modes of participation and 4 kinds of job satisfaction were defined so the hypothesis that vocational education improves job satisfaction was tested 24 different times. Only two of these coefficients were statistically significant at the 0.05 level, barely more than what would be expected by chance. Only one of the eight coefficients testing the impact of having a training related job was statistically significant (Campbell *et al.*, 1982, Appendix Tables E-1 to E-4).

7. Most of the research used supervisory ratings as the criterion of performance but the basic finding is, in fact, strengthened when better work sample measures of performance are employed (Hunter, 1983).

8. These test validities are calculated by dividing observed correlations between the tests and supervisor reports of job performance by the known reliabilities of the tests and the criterion.

9. If students are able to evaluate program quality and avoid programs judged of low quality, enrollment based funding will reward quality. Students, however, are not well informed about program quality, they may not care about quality and their commitment to a particular occupation may be so strong they will stick with it even if the teacher is doing a poor job. An additional problem is that student enrollment choices may be manipulated by teachers with quotas to fill. Especially perverse incentives arise when occupational programs must have some minimum enrollment to receive state funds. Teachers in need of bodies to meet the target are often willing to accept and sometimes actively recruit into their program students who they know do not want or have only a low probability of getting a job in the field.

10. The use of training related placement rates in reimbursement formulas is clearly feasible for it has been implemented in two states, Florida and South Carolina. JTPA's performance standards also have many similarities to what is being proposed here. Tennessee funds its state colleges and universities in part through a performance incentive system (Bogue and Brown, 1982).

11. The outcomes included in the formula would not have to be limited to economic outcomes. Other indicators might also be employed such as: checklists of competencies attained, numbers of participants in skill olympics and the average rating of the submissions, completions of more advanced training by program graduates, evaluations by the teachers in these post-secondary programs, and scores on occupational competency exams or state licensing exams.

12. Reputations of teachers and programs are influenced by absolute levels of student performance — contests won, houses well constructed, and good jobs obtained. Value added — saving students who were headed for failure — is much harder to assess. Attention goes to the students who fail rather than the ones who graduate and find a job despite handicaps or a disadvantaged background. Not surprisingly teachers compete for the opportunity to teach the better students. All of these factors create incentives to cream — that is to recruit the most able and screen out those with learning problems or a bad attitude.

13. The selection of specific parameters for such a formula is a political decision because distributional considerations must be balanced against incentive effects. Each criterion used would need its own set of adjustment factors. Studies of the background and environmental determinants of each potential criterion would be helpful in making these decisions but are not necessary. Performance based funding formulas are feasible for general education as well.

14. In many cases the match between the industry and the field of training will be so close that a training related placement can be assumed without the necessity of a follow up. Where the nature of the job is not clear from the industry code, a card could be sent to the employer requesting a description of the employee's job and possibly also asking for an evaluation of the training the employee had received. If no response is received from the card, an independent survey firm could be contracted to telephone the employer. Where no match turned up in the system, an effort could be made to call the student's parents. The list of students and their job classifications would be sent to the vocational teacher and the school district. This would give the teacher the opportunity to appeal and correct misclassifications.

15. Students who have not signed a contract and who do not have career plans in the field might be allowed to take vocational courses alongside of the "contract" students but state reimbursements would not be available for such students.

REFERENCES

BICE, G.R. and BROWN, R. (1973) *Selected Information and Vocational-Technical Education in Tennessee for the School Year 1972–1973, Information Series No. 20.* Nashville, TN: Tennessee State Department of Education, Division of Vocational-Technical Education. Tennessee University Knoxville, Occupational Research and Development Coordinating Unit, (ED 091 516 CE 001 283).

BISHOP, J. (1982) *The Social Payoff for Occupationally Specific Training: The Employers' Point of View.* Columbus: The National Center for Research in Vocational Education, The Ohio State University, November.

BISHOP, J. (1985) *Preparing Youth for Employment.* Columbus: The National Center for Research in Vocational Education, The Ohio State University.

BISHOP, J. and KANG, S. (1988) *A Signaling/Bonding Model of Employer Finance of General Training*: Center for Advanced Human Resource Studies Working Paper No. 88-08, Cornell University, Ithaca, New York.

BISHOP, J., HOLLENBECK, K., KANG, S. and WILLKE, R. (1985) Training and Human Capital Formation. Columbus: The National Center for Research in Vocational Education, The Ohio State University.

BOGUE, G.E. and BROWN, W. (1982) Performance incentives for state colleges. *Harvard Business Review,* **60** (November–December), 123–128.

CAMPBELL, P.B., ELLIOT, J., HOTCHKISS, L., LAUGHLIN, S. and SEUSY, E. (1987a) Antecendents of Training-Related Placement. Columbus: The National Center for Research in Vocational Education, The Ohio State University.

CAMPBELL, P.B., ELLIOT, J., LAUGHLIN, S. and SEUSY, E. (1987b) The Dynamics of Vocational Education Efforts on Labor Market Outcomes. Columbus; The National Center for Research in Vocational Education, The Ohio State University.

CAMPBELL, P.B. and Basinger, K.S. (1985) Economic and Noneconomic Effects of Alternative Transitions Through School To Work. Columbus: The National Center for Research in Vocational Education, The Ohio State University.

CAMPBELL, P.B., BASINGER, K.S., DAUNER, M.B. and PARKS, M.A. (1986) Outcomes of Vocational Education for Women Minorities, the Handicapped, and the Poor. Columbus: The National Center for Research in Vocational Education, The Ohio State University.

CAMPBELL, P.B., MERTENS, D.M., SEITZ, P. and COX, S. (1986) Job Satisfaction — Antecedents and Associations. Columbus: The National Center for Research in Vocational Education, The Ohio State University.

CAMPBELL, P.B., ORTH, M.N. and SEITZ, P. (1981) *Patterns of Participation in Secondary Vocational Education.* Columbus: The National Center for Research in Vocational Education, The Ohio State University.

CONRY, W.G., JR and DIAMOND, D.E. (1976) *The Impact of Secondary School Occupational Education in Massachusetts.* Lowell, MA: University of Lowell, College of Management Science (ED 122 095).

DAYMONT, T.N. and RUMBERGER, R.W. (1987) The impact of high school curriculum on the earnings and employability of youth. In *Job Training for Youth* (Edited by TAYLOR, R., ROSEN, H. and PRATZNER, F.), Columbus: The National Center for Research in Vocational Education, The Ohio State University.

FEDERAL INSTITUTE FOR VOCATIONAL TRAINING (1986) The Transition of Young People into Employment after Completion of Apprenticeship in the 'Dual System'. West Germany: The Federal Institute for Vocational Training.

FELSTEHAUSEN, J.L. *et al.* (1973) *Follow-Up Report on Illinois "Class of 71" Occupational Program Alumni, Final Report.* Charleston: Eastern Illinois University, Center for Educational Studies (ED 087 866).

GRASSO, J.T. and SHEA, J.R. (1979) *Vocational Education and Training: Impact on Youth.* Berkeley, CA: The Carnegie Council on Policy Studies in Higher Education.

GUSTMAN, A.L. and STEINMEIER, T.L. (1981) The Relation Between Vocational Training in High School and Economic Outcomes. Paper prepared for the Division of Technical Systems in the Office of Technical and Analytic Systems, Office of the Assistant Secretary for Planning and Budget, U.S. Department of Education. Hanover, NH: Darthmouth College.

HOACHLANDER, E.G., CHOY, S.P. and LAREAU, A.P. (1985) From Prescriptive to Permissive Planning: New Directions for Vocational Education Policy. MPR Associates, Inc., Berkeley, California.

HUNTER, J.E. (1983) Causal analysis, cognitive ability, job knowledge, job performance, and supervisor ratings. In *Performance Measure and Theory* (Edited by LUNDY, S., ZEDECK, S. and CLEVELAND, S.) Hillsdale, NJ: Lawrence Erlbaum.

HUNTER, J.E. and HUNTER, R.F. (1984) The validity and utility of alternative predictors and job performance. *Psychol. Bull.* **96**(1), 72–98.

KOHN, M. and SCHOOLER, C. (1978) "The reciprocal effects of substantive complexity of work and intellectual flexibility: a longitudinal assessment. *Am. J. Sociol.* **84**(1), 24–52.

LEVIN, H.M. and RUMBERGER, R. (1983) The low-skill future of high tech. *Technol. Rev.* August/September: 18–21.

LORGE, I. (1945) Schooling makes a difference. *Teachers College Record* **46**, 483–492.

MANGUM, S. and BALL, D. (1986) Military service, occupational training and labor market outcomes: an update. Columbus: Center for Human Resource Research, The Ohio State University, March.

MAYFIELD, E.C. (1964) The selection interview: a reevaluation of published research. Personnel Psychology **17**, 239–260.

MERTENS, D.M., McELWAIN, D., GARCIA, C. and WHITMORE, M. (1980) *The Effects of Participating In Vocational Education: Summary of Studies Reported Since 1968*. Columbus: The National Center for Research in Vocational Education, The Ohio State University.

MERTENS, D.M., SEITZ, P. and COX, S. (1982) *Vocational Education and the High School Dropout*. Columbus: The National Center for Research in Vocational Education, The Ohio State University, September.

MEYER, R. (1982) Job training in the schools. In *Job Training for Youth*, (Edited by TAYLOR, R., ROSEN, H. and PRATZNER, F.). Columbus: The National Center for Research in Vocational Education, The Ohio State University.

MEYER, R. (1981) Vocational Education: How Should It Be Measured? Washington, DC: The Urban Institute.

NATIONAL COMMISSION FOR EMPLOYMENT POLICY (1981) The Federal Role In Vocational Education. 24 August.

PLISKO, V.W. (Editor) (1984) *The Condition of Education*. Washington, DC: National Center for Education Statistics, U.S. Department of Education.

PRESSEY, S. and ROBINSON, F. (1944) *Psychology and New Education*. (New York, Harper & Brothers Publication), p. 544.

REILLY, R.R. and CHAO, G.T. (1982) Validity and fairness of some alternative employee selection procedures. *Personnel Psychology* **35**, 1–62.

SCHMIDT, F.L. and HUNTER, J.E. (1983) Individual differences in productivity: an empirical test of estimates derived from studies of selection procedure utility. *J. appl. Psychol.* **68**, No. 3, 407–414.

SILBERMAN, H.F. (1982) Problems of Cooperation and Coordination in Vocational Education. Chapter XII, *Education and Work: 1982*. Eighty-first Yearbook of the National Society for the Study of Education. Chicago: University of Chicago Press.

Part III
Efficiency of Schools

[15]

Journal of Economic Literature
Vol. XXIV (September 1986), pp. 1141–1177

The Economics of Schooling: Production and Efficiency in Public Schools

By Eric A. Hanushek

University of Rochester

Large parts of this article were written while I was at the Congressional Budget Office. Helpful comments and suggestions were provided by Stanley Engerman, Daniel Koretz, Richard Murnane, John Pencavel, Rudolph Penner, John Quigley, and a referee. Paul Houts provided excellent editorial suggestions. Responsibility for the interpretation of data, of course, rests solely with me.

I. Introduction

IN RECENT YEARS, public and professional interest in schools has been heightened by a spate of reports, many of them critical of current school policy.[1] These policy documents have added to persistent and long-standing concerns about the cost, effectiveness, and fairness of the current school structure, and have made schooling once again a serious public issue. As in the past, however, any renewed interest in education is likely to be short-lived, doomed to dissipate as frustration over the inability of policy to improve school practice sets in.

This frustration about school policy relates directly to knowledge about the educational production process and in turn to underlying research on schools. Although the educational process has been extensively researched, clear policy prescriptions flowing from this research have been difficult to derive.[2]

There exists, however, a consistency to the research findings that does have an immediate application to school policy: Schools differ dramatically in "quality,"

---

[1] During a two-month period in the spring of 1983, no fewer than five notable reports on the nation's schools appeared: National Commission on Excellence in Education 1983; Aerospace Research Center 1983; Business-Higher Education Forum 1983; Education Commission of the States 1983; and Twentieth Century Fund 1983. The Department of Education has responded with two major reports: U.S. Department of Education 1984, 1986. Two more recent reports presenting extensive reform plans are Task Force on Teaching (1986) and The Holmes Group (1986).

[2] Education, being a more recent subject of economists' attention, has been analyzed more extensively by researchers in other disciplines: psychology, sociology, and political science. Much of this work focuses on subjects outside those of interest to economists. However, there are very important points of overlap in measuring scholastic performance, in analyzing the educational production process, and in formulating educational policy. Indeed, although not usually found in economics journals, this related research is an important ingredient in the material discussed here.

but not because of the rudimentary factors that many researchers (and policy makers) have looked to for explanation of these differences. For example, differences in quality do not seem to reflect variations in expenditures, class sizes, or other commonly measured attributes of schools and teachers. Instead, they appear to result from differences in teacher "skills" that defy detailed description, but that possibly can be observed directly. This interpretation of research findings has clear implications for school policy.

This essay reviews existing analyses of the educational process from several different perspectives, one of which is the relevance of the research for school policy. The economics research on schooling is empirical in nature, and an understanding of its findings must begin with an underlying conceptual model of the educational process. A natural starting point is economic models of production theory and firm behavior. Unfortunately, standard textbook formulations or typical industry and aggregate production function specifications provide little direct guidance in educational analysis, because they seldom are designed to deal with the detailed policy questions that have been central to investigations of schooling. Indeed, after modifying the standard framework to accommodate the policy purposes, the measurement issues, the incentive structure of schools, and so forth, the resultant models may be sufficiently different that a new nomenclature is useful. The most important modification involves interpretations of economic efficiency—a concept that has a very clear meaning in textbook analyses of the theory of the firm but that becomes quite cloudy in the world of public schools.

The empirical formulations developed in the research on schooling do provide insights that appear applicable to other micro policy areas where complicated production relationships for services are

central. The results of this review also have immediate implications for other areas of economic study. A variety of public finance investigations, urban housing and location studies, and labor economics analyses include at least tangentially some consideration of school quality and performance—but generally these studies do not incorporate the results of direct analyses of schooling.

A. *Limits of the Study*

This study examines the research on the economics of education and schooling and explores what has been learned and where major gaps remain, focusing on production and efficiency aspects of schools as opposed to the ultimate uses of education. Because there are excellent reviews of "human capital" (Jacob Mincer 1970; Sherwin Rosen 1977), this area is specifically downplayed, even though human capital investment and the economics of education are at times treated as being synonymous.[3] This review also concentrates on public education, for lack of comparable research on the private sector,[4] and on the United States to avoid the problems of drawing inferences from cross-country data where basic educational patterns differ substantially.[5]

---

[3] An additional reason for emphasizing production and efficiency aspects is that, although work on human capital ostensibly deals with investment behavior in schooling, the real focus frequently tends to be on income determination, or schooling as an input to the wage determination process.

[4] Recent work on private schooling, while generating considerable interest, has not looked explicitly at production relationships in private schools. Instead it has stopped at contrasting mean performance in public and private schools. See section IV, below.

[5] There have been a number of studies of schooling in developing countries, much of it emanating from the World Bank. See, for example, Stephen Heyneman and William Loxley (1983), Richard Kollodge and Robin Horn (1985), and Bruce Fuller (1985). These studies frequently involve a much wider range of inputs—such as teachers' education levels ranging from the third grade through college—and therefore are better able to identify and to estimate the effects

Hanushek: The Economics of Schooling   1143

One other prefatory remark may be useful. At least from an economics perspective, distinctions between elementary and secondary schooling and postsecondary schooling seem small. While the private postsecondary schooling sector is somewhat larger, both segments of the educational system are dominated by public supply; the technologies appear very similar, at least on the surface; and, most frequently a year of schooling at any level is treated as being equivalent in the sense that years enter linearly into some other activity or behavior that is being modeled. However, the research and indeed the focus of policy attention in the two sectors have differed markedly. Economic studies of elementary and secondary schooling have concentrated on production processes, public finance questions about governmental support, and, to a lesser extent, labor markets for teachers, cost-benefit analyses of specific programs, and public-private choices. Economic studies of higher education have been largely concerned with distributional questions related to access and costs faced by different groups, with governmental subsidy policies, and with attendance decisions; virtually no attention has been given to production processes or the analysis of specific programs.[6]

---

of fundamental school inputs. On the other hand, the relevant range for policies in developed countries may not even be included in the sample data. The classic study for England is Central Advisory Council for Education 1967.

[6] Exceptions include David Breneman 1976; Lewis Perl 1976; and Timothy Hogan 1981. These studies have tended to concentrate on quantitative variations (for example, numbers of PhDs produced) instead of qualitative variations. Hogan's study is unique in measuring qualitative differences (through subsequent publication records) among PhDs produced.

The division by level of schooling might well be explained by the traditions of other disciplines; those divisions reflect in part differences in cognitive processes with age and in part organizational variations and perspectives. Much of the economic analysis of education has been rather recent and has built upon that of other disciplines.

TABLE 1

EXPENDITURES AND SOURCE OF FUNDING: 1960–83
(ALL ELEMENTARY AND SECONDARY SCHOOLS)

	1960	1970	1980	1983
Expenditures				
(Billion $)	18.0	45.7	108.6	132.9
Percent GNP	3.6	4.6	4.1	4.0
Source of Funds (percent)				
Federal	3.9	7.4	8.7	6.8
State	31.1	34.6	41.5	43.3
Local	52.8	47.5	38.2	38.1
Private	12.3	10.5	11.5	11.8

Source: U.S. Statistical Abstract, 1985.

B. The Elementary and Secondary School Sector

Before discussing the direct analyses of schooling, it is useful to understand the overall dimensions of the sector. The size of the sector and the changes that have taken place frequently are not well understood.[7] Yet the kinds of policies behind these changes relate directly to the character of production in the public schools and the substance of economists' analyses of schools.

Expenditures. The total spending on elementary and secondary schooling in the United States, as shown in Table 1, is currently equal to about 4 percent of gross national product. The largest fluctuations in its relative size reflect simply total enrollments in schools, which peaked in 1970. A steady rise in per pupil expenditures, however, has pushed upward the resources going into elementary and secondary schools.

There have been two major changes over the past 25 years in the source of funding for schools. First, as displayed in Table 1, federal funding jumped during

---

[7] A more detailed analysis of schooling at all levels that also includes data since 1940 can be found in Dave O'Neill and Peter Sepielli (1985).

1144   *Journal of Economic Literature, Vol. XXIV (September 1986)*

TABLE 2

ELEMENTARY AND SECONDARY SCHOOL PUPILS, STAFFING, AND TYPE OF CONTROL: 1960–80

	1960	1965	1970	1975	1980
Enrollment (thousands)					
Total	42,181	48,473	51,272	49,791	45,949
Elementary	29,150	31,570	31,553	29,340	27,779
Secondary	13,031	16,904	19,719	20,451	18,170
Classroom Teachers (thousands)					
Total	1,600	1,933	2,288	2,451	2,439
Elementary	991	1,112	1,281	1,352	1,365
Secondary	609	822	1,007	1,099	1,074
Private School Enrollment					
(Percent of Total Enrollment)					
Total	14.0	13.0	10.5	10.0	10.8
Elementary	16.5	15.5	12.8	12.6	13.0
Secondary	8.4	8.3	6.6	6.4	7.4
Catholic School Enrollment					
(Percent of Private Enrollment)					
Total	89.0	88.5	81.4	68.3	62.6
Elementary	91.1	91.7	82.9	68.2	62.6
Secondary	80.0	77.3	76.9	68.5	62.5

Source: U.S. Statistical Abstract, 1985.

the 1960s. This was followed by a slow growth in federal share during the 1970s and a decline during the 1980s. Second, the financing of local schools was altered extensively during the 1970s by a series of legal and legislative challenges to the use of local property taxes as the principal funding source. This resulted in the steady increase in the level of support from state revenue sources with a commensurate decline in the support of schools from local revenues. Direct private support for schools almost entirely represents expenditures on private schooling; there is a minuscule amount of governmental support for private schooling, and there is a minuscule amount of nongovernmental support for the public schools.

Enrollments. Currently, about 45 million students are enrolled in schools. The peak in elementary school enrollments (grades 1 through 8) occurred in the late 1960s, while high schools peaked in the mid-1970s (Table 2). While student enrollment fell by over 10 percent between 1970 and 1980, the number of classroom teachers actually increased by 7 percent over the same period.[8]

Enrollment in private schools declined in the 1960s and, since then, has remained roughly constant as a proportion of total enrollment. The private school decline largely reflects the decline in Catholic

[8] It is difficult to get total employment figures for elementary and secondary schools, because much of the governmental employment is not separated in the data by level of schooling. Classroom teachers make up 88 percent of the total instructional staff, which includes principals, librarians, and so forth.

Part of the increase in teachers may reflect the requirements of laws related to handicapped students. Federal legislation in 1975 (P.L. 94-142, The Education of All Handicapped Children Act) has been particularly important because of its specific requirements dealing with administrative and school processes.

TABLE 3
SCHOOL COMPLETION: 1950–80

	1950	1960	1965	1970	1975	1980
School Retention						
Percent graduating from high school	50.5	62.1	73.2[a]	75.0	74.3	74.4
Percent entering college	20.5	32.8	38.4[a]	46.1	45.2	46.3
School Completion						
(Population age 25–29)						
Median years completed	12.0	12.3	12.4	12.6	12.8	12.9
Percent 4 years high school or more	52.8	60.7	70.3	73.8	83.1	84.5

Source: U.S. Statistical Abstract, 1970, 1982, 1985.
[a] Data for 1966.

school enrollment. While Catholic schools made up almost 90 percent of private enrollment in 1960, this was down to 63 percent in 1980. Schools affiliated with other religions made up an additional 21 percent of the private school enrollment in 1980, leaving 16 percent of the private school instruction in private schools with no religious affiliation. Private schools remain more important at the elementary school level than at the secondary level.

Performance. In terms of graduation rates and continuation into college, there has been remarkably little change since the mid-1960s. As seen in Table 3, recent data show that an almost constant three-quarters of each age cohort graduates from high school at the normal time, and, with some fluctuations, about 45 percent of each age cohort will enter college immediately. The school completion data for the population age 25 to 29 give a similar view, only the timing is different because of the ages considered. The median years of school completed for the population age 25 to 29 has crept up from 12.3 years in 1960 to 12.9 in 1980. Further, reflecting the increased school attendance of the 1950s and 1960s, the calculated percentage of this age group completing 4 or more years of high school shows a steady rise, reaching 84.5 percent by 1980. Many

people note the steady increases in educational attainment of the workforce without realizing that the graduation and college attendance behavior have been steady since before 1970.

There does remain some disparity between high school graduation rates and the completion percentages; the percentage of 25–29 year olds reporting 4 or more years of high school is 10 percent higher than the estimated graduation rate. This may reflect an increasing tendency to complete high school at later ages. Or, the recall data on school completion may simply be inaccurate. Unfortunately, it is not possible to differentiate among these alternative explanations.

Most of the attention given to schools relates to performance on standardized tests and, more specifically, on the Scholastic Aptitude Test (SAT). (For an excellent current review of evidence on test score declines, see Congressional Budget Office 1986a.) Figure 1 displays the history of average test scores on the verbal and math portions of the SAT. As is well known, beginning in 1963, test scores began a steady decline. Verbal scores fell about one half of a stardard deviation before bottoming out in 1979; math scores followed the same time pattern, although the magnitude of decline was not as large.

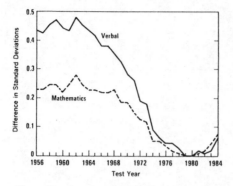

Figure 1.   Average SAT Scores, by Subject,
Differences from Lowest Year

Source: Congressional Budget Office, 1986a.

Note: Average test scores in each year are measured in standard deviations of student performance from mean scores in 1979, the year of lowest average SAT performance. Comparisons in terms of percentile position of the means across years can be calculated approximately from the normal distribution.

Because absolute scores have little meaning, the comparisons are made in terms of standard deviations of student performance, which can be translated into percentile comparisons using the normal distribution. Thus, a fall in mean performance of .48 standard deviations (verbal scores) implies that mean performance at the trough was approximately equivalent to performance at the 32nd percentile in 1963. Similarly, a drop of .28 standard deviations (math scores) implies that mean performance in 1979 was roughly equivalent to performance at the 39th percentile in 1963.

Performance on other tests, however, is much less known. A wide range of different tests, ones designed with different purposes and validated in a variety of different ways, show declines beginning about the same time. There was a pervasive decline at all grade levels, not restricted just to graduating students. Moreover, as described in Table 4, test scores

at lower grades appear to have begun a recovery before the SAT scores. The time patterns of performance on the Iowa tests for different grade levels is shown in Figure 2. Making such intertemporal comparisons is frequently difficult, but the consistency of findings suggests improvements that began in the mid-1970s. The crude evidence points to declines closely related to specific years of schooling or birth cohorts.[9]

Over the past 15 years there has been a consistent narrowing of the gap in test scores between blacks and nonminority students (Congressional budget Office 1986a). This trend appears on virtually all tests, including the SATs. Nevertheless, gaps between minority and nonminority students remain sizable.

Public School Inputs. Dramatic changes in the operations of schools have come along with these changes in student performance. Most notable has been the increase in expenditures per pupil shown in Table 5. The 1983 spending for current services of $2,960 per public school student in attendance was 135 percent *in real terms* above that in 1960. This corre-

---

TABLE 4

ONSET AND END OF THE ACHIEVEMENT DECLINE,
SELECTED TESTS

	Onset	End
Scholastic Aptitude Test (SAT)	1963	1979
American College Testing Program (ACT)	1966	1975
Iowa Tests of Basic Skills—grade 5	1966	1974
Iowa Tests of Basic Skills—grade 8	1966	1976
Iowa Tests of Educational Development—grade 12	1968	1979
Minnesota Scholastic Aptitude Test	1967	na

Source: Congressional Budget Office, 1986a.

---

[9] See Congressional Budget Office (1986b) for a discussion of alternative hypotheses about this time pattern.

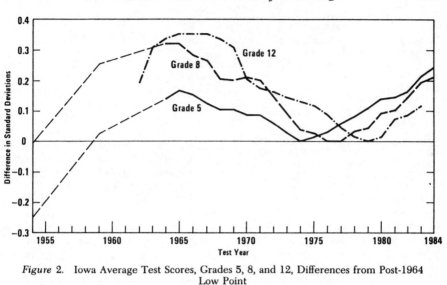

Figure 2.   Iowa Average Test Scores, Grades 5, 8, and 12, Differences from Post-1964
Low Point

Source: Congressional Budget Office, 1986a.
Note: See explanation, Figure 1.

sponds to a compound annual growth rate of real expenditures of 3.8 percent. Total expenditures, which include capital expenditures and interest on debt, showed somewhat lower growth, because capital spending was a decreasing portion of the total. By 1983, total spending per student had reached an average of $3,261.

A very significant component of this growth in per pupil expenditures is the overall fall in pupil-teacher ratios (Table 6). These declines, which were previously seen in the increases in classroom teachers during a period of falling school enrollments, have an enormous effect on expenditures per pupil. In the public schools, pupil-teacher ratios fell over 25 percent between 1960 and 1980, with the decline being somewhat higher in elementary schools. By way of comparison, private schools have also had large falls in pupil-teacher ratios, although some of this may

TABLE 5

PUBLIC SCHOOL EXPENDITURES PER STUDENT IN AVERAGE DAILY ATTENDANCE (ADA): 1960–83

	1960	1966	1970	1975	1980	1983
Current expenditure/ADA	$375	$537	$816	$1,286	$2,230	$2,960
1983 Dollars	$1,262	$1,696	$2,094	$2,381	$2,696	$2,960
Total Expenditures/ADA	$472	$654	$955	$1,503	$2,502	$3,261
1983 Dollars	$1,598	$2,066	$2,451	$2,783	$3,025	$3,261

Source: U.S. Statistical Abstract, 1970, 1981, 1985.

TABLE 6
PUPIL-TEACHER RATIOS: 1960–80

	1960	1965	1970	1975	1980
Public Schools					
Total	25.8	24.6	22.3	20.4	19.0
Elementary	28.4	27.6	24.4	21.7	20.5
Secondary	21.7	20.8	19.9	18.8	17.1
Private Schools					
Total	30.7	28.3	23.0	19.6	17.9
Elementary	36.1	33.3	26.5	21.5	19.3
Secondary	18.6	18.4	16.4	15.7	15.0

Source: U.S. Statistical Abstract, 1982, 1985.

reflect the changing composition of private school enrollment noted above. While it is sometimes asserted that the falls in pupil-teacher ratios simply reflect an attempt to maintain overall teacher employment in the face of declining enrollment, this seems inconsistent with the fact that class size declines begin before total enrollment declines.

The characteristics of teachers have also changed dramatically over time. Perhaps the most dramatic change, shown in Table 7, is the aging of the current teacher force. While one-third of public school teachers in the mid-1960s were in their first four years of teaching, that fell to one-twelfth by 1983. The median experience of teachers reached 13 years of experience, from a low of 8 years.

Reflecting in part this stability in the teacher force and in part state regulations and financial incentives of teacher salary schedules, the percent of all teachers with a master's degree or more doubled between 1966 and 1983. By 1983, over half of all public school teachers held at least a master's degree.

Table 7 also shows that the picture of teachers' salaries is, however, different. Average salaries rose dramatically during the 1960s, but subsequently fell in real terms throughout the 1970s. This fall in average salaries is more dramatic when

combined with the increase in experience and amount of graduate training of teachers, because both of those factors will increase salaries. Data on entry level salaries show a much steeper decline (in real terms). On the other hand, workers in the entire economy lost ground during the inflationary period of the last decade, so that teacher salaries hold up reasonably well against the salaries of private nonagricultural workers. (In Table 7, average teacher salaries are compared to annualized values of average weekly earnings.)

The Puzzle. The data on the schooling sector suggest a number of puzzles. The most important one—and the subject of most of this review—is that the constantly rising costs and "quality" of the inputs of schools appear to be unmatched by improvement in the performance of students. It appears from the aggregate data that there is at best an ambiguous relationship and at worst a negative relationship between student performance and the inputs supplied by schools. Such conclusions cannot, however, be made on the basis of just the aggregate data.

C. Overview

Studies of educational production functions (also referred to as "input-output" analyses or "cost-quality" studies) examine the relationship among the different inputs into and outcomes of the educational process. These studies are systematic, quantitative investigations relying on econometric, as opposed to experimental, methods to separate the various factors influencing students' performance.

The standard textbook treatment of production functions considers only the most stylized examples—say, for example, how much capital and labor to employ in producing some specific output. Knowledge of the production function and the prices for each of the inputs allows a straightforward solution of the "least cost"

TABLE 7

CHARACTERISTICS OF PUBLIC SCHOOL TEACHERS: 1960–83

	1960	1966	1971	1976	1981	1983
Teacher Experience						
1–4 years (percent)	na	32.2	32.3	27.1	14.1	8.3
Greater than 20 years (percent)	na	21.6	18.5	14.3	21.8	25.0
Median (years)	na	9	8	8	11	13
Education						
Master's degree or more (percent)	na	26.1	27.2	36.7	48.9	53.0
Salaries						
Average salary[a]	$5,174	$6,935	$9,470[b]	$12,448	$18,321	$21,790
1983 dollars	$17,406	$21,290	$23,296	$21,786	$20,070	$21,790
Ratio average worker[c]	1.23	1.35	1.43	1.36	1.38	1.49

Source: U.S. Statistical Abstract, 1982, 1985.
[a] Average salary of all instructional personnel (i.e., teachers, principals, guidance counselors, librarians and others associated with instruction).
[b] Estimated.
[c] Ratio of average salary to annualized average weekly earnings in the U.S.

set of inputs—that is, the combination of inputs that would produce any given output at minimum cost. The concept of a production function is a powerful pedagogical tool, and, in its basic form, appears applicable to a wide range of industries—from petrochemicals to education.

In an intermediate microeconomics classroom, production functions are generally assumed to be known precisely by decision makers, to involve only a few inputs that are measured perfectly, and to be characterized by a deterministic relationship between inputs and outputs (that is, a given set of inputs always produces exactly the same amount of output). Furthermore, it is assumed that all inputs can be varied freely.

The realities of education (and virtually all other areas for that matter) differ considerably from such pedagogical assumptions. Indeed, the production function is unknown (to both decision makers and researchers) and must be estimated using imperfect data; some important inputs cannot be changed by the decision maker;

and any estimates of the production function will be subject to considerable uncertainty.

Perhaps the largest difference between applying production functions to education and to other industries, however, has been in its immediate application to policy considerations. Statistical estimates of educational production functions have entered into a variety of judicial and legislative proceedings and have formed the basis for a number of intense policy debates.

The history of educational production function analysis is typically traced to *Equality of Educational Opportunity,* or, more commonly, the "Coleman Report" (James Coleman et al. 1966). The Coleman Report was mandated by the Civil Rights Act of 1964 and was conceived as a study of the distribution of educational resources within the United States by race or ethnic background. The study, however, went far beyond simply producing an inventory of school resources. It created a massive statistical base containing

1150   *Journal of Economic Literature, Vol. XXIV (September 1986)*

survey information for more than one half million students found in some 3,000 separate schools that was employed to ascertain which of the various inputs into the educational process were most important in determining the achievement of students.

Although not the first such study, it is both the best known and the most controversial. In simplest terms, the Coleman Report appeared to demonstrate that differences in schools had little to do with differences in students' performance. Instead, family background and the characteristics of other students in the school seemed much more important. The report's findings generated extensive critiques, policy discussions, and further research (see, for example, Eric Hanushek and John Kain 1972; Samuel Bowles and Henry Levin 1968; and Glen Cain and Harold Watts 1970). Today, even though it remains the most cited analysis of schools, the Coleman Report is commonly held to be seriously flawed, and its importance is more in terms of intellectual history than insights into schools and the educational process.

The production function approach, which began in earnest with the Coleman Report, has not been universally accepted, particularly among educational decision makers. In part, criticism of the approach appears to be a reaction against the specific results. (For example, as described below, these studies tend to suggest that schools are very inefficient in their use of resources.) In part it appears to reflect a general reaction against doing any quantitative evaluation of education and schools. But, it also reflects concern about legitimate analytical problems or misinterpretation of the results of specific studies.

II. *Conceptual and Specification Issues*

The underlying model guiding most analysis is very straightforward. The output of the educational process—that is, the achievement of individual students—is directly related to a series of inputs. Some of these inputs—the characteristics of schools, teachers, curricula, and so forth—are directly controlled by policy makers. Other inputs—those of families and friends plus the innate endowments or learning capacities of the students—are generally not controlled. Further, while achievement may be measured at discrete points in time, the educational process is cumulative; inputs applied sometime in the past affect students' current levels of achievement.[10]

A. *Specification and Measurement of Output*

Clearly, to analyze school production it is essential to employ adequate measures of outcomes. But measuring outputs is not simple. While economic theory concentrates on varying quantities of a homogeneous output, this is not easily translated into an educational equivalent. Education is a service that transforms fixed quantities of inputs (that is, individuals) into individuals with different qualities. Educational studies concentrate—as they should—on "quality" differences.

A majority of studies into educational production relationships measure output by standardized achievement test scores, although significant numbers have employed other quantitative measures such as student attitudes, school attendance rates, and college continuation or dropout rates. The measures used, however, are generally proxies (with varying degrees of validation) for more fundamental outcomes. Some people, including many school practitioners, simply reject this line of research entirely because they believe that educational outcomes are not or cannot be adequately quantified.

---

[10] For further discussion of this model, see Hanushek (1972, 1979).

Interest in and concern about the performance of schools relates directly to the perceived importance of schooling in affecting the ability of students to perform in and cope with society after they leave school. While seldom fully articulated, the theory is that more schooling makes people more productive in the labor market, better able to participate in democracy, better consumers, and so forth—in other words, healthy, wealthy, and wise. Economists, sociologists, and political scientists have conducted a broad range of investigations into postschooling outcomes. In general, empirical studies confirm the correlation between higher levels of schooling and positive attributes after schooling. Indeed, it is commonplace for individual level investigations of behavior to include schooling more or less automatically as a conditioning variable regardless of the topic under investigation.

The analytic problem is that postschooling outcomes cannot be contemporaneously observed with the schooling. Of course, this kind of problem arises elsewhere—for example, in the analysis of environmental effects on health or of changes in social security law on retirement behavior, and a variety of approaches are employed for gleaning information from existing data. By far the most common approach in education is to analyze cross-sectional variations in measures that can serve as proxies for future performance. A natural starting point, thus, is an investigation of how schooling affects labor market performance and other postschooling activities.

From the standpoint of production function analyses, there are two fundamental difficulties with existing research into postschooling outcomes. First, the concentration on *quantity differences*, or pure time spent in schooling activities, as opposed to *quality differences* makes it difficult to relate the analyses directly. Treating all time spent in schooling activi-

ties equally neglects the possibility that time in some school settings might very well have different value from that spent in other settings; yet the differential effectiveness of schools is the heart of production function studies. This concentration on quantity of schooling, which is perfectly explicable in terms of the availability of data, holds equally for the labor market studies generally pursued by economists and for the nonlabor market studies pursued more frequently by researchers in other disciplines. Second, the conceptual underpinnings of the presumed improved performance of the more educated remain unclear. This complicates attempts to measure directly any quality differences among students, because there is little guidance on just what to look for.

The most extensive analyses by economists have related wages of workers to number of years of schooling completed (see, for example, the reviews by Mincer 1970 and Rosen 1977). To be sure, the theoretical modeling behind this work does not restrict attention merely to quantity and, in fact, in many instances can be interpreted as incorporating both quantity and quality differences in schooling. Nevertheless, when it comes to empirical implementation, data shortcomings frequently demand that exclusive attention be given to quantity. This is even the case in models of "human capital production functions" (see Yoram Ben-Porath 1970).

Attempts to incorporate qualitative measures of schooling into labor market studies have been severely limited by availability of data, by the necessity of using fairly peculiar samples, and by reliance on stringent assumptions about school operations. One approach has been to include individual test score information, but this sort of data exists only in rare instances and is usually not representative; see, for example, Zvi Griliches and William Mason 1972; John Hause 1972;

1152 *Journal of Economic Literature, Vol. XXIV (September 1986)*

Hanushek 1973, 1978; Orley Ashenfelter and Joseph Mooney 1968; Daniel Rogers 1969; Randall Weiss 1970; Paul Taubman and Terence Wales 1974; W. Lee Hansen, Burton Weisbrod, and William Scanlon 1970.

These studies produce a wide range of estimates of the test score/earnings relationships; they range from finding no relationship to finding one that dominates any measure of quantity of schooling. In most studies, however, years of schooling and measures of cognitive ability exhibit independent effects on earnings.

Another general line of inquiry has been to incorporate measures of the characteristics of individuals' schools directly into earnings functions. One class of such studies includes average school expenditure data (for example, Paul Wachtel 1976; George Johnson and Frank Stafford 1973; Thomas Ribich and James Murphy 1975; Charles Link and Edward Ratledge 1975; John Akin and Irwin Garfinkel 1977). A second class includes measures of specific school resources or characteristics of teachers in the earnings model (for example, Finis Welch 1966, 1973; Christopher Jencks and Marsha Brown 1975; Jere Behrman and Nancy Birdsall 1983). But such analyses must *assume* that differences in expenditures or in the specific resources provide an index of differences in quality. This is an important question to be addressed through the analysis of educational production functions. Moreover, unless the models also include measures of other inputs into the educational process—such as the family backgrounds or characteristics of other students in the schools, they will obtain biased estimates of the effects of differences in schools.[11] Perhaps for these reasons, the results of

these studies on the effects of quality differences have been inconclusive.

Although the relationship of schooling and labor market performance is central to many policy questions, it is not the only area of interest; see, for example, reviews by Robert Michael (1982) and Robert Haveman and Barbara Wolfe (1984). Studies have examined the role of education in increasing job satisfaction, in maintaining personal health (Michael Grossman 1975), and in increasing the productivity of mothers engaged in household production (Arleen Leibowitz 1974), as well as the effects of the mother's education on the learning of young children. Other studies have considered the effect of education on political socialization and voting behavior (Richard Niemi and Barbara Sobieszek 1977), the relationship between education and criminality (Isaac Ehrlich 1975), the contribution of education to economic growth (Edward Denison 1974), and the effect of education on marriage and divorce (Gary Becker, Elizabeth Landes, and Robert Michael 1977). While these studies have suggested some gross effects of the quantity of schooling on other life outcomes, they virtually have never addressed the question under consideration here: How do such outcomes vary in response to differences in school programs and operations?

In summary, the literature about the relationship between measures of schooling quality and subsequent attainment is ambiguous. The analyses available are often crude empirical forays that are difficult to replicate and to evaluate in a definitive manner. While these studies offer an important perspective on how to observe educational outcomes, they do not currently provide firm guidance about appropriate contemporaneous measures of quality that might be used in production function analysis. (This is not, of course, the primary purpose of such studies.)

As a general research strategy, one might think of approaching the issue in

---

[11] Education occurs both at home and in the schools, and characteristics of families (such as income levels) and characteristics of schools tend to be positively correlated. These correlations, discussed below, imply biased estimates in the analysis of earnings discussed here.

a different way—by considering what attributes of schooling (or individuals) were important for subsequent success and then developing direct measures that could be obtained during the same time period with the schooling. Yet, a fundamental shortcoming of this strategy is the superficiality of the conceptual notions of the mechanisms by which education affects productivity and later experiences. As measured through various standardized tests, cognitive skills are probably the chief contemporaneous measure of educational quality currently available. But this may not be the only, let alone the most important, outcome of schooling in determining the future success of students. One might think that more educated individuals can accomplish given tasks better or more swiftly, but surely this holds for only certain types of jobs. Less education may even be an advantage in jobs requiring manual skills or jobs that are very repetitive.

One rather commonly held presumption is that better educated individuals are able to perform more complicated tasks or are able to adapt to changing conditions and tasks (see Welch 1970; Richard Nelson and Edmund Phelps 1966). This hypothesis has important implications for studying the productivity and outputs of schools, because it provides some rationale for favoring measures of analytical ability. Outside of this area, however, similar conceptual views of the important elements of schooling are even harder to find.

The uncertainty about the source of schooling-earnings relationships is also highlighted by recent attention to "screening" aspects of schooling. Schools may not improve the skills of students but may simply identify the more able. The latter view has been the subject of both theoretical and empirical treatment by economists and sociologists (for example, Ivar Berg 1970; A. Michael Spence 1973, 1974; Kenneth Wolpin 1977; John Riley 1979a, 1979b; Richard Layard and George

Psacharopoulos 1974; Andrew Weiss 1983). Screening implies that the social value of schooling may be considerably less than the private value if schools are merely identifying the more able instead of actually changing their skills.

The screening model also has direct implications for measuring educational outcomes and analyzing educational production relationships. In a screening model, the output of schools is information about the *relative* abilities of students. This would suggest that more attention should be directed toward the distribution of observed educational outcomes (instead of simply the means) and their relationship to the distribution of underlying abilities. Further, it might radically alter the interpretation of some studies, such as those of school dropout rates, because schools with higher dropout rates might actually be providing better information (higher output) than those with lower rates. (This is clearly an interpretation that is very different from that of the authors of these studies.)

Production and screening, however, are not the only models explaining subsequent performance. For example, Jencks et al. (1972) argue that luck and personal characteristics (unaffected by schooling) are the most important determinants of earnings differences. Bowles and Herbert Gintis (1976) believe that differences in earnings arise chiefly from the existing social structure and that schools adjust to rather than determine subsequent outcomes. While these last two theories are not completely convincing, there is not enough available evidence to determine conclusively which, if any, of these four divergent views are valid.

B. *Standardized Test Scores*

At this point, it may be useful to consider standardized test scores more specifically because they are the most commonly used measure in investigating the educational process. As previously men-

1154   *Journal of Economic Literature, Vol. XXIV (September 1986)*

tioned, considerable uncertainty exists about the appropriateness of using test scores as outcome measures. Studies of lifetime outcomes, while conceptually very relevant to measuring school outputs, have not been particularly illuminating; existing empirical evidence is inconclusive about the strength of the link between test scores and subsequent achievement outside of schools. Because cognitive tests given in schools are generally not designed to measure subsequent performance, it is not particularly surprising that they are imperfect.[12]

Nevertheless, performance on tests is being used to evaluate educational programs, and even to allocate funds, and there are some pragmatic arguments for the use of test scores as output measures. Besides their common availability, one argument is that test scores appear to be

valued in and of themselves. To a large extent, educators tend to believe that they are important, albeit incomplete, measures of education. Further, parents and decision makers appear to value higher test scores—at least in the absence of evidence that they are unimportant. In fact, the use of scores on standardized tests as criteria for high school graduation (usually referred to as minimum competency tests) has increased dramatically in recent years and now is mandated by many states.

A more persuasive argument for the use of test scores relates to continuation in schooling. Almost all studies of earnings that include both quantity of schooling and achievement differences find significant effects of quantity that are independent of achievement differences. This implies that measured differences in achievement do not adequately measure all skill differences. At the same time, however, test scores have an important use in selecting individuals for further schooling and thus may relate directly to the "real" outputs through the selection mechanism (cf. Dennis Dugan 1976). The use of tests for predicting future school performance and for selection is also a central issue in the study by Willard Wirtz et al. (1977), which reviews the decline in Scholastic Aptitude Test scores.

Finally, the variety of potential outcomes of schooling suggests that the educational process may have multiple outputs, some of which are very poorly measured by test scores. Moreover, how effective test scores are in measuring the contribution of schooling to subsequent performance probably varies at different points in the schooling process. Specifically, test scores might be more appropriate in the earlier grades, where the emphasis tends to be more on basic cognitive skills—reading and arithmetic—than in the later grades. (Note that virtually all production function studies have been conducted for elementary and secondary

[12] Standardized tests employed by schools lack external validation in terms of labor market skills or other subsequent outcomes. This is not particularly surprising, however, given the primary motivations behind their construction. Most tests are designed to: examine students on specific knowledge; rank students in terms of skills or knowledge; or predict performance. The performance of interest, however, is often future success in schooling. This, for example, is motivation behind the SAT tests. See Congressional Budget Office (1986a, Chapter 2) for an excellent discussion of standardized tests and their use.

The efforts to validate tests are often quite extensive (see, for example, Hunter Breland (1979) on the SAT test), but they are frequently concerned with such things are consistency across tests or correlations with other measures. Alternative standards for validation are described in American Educational Research Association (1985).

Reliability of tests is a second major concern. Does a given test produce the same score if taken at different times by the same individual, and do slightly different wordings of questions covering the same concept yield the same results? None of these relates directly to whether or not tests cover material, knowledge, or skills valued by society.

Finally, although they have come under considerable criticism, a variety of employment tests have been designed and validated with labor market performance. The attacks on these have concentrated on both their inaccuracies and their potential for discriminatory results. Data on performance on these tests have never been available to school researchers.

schools. In postsecondary education, few people believe that test scores adequately measure outputs.)[13]

The objective in measuring outputs of education is to find a quantitative measure that is both readily available and related to long-run goals of schooling. At the individual level, test scores related to ability or achievement have obvious appeal, even though available research provides little guidance about specific kinds of tests or different possible dimensions.[14] When analysis is conducted at the aggregate school level, other possibilities such as school continuation rates or college attendance rates also are available and provide a direct link to differences in quantities of schooling.

C. *Empirical Formulation*

Somewhat ironically, even though educational studies have attempted to provide much more detail about input differences, they have still been faced with

[13] One exception is found in work on economics education where students' knowledge of economics has been investigated in a variety of contexts. See, for example, John Seigfried and Rendigs Fels 1979; John Chizmar and Thomas Zak 1983.

[14] A few miscellaneous issues about output measurement deserve passing attention. First, if one does use test score measurements, there are a number of choices, related simply to the scaling of scores. Tests are often available in "grade level" equivalent, percentile ranking, or raw score forms, all of which provide the same ordinal ranking (except for the possibility of some compression of the rankings). Yet, for most statistical work, one wants a scale that indicates how different individuals function rather than one that simply ranks them. The choice really depends upon the relationship of these estimates of output to the subsequent outcomes and is best seen as a special case of more general questions about the functional form of production functions. Second, there is some movement toward criterion-references tests—tests that relate to some set of educational goals. The crucial issue is the development of goals. The previous discussion argues for goals that relate to performance outside of schools, but it is not obvious that these goals guide much of the current test development work. See also Congressional Budget Office (1986a) for a discussion of different kinds of tests and of validation techniques.

extensive criticism about the specification of the inputs. Part of this criticism arises because the choice of inputs is guided, sometimes quite explicitly, by the availability of data more than by any notions of how the study is best conceived. But most of the criticism undoubtedly stems from the desire to apply findings to actual policy decisions—something not found in more academic investigations of production relations.

The general conceptual model depicts the achievement of a given student at a particular point in time as a function of the cumulative inputs of family, peers or other students, and schools and teachers. These inputs also interact with each other and with the innate abilities, or "learning potential," of the student. Two points deserve emphasis: The inputs should be relevant to the students being analyzed; and the educational process should be viewed as cumulative—past inputs have some lasting effect, although their value in explaining output may diminish over time. Failure to recognize these points has probably caused the greatest problems in interpreting individual studies.

Empirical specifications have varied widely in details, but they have also had much in common. Family inputs tend to be measured by sociodemographic characterics of the families, such as parental education, income, and family size. Peer inputs, when included, are typically aggregate summaries of the sociodemographic characteristics of other students in the school. School inputs include measures of the teachers (education level, experience, sex, race, and so forth), of the school organization (class sizes, facilities, administrative expenditures, and so forth), and of district or community factors (for example, average expenditure levels). Except for the original Coleman Report, most empirical work has relied on data constructed for other purposes, such as the normal administrative records of

1156   *Journal of Economic Literature, Vol. XXIV (September 1986)*

schools that might be supplemented in some manner.

As in most areas of empirical analysis, a wide variety of approaches to estimation exist. Some have concentrated on variations in individual student achievement (for example, Hanushek 1971; Richard Murnane 1975; Anita Summers and Barbara Wolfe 1977), while others have looked at aggregate performance across school buildings or districts (for example, Herbert Keisling 1967; Jesse Burkhead 1967; Byron Brown and Daniel Saks 1975; Frederick Sebold and William Dato 1981). Similarly, studies have both concentrated on variations within a single system (for example, David Armor et al. 1976; Stephen Michelson 1972; Donald Winkler 1975) and on variations across districts (for example, Marshall Smith 1972; Jencks and Brown 1975; John Heim and Lewis Perl 1974). Estimation has largely been done by single equation regression, but a number of studies have gone into simultaneous equation estimation (for example, Anthony Boardman, Otto Davis, and Peggy Sanday 1977; Elchanan Cohn 1975; and Henry Levin 1970).

Each of these approaches has both strengths and weaknesses, and each is helpful in answering some questions but not others. Because the details of these specifications are discussed and critiqued elsewhere (Hanushek 1979), the focus in this discussion is on two fundamental options in analysis. The first is whether estimation is conducted in "level" form or in "value-added" form; the second is whether teacher differences are measured explicitly or implicitly.

Two pervasive problems arise when an achievement measure is simply regressed on a series of available inputs. First, adequate measures of innate abilities have never been available. Second, while education is cumulative, frequently only contemporaneous measures of inputs are available, leading to measurement and specification errors. Each of these problems leads to biases in the estimated effects of educational inputs.[15] The latter problem, the imprecise characterization of the stream of educational inputs, is probably the more severe one in terms of biased estimation of school policy factors, but both are potentially important.[16]

---

[15] There are of course other data and estimation problems, but they are more idiosyncratic both in their appearance and their solution. Perhaps the most common issue not discussed here is the imprecise measurement of the specific school resources relevant to individual students at a given point in time. This problem, which is most severe in individual versus aggregate school estimation, occurs because schools are quite heterogeneous institutions offering a diversity of inputs to specific students, and the exact provision for individuals is often not recorded or available. The answer is straightforward (one should measure inputs more precisely) if unappealing in specific research situations (see Hanushek 1979).

[16] In a regression framework, the effect of omitting an important variable is bias in the estimated regression coefficients with the size of bias being related both to the influence of the variable on achievement and the correlation of the omitted variable with other included variables in the model; see Hanushek and John Jackson 1977. Because it is reasonable to assume that innate abilities are positively correlated with family background (both through genetics and environment), omission of innate abilities probably biases upward the estimated impact of family background on achievement. Yet, because the correlations between innate abilities and school attributes, after allowing for family background factors, is likely to be small, biases there are probably much less.

In terms of historical school inputs, because students regularly change teachers and schools, current inputs are frequently very inaccurate indicators of past inputs. This is also a problem with measuring peer inputs, particularly in the case of integration and the racial composition of schools. Because of student migration, abrupt changes in racial composition through court or administratively ordered desegregation, and other similar factors, the current racial mix may not indicate history.

One attempt to analyze the effect of historical errors in measurement induced by using purely cross sectional measures of school characteristics can be found in Daniel Luecke and Noel McGinn 1975. Most of their evidence pertains, unfortunately, to the estimation of simple correlations or the analysis of variance of the type included in the Coleman Report. By their simple simulations, which are not replicated across different samples, estimated regression coefficients are reasonably close to the theoretically correct values.

Both problems are also helped if one uses the "value-added" versus "level" form in estimation. That is, if the achievement relationship holds at different points in time, it is possible to concentrate on exactly what happens educationally between those points when outcomes are measured. For example, we could consider just the difference in achievement between two different years. This difference in achievement can then be related to the specific inputs over the same, more limited period.[17] Similarly, the importance of these omitted factors (such as innate abilities) is lessened if the model is estimated in value-added form, because any "level" effects have already been included through entering achievement and only "growth" effects of innate abilities have been omitted. (See Boardman and Murnane, 1979, for a discussion of potential biases in alternative specifications.)

For the most part, value-added estimation has been possible only when outputs

have been measured by standardized test scores. This results simply from data availability, because a one-shot data collection effort using school records can still yield intertemporal information through the history contained in normal records (see Hanushek 1971; Murnane 1975; Armor et al. 1976; Summers and Wolfe 1977; Murnane and Phillips 1981).

The second "strategic" issue in estimation is how to characterize teacher and school inputs. In many ways, the most natural approach is to identify a parsimonious set of variables depicting the central inputs, and policy decisions, in the schools. Plausible descriptors of schools include such things as class sizes, backgrounds and experiences of teachers, use of particular curricula, expenditures on administration, and so forth. Indeed, this has been the mode of analysis for the vast majority of studies. It does, however, face a potentially severe problem, although one quite common: If the choice of inputs does not include the most important ones or if the inputs have an inconsistent effect on performance,[18] the regression estimates will be difficult to interpret. But education differs from most other areas in that an alternative is available that provides direct information about the two potential problems.

With large data samples that provide multiple observations of students with the same teacher, it is possible to estimate teacher effects *implicitly, instead of explicitly*. In particular, if one had a sample of "otherwise identical" students who differed only in the teachers that they had, a direct estimate of the effectiveness of

[17] In actual analyses, however, it is generally preferable to include the initial achievement measure as one of the inputs, instead of differencing the dependent variable. There are three reasons for doing this: (1) empirically, output measurements, particularly test scores in different grades, may be scaled differently; (2) levels of starting achievement may influence achievement gain; and (3) correlated errors in achievement measurement may suggest such a formulation (Lee Cronbach and Lita Furby 1970). However, the latter argument suggests that further corrections for errors in the exogenous variables—probably based upon test reliability measures—are also needed because such errors, even if they have zero means, will yield inconsistent estimates (see Hanushek 1986). The relationship between model specification and errors in measurement is discussed extensively by David Rogosa and John Willett (1985). This general formulation of the "value-added" specification lessens the data requirements, but it does so at the expense of some additional assumptions about the relationships. This approach would suffer if prior inputs had a lasting effect over and above any effect on initial achievement levels. This is, for example, one interpretation that could be given to some of the analyses of preschool programs where persistent and long lasting outcome differences are observed even though early IQ effects of preschool disappear. The evidence is, however, very indirect; see Richard Darlington et al. (1980) and John Berrueta-Clement (1984).

[18] Some work in education suggests an inconsistency of effect arising from interactions among different factors. For example, if teachers with a particular background are effective in suburban schools but ineffective in urban schools, simple linear specifications that force common effects across different circumstances might yield very misleading results. Other similar examples, or hypotheses, abound in the educational literature.

1158 *Journal of Economic Literature, Vol. XXIV (September 1986)*

each teacher would be the average performance of all the students each teacher taught. Obtaining samples of identical students is clearly impossible, but statistical analysis can be used to adjust for differences among students.

Consider test score performance. The idea is that a teacher can be judged on the basis of the average test scores of her students, but only after "correcting" for differences in the achievement of the students that occurred *before* the teacher had the particular group of students and only after correcting for differences in education that occur *outside* the classroom. This can be done by estimating a regression model that includes measures of prior achievement of students, family backgrounds, and so forth and that also includes a separate intercept for all students with a specific teacher. Such teacher-specific intercepts, which can be estimated by including a dummy variable for each teacher, are interpreted as the mean achievement of the students of a given teacher after allowing for other differences among the students.[19] This approach allows the implicit evaluation of the effectiveness of teachers while avoiding the requirement of providing a detailed specification of the separate characteristics of teachers that are important.

The approach, which we will call the study of "total teacher effects," does present its own problems. This estimation provides fundamentally less information than a completely specified explicit model, because it is not possible to characterize the kinds of teachers or teaching techniques that are most effective. It also

presents sizable data requirements, which are only infrequently met. Estimation must be conducted in a value-added form to insure that the estimates provide information about teacher effectiveness as opposed to classroom assignment of students or other, nonteacher aspects of education. Further, if all students for a given teacher are together in the same class (such as in the case of a traditional elementary school where students stay with the same teacher for all subjects), the estimates indicate the combined effect of the teacher and the specific classroom composition. Therefore, interpretation of such estimates as just the effectiveness of teachers requires additional information or estimation work.[20] It is also difficult to provide interdistrict estimates, making this approach less suited to addressing any district level policy matters.[21] Nevertheless, in those studies where the approach has been applied (Hanushek 1971; Murnane 1975; Armor et al. 1976; and Murnane and Phillips 1981), important new information has resulted (as described in the following section).

As in other areas of empirical research, compromises are frequently necessary be-

---

[19] Actual estimation can be done in a variety of ways such as through a general covariance program or by differencing all variables from their teacher-specific mean. Some care is required, however, because these estimation techniques are frequently developed for balanced designs, that is, equal numbers of students for all teachers. See Hanushek and John Quigley 1985.

[20] It is possible to include characteristics of the students in the classrooms in the estimation, as long as one can find explicit measures of the characteristics. One attempt at doing so (Hanushek 1971) confirmed that teacher differences were much more important than any measured differences in classroom composition. Another way to disentangle teachers from other classroom characteristics would be to consider the stability of estimated teacher effects over time and across classrooms. Unfortunately, little such work is available. See Hanushek 1986 and, from a different perspective, Rosenshine 1970.

[21] Because of the extensive data requirements, such estimation across districts has not been possible. Even with the required data, the estimation would have to measure any important interdistrict aspects and, without a sizable number of different districts, would not be able to provide very reliable estimates of their independent effect on student achievement. It would, nonetheless, be useful to attempt such a study because it would help validate the results; these value-added studies, while much better than level studies in terms of complete data, still are subject to overall concerns about model specification.

tween what is conceptually desirable and availability of data. Because analysis proceeds on the basis of statistical investigations of "natural experiments," the precise specification and statistical methodology can directly affect the results, and controversy over the interpretation of results, such as with the Coleman Report, must therefore be put within the context of the underlying conceptual model. Frequently, educational production functions are interpreted as if the variables included are conceptually correct and accurately measured, when in fact this may not be the case. The severity of such problems, however, differs significantly from study to study and clearly explains part of the apparent inconsistencies in specific findings.

III. Results

Since the Coleman Report in 1966, some 147 separately estimated educational production functions have appeared in the published literature. While varying in focus, in methodology, and ultimately in quality, these estimates provide a number of insights into schools and school policy.[22]

A. Do Teachers Differ?

Since the publication of *Equality of Educational Opportunity*, the Coleman Report, intense debate has surrounded the fundamental question of whether schools and teachers are important to the educational performance of students. This debate follows naturally from the Coleman Report, which is commonly interpreted as finding that variations in school resources explain a negligible portion of

the variation in students' achievement.[23] If true, this would indicate that it did not matter which particular teacher a student had—something most parents at least would have a difficult time accepting.

A number of studies provide direct analyses of this overall question of differential effectiveness of teachers through the estimation of total teacher effects (described above). The findings of these studies (Hanushek 1971, 1986; Murnane 1975; Armor et al. 1976; and Murnane and Phillips 1981) are unequivocal: *Teachers and schools differ dramatically in their effectiveness.*

While a number of implications and refinements of that work still need addressing, this conclusion is very firm. It also gives a very different impression from that left by the Coleman Report and indeed by a number of subsequent studies. These faulty impressions have primarily resulted from a confusion between the difficulty in explicitly measuring components of effectiveness and true effectiveness. In other words, existing measures of characteristics of teachers and schools are seriously flawed and thus are poor indicators of the true effects of schools; when these measurement errors are corrected, schools are seen to have important effects on student performance.

B. Summary of Expenditure Relationships

While it is important to confirm that teachers differ in effectiveness, it would be more desirable to be able to identify the specific aspects and characteristics of

---

[22] Other reviews and interpretations of this work can be found in James Guthrie et al. 1971; Harvey Averch et al. 1974; R. Gary Bridges, Charles Judd, and Peter Moock 1979; Murnane 1981b; Naftaly Glasman and Israel Biniaminov 1981; and Murnane and Nelson 1984.

[23] The Coleman Report concentrates on explained variance in student achievement. Its conclusions about school effects come directly from noting that the increase in explained variance (R^2) is small when school variables are added to a regression equation already containing other educational inputs. Such results are obviously sensitive to the order in which various inputs are added to the equation (Hanushek and Kain 1972).

teachers and schools that are important. In approaching this question, scholars have disagreed about the factors that should be explicitly measured and included as inputs into the educational production process. However, there is a "core" set of factors—those that determine basic expenditures—that is almost universally investigated. Instructional expenditures make up about two-thirds of total school expenditures. Given the number of students in a school district, instructional expenditures are in turn determined mostly by teacher salaries and class sizes. Finally, most teacher salaries are directly related to years of teaching experience and educational levels completed by the teacher. Thus the basic determinants of instructional expenditures in a district are teacher experience, teacher education, and class size, and most studies, regardless of what other descriptors of schools might be included, will analyze the effect of these factors on outcomes. (These are also the factors most likely to be found in any given data set, especially if the data come from standard administrative records.)

Because of this commonality in specification, it is possible to tabulate easily the effects of these expenditure parameters. An (attempted) exhaustive search uncovers 147 separate "qualified studies" found in 33 separate published articles or books.[24] These studies, while restricted just to public schools, cover all regions of the country, different grade levels, different measures of performance, and differ-

ent analytical and statistical approaches.[25] While some of these factors could lead to differences in results, they are ignored in the overall tabulations of results.[26]

Table 8 presents overall tabulations for the 147 studies. Because not all studies include each of the expenditure parameters, the first column in Table 8 presents the total number of studies for which an input can be tabulated—for example, 112 (of the 147) studies provide information about the relationship between teacher-student ratio and student performance. The available studies provide regression estimates of the partial effect of given inputs, holding constant family background and other inputs. These estimated coefficients have been tabulated according to two pieces of information: the sign and the statistical significance (5 percent level) of the estimated relationship.

According to conventional wisdom, each tabulated factor should have a positive effect on student achievement. More education and more experience on the part of the teacher both cost more and are presumed to be beneficial; smaller classes (more teachers per student) should also improve individual student learning.[27] Having the "correct" sign in a pro-

---

[24] A qualified study is defined as a production function estimate: (1) published in a book or refereed journal; (2) relating some objective measure of student output to characteristics of the family and the schools attended; and (3) providing information about the statistical significance of estimated relationships. A given publication can contain more than one estimated production function by considering different measures of output, different grade levels, or different samples of students (but different specifications of the same basic sample and outcome measure are not duplicated). This is an expanded version of tabulations in Hanushek 1981.

[25] The studies are almost evenly divided between studies of individual student performance and aggregate performance in schools or districts. Ninety-six of the 147 studies measure output by score on some standardized test. Approximately 40 percent are based upon variations in performance within single districts while the remainder look across districts. Three-fifths look at secondary performance (grades 7–12) with the rest concentrating on elementary student performance. Added descriptive information about the universe of studies can be found in Hanushek 1981.

[26] Subsequent analysis does not suggest any bias from looking at all of the studies together. While there are obvious limits to the possible stratifications of the separate studies, further analyses that grouped studies by grade level, by whether individual or aggregate data are used, by measure of output, and so forth yield the same qualitative conclusions.

[27] Tabulated results are adjusted for variables being measured in the opposite direction; for example, the sign for estimated relationships including student-teacher ratios is reversed.

TABLE 8

SUMMARY OF ESTIMATED EXPENDITURE PARAMETER COEFFICIENTS FROM 147 STUDIES OF EDUCATIONAL
PRODUCTION FUNCTIONS

Input	Number of Studies	Statistically Significant			Statistically Insignificant		
		+	−	Total	+	−	Unknown Sign
Teacher/pupil ratio	112	9	14	89	25	43	21
Teacher Education	106	6	5	95	26	32	37
Teacher Experience	109	33	7	69	32	22	15
Teacher Salary	60	9	1	50	15	11	24
Expenditures/pupil	65	13	3	49	25	13	11

Sources: Armor et al. 1976; Richard Beiker and Kurt Anschek 1973; Boardman, Davis, and Sanday 1977; Bowles 1970; Brown and Saks 1975; Burkhead 1967; Cohn 1968, 1975; Eberts and Stone 1984; Hanushek 1971, 1972; Heim and Perl 1974; Henderson, Mieszkowski, and Sauvageau 1976; Jencks and Brown 1975; Katzman 1971; Keisling 1967; Levin 1970, 1976; Link and Ratledge 1979; Maynard and Crawford 1976; Michelson 1970, 1972; Murnane 1975; Murnane and Phillips 1981; Perl 1973; Raymond 1968; Ribich and Murphy 1975; Sebold and Dato 1981; Smith 1972; Strauss and Sawyer 1986; Summers and Wolfe 1977; Tuckman 1971; Winkler 1975. See, Hanushek 1981 for further description of studies.

duction function is clearly a minimal requirement for justifying purchases of a given input, but quantitative magnitudes of estimated relationships are ignored here.[28]

Of the 112 estimates of the effects of class size, only 23 are statistically significant, and *only 9* show a statistically significant relationship of the expected positive sign.[29] Fourteen display a statistically significant *negative* relationship. An additional 89 are not significant at the 5 percent level. Nor does ignoring statistical significance help to confirm benefits of small classes, because the insignificant coefficients have the "wrong" sign by a 43 to 25 margin.[30]

The entries for teacher education and teacher experience in Table 8 tell much the same story. In a majority of cases, the estimated coefficients are statistically insignificant. Forgetting about statistical significance and just looking at estimated signs does not make much of a case for the importance of these factors either.

The one possible exception—teacher experience—at least has a clear majority of estimated coefficients pointing in the expected direction, and almost 30 percent of the estimated coefficients are statistically significant by conventional standards. If experience is really a powerful factor in teaching, however, these results

[28] It would be extremely difficult to provide information of quantitative differences in the coefficients because the units of measure of both inputs and outputs differ radically from one study to another. One attempt to provide quantitative estimates of varying class sizes is Gene Glass and Mary Lee Smith (1979). This work, however, has been subjected to considerable criticism, largely because of the ultimate difficulties in doing such analyses.

[29] Teacher/pupil ratios are treated here as being synonymous with class sizes. This is not strictly the case and, in fact, could be misleading today. Several changes in schools, most prominently the introduction of extensive requirements for dealing with handicapped children in the mid-1970s, have led to new instructional personnel without large changes in typical classes. Because much of the evidence here refers to the situation prior to such legislation and restrictions, it is reasonable to interpret the evidence as relating to class sizes.

[30] Note that not all studies report the sign of insignificant coefficients. For example, 21 studies report insignificant estimated coefficients for teacher-student ratios but do not report any further information.

are hardly overwhelming. Moreover, because of possible selection effects, they are subject to additional interpretive questions. Specifically, these positive correlations may result from more senior teachers having the ability to select schools and classrooms with better students. In other words, causation may run from achievement to experience and not the other way around.[31]

The results are startlingly consistent in finding no strong evidence that teacher-student ratios, teacher education, or teacher experience have an expected positive effect on student achievement. According to the available evidence, one cannot be confident that hiring more educated teachers or having smaller classes will improve student performance. Teacher experience appears only marginally stronger in its relationship.

The final two rows in Table 8 include summary expenditure information, teacher salaries, and expenditures per student.[32] While less frequently available,

these measures—not surprisingly—provide no separate indication of a relationship between expenditures and achievement.[33] Most data do show a strongly positive simple correlation between school expenditures and achievement, but the strength of this relationship disappears when differences in family background are controlled for.

Without systematic tabulation of the results of the various studies, it would be easy to conclude that the findings of the studies are inconsistent. But there is a consistency to the results: *There appears to be no strong or systematic relationship between school expenditures and student performance.* This is the case when expenditures are decomposed into underlying determinants and when expenditures are considered in the aggregate.[34]

There are several obvious reasons for being cautious in interpreting this evidence. For any individual study, incomplete information, poor quality data, or faulty research could distort a study's sta-

---

[31] David Greenberg and John McCall (1974) analyzed a single urban school system in the early 1970s and concluded that race and socioeconomic background of students were systematically related to the selection and transfer of teachers with different education and experience levels. However, Murnane (1981a) suggests, from analysis of a different school system, that declining enrollments and the subsequent surplus of teachers have led to a much greater reliance on institutional rules and much less on individual teacher preferences (which was the hypothesized mechanism in Greenberg and McCall 1974).

Nevertheless, the potential problems arise from achievement affecting selection, and not from family background, race, or other factors that are included on the right-hand side of the estimated model affecting selection. Clearly the severity of the problem is related to the structure of the model estimated and in many instances is serious only in the presence of fairly subtle selection mechanisms (particularly in a "value-added" specification).

[32] Information on salaries and expenditures is less frequently available. Importantly, because expenditures per student are generally measured for districts, any of the 60 analyses for individual districts would find no variation in this input and thus could not include it. Further, the interpretation of both of these measures is sometimes clouded by including them *in addition to* teacher experience, education, and/or class size.

[33] The expenditure and salary estimates are generally more difficult to interpret than the other, real resource measures. Because the prices can vary across the samples in the separate studies, it is sometimes difficult to interpret the dollar measures. Are they indicators of quality differences? of price differences? of costs that vary with the characteristics of the city and students (that is, of "compensating differentials" for various undesirable characteristics)?

In the expenditure estimates, 8 of 13 significant positive results also come from the different estimates of Sebold and Dato (1981). These estimates involve aggregate school districts in California and, importantly, involve very imprecise measures of family backgrounds. For lower grades, a socioeconomic index compiled by teachers is employed; for the higher grades (8 out of 10 separate estimates) the percentage of families on Aid for Dependent Children (AFDC) is the only measure available. With this imprecise measurement, school expenditures may in fact be a proxy for family background.

[34] This also holds up when the sample of available studies is divided along different dimensions: the measurement of outcomes (i.e., test score versus other measures); elementary versus secondary; single system versus multiple systems; value-added versus level; and so forth. While the precise tabulations obviously change with the smaller subsamples, the overall picture remains.

tistical results. Even without such problems, the actions of school administrators could mask any relationship. For example, if the most difficult to teach students were consistently put in smaller classes, any independent effect of class size could be difficult to disentangle from mismeasurement of the characteristics of the students. Finally, statistical insignificance of any estimates can reflect no relationship, but it also can reflect a variety of data problems—those above and others such as high correlations among the different measured inputs. In other words, as in most research efforts, virtually any of the studies is open to some sort of challenge.

Just such uncertainties about individual results led to this tabulation of estimates. If these specific factors were in fact central to variations in student achievement, the tabulations would almost certainly show more of a pattern in the expected direction. The reasons for caution listed above are clearly more important in some circumstances than others, and the inconsistency across these very different studies is still striking. Furthermore, given the general biases toward publication of statistically significant estimates, the paucity of statistically significant results is quite notable. While individual studies are affected by specific analytical problems, the aggregate data provided by the 147 separate estimates seem most consistent with the conclusion that the expenditure parameters are unrelated to student performance (after family backgrounds and other educational inputs are considered).

C. Other Results

In the course of these analyses, a wide variety of other school and nonschool factors have been investigated. First, family background is clearly very important in explaining differences in achievement. Virtually regardless of how measured, more educated and more wealthy parents have children who perform better on average.[35] One particularly interesting subset of these analyses, however, involves investigating more detailed aspects of family structure and size. The large changes in birth rates and divorce rates of the past two decades have created a concern about their potential effects on learning and achievement. Analyses of these issues unfortunately have not been undertaken in any systematic manner within the context of educational production functions.[36]

Second, considerable attention has been given to the characteristics of peers or other students within schools. This line of inquiry was pressed by the Coleman Report and pursued by a number of subsequent studies.[37] This question is especially important in considering school desegregation where the issues revolve around the racial compositions of schools. The educational effect of differing student bodies has also been important in the debate about public versus private schooling, as discussed below. Nevertheless, the findings are ambiguous.

Finally, a wide range of additional measures of schools and teachers has been pursued in the different existing studies. Various studies have included indicators of

[35] There have been vast quantities of studies concentrating on the effects of family background. Unfortunately, few such studies include measures of school factors. Exceptions are Murnane, Rebecca Maynard, and James Ohls (1981) and Hanushek (1986).

[36] General discussions and reviews of the issues can be found in Richard Easterlin (1978) and Samuel Preston (1984). For the most part, these ignore influences of schools on achievement, although it may not be too problematical in a time series context. A preliminary investigation of family factors based upon simple time allocation models can be found in Hanushek (1986).

[37] See, in particular, Hanushek 1972; Winkler 1975; Summers and Wolfe 1977; and Vernon Henderson, Peter Mieszkowski, and Yvon Sauvageau 1976. Part of the ambiguity about the results arises from the possibility of confusing measures of peers with the influence of family background through measurement errors in family characteristics; see Hanushek and Kain 1972. In terms of the public-private school debate, see Coleman, Thomas Hoffer, and Sally Kilgore 1982; Murnane 1984.

1164   *Journal of Economic Literature, Vol. XXIV (September 1986)*

organizational aspects of schools, of specific curricula or educational process choices, and of such things as time spent by students working at different subject matters. Others have included very detailed information on teachers—their cognitive abilities, family backgrounds, where they went to school, what their majors were, their attitudes about education or different kinds of students, and so forth. Similarly detailed information has been included about school facilities and school administrators and other personnel. The closest thing to a consistent finding among the studies is that "smarter" teachers, ones who perform well on verbal ability tests, do better in the classroom, but even for that the evidence is not very strong (Hanushek 1981).[38]

D. *Teacher Skill Differences*

In the typical study of production relationships outside of education, measures of organization and process are seen as irrelevant in estimation. Production functions are interpreted as the relationship between inputs and outputs *mutatis mutandis*. Information about production possibilities is viewed as being publicly available in the form of scientific and engineering knowledge, and production processes are reproducible through blueprints and machinery. The possibility of the actors in production making dynamic choices about process is not considered, and the choice of "best" process is assumed to be automatically made after the selection of inputs. While the appropriate-

ness of this framework is open to question in a wide number of instances, it is particularly questionable in the case of education.

Some aspects of the educational process are inherently difficult to disentangle from the characteristics of individual teachers (such as classroom management, methods of presenting abstract ideas, communication skills, and so forth). This creates serious problems both in applying the general conceptual model of production theory and in interpreting any estimated effects. Many educational decisions are "micro" ones, made mainly by teachers, and they are difficult to observe and measure and, quite possibly, not easy to reproduce. Further, these decisions interact with the characteristics and abilities of the individual teacher. As a shorthand description, these factors will be referred to simply as "skill" differences.[39]

Once the possibility of skill differences in introduced, it is difficult to define just what "maximum possible output" might mean because it is difficult to specify what the "homogeneous" inputs are. In other words it is difficult if not impossible to specify a few objective or subjective characteristics of teachers that capture the systematic differences of both backgrounds of teachers and their idiosyncratic choices of teaching style and methods.[40] This

---

[38] Many states currently require standardized testing of teachers, either for initial or continuing employment. There is little evidence that the commonly used teacher examinations provide much evidence about effectiveness at teaching. See, however, Strauss and Sawyer 1986. Further, if one thought of routinely using test information, such as scores on the verbal ability tests available to researchers, to determine hiring and salary, teachers would most likely concentrate more on the tests, thus lessening any correlations between test performance and teaching skill.

[39] A formal model that captures many of these ideas is presented in Anthony Lima 1981. The concept of skill in production also appears in Richard Nelson and Sidney Winter 1982.

This kind of notion also appears in the explanation for not finding any systematic relationship between process and organizational choices of schools and achievement. The explanation of the apparent insignificance of macro process variables in Armor et al. (1976) is the great variation in implementation of overall process decisions at the classroom level. This is also brought out in detailed analysis of the implementation of innovative techniques at the classroom level (see Paul Berman and Milbrey McLaughlin 1975).

[40] Part of the general specification issue can be found in other situations. For example, measurement of capital stocks of varying vintages clearly aggregates over heterogeneous inputs and therefore intro-

raises questions, discussed below, about how much of standard production theory is usable without some modification.

The empirical implications are that individual variables describing certain partial aspects of teacher skill are unlikely to display systematic relationships with student performance (which is our measure of the performance of teachers). This is just the interpretation of the previously presented results. Individual teacher skill differences are quite important, as estimated implicitly and discussed above. But, teacher skill is not systematically correlated with the explicit measures of teacher characteristics that have been available.[41] Again, the consequences of not measuring teacher inputs explicitly should not be mistaken for the ineffectiveness of teachers.

An important sidelight of such investigations is that decision makers might be able to identify with fair accuracy underlying differences in skills among teachers. Murnane (1975) and Armor et al. (1976) find that principals' evaluations of teachers were highly correlated with estimates

of total effectiveness (that is, adjusted mean gains in achievement by the students of each teacher). For many purposes, this is almost as good as the ability to identify differences among teachers ex ante.

Recognition of skill differences does alter the interpretation of teacher and school inputs. It is still reasonable to consider the impact of measured attributes of teachers, because many school decisions such as hiring and salary are based on a set of these characteristics. The estimated impacts of these measured attributes, however, indicate the inability either to predict or develop more skilled teachers according to the attributes identified. Consider, for example, the almost universal finding that graduate education of teachers bears no systematic relationship to achievement, which can be interpreted as indicating that current teacher training institutions do not, on average, change the skills of teachers. This is somewhat different from saying that *everything* else being equal, more education for teachers has no effect. Similarly, the frequent finding that class size doesn't affect achievement may arise from complicated (and unobserved) interactions with the processes and instructional methods that teachers choose. Therefore, while it is possible that smaller classes could be beneficial in specific circumstances, it is also true that, in the context of typical school and teacher operations, there is no apparent gain.

The concept of teacher skill differences has clear implications for research. At least a part of past research development can be characterized as a search for "the" factor or specification that unifies other results or that at least explains the apparent inconsistencies for specific factors. But if teaching skill involves mixing different objective and subjective characteristics together, sometimes in very different ways across individuals, the search for a simply articulated and measured description of

---

duces error into any estimation of production relationships. However, in such a case one could at least conceptually provide more detailed measurements of the capital stock and eliminate the problems. The situation considered here is more complicated, because the inputs (teachers) are also the managers of the classroom, deciding how to organize the educational experience, how to employ their own education and experiences, and so on. There are perhaps similarities to labor inputs into other production processes, but the argument here is that there is a difference in degree of autonomy and choice exercised by the teacher. There is also a difference in the specificity of the analysis of education, which takes this analysis to a deeper level than most aggregate production functions.

[41] In individual studies, it appears that roughly only half of total teacher performance, estimated as described above by adjusted average performance of a teacher's students, can be explained by any combination of measured teacher and classroom attributes. (Such studies include more extensive measures of teachers than just the expenditure parameters found in Table 8.) See in particular Hanushek (1972) and Murnane and Phillips (1981).

1166   *Journal of Economic Literature, Vol. XXIV (September 1986)*

effective teachers or schools is likely to fail.

E. *Efficiency in Schools*

If we think of schools as maximizing student achievement, the preceding evidence indicates that schools are *economically inefficient*, because they pay for attributes that are not systematically related to achievement. This statement, of course, presumes that schools are attempting to maximize student performance. While such motivation seems reasonable to assume, complicated objectives on the part of school officials would lead to tempering this judgment.[42]

A suggestion of inefficiency on the part of public schools of course does not come as a great surprise to many for two reasons. First, educational decision makers apparently not guided by incentives to maximize profits or to conserve on costs.[43] Sec-

ond, they may not understand the production process and therefore cannot be expected to be on the production frontier. In other words, much of the optimization part of the theory of the firm and competitive markets is questionable in the case of governmental supply in quasi-monopoly situations.[44]

While few people would go so far as to say that school expenditures could not have an important effect on performance, it is at the same time possible to conclude that expenditures are unrelated to school performance as schools are currently operated. The fact that a school spends a lot on each of its students simply gives us little information on whether or not it does well in terms of value added to students.

It is, however, useful to be clear about the issues of efficiency and what can be inferred from the data on schools. Past education discussions have blurred any distinction between economic efficiency (the correct choice of input mix given the prices of inputs and the production function) and technical efficiency (operating on the production frontier). The previous evidence relates directly to economic efficiency. The consideration of technical efficiency is more complicated.

The standard conceptual framework indicates that, if two production processes are using the same inputs, any systematic difference in outputs reflects technical

---

[42] The studies reviewed previously do consider a wide range of measures of student performance. Therefore, a simple objection to test scores as representing the focus of attention by school officials does not suffice to overturn this conclusion.

There are two aspects of "nonmaximizing behavior" that have been analyzed within the context of educational production functions. First, a number of researchers have considered multiple objectives of school officials and have analyzed simultaneous equations models of production. These analyses do not come to qualitatively different conclusions from those presented. Second, a few have attempted to evaluate explicitly the impact of school preferences for specific outcomes. Michelson (1970) considers preferences for different outcomes that vary across schools and suggests that this could obscure relationships estimated for single dimensions. Brown and Saks (1975) consider a model where schools are interested in both the mean and variance of student achievement, although all schools have the same objective function. They suggest again that analyses of just mean test score performance could be biased by the unobserved preferences of districts. Unfortunately, because little information is available about preferences other than performance maximization on the part of schools, it is very difficult to evaluate their influence on the measured efficiency of schools.

[43] It should be pointed out that similar analyses of production functions for private, profit-making industries are not readily available. We are prone to

accept without real evidence that for-profit firms are optimizing such that a tabulation of results for competitive firms would look different from Table 8. We at least know that for-profit firms that are not maximizing are more likely to go out of existence than a public enterprise that is not maximizing.

[44] It must be noted that economic inefficiency does not preclude estimation of production functions. Indeed, such inefficiency aids estimation (at least when done directly and not through cost functions) because it provides observations of the technical relationships under different input mixes. If all schools faced the same prices and operated efficiently, there would be no variation in the data, and estimation would not be possible.

inefficiency.[45] The concept of skill differences, however, simply recognizes that individuals with the same measured characteristics make a series of important production decisions (reflected in behavior, process choices, and so forth) that are difficult to identify, measure, and model. Therefore, it is not surprising that the same measured inputs yield variations in output; at the same time, it is difficult to label such observed variation differences inefficiency.[46] In part the argument is one of semantics: How much of economic theory should implicitly be brought along in analyses of production functions? There are, however, obvious implications for policy and research in terms of the interpretation of findings and the ability to operate on achievement by changing the observed attributes of teachers and schools.[47]

---

[45] Concern about technical inefficiency has led to some, basically nonstatistical, estimation (cf. Dennis Aigner and S. Chu 1968) of the production frontier. Different applications to educational production can be found in Levin (1976) and, with a somewhat different approach, Robert Klitgaard and George Hall (1975). Besides assuming accurate measures of both inputs and outputs, these analyses appear internally inconsistent: They are motivated by the perceived uncertainty about the production process, yet assume that the researcher knows and measures all of the inputs to the production process; see Hanushek (1976). Further, the possibility of nonreproducible skill differences is totally neglected.

[46] The importance of embodied process differences leads Murnane and Nelson (1984) to argue that the whole concept of production functions may not have much usefulness in education and other areas where the actors tacitly make many production decisions. The standard treatment of production functions is clearly strained by the necessity to observe and measure choices of classroom presentation, organization of materials, interactions with students, and so forth; that is, things that constitute how real inputs of teacher's knowledge, experiences, and other characteristics are put together in the production process. One could of course expand the simple notion of production functions to include such matters, but, since our current ability to identify and measure such expanded inputs is quite poor, this would not provide much guidance to empirical analysis.

[47] Note that this discussion is quite different from the consideration of "X-inefficiency" (Harvey Leibenstein 1966). That discussion is best interpreted as simply omitting an important factor that might

IV. *Some Policy Implications*

The conclusion that schools are operated in an economically inefficient manner has obvious implications for school policy. The clearest one is simply that increased expenditures by themselves offer no overall promise for improving education. Further, the components of these expenditures offer little promise. Thus, a simple recommendation: Stop requiring and paying for things that do not matter.

There is little apparent merit for schools to pursue their ubiquitous quest for lowered class sizes.[48] Nor should teachers be required, as they are in many states, to pursue graduate courses merely to meet tenure requirements or to get an additional salary increment. More teacher experience by itself does not seem to have much value.

Each of these statements also has its limits. The evidence for them comes from the current operations of public schools. Yet, policies that take schools outside the bounds observed could lead to different results. For example, class sizes between 15 and 40 students fall well within the data; classes of 2 students or 300 students do not—and they may show significant relationships with achievement. The evidence is also limited to overall, systematic relationships. Quite clearly, small classes might be very beneficial in certain circumstances, depending on the teachers and the subject matter; if there is specific evidence of this, one should clearly act differently. The point is that we have no evidence of this universally, and thus we have no mandate for making massive changes just to be doing something.

Pay of teachers offers another set of pol-

---

simply be labeled entrepreneurial ability. This discussion goes deeper into the measurement and specification of production functions as a generic model.

[48] One pervasive and extremely expensive trend in American education has been the progressive lowering of student-teacher ratios. See Table 6, above, for the recent history of declines.

1168   *Journal of Economic Literature, Vol. XXIV (September 1986)*

icy issues. Two issues receive constant attention: the level of pay and the distribution of pay.[49] We begin with the second issue, the one most directly addressed by the available research. In most school systems, salary schedules are rigidly linked to the education levels completed by the teacher and years of teaching experience. Salary is unrelated to specialty—math teachers are paid the same as English teachers—or to grade level. Is there an alternative, given that this structure does not appear to correlate very closely with productivity? Recent commission reports have increasingly called for instituting "merit pay," an idea that has been around for decades but that has defied widespread implementation.[50] Relating pay to performance is a key element of the comprehensive reforms suggested by the Task Force on Teaching (1986).

The previous evidence suggests that a merit pay system would make sense. It is clear that significant differences exist among teachers. And, while not conclusive, direct tests that correlate estimates of specific teachers' value added[51] with principals' evaluations of the same teach-

ers suggest that principals do reasonably well at identifying good and bad teachers (Murnane 1975; Armor et al. 1976). Thus, the essential elements of merit pay schemes seem present.

The main argument used against merit pay is that objective evaluation is difficult and thus there is always the possibility that political and other influences may creep into pay determination. There is little direct evidence from schools related to this possibility. Of course, the pay of most other workers in the economy is at least partially determined by their supervisors, and there are not obvious reasons to believe that employment relationships in schools are unique.

The more difficult problem is to introduce such a system and get it working. First, the current pay system might be a classic illustration of the inflexible rules that are said to characterize internal labor markets, and they certainly have the effect of reducing any direct competition among teachers. This in turn promotes collaboration among teachers, which might suffer if teachers perceived themselves to be in competition. Second, principals seem to be able to identify good teachers when nothing is at stake, but whether they would make such judgments if their evaluations mattered is unknown. Third, a restructuring of pay would lead to direct conflict with teachers' unions. With little experience and analysis of these issues, however, there is no way to judge their importance.

The second aspect of pay is its overall level. Many people have argued that the rewards of teaching are so low that it is little wonder that the best graduates are not attracted to teaching. Others have used evidence of shortages of particular kinds of teachers—for example math and science teachers—to argue for general pay increases to teachers.

There is clearly no absolute standard for setting teachers' pay, although there is fre-

---

[49] When considering the distribution of pay, it is useful to hold average level constant so as to avoid direct incentive effects on choice of teaching as a profession. For example, if teacher experience is not systematically related to performance, it is not efficient to pay more for greater experience; this does not mean, however, that all teachers should receive the salary of a beginning teacher because that would dramatically lower the lifetime earnings of the average teacher. Clearly, it is not possible to separate these issues completely, but it is useful to deal with the components of level and distribution separately.

[50] The idea of merit pay enjoyed a brief period of national discussion after it was recommended by the National Commission on Excellence in Education in *A Nation at Risk* and after this idea was promoted by the President Reagan. See David Cohen and Murnane (1985, 1986) for a recent discussion of issues in the implementation of merit pay systems. Many school systems have tried "merit pay" systems, but most attempts have not lasted very long.

[51] Value added is measured, as described above, by estimates of the average gain in student performance (adjusted for factors unrelated to the teacher) that are associated with specific teachers.

quently an appeal to some notion of "comparable worth." Average real salaries of teachers rose during the 1960s to the mid-1970s. Indeed they rose faster than average salaries in other parts of the economy. After that, they slid back as did the real income of the average worker. By 1983 the average (nine month) salary for teachers was $20,700; in the same year the median income for a male (female) year-round, full-time worker with four or more years of college was $31,800 ($20,251).[52] Salaries in schools have remained between 15 and 20 percent above the earnings of the average full-time employee in the economy over time. Whether this is too high or too low is difficult to judge.

Raising all salaries would almost certainly attract more able people into teaching. But three factors must be borne in mind. First, the ability to alter the teaching force is constrained by vacancies at schools. Somewhat less than 3.5 percent of all teachers in 1983 were in either their first or second year of teaching.[53] If there is a lag between choosing a profession in college and becoming trained for it (cf. Richard Freeman 1971) and if future turnover remains at current levels, it would be many years after changes in overall salaries took place before any significant change in the teacher force could be dis-

cerned. (Because of changing age patterns in the teaching profession, retirements and thus turnover will undoubtedly increase over the coming decade. Therefore, current rates probably underestimate the potential for change. See Table 7, above.)

Second, as argued by Murnane (1985) current restraints imposed by state certification requirements, inhibit the flow of new people into the profession. These requirements, frequently stated in terms of specific courses, practice teaching time, and so forth, act as an entry barrier to many potential teachers who find that their course of study would be noticeably distorted. (Radical changes in both teacher training and teacher certification are central to reform proposals in Task Force in Teaching, 1986, and the Holmes Group 1986.)

Third, if the salary structure takes into account no information about competing demands for specialties (of which math and science have received the most attention for the past two decades), considerable inefficiency must always be present: Either people in "low demand" areas will be overpaid when compared to what is needed to insure sufficient supply into teaching, or teachers in "high demand" specialties will tend to be of lower quality than those in low demand specialties. (This observation has, of course, been made previously; see Joseph Kershaw and Roland McKean 1962.)

The entire area of state certification and educational regulations is open to considerable question, particularly given the evidence above. While there is wide variation in the specifics, states tend to require teachers to pursue graduate degrees—a dubious restriction given the evidence about lack of effectiveness and an expensive one because school systems then pay these teachers more. By 1983, over half of all teachers had a master's degree or more, up from less than a third only a

[52] The information on salaries in Table 7 included all instructional personnel, in part because principals, guidance counselors, and other school people outside the classroom often start out as classroom teachers. (Classroom teachers make up about 90 percent of all instructional personnel.) Salaries of this larger group seem relevant to someone contemplating a teaching career.
Note that the median incomes include more than just wages and salary. U.S. Bureau of the Census 1985, p. 141; U.S. Bureau of the Census 1985, pp. 158, 162.
[53] The teacher force has gone through large growth and depression periods, related to the demographics of the school-age population. Based on the numbers of children under five (that is, already born but not in schools), there will be some growth in the school-age population, but not an enormous amount.

1170   *Journal of Economic Literature, Vol. XXIV (September 1986)*

decade before.[54] States also set tenure rules, with tenure coming as early as the third year of teaching. And, in a number of programs, states either set explicit class size maximums or provide monetary incentives to have smaller class sizes. None of these practices seems very useful from a public policy view related to student achievement. Instead their primary justification must come in terms of compensating teachers or restricting the supply of teachers.

Many restrictions on hiring, promotions, and so forth also are found in contracts and local regulations (see Lorraine McDonnell and Anthony Pascal 1979). These have a similar inhibiting effect on schools, although it seems possible to eliminate the more harmful ones through the bargaining process. The effects of unions on salaries, expenditures, and other employment conditions is, however, incompletely understood; see, for example, the review by Freeman (1986) and analyses by Jay Chambers (1977) and Randall Eberts and Joe Stone (1984, 1985, 1986).

Finally, along similar lines, it is useful to consider the financing of local school systems. There are again a great many different financing schemes by which states support local schools. Beginning in the late 1960s, local reliance on property taxes and state distribution schemes that did not counteract differences in property tax bases became an active area of judicial attention, legislative concern, and academic research. The 1968 California court case of *Serrano* v. *Priest* opened a virtual outpouring of studies, legal suits, and legislative bills.[55] In simplest terms, a general

equity argument was made that some districts, those with larger tax bases, found it easier to raise money for schools than districts with lower tax bases. As a result, expenditures per student tended to be quite unequal across jurisdictions. The research into expenditure variations across local school districts and their causes has been extensive (see, for example, Robert Berne and Leanna Steifel 1983; Martin Feldstein 1975; Robert Reischauer and Robert Hartman 1973; David Stern 1973; Robert Inman 1978; John Coons, William Clune, and Stephen Sugarman 1970; John Pincus 1974).

Much of this discussion appears motivated by an underlying assumption that poor districts (in terms of property tax bases) are the same as poor students. This, it turns out, is not uniformly the case.[56] But, more than that, the discussion is based entirely on a presumption that expenditures per student are the appropriate focus for policy. Without this presumption, an unwarranted one from the previous evidence, the line of argument—

---

[54] As noted above, such comparisons require some caution in interpretation because the age and experience of the teaching force has changed over time.

[55] The legal issues took several years to be sorted out. Originally suits were brought under the Fourteenth Amendment to the U.S. Constitution on the grounds that students were being discriminated

against "on the basis of the wealth of their neighbors" because the size of the property tax base directly influenced how much money could be raised and spent in the local schools. The U.S. Constitution arguments were not accepted by the U.S. Supreme Court in its 1973 decision in *Rodriguez* v. *San Antonio Independent School District*. Subsequently, a number of successful (and a number of unsuccessful) suits were brought in state courts under education clauses of state constitutions. See John Coons, William Clune, and Stephen Sugarman 1970; John Pincus 1974; James Guthrie 1980; Walter Garms, Guthrie, and Lawrence Pierce 1978.

[56] As an example, New York City and the other large cities of New York State had to develop a new argument, "municipal overburden," in order to join the property-poor plaintiffs in their state school finance suit of *Levittown* v. *Nyquist*. This argument—that large cities had disproportionate other demands on their resources—allowed them to enter on the side of the plaintiffs in suing the state for increased state financing. This was necessary because these large cities tended to have the largest tax bases per student in the state; they also have a disproportionate share of poor people.

legal and academic—becomes quite peculiar.[57]

One might argue that altering existing financing formulae would have only distributional consequences, because expenditure variations do not relate to the performance of different school systems. But this is not the only effect. The politics of redistribution tend to promote increases in total spending on schools. States find it difficult to lower funding for one district in order to raise it for another, and therefore they tend to raise low spending districts up to the level of high spending districts. (This probably explains the general support by teachers unions for school finance "reform.") The responses of states to challenges to their funding of schools are thus frequently to increase the amount of economic inefficiency in the system.

A final policy area that is closely related but not precisely covered by the research discussed above is the public versus private school debate. All of the evidence presented previously relates to public school systems. Perhaps as a response to perceptions that public schools need improving, a variety of measures have been proposed to encourage further private school competition. The notion of educational vouchers, originally proposed by Milton Friedman (1962), has always had some appeal to economists because it would promote more individual choice and competition. A recent version of this—tuition tax credits—has received the endorsement of President Ronald Reagan

and has appeared in his budgetary proposals; it would effectively encourage private schooling through the federal income tax system. Nevertheless, private schools have not been subjected to much direct analysis.

A recent study by Coleman, Thomas Hoffer, and Sally Kilgore (1982) has again brought the issue into discussion. This study basically contrasted the performance of students in public and private schools and concluded that private schools systematically performed better than public schools. This conclusion has been the subject of intense debate, one that remains unresolved. There are two basic questions: First, are the results simply a reflection of selectivity bias arising from parents' choice of school type? Second, does the control of schools (private versus public) identify the most important differences among the sampled schools? The study attempts to measure and to control for a series of background measures of students, but many critics have argued that it does so imprecisely (Arthur Goldberger and Cain 1982; Murnane 1984; Jay Noell 1982). Also, the study makes no attempt to describe the specific characteristics of schools and teachers in either the public or private setting. Therefore, the policy conclusions rest importantly on having a random sample of schools and being able to replicate the private school success through a policy of expanding the private sector. In this area, the evidence is very incomplete.

Individual studies of the educational production process frequently point to other specific conclusions about policies. Nevertheless, because many of these conclusions appear only once and are not replicated in other studies, it does not appear useful to develop them in detail. Instead, given the current state of research, it is appropriate to stop with these general observations.

---

[57] It is possible to interpret the issue as one of "taxpayer equity" instead of "educational equity." The tax rate that is needed to achieve any given funding level for schools does vary widely across districts, and it is particularly sensitive to the amount of nonresidential property in the local tax base. This line of argument has a distinct legal problem associated with it, because most judicial challenges to school funding formulae have arisen from specific mention of educational concerns in state constitutions. Tax equity does not enjoy the same legal status.

V. *Some Research Implications*

The analyses of schools obviously raise a number of unanswered questions that could profit from more research. Because many of these have been discussed elsewhere (see, for example, Hanushek 1979, 1981; Murnane and Nelson 1984), another set of research questions is raised here. Namely, what do these findings have to say about other lines of research by economists?

Through two decades of research, an enormous amount has been learned about the empirical application of production function notions to educational policy questions. Much of this clearly is transferable to other areas—for example, health programs or agricultural production. Perhaps most important is the lesson about evaluation of activities where the idiosyncratic nature of the actors can be key to the results. In a great many areas, particularly ones related to public policy matters, it is necessary to evaluate production efficiency and this, in turn, frequently calls for the analysis of individual skill differences. In these, the straightforward econometric design may yield quite misleading results.

But beyond such areas, one must also consider how the results of the educational analysis relate to analyses of the effects of schooling. In particular, a wide variety of public finance investigations implicitly or explicitly consider how differences in education and schools affect some other types of behavior.

Following the theoretical work of Charles Tiebout (1956) and the empirical work of Wallace Oates (1969), a number of studies have investigated how differences in the attractiveness of jurisdictions come to be capitalized into the price of houses. A substantial portion of these studies has focused on differences in the provision of public services, of which schooling is the most important local one. With few exceptions,[58] the level of schooling provided is given by expenditures, and this is contrasted with the local tax cost of providing such expenditures. But if expenditures per student are not an accurate index of educational provision, this does not adequately capture locational differences.[59] Studies of housing location have also tended to make similar presumptions.

Investigations of labor market performance of individuals have, in their quest to include individual quality differences, used a variety of measures of schooling such as expenditures or characteristics of teachers in given schools (see above). Again, these do not appear to be good indicators of schooling differences.[60]

Finally, the signaling versus production models of schools represents an area where the preceding analysis is most appropriate. Empirical analyses of screening have typically looked for labor market tests of the competing hypotheses. Both models, however, imply higher earnings by more educated people: the screening

[58] Examples of exceptions include Kain and Quigley (1975) and Harvey Rosen and D. J. Fullerton (1977).

[59] Of course, changing school finance formulae, which would have the effect of helping some jurisdictions and hurting others, would affect housing values immediately—unless there were offsetting changes in school quality. See, for example, John Hilley (1983) and Donald Jud and James Watts (1981).

[60] It is important, however, to distinguish the above evidence from the potential use of expenditures in such analyses. The above evidence indicates that expenditures per student do not do particularly well at indicating the value added of schools. On the other hand, by themselves (that is, without controlling for any other factors) expenditures per student are quite generally correlated with student achievement. This results from the fact that higher income families tend both to pay more for schools and to provide more educational input in the homes. Therefore, expenditure differences do tend to measure differences in student achievement, which is what is needed for labor market studies; they just cannot be interpreted as indicating the importance of schools per se. This is quite different from the preceding discussion of capitalization, where the conceptual factor is the value added of local schools and not just the overall performance of students.

model through the information provided about differential abilities, and the production model through changing the abilities of individuals. While some ingenious tests have been proposed (see, for example, Wolpin 1977; Riley 1979), these necessarily fail because the models predict that the observations of individuals in the labor market will have the same basic character. (In technical terms, they are generally unidentified.) The models differ significantly, however, when one looks at the schooling process itself. The signaling version assumes that individuals are basically unaffected by school experience—they simply wait and endure schooling until the information about abilities catches up with their actual abilities. The production model suggests that the schooling experience changes individuals. At least in the polar cases, the weight of available evidence on schools suggests that the production model is more appropriate, because where students end up is strongly affected by the schools they attend. This conclusion breaks down, of course, if one holds to a "mixed" model of schools, because there is no way to make judgments about the absolute differences that come out of the process. Nonetheless, evidence about school production seems most appropriate for addressing these hypotheses.

REFERENCES

AEROSPACE RESEARCH CENTER. *Meeting technology and manpower needs through the industry/university interface: An aerospace industry perspective.* Washington, DC: Aerospace Industries Assoc. of Amer., May 1983.
AIGNER, DENNIS J. AND CHU, S. F. "On Estimating the Industry Production Function," *Amer. Econ. Rev.*, Sept. 1968, 58(4), pp. 826–39.
AKIN, JOHN S. AND GARFINKEL, IRWIN. "School Expenditures and the Economic Returns to Schooling," *J. Human Res.*, Fall 1977, 12(4), pp. 460–81.
AMERICAN EDUCATIONAL RESEARCH ASSOCIATION, AMERICAN PSYCHOLOGICAL ASSOCIATION, AND NATIONAL COUNCIL ON MEASUREMENT IN EDUCATION. *Standards for educational and psychological testing.* Washington, DC: American Psychological Assoc., 1985

ARMOR, DAVID ET AL. *Analysis of the school preferred reading program in selected Los Angeles minority schools.* R-2007-LAUSD. Santa Monica, CA: Rand Corp., 1976.
ASHENFELTER, ORLEY AND MOONEY, JOSEPH D. "Graduate Education, Ability, and Earnings," *Rev. Econ. Statist.*, Feb. 1968, 50(1), pp. 78–86.
AVERCH, HARVEY A. ET AL. *How effective is schooling? A critical review and synthesis of research findings.* Englewood Cliffs, NJ: Educational Technology Publications, 1974.
BARNOW, BURT S. AND CAIN, GLEN G. "A Reanalysis of the Effect of Head Start on Cognitive Development: Methodology and Empirical Findings," *J. Human Res.*, Spring 1977, 12(2), pp. 177–97.
BECKER, GARY S.; LANDES, ELISABETH M. AND MICHAEL, ROBERT T. "An Economic Analysis of Marital Instability," *J. Polit. Econ.*, Dec. 1977, 85(6), pp. 1141–47.
BEHRMAN, JERE R. AND BIRDSALL, NANCY. "The Quality of Schooling: Quantity Alone Is Misleading," *Amer. Econ. Rev.*, Dec. 1983, 73(5), pp. 928–46.
BEIKER, RICHARD F. AND ANSCHEK, KURT R. "Estimating Educational Production Functions for Rural High Schools: Some Findings," *Amer. J. Agr. Econ.*, Aug. 1973, 55, pp. 515–19.
BEN-PORATH, YORAM. "The Production of Human Capital Over Time," in *Education, income, and human capital.* Ed.: W. LEE HANSEN. NY: NBER, 1970, pp. 129–47.
BERG, IVAR. *Education and jobs: The great training robbery.* NY: Praeger, 1970.
BERMAN, PAUL AND McLAUGHLIN, MILBREY W. *Federal programs supporting educational change, Vol. IV: The findings in review.* R-1589/4-HEW. Santa Monica, CA: Rand Corp., 1975.
BERNE, ROBERT AND STIEFEL, LEANNA. "Changes in School Finance Equity: A National Perspective," *J. Educ. Finance*, Spring 1983, 8, pp. 419–35.
BERRUETA-CLEMENT, JOHN R. ET AL. *Changed lives: The effects of the Perry preschool program on youths through age 19.* Ypsilanti, MI: The High/Scope Press, 1984.
BOARDMAN, ANTHONY; DAVIS, OTTO AND SANDAY, PEGGY. "A Simultaneous Equations Model of the Educational Process," *J. Public Econ.*, Feb. 1977, 7(1), pp. 23–49.
BOARDMAN, ANTHONY AND MURNANE, RICHARD. "Using Panel Data to Improve Estimates of the Determinants of Educational Achievement," *Sociology Educ.*, Apr. 1979, 52, pp. 113–21.
BOWLES, SAMUEL. "Toward an Educational Production Function," in *Education, income and human capital.* Ed.: W. LEE HANSEN. NY: NBER, 1970, pp. 11–60.
BOWLES, SAMUEL AND GINTIS, HERBERT. *Schooling in capitalist America.* NY: Basic Books, 1976.
BOWLES, SAMUEL AND LEVIN, HENRY M. "The Determinants of Scholastic Achievement—An Appraisal of Some Recent Evidence," *J. Human Res.*, Winter 1968, 3(1), pp. 3–24.
BRELAND, HUNTER M. *Population validity and col-*

1174   *Journal of Economic Literature, Vol. XXIV (September 1986)*

lege entrance measures. NY: The College Board, 1979.

BRENEMAN, DAVID W. "The Ph.D. Production Process," in JOSEPH T. FROOMKIN, DEAN T. JAMISON AND ROY RADNER, 1976, pp. 3–52.

BRIDGES, R. GARY; JUDD, CHARLES M. AND MOOCK, PETER R. *The determinants of educational outcomes: The impact of families, peers, teachers, and schools.* Cambridge, MA: Ballinger, 1979.

BROWN, BYRON W. AND SAKS, DANIEL H. "The Production and Distribution of Cognitive Skills within Schools," *J. Polit. Econ.*, June 1975, *83*(3), pp. 571–93.

BURKHEAD, JESSE. *Input-output in large city high schools.* Syracuse, NY: Syracuse U. Press, 1967.

BUSINESS-HIGHER EDUCATION FORUM. *America's competitive challenge: The need for a national response.* Washington, DC: Business-Higher Education Forum, Apr. 1983.

CAIN, GLEN G. AND WATTS, HAROLD W. "Problems in Making Policy Inferences from the Coleman Report," *Amer. Soc. Rev.*, Apr. 1970, *35*(2), pp. 328–52.

CENTRAL ADVISORY COUNCIL FOR EDUCATION (ENGLAND). *Children and their primary schools.* London: Her Majesty's Stationery Office, 1967.

CHAMBERS, JAY G. "The Impact of Collective Bargaining for Teachers on Resource Allocation in Public School Districts," *J. Urban Econ.*, July 1977, *4*(3), pp. 324–39.

CHIZMAR, JOHN F. AND ZAK, THOMAS A. "Modeling Multiple Outputs in Educational Production Functions," *Amer. Econ. Rev.*, May 1983, *73*(2), pp. 18–22.

COHEN, DAVID K. AND MURNANE, RICHARD J. "The Merits of Merit Pay," *The Public Interest*, Summer 1985, *80*, pp. 3–30.

_____. "Merit Pay and the Evaluation Problem: Understanding Why Most Merit Pay Plans Fail and a Few Survive," *Harvard Educ. Rev.*, Feb. 1986, *56*(1), pp. 1–17.

COHN, ELCHANAN. "Economies of Scale in Iowa High School Operations," *J. Human Res.*, Fall 1968, *3*(4), pp. 422–34.

COHN, ELCHANAN, WITH MILLMAN, STEPHEN D. *Input-output analysis in public education.* Cambridge, MA: Ballinger, 1975.

COLEMAN, JAMES S. ET AL. *Equality of educational opportunity.* Washington, DC: U.S. GPO, 1966.

COLEMAN, JAMES S.; HOFFER, THOMAS AND KILGORE, SALLY. *High school achievement: Public, Catholic, and private schools compared.* NY: Basic Books, 1982.

CONGRESSIONAL BUDGET OFFICE. *Trends in educational achievement.* Washington, DC: Congressional Budget Office, 1986a.

CONGRESSIONAL BUDGET OFFICE. *Educational achievement: Explanations and implications of recent trends.* Washington, DC: Congressional Budget Office, 1986b.

COONS, JOHN E.; CLUNE, WILLIAM H. AND SUGARMAN, STEPHEN D. *Private wealth and public education.* Cambridge, MA: The Belknap Press of Harvard U. Press, 1970.

CRONBACH, LEE J. AND FURBY, LITA. "How Should We Measure 'Change'—or Should We?" *Psych. Bull.*, July 1970, *74*(1), pp. 68–80.

DARLINGTON, RICHARD B. ET AL. "Preschool Programs and Later School Competence of Children from Low-Income Families," *Science*, April 11, 1980, *208*, pp. 202–04.

DENISON, EDWARD F. *Accounting for United States economic growth 1929–1969.* Washington, DC: Brookings Inst., 1974.

DUGAN, DENNIS J. "Scholastic Achievement: Its Determinants and Effects in the Education Industry," in JOSEPH T. FROOMKIN, DEAN T. JAMISON AND ROY RADNER, 1976, pp. 53–83.

EASTERLIN, RICHARD A. "What will 1984 Be Like? Socioeconomic Implications of Recent Twists in Age Structure," *Demography*, Nov. 1978, *15*(4), pp. 397–421.

EBERTS, RANDALL W. AND STONE, JOE A. *Unions and public schools: The effect of collective bargaining on American education.* Lexington, MA: Lexington Books, 1984.

_____. "Wages, Fringe Benefits, and Working Conditions: An Analysis of Compensating Differentials," *Southern Econ. J.*, July 1985, *52*(1), pp. 274–79.

_____. "On the Contract Curve: A Test of Alternative Models of Collective Bargaining," *J. Labor Econ.*, Jan. 1986, *4*(1), pp. 66–71.

EDUCATION COMMISSION OF THE STATES, TASK FORCE ON EDUCATION FOR ECONOMIC GROWTH. *Action for excellence: A comprehensive plan to improve our nation's schools.* Denver, CO: Education Commission of the States, June 1983.

EHRLICH, ISAAC. "On the Relation Between Education and Crime," in *Education, income, and human behavior.* Ed.: F. THOMAS JUSTER. NY: McGraw-Hill, 1975, pp. 313–37.

FELDSTEIN, MARTIN S. "Wealth Neutrality and Local Choice in Public Education," *Amer. Econ. Rev.*, Mar. 1975, *65*(1), pp. 75–89.

FREEMAN, RICHARD B. *The market for college trained manpower.* Cambridge, MA: Harvard U. Press, 1971.

_____. "Unionism Comes to the Public Sector," *J. Econ. Lit.*, Mar. 1986, *14*(1), pp. 41–86.

FRIEDMAN, MILTON. *Capitalism and freedom.* Chicago: U. of Chicago Press, 1962.

FROOMKIN, JOSEPH T.; JAMISON, DEAN T. AND RADNER, ROY, eds. *Education as an industry.* Cambridge, MA: Ballinger, 1976.

FULLER, BRUCE. *Raising school quality in developing countries: What investments boost learning?* Report No. EDT7, Education and Training Series, The World Bank, Sept. 1985.

GARMS, WALTER I.; GUTHRIE, JAMES W. AND PIERCE, LAWRENCE C. *School finance: The economics and politics of public education.* Englewood Cliffs, NJ: Prentice-Hall, 1978.

GLASMAN, NAFTALY S. AND BINIAMINOV, ISRAEL. "Input-Output Analyses in Schools," *Rev. Educ. Res.*, Winter 1981, *51*(4), pp. 509–39.

GLASS, GENE V. AND SMITH, MARY LEE. "Meta-Analysis of Research on Class Size and Achievement," *Educ. Eval. and Policy Anal.*, 1979, *1*(1), pp. 2–16.

GOLDBERGER, ARTHUR S. AND CAIN, GLEN G. "The Causal Analysis of Cognitive Outcomes in the Coleman, Hoffer and Kilgore Report," *Sociology Educ.*, Apr./Jul. 1982, *55*, pp. 103–22.

GREENBERG, DAVID AND MCCALL, JOHN. "Teacher Mobility and Allocation," *J. Human Res.*, Fall 1974, *9*(4), pp. 480–502.

GRILICHES, ZVI AND MASON, WILLIAM. "Education, Income, and Ability," *J. Polit. Econ.*, May/June 1972, *80*(3), Pt. 2, pp. S74–S103.

GROSSMAN, MICHAEL. "The Correlation Between Health and Schooling," in *Household production and consumption.* Ed.: NESTOR E. TERLECKYJ. NY: NBER, 1973, pp. 147–211.

GUTHRIE, JAMES W., ed. *School finance policies and practices.* Cambridge, MA: Ballinger, 1980.

GUTHRIE, JAMES W. ET AL. *Schools and inequality.* Cambridge, MA: MIT Press, 1971.

HANSEN, W. LEE; WEISBROD, BURTON AND SCANLON, WILLIAM J. "Schooling and Earnings of Low Achievers," *Amer. Econ. Rev.*, June 1970, *60*(3), pp. 409–18.

HANUSHEK, ERIC A. "Teacher Characteristics and Gains in Student Achievement: Estimation Using Micro Data," *Amer. Econ. Rev.*, May 1971, *61*(2), pp. 280–88.

———. *Education and race: An analysis of the educational production process.* Cambridge, MA: Heath-Lexington, 1972.

———. "Regional Differences in the Structure of Earnings," *Rev. Econ. Statist.*, May 1973, *55*(2), pp. 204–13.

———. "Comment," in JOSEPH T. FROOMKIN, DEAN JAMISON AND ROY RADNER, 1976, pp. 191–96.

———. "Ethnic Income Variations: Magnitudes and Explanations," in *American ethnic groups.* Ed.: THOMAS SOWELL. Washington, DC: Urban Inst., 1978, pp. 139–56.

———. "Conceptual and Empirical Issues in the Estimation of Educational Production Functions," *J. Human Res.*, Summer 1979, *14*(3), pp. 351–88.

———. "Throwing Money at Schools," *J. Policy Anal. Manage.*, Fall 1981, *1*(1), pp. 19–41.

———. "The Trade-off Between Child Quantity and Quality: Some Empirical Evidence." Working Paper No. 45, Rochester Center for Economic Research, 1986.

HANUSHEK, ERIC A. AND JACKSON, JOHN E. *Statistical methods for social scientists.* NY: Academic, 1977.

HANUSHEK, ERIC A. AND KAIN, JOHN F. "On the Value of 'Equality of Educational Opportunity' as a Guide to Public Policy," in *On equality of educational opportunity.* Eds.: FREDERICK MOSTELLER AND DANIEL P. MOYNIHAN. NY: Random House, 1972, pp. 116–45.

HANUSHEK, ERIC A. AND QUIGLEY, JOHN M. "Life-Cycle Earning Capacity and the OJT Investment Model," *Int. Econ. Rev.*, June 1985, *26*(2), pp. 365–85.

HAUSE, JOHN C. "Earnings Profile: Ability and

Schooling," *J. Polit. Econ.*, May/June 1972, *80*(3), Pt. II, pp. S108–38.

HAVEMAN, ROBERT H. AND WOLFE, BARBARA L. "Schooling and Economic Well-Being: The Role of Nonmarket Effects," *J. Human Res.*, Summer 1984, *19*(3), pp. 377–407.

HEIM, JOHN AND PERL, LEWIS. *The educational production function: Implications for educational manpower policy.* Institute of Public Employment Monograph 4. Ithaca, NY: Cornell U., 1974.

HENDERSON, VERNON; MIESZKOWSKI, PETER AND SAUVAGEAU, YVON. *Peer group effects and educational production functions.* Ottawa, Canada: Economic Council of Canada, 1976.

HEYNEMAN, STEPHEN P. AND LOXLEY, WILLIAM. "The Effect of Primary-School Quality on Academic Achievement Across Twenty-nine High and Low-Income Countries," *Amer. J. Sociology*, May 1983, *88*, pp. 1162–94.

HILLEY, JOHN. "The Distributive Impact of Education Finance Reform," *Nat. Tax J.*, Dec. 1983, *36*(4), pp. 503–9.

HOGAN, TIMOTHY D. "Faculty Research Activity and the Quality of Graduate Training," *J. Human Res.*, Summer 1981, *16*(3), p. 400–15.

HOLMES GROUP. *Tomorrow's teachers.* East Lansing, MI: The Holmes Group, 1986.

INMAN, ROBERT P. "Optimal Fiscal Reform of Metropolitan Schools: Some Simulation Results," *Amer. Econ. Rev.*, Mar. 1978, *68*(1), pp. 107–22.

JENCKS, CHRISTOPHER S. AND BROWN, MARSHA. "Effects of High Schools on Their Students," *Harvard Educ. Rev.*, Aug. 1975, *45*(3), pp. 273–324.

JENCKS, CHRISTOPHER ET AL. *Inequality: A reassessment of the effects of family and schooling in America.* NY: Basic Books, 1972.

JOHNSON, GEORGE E. AND STAFFORD, FRANK P. "Social Returns to Quantity and Quality of Schooling," *J. Human Res.*, Spring 1973, *8*(2), pp. 139–55.

JUD, G. DONALD AND WATTS, JAMES M. "Schools and Housing Values," *Land Econ.*, Aug. 1981, *57*, pp. 459–70.

KAIN, JOHN F. AND QUIGLEY, JOHN M. *Housing markets and racial discrimination.* NY: NBER, 1975.

KATZMAN, MARTIN. *Political economy of urban schools.* Cambridge, MA: Harvard U. Press, 1971.

KEISLING, HERBERT. "Measuring a Local Government Service: A Study of Efficiency of School Districts in New York State." Unpublished PhD thesis, Harvard U., 1965.

———. "Measuring a Local Government Service: A Study of School Districts in New York State," *Rev. Econ. Statist.*, Aug. 1967, *49*, pp. 356–67.

KERSHAW, JOSEPH A. AND MCKEAN, ROLAND N. *Teacher shortages and salary schedules.* NY: McGraw-Hill, 1962.

KLITGAARD, ROBERT E. AND HALL, GEORGE R. "Are There Unusually Effective Schools?" *J. Human Res.*, Winter 1975, *10*(1), pp. 90–106.

KOLLODGE, RICHARD AND HORN, ROBIN. *Education research and policy studies at the World Bank: A bibliography.* Report No. EDT23, Education and Training Series, The World Bank, Dec. 1985.

LAYARD, RICHARD AND PSACHAROPOULOS,

1176 *Journal of Economic Literature, Vol. XXIV (September 1986)*

GEORGE. "The Screening Hypothesis and the Returns to Education," *J. Polit. Econ.*, Sept./Oct. 1974, *82*(5), pp. 985–98.

LEIBENSTEIN, HARVEY. "Allocative Efficiency vs. 'X-Efficiency,'" *Amer. Econ. Rev.*, June 1966, *56*(3), pp. 392–415.

LEIBOWITZ, ARLEEN. "Home Investments in Children," *J. Polit. Econ.*, Mar./Apr. 1974, *82*(2), Pt. II, pp. S111–31.

LEVIN, HENRY M. "A New Model of School Effectiveness," in *Do teachers make a difference?* U.S. Office of Education. Washington, DC: U.S. Dept. of Health, Education, and Welfare, 1970, 55–78.

———. "Economic Efficiency and Educational Production," in JOSEPH T. FROOMKIN, DEAN JAMISON AND ROY RADNER. Cambridge, MA: NBER, 1976, pp. 149–90.

LIMA, ANTHONY K. "An Economic Model of Teaching Effectiveness," *Amer. Econ. Rev.*, Dec. 1981, *71*(5), pp. 1056–59.

LINK, CHARLES R. AND RATLEDGE, EDWARD C. "Social Returns to Quantity and Quality of Education: A Further Statement," *J. Human Res.*, Winter 1975, *10*(1), pp. 78–89.

———. "Student Perceptions, I.Q., and Achievement," *J. Human Res.*, Winter 1979, *14*(1), pp. 98–111.

LUECKE, DANIEL F. AND MCGINN, NOEL F. "Regression Analyses and Education Production Functions: Can They Be Trusted?" *Harvard Educ. Rev.*, Aug. 1975, *45*(3), pp. 325–50.

MAYNARD, REBECCA AND CRAWFORD, DAVID. "School Performance," in *Rural income maintenance experiment final report*. Madison, WI: Inst. for Research on Poverty, U. of Wisconsin, 1976.

MCDONNELL, LORRAINE AND PASCAL, ANTHONY. *Organized teachers in American Schools*, R-2407-NIE. Santa Monica, CA: Rand Corp., 1979.

MICHAEL, ROBERT T. "Measuring Non-monetary Benefits of Education: A Survey," in *Financing education: Overcoming inefficiency and inequity*. Ed.: WALTER W. MCMAHON AND TERRY G. GESKE. Urbana, IL: U. of Illinois Press, 1982, pp. 119–49.

MICHELSON, STEPHEN. "The Association of Teacher Resources with Children's Characteristics," in U.S. Office of Education. *Do Teachers Make a Difference?* Washington, DC: U.S. GPO, 1970, pp. 120–68.

———. "For the Plaintiffs—Equal School Resource Allocation," *J. Human Res.*, Summer 1972, *7*(3), pp. 283–306.

MINCER, JACOB. "The Distribution of Labor Incomes: A Survey with Special Reference to the Human Capital Approach," *J. Econ. Lit.*, Mar. 1970, *8*(1), pp. 1–26.

MURNANE, RICHARD J. *Impact of school resources on the learning of inner city children*. Cambridge, MA: Ballinger, 1975.

———. "Teacher Mobility Revisited," *J. Human Res.*, Winter 1981a, *16*(1), pp. 3–19.

———. "Interpreting the Evidence on School Effectiveness," *Teachers College Record*, Fall 1981b, *83*(1), pp. 19–35.

———. "How Clients' Characteristics Affect Organization Performance: Lessons from Education," *J. Policy Anal. Manage.*, Spring 1983, *2*(3), pp. 403–17.

———. "A Review Essay—Comparisons of Public and Private Schools: Lessons from the Uproar," *J. Human Res.*, Spring 1984, *19*(2), pp. 263–77.

———. "An Economist's Look at Federal and State Education Policies," in *American domestic priorities: An economic appraisal*. Eds.: JOHN M. QUIGLEY AND DANIEL L. RUBINFELD. Berkeley: U. of California Press, 1985, pp. 118–47.

MURNANE, RICHARD J.; MAYNARD, REBECCA A. AND OHLS, JAMES C. "Home Resources and Children's Achievement," *Rev. Econ. Statist.*, Aug. 1981, *63*(3), pp. 369–77.

MURNANE, RICHARD J. AND NELSON, RICHARD R. "Production and Innovation when Techniques Are Tacit," *J. Econ. Behavior Org.*, 1984, *5*, pp. 353–73.

MURNANE, RICHARD J. AND PHILLIPS, BARBARA. "What do Effective Teachers of Inner-City Children Have in Common?" *Social Sci. Res.*, Mar. 1981, *10*(1), pp. 83–100.

NATIONAL COMMISSION ON EXCELLENCE IN EDUCATION. *A nation at risk: The imperative for educational reform*. Washington, DC: U.S. GPO, Apr. 1983.

NELSON, RICHARD R. AND PHELPS, EDMUND. "Investment in Humans, Technology Diffusion, and Economic Growth," *Amer. Econ. Rev.*, May 1966, *56*(2), pp. 69–75.

NELSON, RICHARD R. AND WINTER, SIDNEY G. *An evolutionary theory of economic change*. Cambridge, MA: The Belknap Press of Harvard U. Press, 1982.

NIEMI, RICHARD AND SOBIESZEK, BARBARA I. "Political Socialization," *Annual Rev. Sociology*, 1977, *3*, pp. 209–33.

NOELL, JAY. "Public and Catholic Schools: A Reanalysis of Public and Private Schools," *Sociology Educ.*, Apr./Jul. 1982, *55*, pp. 123–32.

OATES, WALLACE. "The Effects of Property Taxes and Local Public Spending on Property Values: An Empirical Study of Tax Capitalization and the Tiebout Hypothesis," *J. Polit. Econ.*, Nov./Dec. 1969, *77*(6), pp. 957–71.

O'NEILL, DAVE M. AND SEPIELLI, PETER. *Education in the United States: 1940–1983*, CDS-85-1, Special Demographic Analysis. Washington, DC: U.S. Bureau of the Census, 1985.

PERL, LEWIS J. "Family Background, Secondary School Expenditure, and Student Ability," *J. Human Res.*, Spring 1973, *8*(2), pp. 156–80.

PERL, LEWIS J. "Graduation, Graduate School Attendance, and Investments in College Training," in JOSEPH T. FROOMKIN, DEAN T. JAMISON AND ROY RADNER, 1976, pp. 95–135.

PINCUS, JOHN, ED. *School finance in transition*. Cambridge, MA: Ballinger, 1974.

PRESTON, SAMUEL H. "Children and the Elderly: Divergent Paths for America's Dependents," *Demography*, Nov. 1984, *21*(4), pp. 435–57.

RAYMOND, RICHARD. "Determinants of the Quality

of Primary and Secondary Public Education in West Virginia," *J. Human Res.*, Fall 1968, *3*(4), pp. 450–70.

REISCHAUER, ROBERT O. AND HARTMAN, ROBERT W. *Reforming school finance.* Washington, DC: Brookings Inst., 1973.

RIBICH, THOMAS I. AND MURPHY, JAMES L. "The Economic Returns to Increased Educational Spending," *J. Human Res.*, Winter 1975, *10*(1), pp. 56–77.

RILEY, JOHN G. "Informational Equilibrium," *Econometrica*, Mar. 1979a, *47*(2), pp. 331–59.

———. "Testing the Educational Screening Hypothesis," *J. Polit. Econ.*, Oct. 1979b, Pt II, *87*(5), pp. S227–52.

ROGOSA, DAVID R. AND WILLETT, JOHN B. "Understanding Correlates of Change by Modeling Individual Differences in Growth," *Psychometrika*, June 1985, *50*(2), pp. 203–28.

ROGERS, DANIEL P. "Private Rates of Return to Education in the United States: A Case Study," *Yale Econ. Essays*, Spring 1969, *9*(1), pp. 89–134.

ROSEN, HARVEY S. AND FULLERTON, DAVID J. "A Note on Local Tax Rates, Public Benefit Levels, and Property Values," *J. Polit. Econ.*, Apr. 1977, *85*(2), pp. 433–40.

ROSEN, SHERWIN. "Human Capital: A Survey of Empirical Research," in *Research in labor economics*, Vol. I. Ed.: RONALD G. EHRENBERG. Greenwich, CT: JAI Press, 1977, pp. 3–39.

ROSENSHINE, BARAK. "The Stability of Teacher Effects upon Student Achievement," *Rev. Educ. Research*, Dec. 1970, *40*(5), pp. 647–62.

SEBOLD, FREDERICK D. AND DATO, WILLIAM. "School Funding and Student Achievement: An Empirical Analysis," *Public Finance Quart.*, Jan. 1981, *9*(1), pp. 91–105.

SIEGFRIED, JOHN J. AND FELS, RENDIGS. "Research on Teaching College Economics: A Survey," *J. Econ. Lit.*, Sept. 1979, *17*(3), pp. 923–69.

SMITH, MARSHALL. "Equality of Educational Opportunity: The Basic Findings Reconsidered," in *On equality of educational opportunity.* Eds.: FREDERICK MOSTELLER AND DANIEL PATRICK MOYNIHAN. NY: Random House, 1972, pp. 230–342.

SPENCE, A. MICHAEL. "Job Market Signaling," *Quart. J. Econ.*, Aug. 1973, *87*(3), pp. 355–74.

———. *Market signalling: Informational transfer in hiring and related screening processes.* Cambridge, MA: Harvard U. Press, 1974.

STERN, DAVID. "Effects of Alternative State Aid Formulas on the Distribution of Public School Expenditures in Massachusetts," *Rev. Econ. Statist.*, Feb. 1973, *55*(1), pp. 91–97.

STRAUSS, ROBERT P. AND SAWYER, ELIZABETH A. "Some New Evidence on Teacher and Student Competencies," *Econ. Educ. Rev.*, 1986, *5*(1), pp. 41–48.

SUMMERS, ANITA AND WOLFE, BARBARA. "Do Schools Make a Difference?" *Amer. Econ. Rev.*, Sept. 1977, *67*(4), pp. 639–52.

TASK FORCE ON TEACHING AS A PROFESSION. *A nation prepared: Teachers for the 21st century.* Carnegie Forum on Education and the Economy, 1986.

TAUBMAN, PAUL AND WALES, TERENCE. *Higher education and earnings.* NY: McGraw-Hill, 1974.

TIEBOUT, CHARLES M. "A Pure Theory of Local Expenditures," *J. Polit. Econ.*, Oct. 1956, *64*, pp. 416–24.

TUCKMAN, HOWARD P. "High School Inputs and Their Contribution to School Performance," *J. Human Res.*, Fall 1971, *6*(4), pp. 490–509.

TWENTIETH CENTURY FUND, TASK FORCE ON FEDERAL ELEMENTARY AND SECONDARY EDUCATION POLICY. *Making the grade.* NY: Twentieth Century Fund, 1983.

U.S. BUREAU OF THE CENSUS. *Statistical abstract of the United States, 1985.* Washington, DC: U.S. GPO, 1985.

U.S. BUREAU OF THE CENSUS. Current Population Reports. *Money income of households, families, and persons in the United States: 1983*, Ser. P-60, No. 146. Washington, DC: U.S. GPO, 1985.

U.S. DEPARTMENT OF EDUCATION. *The nation responds: Recent efforts to improve education.* Washington, DC: U.S. Department of Education, 1984.

———. *What works: Research about teaching and learning.* Washington, DC: U.S. Department of Education, 1986.

WACHTEL, PAUL. "The Effect on Earnings of School and College Investment Expenditures," *Rev. Econ. Statist.*, Aug. 1976, *58*(3), pp. 326–31.

WEISS, ANDREW. "A Sorting-cum-Learning Model of Education," *J. Polit. Econ.*, June 1983, *91*(3), pp. 420–42.

WEISS, RANDALL D. "The Effect of Education on the Earnings of Blacks and Whites," *Rev. Econ. Statist.*, May 1970, *52*(2), pp. 150–59.

WELCH, FINIS. "Measurement of the Quality of Schooling," *Amer. Econ. Rev.*, May 1966, *56*(2), pp. 379–92.

———. "Education in Production," *J. Polit. Econ.*, Jan./Feb. 1970, *78*(1), pp. 35–59.

———. "Black-White Differences in the Returns to Schooling," *Amer. Econ. Rev.*, Dec. 1973, *63*(5), pp. 893–907.

WINKLER, DONALD. "Production of Human Capital: A Study of Minority Achievement." Unpublished PhD thesis, U. of California, Berkeley, 1972.

———. "Educational Achievement and School Peer Group Composition," *J. Human Res.*, Spring 1975, *10*(2), pp. 189–204.

WIRTZ, WILLARD ET AL. *On further examination: Report of the Advisory Panel on the Scholastic Aptitude Test Score Decline.* NY: College Entrance Examination Board, 1977.

WOLPIN, KENNETH I. "Education and Screening," *Amer. Econ. Rev.*, Dec. 1977, *67*(5), pp. 949–58.

[16]

Abstract An attempt is made to explore the production set for educational achievement for both "efficient" and "inefficient" schools. The inefficient or average production relationship is obtained by estimating a reduced-form equation for all schools among a sample drawn from a large Eastern city. The efficient set is derived by using a linear programming approach to yield coefficients for those schools that show the largest student achievement output relative to their resource inputs. A comparison of the two sets of technical coefficients suggests that the relative marginal products are probably different. Because of such differences, the optimal combination of inputs for producing educational achievement relative to a given budget constraint will probably vary between achievement-efficient and inefficient schools, and may even vary from school to school. The result is that the use of such production-function estimates for attempting to improve the efficiency of the educational sector may have far less utility than its advocates imply.

MEASURING EFFICIENCY IN EDUCATIONAL

PRODUCTION

HENRY M. LEVIN
Stanford University

The search for efficiency in public sector activities has been gaining substantial momentum in recent years. Rapid rises in the costs of public services, in conjunction with a widespread belief that their quality is deteriorating, has raised concerns in many quarters (Baumol, 1967). Economists have responded by attempting to explore the production of specific public goods, as well as their pricing (Hirsch, 1973: ch. 12; Mushkin, 1972). In many cases, the analytic approaches have

AUTHOR'S NOTE: This paper is adapted from an earlier work that was presented before the 1971 Meetings of the Psychometric Society (Levin, 1971). The author appreciates the comments of the two anonymous referees who provided constructive suggestions. He also wishes to thank both Pak Wai Liu and Kathy Diehl for assistance.

PUBLIC FINANCE QUARTERLY / January 1974, Vol. 2 No. 1

paralleled those used in the study of production in the private sector since the tools of production analysis have been largely forged and honed in that arena. In this paper we will demonstrate some of the problems that arise in understanding production in the public sector by reviewing the usual approach to estimating the production set in elementary and secondary education. We will suggest that the results that have been derived are likely to be misleading, and that they may lead to decreased efficiency if they are adopted as a basis for public policy.

The elementary and secondary educational sector represents an interesting focus for studies that would attempt to understand efficiency in the production of government services. It has represented a substantial portion of public activity (about $43 billion in 1971), and the per pupil costs in constant dollars have risen very rapidly (about 6-7% per year between 1930 and 1970). Moreover, serious questions have been raised about the effectiveness of the educational system and the apparent inability of additional expenditures to improve educational outcomes (Averch et al., 1972).

A large number of studies have been undertaken in the last few years to estimate the "educational production function" (Bowles, 1970; Bowles and Levin, 1968; Burkhead, 1967; Hanushek, 1972; Katzman, 1971; Kiesling, 1967; Levin, 1970a; Michelson, 1970; Perl, 1973; Winkler, 1972). While they have relied upon very diverse sets of data and different measures of inputs, almost all have considered the appropriate measure of educational output to be pupil scores on standardized achievement tests. The general formulation of the production function that seems to underlie most of these studies is represented by equation 1.

$$A_{i\,t} = g\,[F_{i(t)}, S_{i\,(t)}, P_{i\,(t)}, O_{i\,(t)}, I_{i\,t}]\,. \qquad [1]$$

The i subscript refers to the ith student; (t) refers to an input that is cumulative to time t.

$A_{i\,t}$ = a vector of educational outcomes for the ith student at time t.

$F_{i\,(t)}$ = a vector of individual and family background characteristics cumulative to time t.

$S_{i\,(t)}$ = a vector of school inputs relevant to the ith student cumulative to t.

$P_{i\,(t)}$ = a vector of peer or fellow student characteristics cumulative to t.

$O_{i\,(t)}$ = a vector of other external influences (the community, for example) relevant to the ith student cumulative to t.

$I_{i\,t}$ = a vector of initial or innate endowments of the ith student at t.

Although only a few studies specify the general form of the educational production function as in equation 1, most explorations seem to be based upon such a model.[1] In most of the applications, the $A_{i\,t}$ vector is reflected by one or more tests of standardized achievement for each pupil. $F_{i\,(t)}$ includes measures of family socioeconomic status and family structure. $P_{i\,(t)}$ attempts to capture the socioeconomic status of the student environment; and $O_{i\,(t)}$ represents a residual category of community and other educational influences. $I_{i\,t}$ is usually omitted for lack of a reliable measure, and the specification biases created by this omission have been discussed (Levin, 1970a: 65-66). $S_{i\,(t)}$ includes such school resources as the number and quality of teachers and other personnel, facilities, curriculum, and other inputs. It is essentially these school inputs that are of particular interest to economists in their quest for efficiency, for these resources represent the ones that are purchased by the school budget and for which resource allocation decisions can be made.

THE EFFICIENT PRODUCTION OF EDUCATIONAL ACHIEVEMENT

Although the educational production function in equation 1 is stated in a most general form, the efforts to measure it have concentrated principally on one school output, academic achievement. In general, the goals of these studies are to obtain the production set for student test scores and to assess the marginal product to price ratios for all of the inputs in order to recommend better ways of allocating school budgets. For the results of such studies to be valid, we must assume that the estimated production coefficients are unbiased. Yet, possible errors in the equations and in the variables must surely loom as a likely possibility in an area where we know so little about the psychological process of learning and socialization and where measurement is so difficult.

While there are numerous grounds for such errors and their resultant biases, one of the most important of these is the misspecification of output. In short, schools are multi-product firms that are charged with producing many student outcomes in addition to increasing those qualities measured by cognitive achievement scores. The inculcation of attitudes and values has long been an important part of the school agenda. Based upon recent studies of earnings functions that use cognitive achievement scores among their independent variables, one cannot even argue that cognitive skills as measured by test scores are the most crucial determinant of earnings. To the contrary, it appears that variance in achievement scores explains only a relatively nominal portion of differences in success in the labor market (Taubman and Wales, 1973; Griliches and Mason, 1972).

A more insightful analysis of the relationship between educational production and labor market success seems to be reflected in the recent work of Bowles (1972) and Gintis (1972, 1971). These studies suggest that the principal purpose of schools is to reproduce the social relations of production, and that achievement scores are only one component of the productive hierarchy. "The school is a bureaucratic order with hierarchical authority, rule-orientation, stratification of 'ability' (tracking) as well as by age, role differentiation by sex (physical education, home economics, shop) and a system of external incentives (marks, promise of promotion, and threat of failure) much like pay and status in the sphere or work" (Bowles, 1973: 352).

Even an examination of the incentive structures and the information available to school managers suggests that it is not

likely that they are attempting to maximize cognitive achievement. Various studies have shown that school administrators
have very little knowledge on how to improve achievement
scores; they seem to lack substantial management discretion
over their input mix; they do not operate under competitive
forces that would force them to maximize student achievement,
nor does the incentive or reward structure for personnel
correspond to student achievement outcomes; and information
feedback to school managers on the "value-added" to student
test scores that is produced uniquely by school inputs is
unavailable (Levin, 1971). These characteristics of schools are
supported by the findings of Gintis (1971) that grades and
other social rewards of schooling are more consistently correlated with the personality attributes of students than their
cognitive achievement scores.

But, in order to estimate a production function for educational achievement, we must assume that all schools are
operating on the production frontier for this output, so that the
observed relations represent the maximum output that can be
produced with the inputs that are being utilized. The fact that
schools are producing other outputs besides cognitive achievement raises serious questions about this assumption, since it is
reasonable to believe that the production of other outputs
reduces the amount of cognitive learning that will be produced.
In this case, it is obvious that statistical estimates among
existing schools that consider only the achievement score
outcomes of students will not give us estimates of the
production frontier, since more achievement could be obtained
by reducing the levels of all noncomplementary outputs to zero.

The obvious answer to estimating production functions in the
multi-product case is to specify a system of equations that takes
into account all of the outputs of schooling.[2] Unfortunately,
our overall ignorance of the conceptual outputs of schools, of
their measurement and their structural relationships to one
another and to inputs, limits our ability to include nonachieve-
ment outputs in the analysis. The result of these limitations is
that almost every study that has attempted to estimate
educational production functions has considered only educa-

tional achievement as an output.[3] In most cases, the obvious problems involved are either ignored or the assumption is made that all other outputs are produced as perfect joint products in exact fixed proportion to achievement scores. There is no empirical substantiation for this assumption.

The situation is shown in Figure 1, which represents a hypothetical input-input space wherein S_1 and S_2 represent two different school inputs into the production of student achievement. (It is assumed here that other inputs are being held constant; of course, this example can be generalized algebraically for n inputs.) Each observation represents the combination of S_1 and S_2 that a particular school is using to produce a given amount of achievement output, Ao. That is, each school in the sample is using a different input mix even though the apparent output is the same.

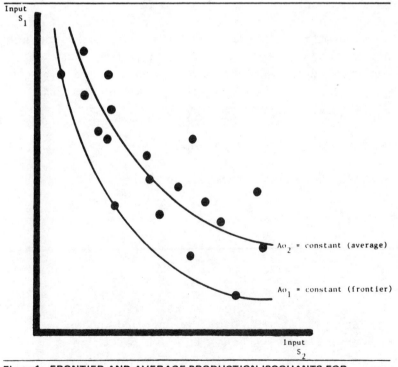

Figure 1: **FRONTIER AND AVERAGE PRODUCTION ISOQUANTS FOR STUDENT ACHIEVEMENT**

The Economic Value of Education

Isoquant Ao_1 represents the production frontier defined as the locus of all observations that minimize the combinations of S_1 and S_2 required to produce constant product Ao. Presumably, these schools are producing only the socially minimal required levels of other school outputs.[4] Since Ao_1 is a mapping of the most efficient points for producing achievement A_o, it is the production frontier. All observations to the northeast of Ao_1 are of inefficient schools that are using higher input levels to produce the same achievement.[5] Now assume that we fit the observations statistically via normal regression procedures. We obtain the statistical equivalent of Ao_2 for all schools (both efficient and inefficient ones). Of course all points on Ao_2 are farther from the origin than those on Ao_1, showing that the average production relationship is a less efficient one than the frontier relationship.

Since virtually all estimates of educational productions have been based on the performance of both average and efficient schools rather than efficient ones only, the existing statistical studies of educational production are not production function studies in the frontier sense. Moreover, their results may suggest erroneous conclusions about which combination of inputs (program) maximizes achievement for a given budget constraint. For example, assume the two-input production function:

$$A = h(S_1, S_2). \qquad [2]$$

In equilibrium we would wish to satisfy the conditions set out in equation 3, where P_1 and P_2 represent the prices of S_1 and S_2 respectively.

$$\frac{\partial Y/\partial S_1}{P_1} = \frac{\partial Y/\partial S_2}{P_2} \quad \text{or} \quad \frac{h_1'}{P_1} = \frac{h_2'}{P_2} \qquad [3]$$

Now consider two different values for h_1' and h_2'. At the frontier, $h_1' = \hat{h}_1'$, and for the average of all schools, $h_1' = \bar{h}_1'$. The symbols for h_2' can be defined in the same way.

$$\frac{\hat{h}_1'}{\hat{h}_2'} = \frac{\bar{h}_1'}{\bar{h}_2'} = \frac{P_1}{P_2} \qquad\qquad [4]$$

Equation 4 reiterates the necessary conditions for a maximum, both for frontier estimates and for average estimates of the production function. In both cases we wish to select the combination of inputs that equates the ratios of marginal products (first derivatives) to the ratios of prices.

EFFICIENCY IMPLICATIONS OF THE ESTIMATES

If we estimate only the average production function or only the frontier one, can the optimal ratio of inputs derived from one estimate also apply to the other? The answer to this question clearly depends on whether there are differences in the structural parameters associated with each input.

For example, it is possible that the inefficiencies of non-frontier schools are neutral among inputs so that at every level of input and for every combination of inputs the ratios of the marginal products are identical for both frontier and average functions. That is, equation 5 holds.

$$\hat{h}_i' = \gamma \bar{h}_i' \qquad (i = 1,2) \qquad\qquad [5]$$

$$\gamma \geqslant 1$$

This can be represented by Figure 2, where Ao_1 signifies the production isoquant for Ao for all efficient schools and Ao_2 represents the same level of output for the entire set of schools, efficient and inefficient. B_1 B_2 and C_1 C_2 represent budget or isocost lines reflecting the various combinations of S_1 and S_2 obtainable for two given cost constraints, B and C, where $C > B$. The slope of the isocost lines is determined by the ratio of the prices, P_2 / P_1. Thus, E and F represent equilibrium points which reflect equation 4. That is, the combination of S_1 and S_2 that

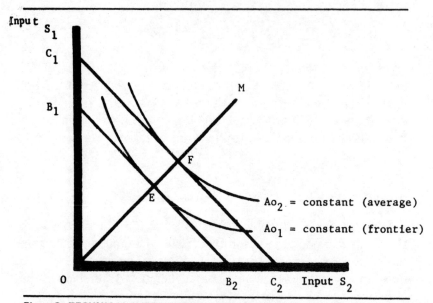

Figure 2: TECHNICAL INEFFICIENCY THAT IS NEUTRAL AMONG INPUTS

obtains Ao for budget constraint B is determined by the tangency of Ao_1 to $B_1 B_2$ at point E for efficient or frontier schools and of Ao_2 to $C_1 C_2$ at point F for schools on the average.

It can be shown that the relative intensities of the two inputs will be identical for both groups of schools if a ray drawn from the origin intersects both points of tangency. O M satisfies that condition, so the same ratio of S_1/S_2 is optimal for both groups of schools. Whether we use the estimates of frontier schools or of all schools, the findings on the optimal combinations of S_1 and S_2 will be binding for both. In such a case it does not matter which group we use to estimate the production function, although the absolute product will be higher for the set of schools at the frontier for any input level.

On the other hand, there is a case in which equation 5 does not hold. This can be shown in Figure 3, and it is also evident in Figure 1. Here the relative inefficiency in the use of S_1 appears to be greater than that for S_2. For example, if S_1 represents

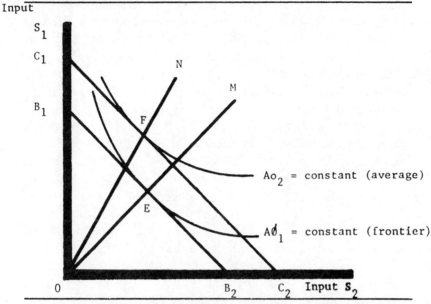

Figure 3: **TECHNICAL INEFFICIENCY THAT IS BIASED BETWEEN INPUTS**

physical school facilities and S_2 represents teachers, Figure 3 suggests that the organizational arrangements in inefficient schools are relatively more harmful to the productivity of the facilities than to that of the teachers. In this case a ray drawn through the origin representing a constant ratio of inputs will not intersect both points of tangency. That is, the optimal ratio of S_1/S_2 for frontier schools will be different from that for inefficient schools. In this event, the results obtained for one group of schools (e.g., frontier ones) cannot be applied to another group (e.g., nonfrontier ones). Rather, each set of schools will have its own optimal combination of S_1/S_2 depending on its relative efficiency.

AN EMPIRICAL APPLICATION

One major difficulty in demonstrating some of the empirical implications of the foregoing analysis is that the necessary relationships are much easier to obtain mathematically than they are statistically. The particular problems in deriving educational production functions have been described else-where, so they will not be detailed here (Bowles, 1970; Levin, 1970a; Michelson, 1970). It is useful to note, however, that the statistical work in this area is subject to both errors in the equations and errors in the variables. In the former case, the proper specification of the model is still in the exploratory stage. The structure of the model, the specific variables to be included, and the relationship of the variables to one another have not been well established, and there are many gaps in our knowledge. Moreover, most of the operational variables used in the models are subject to varying degrees of measurement error.

Thus, no strict application of the findings to public policy is warranted. Rather, the empirical aspects are meant to suggest new directions and to provoke new thought on the process of evaluation. The results derived must surely be subject to replication and further analysis before they can be considered acceptable for policy consideration.

The data used in this analysis represent a subsample drawn from the Survey on Equal Educational Opportunity, conducted by the U.S. Office of Education for the school year 1965-1966. Specifically, the subsample is composed of some 597 white sixth graders who had attended only the schools in which they were enrolled at the time of the survey (see Levin, 1970a, and Michelson, 1970 for details). Since the data were reanalyzed and recoded extensively for the purpose of estimating present relationships, they differ in important ways from the data used in other studies that have drawn information from the same survey. Twenty-nine schools are represented in the sample, and the teacher characteristics identified are averages for each school for all teachers who were assigned to grades three through five. These averages were intended to reflect the teacher characteristics that had influenced student behavior up to the time of the survey. Moreover, it was assumed that the observed measures of family background and other educational influences were related systematically to the cumulative impact of each of these variables.

TABLE 1
LIST OF VARIABLES

Variable	Item Measured	Coding
Verbal score	Student performance	Raw score

	Efficacy	Index compiled from questions 33-40 in the Sixth-Grade Student Questionnaire of the Equal Opportunity Survey
		"I can do many things well."
		   (Yes/No/Not Sure)
		"I sometimes feel I just can't learn."
		   (Yes/No)
		The higher the value of the index, the greater the perceived efficacy of the student.

	Educational expectations of parents	Index based on three questions: (1) How good a student does your mother want you to be? (2) How good a student does your father want you to be? (3) Did anyone at home read to you when you were small, before you started school? (and how often?)
	Student motivation	Grade level the student wishes to complete
Sex	Male-female differences	Male = 0 Female = 1
Age	Overage for grade	Age 12 or over = 1 Less than 12 = 0

Possessions in student's home	Family background (socioeconomic status)	Index of possessions:
		   television
		Yes = 1 telephone
		No = 0 dictionary
		for each encyclopedia
		item. Index automobile
		is sum. daily newspaper
		   record player
		   refrigerator
		   vacuum cleaner

Family size	Family background	Number of people in home
Identity of person serving as mother	Family background	Real mother at home = 0 Real mother not living at home = 1 Surrogate mother = 2

Levin / EFFICIENCY IN EDUCATIONAL PRODUCTION [15]

TABLE 1 (Continued)

Variable	Item Measured	Coding
Identity of person serving as father	Family background	Real father at home = 0 Real father not living at home = 1 Surrogate father = 2
Father's education	Family background	Number of years of school attained
Mother's employment status	Family background	Has job = 1 No job = 0
Attended kindergarten	Family background	Yes = 1 No = 0
Teacher's verbal score	Teacher quality	Raw score on vocabulary test
Teacher's and Parents' Income	Teacher socioeconomic status	Father's occupation scaled according to income (thousands of dollars)
Teacher experience	Teacher quality	Number of years of full-time experience
Teacher's undergraduate institution	Teacher quality	University or college = 3 Teacher institution = 1
Satisfaction with present school	Teacher's attitude	Satisfied = 3 Maybe prefers another school = 2 Prefers another school = 1
Percentage of white students	Student body	Percentage estimated by teachers
Teacher turnover	School	Proportion of teachers who left in previous years for reasons other than death or illness
Library volumes per student	School facilities	Number of volumes divided by school enrollment

The equation used to explore differences between frontier and average estimates is a linear equation based on equation 1. Linearity not only violates our assumptions about the second derivative, but it also runs counter to our intuition about the real world. Nevertheless, the difficulties of estimating particular nonlinear functions and the risk of creating even greater specification biases in the coefficients by imposing another arbitrary functional form suggest that the linear equation might yield reasonable first approximations to the estimates that we seek. Following this procedure, of course, limits our comparison of the frontier and average estimates to the linear marginal products and price ratios.

The variables in the equation are shown in Table 1. These variables are taken from the reduced-form equation for verbal achievement derived from a four equation system encompassing three simultaneous equations and one that represents a recursive relationship. Once that system is estimated, one can solve for the reduced-form equation for any of the three endogenous variables. Since the estimation of that system is discussed elsewhere (Levin, 1970a), this paper is concerned only with the reduced form of the verbal equation. This equation was fitted to the entire sample of observations; thus, it represents the average production relationship for the sample of schools. Results are shown for this estimate in the right-hand column of Table 2.

OBTAINING FRONTIER ESTIMATES

The same set of data and variables can be used to obtain estimates of the equation for only the most efficient observations. There are several ways of doing this; the one used here is the programming approach in input-output space suggested by Aigner and Chu (1968; the linear programming application draws upon the approach of Timmer, 1969). Since the individual observations are of students rather than schools, we wish to seek those students who show a particular outcome with the lowest application of resources.[6] Operationally, we wish to minimize equation 6.

$$\sum_{i=0}^{n} \hat{a}_i \bar{X}_i \qquad [6]$$

where $\hat{a}_i$ is the parameter for the ith input, $\overline{X}_i$ is the mean of input X_i, and $\overline{X}_o = 1$ in order to obtain a constant term. More specifically, the problem is to minimize equation 6, which can be rewritten as 7 subject to the constraints of 8 where there are n inputs and m students.

$$\text{Min.} \quad \hat{a}_o + \hat{a}_1 \overline{X}_1 + \ldots + \hat{a}_n \overline{X}_n, \qquad [7]$$

subject to:

$$\hat{a}_o + \hat{a}_1 X_{11} + \ldots + \hat{a}_n X_{n1} \geqslant A_1 \qquad [8]$$

$$\hat{a}_o + \hat{a}_1 X_{im} + \ldots + \hat{a}_n X_{nm} \geqslant A_m$$

$$\hat{a}_i \geqslant 0$$

Since this is essentially a linear programming problem, there will be as many "efficient" observations as there are inputs into the production function (assuming that no two observations are identical). Unfortunately, some of the observations will appear to be "efficient" when in fact they represent measurement errors. Thus, it is impossible to know a priori whether a particular observation is efficient or whether it is spurious. Therefore, extreme observations have been discarded in order to eliminate what might be spurious points. This is particularly important for the frontier estimates, since very few observations determine the structural coefficients.

Table 2 contrasts the frontier "estimates" with the estimates for the average function. Figures in parentheses beneath each coefficient for the average function signify the t-statistics of those coefficients. Each of the coefficients represents the first derivative or marginal product of the function.[7] Four linear programming runs were used to obtain frontier estimates. Run 1 eliminated no observations; run 2 discarded the nine most "efficient" points; run 3 eliminated 23 observations; and run 4

TABLE 2
FRONTIER AND AVERAGE PRODUCTION RELATIONS FOR WHITE SIXTH GRADERS, EASTMET CITY

Variable	Frontier Function				Average Function
	Run 1	Run 2 (−9)	Run 3 (−23)	Run 4 (−38)	
Personal Variables					
Sex	0.0	1.649	0.982	0.01956	0.817 (1.41)
Age	−7.714	−4.642	−4.769	−5.553	−6.010 (−4.49)
Family size	−0.502	−0.500	−0.089	−0.770	−0.552 (−3.50)
Father's identity	0.0	0.0	−0.283	−0.420	−0.327 (0.64)
Mother's identity	−0.878	−1.342	−1.190	−1.202	−0.433 (−1.90)
Father's education	0.509	0.179	0.0	0.103	0.273 (3.22)
Mother's employment	−1.726	−2.293	−1.089	−0.951	−0.509 (−1.31)
Possessions	1.865	1.464	1.070	1.020	1.229 (5.201)
School Variables					
Kindergarten	0.0	2.866	1.920	2.106	2.372 (2.47)
Teacher's verbal ability	0.810	0.218	0.695	0.791	0.250 (1.70)
Teacher's parents' income	0.0	0.0	0.0	−0.000	−0.118 (−0.64)
Undergraduate institution	3.736	5.269	1.991	8.307	6.525 (2.09)
Teacher experience	0.0	0.392	0.368	0.616	0.787 (4.93)
Teacher satisfaction	3.630	7.078	4.666	3.608	1.960 (1.50)
% white students	0.0	−0.500	−0.264	−0.178	−0.047 (−.03)
Library volumes per student	0.0	0.571	0.509	0.156	0.565 (1.53)
Teacher turnover	0.0	0.0	0.0	−0.035	−0.101 (−1.27)
	0.0	0.0	0.944	−4.051	−7.902 (.84)

Levin / EFFICIENCY IN EDUCATIONAL PRODUCTION [19]

discarded the 38 most extreme points (about 6% of the sample). We will compare the frontier function from run 4 and the average function, and at the same time will examine two properties of the estimates: (1) the relative magnitudes of the coefficients; and (2) the implications for allocative or price efficiency.

Recall that in order for findings of optimal input intensities to yield the same relative applications of inputs for both average and frontier schools, the marginal products for both functions must bear a constant relation to each other as reflected in equation 5. Table 3 shows the ratios of marginal products for the two sets of estimates for all of the school variables. According to this table, there is no systematic relationship between the two sets. At the frontier, such inputs as the teacher's verbal facility and the proportion of white students to others show marginal products that are more than three times their counterparts derived for the sample as a whole. On the other hand, such variables as teacher turnover, teacher experience, and library volumes per student show much smaller coefficients for the frontier function.

In summary, it appears that when student achievement is used as the criterion of educational output, so-called frontier schools are more efficient in the use of some inputs and less efficient in the use of others. Standard errors of the coefficients

TABLE 3

RATIO OF MARGINAL PRODUCTS AT THE FRONTIER TO MARGINAL PRODUCTS FOR THE ENTIRE SAMPLE

School Variables	MP (frontier) MP (average)	School Variables	MP (frontier) MP (average)
Kindergarten	.888	Teacher satisfaction	1.841
Teacher's verbal ability	3.164	Percentage of white students	3.787
Teacher's parents' income	.001 (.0005)	Library volumes per student	.276
Undergraduate institution	1.273	Teacher turnover	.347
Teacher experience	.783	Constant	.513

tend to be high relative to the differences in coefficients. Even so, the coefficient for teacher's verbal ability is significantly different between the two estimates, and other differences are on the margin of significance. This in turn suggests that the production isoquants for schools of different efficiencies with regard to the production of student achievement may be intersecting within the relevant ranges of factor substitution. This characteristic is probably attributable to differences in output mixes that are ignored in this type of analysis. Nevertheless, any optimal combination of inputs for any set of schools or any individual school for the production of achievement is likely to be less than optimal for any other set of schools or individual school that are pursuing a different combination of objectives. In other words, for any given array of prices $(P_1 \ P_2 \ \ldots, \ P_n)$, the optimal set of input proportions will vary from school to school depending upon its other priorities.

For purposes of generalizing about the optimal strategies for increasing student verbal scores, this is the worst of all possible worlds. That is, whereas we might be able to derive the optimal input structure for frontier schools or for schools on the average as represented by equilibrium conditions stated in equation 4, it is likely that the desirable combination of input intensities may differ between the two sets of schools (and may even differ significantly from school to school).

An illustration of this is found in Table 4, which shows the estimated ratios of prices for two inputs (teacher verbal score and teacher experience) as well as the two sets of marginal

TABLE 4

RELATIVE PRICES AND MARGINAL PRODUCTS FOR TEACHER VERBAL SCORE AND TEACHER EXPERIENCE

	(1) Teacher Verbal Score	(2) Teacher Experience	(3) Ratio of (1) to (2)
Price (salary increment)	$24.00	$79.00	0.303
Marginal Product at Frontier	0.791	0.616	1.284
Marginal Product on Average	0.250	0.787	0.317

products for those inputs. The prices reflect the increments to annual teacher salaries for each of the teacher attributes; they were derived from an equation relating teacher attributes to earnings in the Eastmet teacher market (Levin, 1970a, 1968). The marginal products associated with a unit change in the two inputs are taken from Table 2. In equilibrium the ratios of the marginal products of the inputs should be equal to the ratios of their respective prices. For the average production estimates these ratios are almost identical, so that allocative or price efficiency is implied even though the average estimates are assumed to be based on technically inefficient (nonfrontier) schools.

On the other hand, the frontier estimates show a ratio of marginal products four times as great as the price ratio for the two inputs. This suggests that the utilization of more verbally able teachers yields four times as much output per dollar as the utilization of additional teacher experience. If this is correct, the schools on the frontier could increase total output by reallocating their budgets in favor of teachers' verbal scores rather than their experience.

CONCLUSIONS

The significant aspect of this analysis is that the combination of inputs which maximizes output for any set of prices differs between the two estimates. If these differences persist among schools of different apparent efficiencies in the production of achievement, the hope of obtaining general decision rules that can be applied across schools seems to be frustrated. That is, the lack of similarities among the production techniques used by different schools may mean that neither average nor frontier findings can be applied to any particular school. Indeed, in the extreme case, each individual school is on its own production function (which varies according to the outputs being pursued), and evaluation results for any group of schools will not be applicable to individual schools in the sample.

While measurement of educational production may be a useful exercise in itself, it is not clear that such studies can help us to improve the efficiency of the educational sector. In particular, our focus on a single and measurable output, student achievement, not only limits the analysis considerably; but it may provide policy recommendations that would reduce the economic efficiency of the educational industry if they were adopted. Perhaps the only generalization that one can make from this pessimistic overview is that the analysis of production of public activities is fraught with difficulties that are unusually severe given the present analytical state of the art. The implications of estimates of public sector production functions for improving social efficiency should probably be stated with far greater modesty than they have been. They may be totally misleading.

NOTES

1. This formulation is based on Hanushek (1972). See his discussion of its components (1972: ch. 2).

2. For a discussion of the problems in specifying the multi-product case in studies of production, see Pfouts (1961), Salter (1960), and Carlson (1956). Normally this problem is avoided in estimating production functions in the private sector, since the measure of output is valued in monetary terms. Thus, different market outputs can be weighted according to their prices in order to obtain a single monetary index of total market output. Of course, this procedure is based upon the normal assumptions of profit maximization. It does not account for nonmarket outputs.

3. Exceptions to this are the multi-product estimations of Levin (1970a) and Michelson (1970). Work in this area is also being carried out in 1973 by Otto Davis and his associates at Carnegie-Mellon University.

4. In theory, schools on the frontier for student achievement are producing no other outputs. That is, the production of other outputs is assumed to detract from the production of student achievement. But, in fact, it is likely that there is a socially minimal level of other outputs (such as citizenship, work attitudes, and so on) that all schools produce. In this case, the schools that appear to be on the achievement frontier are on a "modified" frontier which assumes a socially minimal level of other outputs. That is, short of an experiment we are unable to obtain production data on schools that are producing only student achievement.

5. Inefficiency is used here in a very narrow way. Specifically, it refers to the case in which more of a particular output could be obtained by reallocating existing resources from other outcomes to the one under scrutiny. The case of "technical inefficiency" or "x-inefficiency" is just a misnomer for this condition. Under conditions of technical inefficiency, it appears that more output could be obtained with the same level of inputs. But, as we have shown elsewhere (Levin and Müller, 1973), the physical laws of production must surely behave according to the principles of conservation of mass and energy so that nothing is "lost" in the production process. One is always on the production frontier in that there is a mapping of outputs on inputs for any production process. When a steel mill is producing less steel for a given set of inputs than another mill, it is producing more heat energy or worker

leisure or other outputs. It just happens that the most-valued or preferred output from the perspective of the analyst is steel rather than heat energy or worker leisure. Thus, so-called technical inefficiency can always be shown to reduce to allocative or price inefficiency since it is a function of values rather than energy losses in a physical sense. For reference to the concept of technical efficiency or x-efficiency, see Farrell (1957) and Leibenstein (1966). In our view, their conception is erroneous for reasons mentioned above and outlined more systematically in Levin and Müller (1973).

    6. The normal approach to estimating educational production functions is to use individual students as units of observation, rather than school averages. There are a variety of reasons for this including the fact that there is a great deal more variance in standardized achievement scores within schools than among them, and that collinearity increases markedly at the higher level of aggregation. In all cases the school characteristics are aggregated to classroom or multi-classroom level. Strictly speaking, the linear programming solution obtains coefficients for frontier students rather than frontier firms. Since both average and frontier functions are obtained from samples of individuals, the approach is consistent. For a useful discussion of the choice of individual students as units of observation, see Michelson (1970: 125-128).

    7. Since $a_i \geq 0$, those variables that showed negative coefficients for the average function represented problems for the programming estimates. The array for each such variable was multiplied by -1 for the programming estimates, and the signs were reversed in turn when reporting the results in Table 2. The author is indebted to Richard C. Carlson for computing the programming estimates (Carlson, 1970).

REFERENCES

AIGNER, D. J. and S. F. CHU (1968) "On estimating the industry production function." Amer. Economic Rev. 58 (September): 826-839.

AVERCH, H., S. CARROLL, T. DONALDSON, H. KIESLING, and J. PINCUS (1972) How Effective is Schooling? A Critical Review and Synthesis of Research Findings. Santa Monica, Calif.: RAND Corporation.

BAUMOL, W. (1967) "Macroeconomics of unbalanced growth: the anatomy of urban crisis." Amer. Economic Rev. 52 (June): 415-426.

BOWLES, S. S. (1973) "Understanding unequal economic opportunity." Amer. Economic Rev. Papers and Proceedings 63 (May): 346-356.

——— (1972) "Unequal education and the reproduction of the social division of labor," pp. 36-66 in M. Carnoy, Schooling in a Corporate Society. New York: David McKay.

——— (1970) "Towards an educational production function," pp. 11-60 in W. L. Hansen (ed.) Education, Income, and Human Capital. New York: National Bureau of Economic Research.

——— and H. M. LEVIN (1968) "The determinants of scholastic achievement—a critical appraisal of some recent evidence." J. of Human Resources 3 (Winter): 3-24.

BURKHEAD, J. et al. (1967) Input and Output in Large City High Schools. Syracuse, N.Y.: Syracuse Univ. Press.

CARLSON, R. C. (1970) "Educational efficiency and effectiveness." Presented at the Stanford University Seminar in Economics of Education, May.

[24] PUBLIC FINANCE QUARTERLY

CARLSON, S. (1956) A Study on the Pure Theory of Production. New York: Kelley & Millman.

FARRELL, M. (1957) "The measurement of productive efficiency." J. of the Royal Statistical Society 120, 3: 253-281.

GINTIS, H. (1972) "Toward a political economy of education." Harvard Educ. Rev. 42 (February): 70-96.

――― (1971) "Education, technology and the characteristics of worker productivity." Amer. Economic Rev. 61 (May): 266-279.

GRILICHES, Z. and W. MASON (1972) "Education, income, and ability." J. of Pol. Economy (May/June Supplement): S.74-S.103.

HANUSHEK, E. (1972) Education and Race. Lexington, Mass.: D. C. Heath.

HIRSCH, W. Z. (1973) Urban Economic Analysis. New York: McGraw-Hill.

KATZMAN, M. (1971) The Political Economy of Urban Schools. Cambridge, Mass.: Harvard Univ. Press.

KIESLING, H. J. (1967) "Measuring a local government service: a study of school districts in New York State." Rev. of Economics and Statistics 49 (August): 356-367.

LEIBENSTEIN, H. (1966) "Allocative efficiency vs. 'X-efficiency.'" Amer. Economic Rev. 56: 392-415.

LEVIN, H. M. (1971) "Frontier functions: an econometric approach to the evaluation of educational effectiveness." Stanford, Calif.: Stanford Center for Research and Development in Teaching R. and D. Memo 80.

――― (1970a) "A cost-effectiveness analysis of teacher selection." J. of Human Resources 5, 1: 24-33.

――― (1970b) "A new model of school effectiveness," ch. in Do Teachers Make a Difference? Washington, D.C.: U. S. Department of Health, Education, and Welfare Office of Education.

――― (1968) "Recruiting teachers for large-city schools." Washington, D.C.: Brookings Institution. (mimeo)

――― and M. MULLER (1973) "The meaning of technical efficiency." Stanford University. (unpublished)

MICHELSON, S. (1970) "The association of teacher resourcefulness with children's characteristics," ch. 6 in Do Teachers Make a Difference? Washington, D.C.: U.S. Department of Health, Education, and Welfare Office of Education.

MUSHKIN, S. [ed.] (1972) Public Prices for Public Products. Washington, D.C.: Urban Institute.

PERL, L. J. (1973) "Family background, secondary school expenditure, and student ability." J. of Human Resources (Spring): 156-180.

PFOUTS, R. W. (1961) "The theory of cost and production in the multi-product firm." Econometrica 29: 650-658.

SALTER, W.E.G. (1960) Productivity and Technical Change. Cambridge, Mass.: Cambridge Univ. Press.

TAUBMAN, P. J. and T. J. WALES (1973) "Higher education, mental ability, and screening." J. of Pol. Economy 81 (January/February): 28-55.

TIMMER, C. P. (1969) "On measuring technical efficiency." Ph.D. dissertation. Harvard University.

WINKLER, D. R. (1972) "The production of human capital: a study of minority achievement." Ph.D. dissertation. University of California (Berkeley).

Part IV
Education and Economic Development

[17]

Education and Economic Development:
The First Generation

Martin Carnoy

Stanford University and Center for Economic Studies

While economists have long recognized schooling as contributing to individual occupational position and wage differentiation (Adam Smith, for example, discussed schooling in this context), the analysis of the role of education in economic development is appropriately characterized as a child of the last quarter century.

In the mid-1950s, the interest in expenditures on education as a possible source of increasing output grew out of the failure of traditional development models, in which inputs were defined as homogeneous labor and capital, to explain more than about half of the total increase in economic output during a growth period. The early works on education and economic development therefore concentrated on establishing education as an input into the growth process—a form of increasing the productive "quality" of labor. More recently, however, serious questions have been raised about what expenditures on schooling actually do to increase output, or, for that matter, whether more schooling raises output at all. Finally, some economists began to ask whether economic growth is the only development objective concerning the political economy and whether, indeed, the most important function of education is not its distribution role, within and between generations of workers.

In this essay, I review this rich and varied theoretical and empirical literature on education and development which appeared in such abundance in the pages of this journal and elsewhere. It is clearly impossible to do more than touch the surface of this richness: I have chosen, for better or worse, those topics which seem to clarify where the subject has been and where it is going.

Education as an Input into Economic Growth
Development economists found in the fifties that increases in labor and capital, as measured by man-hours of work and the value of capital, explained only a part of a country's growth rate. The "residual" of un-

Martin Carnoy

explained growth was at first ascribed to technology,[1] but later this general term was broken down to include improvements in the quality of capital[2] and the investment in human beings.[3] In a series of pioneering studies, Schultz developed the idea that expenditures on education were not primarily consumption but rather an investment in the increased capacity of labor to produce material goods. Hence, formal schooling was at least in part an investment in human capital, an investment with economic yield in terms of higher product per workers, holding physical capital constant.

At the same time, Denison applied measurements on investment in human capital and others' estimates of the economic return to such investment in an effort to account for unexplained growth in the postwar U.S. economy. Denison found that expenditures on education seemed to explain about 23 percent of the 1909–29 growth rate in per-person employed income and 42 percent between 1929 and 1957, while increased capital per worker accounted for 29 and 9 percent in the two periods. Denison concluded that additional education played a significant role in increasing U.S. material growth, particularly after the first period of rapid physical capital increase.

This concept may have rankled some educators who saw education primarily as a means for elevating culture and civilization, not for bettering labor for production.[4] Nevertheless, human-capital theory ultimately provided a rationale for a massive expansion of schooling in the Third World: If expenditures on such schooling contributed to economic growth, governments could satisfy demands by their populations for schooling while simultaneously contributing to the overall material growth of the economy.[5]

[1] Robert Solow, "Technical Change and the Aggregate Production Function," *Review of Economics and Statistics* 39 (August 1957): 312–20.

[2] Edward F. Denison, *The Sources of Economic Growth in the United States and the Alternatives before Us* (New York: Committee for Economic Development, 1962); Zvi Griliches and Dale Jorgenson, "Sources of Measured Productivity Change: Capital Input," *American Economic Review* 61 (May 1966): 50–61.

[3] Theodore W. Schultz, "Investment in Man: An Economist's View," *Social Service Review* 33 (June 1959): 110–17, and "Investment in Human Capital," *American Economic Review* 51 (March 1961): 1–17.

[4] So T. W. Schultz wrote, "Those who value schooling highly, which includes most of those who are part of the educational establishment, are likely to look upon an effort such as this as an intrusion which can only debase the cultural purposes of education. In their view, education lies beyond the economic calculus, because they believe that education is much more than a matter of costs and returns" (Theodore W. Schultz, *The Economic Value of Education* [New York: Columbia University Press, 1963]).

[5] Further rationale was provided by another type of study. Frederick Harbison and Charles Myers (*Education, Manpower and Economic Growth* [New York: McGraw-Hill Book Co., 1964]), for example, argued that secondary and higher education per capita were highly correlated with per capita income. Therefore, they reasoned, increasing the per capita level of intermediate and higher education would lead to higher levels of income per capita.

Economic Development and Cultural Change

In the second wave of empirical work on education as human capital, the cost of (investment in) education was related to the increase in income (productivity) realized, on the average, by individuals in the labor force to show how much expenditures on education were worth compared to other investments in the economy. Studies by Hansen, Becker and Hanoch for the United States, Blaug for England, and Carnoy for Mexico and other Latin American countries indicated that the rate of return to education as an investment was high compared with investment in physical capital.[6] On the other hand, Gounden's data for India[7] suggested just the opposite: physical capital seemed to be a better investment in India than education. No matter what they showed, however, the implication of these studies was (like Denison's work) that income differences among groups of people with different amounts of schooling in the labor force could be used to estimate the expected value of education, not only to the marginal individual taking more schooling, but to the aggregate economy in the form of increased output produced by those with more education. These economists were arguing that increasing the level of education increased the level of material output; for every additional dollar, peso, or rupee invested at the margin, gross national product (GNP) would increase approximately by the rate of return to education times labor's share in GNP.

One of the first questions to be asked by these same analysts, however, was whether the entire income difference among groups with different levels of schooling could be ascribed to schooling. Mincer[8] noted that differences in earnings not only differed for those with differential schooling, but that the differences seemed to increase with age. He argued that this was due to investment in on-the-job training and that those with more schooling had, as part of the return to their investment, greater access to on-the-job training opportunities than those with less schooling.

Denison had introduced the concept of correcting earnings differences for nonschooling, nontraining variables like IQ by adjusting his estimates of such differentials by an "alpha coefficient" of 0.6; this

[6] W. Lee Hansen, "Total and Private Rates of Return to Investment in Schooling," *Journal of Political Economy* 71 (April 1963): 128–40; Gary S. Becker, *Human Capital* (New York: Columbia University Press, 1964); Giora Hanoch, "An Economic Analysis of Earnings and Schooling," *Journal of Human Resources* 2 (Summer 1967): 310–29; Mark Blaug, "The Private and Social Returns on Investment in Education: Some Results for Great Britain," *Journal of Human Resources* 2 (Summer 1967): 330–46; Martin Carnoy, "Rates of Return to Schooling in Latin America," *Journal of Human Resources* 2 (Summer 1967): 359–74, and "Earnings and Schooling in Mexico," *Economic Development and Cultural Change* 15 (July 1967): 408–19.

[7] Nalla A. M. Gounden, "Investment in Education in India," *Journal of Human Resources* 2 (Summer 1967): 347–58.

[8] Jacob Mincer, "On-the-Job Training: Costs, Returns and Some Implications," *Journal of Political Economy* 70, suppl. (October 1962): S50–S79.

Martin Carnoy

assumed that 60 percent of income (productivity) differences was due to schooling alone. Morgan and David[9] adjusted earnings differentials of white male heads of nonfarm households in the U.S. labor force for measures of religion, personality, father's education, labor market conditions, mobility, and supervisory responsibilities. The adjustment was intended to separate the effect of schooling on earnings from motivation and ability. They found that, although the adjustment varied by level of schooling and age, for those less than 35 years old the 60 percent adjustment used by Denison seemed generally to hold.

Later studies by sociologists like Blau and Duncan and by economists like Griliches and Mason and Hause in the United States and Carnoy in Mexico[10] using different statistical techniques tended to confirm further that of the explainable differences in earnings among individuals of the same race and sex, the part explained by schooling was the largest. Eckhaus and Chiswick and Mincer in the United States and Thias and Carnoy in Kenya showed that the employment factor was also crucial in understanding why individuals earned differentially.[11] Correcting for the differential unemployment rate among individuals with different levels of schooling, these studies indicated that the role of schooling in earnings was greatly reduced, particularly at certain levels of schooling. Their studies cast some doubt on the previously high estimate of the "productive" value of schooling, since annual income is a function of the amount of time worked and wages paid per unit of time. It is the latter which supposedly reflects productivity differences (although it could be argued that more schooling makes people prefer to work more).

The Reaction: Schooling as an Allocator of Economic Roles

The concept that the correlation of schooling with earnings reflected a causal relation between schooling as an investment good and the higher productivity of labor was not universally agreed upon. First, as I mentioned, some educators probably felt that the principal function

[10] Peter Blau and Otis Dudley Duncan, *The American Occupational Structure Journal of Economics* 77 (1963): 423–37.

[10] Peter Blau and Otis Dudley Duncan, *The American Occupational Structure* (New York: John Wiley & Sons, 1967); Zvi Griliches and William Mason, "Education, Income, and Ability," *Journal of Political Economy* 80, suppl. (May/June 1972): S74–S103; John Hause, "Earnings Profile: Ability and Schooling," *Journal of Political Economy* 80, suppl. (May/June 1972): S108–S138; Carnoy, "Earnings and Schooling in Mexico," pp. 408–14.

[11] Richard Eckaus, *Estimating the Returns to Education: A Disaggregated Approach* (Berkeley, Calif.: Carnegie Corp., 1973); Barry Chiswick and Jacob Mincer, "Time Series Change in Personal Income Inequality in the United States from 1939, with Projections to 1985," *Journal of Political Economy* 80, suppl. (May/June 1972): S34–S66; Hans Thias and Martin Carnoy, *Cost-Benefit Analysis in Education: A Case Study of Kenya* (Washington, D.C.: World Bank, 1972).

of schooling was to prepare better, happier citizens, not inputs into the production process. Similarly, some economists felt that the observed correlation could be explained by the conception of schooling as a consumption good: an individual with higher income tended to have a higher-income family who purchased more schooling for their children. In this consumption interpretation, of course, more schooling did not result in more income, but rather more income resulted in more schooling consumed.[12] Thus, schooling was not seen principally as a policy variable in increasing economic growth.

However, more sophisticated statistical analysis—Blau and Duncan and Duncan, Featherman, and Duncan, for example[13]—indicated that even when parents' education and occupation (highly correlated with family income) were accounted for, an individual's schooling was still a significant explainer for his occupational position and earnings. This implied that additional schooling is a factor in additional earnings even when the possible correlation between socioeconomic family position and schooling taken by children is adjusted for. Although this did not prove that schooling was not primarily a consumption good, it strengthened the argument that there was a direct relation between schooling and earnings (more schooling leading to higher earnings) that had to be explained in some way.[14]

Another discussion which questioned the contribution of schooling to growth revolved around the earnings/productivity relation. Given

[12] There are a number of studies which attempt to measure the income elasticity of schooling expenditures. See, for example, Sherman Shapiro, "An Analysis of the Determinants of Current Public and Societal Expenditures per Pupil in Elementary and Secondary Schools, Decennially, 1920–1950" (Ph.D. diss., University of Chicago, 1962); and Z. Hirsch, *Analysis of the Rising Costs of Public Education*, Congressional Joint Economic Committee, 86th Cong., 1st sess. (Washington, D.C.: Government Printing Office, 1959).

[13] See Blau and Duncan (n. 10 above); Otis Dudley Duncan, David L. Featherman, and Beverly Duncan, *Socioeconomic Background and Achievements* (New York: Seminar Press, 1972).

[14] Samuel Bowles ("Schooling and Inequality from Generation to Generation," *Journal of Political Economy* 80, suppl. [May/June 1972]: S219–S251) has argued that such studies generally underestimate the effect of social class on present earnings and occupational status relative to the effect of schooling on those variables for two reasons: (1) There is a bias in remembering parents' education and occupation relative to the amount of schooling a person took. People with high education tend to remember their parents as having less education and lower-status occupations than they actually had, and those with less schooling tend to remember their parents with higher education and status than they actually had, thus reducing the variance in social class relative to the variance in the education of the interviewee. (2) The use of parents' education and occupation is only a proxy for the parents' class position; parents' income and wealth are better predictors of the effect of social class and a person's earnings than parents' education or occupation. Indeed, William H. Sewell and Robert M. Hauser's recent work (*Education, Occupation, and Earnings: Achievement in the Early Career* [Madison: University of Wisconsin, Department of Sociology, 1974]) on Wisconsin data bears out this second contention.

Martin Carnoy

that more schooling leads to higher earnings for the individual, does this mean that increasing schooling produces higher productivity? Do earnings equal productivity? Vaizey[15] and others were willing to concede that the individual saw schooling as an investment; that is, that he correctly expected to earn more if he went further in school, but that this did not necessarily imply that schooling actually produced more aggregate output. Education could be an allocator of the share of output going to labor, assigning more earnings to those with more schooling and less earnings to those with less, even though the marginal product of both groups could be approximately equal. In that model, higher investment by society in schooling would not necessarily produce more goods for distribution among the labor force, but the pattern of investment among individuals and groups of individuals would be important in determining who received the share of output going to labor. Neither would a higher average level of schooling lead to higher income per capita.

Support for this argument came indirectly from two sources. The first was Ivar Berg's work (followed by Fuller's work on India)[16] which showed that within carefully defined occupational categories, schooling and physical productivity of workers were not significantly correlated. The second was Thurow's study of the relation between the marginal productivity of labor as derived from aggregate production-function estimates and wages paid to labor.[17] Thurow's comparison indicated that in the United States workers received, on the average, earnings less than their marginal product (on the average 63 percent of productivity), while workers in less union-organized and lower average-education sectors (nonfarm, nonmanufacturing) received, on average, less earnings relative to marginal product (60 percent) than workers in manufacturing (80 percent). Both studies, of course, only suggested that the correlation between schooling and productivity, if it could be measured properly, would be less than the correlation between schooling and income. If the suggested relation were borne out, the contribution of schooling to growth, by implication, was less than indicated by estimates based on earnings differences.

However, Berg's, Fuller's, and Thurow's work have methodological problems serious enough to cast doubt on their conclusions. Berg's and Fuller's correlation of productivity and schooling within an occu-

---

[15] John Vaizey, *The Economics of Education* (London: Faber & Faber, 1961).

[16] Ivan Berg, *Education and Jobs: The Great Training Robbery* (New York: Praeger Publishers, 1970); William Fuller, "Education, Training, and Worker Productivity: Study of Skilled Workers in Two Firms in South India" (Ph.D. diss., Stanford University, 1970).

[17] Lester Thurow, "Disequilibrium and the Marginal Productivity of Capital and Labor," *Review of Economics and Statistics* 50 (February 1968): 23–31.

Economic Development and Cultural Change

pation yields good productivity comparisons in the sense that it can be measured in physically comparable units, but it necessarily excludes those workers at the lower end of the occupation's schooling spectrum who are in lower-paying and, supposedly, less-productive occupations where the average level of schooling is also lower. At the same time, it excludes those workers at the higher end of the occupation's education spectrum who are in higher-paying, more "productive" jobs where the average levels of schooling are also higher. Put another way, within a single occupation we will usually find workers with a fairly wide range of schooling but a fairly low variance of income relative to the overall earnings variance in the labor force. We have to assume that the workers with much less or much more than the occupation's average schooling are extraordinary in some way which may be related to their productivity and earnings but which is not picked up by the schooling variable. Since, on average, those with different amounts of schooling are in different occupations producing different goods, it is virtually impossible to estimate the relation between physical productivity and schooling. On average, people with more schooling receive higher incomes than those with less schooling because they produce goods which are defined as "worth" more.

Thurow's methodology is also questionable. His results indicate that even in terms of the value of goods produced, more-skilled and better-organized workers are doing better relative to their marginal product than less-skilled and/or less-organized workers. But he faces the counterargument that estimates of aggregate production functions are not a meaningful reflection of what is happening in any real economic sense.[18] Thurow's estimates of marginal productivity may or may not measure the productivity of different groups, and hence his comparisons with average wages may be valid or not.

In later work, Thurow and Robert Lucas[19] contended that education and training are not important factors in determining potential productivity of workers because "productivity" is an attribute of jobs, not people. Jobs associated with a lot of modern capital equipment are high-productivity jobs, and workers queue up for them. Once a worker is hired, the cognitive skills necessary to raise his productivity up to the productivity of the job are learned through formal and informal training programs. The chief criterion which employers use in selecting

[18] Mark Blaug, "Neo-Keynesian Theory of Value and Distribution: Revolution or Dead End?" mimeographed (London: University of London, Institute of Education, 1974).

[19] Lester Thurow and Robert Lucas, "The American Distribution of Income: A Structural Problem," in *Hearings before the Joint Economic Committee* (Washington, D.C.: Government Printing Office, 1972).

Martin Carnoy

workers for jobs is "trainability": Those who possess background characteristics which employers feel reduce training costs go to the head of the queue and receive the best work.

The "queue" concept of education in the labor market sees the correlation between schooling and earnings as unrelated to any specific knowledge that schooling imparts to workers which makes them more productive; rather, schooling provides a convenient device for employers to identify those workers who can be trained more easily, based, it seems, primarily on noncognitive values and norms acquired by students as they go further in school. Is this a contribution to worker productivity? Or is it a subsidy to employers to make it easier for them to select workers for various jobs—a transfer of resources from the public sector to owners of capital?

Similarly, Arrow[20] suggested that schooling may act as a mechanism to screen "desirable" from less-desirable employees. The "screening" hypothesis and the "queue" concept both implied that education did not contribute directly to economic growth but served as a means to sort people for jobs, higher- and lower-productivity jobs paying higher and lower wages. Although some economists retorted that screening did contribute to higher output because it made employers' labor search costs lower, Arrow showed that such a transfer to employers made the economy no better off. This left the discussion back at the level of determining whether there were persuasive reasons to believe that education did contribute directly to higher worker productivity or whether it was primarily a sorter of individuals for differentially paying jobs.

The argument for schooling contributing to growth lay in the productivity-raising skills that schooling allegedly provides to students as potential workers. Unlike the queue theory, in which more schooling made students more trainable as workers, the screening argument rested on the certificates awarded to students as they went further in school. For the screen to function, some types of criteria have to be used, but these need not be cognitive, productivity-raising, or even trainability ones.

Bowles and Gintis[21] took another view. They suggested that young people were allocated to different occupations and earnings in large part

[20] Kenneth Arrow, "Higher Education as a Filter," Technical Report no. 71 (Stanford, Calif.: Institute for Mathematical Studies in the Social Sciences, Stanford University, 1972).

[21] Samuel Bowles, "Unequal Education and the Reproduction of the Social Division of Labor," in *Schooling in a Corporate Society*, ed. Martin Carnoy, 2d ed. (New York: David McKay Co., 1975); Herbert Gintis, "Education, Technology, and Worker Productivity," *American Economic Association Proceedings* 61 (May 1971): 266–71.

Economic Development and Cultural Change

on the basis of parents' social class (income, occupation, education), and that the principal function of schooling was to legitimize this repro-duction of the unequal class structure through a facade of meritocracy. Thus, the Bowles-Gintis view contended that schooling was more than a screening device for labor as an input to production (a benefit to employers as entrepreneurs); it was an institution which served em-ployers' class interest in perpetuating the capitalist social hierarchy. In this view, the growth function of schooling is not rejected: Bowles and Gintis argue that there is a cognitive component to schooling, but that this cognitive component is overshadowed by the importance of class values and norms in school output and in assigning groups of individuals to various economic roles. But Carnoy points out that the function of schooling as an ideological arm of the State, reinforcing and reproducing the social structure, may have a negative effect on economic growth, since it places priority on distribution of power (profit) and hierarch-ical rules rather than maximization of output.[22]

Where does all this leave us? Does schooling contribute to increased output, or does it allocate people to jobs with higher training, produc-tivity, and earnings possibilities? Is it a subsidy to employers? Does it legitimize an unequal social structure and hence contribute to higher output through helping to produce acceptance of unequal work roles and hence political stability (or to lower output through political sta-bility)?

We can imagine how schooling could contribute to economic growth: the breaking of abstract codes in a systematic way (reading and arithmetic) allegedly helps develop deductive and inductive logic which, in turn, helps people solve problems associated with production. More important, even though such logical capability may not contribute directly to increased production, it may make the physical capital with which people work more productive, since workers probably would be more aware of the nature of, and the care required by, machinery. More schooling—especially centrally controlled, or common, schooling—also probably makes for better communication among workers and between workers and supervisors. If people have shared a common communica-tive experience with a common knowledge base (the school), workers from different family backgrounds, age groups, or cultures should be able to relate at least at that common experiential level. Welch suggests that the main contribution of education in production is yet something different: it makes producers better decision makers in the allocation of resources, including time.[23] Welch's model implies that the greater the

[22] Martin Carnoy, *Education as Cultural Imperialism* (New York: David McKay Co., 1974).

[23] Finis Welch, "Education in Production," *Journal of Political Economy* 78 (January/February 1970): 35–59.

Martin Carnoy

decision making associated with a job, the greater would be the potential effect of education on productivity.[24]

We can also understand the basis for the screening or "legitimization" argument: there is, after all, no way to prove that those with higher wages produce more than those with lower wages. It is a persuasive point that more schooling requires the expenditure of real resources, so that society would be wasteful and irrational to spend such resources if they did not result in some positive return. But the return might not be in the form of higher total output: "Society" is defined as a particular subset of the population, and that subset may profit from a shift of product among groups, such as between those who are less and those who are more educated or between workers and capitalists. Schooling, in the screening argument, helps perform this shift, and the return to schooling may represent not a net contribution to total output, but the transfer of labor's product from the less schooled to the more schooled. Thus, we could observe a positive return (as measured by wage differences) to expenditures on schooling as a result of people with lower wages being paid less than their product and people with higher wages being paid more than their product, and schooling not contributing to a net increase in total product. Higher-schooled groups would have succeeded in such a case to use schooling to shift consumption power from the less-schooled to the more-schooled groups through wage and income policies.

Finally, it is also possible that the principal function of schooling in economic growth lies in its legitimization of the existing, or some emerging, social order. The acceptance by the masses of a particular social structure could have a positive effect on economic output. However, if the accepted economic organization—acceptable in part because schools have helped legitimize that organization—is not maximizing total output but only the income of certain groups, schooling could have a negative effect on economic growth.[25]

Schooling probably does all of these things, but the main discussion centers on which of these functions best characterizes the role of schooling.[26] The question is not so much whether or not schooling contributes to growth, but how much it contributes. We conclude that the contribution is probably smaller than the early human-capital theorists

---

[24] All of these possible effects of schooling on productivity form the implicit bases for the studies of correlation between education in the labor force and the level of gross national product (M. J. Bowman and Arnold Anderson, "Concerning the Role of Education in Development," in *Old Societies and New States*, ed. Clifford Geertz [Glencoe, Ill.: Free Press, 1963]; and Harbison and Myers [n. 5 above]).

[25] Carnoy, *Education as Cultural Imperialism.*

[26] Mark Blaug, "The Correlation between Education and Earnings: What Does It Signify?" *Higher Education* 1 (February 1972): 53–76.

Economic Development and Cultural Change

and development economists thought. The correlation between earnings and schooling picks up many other influences on earnings which are also correlated with schooling. There is also little evidence that earnings and productivity are isomorphic—indeed, it is likely (on political grounds) that societies in which the higher educated are more powerful socially and politically reward those with higher education more relative to their productivity and those with less education less relative to their productivity even if, in neoclassical terms, this prevents an "optimum" allocation of resources.

Education and Income Distribution

This leads us to a different point: Should economic development be interpreted only as aggregate economic growth per capita? Economists in the last decade became increasingly interested in the distribution aspect of development. A number of studies found, for example, that increased output per capita did not necessarily mean that all groups in the economy participated in that increase.[27] This raised serious questions about the meaning of a development process which may only benefit a minority of the labor force and population and a definition of development—aggregate economic growth per capita—which does not distinguish between those situations in which all groups participate in an income increase and those where the income increase is highly concentrated in a small percentage of the population. Furthermore, the achievement of rapid growth of material output in low-income, non-European societies that placed distribution considerations on a par with (or even above) growth considerations, such as China, and now Cuba, placed alternative models of development in direct competition with each other, a competition in which the distribution of output played a key role.[28]

What function does schooling play in income distribution? The literature on screening and the queue theory indicates that schooling may designate who gets the high- and low-paying jobs in an economy. But the variation of income among jobs in that concept of the role of schooling would not be affected by the distribution of schooling in a society: income distribution is a function of the types of jobs available

[27] David Barkin, "Acceso a la educación superior y beneficios que reporta en Mexico," *Revista del Centro de Estudios Educativos* 1, no. 3 (1971): 47–74; Albert Fishlow, "Brazilian Income Size Distribution: Another Look," mimeographed (Berkeley: University of California, 1973).

[28] John W. Gurley, "The New Man in the New China," *Center Magazine* 3 (May 1970): 25–33; Martin Carnoy and Jorge Werthein, "Cuba: Economic Change and Educational Reform, 1955–1974," mimeographed (Palo Alto, Calif.: Center for Economic Studies, 1975).

Martin Carnoy

and the incomes attached to those jobs. The legitimization/reproduction of class structure argument also implies a distribution role for schooling, primarily in maintaining groups of people in the same relative income position from generation to generation.

In order to sort out these relationships and what we know about them, the discussion should be divided into two issues: the effect of education on intergenerational changes in relative income position (mobility), and its relation to *intra*generational changes in income distribution.

The first of these issues has been the object of many studies, particularly by sociologists.[29] In the most recent of these studies in the United States, Sewell and Hauser found that education and occupational status of parents are highly correlated with children's educational attainment, but that, while the overall effect of parents' status and income is the single most important variable explaining a person's current income, his educational attainment is almost as important. The overall explainability of earnings variation by parents' socioeconomic status and by a person's IQ and educational attainment is very low (less than 10 percent). This was Jencks's argument as well. On the other hand, a person's occupational status seems to be largely explained by educational attainment, not parents' social status.[30] If these results are correct, schooling appears to increase mobility, even when parents' social class background is accounted for both in explaining how much schooling is taken and in the income equation.

In low-income countries, the effect of schooling on earnings appears to be greater than in the United States;[31] but very few of the low-income-country studies carry out an analysis where the effect of parents' social

[29] J. E. Floud, A. H. Halsey, and F. M. Martin, *Social Class and Educational Opportunity* (London: William Heinemann, Ltd., 1957); Robert Havighurst and Aparecida J. Gouveia, *Brazilian Secondary Education and Socio-Economic Development* (New York: Praeger Publishers, 1969); Christopher Jencks et al., *Inequality* (New York: Basic Books, 1972); see also Sewell and Hauser (n. 14 above).

[30] Sewell and Hauser.

[31] Martin Carnoy, "Earnings and Schooling in Mexico," pp. 408–19; Thias and Carnoy, pp. 124–42; Martin Carnoy, Richard Sack, and Hans Thias, *Systems Analysis in Education: A Case of Tunisian Secondary Schools* (Washington, D.C.: World Bank, in press); Alejandro Toledo, "Education, Employment, and the Distribution of Labor Income in Peru, 1961 and 1972" (paper presented at OECD Development Center Conference on Education and Employment, Paris, July 1975); Claudio Castro, "Investment in Education in Brazil: A Study of Two Industrial Communities" (Ph.D. diss., Vanderbilt University, 1970); Jacques Rocha Velloso, "Human Capital and Market Segmentation: An Analysis of the Distribution of Earnings in Brazil, 1970" (Ph.D. diss., Stanford University, 1975); Pak Wai Liu, "Education and Socioeconomic Status in Labor Market Segmentation: A Case Study in Singapore" (paper presented at OECD Development Center Conference on Education and Employment, Paris, July 1975).

Economic Development and Cultural Change

class background is related to both child's school attainment and child's income. In those cases where this is done (Tunisia and Singapore, for example), the results indicate that the effect of schooling on earnings is much greater than in the United States. And schooling and social class variables together explain a higher fraction of variance in low-income countries. In the studies where the social-class-of-parents variable does not enter, schooling alone as an explanation of earnings is more important than in U.S. estimates.

These results lead us to believe that, much more than in high-income countries, schooling and socioeconomic-background variables in developing economies are together highly related to earnings and occupational position. In other words, there appears to be less of a "chance" factor in a person attaining his or her economic position in the low-income situation. Although there is not very much information about whether parents' social class in low-income countries is important in explaining the amount of schooling taken by children, recent work in Brazil indicates that parents' social class explains about 50 percent of the variance in individual educational attainment.[32] Work in Kenya also shows a high correlation between father's income and the amount and kind of schooling taken.[33] As far as intergenerational mobility is concerned, then, schooling undoubtedly contributes in developing societies to such mobility, but parents' social class seems to be very influential in determining how much schooling a person gets. Schooling to an important degree appears to confirm a person's parents' social class and legitimizes the passing of that social position from one generation to the next. The relation varies from country to country: I tend to believe that this role of schooling is more pronounced in Latin America, for example, than in Africa, where multiple social structures still exist (tribal vs. colonial). But even in Africa, as Mwaniki's work indicates, new social structures based on European-type peasant/worker/urban bourgeoisie divisions are developing rapidly.

The issue of schooling's role in intragenerational variation in income is much more complex. As early as the mid-1950s, Kuznets argued in his presidential address to the American Economic Association[34] that he felt that the distribution of income became more equalized as an economy reached higher levels of income per capita (see also Mincer,

[32] Isaura Belloni and Glaura Miranda, "The Determinants of Educational Attainment in Minas Gerais, Brazil" (paper presented at ECIEL Conference, Lima, Peru, August 1975).

[33] Dinguri Mwaniki, "Education and Socio-Economic Development in Kenya: A Study of the Distribution of Resources for Education" (Ph.D. diss., Stanford University, 1973).

[34] Simon Kuznets, "Economic Growth and Income Inequality," *American Economic Review* 45 (May 1955): 1–28.

Martin Carnoy

and the Kuznets article which appeared in *EDCC* in 1959).[35] One of
the principal reasons for this equalization, in Kuznets's view, was the
higher education of the labor force in higher-income economies. In other
words, an increased level of schooling in the labor force contributes to a
more equal distribution of earnings.

In part, Kuznets came to this conclusion because he felt that a
more educated labor force is more likely to agitate politically for a more
equal wage structure, but there are also good economic reasons in the
neoclassical framework for believing that higher average schooling will
contribute to a lower variance in earnings: if there is a direct connection between education and productivity, and between productivity and
earnings, raising the average level of schooling could eventually reduce
the variance of years of schooling in the labor force. There probably is
an upper limit on how much schooling people would be willing to take,
since there are fewer and fewer years in which to collect increased
earnings from such additional schooling, and since governments seem
increasingly committed to providing a minimum level of schooling to its
young population, with that minimum rising as the average level of
schooling in the labor force rises. These two effects reduce the variance
of schooling in the labor force over time and should, if the connection
between education, productivity, and earnings holds, also reduce the
variance in productivity and hence in earnings. The reduction in the
variance of schooling in the labor force can be affected directly by concentrating investment in lower levels of schooling.[36] In any case, varying
the distribution of schooling in the labor force should have a direct
effect on the distribution of earnings if the causal connection between
these two variables really exists.

In his study of the drastic decrease in income equality in Brazil
between 1960 and 1970, Langoni[37] explains the change in precisely
this way: the distribution became more unequal in part because the distribution of schooling became more unequal—Brazilian university education expanded much more rapidly than primary school. Indeed, Langoni goes along with Kuznets on another implicit assumption (made
explicit in Langoni's work): not only was the change in distribution of
schooling partly responsible for the change in earnings distribution, but
the pattern of the expansion of education was a "natural" phenomenon
in the economic growth process. So, just as Kuznets uses "natural"

[35] Simon Kuznets, "Quantitative Aspects of the Economic Growth of Nations.
IV. Distribution of National Income by Factor Shares," *Economic Development
and Cultural Change,* 7, no. 3, pt. 2 (April 1959); Jacob Mincer, "Investment
in Human Capital and Personal Distribution of Income," *Journal of Political Economy* 66 (August 1958): 281–301.

[36] Fishlow (n. 27 above).

[37] Carlos Langoni, *A Distribuçaõ da renda e desenvolvimento econômica
do Brasil* (Rio de Janeiro: Editora expressaõ e cultura, 1973).

Economic Development and Cultural Change

forces in the economic growth process to predict an evolution to more equal income distribution, Langoni uses them to explain an increasingly unequal income distribution.

But if productivity is primarily a function of jobs, not characteristics of workers, as in the queue theory, the effect on income distribution of changing the distribution of schooling in the labor force should be negligible. It would be the job or income structure itself which would have to be changed in order to influence income distribution. Education would serve to allocate people to jobs with various earnings attached to them. In a case where their distribution were highly unequal, the value of additional schooling would be high, and in the case where their distribution were more equal, the value of additional schooling would be correspondingly lower. Again, in the Brazilian case, Malan and Wells[38] present evidence that the increased inequality of Brazilian incomes did not occur during the rapid growth period of the late sixties, but rather in a single year, 1965–66, when the Brazilian government intervened directly in the wage structure by holding wages fixed during an inflationary period and allowing salaries of higher paid workers to raise more rapidly than prices. Although no other country has had an empirical debate of this sort, data for Chile[39] also indicate that changes in the distribution of schooling during the 1960s apparently had a negligible effect on income distribution, while direct government wage policy during three successive regimes (1964–75) significantly increased inequality (1966–70), reduced inequality (1970–73), and drastically increased inequality (1973–75).

United States data, furthermore, point to unemployment as a key factor in income distribution, apparently more important than either the level of education or its distribution.[40] The fact that employment (number of days worked annually) is a function of policies which have little to do with schooling (business cycles, the direct intervention of the state in fiscal and monetary policy, or even direct controls over investment and employment) again suggests that the distribution of income, while possibly related to the distribution of education in the labor force, is more closely related to government macroeconomic strategy directly related to incomes policies: If a government is dedicated to ensuring full employment and reducing the variance of earnings in the labor force as

[38] Pedro Malan and John Wells, "Distribuçaõ da renda e desenvolvimento econômico do Brasil," *Pesquisa e planejamento economico,* vol. 3 (December 1973).

[39] Christian Eyzguirre Johnston, "Educación y distribución del ingreso" (thesis presented to the Faculty of Economics, University of Chile, December 1973); Andre Gunder Frank, "An Open Letter about Chile to Arnold Harberger and Milton Friedman," *Radical Review of Political Economics* 7 (Summer 1975): 61–76.

[40] Chiswick and Mincer (n. 11 above), pp. S34–S36.

Martin Carnoy

part of its development policy (Israel and Sweden, for example), the income distribution will be more equal than in economies where the government is primarily concerned with shifting income to professionals and administrators (Brazil and Mexico, for example). It is likely that, in both cases, educational investment will be oriented to be consistent with the overall incomes policy (although in Chile between 1964 and 1973 it was not), so it may be a moot point to separate the effect of education from the direct intervention of the state. Nevertheless, in the studies I have cited, education seems to play a rather limited role.

It is important to note that in most of the literature on both inter-generational and intragenerational education/earnings relations, the dependent variable being discussed is wages and salaries (earnings)—not income. But wages and salaries represent only a fraction of the total product of the economy—about 65–75 percent in the United States,[41] 70–75 percent in western Europe,[42] and perhaps as low as 55 percent or less in Latin America. Even if changing the distribution of wages and salaries through an educational policy could work, it would therefore affect less than three-fifths of the total income distribution in low-income countries unless other measures were taken to equalize wealth. Similarly, making the access to wages and salaries less dependent on father's education and earnings (through making access to education more equal for various groups, for example) would probably have little effect on the access to nonwage/salary income derived from capital wealth (land and physical capital). While there are large variations in wage and salary income in every nonsocialist country, these variations are considerably smaller than the distribution of all income (which includes income from physical wealth).

Where Does the Theory Go from Here?

Analysis of the role of education in economic development has proceeded rapidly in the last 15 years. While there are a number of conflicting hypotheses concerning the relationship between education and growth and between education and the distribution of wages and salaries, we have learned quite a lot about the possible nature of these relationships. The principal confrontation now taking place is in the interpretation of a large body of data and the emphasis on some empirical results rather than others.

A major deficiency to date is that both the theory of education's role in societal change and empirical studies of that role have been

[41] Kuznets, "Quantitative Aspects of the Economic Growth of Nations"; Fritz Machlup, "Micro- and Macro-Economics," in *Essays in Economic Semantics,* ed. Merton H. Miller (Englewood Cliffs, N.J.: Prentice-Hall, Inc., 1963).

[42] Edward Denison and Jean Pierre Poullier, *Why Growth Rates Differ* (Washington, D.C.: Brookings Institution, 1967).

Economic Development and Cultural Change

rather ahistorical. The understanding and knowledge we have gleaned
have derived almost entirely from cross-sectional studies at a single
point in time. In part this is true because the issue is so young and
data have not been gathered over past time; but in part, the problem
also lies in the ahistorical nature of U.S. social science. In the future,
then, to delve deeper into the role of schooling requires more historical studies of education. These can be classified into (*a*) longitudinal
studies, using data collected on individuals or groups over time; and
(*b*) historiography, which studies the expansion of education in the
past and the role it played in social change.

Longitudinal Studies

Longitudinal work has, of course, already been done, and its results
have generally confirmed cross-sectional studies. Husén[43] analyzed follow-up data on a group of Swedes in Malmö who were first tested in
1938, when they were 10 years old. His "26-year follow-up," begun
in 1964, showed that schooling was the single most important factor
explaining economic success of individuals in this group, but that the
amount of schooling taken is heavily influenced by the social class
background of students. In later work with the same sample, Fägerlind[44] found that the effect on earnings of education and its social class
and IQ precedents increases as individuals get older.

Other longitudinal work is proceeding in the United States based
on a sample taken by Parnes and his associates at Ohio State and the
Project Talent survey taken in the early sixties.[45] Although follow-up
studies will be rare in low-income countries because of the greater
scarcity of base data and the high cost of such studies, the International
Labor Organization's World Employment Project is, for example, following up a survey of Tunisian secondary school students taken in
1969.[46] Although neither the United States nor Tunisian analyses span
the length of time covered by the Swedish data, they can reveal the
effect of schooling on individuals' early employment and income and,
in the case of the Parnes data, on schooling's role in what happens to
people in mid-career.

Another type of "longitudinal" study which has already yielded
some results but will be more important in the future is the analysis
of cross-section results over time, using comparable samples. Welch,

[43] Thorsten Husén, *Talent, Opportunity, and Career* (Stockholm: Almquist
& Wiksell, 1969).

[44] I. Fägerlind, *Formal Education and Adult Earnings* (Stockholm: Almquist
& Wiksell, 1975).

[45] Herbert Parnes, "Longitudinal Surveys: Prospects and Problems," *Monthly
Labor Review* 95 (February 1972): 11–15; Hause (n. 10 above), pp. S108–S138.

[46] Carnoy et al. (n. 31 above).

Martin Carnoy

Freeman, Fuchs, and Carnoy and Marenbach[47] are just several examples in the United States of studies which utilized surveys to make such intertemporal comparisons of the economic payoff to various groups in the labor force (blacks, women, and white males), and of the possible role of schooling in affecting economic position. Chiswick and Mincer in the United States and Langoni, Malan and Wells, and Velloso in Brazil have similarly analyzed the role of schooling in a changing income distribution over time. We will soon have additional studies in Peru and Mexico.[48]

The important contribution that longtitudinal studies will make to our understanding of education in development is their analysis of change over time within a single country. When we make estimates from cross-sectional studies, inferences from such estimates require the assumption that different groups of individuals or countries will follow the same process through time as other groups which have higher education and higher earnings or more or less equal income distribution. While the assumption may be a valid one, we have little knowledge of the process of getting from one point to another; the theory of economic development is, after all, primarily a theory of process. Some of the most important unanswered questions about schooling and economic development deal with the effect on those individuals and groups who get more schooling.

Such empirical studies, however, do share one serious deficiency with cross-section analysis: both rely on correlations for understanding causality. They do not usually tell us, for example, whether the correlation between education and earnings is an education-productivity relation; they do not reveal whether the relation between the distribution of earnings and education is the result of productivity effects of simultaneous income distribution and schooling distribution policies by the same government.

To study these issues, future projects should examine the historical role of education in the development process. The economic history of education (as it might be called) will give us a clearer picture of how and why education was expanded in a particular place and period of history and, at the same time, help us understand general development policy (including wage policy) in the period being studied.

[47] Finis Welch, "Education and Racial Discrimination," in *Discrimination in Labor Markets*, ed. O. Ashenfelter (Princeton, N.J.: Princeton University Press, 1974); Richard Freeman, "Changes in the Labor Market for Black Americans, 1948–72," in *Brookings Papers on Economic Activity, 1:1973* (Washington, D.C.: Brookings Institution, 1974); Victor Fuchs, "Recent Trends and Long-Run Prospects for Female Earnings," *American Economic Review* 64 (May 1974): 236–42; Martin Carnoy and Deiter Marenbach, "The Rate of Return to Education in the United States, 1939–69," *Journal of Human Resources* 10 (Summer 1975): 312–31.

[48] Toledo (n. 31 above); Jose Lobo, "Education and Income Distribution in Mexico, 1960–70" (Ph.D. diss., Stanford University, 1977).

Economic Development and Cultural Change

Histories of education have been written, of course (although not many outside of the United States and western Europe), but these usually take a "cultural" point of view, that is, that education was spread as an end in itself to liberate people from ignorance or to bring them into a new, more civilized culture. Recently, sociologists, economists, and revisionist historians have questioned this approach by writing new interpretations of educational expansion within the context of economic and social change. Katz, Spring, Karier, Tyack, and Bowles and Gintis for the United States; Foster for Ghana; Quick for England; and Carnoy for the Third World in general all provide us with insight into the role of education in the process of economic and social change.[49] They claim that education serves the needs of the economic and social system, particularly the dominant economic groups in that system and the bureaucracy of the educational system itself.[50] Foster stresses individual investor sovereignty when faced by a set of educational choices within a given social structure. Other studies[51] emphasize the correspondence between allowable individual educational decisions and the economic/social needs of a dominant class of capitalists or capitalist intermediaries.

These are different views of educational expansion, but the important point here is not so much their difference; rather, it is the theoretical framework they develop for social scientific education/economic growth studies. In the future, much of the controversy about the relation between schooling and development will occur through the historiographic literature, both that literature which deals with the more distant past and that of the near present (such as Spring[52] on post–World War II in the United States and Malan and Wells on Brazilian income distribution in the 1960s). We have to have carefully supported theories of why educational reforms occurred and what effect these reforms had for different groups in the economy. We also must have a better understanding of the meaning of economic growth during particular historical periods. Which groups' income or share of product rose and

[49] Michael Katz, *The Irony of Early School Reform* (Cambridge, Mass.: Harvard University Press, 1968), and *Class, Bureaucracy, and Schools* (New York: Praeger Publishers, 1971); Joel Spring, "Education and the Corporate State," *Socialist Revolution* 2 (March/April 1972): 80–81; Clarence Karier, "Testing for Order and Control in the Corporate State," mimeographed (Urbana-Champaign: University of Illinois, 1972); David Tyack, *The One Best System* (Cambridge, Mass.: Harvard University Press, 1975); Samuel Bowles and Herbert Gintis, *Schooling in a Capitalist Society* (New York: Basic Books, 1975); Philip Foster, *Education and Social Change in Ghana* (London: Routledge & Kegan Paul, 1965); Patricia Mary Quick, "Education and Industrialization: Elementary Education in Nineteenth Century England and Wales" (Ph.D. diss., Harvard University, 1974); Carnoy, *Education as Cultural Imperialism*.

[50] Tyack.

[51] Bowles and Gintis; Carnoy, *Education as Cultural Imperialism*.

[52] Joel Spring, *The Sorting Machine* (New York: David McKay Co., 1976).

Martin Carnoy

which stayed constant or fell? Was this differential income growth, for example, related to differential schooling?

There are two subfields of these historical studies which will be especially crucial to our understanding of the education/development issue. The first is studies of the role of the state in economic development. The second is the study of labor markets. Neoclassical economic theory has left us with deficiencies in both these areas—in understanding the state because neoclassical theory views the state as largely distorting, for obscure political reasons, the optimum allocation of resources by the free market; and in understanding the labor market institutions because in neoclassical theory the labor market is a derivative of the market for goods and the number of people available for various kinds of jobs. Whether or not the state should provide free education, a source of debate among neoclassical economists in the past (see Blaug[53] for a review of that debate), the fact is that the state is, and has been for a long time, massively involved with trying to control formal schooling in most countries. What is the relationship among the state, the private production sectors, and education in capitalist societies? between the state and various social class groups? between the state and the educational bureaucracy it created? between state economic planning and the educational bureaucracy in socialist societies? The way the state provides education may have a lot to do with intergenerational mobility and changes in the distribution of income over time; thus, understanding the process of public investment in education would be a major contribution to development theory.

Naturally, this assumes that education not only has an effect on individual income but on overall income distribution. A key to testing this assumption and also the relationship between education and productivity is in more extensive historical and time-series studies of the nature of labor markets. Again, such studies have appeared in the past in already industrialized countries, but they have rarely included workers' education as a variable. Recently, the theory of labor markets (including formal schooling in the labor force as a variable) has been the focus of an important debate among economists,[54] and this debate will undoubtedly spread to the lower-income countries.[55] The opera-

[53] Mark Blaug, *An Introduction to the Economics of Education* (London: Penguin Press, 1970).

[54] David Gordon, *Theories of Poverty and Unemployment* (Lexington, Mass.: Heath Lexington Books, 1972); Peter Doeringer and Michael Piore, *Internal Labor Markets and Manpower Training* (Lexington, Mass.: Heath Lexington Books, 1971); Michael Reich, David Gordon, and Richard Edwards, "Labor Market Segmentation in American Capitalism" (paper presented at the Conference on Labor Market Segmentation, Harvard University, March 1973); Michael Carter and Martin Carnoy, "Theories of Labor Markets and Worker Productivity," mimeographed (Palo Alto, Calif.: Center for Economic Studies, 1974).

[55] Velloso (n. 31 above); Liu (n. 31 above).

Economic Development and Cultural Change

tion of such markets is at the center of the discussion of whether education increases productivity and hence contributes to growth, or whether the state's involvement in schooling is primarily a means of subsidizing the return to capital (the screen) or primarily a means of reproducing the capitalist (or postcapitalist) organization of production, and hence does not contribute much to growth but does maintain the hierarchy of power largely unchanged from generation to generation.

It is future longitudinal and historical research, with its focus on the role of the state in providing public education and on the functioning and structure of labor markets, which will help us more fully grasp what education really does in the process of economic and social development.

[18]

Earnings, Schooling, Ability, and Cognitive Skills

By M. BOISSIERE, J. B. KNIGHT, AND R. H. SABOT*

Conventional estimates now available for a large number of countries generally indicate that the social returns to education are positive, large, and competitive with returns to investment in physical capital.[1] That such estimates are good guides for public resource allocation has, however, been questioned. The heart of the problem lies in the interpretation of the positive relationship between the education and the earnings of workers: whether, as the conventional estimates assume, the coefficient of the education variable in the earnings function measures the effect on the productivity of workers of human capital acquired in school. It has been hypothesized that education in part, or instead, represents screening for native ability and motivation, or credentialism, and that as a consequence conventional measures of the social benefit of education are substantially upward biased.[2]

In this paper we attempt to distinguish the influence on earnings of cognitive achievement, native ability, and years of education as a means of adjudicating the human capital, screening, and credentialist hypotheses. Our econometric analysis is based on two rigorously comparable micro data sets from Kenya and Tanzania, generated by surveys of the urban wage-labor force specifically for this study. These data sets contain the usual variables found in earnings function estimates of the benefits of schooling—individual earnings, years of education, and years of employment experience. In addition, they contain two variables—measures of the worker's cognitive skills and of his or her reasoning ability—not previously found in studies of developing countries and only rarely found in studies of the education-earnings relationship in developed countries.[3] With these variables we can estimate the direct effects on earnings of cognitive skills, ability, and years of schooling. By using them to estimate educational production functions and educational attainment functions, and linking these functions with the earnings function in a recursive framework, we can also assess the various indirect effects on earnings of ability and years of schooling. Having data sets from two countries very similar with respect to size, resource endowments, structure of production and employment, and level of development means that not only can we subject our results to the usual statistical tests, but we can also assess their replicability.

Both Kenya and Tanzania have nearly achieved the objective of universal primary education while university enrollments remain at less than 1 percent of the relevant age group. The important policy issues re-

*Boissiere: Development Research Department, The World Bank, 1818 H Street, Washington, D.C. 20433; Knight: Institute of Economics and Statistics, Oxford University; Sabot: Williams College, Williamstown, MA 01267. We are grateful to the Educational Testing Service of Princeton for the design of tests used in this study and to J. Armitage, J. Behrman, J. Hausman, D. Hendry, D. Jamison, and an anonymous referee for their insights and advice. Helpful comments were also received from participants in seminars at Oxford and Yale universities. The views presented here are our own; they should not be interpreted as reflecting those of the World Bank.

[1] George Psacharopoulos (1973; 1981) contains a listing of 44 countries in which rate of return studies had been conducted and of the estimates obtained.

[2] For instance, Kenneth Arrow (1973), Mark Blaug (1976), Samuel Bowles and Herbert Gintis (1976), John Riley (1979), Michael Spence (1976), and Lester Thurow (1975).

[3] For attempts to control for ability and/or for cognitive achievement in studies for the United States, see Jere Behrman et al. (1980), Gary Chamberlain and Zvi Griliches (1977), Griliches and William Mason (1972), Michael Olneck (1977), Paul Taubman and Terence Wales (1974), Taubman (1975), and David Wise (1975); see also the survey articles by Griliches (1977; 1979). In most instances the data refer to special subgroups in the population and clear distinction cannot be made between natural ability and cognitive skills acquired in school.

garding mass education in East Africa arise at the secondary level. We are therefore concerned to evaluate the benefits of secondary education. The public educational system in both countries is meritocratic and years of education may thus provide good signals of ability. The public sector is an influential employer of urban labor in East Africa, accounting in 1980 for 39 and 61 percent of the total in Kenya and Tanzania, respectively. Moreover, institutional arrangements suggest that access to public sector employment grades and entry pay are influenced by educational qualifications. Explanations of the earnings-education relationship in terms of screening or credentialism cannot therefore be dismissed in the present context.

Section II presents our recursive model of ability, years of education, cognitive achievement, and earnings. Section III discusses our data. Estimates of the model are presented —earnings functions in Section IV and educational production and attainment functions in Section V—and their implications for the human capital, screening and credentialist hypotheses are discussed.

I. The Model

In the conventional measurement of the social rate of return to (say) secondary education, the benefit stream is estimated by means of an earnings function, of which the following, for a sample of primary and secondary school completers, is an example:

$$(1) \quad \ln W = a + bS + cL + dL^2 + u$$

where $\ln W$ = log of (pre-tax) earnings of the individual, S = dummy variable signifying that the individual has precisely completed secondary education, individuals with a complete primary education forming the base subcategory,[4] L = the number of years of employment experience of the individual, and u = a disturbance term.

[4]Schooling is introduced as a dichotomous rather than a continuous variable for reasons of survey design, to be discussed below.

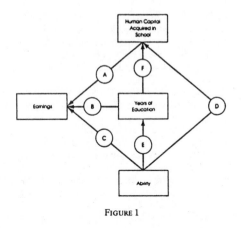

FIGURE 1

The term S is interpreted as a proxy for the cognitive skills or other marketable traits acquired in secondary education. The cross-section earnings function is used to simulate two time-series, $\hat{W}_p$ and $\hat{W}_s$, representing the predicted earnings, over their expected working-lives, of primary and secondary school leavers, respectively. The difference between the educational groups in predicted lifetime earnings is then used as the estimate of the social benefits of secondary education, from which the rate of return can be calculated.

The criticism of the assumptions underlying this approach can be illustrated in terms of Figure 1, which presents a simple structural model of the relationships among earnings, years of education, natural ability, and human capital. For these four variables, the figure depicts those which are determinants of human capital (the vertical arrows), of earnings (the horizontal arrows), and of both. Of the six links depicted, equation (1) includes only B, the relationship between years of education and earnings. The coefficient on S in (1) will be an unbiased estimate of the effect on earnings of skills acquired in school only under certain stringent conditions.

The first condition is that years of education must—through the relation F—provide an accurate measure of the human capital acquired in school. The market value of this human capital, determined by marginal product, must then determine earnings via A. However, years of education, being one input into the educational production function, may be a poor guide to the output from the function. Second, years of education must influence earnings only indirectly, through $F + A$. If there is a direct relationship, through B, which is positive, the coefficient on years of education overstates the human capital effect. The loose amalgam of hypotheses concerning the payment for educational qualifications irrespective of their economic value, generally known as "credentialism," stresses the direct effect of years of education on earnings. According to this view, schools provide students with a credential which is personally valuable but not productive. For instance, the government may determine wages and establish education-based hiring and payment criteria, or private employers may discriminate in favor of the educated with whom they share similar socioeconomic backgrounds.

The third condition is that, if ability is correlated with years of education (E), it must have no direct (C) or indirect (via $E + B$) effect on earnings: positive relationships imply that the coefficient on S in (1) overstates the effect on earnings of skills acquired in school, that is, the effect of ability is wrongly attributed to years of education. Employers may reward ability on an individual basis or, according to the theory of educational screening for ability, they may use years of education as a means of identifying workers who are potentially more productive, drawing on two stochastic relationships, E and C. Educational attainment "signals" workers with greater average ability, and it is this ability, rather than what is actually learned in school, that is rewarded. There is, however, a way in which ability can strengthen the human capital relationship between earnings and education. If educational selection criteria are meritocratic in the sense that they promote the more able (relation E), then years of education are more efficiently transformed into cognitive skills (on account of D): $E + F + A$ and $D + A$ influence but do not bias the estimate of the effect on earnings of skills acquired in school.

To capture the complex relationships depicted in Figure 1 we take cognitive skills to be a measure of human capital and reasoning ability to be a measure of predetermined natural ability, and posit a recursive model represented in the following three equations:

$$(2) \qquad S = a_0 + a_1 R + a_2 E + a_{3i} F_i + v$$

$$(3) \qquad H = b_0 + b_1 R + b_2 S + b_3 G + b_4 B + y$$

$$(4) \quad \ln W = c_0 + c_1 S + c_2 R$$
$$+ c_3 H + c_4 L + c_5 L^2 + z$$

where R = reasoning ability, E = an indicator of the aggregate probability of attending secondary school when the individual was aged 14, F_i = indicators of parental educational background, H = cognitive achievement, G = an indicator of attendance at a government (as opposed to private) school, B = an indicator of urban (as opposed to rural) birth, and v, y, z = disturbance terms.[5]

Equation (2) reflects the influence of natural ability on educational attainment within a subsidized and competitive educational system (relation E in Figure 1). Equation (3) is an educational production function, incorporating relations D and F; it is similar in form to those used in most such studies.[6] The earnings function specified in equation (4) includes relations A, B, and C. As opposed to the "conventional human capital model" in (1), we refer to (4) as the "expanded human capital model."

II. The Data

The data for this investigation come from rigorously comparable surveys administered by a team (including the authors) in the two countries within a few months of each other in 1980. The full samples were randomly

---

[5] Full definitions of variables are provided and the system is tested for recursiveness in the subsequent sections.

[6] See the reviews of Eric Hanushek (1979) and L. Lau (1979).

selected on an establishment basis, using a two-stage procedure, from among the wage-labor force of Nairobi and of Dar es Salaam. Establishments from all sectors of the urban economy—public and private, manufacturing and nonmanufacturing—are represented.[7] The main questionnaire was administered to the full sample, and provides the information on earnings,[8] education, employment experience, and other personal characteristics. Not all the respondents were given the three tests that yielded our measures of reasoning ability, literacy, and numeracy: testing was confined to a random subsample of primary- and secondary-completers.[9] Whereas the full samples each contained some 2,000 employees, the subsamples numbered 205 in Kenya and 179 in Tanzania. The analysis using the test results is necessarily confined to the subsamples. The survey design thus requires that schooling be entered as a dichotomous rather than a continuous variable.

Reasoning ability was tested by means of "Raven's Progressive Matrices" (see J. C. Raven, 1956). This test involves the matching of pictorial patterns, for which literacy and

numeracy provide no advantage; it has been widely used in developing countries.[10] The tests of reading achievement and mathematics were designed by the Educational Testing Service of Princeton specifically for use in these surveys. The designs were based on questions in national primary-leaving and Form IV examinations and on other guides to the content of the academic curriculum, which is much the same in Kenya as in Tanzania. The major difference is that use of Swahili is stressed more in Tanzania; questions were therefore set in both English and Swahili for respondents to choose the language they preferred. The sum of the scores on the literacy and numeracy tests is used as the measure of cognitive skill.[11] The frequency distributions of test scores for each sample as a whole and for primary- and secondary-leavers reveal considerable variance on each test, a desirable characteristic for dependent and independent variable alike. All three tests appear to have been appropriate for the target groups: there are very few perfect scores and no zero scores, suggesting that the results do not suffer from the common problem of truncation of the ability or achievement distribution that arises when questions are too easy or too difficult.

Although these measures represent a distinct advance, their limitations should be recognized in the interpretation of the results to come. Because secondary schools select entrants partly on the basis of performance in primary-leaving examinations, the difference between primary- and secondary-leavers in mean achievement scores may exaggerate the value added by secondary education. However, our test of whether selection by cognitive achievement for secondary school qualifies our assumption of recursiveness proved negative. Noncognitive traits, such as attitudes and interests, may also be acquired in school and may be valued in the labor market. Natural ability may

---

[7] Neither very small establishments (< 5 employees) nor establishments in urban and rural areas outside the capital cities were included in our samples. Since selectivity by unmeasured personal characteristics in the surveyed capital city establishments is likely to be stronger at the primary than at the secondary level, however, any consequent sample selection bias is likely to understate the benefits of cognitive skill acquisition, so strengthening the argument of this paper.

[8] Sometimes referred to below as wages. As data are generally available only on earnings per month and not on hours worked, it is not possible to estimate separate wage and hours functions, nor to establish whether higher cognitive skill causes people to work more productively as opposed to longer hours. However, the influence of longer hours is unlikely to have been important: only 20 percent of the sample had worked overtime in Kenya, and 31 percent in Tanzania; the percentages for nonmanual employees being 10 and 23 percent, respectively. Whether overtime was worked appeared to depend mainly on the nature of the job and the characteristics of the employer.

[9] It took half an hour per respondent to complete the questionnaire and an hour per respondent to administer the tests. Given its small size, the subsample was stratified by education to ensure sufficient observations in strata of particular interest.

[10] See, for example, E. L. Klingelhofer (1967), M. Wober (1969), and U. Sinha (1968).

[11] The ability score is marked out of 36, the achievement score out of 63 (34 for numeracy and 29 for literacy).

1020 *THE AMERICAN ECONOMIC REVIEW* *DECEMBER 1985*

involve not only reasoning power, but also such unmeasured but marketable qualities as drive, determination, and dynamism. If the test scores are too narrow as measures of natural ability and human capital formation, the R and H coefficients are likely to understate their importance. Insofar as the omitted variables are positively correlated with educational attainment, the coefficient on S is likely to overstate the importance of credentialism. Finally, the ability that we measure may not be due entirely to heredity and home environment: education may have enhanced reasoning power.[12] However, the fact that the weighted subsample mean values of R are not significantly different (27.8 in Kenya and 26.4 in Tanzania), whereas those of H are significantly different (40.0 and 30.3, respectively), on account of the greater quantity and quality of secondary education in Kenya,[13] suggests that R is not acquired in school.

III. The Expanded Human Capital Earnings Function

Estimates of the conventional human capital earnings function (equation (1)) for Kenya and Tanzania are shown in column 1 of Table 1.[14] In Kenya workers are paid a premium of 4.2 percent per year of employment experience, and secondary-leavers are paid 61 percent more than primary-leavers. In Tanzania the returns to experience are higher (5.5 percent), but because of Tanzania's vigorously imposed pay policy the gain from secondary education, though substantial, is lower (32 percent).[15]

---

[12] In that case, the coefficient on ability is liable to be upward biased and that on achievement downward biased.

[13] See Knight and Sabot (1984).

[14] The equations were also estimated with a squared experience term, but whereas the coefficient was negative as expected, it was not significantly different from zero.

[15] The Tanzania government has compressed the structure of wages in the dominant, public sector. In the relatively unfettered private sector, the premium on secondary education is higher than in the public sector and, indeed, higher than in Kenya. We recognize that the competitive market value of secondary education in Tanzania is greater than our estimates suggest. See Knight and Sabot (1983).

A. Do Cognitive Skills and Ability Matter?

Column 2, Table 1, permits a comparison of estimates of the conventional and expanded human capital earnings functions in Kenya and Tanzania. In neither country are the estimated returns to experience affected by the introduction of variables measuring (cognitive) achievement and (reasoning) ability. By contrast, the premium on secondary education declines by nearly two-thirds in both countries, and in Tanzania it is no longer significantly different from zero. In neither country is the independent influence of ability on earnings either large or significant. By contrast, in both countries the coefficient on the achievement score is positive, significant, and large relative to the coefficient on the ability score.[16]

B. Do Cognitive Skills Matter for Manual as Well as for Nonmanual Workers?

The results of the stratified regressions (cols. 5 and 6) show that in both countries the payment for cognitive skills is not confined to white-collar workers: manual workers are also rewarded for literacy and numeracy. Although the coefficient on H is higher for nonmanual (0.017) than for manual workers (0.013) in Kenya and also in Tanzania (0.012 and 0.008, respectively), F-tests indicate that in neither country is the difference in the coefficient on H significant as between occupations. It seems that accomplishment in the basic skills of reading and numbering enables mechanics, machinists, and fork-lift drivers as well as accountants, clerks, and secretaries to do a better job.[17] By contrast, in no case is the coefficient on R significant.[18]

---

[16] This result holds when either the literacy or numeracy score replaces the combined score.

[17] In only one of the four cases (manual workers in Tanzania) is the coefficient on achievement not significant at the 5 percent level.

[18] When the samples are stratified instead by educational levels, F-tests indicate precisely equivalent results for the achievement variable. The effect of ability on earnings remains small by comparison with the effect on achievement, and not significantly different from zero in three of the four cases.

VOL. 75 NO. 5   *BOISSIERE ET AL.: EARNINGS AND SCHOOLING*   1021

TABLE 1—HUMAN CAPITAL EARNINGS FUNCTIONS WITH AND WITHOUT MEASURES OF ABILITY
AND COGNITIVE ACHIEVEMENT[a]

	Whole Subsample (1)	Whole Subsample (2)	Primary Leavers (3)	Secondary Leavers (4)	Manual Workers (5)	White-Collar Workers (6)
Kenya						
L	.042	.045	.031	.062	.036	.049
	(8.40)	(9.84)	(4.49)	(10.20)	(6.02)	(8.64)
S	.476	.192	–	–	.065	.030
	(6.70)	(2.47)			(0.650)	(0.23)
H	–	.020	.019	.023	.013	.017
		(6.18)	(3.98)	(5.40)	(3.21)	(3.55)
R	–	.006	– .000	.014	.003	.011
		(1.32)	(0.02)	(2.17)	(0.50)	(1.46)
Constant	6.297	5.459	5.811	5.171	5.866	5.705
R^2	.29	.44	.39	.50	.32	.49
N	205	205	71	134	116	88
Tanzania						
L	.054	.055	.049	.066	.044	.061
	(9.70)	(10.10)	(7.13)	(7.06)	(4.88)	(7.82)
S	.280	.112	–	–	.141	.068
	(4.30)	(1.42)			(0.85)	(0.58)
H	–	.013	.009	.013	.008	.012
		(3.22)	(1.66)	(2.29)	(1.16)	(2.25)
R	–	.001	– .001	.010	– .004	.013
		(0.15)	(0.21)	(1.01)	(0.64)	(1.51)
Constant		5.752	5.908	5.476	5.027	5.423
R^2	.38	.43	.34	.47	.24	.46
N	179	179	107	72	87	88

[a] The dependent variable is ln W. The t-statistics are shown in parentheses.

C. *Could Cognitive Skills Represent Anything But Human Capital?*

Administered wage scales might explain why employers would pay a premium to workers with more years of education even if they were not more productive. Screening for ability might similarly explain such a premium even if the cognitive skills acquired in school had no economic value. Neither of these accounts, however, could also explain why cognitive skills are rewarded within an educational stratum.

Whereas employers could ascertain the length of education of job applicants, they did not have our test scores to provide them with independent measures of numeracy and literacy. Grades of pass in the national secondary-leaving examination do provide employers with a ready indication of cognitive achievement and ability. There is evidence for Kenya, where competition for jobs among secondary-leavers is intense, that examina-

tion scores are used as a selection criterion. We therefore expect, and find, a significantly positive relation between grade of pass and starting wage.[19] Similarly, our achievement test score bears a positive and significant relationship to the starting wage in Kenya. If, however, these results reflected the favoring of good examinees for reasons of "fairness" or for screening purposes, rather than simply for their cognitive skills, we would expect the relation to decline as employment experience lengthens. On the contrary, in Kenya, achievement as measured by scores on our test is a markedly better predictor of current than of starting wages.[20]

[19] In a Kenya earnings function for secondary-leavers in which the worker's (constant price) starting wage is the dependent variable.

[20] The substitution of ln starting for ln current wage as the dependent variable in column 2 of Table 1 results in a reduction in the coefficient on H from .020 to .011,

In Tanzania, where secondary-leavers are in scarcer supply, there is no significant relation between starting wage and grade of secondary school pass or achievement score.[21] Yet the current returns to cognitive achievement for secondary-levers are positive and significant in both countries. Whereas in neither country do employers have ready equivalent measures of the cognitive skills of primary-leavers, in both countries the returns to cognitive achievement are of the same order of magnitude to primary- and to secondary-leavers. It would seem that employers discover the cognitive skills of their workers on the job, and that they are willing to pay for these skills.

D. *Why Do Secondary-Leavers Earn More than Primary-Leavers?*

The coefficients on the independent variables can only be suggestive of their relative importance. This, and subsequent exercises, provide measures of the relative effects of the independent variables in the earnings function on the structure and dispersion of earnings. The gross difference in (geometric) mean wages (G) between primary- and secondary-leavers (24 percent in Kenya and 30 percent in Tanzania) is decomposed.[22] The earnings of primary-leavers (denoted by the subscript p) are determined by the earnings function for primary-leavers, and by their characteristics, represented by the vector Z_p: $W_p = F_p(Z)_p$; similarly, $W_s = F_s(Z_s)$ where s denotes secondary-leavers. A bar indicates the mean value of a variable:

$$(5) \quad G = \overline{W}_s - \overline{W}_p = F_s(\overline{Z}_s) - F_p(\overline{Z}_p)$$
$$= F_s(\overline{Z}_s - \overline{Z}_p) + \left(F_s(\overline{Z}_p) - F_p(\overline{Z}_p)\right).$$

The former is the component "explained" by the differences in the mean characteristics of the two groups, and the latter is the "unexplained" component which results from differences in the constant term and coefficients of the earnings functions.[23]

We simulate the effect on the predicted wage of a representative primary-leaver (with the mean characteristics of his group) of imposing, each in turn, the characteristics of a representative secondary-leaver. In the case of achievement, for instance, the effect is to raise $\overline{W}_p$ in the proportion $c_{3p}(\overline{H}_s - \overline{H}_p)$. The effect of the difference in length of education is obtained from the unexplained residual in (5), which reflects group differences in earnings functions. The relative contributions to this premium that are made by group differences in cognitive skills, ability, years of education, and employment experience are shown in Table 2.

Secondary-leavers do not earn more because of differential experience on the job: they have *less* experience than primary-leavers, markedly so in Kenya and marginally so in Tanzania.[24] Nor does the small difference in ability as between the two educational groups explain why secondary-leavers earn more. The direct returns to ability are so low that giving primary-leavers the ability levels of secondary-leavers would increase their earnings by some 0–7 percent in Kenya and by 0–4 percent in Tanzania.[25] Giving primary-leavers four more years of education would, *ceteris paribus*, substantially increase their earnings, by 15–24 percent in Kenya and 8–18 percent in Tanzania. This could be a reflection of credentialism or of screening, but it could alternatively be the result of unmeasured noncognitive skills acquired in secondary education. The largest

i.e., the percentage response of current wage to a unit increase in H is nearly twice as great as that of starting wage.

[21] Using the same specification for Tanzania as for Kenya.

[22] By means of a technique taken from the literature on labor market discrimination; Alan Blinder (1973) and Ronald Oaxaca (1973) are pioneering examples. We decompose the differences in geometric mean wages, i.e., in antilog mean ln W, because the earnings function has ln W as dependent variable.

[23] Alternatively, the decomposition can be based on $F_p(Z_s)$ instead of $F_s(Z_p)$.

[24] Reflecting not only their later entry to the labor force but also the expansion of secondary education, and the more rapid expansion in Kenya than Tanzania.

[25] In each case, the lower end of the range is the estimate yielded by the earnings function for primary-leavers, whose returns are generally lower, and the upper end is that yielded by the earnings function for secondary-leavers.

TABLE 2—THE EFFECT OF INTRODUCING THE CHARACTERISTICS OF A REPRESENTATIVE SECONDARY-LEAVER
ON THE PREDICTED WAGE OF A REPRESENTATIVE PRIMARY-LEAVER

	Mean Value		Change in Predicted Wage Using:					
			Primary-Leaver Coefficients			Secondary-Leaver Coefficients		
	Secondary-Leavers	Primary-Leavers		$\Delta \overline{W}_s$			$\Delta \overline{W}_p$	
	$\overline{Z}_s$	$\overline{Z}_p$	$\Delta \ln \overline{W}_s$	Shillings	Percent	$\Delta \ln \overline{W}_p$	Shillings	Percent
Kenya								
W	1141.0	918.0						
$\ln W$	7.040	6.822						
H	46.3	32.3	.266	280	30.5	.322	349	38.0
R	30.3	25.7	.000	0	0.0	.064	61	6.6
L	6.4	12.6	−.192	−194.6	−21.2	−.384	−429	−46.8
S	−	−	.143	141.3	15.4	.215	220	24.0
Tanzania								
W	843.0	649.0						
$\ln W$	6.737	6.475						
H	37.5	24.7	.115	79	12.2	.166	117	18.1
R	29.0	25.0	−.004	−3	−0.4	.040	27	4.1
L	7.2	7.5	−.015	−10	−1.5	−.020	−13	−2.0
S	−	−	.165	116	17.9	.075	51	7.8

Notes: The change in the predicted geometric mean wage of primary- or secondary-leavers as the result of the addition or subtraction of four years of secondary education is derived as a residual (the remaining difference in geometric mean wages of the two groups) after eliminating the differences due to differences in the mean characteristics.

The percentage change in the geometric mean wage is calculated from the change in $\ln \overline{W}$ in a way analogous to the dummy variable in semilogarithmic earnings functions explained by Halvorsen and Palmquist.

The differences between primary- and secondary-leavers in the mean values of H and R are significant at the 1 percent level in both countries.

$\Delta \ln \overline{W}_s = F_p(\overline{Z}_s - \overline{Z}_p)$ and $\Delta \ln \overline{W}_p = F_s(\overline{Z}_s - \overline{Z}_p)$.

increase in wages would result from giving primary-leavers the higher achievement levels of secondary-leavers: 31–38 percent in Kenya and 12–18 percent in Tanzania.

E. Do High-Achieving Primary-Leavers Earn More than Low-Achieving Secondary-Leavers?

Columns 1 (Kenya) and 5 (Tanzania) of Table 3 show substantial variation in cognitive development within educational strata. The average achievement test score of the top third of primary-leavers is double that of the bottom third in both countries. Among secondary-leavers, the average score of the top third is half as much again as the bottom third in Kenya, and double that of the bottom third in Tanzania. In both countries, the literacy and numeracy of the top third of primary-leavers is roughly equal to that of the middle third of secondary-leavers.[26]

To estimate the impact on earnings within each educational group of the within-group variance of cognitive achievement, the estimated stratified earnings functions are used to predict earnings for different levels of cognitive achievement. In the case of primary-leavers:

$$(6)\ (\widehat{\ln W_{PH}})_i = c_{0p} + c_{2p}\overline{R}_p + c_{4p}\overline{L} + c_{3p}H_{pi}$$

$$(7)\ (\widehat{\ln W_{PR}})_i = c_{0p} + c_{3p}\overline{H}_p + c_{4p}\overline{L} + c_{2p}R_{pi}$$

where H_{pi} and R_{pi} represent the achieve-

---

[26] It seems that cognitive skills are not the only basis for access to secondary education.

TABLE 3—PREDICTED WAGES OF PRIMARY- AND SECONDARY-LEAVERS WITH VARYING LEVELS
OF COGNITIVE ACHIEVEMENT AND REASONING ABILITY

		Kenya				Tanzania			
		By Achievement		By Ability		By Achievement		By Ability	
		$\bar{H}_i$ (1)	$\bar{Y}_i$ (2)	$\bar{R}_i$ (3)	$\bar{Y}_i$ (4)	$\bar{H}_i$ (5)	$\bar{Y}_i$ (6)	$\bar{R}_i$ (7)	$\bar{Y}_i$ (8)
Primary-Leavers									
Bottom	10%	13.1	532	10.9	807	11.9	571	9.1	657
Bottom	1/3	21.4	623	16.0	806	16.8	598	16.7	651
Middle	1/3	31.2	751	26.0	804	24.6	643	26.1	643
Top	1/3	45.0	978	32.2	803	32.0	689	31.1	639
Top	10%	51.6	1,109	34.0	803	40.7	747	33.4	637
Secondary-Leavers									
Bottom	10%	28.1	864	17.4	1,083	20.1	681	13.4	732
Bottom	1/3	36.1	1,036	24.2	1,196	25.6	725	21.4	792
Middle	1/3	47.2	1,333	31.5	1,323	37.3	847	29.9	862
Top	1/3	54.0	1,556	34.9	1,387	48.5	983	33.8	896
Top	10%	55.9	1,624	35.3	1,395	52.6	1,039	35.5	911

ment and ability scores of each primary-leaver i and a circumflex indicates a predicted value.

Columns 2 and 6 show the predicted mean wages of primary- and secondary-leavers of varying levels of achievement but of the same levels of ability and experience. Secondary-leavers who scored in the top third on the achievement test are predicted to earn some 50 percent more than those in the bottom third in Kenya, and some 35 percent more in Tanzania; roughly the same percentages apply to primary-leavers. In both countries, it would seem, how much you learn in primary or in secondary school has a substantial influence on your performance at work. Moreover, the predicted wage of primary-leavers who scored in the top third is nearly as high as that of secondary-leavers who scored in the bottom third. In East Africa, mere attendance at secondary school is no guarantee of success in the labor market: it is necessary to learn one's school lessons.

F. *Do More Able Primary-Leavers Earn More than Less Able Secondary Leavers?*

There is substantial variation in reasoning ability within the two educational strata (cols. 3 and 7, Table 3). As with achievement, the ability of the top third of primary-leavers is roughly equal to that of the middle third of secondary-leavers. In contrast to variation in achievement, however, variation in ability has no effect on the predicted earnings of primary-leavers and little on those of secondary-leavers. Moreover, whereas the ability scores of the ablest 10 percent of primary-leavers are roughly double those of the least able 10 percent of secondary-leavers, their predicted wages are lower (cols. 4 and 8). In neither country is being among the most able of your peers a sufficient condition for successful performance in the labor market.

G. *How Much Inequality is Due to Cognitive Skills?*

The effects of ability, cognitive development, or years of education on the dispersion of earnings may differ in relative importance from their effects on the structure of earnings. The latter depends only on the size of the coefficients in the earnings function. The former depends also on the proportion of employees with a particular characteristic (in the case of the dummy variable), or the extent to which employees differ in possession of that characteristic (in the case of

TABLE 4—THE RELATIVE CONTRIBUTIONS OF WORKER CHARACTERISTICS TO THE DISPERSION
OF EARNINGS; THE MEAN CHARACTERISTICS OF WORKERS BY EARNINGS QUINTILE

Contribution to Variance:	Kenya			Tanzania		
	Absolute	Percentage of Total	Percentage of Restricted Total	Absolute	Percentage of Total	Percentage of Restricted Total
L	.031	32.0	–	.095	72.0	–
S	.011	11.3	16.7	.011	8.3	29.8
H	.049	50.5	74.2	.025	18.9	67.6
R	.006	6.2	9.1	.001	.8	2.7
Total	.097	100.0	100.0	.132	100.0	100.0

Earnings Quintile:	Lowest	Second	Third	Fourth	Highest	Lowest	Second	Third	Fourth	Highest
$\bar{L}$	6.45	8.64	6.62	7.73	13.28	3.16	5.73	7.68	8.69	12.07
$\bar{S}$	.43	.45	.78	.70	.74	.23	.38	.38	.32	.61
$\bar{H}$	31.69	38.00	44.60	43.82	46.61	26.00	28.98	29.43	27.56	36.16
$\bar{R}$	25.32	27.57	29.71	29.80	29.21	25.41	25.14	27.60	26.10	27.54

continuous variables); and where in the distribution of pay those who possess the characteristic or possess it in varying degrees are found.

To measure relative contributions to dispersion, we adopt the following procedure: using equation (4), written here as $\ln W_i = a + \sum_j b_{ij} Z_{ij}$, where Z_{ij} is the set of independent variables ($j = 1 \ldots n$), we predict the earnings of each employee ($\hat{W}_i$). Each independent variable (j) is in turn set equal to its mean value, and predicted earnings ($\hat{W}_{ij}$) are estimated using the set of other characteristics possessed by each employee. Here $\hat{W}_{ij}$ represents the predicted value of W for each individual (i) when his endowment of j equals that of all other individuals. The variances of $\hat{W}_i$ and $\hat{W}_{ij}$ are calculated, and the contribution of Z_j to the explained variance of earnings is estimated as $\text{var}(\hat{W}_i) - \text{var}(\hat{W}_{ij})$. The relative contribution of each individual variable is calculated by expressing its contribution as a percentage of $\sum_j (\text{var}(\hat{W}_i) - \text{var}(\hat{W}_{ij}))$.[27] In effect we are attempting to answer the following counterfactual question: what would be the effect on the inequality of pay if, while mean earnings were held constant, the dispersion due to a particular characteristic such as cognitive achievement was eliminated?

The relative contribution to inequality of each independent variable in the expanded human capital earnings function for the unstratified sample is shown in Table 4. The contribution of employment experience to the variance of earnings is markedly greater in Tanzania than in Kenya.[28] The contribution of the ability variable to the variance of earnings is small in both countries, partly because of its negligible coefficient and partly because high and low earners have similar ability scores. The contribution of years of education is larger, reflecting the size of its coefficient and the tendency for the proportion with secondary education to rise with earnings quintile. In Kenya achievement accounts for three-quarters of the variance in earnings explained jointly by ability, education, and achievement; in Tanzania the share is two-thirds. Not only are cognitive skills highly rewarded, but there are few highly literate and numerate workers, be they

[27] For further explication of this method of decomposing inequality and a comparison with other methods, see Behrman, Knight, and Sabot (1983).

[28] In Tanzania mean experience rises monotonically, from 3.1 years in the lowest to 12.1 years in the highest earnings quintile. This is not the case in Kenya; i.e., high levels of experience are associated with low as well as with high incomes, possibly because of the inverse correlation between education and experience: the more educated, who are more plentiful in Kenya, have received preference over the more experienced but less educated in access to jobs.

primary- or secondary-leavers, in the low-earnings quintiles.

IV. The Educational Production and Attainment Functions and Indirect Effects on Earnings

Having shown that length of education has a relatively small and ability a negligible direct influence on earnings, we now examine a possible indirect influence through their effects on cognitive achievement. The simple correlations between S and H and between R and H are strong and positive. The mean achievement scores are significantly higher for secondary- than for primary-leavers (43 percent higher in Kenya and 52 percent in Tanzania), and there is a monotonic relationship between ability groups and their mean levels of achievement.

An educational production function, based on equation (3), is presented in Table 5 using a linear specification.[29] In both countries, cognitive achievement bears a highly significant positive relationship to educational level and to ability. In Kenya, secondary education raises H by 11.75 points, or by 35 percent at the mean; very similar results are obtained for Tanzania. The elasticity of response of cognitive skill to reasoning ability at the mean is roughly 0.4 in both countries. In Kenya the coefficient on G (a dummy variable taking a value of 1 if the secondary school attended by a secondary-leaver, and the primary school attended by a primary-leaver, was a government school, and 0 otherwise) is significantly positive. In both countries the coefficient on B (a dummy variable indicating birth in an urban area, birth in a rural area being the omitted category) is almost significantly negative.[30]

[29]A log-linear specification (with the continuous variables H and R in natural logarithms) was also estimated but was inferior in terms of the percentage standard error of H (29 percent in Kenya and 31 percent in Tanzania) and the significance of some coefficients. The ensuing simulation analysis is based on the linear specification but the results are not sensitive to the choice of specification.

[30]This counterintuitive result may reflect greater selectivity in access to schooling and to the urban labor market among the rural born.

TABLE 5—EDUCATIONAL PRODUCTION FUNCTIONS

Variable	Kenya·	Tanzania
S	11.754	10.939
	(8.50)	(8.84)
G	3.366	0.995
	(2.49)	(0.76)
B	−3.567	−2.651
	(1.78)	(1.82)
R	0.560	0.487
	(5.55)	(5.58)
Constant	15.49	12.34
$\bar{H}$	39.98	30.33
R^2	0.42	0.44
Standard Error	8.77	7.76
Percentage Standard Error	21.1	26.2

Notes: The dependent variable is H; *t*-statistics are shown below the coefficients in parentheses; the mean values of variables, here and elsewhere, are derived from the subsamples weighted according to the proportions in which primary- and secondary-completers are found in the full samples.

An educational attainment function, based on equation (2), was estimated by means of probit analysis. The results are very similar in the two countries, being

$$\hat{p} = \phi(-1.816 + .049R + .070E$$
$$(4.051) \quad (3.075) \quad (3.918)$$

$$+ .184F_1 + .530F_2) \qquad \chi^2 = 46.54$$
$$(.752) \quad (1.975)$$

$$\hat{p} = \phi(-1.760 + .067R - .248E$$
$$(3.357) \quad (3.889) \quad (2.484)$$

$$+ .133F_1 + .929F_2) \qquad \chi^2 = 30.92$$
$$(.515) \quad (3.426)$$

in Kenya and Tanzania, respectively, where $\hat{p}$ is the probability of going on to secondary school, E is the number of secondary school places as a proportion of the number of 14-year olds when the respondent was aged 14, F_1 indicates that one parent and F_2 that both had received education, $\phi(\cdot)$ denotes the cumulative unit normal distribution, and

VOL. 75 NO. 5   BOISSIERE ET AL.: EARNINGS AND SCHOOLING   1027

the figures in parentheses are t-statistics. The probability of going on to secondary school was positively and significantly related to the ability score, it was raised significantly if both parents had been educated, and it was significantly affected by the secondary enrollment ratio—positively, as expected, in Kenya but negatively in Tanzania. The reason for this negative sign is that although E rose over time, the proportion of primary school completers continuing to secondary school actually fell. With all independent variables at their mean values, an increase in the ability score from the mean of the bottom to that of the top-ability tercile would raise the probability of secondary school attendance by .25 in Kenya and by .35 in Tanzania. Ability therefore has two indirect effects on earnings: not only via relation D but also via relation E in Figure 1.

Before combining the three functions for simulation analysis, we test whether the estimated model is recursive; that is, whether the estimates are consistent and not subject to simultaneous equation bias. If some unmeasured characteristics, such as drive and determination, contributed to educational attainment, to cognitive achievement, and to earnings, the error terms (v, y, and z, respectively) in equations (2), (3), and (4) would be correlated, as would educational attainment and y, educational attainment and z, and cognitive skill and z. Applying a specification test developed by Jerry Hausman (1978), we added the predicted value of educational attainment ($\hat{S}$) for each individual as an independent variable in (3) and in (4), and the predicted value of cognitive skill ($\hat{H}$) as an independent variable in (4).[31] Our findings that the coefficients are not significantly different from zero in five of the six cases and just significantly so in the sixth makes it difficult to reject the null hypothesis that the equation system is recursive.[32]

A further test of recursiveness between equations (2) and (3) was conducted. Equation (3) was estimated using instrumental variables, and the estimated coefficients were used to generate $\hat{H}$ for each individual at the end of primary school (i.e., with $S = 0$). Equation (2) was then estimated with $\hat{H}$ as an additional independent variable. The coefficient on $\hat{H}$ is not significant in either country suggesting that simultaneity on account of selection for secondary school by cognitive achievement is unlikely.[33]

The indirect effects of ability are measured and compared with the direct effect in Table 6. Two ability levels are considered in each sample, corresponding to the mean values of R for the top- and bottom-ability terciles; all other characteristics of the sample are kept at their mean values. Within the three-equation system, we then trace the difference in predicted wages between the two ability levels which is due to relations C, D, and E in Figure 1. The full consequence of the assumed ability difference—incorporating all three effects—is to create a difference in predicted wages equal to 32 percent of the sample mean in Kenya and 16 percent in Tanzania (the final row of the table). The direct effect of ability differences on earnings, working through the earnings function alone, accounts for only one-fifth of the predicted full wage difference in Kenya and for much less in Tanzania (relation C). The indirect effect of ability on cognitive skill acquisition and hence on earnings represents

---

[31] S and H are generated using (2) and (3), respectively, plus the other exogenous variables in the three-equation system.

[32] The coefficients are -1.518 (t-value $= .373$), $-.058$ (.210), and $-.011$ (.748) in Kenya, and 4.243 (1.430), .433 (2.036), and $-.011$ (.647) in Tanzania. The possibil-

ity of simultaneity between equations (2) and (4) in Tanzania makes the Tanzanian results less reliable. However, the fact that the coefficient on $\hat{S}$ is significantly positive implying that the coefficient on S is biased downwards, suggests that the bias is not due to simultaneity. The extreme rationing of secondary enrollment in Tanzania ensures that the private demand remains strong—as revealed by the private rate of return and subjective responses to survey questions—despite government compression of the earnings structure (fn. 17). The suggestion that the significant positive coefficient is due to the less perceptive acquiring unprofitable education and receiving lower income, is therefore implausible.

[33] The coefficient was actually negative, being -0.090 (standard error $= 0.053$) in Kenya, and -0.063 (0.079) in Tanzania.

TABLE 6—THE DIRECT AND INDIRECT EFFECTS OF ABILITY ON EARNINGS

Mean Values for the Top and Bottom Terciles Classified by Reasoning Ability	Kenya				Tanzania			
			Difference				Difference	
	Top Tercile	Bottom Tercile	Absolute	As Percentage of Total[a]	Top Tercile	Bottom Tercile	Absolute	As Percentage of Total[a]
R	33.8	19.8	14.0		33.3	18.5	14.8	
p	0.77	0.52	0.25		0.54	0.19	0.35	
H (all effects):	45.8	34.9	10.9		34.7	23.7	11.0	
Predicted Wages Showing the Effect of:[b]								
Relation C	1,064	979	85	24	749	739	10	7
Relation D	1,089	929	160	44	772	704	68	48
Relation E	1,127	1,012	115	32	765	700	65	45
Relation E' (human capital only)	1,076	1,014	62	17	754	718	36	25
Relations C, D, E (all effects)	1,250	890	360	100	804	661	143	100

[a] As the sum of the separate effects is not exactly equal to their combined effect, each is expressed as a percentage of the sum.

[b] The measure of each effect is derived from equations (2), (3), and (4). It shows the effect on the wage of replacing the mean value of ability for the subsample ($\bar{R}$) by the mean value for the upper or lower tercile ($\bar{R}_t$). The multiplicands are as follows: Relation C: c_2; Relation D: $c_3 \cdot b_1$; Relation E: $c_1 \cdot p(a_1) + c_3 \cdot p(a_1) \cdot b_2$; Relation E': $c_3 \cdot p(a_1) \cdot b_2$; Relations C, D, E: $c_2 + c_3(b_1 + p(a_1) \cdot b_2) + c_1 \cdot p(a_1)$ (for instance, in the case of relation C: $(\ln W)_t - (\overline{\ln W}) = c_2(\bar{R}_t - \bar{R})$).

38 percent in both countries (relation D), and the indirect effect of ability via educational attainment about a third (relation E). At least half of this effect works through human capital acquisition (relation E') rather than credentialism.

It is also possible to distinguish the different effects of secondary school attendance on earnings. The directly observed effect (relation B in Figure 1) is derived from the coefficient c_1 in equation (4). The value is 0.19 in Kenya and 0.11 in Tanzania, implying that the wage is raised by 21 and 12 percent, respectively, by what we termed credentialism. The other effect (relations F and A in Figure 1) is derived from a combination of equations (3) and (4). The coefficient b_2 in the former shows the effect of secondary schooling on cognitive skills, and c_3 in the latter the effect of cognitive skills on earnings. Their product $b_2 \cdot c_3$ (0.22 in Kenya and 0.14 in Tanzania) indicates that human capital acquisition in secondary school raises earnings by 25 and 15 percent, respectively.

The human capital effect of a secondary education thus exceeds the credentialist effect. In summary, use of the three-equation system has shown that the indirectly measured effects of differences in reasoning ability and in educational attainment both exceed the direct effects.

V. Conclusions

Our survey data from East Africa have permitted a sharper test than hitherto of the competing explanations—credentialism, ability, screening, or human capital—of why workers with secondary education earn more. The direct returns to reasoning ability in the labor market are small, those to years of education are moderate, and those to literacy and numeracy—dimensions of human capital—are large. The returns to cognitive achievement are not significantly lower for manual than for nonmanual workers.

The returns to cognitive skills cannot but be a payment for human capital. The direct

VOL. 75 NO. 5   BOISSIERE ET AL.: EARNINGS AND SCHOOLING   1029

returns to years of education, on the other hand, could reflect credentialism or screening or human capital acquired at school or at home; that is, their interpretation is inconclusive. It appears that literate and numerate workers are more productive, and that education is valuable to workers because it can give them skills that increase their productivity. These conclusions have generally satisfied the usual statistical tests. Their robustness derives no less from the fact that they all apply to both Kenya and Tanzania.

The main effects of length of education and reasoning ability on earnings are indirect, operating through the development of cognitive skills. More educated or brighter workers tend to be more literate and numerate. The main reason why secondary-leavers earn more on average than primary-leavers is their higher average level of cognitive achievement. However, there is substantial variation in cognitive achievement, and also in reasoning ability, within the two educational groups. Whereas primary-leavers of high ability earn less than less able secondary-leavers, this is generally not the case for cognitive skills. Within each educational group, high achievers earn a great deal more than low achievers. Just as cognitive achievement is the main determinant of the structure of earnings, so also—far more than reasoning ability and school attendance—does it account for much of the inequality of earnings among workers. Because inequality is primarily due to differences in productivity based on cognitive skills, the efficiency cost of reducing inequality may be high.

Our analysis provides strong support for the human capital interpretation of the educational structure of wages. Whether these conclusions should be generalized beyond East Africa to the many other countries in which rates of returns have been estimated is, however, open to question. Kenya and Tanzania have much lower incomes, and cognitive skills are in shorter supply, than in most developing counties, particularly those of Asia and Latin America. As economic development proceeds, the growth of educated labor may outstrip the growth of the economy. In that case, the returns to cogni-tive achievement may decline, while for political and institutional reasons the returns to years of education may remain high.

REFERENCES

Arrow, Kenneth J., "Higher Education as a Filter," *Journal of Public Economics*, July 1973, *2*, 193–216.

Behrman, Jere R. et al., *Socioeconomic Success: A Study of the Effects of Genetic Endowments, Family Environment and Schooling*, Amsterdam: North-Holland, 1980.

Behrman, Jere, Knight, J. B. and Sabot, R. H., "A Simulation Alternative to the Comparative R^2 Approach to Decomposing Inequality," *Oxford Bulletin of Economics and Statistics*, August 1983, *45*, 307–12.

Blaug, Mark, "Human Capital Theory: A Slightly Jaundiced View," *Journal of Economic Literature*, September 1976, *14*, 827–55.

Blinder, Alan S., "Wage Discrimination: Reduced Form and Structural Estimates," *Journal of Human Resources*, Fall 1973, *8*, 436–55.

Bowles, Samuel and Gintis, Herbert, *Schooling in Capitalist America*, London: Routledge and Kegan Paul, 1976.

Chamberlain, Gary and Griliches, Zvi, "More on Brothers," in Paul Taubman, ed., *Kinometrics: Determinants of Socioeconomic Success within and between Families*, Amsterdam: North-Holland, 1977.

Griliches, Zvi, "Estimating the Returns to Schooling: Some Econometric Problems," *Econometrica*, January 1977, *45*, 1–22.

_____, "Sibling Models and Data in Economics: Beginnings of a Survey," *Journal of Political Economy*, October 1979, Suppl., *87*, S37–64.

_____ **and Mason, William M.,** "Education, Income, and Ability," *Journal of Political Economy*, May/June 1972, Suppl., *80*, S74–103.

Halvorsen, Robert and Palmquist, Raymond, "The Interpretation of Dummy Variables in Semilogarithmic Equations," *American Economic Review*, June 1980, *70*, 474–75.

Hanushek, Eric A., "Conceptual and Empirical

Issues in the Estimation of Educational Production Functions," *Journal of Human Resources*, Summer 1979, *14*, 351–88.

Hausman, Jerry, "Specification Tests in Econometrics," *Econometrica*, November 1978, *46*, 1251–71.

Klingelhofer, E. L., "Performance of Tanzanian School Pupils on the Raven's Matrices Test," *Journal of Social Psychology*, August 1967, *72*, 205–16.

Knight, J. B., and Sabot, R. H., "Educational Expansion, Government Policy and Wage Compression," The World Bank, 1983.

_____ and _____, "Educational Policy and Labor Productivity: An Output Accounting Exercise," The World Bank, 1984.

Lau, L., "Educational Production Functions," in Report of a Committee of the National Academy of Education, *Economic Dimensions of Education*, Washington, 1979.

Oaxaca, Ronald, "Male-Female Differentials in Urban Labor Markets," *International Economic Review*, October 1973, *3*, 673–709.

Olneck, Michael R., "On the Use of Sibling Data to Estimate the Effects of Family Background, Cognitive Skills and Schooling: Results from the Kalamazoo Brothers Study," in Paul Taubman, ed., *Kinometrics: Determinants of Socioeconomic Success within and between Families*, Amsterdam: North-Holland, 1977.

Psacharopoulos, George (assisted by Keith Hinchcliffe), *Returns to Education. An International Comparison*, Amsterdam: Elsevier, 1973.

_____, "Returns to Education: An Updated International Comparison," *Comparative Education*, March 1981, *17*, 321–41.

Raven, J. C., *Guide to the Coloured Progressive Matrices (Sets A, Ab, B)*, London: H. K. Lewis and Company, 1956.

Riley, John G., "Testing the Educational Screening Hypotheses," *Journal of Political Economy*, October 1979, Suppl., *87*, S227–52.

Sinha, U., "The Use of Raven's Progressive Matrices Test in India," *Indian Educational Review*, January 1968, *3*, 118–32.

Spence, Michael, "Competition in Salaries, Credentials, and Signalling Prerequisites for Jobs," *Quarterly Journal of Economics*, February 1976, *90*, 51–74.

Taubman, Paul, *Sources of Inequality of Earnings*, Amsterdam: North-Holland, 1975.

_____ and Wales, Terence, *Higher Education and Earnings: College as an Investment and as a Screening Device*, New York: McGraw-Hill, 1974.

Thurow, Lester C., *Generating Inequality*, New York: Basic Books, 1975.

Wise, David A., "Academic Achievement and Job Performance," *American Economic Review*, September 1975, *65*, 350–66.

Wober, M. "The Meaning of Stability of the RPM Among Africans," *International Journal of Psychology*, 1969, *4*, 310–24.

[19]

World Development Vol. 7 pp. 995–1004
Pergamon Press Ltd. 1979. Printed in Great Britain

International Comparisons of Educational and Economic Indicators, Revisited

KIONG-HOCK LEE
University of Malaya

and

GEORGE PSACHAROPOULOS
London School of Economics

Summary. – Educational planning today, especially in developing countries, is still largely based on international comparisons of the relationship between educational and economic performance indicators in more advanced countries. In this paper we examine cross-sectional data one decade apart for a large number of countries and conclude that this relationship is very weak. In particular, enrolments in vocational schools and the number of doctors in the population, two indicators often mentioned in educational plans, vary widely from one country to another and exhibit low correlations with the other variables examined. The results of our analysis suggest caution in the use of international comparisons for analytical purposes, although it is accepted that such comparisons are difficult to resist on political grounds.

1. INTRODUCTION

In the old days of educational planning one of the techniques used was what has since been known as 'international comparisons'. Under this 'technique' the planner in a country at the X stage of economic development observed the educational parameters (usually enrolments) in another country at a more advanced economic stage and was setting target enrolments for his own country to achieve by the target year of the plan. Since that time a number of analyses have been conducted (ranging from the crudest to very sophisticated ones) attempting to document international patterns of economic and educational development.[1]

In spite of the fact that these efforts have failed to produce persuasive statistical evidence on any pattern, let alone the thorny issue of the direction of causation (i.e. on whether education is a lead or lag variable), international comparisons are still used nowadays in the making of educational plans.

The use of international comparisons in this respect takes mainly two forms. First, in the absence of domestic statistical data (either cross-sectional or time-series), the technocrat who elaborates the educational plan is tempted to borrow parameters from other countries.

The 'parameters' could refer to the number of doctors per 1000 population or to the amount of value added per university graduate in the manufacturing sector of the economy. Second, administrators in countries that attempt to 'plan' their educational system (i.e. the majority of developing countries) are very much impressed by and try to imitate prestige educational statistics observed in countries at more advanced levels of economic development. Suffice to mention as an example in this respect the percentage of GNP or the state budget spent on education. If a neighbouring, higher *per capita* income country spends 5% of GNP on its educational system, social pressure is put upon the politicians in poorer countries to replicate this statistic.

In this essay we look at some recently published world statistics and conclude – yet again – that international comparisons of educational and economic indicators, no matter how tempting they might be, should *not* be used for planning the expansion of an educational system.

2. THE DATA

The data refer to a set of educational and economic indicators for 1960 and 1970 in 114 countries, as reported in IBRD (1976) and UNESCO (1976). The educational indicators are:

> *LIT* : the percentage of adults who are literate;
>
> *P,S,H* : the percentage enrolment ratio in primary, secondary and higher education, respectively;
>
> *V* : the percentage enrolment in vocational education relative to total enrolment in secondary education.

The economic indicators are:

> *YP* : *per capita* income (GNP) in 1973, measured in $US;
>
> *LAGR* : the percentage of the labour force employed in agriculture;
>
> *GY* : the average annual growth rate of GNP at constant market prices during the 1960s.

Finally, the following social indicator has been included in the analysis because it relates to educational planning:

> *PDOC* : the number of people in the population per one medical doctor.

Tables 1 and 2 show the means and coefficients of variation of these variables for 1960 and 1970. The full set of countries ($N = 114$) has been split into three development groups as indicated on top of the tables.[2] Before proceeding with the analysis, two points are in order.

First, it is a widely held belief that international data of the kind used here are 'bad' mainly because of the incomparability of definitions of the same variable across countries. In this essay we make no claim on how good or bad the data are. These are *the* very data available to technocrats and administrators around the world, so these are the appropriate data to use in this analysis.

Second, there exists a great controversy on whether education is a lead or lag variable in economic development; for this reason we shall proceed in two steps: (a) correlation analysis in a comparative statics framework, and (b) over-time changes of the parameters in a dynamic framework.

3. STATIC ANALYSIS

Before we look at any correlations between the different variables across countries, it is interesting to note the high coefficient of variation of some of the variables in Tables 1 and 2.

A high value of this coefficient (e.g. unity or above) means that one can place little confidence on the mean in question. In other words, a country attempting to borrow such a parameter from another country might be copying a non-typical value which has no meaning for planning purposes. The size of the coefficients of variation are reduced when the total sample of countries is split into development groups. However, the variance of some of the variables relative to their means continues to be high. For example, the coefficient of variation of population per doctor in the 1970 data set is well above unity for all country groups. This means that one cannot confidently use the observed doctor–population ratio in another country to set targets for the amount of doctors his own country should have.

Tables 3 and 4 present simple correlation matrices between educational and economic performance indicators in 1960 and 1970, respectively. Although enrolment ratios correlate significantly with the level of development (as measured by *per capita* income or the percentage of labour in agriculture) this relationship becomes weaker once the sample is subdivided into country groups. Among the group of developing countries with *per capita* incomes of less than $750, primary-, secondary- and higher-education enrolment ratios and literacy are significantly correlated with the level of economic development in 1960 and 1970. This represents a significant contrast relative to the other two groups of countries. In the case of the intermediate countries, with *per capita* incomes lying between $750 and $2000, none of the educational variables was significantly correlated with the level of economic development in both periods. For the group of advanced countries with *per capita* incomes of at least $2000, only the secondary- and higher-education enrolment ratios were significantly correlated with the level of economic development in 1960 and 1970, respectively. It should be underlined that in no case was *vocational* enrolment significantly associated with the level of economic development as measured by *per capita* income.

The only educational variable that relates to economic growth in the 1960 data set is *primary* education and *literacy*. In the 1970 data set, secondary- and higher-education enrolment ratios are significantly related to economic growth in only the poorest country group. It should again be underlined that in no case was *vocational* enrolment significantly correlated with economic growth. Further, in the case of the intermediate and advanced groups of

Table 1. *Means and coefficients of variation of variables*, 1960

Variable		Country group		
	All	YP <$750	YP $750–$2000	YP >$2000
YP	1221 (1.33)	288 (0.65)	1186 (0.31)	4338 (0.27)
GY	5.2 (0.51)	4.8 (0.42)	6.7 (0.37)	5.0 (0.38)
LAGR	51.2 (0.52)	67.9 (0.27)	37.6 (0.45)	24.3 (0.86)
PDOC	11,400 (1.83)	19,600 (1.32)	2200 (0.68)	1500 (1.33)
LIT	57.0 (0.54)	43.4 (0.56)	66.4 (0.41)	73.0 (0.53)
P	72.5 (0.47	56.6 (0.56)	89.3 (0.21)	101.2 (0.25)
S	21.5 (1.04)	8.8 (0.97)	24.2 (0.55)	54.1 (0.38)
V	20.5 (0.82)	16.6 (0.63)	18.9 (1.01)	32.0 (0.71)
H	3.8 (1.34)	1.4 (1.5)	4.6 (0.87)	9.5 (0.71)
Number of countries	114	68	21	25

Source: All data are from IBRD (1976) except enrolment ratios for higher education which are from UNESCO (1976).
Note: Numbers in parentheses are coefficients of variation.

Table 2. *Means and coefficients of variation of variables*, 1970

Variable		Country group		
	All	YP <$750	YP $750–$2000	YP >$2000
LAGR	46.3 (0.59)	63.0 (0.30)	32.9 (0.54)	17.4 (1.07)
PDOC	11,268 (1.58)	17,692 (1.18)	2905 (1.78)	1962 (1.66)
LIT	63.1 (0.50)	45.0 (0.59)	75.4 (0.28)	90.2 (0.26)
P	83.8 (0.39)	71.2 (0.48)	102.6 (0.22)	101.0 (0.20)
S	32.5 (0.85)	16.1 (0.80)	41.6 (0.38)	65.2 (0.43)
V	17.4 (0.89)	11.6 (0.82)	20.7 (0.88)	30.8 (0.56)
H	6.7 (1.21)	2.8 (1.32)	8.2 (0.71)	16.7 (0.62)

Source: As in Table 1.

Table 3. *Zero-order correlations between educational and other social indicators, 1960*

	YP	GY	LAGR	PDOC
A. All countries				
LIT	0.351*	0.045	−0.719*	−0.427*
P	0.611*	0.286*	−0.772*	−0.577*
S	0.888*	0.112	−0.802*	−0.449*
V	0.415*	−0.066	−0.242*	−0.098
H	0.754*	0.111	−0.648*	−0.350*
B. YP <$750				
LIT	0.542*	0.061	−0.711*	−0.459*
P	0.684*	0.397*	−0.737*.	−0.494*
S	0.577*	0.270	−0.764*	−0.518*
V	0.172	0.014	0.021	0.200
H	0.388*	0.292	−0.330*	−0.442*
C. YP $750–$2000				
LIT	0.121	−0.577*	−0.505*	−0.743*
P	0.195	−0.284	−0.318	−0.282
S	0.316	−0.120	−0.275	−0.466*
V	0.144	−0.183	0.197	−0.523*
H	0.231	−0.199	−0.419*	−0.326
D. YP >$2000				
LIT	−0.291	0.425	−0.728*	−0.577*
P	0.021	−0.022	−0.669*	−0.736*
S	0.445*	−0.021	−0.754*	−0.632*
V	0.125	−0.148	−0.163	−0.171
H	0.412	−0.151	−0.491*	−0.330

Note: *Statistically significant at the 95% level of probability.

Table 4. *Zero-order correlations between educational and other social indicators, 1970*

	YP	GY	LAGR	PDOC
A. All countries				
LIT	0.651*	0.226*	−0.838*	−0.625*
P	0.435*	0.324*	−0.644*	−0.651*
S	0.856*	0.150	−0.800*	−0.535*
V	0.514*	0.076	−0.461*	−0.225*
H	0.783*	0.106	−0.657*	−0.410*
B. YP <$750				
LIT	0.615*	0.478*	−0.649*	−0.613*
P	0.631*	0.396*	−0.578*	−0.604*
S	0.597*	0.311*	−0.623*	−0.602*
V	0.231	0.081	−0.260*	−0.013
H	0.496*	0.246*	−0.352*	−0.435*
C. YP $750–$2000				
LIT	0.176	−0.458*	−0.617*	−0.725*
P	−0.021	−0.132	0.071	0.317
S	0.352	−0.149	−0.403*	−0.500*
V	0.203	−0.196	0.022	−0.456*
H	0.093	−0.370	−0.318	−0.423*
D. YP >$2000				
LIT	−0.088	−0.048	−0.905*	−0.996*
P	0.224	−0.193	−0.752*	−0.853*
S	0.331	−0.107	−0.600*	−0.718*
V	0.066	0.134	−0.146	−0.341
H	0.455*	−0.134	−0.496*	−0.375

Note: *Statistically significant at the 95% level of probability.

countries almost all educational variables were negatively correlated with economic growth; this is in direct contrast to the case of developing countries.

When the percentage of the labour force employed in agriculture is used as the indicator of the level of economic development, more significant correlations are found. However, it should be noted that current enrolment ratios may not accurately reflect the current stock of human capital hence little significance can be attached to these correlation coefficients. *Literacy* may be a more accurate indicator of the current stock of human capital and hence more weight might be attached to the significant correlations between the current literacy ratio and current levels of economic development as given by the percentage of the labour force employed in agriculture. However, it should be noted that vocational enrolment was found to be insignificantly correlated with this indicator of the level of economic development in all cases but one, i.e. the case of the poorest group of countries in 1970.

4. OVER-TIME CHANGES

Table 5 reports the means of 1960—1970 *differences* of the value of each variable in each country group. For example, the first entry in this table means that, on the average, the proportion of the labour force employed in agriculture the world over has dropped by 5.5% in

the decade of the 1960s. This decline has been faster (equal to 6.3%) in the more advanced countries. Again, the coefficients of variation of most variables are on the high side, especially those referring to doctors and vocational education.

Table 6 presents simple correlation coefficients between over-time variables *changes* which now *could* be assigned a causal link. The difference test produces still weaker correlations relative to the static case examined in the previous section. Literacy appears to be significantly linked to economic growth in two country groups — the intermediate and advanced groups — whereas vocational education is insignificant throughout this table.

5. DISCUSSION OF THE RESULTS

From the empirical findings above, there appears to be some relationship between educational development and the indicators of economic performance; this is particularly true for the poorest group of countries. The question here is whether any significance can be attached to these apparent relationships. The answer to this question will affect the policy issue on whether a country can meaningfully plan its educational system on the basis of international comparisons.

The statistical technique used in this analysis, and in many studies of a similar nature, measures the degree of association (correlation) between

Table 5. *Means and coefficients of variation of variable differences, 1970—1960*

Variable		Country group		
	All	YP <$750	YP $750–$2000	YP >$2000
Change in *LAGR*	−5.5 (0.87)	−4.7 (0.89)	−6.7 (0.97)	−6.3 (0.68)
Change in *PDOC*	−3,300 (3.08)	−6,042 (2.22)	−444 (1.39)	0 (0.00)
Change in *LIT*	12.2 (1.33)	13.3 (0.76)	8.7 (0.91)	19.0 (2.1)
Change in *P*	11.7 (1.43)	15.4 (1.00)	13.3 (1.28)	0.6 (2.63)
Change in *S*	11.2 (0.76)	7.4 (0.80)	17.4 (0.46)	16.2 (0.59)
Change in *V*	−2.0 (4.90)	−4.4 (2.41)	1.8 (3.39)	1.2 (7.00)
Change in *H*	3.4 (1.10)	1.7 (1.12)	4.0 (0.75)	7.6 (0.61)

Source: As in Table 1.

Table 6. *Zero-order correlations between changes in educational and other social indicators, 1960–1970*

	GY	Change in LAGR	Change in PDOC
A. All countries			
Change in *LIT*	−0.048	−0.043	0.008
Change in *P*	0.048	−0.074	−0.045
Change in *S*	0.204	−0.248*	0.321*
Change in *V*	0.123	−0.074	0.322*
Change in *H*	0.107	−0.175	0.242*
B. YP <$750			
Change in *LIT*	0.151	−0.135	0.075
Change in *P*	0.071	−0.056	0.094
Change in *S*	0.286*	0.040	0.345*
Change in *V*	0.029	−0.064	0.373*
Change in *H*	0.290	−0.109	0.281*
C. YP $750–$2000			
Change in *LIT*	0.673*	−0.266	−0.237
Change in *P*	0.137	−0.273	−0.225
Change in *S*	−0.096	−0.450*	0.463*
Change in *V*	−0.016	0.318	−0.115
Change in *H*	−0.358	−0.296	0.256
D. YP >$2000			
Change in *LIT*	−0.475*	0.508*	0.073
Change in *P*	−0.191	−0.093	−0.199
Change in *S*	−0.169	−0.202	−0.379
Change in *V*	0.275	−0.244	−0.190
Change in *H*	−0.070	0.049	0.088

Note: *Statistically significant at the 95% level of probability.

two variables but it cannot be used to prove that a causal link exists between any two variables. It is wrong to infer causation from a measure of association. Nevertheless, the observed relationships are not wholly accidental and they do offer clues to some important lessons which may be useful to the educational planner.

In the following discussion we concentrate on the relationship between the educational variables and *per capita* income (GNP) which serves as the indicator of the level of economic development for two principal reasons. First, both *per capita* income and the percentage of labour in agriculture give rather similar results; this is as expected since there is a significant correlation between the two variables (equal to −0.74). Second, *per capita* income is preferred to the percentage of labour in agriculture because planners in developing countries tend to think more in terms of the former than in terms of the latter as an indicator or measure of the level of economic development.

Concentrating on *per capita* income (1973), it is unlikely that the chain of causation will run from *per capita* income to the educational enrolment ratios of 1960 and 1970. The likely

chain of causation is from the educational enrolment ratios to *per capita* income in 1973 via education's positive effects on the stock of human capital.

But, if there is a strong correlation between 1973 *per capita* income and past *per capita* income levels, then less confidence can be placed on the likely chain of causation from education to *per capita* income. It would then appear that the significant correlation coefficients, especially for the enrolment ratios of 1970 for the group of developing countries, may in fact be nothing more than a reflection of basic national policies of these countries. Virtually all developing countries seek to attain universal primary education and literacy, and to supply the inputs (students) to the higher levels of education. In other words, the observed significant correlations may only be a reflection of existing national policies to imitate the developed countries; the observed patterns may in fact have been self-generated by the developing countries. The zero-order correlation coefficients between the education variables for 1970 and *per capita* income in 1960 given in Table 7 seem to support this. The coefficients have the expected sign and are significant for

INTERNATIONAL COMPARISONS OF EDUCATIONAL AND ECONOMIC INDICATORS   1001

Table 7. *Zero-order correlations between education variables in* 1970 *and* per capita *income in* 1960

	P70	S70	V70	H70	Number of cases
A. All countries	0.405*	0.795*	0.449*	0.834*	93
B. $YP < $750	0.469*	0.432*	0.266*	0.450*	54
C. YP $750–$2000	0.008	0.095	0.078	0.217	19
D. $YP > $2000	0.210	0.216	0.203	0.776*	20

Note: *Statistically significant at the 95% level of probability.

Table 8. Per capita *income elasticities in* 1973 *with respect to enrolments in* 1960 *and* 1970

Country group	P60	S60	V60	H60	R^2
A. All countries	−0.155	0.919*	0.160*	0.252	0.782
B. $YP < $750	0.416	0.284*	0.242	−0.010	0.459
C. YP $750–$2000	−0.082	0.226	0.005	0.082	−0.081
D. $YP > $2000	1.223	0.525	0.101	0.358	0.190

	P70	S70	V70	H70	
A. All countries	0.308	1.013*	0.201*	0.311*	0.730
B. $YP < $750	0.506*	0.161	0.129	0.089	0.436
C. YP $750–$2000	0.038	0.279	0.060	0.008	0.095
D. $YP > $2000	0.998	0.443	0.083	0.231	0.083

Note: *Statistical significance of the underlying regression coefficient at the 95% level of probability or better.

the group of developing countries. Again, note the insignificance of the correlation coefficient for vocational education in developed countries. In Table 8, we also report elasticities of *per capita* income in 1973 with respect to enrolments in 1960 and 1970. It is worth noting the relatively high R^2s when the regressions are fitted to the whole sample or to the low-income group, whereas education does not explain much of the variation in *per capita* income in the more advanced countries.

Attaching some significance to the chain of causation which runs from education enrolment ratios in 1960 and 1970 to *per capita* income in 1973, the following obervations should be of relevance to educational planners. The empirical results seem to indicate that at low levels of economic development (*per capita* income less than $750) educational development contributes significantly to economic development. This can be expected if education, even of a low quality, adds to the productivity of the labourer. In this case, any educational development giving the labourer, who would otherwise be 'unedu-cated', some formal education would in fact contribute towards higher national output.

At the intermediate and advanced economic levels, educational development does not seem

to be markedly associated with economic development. Two explanations appear plausible. First, countries at the intermediate and advanced levels of economic development have more or less achieved 'universal' education especially at the primary level (see Figure 1). Any enrolment

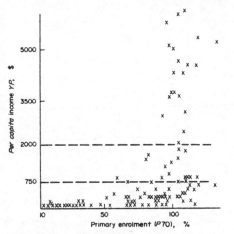

Figure 1. *The relationship between* per capita *income and enrolments in primary education.*

beyond these levels of 'universal' education, especially at the secondary- and higher-education levels, may be considered 'education-producing' rather than 'wealth-producing'. Second, for the intermediate and advanced groups of countries, enrolment ratios may be poor measures or indicators of the quality of education, and hence, of the actual and potential stock of human capital. This is particularly relevant where 'universal' education has already been achieved. Enrolment ratios fail to reflect quality differences. It seems unlikely that the quality of education in a developing country will be comparable to that of an intermediate or advanced country.

A similar problem exists with literacy rates. Given the national policies of universal education in developing countries the usefulness of literacy rates as an explanatory variable for differences in the level of economic development can be expected to decline over time. Also, the significance attached to literacy rates can also be expected to diminish. At present it appears that in the 1960–1970 period a literacy rate of about 75% is essential if *per capita* income is to exceed $750 (see Figure 2).

Consider now the relationship between educational development and economic performance as measured by the average rate of growth of GNP in the decade of the 1960s. Tables 3 and 4 show that primary enrolment and literacy are significantly related to economic performance for all except the advanced group of countries. Although some confidence may be attached to the chain of causation running from

primary enrolment and literacy in 1960 to economic performance, less confidence can be placed on a chain of causation running from educational enrolment ratios and literacy rates in 1970 to economic performance; if at all, the probable chain of causation would be from economic performance to educational development. In other words, a more rapid rate of economic growth may facilitate the development of education. For the advanced countries the absence of any significant correlation may again be attributed to the idea that enrolment ratios may be a poor indicator or measure of the quality of education and hence the actual and potential stock of human capital.

The United Nations declared the 1960s as the 'First Development Decade' and set a target growth rate of 5% per annum in real terms for the member countries, and in particular for the developing countries. On this basis the countries were divided into two groups:

(a) Low-growth countries with average rates of growth of GNP in the 1960s less than 5%;
(b) High-growth countries with average rates of growth of GNP equal to or more than 5%.

It is interesting to note that for the low-growth group of countries, primary enrolment and literacy are significantly correlated with the average rate of growth of GNP (see Table 9). In contrast, none of the correlations are significant for the high-growth countries, and further, six of the 10 correlation coefficients had an unexpected negative sign. Table 10 shows that over 65% of the low-growth countries are

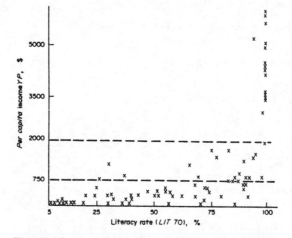

Figure 2. *The relationship between* per capita *income and the literacy rate.*

Table 9. *Zero-order correlations between educational variables and the average rate of growth of GNP in the 1960s*

Variable	$GY < 5\%$	$GY > 5\%$
A. 1960		
LIT	0.109	0.039
P	0.427*	0.033
S	0.145	0.059
V	0.277	−0.259
H	0.091	−0.002
B. 1970		
LIT	0.364*	−0.102
P	0.422*	−0.008
S	0.203	0.047
V	0.266	−0.112
H	0.140	−0.147

Note: *Statistically significant at the 95% level of probability.

developing countries; the intermediate and advanced countries account for just over 11% and about 24% of the total number of low-growth countries, respectively. This is quite a contrast to the case of the group of high-growth countries; here the developing countries represent only 50% of the total number of high-growth countries but the intermediate countries represent almost 37%, and the advanced countries a much smaller 13%.

Hence, it appears that high educational development, as measured by high enrolment ratios, does not necessarily imply high rates of economic growth. A plausible explanation for this weak link is that enrolment ratios and literacy rates are poor indicators of the stock of human capital. The quality of education may far outweigh the quantity of education on the road towards rapid economic growth.

Alternatively, a weak link could imply that other factors apart from education, say physical capital and technical change, are more important at the intermediate and advanced levels of economic development.

6. CONCLUSIONS

In this essay, we have looked at the data most readily available to and most likely to be used by technocrats and administrators in their attempt to compare their country's standing in the international league of education and economic performance. The analysis we have conducted supports the following propositions:

(a) Educational and economic indicators vary widely from one country to another, even at the same level of economic development. Therefore, it is very difficult for the administrator or technocrat to choose which country should be imitated, i.e. from which country one should borrow the value of the educational parameter he is after.

(b) Correlations between educational and economic performance indicators are very weak. Therefore the administrator or technocrat should not be under any illusion that by adopting a more advanced country's enrolment ratio his own country may develop faster in the future.

(c) In particular, two indicators often mentioned in educational plans show high coefficients of variation and low correlations among the variables examined. These are:
– enrolments in vocational schools, and
– the number of doctors per 1000 population.

Different countries should not try to imitate

Table 10. *Distribution of sample by the average rate of growth of GNP and the level of economic development*

	YP <$750		YP $750–$2000		YP >$2000		Total column percentage	
A. GY <5%								
Number of countries	47		8		17		72	
Row percentage		65		11		24		65
Column percentage		71		36		77		
B. GY >5%								
Number of countries	19		14		5		38	
Row percentage		50		37		13		35
Column percentage		29		64		23		
Total	66		22		22		110*	
Row percentage		60		20		20		100

Note: *Sample size is less than 114 because of missing values.

one another regarding these parameters because, as the above analysis shows, this makes little sense.

(d) The only educational indicators that perform better than others in the correlations are enrolments in primary education and literacy. Since these are not policy variables for advanced countries, we propose that developing countries shift their attention from vocational schools and technical schools, and concentrate on increasing the participation of the population in basic education and functional literacy programmes. (This proposal is of course addressed to those who, no matter what the evidence says, will continue to use international comparisons.)

NOTES

1. For example, Anderson and Bowman (1963), Harbison and Myers (1964), Layard and Saigal (1966), Blaug (1970) and OECD (1970).

2. For obvious reasons, the oil-rich countries of Kuwait, Libya, Qatar and Saudi Arabia have been excluded from this analysis.

REFERENCES

Anderson, C. A. and M. J. Bowman, 'Concerning the role of education in development', in C. Geertz (ed.), *Old Societies and New States* (The Free Press of Glencoe, 1963).

Blaug, M., *An Introduction to the Economics of Education* (Penguin, 1970).

Harbison, F. and C. A. Myers, *Education, Manpower and Economic Growth* (McGraw-Hill, 1964).

International Bank for Reconstruction and Development, *World Tables* 1976 (IBRD, 1976).

Layard, P. G. R. and J. Saigal, 'Educational and Occupational characteristics of manpower: an international comparison', *British Journal of Industrial Relations* (July 1966).

OECD, *Occupational and Educational Structures of the Labour Force and Levels of Economic Development* (OECD, 1970).

UNESCO, *Statistical Yearbook* 1975 (UNESCO, 1976).

[20]

Excerpt from *Education and Economic Development Since the Industrial Revolution*, 29–45

Education and economic Growth: Another axiom of indispensability? From human capital to human capabilities

David Mitch
University of Maryland,

"The most important implication of this study is that no single innovation was vital for economic growth in the nineteenth century."

Robert Fogel (1964, 234)

"The proposition that education is requisite for economic 'growth' is today virtually a platitude."

C. Arnold Anderson and Mary Jean Bowman (1976, 3)

In a pioneering and controversial piece of cliometric history, Robert Fogel challenged the view held by many economic historians that the railroad was critical for American economic growth in the nineteenth century. Fogel dubbed this view "the axiom of indispensability." The root cause of his challenge was "the implicit assertion that the economy of the nineteenth century lacked an effective alternative to the railroad and was incapable of producing one" (1964, 10).

During the early 1960s, while Fogel was challenging the railroad's importance for American economic growth, many economists were pointing to the importance of education for economic growth. Some economists and historians gave education the status of a prerequisite for economic growth by arguing for the existence of education thresholds. The basic principle of an education threshold, in this view, is that some standard of educational attainment must spread throughout a population if an economy is to progress, in terms of one or another measure of economic development income per capita, the proportion of the labor force in manufacturing, an so on. [1] By the mid-1970s, many economists

---

[1] For one especially influential argument for the existence of education thresholds, see Bowman and Anderson (1963, 252, 255).

had come to doubt the extent to which education increased labor productivity.[2] And, some historians had come to argue that before the twentieth century, only a small percentage of the work force would have had occasion to use of even basic literacy.[3]

Despite these doubts, the notion of an educational threshold has continued to be influential among economic historians and development economists. Some writers have reconciled evidence challenging the productive value of education with the presence of and education threshold by claiming that it is primarily educational expansion *beyond* the threshold level that is unproductive. For example, Tranter (1981, 224) writes of the English industrial revolution that a national literacy rate above 40 percent played a significant role in "initiating" England's industrialization but was of uncertain value for its "continued progress."

Fogel's grounds for questioning the railroad's indispensability would also seem to apply to education thresholds. The notion of an education threshold presumes that there are no substitutes or only very costly ones for the role that education serves in setting the stage for economic growth.[4] Can this presumption be justified? Economic historians Richard Easterlin (1981), Rondo Cameron (1951, 1985), and Lars Sandberg (1979, 1982) have provided some justification. One can distinguish two basic factors in their explanations: 1) the role of education in allowing an economy to tap into science-based technological advance, and 2) the role of education in facilitating commercial development, such as the development of banking and financial networks. To fully incorporate all the factors mentioned by these authors, the second category should be defined quite broadly so as to include the role of education in promoting geographic and occupational mobility mentioned by Easterlin and Sandberg as well as the supply of entrepreneurship mentioned by Cameron and Sandberg. It should also be noted that Easterlin, Sandberg, and Cameron interpret the term "prerequisite" not as a strict requirement, such as a literacy threshold, but in the sense of Gerschenkron (1972) as some general function that facilitates a certain course of economic development. Thus, while Sandberg (1982) argues for the importance of education in economic growth, he acknowledges the possibility of substitution and points to late nineteenth century Russia as an economy that experienced rapid industrialization despite the low education of its work force.

This essay will consider the role of education in technological advance and commercial development and whether or not some minimum level of educational attainment in a work force is a prerequisite for economic growth. Both economies that appear to have been aided by relatively high levels of educational attainment and those that appear to have been hindered by low levels of educational attainment will be considered. The essay will examine, in turn, the

---

[2] See the surveys by Blaug (1976) and idem (1985).

[3] See for example, Sanderson (1972); Schofield (1973). For a general survey touching on this issue with respect to Western countries see Graff (1987, chap. 7).

[4] For a challenge to the notion of education thresholds see Blaug (1985, 25-26).

3.   *David Mitch*   31

role of education in technological advance and in commercial development. The last section will turn to the general hypothesis —embodied in a challenge to the presence of educational thresholds— that experience and the nonformal development of human capabilities can substitute for the contribution of education to economic growth.

Formal education as a prerequisite for the advance and diffusion of science-based technology

One compelling explanation for why education has become indispensable for economic growth over the last century is that technological advance has increasingly come to underlay economic growth and that this technological advance in turn has been fueled by developments in basic science.[5] The importance of education would derive from the likelihood that a sizable proportion of an economy's workforce must have received formal education of one sort or another or it would be unable to use science-based technology. In assessing the plausibility of this argument, it is useful to consider developments over the last century in industry and agriculture separately. On the one hand, economic decision making in agriculture seems to be more commonly decentralized, implying that larger proportions of the agricultural work force than of the industrial work force are involved in technological decisions. On the other hand, it has been argued that technological choices in agriculture are more subject to the influence of local physical conditions, such as climate and soil types, implying that these choices benefit less form the application of general scientific and technical principles.

Industry

In the case of manufacturing activity, there is clear justification for the premises that growth has been fueled by technological advance and that this advance has been based on scientific principles. Admittedly, there are cases of economic growth fueled primarily by forces other than technological change —whether on the supply side owing to, say, capital accumulation or on the demand side owing to bouyant export markets. One can also conjecture that significant technological advance could have continued into the twentieth century even without the application of scientific principles. Still, despite these reservations, with the emergence of the so-called second industrial revolution in the last quarter or the nineteenth century which was based on the application of principles of chemistry and electricity, the case would seem reasonably strong that an economy's ability to apply scientific principles to economic production considerably enhanced its ability to grow even if other forces were also contributing to economic growth.

---

[5]   The case has been made in Kuznets (1966, 9, 289, 290); Cameron (1951); Easterlin (1981); and Landes (1972).

The oft-told tale of the triumph of German industry over British in the late nineteenth century clearly illustrates the role of education in the use of science-based technology. It is commonly argued that in the production of chemicals, dyes, iron and steel, and machine tools in that period, the cutting edge of technology was based on the application of scientific principles rather than on the rule of thumb. The growing technological superiority of the Germans over the British in these activities has been attributed to the fact that the British persisted in using of rule of thumb methods and incremental tinkering to accomplish improvement and adaptation, while the Germans developed an extensive system of university and polytechnic education with close ties to industry.[6]

Japan's rapid acceleration in industrialization after World War II can also be attributed to the country's ability to tap into science-based technical change. Although the industrial sector had been growing during the late Meiji and interwar periods, this growth was largely in traditional industries such as textiles and crude metallurgy. For this reason, Landes (1965, 110) has argued that technical and scientific education was not of much importance during this early period of industrialization. After World War II, however, Japan's industrialization was spurred by a surge in growth in science-based industries, including metal engineering, chemistry, and electronics. Although immediately after World War II, Japanese industries using advanced Western technology had to rely on foreign experts and send their own workers abroad for training, they were able to establish relatively quickly a pool of native Japanese with the requisite scientific and technical expertise to use the new technology.[7] One factor that may have set the stage for this was the marked rise in literacy and primary school attendance that began during the Meiji period and continued through World War I.[8]

Although there one can reasonably argue that in recent times, the availability of some scientific and technical expertise has enabled economies to tap into science-based technological change and to adapt it to local circumstances, the question arises as to whether the educational demands of science-based technology affects only a relatively small proportion of the industrial work force.[9]

Science-based technical advance will not obviously increase the demand for educated labor beyond an elite group of highly educated scientists and engineers. It could be argued, for example, that an economy can choose between skill-using and skill-saving or education-using and education-saving technical change depending on how scarce or abundant these qualities are in the local work force.[10] Even if one dismisses the possibility of induced technical change in response to factor scarcity, it is not clear that exogenous technical change will

---

[6]   For comparisons of English and German technical advance in manufacturing in the late nineteenth century see Musgrave (1967); Landes (1972, chap. 5); Aldcroft (1975).

[7]   See, for example, Bronfenbrenner (1961, 8, 11) and Taira (1978, 205).

[8]   See, for exemple, Allen (1965, 108) and Ohkawa and Rosovsky (1973).

[9]   This issue was raised by Parker (1961, 1).

[10]   This argument is made by Wright (1986).

have a bias one way or the other in terms of skill and education requirements for the vast bulk of the work force. Indeed, some have argued that by the mid-twentieth century technical change has become "deskilling" —though one should note in this context that the demand for skills and the demand for formal education may move in different directions. For example, Russia in the late nineteenth and early twentieth centuries experienced rapid industrialization using advanced science-based techniques although most of its industrial work force had a low level of education; however, Sandberg (1982, 696) argues that the low level of education considerably slowed down Russia's rate of industrialization.

One can make a case, however, for educating lower-level managers and foremen in the use of advanced technology. Landes (1972, 150-51, 324-25, 343) in particular has argued that as technical advance began to incorporate more scientific principles, the value of mastery of formal science penetrated down to lower supervisory levels and shopfloor foremen. And Landes (1972), Kocka (1978, 535, 570-74), and Lee (1978, 457) have argued that in Germany, supervisors and artisans increasingly obtained formal training in science.

However, it can also be argued that for the middle levels of the work force, the skills they have acquired on the job have been more valuable than those they have acquired through formal schooling. Successful industrializers commonly drew on a stock of workers skilled in more traditional artisanal methods, while economies that had difficulty industrializing may have encountered problems because of the restricted supply of workers whose skills were acquired on the job.[11]

It is for the common operative —composing the bulk of the industrial workforce— that the case for the importance of education in promoting science-based technology is weakest. Even in Germany in the late nineteenth century, where science made a major contribution to technological advance in manufacturing, it is not at all clear that even minimal literacy was important to the ordinary operative; Musgrave (1967, 151) indicates that it was not until after 1920 that German iron and steel producers recognized a need on technical grounds to train lower level operatives. The majority of Germany's industrial work force were not in activities driven by science based technology.[12] And, as already noted, technical change could conceivably have developed substitutes for educated labor, if it was relatively scarce at the lower operative level.

Arguments that stress importance of educated workers for the use of science-based technology tend to shift ground away from strictly technological considerations when they come to consider the ordinary industrial operative. It is argued, for example, that widespread primary education and literacy contribute to industrialization because they facilitate social mobility and, thus, improve the

---

[11]   For illustrations of the role of informally acquired skills in countries that successfully industrialized see Lee (1978, 454-56); Taira (1978, 189); Bronfenbrenner (1961, 11); and Jorberg (1973, 409). For illustrations of the problems generated by the lack of informally acquired skills in countries that failed to industrialize see Crisp (1978, 363, 395, 399); Morris (1983, 582-83).

[12]   See Hoffmann (1965, 196-7).

recruitment of talent for skilled and supervisory positions.[13] But increased social mobility is not strictly necessary for science-based technological advance. A second argument is that through education, workers acquire various behavioral —in many versions of this argument noncognitive— characteristics that are thought to be necessary for an industrial work force.[14] This argument leads to questions about whether the behaviors that schools are alleged to instill are critical to industrialization, whether schools are effective in instilling them and whether other social institutions —religion, cultural traditions, the family, even the organization of work itself— could substitute for schooling and perhaps even produce more effective results. For exemple, Morris's (1960) comparative study of the recruitment of the textile labor forces found that uneducetated factory operatives recruited form traditional societies in India presented no greater problems to their employers than their counterparts in Britain and the United States.

In sum, in the case of industry, there are reasons to believe that the increasing role of science in generating technological advance in the late nineteenth century increased the importance of formal education down to lower-level supervisors and shopfloor foremen. However, these workers' on-the-job experience may have been as or more important in enabling them to master changing technical advance in industry. And the case for the importance of education is no stronger on strictly technical grounds for those who work on a mass production assembly line than for those who work in the artisan's workshop.

Agriculture

The impact of the rise of science-based technology in industry on the demand for educated workers is attenuated by the tendency toward economies of scale and the increasing importance of the factory and other forms of organization that have tended to centralize decision-making responsibility. In agriculture, insofar as peasant farm operators have persisted in many economies, decision making has tended to remain decentralized, which implies that decisions concerning technological advance rest with a much larger proportion of the agricultural work force than of the industrial work force. Moreover, the impact of science-based technological advance on the demand for educated labor may have been much more extensive in agriculture than in industry.

In the last several hundred years, there have been marked technical advances in agriculture throughout he world. Although technological advance has clearly increased agricultural productivity, it is only in the twentieth century that agricultural technical advance has been clearly science-based. The new cropping rotation patterns, fertilizers, and crop varieties that characterized improved agricultural practice up through the early twentieth century were not based on formal scientific principles taken from chemistry, biology, or physics.[15]

---

[13]   See for example Landes (1972, 340, 347, 348); Sandberg (1982); Morris (1983, 583, 653); and Easterlin (1981, 14).

[14]   See for example Graff (1979, 232-33); Lee (1978, 464) and Easterlin (1981, 9-10).

[15]   See Dovring (1965).

3. David Mitch   35

Moreover, while literacy may have raised the probability of new techniques being adopted, one cannot assert that it was strictly required for their diffusion. The role of personal contact was frequently more important than diffusion by print or writing.[16] Even proponents of the importance and value of education, such as Schultz (1975, 834-5, note 11) and Wharton (1965, 203) recognize that illiterates are able to adopt new crop varieties. The rapid spread of the potato among cultivators in Ireland in the seventeenth century illustrates how illiterates could rapidly adopt new agricultural techniques.[17]

Factors other than education may have more decisive influences on the adoption of new crop varieties. Local variations in climate and soil, as noted above, restrict the generality of technical discoveries and improvements in agriculture.[18] Also, new technical developments in agriculture were frequently capital-intensive or at least required sizable capital investments that precluded their widespread adoption. Institutional factors, such as the extent of land reform and the nature of tenancy, have probably also been important determinants of the extent of technical advance.

The experience of countries with both relatively educated and poorly educated farm work forces illustrates the restricted influence of education on technical advance, the limited scientific basis of agricultural advance, the role of personal contact, and the influence of institutional arrangements and capital constraints on the rate of technical advance in agriculture.

The agricultural advances which occurred in Germany and Scandinavia in the late nineteenth century seem on the surface to confirm the importance of education. In Germany, the sugar beet and new crop rotation systems were introduced; in Scandinavia, the cream separator and other dairying improvements were introduced, and more generally, advanced crop rotations were instituted, new fertilizers were used, and mechanization began to spread.[19] In both areas these advances coincided with extensive activities in education explicitly aimed at agriculture or rural areas.[20]

However, it is not at all clear that basic literacy, let alone higher education, was a prerequisite for agricultural advance but other noneducational prerequisites do seem to have been present. In Germany and Norway, peasant agriculture appears to have made very limited progress in the late nineteenth century despite widespread literacy and educational activities in rural areas.[21] Agricultural innovation in Germany only seems to have been profitable with the assistance of protective tariffs.[22] The cooperative movement in Denmark and else-

---

[16]   See, for example, Macdonald (1979, 30-39).
[17]   See Salaman (1949, p.189 and chap.12).
[18]   See Parker (1972, 75-76) and Hayami and Ruttan (1971, 289-90). Also See Evenson (1974).
[19]   On Germany see Clapham (1936, 216 ff); Perkins (1981); on Scandinavia see Milward and Saul (1973, 492 ff); Jorberg (1973, 449-57).
[20]   Clapham (1936, 216). For Denmark see Milward and Saul (1973, 509) and Jorberg (1973, 396).
[21]   On Germany see Clapham (1936, 216, 219). On Norway see Milward and Saul (1973, 520) and Jorberg (1973, 402).
[22]   See Dovring (1965, 656); Perkins (1981).

where in Scandinavia seems to have facilitated agricultural advance.[23] The cooperative movement in Denmark has been associated with the folk high schools, but this can be attributed to the role of community ties that could be developed outside of educational systems.[24] In Japan, technical progress in agriculture was clearly well under way before the advent of scientific agricultural research. Both the development and the diffusion of new techniques took place through the network of so-called veteran farmers who then diffused their methods through community networks; at times they were legally required to do so. This diffusion did not require literacy and was under way before literacy was widespread in rural areas.[25]

In late nineteenth century Russia, the postbellum American South, and late nineteenth— and twentieth-century India, climate, soil conditions, poverty, lack of agricultural reform, "cultural isolation", and the high capital requirements of new techniques were more of a barrier to the spread of new agricultural innovations than was the lack of formal education in rural areas.[26] Although some studies of Russia indicate that literate peasants were more likely to adopt new techniques than those who were not, studies of India have yielded conflicting results on whether literacy per se raised the probability that new techniques were adopted.[27] Moreover, in the case of Russia, there are indications that the *zemstvo* and other regional and community institutions played an important role in encouraging the adoption of new agricultural techniques and that these institutions could overcome the inertia often associated with illiteracy.[28]

The increasing scientific basis for technological advance over the last century or so has clearly increased the demand for educated laborers in some segments of the work force. But how extensive those segments are remains uncertain. In industry, the majority of the workforce was probably unaffected. In agriculture, the value of formal education in the process of technical advance may have influenced a greater share of the workforce than in industry. However among those workers who did perceive an increasing value to education because of the influence of technical advance, this influence may have been greater in industry than in agriculture. In neither sector was it necessary for a majority of the work force to be literate for science-based technical change to progress. The case for widespread mass education rests on the cultivation of characteristics other than cognitive knowledge of a given set of techniques. And even on this issue, other social institutions could substitute for the effects of education.

---

[23]   See Milward and Saul (1973, 504-505).

[24]   Milward and Saul (1973, 508-509). Also see Jorberg (1973, 396).

[25]   See Allen (1965, 80-81); Hayami and Ruttan (1971, 157, 160-61); Rosovsky (1972, 231); Hayami (1975); Smith (1959, 87).

[26]   See Symons (1972, 56-57); Volin (1970, 61, 64, 67-68, 69); Gerschenkron (1965, 743, 777). For the American South see Rubin (1975); Scott (1970, 210 and chap. 8). For India see Divekar (1983, 346) and Maddison (1971, 108-109).

[27]   On Russia see Volin (1970, 64). On India see Villaume (1978, 41, 60); Shono (1975, 98).

[28]   Volin (1970, 67-68).

Education as a prerequisite for commercial and financial development

No matter what the role of education in facilitating technological progress, it seems obvious that the work force must have at least minimal levels of formal education for an economy to develop commercially. It is common to associate economic growth and development with a growing scale and complexity of market activity, including the increased orientation of economic activity toward market sales, the growth and development of capital markets, and the increasing integration and coordination of economic activity under the supervision of bureaucratic hierarchies rather than through market exchanges. The development of commerce would seem to place increasing value on education because of the increasing proportions of the labor force involved in management, entrepreneurship, and clerical work. It is suggestive of the demands of commercial activity for at least minimal literacy skills that in Western Europe between the tenth and fifteenth centuries —where literacy rates at this time among the general adult population were probably well under 10 percent— the first stirrings of rising literacy and educational activity seem to have occurred among those involved in commerce and administration. The commercial revolution in Italy provides an especially notable example of these forces at work.[29] There is disagreement on the extent to which commercial development influences economic development more generally.[30] But commercial and financial development is significant enough to warrant examining whether education is a prerequisite for this development.

Compared with the role of education in technological advance, in would seem that education is important to, but not strictly necessary for, commercial development. Sandberg, for example, allows that government activity can substitute for a poorly developed financial system that is the result of low levels of education, although he also argues that it is not a perfect substitute.[31] Commercial activity and various financial networks have developed in extensively illiterate societies. [32] And illiterates are by no means necessarily irrational or incapable of pursuing profit opportunities.[33] The main issue, then, is the size of the impact of education on commercial development.

In considering the extent to which education facilitates commercial and financial development, one can begin with the function of literacy and formal education in keeping accounts and records. Although one can point to examples of illiterates who have devised primitive accounting systems, as the scale and complexity of commercial transactions develop, literacy would seem to become

---

[29] See Graff (1987, chaps. 3 and 4) and Hyde (1979).

[30] See Goldsmith (1969, 408-9).

[31] See Sandberg (1982, 681, 685, 695, 696).

[32] See for example the descriptions of traders in India, W. Africa and Southeast Asia in Headrick (1988, 352); Geertz (1956, 103); Carstensen and Morris (1978, 262-65); and Dewey (1962, 71).

[33] See for example Macpherson (1972, 158-9); and Catanach (1970, 244).

increasingly important.[34] However, in the past, several factors probably temper-
ed the importance of literacy in keeping accounts. First, until the twentieth
century, accounting appears to have played quite a limited role in economic
decision making.[35]

Second, a relatively small percentage of the labor force would have been
required to keep accounts and records, even in a relatively developed commercial economy. Lewis (1965, 5-6) estimates that to meet the accounting and
administrative needs of contemporary developing economies, it would be adequate if 10 percent of a given age cohort in developing countries received
secondary education. And in England in 1901, clerks were only 4 percent of the
labor force.[36] Even illiterates can be actively involved in a supervisory role in
commercial activity if they can delegate record keeping to trusted subordinates.[37]

The modest importance of keeping accounts or the role of widespread literacy
in dealing with the keeping of accounts is suggested by the extent to which
piece-rate payment schemes have emerged among groups with high rates of illiteracy.[38] Although literacy would enable workers who are paid by the piece to verify
on written accounts the accuracy of their payment, it appears that this advantage
was not decisive enough to motivate piece-rate workers to acquire literacy.

Beyond its value in keeping accounts, more general characteristics associated with education may have been important. Sandberg has emphasized the role
of literacy and education in facilitating the development of banks and other
financial intermediaries. In particular, he has argued that illiterates in nineteenth-century Europe were less likely to trust paper money, bank deposits, or
bills of exchange.[39] A number of authors have asserted that low literacy rates in
the postbellum American South and in India restricted the spread of bank
deposits as substitutes for bank notes as well as the more general development
of the banking system.[40] However, Lampe (1972, 123, 137-8) has reported for
Serbia in the late nineteenth century, where the literacy rate among peasants
was only 15 percent, no clear connection between literacy and people's willingness to use banknotes or between literacy and the general development of the
banking system. And White (1987, 19) found no correlation between literacy
and willingness to accept bank note issues in France during the Revolution.

Other aspects of commercial development have also been associated with
education: the supply of entrepreneurial ability, commercial ability, market

---

[34]   For examples of accounting systems used by illiterates see Jain (1929, 66-67). For an example from
       Java see Dewey (1962, 71). On the importance of literacy increasing with the complexity of
       transactions see Belshaw (1965, 66-67). For examples of the problems that could be encountered
       in extending credit to illiterates, see Jain (1929, 206-7); and Catanach (1970, 201).

[35]   See Pollard (1965, 288); Salsbury (1980, 608b); and Chandler (1977).

[36]   Anderson (1976, 2).

[37]   See for example Geertz (1956, 103).

[38]   See for England, Church (1986, 556); and Mitchell (1984, chap. 8 especially 168-70).

[39]   Sandberg (1982, 681, 683, 684, 693).

[40]   Ransom and Sutch (1972, 647); Sinha (1927, 204, 207-208); Jain (1929, 206-209, 244); Catanach
       (1970, 201).

orientation, geographic and social mobility, adaptability to change, and allocative ability. There are varying amounts of evidence that people with a formal education are more likely to possess these characteristics.[41] However, there is also evidence to suggest that literacy is by no means a prerequisite for possessing any of these characteristics.[42] The existence of extensive trading activity among illiterates in various twentieth-century Asian and African societies was previously mentioned. Indeed, one can even attempt an appeal to Adam Smith's (1776, book 1,chap. 2) proposition that the "propensity to truck, barter, and exchange" is innate to human nature, even among primitive societies.

As with technological advance, it is important to consider what proportion of the labor force needs to acquire education if commercial development is to proceed. It could be argued that one long-run trend in the organization of commerce has tended to increase the importance of at least basic literacy and also, most likely, higher levels of education in the labor force. This trend is the tendency for transactions that were formerly accomplished by market exchange to be done instead within bureaucratic hierarchies. Such hierarchies seem to rely far more on coordination by impersonal communication and, in particular, on the use of records and accounts than do market exchanges by relatively small-scale traders.

However, both the trend toward the dominance of managerial hierarchies in business and the efficiency advantages of this trend have been disputed by Rosenberg and Birdzell (1986, 280). They maintain that in the twentieth-century U.S. economy, the majority of the labor force has continued to work in relatively small enterprises. They also maintain that it is advantageous for an eonomy to maintain a diversity of firm sizes, even within the same general industry.[43] The possibility of this advantage suggests that using small market transactions in place of bureaucratic coordination is one way an economy could compensate for low levels of literacy in the conduct of its commercial activity.

In taking a skeptical view of the role of formal education in the development of commerce, I would not want to deny that role is a positive one. What I question is the importance of that role. And as with technological advance, any competencies and attitudes facilitating commercial activity that formal schooling may cultivate seem to be part of a broader complex of behaviors that can be cultivated in other ways.

Alternatives to formal education in the development of human capabilities

Throughout this essay a common theme has been the possibility of substituting for formal education various kinds of more spontaneous or informal experiences. These may develop human capabilities in ways that might contribute to economic growth, whether through inventive ability, the adoption of technology,

---

[41] See for example Sewell (1985, 253-57). For evidence from nineteenth-century England that literacy is associated with upward social mobility see Vincent (1989) and Mitch (n.d.).

[42] For evidence of occupational and geographical mobility among illiterates, see Sanderson (1972); Vincent (1989); Mitch (n.d.) and Wright (1986, 255).

[43] Rosenberg and Birdzell (1986, 280 and chap. 9). For a similar argument, see Carstensen and Morris (1978, 264-65).

commercial and entrepreneurial skills, or more general allocative ability and adaptability to change. Such a possiblity gives rise to the question of why the human capabilities generated outside of formal schooling would vary over time or space. Solow and Temin (1978, p.13-14) point out that if skills are generated purely by experience and that if each worker acquires skills as he ages, then the pool of skills in the labor force would be determined solely by its age distribution and the number of workers. If the age distribution is unchanged, then there is no reason to expect the mean level of skill per worker to change over time. For the economist, the attractiveness of focusing on education as a way to improve human capabilities is that it does involve scarce resources, it is capable of at least proximate measurement, and it can be treated primarily as another input into the productive process. For neoclassical economists, a focus on education is thus preferable to turning to other aspects of experience that might influence human capabilities, such as culture, values, attitudes, and norms that would lead into sociological and institutional analysis along the lines of Clarence Ayres and Max Weber. What other than formal education, might also influence the development of human capabilities in economic activity?

Solow and Temin (1978, 14) themselves suggest some possibilities. They point out that the occupational composition of the labor force will influence the character of the learning and experience acquired on the job. It is reasonable to suppose that some occupations will be more conducive to learning by doing than others and, thus, the distribution of the labor force between these types of occupations will influence the acquisition of economically productive skills.[44] Solow and Temin (1978) also note that different kinds of work organization use different methods of training workers and this can influence what kinds of skills a labor force acquires. Under the heading of occupational composition one can also place Adam Smith's emphasis on the division of labor as an influence on the development of skills, along with his famous dictum that the division of labor is limited by the extent of the market.

Another influence on the development of skills that Solow and Temin (1978) mention is urbanisation because of the improved links that the city provides to others who have accumulated skills and knowledge.[45] Another factor is the impact on skill development of the distribution and organization of power in a society. Slavery and serfdom, for example, would seem to impede the acquisition of economic decision-making ability and the choice by individual workers of what skills and occupations to pursue.[46] The qualities of autonomy, diversity, and experimentation that Rosenberg and Birdzell (1986, 33) argue have been the source of economic prosperity in Western countries were likely to have excercised a significant part of their influence through their impact on the development of human skills and capabilities.

---

[44]   For a growth model based on this premise see Stokey (1988).

[45]   This theme is emphasized in the growth model developed by Lucas (1988, 35-39), building on the ideas of Jane Jacobs on the influence of cities.

[46]   For arguments along these lines see Jones (1988).

The role of these considerations can be illustrated by the contrast between Japanese farmers at the end of the Tokugawa period and ex-slave sharecroppers in the postbellum South. In neither society was formal education widespread, yet there were marked differences between then in the economically productive skills and capabilities they possessed. James Nakamura (1981, 266) has argued that changes in the feudal order in Tokugawa Japan encouraged the penetration of markets and led to what he terms the "less formal bases of human capital accumulation" in rural areas before the diffusion of literacy or primary schooling commenced. This, in turn, he suggests, set the stage for rapid economic growth in Japan during the Meiji period and later. In contrast, Ransom and Sutch (1973, 136) point to the difficulties that newly emancipated ex-slaves in the rural U.S. South encountered when they tried to establish themselves as share croppers and master the economic decision making required to run a farm because they lacked familiarity with economic markets and with management decisions. They mention illiteracy or lack of formal education only as a "compounding" problem.

The list of factors and brief examples just provided admittedly provide no more than a few hints as to how to go about examining what aspects of a society may develop the economic capabilities of its labor force. One may want to question the feasibility of such an examination. Imagining alternatives to a single physical innovation such as the railroad was not an easy task, some would argue a task that, in principle, cannot be performed successfully, Imagining alternatives to the more amorphous concept of formal educatión may be even more unmanageable. Nevertheless, as Fogel pointed out about assessments of the railroad, making a statement about the contribution of education to economic growth entails making a statement about what an economy would be like without an educated labor force. Furthermore, considering factors other than formal education that may develop the economic capabilities of the labor force emphasizes the variety of ways human potential can affect an economy's performance. In this respect, considering the possibility of substitutes for formal education is an extension more than a refutation of the notion that education contributes to economic growth.

WORKS CITED

ALDCROFT, D. H.: (1975) "Investment in and Utilisation of Manpower: Great Britain and her Rivals, 1870-1914" in Barrie M. Ratcliffe ed. *Great Britain and her World, 1750-1914* Manchester: Manchester University Press.

ALLEN, G. C.: (1965) *Japan's Economic Expansion* London: Oxford University Press.

ANDERSON, C. ARNOLD and BOWMAN, MARY JEAN: (1976) "Education and Economic Modernization in Historical Perspective" in L. Stone ed. *Schooling and Society* Baltimore: Johns Hopkins University Press.

ANDERSON, GREGORY: (1976) *Victorian Clerks* Manchester: Manchester University Press.

BELSHAW, CYRIL S.: (1965) *Traditional Exchange and Modern Markets* Englewood Cliffs, N. J.: Prentice-Hall.

BLAUG, MARK: (1976) "The Empirical Status of Human Capital Theory: A Slightly Jaundiced Survey" *Journal of Economic Literature* 14.

BLAUG, MARK: (1985) "Where are We Now in the Economics of Education" *Economics of Education Review* 4.

BOWMAN, M. J. & ANDERSON, C. A.: (1963) "Concerning the Role of Education in Development" in C. Geertz ed. *Old Societies and New States: The Quest for Modernity in Africa and Asia* Glencoe, Ill.: Free Press.

BRONFENBRENNER, MARTIN: (1961) "Some Lessons of Japan's Economic Development, 1853-1938" *Pacific Affairs* 34.

BRONFENBRENNER, MARTIN: (1985) "A New View of European Industrialization" *Economic History Review* 38.

CAMERON, RONDO: (1951) "The Diffusion of Technology as a Problem in Economic History" *Economic Geography* 51.

CARSTENSEN, f. and MORRIS, M. D.: (1978) "Credit, Infrastructure, and Entrepreneurial Opportunity Developing Regions" *Journal of Economic History* 38.

CATANACH, I. J.: (1970) *Rural Credit in Western India, 1875-1930* Berkeley: University of California Press.

CHANDLER, ALFRED: (1977) *The Visible Hand* Cambridge, Mass.: Harvard University Press.

CHURCH, R. A.: (1986) *History of the British Coal Industry Vol. 3 1830-1913: Victorian Pre-eminenc* Oxford: Clarendon Press.

CLAPHAM, J. H.: (1936) *The Economic Development of France and Germany* 4th edition. Cambridge: Cambridge University Press.

CRISP, OLGA: (1978) "Labour and Industrialization in Russia" *The Cambridge Economic History of Europe* vol. VII Pt. II. Cambridge: Cambridge University Press.

DEWEY, ALICE: (1962) *Peasant Marketing in Java* New York: Free Press of Glencoe.

DIVEKAR, V. D.: (1983) "Western India" in *The Cambridge Economic History of India* vol. 2 Cambridge: Cambridge University Press.

DOVRING, FOLKE: (1965) "The Transformation of European Agriculture" *The Cambridge Economic History of Europe.* Cambridge: Cambridge University Press.

EASTERLIN, RICHARD: (1981) "Why Isn't the Whole World Developed?" *Journal of Economic History* 41.

EVENSON, ROBERT: (1974) "International Diffusion of Agrarian Technology" *Journal of Economic History* 34.

FOGEL, ROBERT: (1974) *Railroads and American Economic Growth* Baltimore: Johns Hopkins University Press.

GEERTZ, CLIFFORD: (1956) *The Social Context of Economic Change: An Indonesian Case Study.* Cambridge, Mass.: Center for International Studies, Massachussetts Institute of Technology.

GERSCHENKRON, ALEXANDER: (1972) "Reflections on the Concept of Prerequisites of Modern Industrialization" *Economic Backwardness in Historical Perspective* Cambridge, Mass.: Harvard University Press.

GERSCHENKRON, ALEXANDER: (1965) "Agrarian Policies and Industrialization: Russia, 1861-1917" *The Cambridge Economic History of Europe* Vol. VI, Pt. II. Cambridge: Cambridge University Press.

GOLDSMITH, RAYMOND: (1969) *Financial Structure and Development* New Haven: Yale University Press.

GRAFF, HARVEY: (1979) *The Literacy Myth* New York: Academic Press.

GRAFF, HARVEY: (1987) *Legacies of Literacy* Bloomington: Indiana University Press.

HAYAMI, Y.: (1975) *A Century of Agricultural Growth in Japan*. Minneapolis: University of Minnesota Press.

HAYAMI, Y. and RUTTAN, V.: (1971) *Agricultural Development. An International Perspective* Baltimore: Johns Hopkins University Press.

HEADRICK, DANIEL: (1988) *Tentacles of Progress. Technology Transfer in the Age of Imperialism, 1850-1940*. New York: Oxford University Press.

HOFFMANN, WALTHER: (1965) *Das Wachstum der Deutschen Wirtschaft Seit der Mitte des 19. Jahrhunderts*. Berlin: Springer Verlag.

HYDE, J. K.: (1979) "Some Uses of Literacy in Venice and Florence in the Thirteenth and Fourteenth Centuries" *Transactions* Royal Historical Society, 5th Series 29.

JAIN, L. C.: (1929) *Indigenous Banking in India* London: Macmillan.

JONES, ERIC: (1988) *Growth Recurring* New York: Oxford University Press.

JORBERG, LENNART: (1973) "The Nordic Countries, 1850-1914" in Carlo Cipolla ed. *The Fontana Economic History Of Europe*. Vol. 4 Pt. II. London: Collins/Fontana Books.

KOCKA, JURGEN: (1978) "Entrepreneurs and Managers in German Industrialization" *The Cambridge Economic History of Europe*. Vol. VII Pt. I Cambridge: Cambridge University Press.

KUZNETS, SIMON: (1966) *Modern Economic Growth. Rate, Structure, and Spread* New Haven: Yale University Press.

LAMPE, JOHN: (1972) "Serbia, 1878-1912" in R. Cameron ed. *Banking and Economic Development. Some Lessons of History* New York: Oxford University Press.

LANDES, DAVID: (1965) "Japan and Europe: Contrasts in Industrialization" in W.W. Lockwood ed. *The State and Economic Enterprise in Japan* Princeton: Princeton University Press.

LANDES, DAVID: (1972) *The Unbound Prometheus* Cambridge: Cambridge University Press.

LEE, J. J.: (1978) "Labour in German Industrialization", *The Cambridge Economic History of Europe* vol. VII, Pt. I.

LEWIS, W. ARTHUR: (1965) *Education and Economic Development* University of Saskatchewan University Lectures n.° 6 University of Saskatchewan.

LUCAS, ROBERT: (1988) "On the Mechanics of Economic Development", *Journal of Monetary Economics* 22.

MACDONALD, S.: (1979) "The Diffusion of Knowledge among Northumberland Farmers, 1780-1815" *Agricultural History Review* 27.

MACPHERSON, W. J.: (1972) "Economic Development in India under the British Crown" in A. Youngson ed. *Economic Development in the Long Run* London: George Allen & Unwin.

MADDISON, ANGUS: (1971) *Class Structure and Economic Growth* London: Allen & Unwin.

MILWARD, A. and SAUL'S.: (1973) *The Economic Development of Continental Europe, 1780-1870* London: George Allen & Unwin.

MITCH, DAVID: (n.d.) "Not Driven But Won: Private Choice and Public Policy in the Rise of Literacy in Victorian England" manuscript.

MITCHELL, B. R.: (1984) *Economic Development of the British Coal Industry, 1800-1914* Cambridge: Cambridge University Press.

MORRIS, MORRIS D.: (1960) "The Recruitment of an Industrial Labor Force in India, with British and American Comparisons" *Comparative Studies in Society and History* II.

MORRIS, MORRIS D.: (1983) "The Growth of Large-Scale Industry to 1947" *The Cambridge Economic History of India* vol. II. Cambridge: Cambridge University Press.

MUSGRAVE, P. W.: (1967) *Technical Change, the Labour Force and Education: A Study of the British and German Iron and Steel Industries 1860-1964*. Oxford: Pergamon Press.

NAKAMURA, JAMES: (1981) "Human Capital Accumulation in Premodern Rural Japan" *Journal of Economic History* 41.

OHKAWA, K. and ROSOVSKY, H.: (1973) *Japanese Economic Growth* Stanford: Stanford University Press.

PARKER, WILLIAM: (1961) "Economic Development in Historical Perspective" *Economic Development and Cultural Change* 10.

PARKER, WILLIAM: (1972) "Technology, Resources, and Economic Change in the West" in A. J. Youngson ed. *Economic Development in the Long Run* London: George Allen & Unwin.

PERKINS, J. A.: (1981) "The Agricultural Revolution in Germany, 1850-1914" *Journal of European Economic History* 10.

POLLARD, SIDNEY: (1965) *The Genesis of Modern Management* Cambridge, Mass.: Harvard University Press.

RANSOM, ROGER and SUTCH, RICHARD: (1972) "Debt Peonage in the Cotton South after the Civil War" *Journal of Economic History* 32.

RANSOM, ROGER and SUTCH, RICHARD: (1973) "The Ex-Slave in the Post-Bellum South" *Journal of Economic History* 33.

ROSENBERG, NATHAN and BIRDZELL, L. E.: (1986) *How the West Grew Rich* New York: Basic Books.

ROSOVSKY, H.: (1972) "What are the Lessons of Japanese Economic History?" In A. Youngson ed. *Economic Development in the Long Run* London: George Allen & Unwin.

RUBIN, JULIUS: (1975) "The Limits of Agricultural Progress in the Nineteeth Century South" *Agricultural History* 49.

SALAMAN, REDCLIFFE: (1949) *The History and Social Influence of the Potatoe* Cambridge: Cambridge University Press.

SALSBURY, STEPHEN: (1980) "American Business Institutions Before the Railroad" in Glenn Porter ed. *Encyclopedia of American Economic History* New York: Charles Scribner's.

SANDBERG, LARS: (1979) "The Case of the Impoverished Sophisticate: Human Capital and Swedish Economic Growth Before World War I" *Journal of Economic History* 39.

SANDBERG, LARS: (1982) "Ignorance, Poverty and Economic Backwardness in the Early Stages of European Industrialization: Variations on Alexander Gerschenkron's Grand Theme" *Journal of European Economic History* 11.

SANDERSON, MICHAEL: (1972) "Literacy and Social Mobility in the Industrial Revolution in Lancashire" *Past and Present*.

SCHOFIELD, ROGER: (1973) "Some Dimensions of Illiteracy, 1750-1850" *Explorations in Economic History* 10.

SCHULTZ, T. W.: (1975) "The Value of the Ability to Deal with Disequilibria" *Journal of Economic Literature* 13.

SCOTT, ROY V.: (1970) *The Reluctant Farmer: The Rise of Agricultural Extension to 1914* Urbana: University of Illinois Press.

SEWELL, WILLIAM: (1985) *Structure and Mobility* Cambridge: Cambridge University Press.

SHONO, P. V.: (1975) *Agricultural Development in India* Delhi: Vikas Publishing House.

SIMHA, H.: (1927) *Early European Banking in India* London: Macmillan.

SMITH, ADAM: (1776) *The Wealth of Nations*.

SMITH, THOMAS: (1959) *The Agrarian Origins of Modern Japan*. Stanford: Stanford University Press.

SOLOW, ROBERT and TEMIN, PETER: (1978) "Introduction: Inputs for Growth" *The Cambridge Economic History of Europe* Vol. VII Pt.I Cambridge: Cambridge University Press.

STOKEY, NANCY: (1988) "Learning by Doing and the Introduction of New Goods" *Journal of Political Economy* 96.

SYMONS, LESLIE: (1972) *Russian Agriculture: A Geographic Survey* New York: Wiley.

TAIRA, KOIJI: (1978) "Factory Labour and the Industrial Revolution in Japan" in *The Cambridge Economic History of Europe* Vol. VII Pt. 2. Cambridge: Cambridge University Press.

TRANTER, N. L.: (1981) "The Labour Supply 1780-1860" in R. Floud and D. McCloskey eds. *The Economic History of Britain since 1700* Vol. I Cambridge: Cambridge University Press.

VILLAUME, JOHN MICHAEL: (1978) "Literacy and the Adoption of Agricultural Innovations" Ed. D Thesis, Harvard University.

VINCENT, DAVID: (1989) *Literacy and Popular Culture* Cambridge: Cambridge University Press.

VOLIN, LAZAR: (1970) *A Century of Russian Agriculture from Alexander II to Kruschev* Cambridge, Mass.: Harvard University Press.

WHARTON, CLIFTON: (1965) "Education and Agricultural Growth: The Role of Education in Early-Stage Agriculture" in C. A. Anderson and M. J. Bowman eds. *Education and Economic Development* Chicago: Aldine.

WHITE, EUGENE: (1987) "Free Banking during the French Revolution" Working Paper, Department of Economics, Rutgers University.

WRIGHT, GAVIN: (1986) *Old South New South* New York: Basic Books.

THE JOURNAL OF ECONOMIC HISTORY

VOLUME XLI   MARCH 1981   NUMBER 1

Why Isn't the Whole World Developed?

RICHARD A. EASTERLIN

The worldwide spread of modern economic growth has depended chiefly on the diffusion of a body of knowledge concerning new production techniques. The acquisition and application of this knowledge by different countries has been governed largely by whether their populations have acquired traits and motivations associated with formal schooling. To judge from the historical experience of the world's twenty-five largest nations, the establishment and expansion of formal schooling has depended in large part on political conditions and ideological influences. The limited spread of modern economic growth before World War II has thus been due, at bottom, to important political and ideological differences throughout the world that affected the timing of the establishment and expansion of mass schooling. Since World War II there has been growing uniformity among the nations of the world, modern education systems have been established almost everywhere, and the spread of modern economic growth has noticeably accelerated.

With the coming of the modern age formal education assumed a significance far in excess of anything that the world had yet seen. The school, which had been a minor social agency in most of the societies of the past, directly affecting the lives of but a small fraction of the population, expanded horizontally and vertically until it took its place along with the state, the church, the family and property as one of society's most powerful institutions.

George S. Counts[1]

IT is now a full two centuries since the coming of the modern technological age was signalled by James Watt's invention of the single acting steam engine. In this period output per capita and per unit of labor input have risen at long-term rates never before seen in human history—first in northern and western Europe and Northern America, subsequently

Journal of Economic History, Vol. XLI, No. 1 (March 1981). © The Economic History Association. All rights reserved. ISSN 0022-0507.

Presidential address to the Economic History Association, Boston, Sept. 12, 1980. The author is Kenan Professor of Economics, University of Pennsylvania. He is grateful for comments on this paper to Eileen M. Crimmins, for suggestions at an earlier stage to Vartan Gregorian and Kenneth C. Land, and for helpful assistance to Abbe Cohen, Andrew M. Easterlin, Lisa M. Ehrlich, Georgeia S. Hutchinson, Denise H. Rosin, and Aline S. Rowens. Special thanks are due to Michael Waldman for his thoughtful help and comments. The author's thinking on this subject owes much to the work and example of Simon Kuznets.

[1] *Encyclopedia of the Social Sciences* (New York, 1931), vol. V, p. 410.

in Japan, southern and eastern Europe, and parts of Latin America and Oceania.[2] So great is the contrast with prior experience that it has led Simon Kuznets to designate this period as a new epoch in world history, the epoch of modern economic growth.[3] Yet, after two centuries, the great majority of the world's population continues to live in conditions not much different from those at the start of this epoch.

Given the startling contrasts in national experience, an objective look at the history of the past two centuries would not, I think, place in the foreground the questions that now dominate the study of economic history. The current preoccupation of Western scholars with American and European—largely northwestern European—economic history can only seem provincial, for the striking feature about these areas is the fundamental similarity in their experience. Rather, the foremost question of modern economic history, the one that challenges explanation, is why the spread of economic growth has been so limited: why isn't the whole world developed? Beyond this, there is the question of the future: *will* the whole world become developed? If so, how soon? What is the outlook for the "epoch of modern economic growth"?

No one can pretend to know the answers to these questions—but it is worth talking about them, if only to build a case for redirection of research in economic history. Let us begin with the question about the past: why has the spread of economic growth been so limited?

I

The heart of the whole process of industrialization and economic development is intellectual: it consists in the acquisition and application of a corpus of knowledge concerning technique, that is, ways of doing things.

David Landes[4]

In thinking about the past, let us imagine, to start with, a world not unlike that of the late eighteenth century—a world of low and roughly equal levels of economic productivity everywhere, and with fairly limited international contacts through trade, migration, and investment. Suppose now that in one nation economic productivity starts rising rapidly and steadily, because of an unprecedented rate of technological progress. Before long, a second nation sets off on a similar course as technological change also accelerates dramatically, and, then, a third. After a century or so, the total number of nations so embarked remains—on a worldwide scale—small, though increasing.

Consider now a few implications of this development. In the course of

[2] Richard A. Easterlin, "Economic Growth: Overview," *International Encyclopedia of the Social Sciences* (New York, 1969), vol. IV, pp. 395–408.
[3] *Modern Economic Growth: Rate, Structure and Spread* (New Haven, 1966), chap. 1.
[4] "The Creation of Knowledge and Technique: Today's Task and Yesterday's Experience," *Daedalus*, 109 (Winter 1980), 111.

Presidential Address 3

time, large and growing disparities would emerge between income levels in those nations enjoying the fruits of rapid technological progress and those that are not. International trade and investment would expand greatly as a result of sharp shifts in comparative advantage caused by differential technological progress, and also because international transfer costs would fall substantially if, as seems likely, those nations benefiting from new technology apply it to problems of international as well as domestic transport. The resulting increased flow of goods and resources internationally would have some beneficial effect on income levels generally, but such effects would be relatively small compared with the dominating effect on income levels of major differences in the rate of technological change.

This, I suggest, is the essence of what has occurred in the past two centuries.[5] During this period international income differences have grown at unprecedented rates, as have foreign trade and investment. The prime mover in this drama has been the sharp acceleration in the rate of technological change in a relatively small number of nations.

If this view is correct, then it follows that explaining why modern economic growth has spread so slowly becomes a question of explaining why rapid technological change has been limited to so few nations. To answer this, one must first consider whether rapid technological change, when it occurred, was based on a new technology in each country that was indigenous or borrowed. On this, the view that a common technology diffused from one country to the next is certainly the more realistic one. This is evidenced by the classic studies of W. O. Henderson and David Landes of the spread of industrial technology in Europe; in the accounts of the modernization of Japan by scholars such as Tuge and Saxonhouse; and in Strassman's studies of contemporary experience.[6] It is evidenced as well by the striking likeness of modern industrial technology among the various high productivity nations themselves. Only in regard to agriculture, where local environmental conditions play an important part in produc-

[5] For similar views see Kuznets, *Growth*; Rondo Cameron, "The Diffusion of Technology as a Problem in Economic History," *Economic Geography*, 51 (July 1975), 217–30; William N. Parker, "Economic Development in Historical Perspective," *Economic Development and Cultural Change*, 10 (Oct. 1961), 1–7; William Woodruff, *Impact of Western Man* (New York, 1967); Paul Bairoch, *The Economic Development of the Third World since 1900* (Berkeley and Los Angeles, 1975); John Robert Hanson, *Trade in Transition: Exports from the Third World, 1840–1900* (New York, 1980); William Ashworth, *A Short History of the International Economy, 1850–1950* (London, 1952). A valuable framework for the study of international political development is presented in Stein Rokkan, "Dimensions of State Formation and Nation Building: A Paradigm for Research on Variations within Europe," in Charles Tilly, ed., *The Formation of National States in Western Europe* (Princeton, 1975), pp. 562–600.

[6] William O. Henderson, *Britain and Industrial Europe*, 3d ed. (Leicester, 1972); David S. Landes, *The Unbound Prometheus: Technological Change and Industrial Development in Western Europe from 1750 to the Present* (Cambridge, 1969); Hideomi Tuge, ed., *Historical Development of Science and Technology in Japan* (Tokyo, 1961); Gary Saxonhouse, "A Tale of Japanese Technological Diffusion in the Meiji Period," this JOURNAL, 34 (March 1974), 149–65; W. Paul Strassman, *Risk and Technological Innovation* (Ithaca, 1959).

4   *Easterlin*

tion, might one hesitate to stress the borrowed over indigenous elements
in modern technological change. But even in agriculture, one finds that
many of the principles of modern technology, such as irrigation, seed selection, livestock breeding, fertilizer, and, more recently, development of
hybrids and use of pesticides, exhibit quite similar features among nations. Thus it seems reasonable to conclude that the question of explaining differential technological change among nations in the modern period
is a matter chiefly of explaining the limited diffusion of a common technology.

Much of the research on technological diffusion has been admirably
synthesized and critiqued by Nathan Rosenberg.[7] One strong impression
that emerges from reading this literature is the extent to which the transfer
of technology is a person-to-person process. As Rosenberg points out,
"the notion of a production function as a 'set of blueprints' comes off very
badly . . . if it is taken to mean a body of techniques which is available
independently of the human inputs who utilize it."[8] According to Svennilson, "much of the detailed knowledge that is born in the course of industrial operations, can more easily and in part exclusively be transferred by
demonstration and training in actual operations."[9] Similarly, to Arrow, "it
seems to be personal contact that is most relevant in leading to . . . adoption [of an innovation]."[10]

This emphasis on the personal element in the transfer of technology
suggests that understanding of it might usefully be approached by analogy with a situation in which most of us here have some relevant experience, namely, as an educational process, in which a new and difficult subject—"modern" technology—must be taught and learned. From this point
of view, explanation of the limited spread of modern economic growth
turns into a question of identifying the factors that have constrained the
dissemination of a new type of knowledge—that of modern technology.

                                      II

Education produces large, pervasive, and enduring effects on knowledge and receptivity to
knowledge.

                                                     Herbert H. Hyman et al.[11]

---

[7] Nathan Rosenberg, "Factors Affecting the Payoff to Technological Innovation," unpublished
document prepared for the National Science Foundation (1974). See also David J. Teece, *The Multi-
national Corporation and the Resource Cost of International Technology Transfer* (Cambridge, MA,
1976).

[8] Nathan Rosenberg, "Economic Development and the Transfer of Technology: Some Historical
Perspectives," *Technology and Culture*, 11 (Oct. 1970), 555, emphasis added.

[9] Ingvar Svennilson, "Technical Assistance: The Transfer of Industrial Know-how to Non-Indus-
trialized Countries," in Kenneth Berill, ed., *Economic Development with Special Reference to East Asia*
(New York, 1964), p. 408, emphasis in original.

[10] Kenneth J. Arrow, "Classification Notes on the Production and Transmission of Technological
Knowledge," *American Economic Review: Papers and Proceedings*, 52 (May 1969), 33; see also Daniel
Lloyd Spencer, *The Technological Gap in Perspective* (New York, 1970).

[11] Herbert H. Hyman, Charles R. Wright, and John Shelton Reed, *The Enduring Effects of Education* (Chicago, 1975), p. 109.

Viewing the transfer of technology as an educational process leads naturally to questions about teachers and students. If new technological knowledge spread slowly, did the fault lie on the teachers' side or the students'?

One reason for minimizing the teachers' responsibility is that when entrepreneurs or governments in low productivity nations wanted teachers, they seem to have been able to beg, borrow, buy, or steal them, as well as send their nationals to the high productivity nations for instruction. After the Meiji Restoration, for example, Japan imported numerous foreign scholars and technological experts and sent students to the West.[12]

The more important question lies on the side of the students. What is it that makes for effective learning? Learning is, as we all know, partly a matter of inherent intelligence; partly of aptitudes; and partly of incentives. What we all seek are bright, well-trained, and highly motivated students.

I think we can safely dismiss the view that the failure of modern technological knowledge to spread rapidly was due to significant differences among nations in the native intelligence of their populations. To my knowledge there are no studies that definitively establish differences, say, in basic IQ among the peoples of the world.

A more persuasive case might be made with regard to incentives for learning; institutional differences among countries undoubtedly created variations in the incentives for mastering the new technology. In their studies of the historical development of property and other institutions, Jonathan Hughes, Douglass North, Robert Thomas, and others are, in this respect, filling an important gap in knowledge about incentive structures.[13] But it is important to recognize that the new technology itself created incentives for learning via the competitive pressures exerted through international trade. Thus the rapid response by producers in parts of Continental Europe and the United States to the British industrial revolution was partly induced by the growing flood of imported British manufactures in their markets. The new technology also created pressures for its more widespread adoption by endowing its possessors with superior military capability. The threat to political sovereignty thus posed was a strong incentive for governments in low productivity countries to initiate and promote programs of technological modernization, as in Japan. In the course of time such economic and political pressures were felt in many nations throughout the world; yet often the new technology failed to be taken up. The question is, why?

The answer, I suggest, has to do in important part with differences

[12] Tuge, *Science*; for early data on Japanese students studying abroad, see Reinhold Schairer, *Die Studenten im internationalen Kulturleben: Beitrage zur Frage des Studiums in fremdem Lande* (Munster in Westfalen, 1927), chap. 1. See also Henderson, *Europe*.

[13] Douglass C. North and Robert Paul Thomas, *The Rise of the Western World: A New Economic History* (Cambridge, 1973); Jonathan R. T. Hughes, *Social Control in the Colonial Economy* (Charlottesville, 1976).

6   *Easterlin*

among countries in the extent of their population's formal schooling: the
more schooling of appropriate content that a nation's population had, the
easier it was to master the new technological knowledge becoming available. Moreover, as I shall note subsequently, substantial increases in formal schooling tend to be accompanied by significant improvement in the
incentive structure. Hence increased motivation often accompanied increased aptitudes for learning the new technology.

The notion that learning potential depends on prior education should
come as no surprise here, for it is a guiding principle in most schools and
colleges. Given intelligence and motivation, one prefers students with better academic records from better schools, and with more training in relevant subjects. If one's concern is to explain why some nations were rapid
learners and others slow, it seems only reasonable to ask what sort of differences there were in the educational systems that prepared their populations for acquiring new knowledge.

As a first step toward establishing the facts, Figure 1 presents historical
data for twenty-five of the largest countries of the world—in 1960 they accounted for over three-fourths of the world's population—on a very crude
indicator of educational development, the primary school enrollment rate.
These countries, I believe, are reasonably illustrative of experience more
generally.[14] The primary school enrollment rate at any date is simply the
number enrolled in primary school per 10,000 total population. It is subject to both conceptual and measurement biases, most notably to variations in the proportion of school age population to the total.[15] It can, however, reasonably be taken as an index of differences among nations and
trends over time in their population's exposure to formal schooling.
Roughly speaking, values less than 400 signify relatively little exposure of
a nation's population to formal schooling; values in the 400–800 range, a
moderate exposure; and values greater than 800, substantial. To facilitate
comparisons among countries in the figure, the section of each graph
bracketed by an enrollment rate of zero to 400 in the period through 1940
has been shaded. Differences among countries in peak values and the
trend in these values are of little analytical significance because they reflect chiefly variations in the proportion of school age population. For this
reason, and to reduce confusion in the figure, a country's curve was not
plotted after it reached a fairly high level.[16]

[14] The countries chosen were those with 1960 populations greater than 18 million. Because of insufficient historical data, Poland, Pakistan, and Viet Nam are omitted.

[15] Among other comparability problems are the occasional use of attendance rather than enrollment data, variations in the time of year for which enrollment is reported, differences in the length of
the school day and school year, and differences in schools included in the "primary" category (e.g.,
kindergartens).

[16] For other studies of enrollment rates see UNESCO, *World Survey of Education*, vol. 2 (New
York, 1958), pp. 42–60; Alexander L. Peaslee, "Education's Role in Development," *Economic Development and Cultural Change*, 17 (April 1969), 293–318. Although enrollment is used here in preference to literacy because it is a more reliable indicator of the expansion of formal mass schooling,
valuable work has been done to develop historical literacy data. See Peter Flora, "Historical Processes

The first impression that emerges from the graph is the very limited extent of formal schooling in most nations throughout most of the period covered in the graph. In 1850, only a little more than a century ago, virtually the entire population of the world outside of northwestern Europe and Northern America had little or no exposure to formal schooling. Even by 1940 this was still largely the case in Africa, most of Asia, and a substantial part of Latin America.

Does the graph offer any support for the idea that spread of the technology of modern economic growth depended on learning potentials and motivations that were linked to the development of formal schooling? The answer, I believe, is generally yes. Within Europe the most advanced nations educationally, those in northern and western Europe, were the ones that developed first. Not until the end of the nineteenth century did most of southern and eastern Europe start to approach educational levels comparable to the initial levels in the north and west, and it was around this time that these nations began to develop. With regard to the overseas descendants of Europe the picture is the same: the leader in schooling is the leader in development, the United States. Within Latin America, Argentina, the most developed nation there today, took the lead in educational growth in the last half of the nineteenth century. In Asia, Japan's nineteenth-century educational attainment is clearly distinctive, and this was true even before the Meiji Restoration, though important reforms were introduced in 1872.[17] In contrast, note the persistently low educational levels until very recently in Turkey, a nation subject in many ways to external economic and political pressures similar to those experienced by Japan, but failing until recently to show substantial technological modernization.

There is, of course, the matter of cause and effect: are we looking here at the effect of education on economic growth, or vice-versa? Is the growth of schooling merely induced by the process of economic growth itself? In theory, economic growth is a cause of educational growth, but it is only one factor and not clearly the dominant one. Some empirical evidence suggesting that the growth of formal schooling often occurred largely independently of economic development is offered by Figure 1 itself. Note that in the United States and Germany development of widespread for-

---

of Social Mobilization: Urbanization and Literacy, 1850–1965," in Shmuel N. Eisenstadt and Stein Rokkan, eds., *Building States and Nations*, vol. I (Beverly Hills, 1973), pp. 213–58; Carlo M. Cipolla, *Literacy and Development in the West* (Baltimore, 1969); UNESCO, *Progress of Literacy in Various Countries* (Paris, 1953); UNESCO, *World Illiteracy at Mid-Century* (Paris, 1957); James F. Abel and Norman J. Bond, "Illiteracy in the Several Countries of the World," *Department of the Interior Bureau of Education Bulletin* No. 4 (1929), pp. 1–68.

[17] Ronald P. Dore, *Education in Tokugawa Japan* (Berkeley and Los Angeles, 1965); Herbert Passin, *Society and Education in Japan* (New York, 1965). A number of writers stress the role of education in Japanese economic growth. See, for example, Kazushi Ohkawa and Henry Rosovsky, "A Century of Japanese Economic Growth," in William W. Lockwood, ed., *The State and Economic Enterprise in Japan* (Princeton, 1965), pp. 58–59, and Yasukichi Yasuba, "Another Look at the Tokugawa Heritage with Special Reference to Social Conditions," unpublished paper, The Center for Southeast Asia Studies, Kyoto University, October 1979.

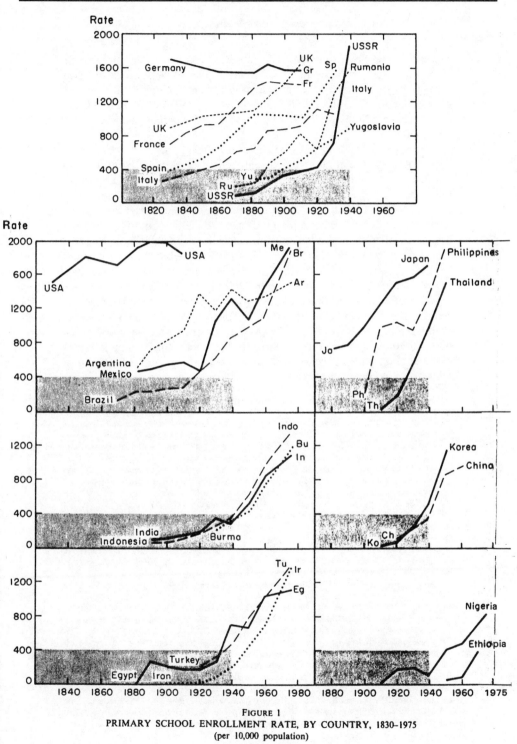

FIGURE 1
PRIMARY SCHOOL ENROLLMENT RATE, BY COUNTRY, 1830–1975
(per 10,000 population)

Source: Appendix Table 1.

mal schooling clearly preceded the onset of modern economic growth.
Note, too, that for a number of countries the schooling curves show
abrupt upswings that are not matched by concurrent surges in economic
development—examples are Rumania between 1880 and 1910; the Philippines between 1900 and 1920; and Mexico and Thailand between 1920
and 1940.

Even if one were to agree that in a general way theory and evidence are
consistent with the notion that formal schooling fosters attributes in a
population that are conducive to the acquisition of modern technology,
there remain important questions about the type of schooling and attributes. Is it true, for example, that "the spread of technological knowledge,
narrowly considered, is not a matter of mass education, but of the training
of a small elite"?[18] If mass education is important, does it have its effect
via training in functional skills such as "the three R's," through "screening," or via political socialization, either of a broad sort, or more narrowly, in instilling a discipline appropriate to factory work?[19] Or is the
function of education, as some sociological studies suggest, one chiefly of
creating a basic change in human personality—a "modern man" who acquires aspirations and attitudes especially favorable to the adoption of
new technology?[20] According to these studies even a small amount of formal schooling has an effect of this sort, although the greater the amount of
schooling the greater the effect.[21]

[18] William N. Parker, "Perspective," p. 1. For valuable discussions of some of the issues in this
paragraph see C. Arnold Anderson and Mary Jean Bowman, eds., *Education and Economic Development* (Chicago, 1965); C. Arnold Anderson and Mary Jean Bowman, "Education and Economic
Modernization in Historical Perspective" and Lawrence Stone, "Introduction," both in Lawrence
Stone, ed., *Schooling and Society* (Baltimore, 1976), pp. xi-xvii, 3–19; Mary Jean Bowman and C. Arnold Anderson, "Concerning the Role of Education in Development," and Martin Carnoy, "Education and Economic Development: The First Generation," *Economic Development and Cultural
Change: Essays in Honor of Bert F. Hoselitz*, 25 (Supplement, 1977), 428–48; Frederick Harbison and
Charles A. Meyers, *Education, Manpower, and Economic Growth* (New York, 1964); Cameron, "Diffusion"; The World Bank, *World Development Report* (Washington, D. C., 1980), chap. 5.

[19] James S. Coleman, ed., *Education and Political Development* (Princeton, 1965); Samuel Bowles
and Herbert Gintis, *Schooling in Capitalist America* (New York, 1976); Martin Carnoy, *Education as
Cultural Imperialism* (New York, 1974); Robert Dreeben, *On What Is Learned in School* (Reading,
MA, 1968); Philip Foster, *Education and Social Change in Ghana* (Chicago, 1965); Harvey J. Graff,
The Literacy Myth (New York, 1979); Michael B. Katz, *Class, Bureaucracy, and Schools* (New York,
1971).

[20] Alex Inkeles and David H. Smith, *Becoming Modern* (Cambridge, 1974); Alex Inkeles, "The
School as a Context for Modernization," *International Journal of Comparative Sociology*, 14, no. 3–4
(Sept.-Dec. 1973), 163–79; David C. McClelland, "Does Education Accelerate Economic Growth?"
Economic Development and Cultural Change, 14 (April 1966), 257–78; William Form, "Comparative
Industrial Sociology and the Convergence Hypothesis," *Annual Review of Sociology*, 5 (1979), 1–25.

[21] Inkeles and Smith, *Becoming Modern*, chap. 9. Formal education is, to be sure, not the only institution to create modern men; some of the new economic institutions accompanying modern economic
growth—most notably, the factory—also work in this way. Thus, there is the possibility of growth "by
pulling up on one's own bootstraps"—factories once established create personality changes conducive
to further economic growth. But the population exposed to factory experience is much more limited
than that potentially reached by a formal school system. Moreover, the evidence indicates that the
impact of formal schooling in creating the personality traits of "modern man" is much greater than
that of any other institution—more than twice as great, for example, as that of the next most important institution, the factory.

10   *Easterlin*

The present state of knowledge does not, I think, provide satisfactory answers to what types of education have what specific effects on economic growth, and clearly the answers need not be mutually exclusive. It seems likely, however, that a substantial primary education system is essential for sustained economic growth. The reason for this is clear if one contrasts the process of achieving higher income levels with that of raising life expectancy. Thanks to modern public health and medical technology, it has proven possible to improve life expectancy markedly even among large populations through measures such as use of pesticides, water purification, and establishment of sewage systems that require knowledge and action by only a relatively few technologists. In contrast, raising productivity levels involves active participation in new production methods by large numbers of the population—by workers in agriculture, industry, transportation, and so on. This is not to say that secondary and higher education can be ignored; clearly one needs technologists as well as mass education. But increases at higher levels of education typically go together with the expansion of primary education.[22] On the other hand, education of the elite without mass education is unlikely to foster economic growth.[23]

It also seems that the content of education conducive to economic growth is that of a secular and rationalistic type. While such content has usually characterized an expansion in mass education, this has not always been true. Among the countries in Figure 1, Spain stands out as a country whose rate of educational development seemingly exceeded its economic growth. A closer look at Spanish education, however, reveals that until the twentieth century it remained closely controlled by the Roman Catholic Church: "the children of the masses received only oral instruction in the Creed, the catechism, and a few simple manual skills. . . . [S]cience, mathematics, political economy, and secular history were considered too controversial for anyone but trained theologians."[24] One consequence of this is that literacy in Spain fails to show an increase commensurate with what one might expect from the data on primary school enrollment; even by 1900 almost two thirds of the population remained illiterate.

III

It is necessary that we enter into a new phase of the Revolution which I shall call the psychological revolutionary period; we must enter into and take possession of the minds of children, the consciences of the young, because they do belong and should belong to the

---

[22] For example, for 90 countries in the period 1970-74, the adjusted R^2 between primary and secondary enrollment rates is .51; between primary and higher, .41. Data are from UNESCO, *Statistical Yearbook, 1976* (Paris, 1977).

[23] In the nineteenth century, educational modernization in the Ottoman Empire, to the extent it occurred, stressed education of the elite; see Andreas M. Kazamias, *Education and the Quest for Modernity in Turkey* (Chicago, 1966). The 1950s data for India presented by Harbison and Meyers suggest a disproportion of secondary and higher education relative to primary (*Manpower*, p. 47).

[24] I. N. Thut and Don Adams, *Educational Patterns in Contemporary Societies* (New York, 1964), p. 62.

Revolution.... It is absolutely necessary to drive the enemy out of that entrenchment
where the clergy has been, where the Conservatives have been—I refer to Education.

Mexican General and ex-President Plutarco Calles, 1934[25]

In simplest terms, the argument to this point is that the spread of the
technology underlying modern economic growth depended in large part
on the extent to which the populations in different countries had acquired
appropriate traits and motivation through formal schooling. But even if
the plausibility of this view be tentatively granted, it only leads to a more
fundamental question: how can one explain the immense differences
among the countries of the world in the timing and growth of formal education?

If, to answer this question, one follows the approach of the new economic history, then the appropriate guidelines are those currently offered
by economic theory. This theory centers on decision-making in one social
institution, the family, and sees the expansion of schooling as a voluntary
response to growing payoffs to education generated by economic growth.
Government, if it comes into the picture at all, is seen largely as implementing or ratifying private household decisions through public action.

There can be no question that serious research on economic incentives
should form a part of research into the causes of expansion of mass education.[26] But the seemingly sizable payoffs to child labor that prevailed in
many developed countries in certain phases of their modern economic
history should caution against expecting too much from it. Research is
needed also on motives and decisions affecting education by social institutions other than those relating to the family. Education is, as we are all
aware, a powerful instrument for influencing the minds of individuals in
their formative years; indeed, if we did not believe this, I doubt that most
of us would be doing as professionals what we are now doing. This elementary fact has hardly escaped the attention of those in society interested in obtaining or maintaining political, social, and economic power.[27]
The result has been that the establishment and growth of mass education
has often been the product chiefly not of market forces but of political
conflict in which major groups in a culture—groups that frequently vary
from one society to the next—are ranged against each other. At the risk of
oversimplification, let me try to illustrate this point in terms of Figure 1.

The most obvious shift in political power with which growth of mass
education has been linked is the establishment of independence from a
former colonial power. This is suggested by the histories of a number of

[25] As quoted in J. Lloyd Mecham, *Church and State in Latin America* (Durham, NC, 1934), p. 406.

[26] See, for example, David Mitch, "The Impact of a Growing Demand of Literate Workers on the
Spread of Literacy in Nineteenth Century England," presented at the Workshop in Economic History, University of Chicago, no. 7980-2 (Oct. 1979).

[27] This has been explicitly recognized in recent economic history research. See, e.g., Alexander
James Field, "Economic and Demographic Determinants of Educational Commitment: Massachusetts, 1855," this JOURNAL, 39 (June 1979), 439–57.

countries in southeastern Europe in the period prior to World War I (exemplified in Figure 1 by Rumania and Yugoslavia), in the mid-East in the 1920s and 30s (as illustrated by Egypt), and in Asia and Africa after World War II (see India, Indonesia, Burma, and Nigeria).[28] This observation implies that colonialism was a major deterrent to the growth of mass education, and thus lends support to the "imperialism" explanation for underdevelopment. Detailed empirical studies of colonial policy such as that currently in progress for the United Kingdom by Lance E. Davis and Robert Huttenback are needed to pursue this issue.[29] But the data in Figure 1 suggest reasons against a too hasty generalization of this sort. First, there are cases—though not many—where colonial governments promoted mass education. The clearest illustration is the American takeover of the Philippines from Spain; perhaps another example is Japanese policy in Korea.[30] Second, in Latin America decolonization in the nineteenth century was not followed by a great upsurge in mass education; hence colonialism cannot be the scapegoat there. Third, there is the counterfactual issue: in the absence of colonial rule would mass education have been promoted vigorously by independent governments? It is noteworthy that the historical record for Iran and Turkey in Figure 1 does not differ clearly from that for Egypt; and that the same is true of the record for China compared with India, and of Ethiopia vis-à-vis Nigeria. Even a casual glance at historical experience makes clear the need to consider other factors that have impeded mass education besides colonialism.

One factor that comes quickly to mind is absolute monarchy. The independent countries I have just mentioned—Turkey, Iran, China, and Ethiopia—were all absolute monarchies, and in none of these did a substantial trend toward mass education set in until after autocratic rule was terminated. To judge from Figure 1 the same is true of Russia and Thailand. Absolute monarchs seem usually to have regarded mass education as potentially subversive of their power; in contrast, communist governments have vigorously promoted mass education as an instrument of political socialization.[31]

Another deterrent to mass education appears to have been a situation in which the Roman Catholic Church exercised substantial secular power. This has already been touched on in the case of Spain; in Latin America, it is perhaps the dominant factor. The rapid rise in mass education in Ar-

---

[28] Flora notes the close association in a number of countries between the date of independence and the date when compulsory education was established. See Flora, "Mobilization," pp. 230–37.

[29] Lance E. Davis and Robert A. Huttenback, "Public Expenditures and Private Profit: Budgetary Decisions in the British Empire, 1860–1912," *American Economic Review*, 67 (Feb. 1977), 282–88..

[30] Carl H. Landé, "The Philippines," in James S. Coleman, ed., *Political Development*, pp. 313–52; Shinkichi Etô, "Asianism and the Duality of Japanese Colonialism, 1879–1945," in L. Blussé, H. L. Wesseling, and G. D. Winius, eds., *History and Underdevelopment* (Paris, 1980); Andrew J. Grajdanzev, *Modern Korea* (New York, 1944).

[31] On Russia and the USSR, see Nicholas Hans, *History of Russian Educational Policy, 1701–1917* (New York, 1964), p. 65, and Jeremy R. Azrael, "Soviet Union," in Coleman, ed., *Political Development*, pp. 233–71.

gentina after 1880 and in Mexico after 1920 both occurred in conjunction with a substantial shift in power from church to state.[32] In the Middle East, Islam frequently appears to have been a negative influence in the development of formal schooling.[33]

For the countries where mass education was already fairly well established by the early nineteenth century—represented in Figure 1 by Germany, England, France, and the United States—sufficient data are not available for analyzing the historical patterns of growth. One can ask, however, what set these countries apart from the rest of the world so early and contributed to their relatively high levels of schooling? Three influences stand out in the literature—Protestantism, humanism, and central government efforts at national integration. One of the main tenets of early Protestant thought, as shaped by leaders like Calvin and Luther, was that "the eternal welfare of every individual depends upon the application of his own reason to the revelation contained in the Scriptures"; in practice, this led to advocacy of formal schooling in the vernacular language so that each individual would have personal access to the Bible.[34] Humanism, which reached fullest expression with the philosophers of the eighteenth-century Enlightenment, preached the ultimate perfectibility of humanity and thus also fostered a view favorable to mass education.[35] Finally, some governments saw in mass education a means of securing allegiance to the central government at the expense of local authorities or the church.

The weight of these influences differed from country to country and not all operated in each. The role of Protestantism was strongest in Germany and the United States, weaker in England where the established Protestant religion was an Anglican version of Roman Catholicism and the vigorous proponents of education were the non-conformists; and weakest of all in France, which was predominantly Roman Catholic, although the separation of church and state was achieved fairly early. Humanism was strongest in France[36] and the United States, perhaps somewhat less so in England, and least influential in Germany. Nationalism and national in-

[32] Mecham, *Church*, pp. 245–47, 376–77, 388–93. In Brazil, however, the church does not seem to have played as critical a role in the growth of mass education; there a shift in political control from conservatives to liberals appears to have been more important. See E. Bradford Burns, *A History of Brazil* (New York, 1970), pp. 290, 302–03.

[33] On Turkey, see Kazamias, *Turkey*, pp. 73–74; Iran, Hafez Farman Farmayan, "The Forces of Modernization in Nineteenth Century Iran: A Historical Survey," in William R. Polk and Richard L. Chambers, eds., *Beginnings of Modernization in the Middle East* (Chicago, 1968), p. 123. In Egypt, Islam seems to have been less of an obstacle to educational change; see P. J. Vatikiotis, *The Modern History of Egypt* (New York, 1969), pp. 69–70.

[34] Paul Monroe, *A Text-Book in the History of Education* (London, 1907), p. 407. Japan seems to have had its own version of the "Protestant ethic"; see Robert N. Bellah, *Tokugawa Religion* (New York, 1957).

[35] Carl L. Becker, *The Heavenly City of the Eighteenth-Century Philosophers* (New Haven, 1932).

[36] Cf. Thut and Adams, *Educational Patterns*, p. 113: "In the end, Frenchmen committed themselves to the ideas derived from humanism, rather than from Roman Catholic or Protestant theologies, a development which had profound educational consequences."

14   *Easterlin*

tegration was a potent force in Germany and perhaps France, but largely absent in England and the United States. Occasionally England's laissez-faire philosophy is used to explain its lag in educational growth relative to other countries in northwestern Europe such as Germany, but the United States, which also lacked a national education policy, clearly calls this view into question. The factor that sets the English off most clearly from both Germany and the United States is the differential nature of Protestantism—the much larger representation in the latter countries of what in England would be called non-conformist religions, religions in the tradition of Calvin and Luther.[37]

Earlier, in touching on the question of incentives for learning, I suggested that the expansion of formal schooling often signalled a positive shift in the incentive structure. The reasoning underlying this should now be clear. A major commitment to mass education is frequently symptomatic of a major shift in political power and associated ideology in a direction conducive to greater upward mobility for a wider segment of the population. This is not to imply that it signals complete democratization of opportunity, but it often represents a sizable break with conditions of the past. From this point of view the absence of mass education systems for so long in so many countries of the world is indicative of a double impediment to the spread of the technology underlying modern economic growth: limited incentives as well as limited aptitudes in the population generally.

Major advances in mass education are thus likely to signal sizable changes both in incentive structures and aptitudes favorable to modern economic growth. At the same time they are symptomatic of powerful new political and ideological forces at work in the cultures of the various countries. The educational system is therefore a key link between modern economic growth, on the one hand, and a society's culture, on the other; study of the evolution of mass education provides an important clue as to when the net balance of the principal cultural forces in a society shifts in a direction favorable to economic growth.

Some may object that the study of educational systems and the forces that shape them leads away from the traditional concerns of *economic* his-

---

[37] The leading role of non-conformists in the British industrial revolution is emphasized in Everett E. Hagen, *On the Theory of Social Change* (Homewood, Ill., 1962), chap. 13. Valuable discussions of early American education growth are Lawrence A. Cremin, *American Education: The Colonial Experience, 1607–1783* (New York, 1970); Bernard Bailyn, *Education in the Forming of American Society* (New York, 1960); Albert Fishlow, "The American Common School Revival: Fact or Fancy?" in Henry Rosovsky, ed., *Industrialization in Two Systems: Essays in Honor of Alexander Gerschenkron* (New York, 1966). On England, see Marius B. Jansen and Lawrence Stone, "Education and Modernization in Japan and England," *Comparative Studies in Society and History*, 9 (Jan. 1967), 208–32; Stanley J. Curtis and M.E.A. Boultwood, *An Introductory History of English Education since 1800* (London, 1977); Roger S. Schofield, "Dimensions of Illiteracy, 1750–1850," *Explorations in Economic History*, 10 (Summer 1973), 437–54; E. G. West, "Literacy and the Industrial Revolution," *Economic History Review*, 2nd ser., 24 (Aug. 1978), 369–83.

tory.[38] To this, one may reply that if this is what the problem demands, then traditional orientations have to go. In a broader sense, however, it can be argued that such study is, in fact, a return to traditional economic history, to economic history in the spirit of scholars like Marx, Sombart, Weber, and Tawney.

IV

The intention of the government is within the shortest possible time to uplift the social conditions of the [Sakuddei]. But of course without shocks, this you can know for sure, without shocks, and bit by bit bringing them into contact with the general development of the Indonesian society. We want to bring them up in the state that they can understand us you know. . . . that what is health for, [*sic*] what hygiene for, what is a school for . . . just the elementary conditions that I think is standard for every normal society in this modern world.

Harun Zain, Governor of West Sumatra[39]

Peking Paper Says Getting Rich Is Now an Accepted Socialist Goal.
International Herald Tribune, Jan. 2, 1980, p. 3

So far I have speculated about the spread of modern economic growth in the past. But what of the future? Will modern economic growth and its underlying technology continue to spread? Will the majority of the world's population in Asia, Africa, and Latin America be joining before long the minority? The answer suggested by my reasoning and by contemporary experience is yes. Since World War II growth of mass education has become a widespread phenomenon in the Third World, as is demonstrated by Figure 1. And in this period rates of economic growth have surged sharply upward in many Third World countries.[40] The diffusion of modern economic growth throughout the remainder of the world is already well under way. My guess is that once the developing countries have completed their demographic transitions—in many cases, probably by the end of this century—their long-term per capita growth rates will be at least as high as those that the developed countries have so far experi-

[38] Note, however, the numerous references above to recent economic history research on education. Gallman's recent presidential address also argues for a merger of the new social and economic history; Davis's, of the new political and economic history; see Robert E. Gallman, "Some Notes on the New Social History," this JOURNAL, 37 (March 1977), 3–12; and Lance E. Davis, "It's a Long, Long Road to Tipperary, or Reflections on Organized Violence, Protection Rates, and Related Topics: The New Political History," this JOURNAL, 40 (March 1980), 1–16.

[39] From *The Sakuddei* television program as it appeared in the Odyssey series, produced and copyrighted by Public Broadcasting Associates, Inc., 1980. The original *Sakuddei* program was produced and copyrighted by Granada Television. The Sakuddei is a tribal clan living on an island off the west coast of Sumatra.

[40] David Morawetz, *Twenty-Five Years of Economic Development, 1950 to 1975* (Washington, D.C., 1977); Robert Summers, Irving B. Kravis, and Alan Heston, "International Comparison of Real Product and Its Composition: 1950–77," *The Review of Income and Wealth*, Series 26, No. 1 (March 1980); Everett E. Hagen and Oli Hawrylyshyn, "Analysis of World Income and Growth, 1955–1965," *Economic Development and Cultural Change*, 18, no. 1, part II (Oct. 1969).

16   *Easterlin*

enced, and that another century, in addition to the two so far experienced, will largely complete the transition to modern economic technology and organization throughout the world, though sizable international income differences may persist. This reasoning assumes, of course, that the international political structure will be able to withstand the new strains caused by the shifts in political power arising from the further spread of economic development.

If this comes to pass, what will the world be like when the triumph of this new epoch of economic history is complete? Will "the economic problem" have been put to rest and humanity turn to more important pursuits, as John Stuart Mill once contemplated? Will humanity have made the great leap into freedom that Marx envisaged?

To answer this requires, at a minimum, a projection of both human wants and economic technology. Will material wants continue to grow, and, if so, will they be supported by an ever-expanding technology? Or will we wind down into a stationary state of comfortable satisfaction with material need banished from the earth?

The answers to these questions are, I believe, already at hand. The evidence is that there is no satiation of human wants; rather, that the mechanism of economic growth causes the luxuries of one generation to become the necessities of the next, and thus leads to ever higher material aspirations.[41] Nor is there reason to expect a declining rate of technical progress, because the march of science, on which technology ultimately rests, is steadily onward.[42] While it would be pleasant to envisage a world free from the pressure of material want, a more realistic projection based on current evidence for the now developed countries is of a world caught on a "hedonic treadmill," a world in which generation after generation thinks it needs only another 10 or 20 percent more income to be perfectly happy. This will be, moreover, a monocultural world, East and West, capitalist and communist, for the personality traits that are formed in the process of modern economic growth ultimately prevail over cultural and ideological differences—in short, the hedonic treadmill becomes universal.

Evidence of growing cultural homogeneity in other respects is clearly apparent in recent research. I quote a summary of recent findings in sociology:

Western scientific-technical concepts of reality have penetrated almost everywhere. Rapidly expanding education systems universally promote science, technology, and mathematics, implicitly advancing a conception of natural reality as law-like, strictly causally ordered, and manipulable. This conception is also built into institutions of scientific research, national planning, and national industrialization.

---

[41] Richard A. Easterlin, "Does Economic Growth Improve the Human Lot? Some Empirical Evidence," *Nations and Households in Economic Growth: Essays in Honor of Moses Abramovitz* (New York, 1974); Richard A. Easterlin, "Does Money Buy Happiness?" *The Public Interest*, no. 30 (Winter 1973).

[42] Derek J. de Solla Price, *Science since Babylon* (New Haven, 1961), chap. 5.

Descriptions of transcendental authority also become more uniform. Universalistic and unitary conceptions of God (or equivalently, of history) prevail. Indigenous, localized religious systems applying only to particular groups die out or are transformed to resemble more widespread systems.

Finally, descriptions of the nature of man and society converge. Individuals are seen as both malleable and as possessing many economic and social rights that are remarkably similar, in the abstract, from country to country. Obligations to maintain economic progress and social justice are defined in uniform terms. To a remarkable degree, every sort of state defines for itself uniform long-run economic and social goals.[43]

This, then, is the future to which the epoch of modern economic growth is leading us: a world in which ever-growing abundance is always outpaced by material aspirations, a world of increasing cultural uniformity.

At some point, we may look back and ask what produced this world— how we got where we are. Such inquiry will show, I believe, that the proximate roots of the epoch of modern economic growth lie in the growth of science and diffusion of modern education. In a more fundamental sense, however, it will show that the source of this epoch is the secular, rationalistic, and materialistic trend of intellectual thought that evolved from the Renaissance and Reformation—that in rejecting the authority of the medieval Church, humanity ultimately took up a new "religion of knowledge," whose churches are the schools and universities of the world, whose priests are its teachers, and whose creed is belief in science and the power of rational inquiry, and in the ultimate capacity of humanity to shape its own destiny. The irony is that in this last respect the lesson of history is otherwise: that there is no choice. The epoch of modern economic growth—a world of nations blindly developing—is itself the proof of this.

[43] John W. Meyer, John Boli-Bennett, and Christopher Chase-Dunn, "Convergence and Divergence in Development," in Alex Inkeles, ed., *Annual Review of Sociology,* 1 (Palo Alto, 1975), p. 228.

APPENDIX TABLE 1
ESTIMATED PRIMARY SCHOOL ENROLLMENT RATE
BY COUNTRY, 1830–1975
(per 10,000 population)

Year

Country	1830	1840	1850	1860	1870	1882	1890	1900	1910
USA	1500		1800		1702	1908	1985	1969	1828
UK	900		1045			1107	1261	1407	1648
France	700	846	930	930	1125	1382	1450	1412	1414
Germany	1700		1600	1559		1547	1642	1576	1570

Country	1830	1840	1850	1870	1882	1890	1900	1910	1920	1930	1939
Italy	300		463	611	681	874	881	927	1113	1056	1313
Spain	400	537	663	851	1049	1058	1038	1026	1232	1535	

Country	1870	1882	1890	1900	1910	1920	1930	1939
Rumania	214	261	467	617	839	642	1307	1581
Yugoslavia		303	300	420	512	674	772	888
USSR	98	133	231	348	395	417	734	1873

Country	1870	1882	1890	1900	1910	1920	1930	1939	1950	1960	1975
Argentina		511	709	808	944	1356	1172	1417	1286	1339	1399
Mexico		457	487	544	563	456	1074	1314	1072	1460	1905
Brazil		207	218	258	271	455	618	854	979	1087	1866
Burma							206	316	427	731	1127
India	119		94	107	147	192	343	279	513	854	1082
Indonesia			57	62	96	161	267	338	613	964	1345

	1882	1890	1900	1910	1920	1930	1939	1950	1960	1975
Japan	722	772	984	1240	1508	1550	1695	1891		
Philippines			188	970	1038	936	1267			
Thailand				9	179	552	939	1490		
Egypt	4	264	215	171	171	269	687	662	1038	1107
Iran			3	6	10	82	213	457	701	1353
Turkey					201	318	464	776	1026	1376
China					115	222	329	861	948	
Korea				27	72	246	501	1151		
Nigeria				12	176	191	103	399	479	820
Ethiopia								49	81	366

Source: A: Arthur S. Banks, *Cross-Polity Time Series Data* (Cambridge, 1971); B: *The Statesman's Yearbook 1883–1960* (London, 1883–1960); C: E. Levasseur, *L'Enseignement primaire dans les pays civilisés* (Paris, 1897); D: Richard A. Easterlin, "A Note on the Evidence of History," in C. Arnold Anderson and Mary Jean Bowman, eds., *Education and Economic Development* (Chicago, 1965), pp. 422–29; E: Andrew J. Grajdanzev, *Modern Korea* (New York, 1944); F: UNESCO, *Statistical Yearbook 1977* (Paris, 1978) and United Nations, *Demographic Yearbook 1977* (New York, 1978).

Source of data for 1975 is F; for all other dates A, except as follows: USA 1830, 1850–D; UK 1830, 1850–D; France 1830–D, 1840–1860–C; Germany 1930, 1850–D, 1860–C; Italy 1830–D, 1860, 1870–C; Spain 1830–D, 1850–C; Rumania 1870, 1890–C; USSR 1890–C; Argentina 1882–C; Burma 1930–1950–B; India 1890–1930–B; Indonesia 1890–1939–B; Philippines 1900–1939–B; Thailand 1910–1939–B; Egypt 1882–1939–B; Iran 1900–1939–B; Korea 1910–1939–E; Nigeria 1910–1950–B.

[22]

World Development, Vol. 10, No. 3, pp. 167–185, 1982
Printed in Great Britain.

0305-750X/030167–19$3.00/0
© 1982 Pergamon Press Ltd.

The Impact of Primary Schooling on Economic Development: A Review of the Evidence

CHRISTOPHER COLCLOUGH*

Institute of Development Studies at the University of Sussex, Brighton

Summary. — The contribution of primary schooling to economic development is greater than has conventionally been perceived. This review of recent research shows that primary schooling increases labour productivity in both urban and rural sectors, and that the economic returns to such investment are typically high. In addition, it reduces fertility, improves health and nutrition, and promotes other behavioural and attitudinal changes which are helpful to economic development. Investment strategies which give primary schooling an important place would be more conducive of growth-with-equity than many alternatives. Priorities for government and donor policies are indicated, as are those for future research.

1. INTRODUCTION

Although the distinction between the consumption and investment aspects of educational expenditure has been familiar since the time of Adam Smith, major interest in the economic value of education was not kindled until as recently as 20 years ago. At that time, a series of aggregate production function studies suggested that a large part of the growth of the US economy during the first half of the 20th century was attributable to increases in the stock of human capital (Denison, 1962). It seemed to be a matter of easy logic to translate the implications of this work to the developing world where skilled manpower was in critically short supply. Many such countries remained highly dependent upon the skills of non-citizen workers, particularly in senior positions in industry and government. Attention quickly shifted away from a lack of capital resources towards questions of 'absorptive capacity' and shortages of human skills as an explanation of disappointing growth performance. At the same time, the assumption was made that 'skilled' manpower was broadly synonymous with 'schooled' manpower: by implication, Western modes of education were to become universal modes of skill creation, and educational investment would have to occupy a central part of investment strategy if growth was to proceed.

Of course, the facts about educational enrolments in the Third World broadly supported these views. For example, in the early 1960s,

Africa was in quantitative terms the most underschooled continent in the world: primary education then covered barely two-fifths of the relevant age group, secondary education covered only 3%, and university and other tertiary education, a mere fifth of 1%. In these circumstances it is hardly surprising that the need for quantitative expansion appeared overwhelming. Reflecting this mood, the 1961 round of UNESCO Regional Conferences for Ministers of Education, held in Karachi, Addis Ababa and Santiago, adopted ambitious expansionary targets. Subsequently, the quantitative increases in enrolments throughout the developing world have been enormous. It can be seen from Table 1 that enrolments at primary level more than doubled in Africa and Latin America between 1960 and 1975, whilst in Asia they increased by almost 80%. Growth at secondary and tertiary levels has been much faster — partly, how-

---
* The research for this article was supported by the World Bank, and an earlier version was issued as 'Primary schooling and economic development: a review of the evidence', World Bank Staff Working Paper No. 399 (1980). Comments from S. Cochrane, D. Davies, R. Dore, P. Fallon, M. Godfrey, S. Heyneman, P. Isenman, D. Jamison, T. King, A. Little, J. Oxenham, R. Prosser and P. Williams are gratefully acknowledged. None of them is responsible for remaining deficiencies. The views and interpretations in this paper are those of the author, and do not necessarily reflect those of the World Bank.

Table 1. *Estimated total enrolment by level of education in the developing world*
(thousands)

Region	Year	Total†	First level	Second level	Third level
Africa	1960	21,378	19,458	1739	180
	1965	29,903	26,539	3058	306
	1975	53,760	44,498	8379	883
Asia*	1960	118,973	89,687	26,581	2704
	1965	160,692	116,507	39,529	4656
	1975	230,371	160,063	61,691	8618
Latin America	1960	31,289	26,628	4088	572
	1965	42,167	34,424	6829	914
	1975	72,941	57,071	12,288	3582

Source: UNESCO (1977).
* Not including China and the Democratic People's Republic of Korea.
† Not including pre-primary, special and adult education.

Table 2. *Annual average increase in enrolment in the developing world,*
1960–1975 (%)

Region	Years	Total†	First level	Second level	Third level
Africa	1960–1965	6.9	6.4	12.0	11.2
	1965–1975	6.0	5.3	10.6	11.2
Asia*	1960–1965	6.2	5.4	8.3	11.5
	1965–1975	3.7	3.2	4.6	6.4
Latin America	1960–1965	6.1	5.3	10.8	9.8
	1965–1975	5.6	5.2	6.1	14.6

Source: UNESCO (1977).
*† See Table 1.

ever, reflecting the initially lower base — with rates of increase in enrolments in excess of 10%/year being typical (Table 2).

This change in the structure of school enrolments has had important budgetary implications for many countries. Secondary and tertiary provision is generally much more expensive than primary schooling — mainly because of higher salaries and more favourable teacher/pupil ratios at the higher levels. The broadening of the apex of the educational pyramid has therefore often meant that expenditures have risen considerably faster than total enrolments. Thus, in spite of the fact that the unit costs of secondary and tertiary education have tended to fall relative to primary education (Table 3), many countries are now facing a severe budgetary constraint in education which is forcing a reassessment of priorities.

Questioning of the recent pattern of school expansion has also been prompted by other factors. Over the last 20 years the structure of em-

ployment opportunities in the Third World has changed profoundly. Although graduate unemployment in India was emerging prior to 1947, elsewhere this was an unusual phenomenon even as late as 1960. During the following decade, however, unemployment of secondary school leavers became widespread in the urban centres, and in a proportional sense, often became more acute than open unemployment amongst those with less education (Table 4). More recently, in many countries even university graduates have found it difficult to find the sort of jobs which their qualifications would normally justify and had previously led them to expect. These rising unemployment rates for the educated should not be taken to imply an overall shortage of jobs which educated workers can do, but rather a shortage of those they are *prepared* to do. Of course, in time their expectations do adjust downwards. One result of this adjustment is an improvement in the average educational qualifications of those in formal employment, and ac-

Table 3. *Ratios of expenditure per student (first level = 100), selected countries and years*

		First level	Second level	Third level
Africa				
Ghana	1965	100	1201.8	21,814.9
	1970	100	1015.0	16,837.2
	1975	100	173.0	4853.7
Kenya	1965	100	1046.3	10,907.8
	1970	100	685.9	5164.8
Nigeria	1970	100	483.1	9298.8
	1974	100	588.9	29,735.5
Asia				
India	1965	100	505.0	2343.7
	1970	100	476.0	2086.9
	1975	100	–	432.3
Thailand	1965	100	275.5	1763.8
	1970	100	286.6	2603.5
	1975	100	149.2	894.8
Latin America				
Mexico	1965	100	200.5	1560.2
	1970	100	312.0	763.1
	1975	100	268.4	614.2
Colombia	1965	100	180.5	3168.6
	1970	100	205.3	2509.6
	1975	100	141.1	503.2
Argentina	1965	100	190.0	429.7
	1970	100	346.1	851.5
	1975	100	435.1	670.8

Source: Calculated from UNESCO (1977).

cess to jobs which previously 'required' only secondary school qualifications becomes impossible without, say, a university degree. Depending upon economic and social conditions, this upgrading of hiring standards may or may not be justifiable on efficiency grounds. Nevertheless it is clear that in most countries so affected its mainsprings are changes in the relative supplies of labour with various levels of schooling, rather than in the technical complexity of the jobs concerned or other demand-induced changes. Under these circumstances, the 'skilled-manpower' arguments for rapid secondary and tertiary expansion become less convincing to economic planners than they were some years ago.

For the same reasons, there has been increased concern expressed at both the national and international levels that the primary span of education still excludes large numbers in the eligible age group. Although individual circumstances differ, and – in this sense – countries in Latin America are generally well ahead of those elsewhere, there are many countries with an acute (and worsening) secondary school-leaver problem in which still less than two-thirds of the eligible age group are attending primary schools. This situation has served to sharpen the emphasis given to equity considerations in the allocation of educational resources – although often with disappointing results in the face of the strong social demand for schooling which, for good private maximizing reasons, remains focused upon the top end of the school system.

But the reassertion of interest in primary schooling is not only based upon equity arguments. After all, education (and literacy) through schooling as a human *right*, pre-dated its recognition/perception as human *capital*, and most government plans – if not always their practice – adopt this as a *sine qua non* of educational strategy. There is, rather, a view that the literature on educational planning has insufficiently stressed the real benefits of primary schooling. Recent research has produced a considerable amount of evidence to suggest that primary schooling makes a significant con-

Table 4. *Education and unemployment: selected countries*[*]

	Rates of unemployment			
Bogota, Colombia, April 1967	Illiterate	1–5 years education	6–11 years education	12 or more years education
Males	11.5	15.3	14.9	13.2
Females	4.1	22.0	16.3	11.3
Buenos Aires, Argentina, 1965, total labour	Illiterate	Primary	Secondary	Post-secondary
force	3.8	4.8	5.7	3.3
Venezuela, 1969, urban areas	4.3	7.0	10.2	2.3
India, 1960/1961, urban areas	Illiterate	Below matriculation	Matriculation	Graduates
	1.2	2.7	7.0	2.8
Malaysia, 1965, urban areas, 15–24 labour force	Illiterate	Primary	Secondary grades I–IV	Higher certificate and above
Males	10.4	19.5	30.9	15.5
Females	17.2	32.4	69.7	27.5
Syria, 1967, all areas, total labour force	Illiterate	Literate	Elementary to secondary	Graduate
	4.3	5.2	11.7	4.4
Sri Lanka, all areas	Primary or less[†]	Some secondary	Ordinary certificate	Higher
1963	4.0–6.1	16.8	23.5	2.8
1971	4.6–3.0	22.0	32.1	12.8
Philippines, all areas, 1971	Primary or less[†]	Junior secondary	Senior secondary	Higher
	4.4–6.8	13.7	15.3	12.2

Sources: Turnham (1970), pp. 62–63; Richards and Leonor (1981), pp. 48–49.
[*] The data show the proportion of each category of educated labour who were unemployed, and suggest that the probability of being unemployed, in the countries shown, increased with the level of schooling possessed – at least up to higher secondary levels. This does not mean that unemployed secondary school leavers comprised the largest group. In fact the reverse was true, because of the much larger number of people in the labour force who had had little or no schooling.
[†] The range shown indicates the rates which were estimated for illiterates and for those with 4 or more years of primary schooling, respectively.

tribution to economic and social development, and that these benefits have been given insufficient attention over the past few years. This paper attempts, briefly, to summarize this evidence and to draw out some of its implications.[1] In doing so, it is necessary to include within our purview some results of work on post-primary schooling. This is for two reasons: first, many studies have been comparative in nature, and have pointed to different social and economic effects arising from schooling at different levels;

and second, some research on the schooling process *per se* is of relevance to a discussion of the effects of primary schooling even when its main focus is at the post-primary level. The remainder of this paper is in three sections. Section 2 examines those outcomes of the schooling process which affect subsequent work activities; Section 3 considers those that are independent of such activities; and the final section brings together the conclusions and implications of the results discussed.

2. SCHOOL OUTCOMES AND WORKER PERFORMANCE

(a) *Education and productivity: the theoretical debate*

Theoretical formulations of the relationship between years spent in school and subsequent worker productivity have been mainly concerned to account for two types of empirical phenomena which are widely observed in the formal-sector labour market, at all stages of development, in both capitalist and socialist countries. Although our concerns are much wider than the impact of schools on formal skills and output, it is necessary to review the main elements of this debate. The first of these phenomena is that the main criteria used by most employers when hiring recruits at the bottom of the occupational ladder are the level and type of education they have received; as part of this process, eligibility for employment is often codified in terms of the minimum levels of formal education or training required. Second, a characteristic of the wage and salary structure of most countries is that persons with more education tend to receive higher remuneration than those with less, whether in the same occupation or not.

The interpretation given to these phenomena, however, varies amongst different theoretical schools. The traditional view of human capital theorists has been that schooling raises labour productivity through its role in increasing the cognitive abilities of workers. At the lower occupational levels, basic numeracy and literacy, and at the higher levels, a greater capacity for logical and analytical reasoning, for self-expression, and sounder technical knowledge, have been held to have a fundamental impact upon effectiveness at work, and to provide the mechanism whereby the link between education and personal income became established (Becker, 1964, especially Chap. 2). Thus, the view that higher labour productivity is a positive function of the amount of schooling received is the fundamental premise of human capital theory — even if higher educated workers *are* more productive, if these characteristics are formed other than by means of the schools, the economic rationale for investment in schooling is undermined.

One of the most coherent challenges to this argument has recently come from a series of studies conducted in the USA. These present detailed analyses of a number of sets of data collected from national sample surveys. They focus upon the socio-economic correlates of lifetime earnings and of occupational status for men aged between 25 and 64 years. Together, they form the most comprehensive empirical analysis of the determinants of inequality (Jencks *et al.*, 1972) and of individual occupational success (Jencks *et al.*, 1979) yet completed. With regard to the effects of education, their main conclusions are as follows.

In the USA, when an individual first enters the labour market, the highest year of school or college he has completed is the best single predictor of his eventual occupational status. In spite of this, however, controlling adult test scores in addition to years of schooling has little extra effect upon the occupational value of education. This suggests that schooling does not enhance people's chances of entering a high-status occupation primarily by improving their cognitive skills, because the latter — as measured by test scores or high school grades — are not rewarded independently of years of schooling (Jencks *et al.*, 1979, p. 225). At higher levels of education, there is some additional evidence that college and graduate school grades are only minimally related to worker performance within particular occupations (Jencks *et al.*, 1972, p. 187). Thus, the economic benefits of extra education seem not to derive from increases in cognitive ability, as proxied by test scores, and school grades have no significant effects on earnings, once education is controlled (Jencks *et al.*, 1979, p. 228).

These results have led some to argue that it is not the increase in cognitive abilities given by schooling which is valued by employers — rather it is the changes in the non-cognitive domain which are rewarded (Bowles, 1971; Gintis, 1971; Bowles and Gintis, 1976). It is argued that there is a correspondence between the values, attitudes and behaviour inculcated by the schools and the traits required by employers. Although these traits may vary for posts at different levels of organization, so too do the traits formed by different levels of schooling; at the lower levels, those of punctuality, obedience and respect for authority may be emphasized, but as one moves up through the school system the emphasis shifts to the encouragement of initiative, self-reliance and the ability to make decisions. This, then, may provide an explanation for why hiring and promotional standards are heavily influenced by years spent in school, rather than upon grades received before leaving.

In some ways the 'correspondence' explanation for the link between education and earnings is not very different from, and is broadly compatible with the 'human-capital' explanation. Both argue that schooling institutes and nourishes changes in individuals which are valued by employers; for both, formal schooling is still needed to enhance the productivity of future workers, at least given the way that production is presently organized. Thus, these theories differ more in emphasis than in the fundamental functional relationships they hold to exist.

There is a final possible explanation, however, for the demonstrated relationship between schooling and earnings which does present a broadside attack on the view that schooling provides significant economic returns. This is the view that schooling merely serves as a screening device — as a means of choosing between people of widely different capabilities, competing for a small number of jobs. In this interpretation, educational credentials act merely as surrogates for other qualities — such as intelligence and motivation — which will affect future productivity: but although they adequately predict future performance, they make no direct contribution to it.

Although this may seem unlikely, evidence against this hypothesis is extremely difficult to find. Jencks *et al.* (1979) conclude that although completion of the main stages of education associated with gaining a certificate has a particularly high economic return, every year of schooling completed — with or without a certificate — brings salary benefits. Thus Berg's (1971) argument that schooling is only economically valued because it leads to formal credentials appears incorrect. In response, however, it could be argued that employers simply use years of school attended as a means of making marginal choices between individuals when certificates have not been obtained — that they are used as 'surrogate' credentials in those circumstances. This evidence, therefore, is not inconsistent with the hypothesis that the screening function of schooling is dominant.

On a different theme, some writers (Blaug, 1973, p. 37; Layard and Psacharopoulos, 1974) have argued that the screening hypothesis would predict that the private returns to schooling should fall with increased job experience — which they do not. Basically, their argument is that as employers learn which of their educated workers are more productive, and which are less so, the strong association between schooling and earnings should be undermined by promotion practices. But this argument seems incorrect: such learning on the part of employers should lead to greater *variance* in the earnings of more experienced educated workers, compared to those with less experience, but not necessarily to any change in *mean* education—

earnings relationships for workers with different amounts of job experience. In fact, if education does effectively predict future productivity (which the screening hypothesis asserts) we should expect promotion practices to preserve, rather than to undermine earnings differentials between educated and uneducated workers. Only if it did the opposite — that is, if the more educated did *not* receive more of the promotions when employers had had a chance to get to know them better — would the screening argument become inadequate. And under those circumstances, of course, both the human capital and the correspondence explanations would equally be under attack.

In their strict form, all three of these theories, or explanations, are likely to be incorrect. However, all three are important in explaining *part* of the reality. Some minimum level of cognitive ability is necessary for doing most jobs in the formal sector, and some minimum set of attitudes and values is required if employees are to cope reasonably with the social and psychological demands of employment in hierarchical structures. If the schools produce these characteristics in their students, it is not surprising that we notice a general trend in salaries to reward these skills. At the same time, it is well known that the minimum level of schooling required by employers for given jobs rises when the rate of growth of school outputs is faster than that of salaried employment. Thus, in many if not most societies, there is not necessarily any technical (or production function) relationship between the education required for job-eligibility, and the occupational skills needed for effective performance. There probably is, however, some minimum level of schooling that is absolutely essential for certain jobs, because of their need for workers with an ability to use or to acquire the necessary expertise.

It will already be clear that the theoretical debate about education and work has been primarily concerned with phenomena in the formal-sector labour market. Its evidence and analysis has focused upon the salient features of wage and salary structures, hiring standards, and recruitment practices of formal employers, and of the requirements of work within the formal sector. Whilst we may wish, within the confines of that debate, to grant that *some* positive and causal relation between schooling and worker performance is likely, we also need to pose much wider questions than this: first, *how* does schooling act to increase productivity? Second, how do the effects of schooling vary at primary, as compared with post-primary levels? Third, are its effects upon output confined only

THE IMPACT OF PRIMARY SCHOOLING ON ECONOMIC DEVELOPMENT 173

to the formal sector, or does it have a wider impact upon agricultural and informal-sector work? It is these questions to which we now turn.

(b) Measurable effects of schooling: cognitive and non-cognitive change

The theoretical positions which accept that schooling is important to productivity growth variously imply that this is because of the cognitive or non-cognitive ('affective') changes brought about by school. It is clear that such changes in individuals do occur as a result of the schooling process, but it is less clear that school is the only, or indeed the best, means of achieving such changes. Evidence from all countries shows that cognitive abilities are enhanced by schooling, and that, however inefficiently, the major manifest aim of education is thereby promoted by formal schooling. Measures designed to test cognitive abilities normally employ standardized tests to measure retention of specific subject matter. Although such tests so often test memory, rather than analytic ability, there is a strong direct relationship between years spent in school and performance on such tests in all countries (Postlethwaite, 1973). Nevertheless, the efficiency with which schools achieve such outcomes for their students varies enormously between rich and poor countries, between regions within one country, and between different schools. It will become clear that the reasons why there are such significant differences between cognitive outcomes are exceedingly complex, and often seem not to be due to factors that are internal to the school. For the moment, however, it should be noted that more schooling does mean higher cognitive achievement in general — at least in terms of the way this variable is conventionally measured.

Perhaps the most interesting work on the non-cognitive changes arising from schooling has emerged from studies of the determinants of individual modernity (Inkeles and Smith, 1974; Inkeles and Holsinger, 1974). This work has included a major empirical study, covering 6000 individuals in six developing countries, which investigated the socio-economic correlates of values and attitudes held by 'modern men'. A modernization scale was developed by the authors which allowed ranking of the respondents on a scale from 0–100, based upon answers to 166 mainly multiple choice questions, grouped in various ways. The pattern which emerges in all countries gives striking evidence

for the existence of a modernity 'syndrome', the main elements of which respond to external influences in basically the same way. The authors find that in so far as men change under the influence of modernizing institutions, they do so by incorporating the norms implicit in such organizations into their own personality, and by expressing those norms through their own attitudes, values and behaviour.

The school appears to be fundamental to this process. In the six countries studied, education was the single most important variable in explaining the variance of scores on the modernization scale. The median gap between the highest and lowest individual scores in the countries studied was 64 points. The authors calculate that after controlling for work experience, exposure to the media, and for all measurable early and late socialization variables, each year of schooling improved a man's score by about 2 points on the scale. This implies that education alone — on the basis of a 16-year cycle — was capable of producing half of the maximum observed change in attitudes and values, as measured by the modernity scale (Inkeles and Smith, 1974, p. 139). This result is in spite of the fact that none of the questions which went into determining the modernity ranking directly tested items which were objects of the school curriculum to impart. The effect of schooling was found to be cumulative and continuous, and even very small amounts of schooling had a positive effect as measured by the modernity scale.

The changes in attitude and values promoted by schooling have been recognized for many years. Indeed the school has been used in some societies as an explicit means of changing earlier ideals and values to ones more supportive of those societies' chosen paths of development. This has perhaps been most common during periods of socialist transformation, as in Cuba, China and Tanzania. The limited evidence available, however, suggests that educational reforms take a considerable time to affect popular attitudes and values, and that they can in any case have little effect unless they are supported by broader economic and social reforms in economy and society (Colclough, 1978; Shirk, 1979). Thus, the school is not the only vehicle for non-cognitive development. Indeed, Inkeles and Smith (1974) found that factory work brought about — year-for-year — almost as significant a change in attitudes as did schooling in the six countries studied. Some would go further to argue that the kind of non-cognitive changes promoted by schooling are inimical to personal and societal development (Illich, 1972) — that school actually holds back, rather than liberates the creative capatitities of individuals. From some ideological perspectives this may well be true. Empirically, however, the non-cognitive results of schooling are generally welcomed, and national ideologies of both right and left have used the school system as a means of strengthening — if not of leading — their attempts at nation-building.

With regard to the cognitive changes promoted by schooling, there are some additional caveats which should be considered. The question here is whether the differences in cognitive abilities promoted by different amounts of schooling are always great enough to justify universalizing access to all levels of the system. Whilst cognitive development may be almost impossible without the literacy and numeracy given by 4—6 years of schooling, the incremental progress made in subsequent years may be subject to rapidly diminishing returns. Whitla (1977), for example, shows that 4 years of college education does not improve learning ability for students confronting material *outside* their subject of specialism, although the reverse is true for new material within their own domain. Does this imply that particular modes of thought and discourse facilitate further learning within each mode at least up to a certain point, but that once new modes are tried, the increment of ability is cancelled? Cole *et al.* (1978) believe that this is likely to be true. They provide evidence to suggest that differential performance between more and less educated people on standardized tests of memory and analytic ability is revealed mainly in tasks whose form and content are like those practised in school. The question remains as to how this school-related competence is transferred to other contexts. De Moura Castro (1975) suggests that limited transferability of such skills may account for the differential progress at school of people with different socio-economic backgrounds, which, he finds, is *not* mirrored by their differential progress during later working careers. This evidence, then, would suggest that schooled people will do better and better so long as the idiom remains that of the school; but if the idiom is changed, non-schooled people may do just as well. Labour market segmentation may explain why such relationships are not more immediately obvious empirically. Nevertheless if higher cognitive abilities are thought *not* to bring productivity benefits on these grounds, there remain some uncomfortable facts to account for. This will become clear from what follows.

(c) *Evidence on the profitability of investment in primary and post-primary education*

(i) *The formal sector*

If we grant that both the theoretical arguments, and the ways in which employers in fact behave, do suggest that schooling makes people more productive during their future working life, the question arises as to how the returns to various levels of schooling compare. Most approaches to this question have focused upon the distribution of earnings — mainly within the formal sector — by level of education. This has involved the application of standard investment appraisal techniques to compare the costs and benefits of expenditures on various levels of education. Although there are deep problems raised by the assumptions which such studies have typically made, they nevertheless provide the only real evidence upon the relative economic value of different levels of schooling for work in the formal sector in developing countries. For our purposes, therefore, their implications must be discussed.

Most of such studies aim to calculate the rate of interest (or return) which would equate the discounted costs associated with a particular set of educational expenditures with their discounted benefits. There is an important distinction between private and social rates of return to education. Private rates usually compare the privately incurred costs of attending a particular programme — the costs of books, school uniforms, fees, and expected earnings foregone — with the private benefits. These are usually taken as the difference between the post-tax earnings stream associated with graduates from this level of education and the similar stream that could be expected by the individual if the programme were not undertaken. Calculations of social rates, on the other hand, use the same methodology, but include, in addition to the private costs, all public expenditures or subsidies associated with the length of education in question (with the exception of student grants) and take pre-tax earnings differentials as a measure of benefits. Such studies have been completed for over 30 developed and developing countries, the main findings of which have been summarized and compared by Psacharopoulos (1973). Some results are shown in Table 5.

For present purposes, there are two important conclusions which can be drawn from Table 5. First, in the developing countries covered by these studies, the mean private returns to each educational level are high, and considerably greater than the mean social returns. This

Table 5. *Private and social rates of return by educational levels in less developed countries**

	Primary	Secondary	Higher
Private rate†	29.9 (9)	18.5 (14)	22.0 (14)
Social rate†	25.0 (17)	15.2 (18)	12.4 (8)

Source: Calculated from Psacharopoulos (1973), Tables 4.1 and 4.4. See also his more recent study (Psacharopoulos, 1980) which produces closely similar results, based upon a slightly larger sample of countries.
* All countries had a GNP *per capita* of less than US $1000 in 1968.
† The number of country observations are in parentheses.

demonstrates that there is a net public subsidy to education, even after taking account of the future taxation of the educated. This private 'calculus' also shows why the popular political pressures to expand the upper levels of the formal system are so high even in the presence of mounting unemployment at those levels: the probability of remaining unemployed would have to be quite high before undertaking higher education became unattractive.

The second, and more important point, is that both the private and social returns to primary schooling appear to be considerably greater than those at higher educational levels. This is one of the most consistent findings of rate-of-return studies: in only three of the country studies covered by Table 5 were the rates of return to primary schooling somewhat lower than those to higher educational levels. This seems to imply, then, that at least in terms of profitability, and given the existing quality of education and the wage structure at each level, too much is being spent upon the higher levels of the system, and not enough resources are going to the primary schools.

There are, however, some aspects of the economic structure of developing countries which introduce a strong bias into the results of these studies, and which must be considered before accepting this conclusion about the relative neglect of primary education. First, most of the rates of return from which those shown in Table 5 were derived were unadjusted for unemployment. Since open unemployment amongst the educated is widespread in the developing world, such adjustments would have the effect of reducing the rates of return shown. The rates at the primary level would thus be affected, but in many countries of Asia and Africa the rates at secondary and higher levels would be reduced to an even greater extent. Although each level would be differently affected, the evidence suggests that the adjust-

ments would not in general alter the conclusion that primary schooling is associated with the highest rates of return.[2]

Second, a major problem with the cost—benefit approach to investment in education is that it typically ascribes all of the earnings differentials associated with graduates from different levels of the school system (within age—sex groupings) to these school-related differences. Clearly this is unrealistic. At least part of the earnings differential must be atributed to factors like ability, socio-economic background, and achievement motivation. Where data allow it, the better studies derive earnings functions after keeping these factors constant, using multiple regression analysis (Blaug, 1971; Carnoy, 1967; Thias and Carnoy, 1972). Most, however, have simply applied a downward adjustment factor to the earnings profiles — often called the 'alpha coefficient' (Blaug, 1965) — which, on the basis of early evidence has often been estimated at a value of 0.6.[3] Other work, however, suggests that the lower the levels of schooling compared, the smaller the proportion of the income differential is due to education and the more is due to other factors like socio-economic background (Thias and Carnoy, 1972). This result is confirmed by Jencks *et al.* (1979), who also find that, at least in the USA, after controlling for other factors — including socio-economic status and ability — the amount of these differentials explained by schooling alone is smaller than many studies have suggested, at least during the first and second cycles of formal schooling (Jencks *et al.*, 1979, pp. 182–183). On the other hand, as discussed later in this article, in peasant societies the net impact of schooling on future earning capacity may be much more powerful than in developed countries. Thus, the wisdom of using research results based upon conditions in the USA is questionable, and the rates shown in Table 5 may not, in fact, be overestimates. In any event, even if we had the necessary data, it is doubtful that the proper adjustments to take account of non-school variables would be significant enough to change the rank ordering of rates of return suggested in Table 5. Accordingly, the conclusion that primary education brings higher economic returns than investments in higher levels of schooling in the Third World would probably be unaffected by such data adjustments.

Finally, and more fundamentally, is the problem that these rates of return studies use market wages and salaries as means of determining educational benefits. Thus, if we are to attach operational significance to the observed differences between the social rates of return to primary, as compared with higher levels of education, we are required to accept the view, not merely that there is *some* direct relationship between earnings and labour productivity, but that these market wages truly reflect the different contributions to total output which would be given by employing additional workers at each level of schooling. This assumption of proportionality between market wages and the marginal productivity of different categories of labour carries with it a whole appendage of assumptions relating to the operation of free markets under competitive conditions, many of which have been seriously challenged as to their applicability in the typical economic circumstances of less developed countries.[4] These criticisms will not be repeated here.[5] For present purposes, it would, however, be useful to ask how the rate-of-return estimates might be affected if formal-sector wages in less developed countries were determined more by competitive forces than they seem to be at present.

All the available data on wage differentials in poor countries suggest that the difference in remuneration between the highest and least well-paid jobs is much greater than in richer countries. This is also true of average earnings when cross-classified by workers at different educational levels. For example, in those African countries where data are available, average earnings at each of the main exit points from the school—university system are between two and five times greater than those at the next lower level. Moreover, average earnings after university or college education are 20—30 times greater than those of employees who have had no formal schooling.[6] These compare with differentials in Western European countries which are typically no more than two- to threefold for employees at the highest and lowest levels of education (UNECA, 1978; Colclough, 1974; Blaug, 1970).

Most observers agree that such differentials are much greater than can be explained merely by productivity differences. Even if, historically, salaries in the senior jobs of the formal sector were competitively determined in a situation of acute manpower shortage [a view which, itself, is not altogether plausible, given the widespread adoption of metropolitan salary structures at clerical levels and above; see Bennel (1978)], the slow responsiveness of real wages to the subsequent dramatic changes in the supply situation suggests that wage determination in developing countries is not strongly (or quickly) influenced by conditions implicit in the assumptions of the competitive model.

All of this, then, is to say that the use of market wages in rate-of-return studies — whether or not adjusted for unemployment and the effect upon salaries of non-school factors — is likely to result in an overestimation of the real production benefits of investing in higher, as opposed to lower, levels of schooling. Differentials using 'shadow'[7] wages — which cannot be accurately estimated — would be much narrower than those of market wages. Thus if it were possible to incorporate shadow wages in the calculations, the relative production efficiency of lower, relative to higher, levels of schooling would probably be further enhanced, and the results of the comparisons between educational levels given by Table 5 would then be strengthened rather than weakened. Such considerations suggest that the conclusion that there has been underinvestment in primary schooling in the poorer countries — at least as regards the maximization of production in the formal sector — is relatively robust.

(ii) *Productivity benefits outside the formal sector*

As more and more countries move towards universalizing access to primary schooling, an increasing number of primary leavers will remain in the rural areas to gain their livelihood. Typically, the proportion of the population so affected will be between half and two-thirds of the post-primary age group. Thus, if primary schooling is of some benefit to those who remain outside formal employment, rather than being of no benefit, as most economic models have assumed, the economic arguments in favour of increasing the provision of schooling are thereby enhanced.

Recent work does suggest that the primary span of education has positive effects upon farmer productivity. Lockheed *et al.* (1980) review 18 studies conducted in 13 low-income countries concerning the extent to which the educational level of small farmers affects their production efficiency. These studies include analyses of 37 data sets collected over the last 12 years that allow statistical estimation of the effects of education, with other variables controlled. This work supports the following generalizations.

First, in four-fifths of the cases examined, the relationship between years spent in school and agricultural output was positive, and in most of these cases the relationship was statistically significant. The authors estimate that 4 years of schooling, on average, increased output by about 8%, after holding all other factors constant.

Second, the most important determinant of whether or not education has a positive effect upon output is whether or not the farmer is living in a 'modernizing' environment. Specifically, the effect of education appears to be strong and positive only in areas where innovations in the technology used were able to be applied, such as new crop varieties, or access to more sophisticated equipment.

This is no less than we might expect. It suggests that education is particularly likely to increase the output of traditional farmers if other complementary attempts are made to change the farming environment — by the provision of roads or of access to marketing facilities, fertilizer, better crop varieties and so on. Data are not yet available to allow analysis of which of these other 'modernizing' influences are more or less critical for achieving — with education — a growth in farmer incomes. Nevertheless, as part of a package of other investments, education seems able to increase farmer productivity: the evidence suggests that 4 years schooling is capable of enhancing the output of modernizing farmers by as much as 10%/year, as compared to uneducated farmers in the same area, keeping land, capital and labour time constant. Although these results are promising, it has to be noted that in most of the studies surveyed the education variable was measured very simply by years of schooling. Thus, some of the apparent increases in output associated with education may arise from other omitted variables (such as inherited ability) which may be correlated with but not causally related to the number of years spent in school.

With regard to non-agricultural work, there is substantial evidence from the Third World that the more schooled individuals have a higher propensity to migrate from rural or urban areas, and that such migration is mainly influenced by economic motives (Caldwell, 1969; Berry and Sabot, 1978, p. 1204). Not unrelated to this phenomenon is the fact that schooling tends to increase the rates of labour force participation of both men and women (Standing, 1978). But whether such trends translate into increased rates of urban employment or of unemployment depends crucially upon local labour market conditions. We have seen that the structure of school expansion over the last 20 years has been associated, in some countries, with higher rates of unemployment amongst the more schooled participants in the labour force compared to those with less education. In part, this is because higher levels of schooling increase the potential income gains from an extended job-search; some would also argue that, quite separately, they make people less willing to take low-status work in the informal sector (Standing, 1978, p. 146). This may

be true. But the evidence for these relationships with regard to primary education appears less strong: in many countries hiring standards for most formal jobs have moved above the primary level; in such circumstances the benefits of 'waiting' are reduced for primary graduates. Moreover, in some countries there appears to be evidence of a positive relationship between years spent in primary school and the frequency of participation in informal sector work [see, for example, Botswana (1974, p. 38)]. In general, further expansion of primary schooling appears unlikely to have the dramatic effect upon levels of urban unemployment that some observers fear. As schooling continues to expand, for most countries, such arguments have relevance only at higher levels of the system.

In addition to the impact of primary schooling upon rates of participation, a second question concerns the productivity gains, if any, that it brings for workers in the urban informal sector. The evidence on this matter is at present less than satisfactory. Very few studies have been able to investigate earnings functions that incorporate adequate education variables. There is some evidence from the urban informal sector in Colombia that earnings differentials by education among age—sex groupings are substantial — although rather less than are found in the formal sector (Bourguignon, 1979; Kugler et al., 1979). But these studies do not attempt to specify a complete model, and the differentials observed may be substantially influenced by other omitted variables. Other studies of the impact of education on urban poverty [such as Jallade (1977)] are hampered by their lack of a clear delineation between elements of household incomes gained from formal- and informal-sector work. Such research tends to show a substantial rate of return to primary schooling for the poorer households — albeit lower than that for richer groups. But this result may be in part influenced by the poorer households having more restricted access to formal-sector wages, rather than being an exclusive reflection of the earnings benefits of primary schooling gained in the informal sector. Thus, while the available evidence gives cause for optimism, it remains circumstantial at present, and in this sense there is a gap in the research results that are currently available.

3. OTHER EFFECTS OF PRIMARY SCHOOLING

(a) *Non-economic effects*

The evidence reviewed so far suggests that there is a strong theoretical and empirical basis for believing that schooling helps to make people more productive at work. In this regard, primary schooling appears to bring productivity benefits that are significant, and which have perhaps been underplayed in the past: there is a clear economic case for investing in primary education, which is quite separable from notions of equity, social demand or individual human rights. There are however additional benefits of schooling which narrow economic approaches so often fail to capture. These arise from the interactive or strengthening effects of schooling upon objectives of various aspects of social policy, including family size, health, nutrition, literacy and awareness of national culture. For example, a recent comprehensive survey of the evidence (Cochrane, 1979a) shows that the amount of schooling received by females indirectly affects their fertility in three main ways. First, it affects the 'biological supply' of children: by raising the age at marriage and reducing the proportion of women who are married, education is associated with a reduced exposure to pregnancy for women; on the other hand education also tends to raise fecundity by improving health, and by breaking down traditional taboos relating to post-partum abstinence. Second, the demand for children tends to reduce with schooling: the perceived benefits of having more children fall, and the perceived costs appear to rise — mainly because of the enhanced earnings prospects which schooling brings. Third, the knowledge of how to regulate fertility through contraception increases with schooling, thus better enabling parents to have the number of children they want.

These factors obviously interact in various complex ways, resulting in no simple or universally observable relationship between the amount of schooling received and levels of individual fertility. However, the evidence from poor countries shows that increases in schooling are typically associated with first an increase and subsequently a decline in fertility. There are two important points to make about this relationship. First, in those cases where there *is* an initial rise in fertility levels as the education of females increases, the onset of a decline in fertility starts before the end of primary schooling. For eight studies where data on fertility of females by age and level of education exists, and where education was associated with first a rise and then a fall in fertility, the mean years of schooling at which a peak in fertility occurs seems to be between 3 and 4 years (Cochrane, 1979a, pp. 36—39). Second, the frequency of this curvilinear, as opposed to uniformly inverse, relationship also appears to decrease with in-

creases in the average educational level of societies: in countries with high illiteracy, the occurrence of such a relationship appears to be almost twice as frequent as in those with relatively low illiteracy.

For our purposes, this work suggests that fertility levels could be reduced in the poorest countries by making primary schooling accessible to all. Moreover, the effects upon individuals of more schooling appear to be greater when it is widely available than when it is confined to only a few. Here the externalities appear to be substantial: this may be because in illiterate societies the attitudes towards contraception are hostile, and individual females are less easily able to change their behaviour — even if they have the knowledge of how to do so — than in societies where predominant attitudes are more supportive. Whatever the reasons, however, this evidence significantly strengthens the case for universalizing primary schooling in poor communities.

The effects of education on health are no less complex. But the evidence for their existence is equally compelling. In principle, schooling can be expected to affect people's health in two main ways: first, for households at a given income level, schooling should increase their ability to improve the nutritional content of diets, and to initiate earlier and more effective diagnosis of illness; second, the increased household income brought by schooling, via its productivity effects, should lead to increase expenditures on food, housing and medical care particularly amongst poorer households[8] — bringing improved family health as a consequence. Thus, it is reasonable to expect better family health amongst both adults and children in more schooled households.[9] Most of the available evidence on these matters concerns the relationship between parental education and infant and child health. This is for two main reasons: first, children's health is more sensitive to current diet and surroundings than that of adults — thus, the impact of nutritional and environmental disadvantage is more easily measured amongst this group; second, there are strong grounds for imputing causality between more schooling and better health based upon correlations between the education of parents and the health of their children, in the sense that a causal relation could not in this case work the other way around. By contrast, it *would* be possible to question the direction of causality in the case of correlations between the schooling possessed by adults and their *own* health.

Recent reviews of the evidence suggest that

such relationships exist. These studies show that there is a strong correlation across countries between life-expectancy — which is mainly influenced by variations in infant and child mortality — and literacy (Cochrane, 1980). Moreover, with regard to data relating to up to 29 developing countries, both bivariate analysis (Cochrane, 1979b) and multivariate studies (O'Hara, 1979) show that infant and child mortality are lower the higher the mother's level of schooling. The evidence suggests that a wife's education has a larger total effect on mortality than that of her husband, but that the combined effects of both parents being literate (as compared to having no schooling) may be such as to reduce mortality by up to 27/1000. Finally, there is evidence that maternal education not only reduces child mortality, but also improves the health of the survivors: children of more schooled mothers tend to be better nourished. It is also possible that they tend to suffer illness less frequently and less severely than other children, but the evidence for this is as yet insufficiently strong (Leslie and Cochrane, 1979). Thus, there is a large amount of evidence, drawing on research conducted in many countries, which consistently shows that parents with greater amounts of primary schooling have healthier, longer-living children. Efforts to increase the coverage of primary schooling should, therefore, have positive long-run effects upon family health.

The schools' influence on individual modernity also has considerable relevance for economic and social change. Inkeles and Smith (1974) found that 'those who had been in school longer were not only better informed and verbally more fluent. They had a different sense of time, and a stronger sense of personal and social efficacy; participated more actively in communal affairs; were more open to new ideas, new experiences and new people; interacted differently with others, and showed more concern for subordinates and minorities. They valued science more, accepted change more readily, and were more prepared to limit the number of children they would have.' The interaction and strengthening of those individual changes which occur as communities as a whole become more schooled, may well explain a good part of the external or associative benefits of schooling. We have seen that these effects are significant for fertility behaviour, for agricultural innovation, and that similar effects on health and nutrition exist. Equally, other correlates of widely available schooling, such as exposure to mass media, have an interactive effect upon the direct ben-

efits of schooling such as the retention of literacy (Simmons, 1976).

Finally, numeracy and literacy are not only critical to the improvement of productivity at work and in the home, but also to the enhancement of satisfaction in leisure. In societies where illiteracy is widespread, the population has only restricted access to a wide range of potential consumption benefits. A high level of national literacy greatly enhances the possibilities for communication by the media, and — accordingly — the amount of popular participation in cultural and political life. Information can be made more easily accessible, which, in turn, can change people's perceptions and help to clarify the alternatives which face them. The evidence we have reviewed relating to the ways in which literacy appears to encourage adaptability and willingness to innovate, is no less important from a welfare point of view in the context of the family or of social and political life in a wider sense.

This is not to argue that the schools, as they are presently organized, are necessarily the most efficient means of accomplishing these ends. Indeed, the constraints imposed by existing links between the schools and the formal economy produce considerable distortions and inefficiencies in the learning process (Colclough, 1977). Moreover, most studies investigating the effects of schooling proxy both the form and content by a simple measure of 'years enrolled'. It may be, then, that the benefits — particularly for rural workers — could be increased by changing the content of schooling, with few, if any, costs for those who progress to higher educational levels, and subsequently join the formal sector. However, in the absence of evidence that alternative approaches (dual systems, nonformal education, integration of education and production etc.) would achieve present learning objectives more effectively, the balance of research suggests that policies to extend the coverage of primary schooling would bring significant economic and social benefits in both urban and rural sectors.

(b) Distributional effects of quantitative expansion and qualitative change

In the rural areas of most developing countries the enrolment ratios for the primary cycle are lower than in the towns. There are not only fewer school places, but also higher economic demands on children, such as minding cattle and finding water or firewood, while their parents are less able to pay the necessary fees. Many children have to walk long distances to school, and tend to drop out sooner if they are suffering from malnutrition. Data which show that the children of richer groups are overrepresented in the school systems of developing countries are available from a large number of studies.[10] Thus, whilst research suggests that socio-economic background seems not to inhibit cognitive achievement in poor countries, the other constraints associated with economic deprivation do affect the ability of even bright and motivated children to enroll in and continue in school.

Since in most countries it is secondary and higher education which is now the main route to well-paid formal employment, the favoured access of the rich to these higher levels of schooling, and thence to more privileged positions in the labour market, tends to promote a growing concentration in the distribution of income over time. Thus policies to improve the access of the poorer groups to primary schooling — which would need to involve not only the provision of more school places in isolated areas, but policies designed to reduce the costs of school attendance — would reduce this trend towards an increasing concentration of human capital. Even though the total number of *jobs* would not increase, such policies would promote more equality of opportunity, and promote some movement towards a more equal distribution of income over time.

Thus, the arguments for expanding the primary span of schooling to cover the whole of the eligible age group seem to be strong from the point of view of distributional goals. But in some countries of the Third World universal primary education has already been achieved, and in several others it is rapidly being approached. In such cases the relevant questions relate more to the costs and benefits of improving and standardizing the quality of primary schooling than to its further quantitative expansion. In any primary school system a wide range of actual unit costs exist: there are schools with many textbooks, well-trained teachers, high-quality buildings and equipment; and there are many others with few or none of these things. What, then, are the likely benefits of increasing expenditure upon primary schooling aimed at reducing these imbalances? Would such a strategy improve the quality of student outputs sufficiently to justify the increased units costs?

At first sight, work on the determinants of cognitive achievement conducted over the last two decades in rich countries does not augur well for strategies based upon equalizing school inputs. One of the first major reviews of the available evidence in the USA (Coleman *et al.*, 1966) concludes that schools bring little influence to bear on a child's achievement that is independent of his/her background and general social context; and this very lack of an independent effect means that the inequalities imposed on children by their home, neighbourhood, and peer environment are carried along to become the inequalities with which they confront life at the end of school. Jencks' later review (1972) also found little evidence that school resources have a powerful effect upon student outcomes — although some school factors were sometimes important, they were not consistently so. Background factors, on the other hand, were always important: the socio-economic status of a student's family — his/her parents' income, education and occupation — invariably proves to be a significant predictor of his/her educational outcome.

These results from the USA also tend to be confirmed by the recent International Evaluation of Educational Achievement (IEA) studies, which attempted to investigate the factors determining school achievement in 23 countries. Here too, school factors such as the type of school, the teacher's experience, and school equipment were not generally significant in predicting achievement test scores within countries. The home background of the student, however — including father's and mother's education, father's occupation, the number of books in the home and family size — was significant. The director of the IEA studies concludes that they 'provide little guidance for the improvement of educational enterprise. They point out the very decided importance of the input into any school system in determining its outcomes; but, as in the massive study of schools in the United States included in the Coleman report, the IEA results do little to accentuate the importance of differences between schools in their effects upon students' (Postlethwaite, 1973).

There is, however, great danger in assuming that the results of these studies are automatically applicable in developing countries. Even the IEA data included only four poorer countries amongst the 23 case studies. In circumstances where the richest 24 countries in the world were spending more than 40 times more per student in 1970 than the poorest 30 countries in the world the qualitative differences in educational provision within the developed world are much less than those across a sample of countries which includes representatives from both the richest and the poorest groups.[11] In this sense, both the IEA and the USA data support results that are consistent with the view that schooling in rich countries is relatively standardized, so that the inter-school variations in quality are much less marked than the variation in home and financial backgrounds. In these circumstances, it is not surprising that the learning and cultural environment provided by the family emerges as having a strongly dominant effect upon school outcomes.

Equally, more recent research from the UK suggests that *some* types of school advantages do affect the cognitive outcomes of pupils. Rutter *et al.* (1979) find that whilst differences in the physical facilities provided at secondary schools (size, age of buildings, space, equipment) were unimportant in determining outcomes, differences in social organization and teacher styles *were* significant. They find that 'factors as varied as the degree of academic emphasis, teacher actions in lessons, the availability of incentives and rewards, good conditions for pupils, and the extent to which children were able to take responsibility are all significantly associated with outcome differences between schools' (Rutter, 1979, p. 178). Thus, whilst the data from the USA suggest that class sizes between 25 and 40 pupils do not significantly affect the teacher's ability to cope, the issue for many developing countries is whether this remains true for classes of 60–70 pupils. It would seem obvious that there is some critical minimum group of inputs to the schooling process which determines limits for the size of classes, the quality of teachers and physical facilities, and the availability of textbooks, if learning is to be possible, let alone efficient.

Support for this view is now available from research studies conducted in a range of developing countries. Although an early review of the evidence concluded that the determinants of school achievement in rich and poor countries were basically the same (Alexander and Simmons, 1978) more recent work suggests that socio-economic background explains far less of the variance in school achievement, and that school-related factors explain far more, in developing than in industrialized societies [see Shuluka (1974), Kann (1978), Heyneman (1976, 1979), and Heyneman and Loxley (1981)]. Although most studies have so far included only a small number of developing countries their results do suggest that the lower the income of a country the lower is the effect of socio-economic status upon the academic achievement of students, and the higher is the effect of teacher and school quality upon such achievement [see, particularly, Heyneman and

Loxley (1981, p. 32)]. It may be, of course, that the school-related variables are important only until some minimum level of quality has been reached, after which further qualitative improvement ceases to have much effect upon cognitive achievement. Much more work is required on the margins of tolerance for variations in these inputs in selected Third World countries. Meanwhile it is clear that conditions in primary schools in the poorer areas of the poorest countries are so bad that resources spent on improving their quality are almost certainly needed if the cognitive ability of their student output is to be enhanced.

4. CONCLUSIONS AND IMPLICATIONS

The main case for investment in primary schooling is that it makes people more productive at work and in the home. It goes well beyond the attainment of short-run consumption or equity goals, and, far from being an obstacle to higher rates of economic growth, it helps to achieve them. In addition, primary schooling facilitates the attainment of other objectives of social policy, particularly in the fields of fertility control, improvements in health, nutrition, literacy and communications, and the strengthening of national culture.

The evidence suggests that the economic and social returns to investment in primary schooling in most developing countries are higher, at the present time, than other forms of educational investment. Moreover, in some of the poorest countries, where real rates of return on industrial and infrastructure projects are often small or even negative, the returns to investment in primary schooling appear to be very high indeed, and more attractive than many alternatives. In countries where a large proportion of the working population is dependent upon farming, and where rates of illiteracy are very high, primary schooling thus provides an investment opportunity which should have high priority on economic grounds.

An investment strategy which gives a central place to primary schooling will not only facilitate growth, but it will do so in a more equitable way than many alternatives. Even in industrial projects which enjoy high financial rates of return, issues of taxation, ownership and control are crucial, if these financial surpluses are subsequently to be of some benefit to poor people. By contrast, measures to extend and improve primary schooling involve direct expenditure on the poorest population groups. These expenditures subsequently increase the productivity of such people, and the returns to the investment flow mainly to the individuals involved and to the communities in which they live. Investment in primary schooling thus provides a means of tackling the poverty problem directly. It represents not only a more attractive investment in many countries, but also a less risky means of increasing the incomes of the poorest people.

The evidence shows that the benefits of primary schooling arise from the cognitive and non-cognitive behavioural changes which the schooling experience brings. With regard to the latter, it appears that changes in attitudes and behaviour are presently achieved even in the context of school systems of very low quality. The implication is that even if resources are scarce, and if the affordable quality of schooling is low, a further extension of the coverage of primary education can still be expected to bring benefits. In this sense, the evidence from fertility studies, and from studies of farmer productivity, suggest that the individual behavioural changes that result from schooling are stronger when literacy is widely spread than when it is more concentrated. There seems to be, then, an interactive effect between individual and community attitudes and values which significantly strengthens the economic and social case for universalizing access to primary schooling.

This is not to say that governments can be satisfied with quantitative expansion alone: the qualitative differences in school facilities as between rich and poor countries are serious indeed. For example, in 1975 the OECD countries were able to spend, on primary schooling, 33 times more per pupil than were the 36 poorest countries in the world (World Bank, 1979, p. 49). The data from the IEA studies suggest that the qualitative gap between schools in rich and poor countries which these expenditure patterns lead to in part accounts for the large differences in measured cognitive achievement between children in the two groups of countries who are at the same stage in their school career. It should be emphasized, however, that the much lower *per capita* expenditures on schooling in the Third World are not the result of lower priorities given to school finance: the proportion of GNP and of the government budget allocated to educational expenditures is not very different between typical rich and poor countries. The expenditure differences arise rather, from an acute budgetary constraint in education which is facing many governments in the Third World. In these circumstances rapid improvement in the quality of primary schooling — though badly needed — will prove very difficult in the absence of greatly increased external support.

Whilst the pressing need for much more widely available and higher-quality primary schooling is already recognized in many countries of the Third World, the implications of this for donor agencies are somewhat problematic. The need is not so much for school buildings — although where they *are* needed they can and should be built on a very low unit-cost basis — as for teacher-training facilities, for school books and equipment, for innovation with regard to school curricula, and for money to pay teachers' salaries. The last of these is extremely important, since upgrading the qualifications of the primary school teaching profession carries with it, in most countries, an immediate, and considerable, impact on the salary bill. Support for these items from donor countries and agencies would be highly desirable. But in most cases the provision of such resources would require attitudinal and bureaucratic changes, together with some restructuring of existing lending priorities. Moreover, if a resource transfer in support of primary schooling were to be really significant, it is likely that some willingness to finance teachers' salaries and other local costs would also be required. These are contentious issues of policy in most donor agencies. But the evidence of this paper suggests that innovation along these lines could provide major benefits — particularly for the poorest countries and for the poorest groups in their populations.

Finally, whilst the case for investing in primary schooling is a strong one — and much firmer than has been conventionally assumed — there are some gaps in our knowledge which need to be filled. The most important *general* need is for more studies focusing upon the impact of primary schooling on worker productivity outside the formal sector. The existing studies analysing its impact upon farmer productivity are very encouraging. But there are ways in which their methodology could usefully be refined in future. In particular, less crude measures of the amount of schooling received are required, and some independent measures for the abilities — independent of schooling — of the sampled populations would be an advantage in interpreting their results. Perhaps the greatest gap in this area, however, concerns the productivity impact of schooling on informal-sector workers outside agriculture. More household income surveys are required from the peri-urban communities of developing countries to provide data on education—income relationships in the informal sector. Although initial results give grounds for optimism as to the beneficial effects of primary schooling, more work is required before these conclusions can be confidently accepted.

There are two other priority areas for further research. The first relates to the effects of primary schooling on health. Whilst good evidence exists, as we have seen, to show that schooling helps to reduce mortality and improve nutrition, the available studies are ambiguous as to its effects upon the frequency and duration of illness. This is more a product of a lack of relevant evidence at present, than of studies showing a neutral or negative impact, and more research in this area is likely to show that health as measured by morbidity is improved by exposure to schooling.

The final area in which more work is required concerns the whole issue of qualitative change in schooling and its influence on school outcomes. We have argued, on the basis of the available evidence, that the positive effects of improvements in school quality in poor countries are likely to be much greater than is typically found in Europe and North America, because of high school standards which have already been reached in the more developed world. Although this is so, further work aimed at clarifying these issues would be extremely helpful. The public expenditure constraint in education is now tightening at a time when the social demand for increased access to schooling has never been greater. At best, therefore, in most developing countries, public expenditure per pupil on primary schooling will grow only very slowly in real terms. Under these circumstances the question of how best to improve the quality of primary schooling becomes very important. Should the priority be to increase the number of trained teachers or to improve the quality of their training? Should it be to abandon double-shift teaching or to reduce average class size? Should it be to increase the quantity or the quality of school books and equipment? Hardly any research has yet been done on these difficult questions in a Third World context, even though they represent critical decisions faced by most ministries of education at the present time. Thus, whilst this paper has shown that considerable progress has recently been made in identifying the behavioural outcomes of the primary schooling experience, on balance, research should now concentrate more upon exactly how these effects are brought about, and — by implication — upon how the positive impact of limited resource inputs to primary schools can be maximized.

NOTES

1. The evidence reviewed in this paper largely excludes cross-national correlation studies of education and economic development. This is partly because earlier work in this tradition was generally subject to serious identification problems, and also because much of it did not focus on primary schooling. For recent reviews of this literature, see Bowman (1980) and Wheeler (1980).

2. See Table 4, which shows higher rates of unemployment amongst those with secondary and tertiary education, than those with primary education, in selected countries. See also the detailed evidence of the country studies given in Psacharopoulos (1973), Chap. 3.

3. This would imply that 60% of the observed income differentials were attributable to education alone.

4. This is not to say that the relevance of the assumptions of the competitive model are not being increasingly questioned also in the context of the changing economic and power structures of developed market economies.

5. For a review of the evidence that labour markets in less developed countries are more imperfect than those of richer nations, see Turner (1965). The limitations of rate-of-return analysis in these circumstances are discussed in Jolly and Colclough (1972).

6. It should be emphasized that these differentials are *averages*. Selection of individual jobs, or even occupation groups, can reveal much greater differences than these.

7. Imputed marginal products.

8. This is mainly because of higher income elasticities of demand for food amongst the poorer groups.

9. For a theoretical treatment of the plausible effects of education on health, see O'Hara (1980).

10. See those for Brazil (Jallade, 1977), India (Bhagwati, 1973; Dasgupta, 1973), Tunisia (Simmons, 1974) and Botswana (Campbell and Abbott, 1976; Kann, 1978).

11. See also Schiefelbein (1973) on this point.

REFERENCES

Alexander, L. and J. Simmons, 'The determinants of school achievement in developing countries: a review of research', *Economic Development and Cultural Change*, Vol. 26 (January 1978), pp. 341–358.

Becker, G., *Human Capital* (New York: National Bureau of Economic Research, 1964).

Bennel, P., 'The historical legacy of colonial civil service salary structures in anglophone Africa: a case study', IDS Working Paper (Brighton: mimeo, 1978).

Berg, I., *Education and Jobs: The Great Training Robbery* (Boston: Beacon Press, 1971).

Berry, A., 'Education, income, productivity and urban poverty' (Washington: World Bank, mimeo, 1980).

Berry, A. and R. H. Sabot, 'Labour market performance in developing countries: a survey', *World Development*, Vol. 6, No. 11/12 (1978).

Bhagwati, J., 'Education, class structure and income inequality', *World Development*, Vol. 1, No. 5 (1973).

Blaug, M., 'The rate of return on investment in education in Great Britain', *The Manchester School* (September 1965).

Blaug, M., *An Introduction to the Economics of Education* (London: Allen Lane, Penguin, 1970).

Blaug, M., *The Rate of Return to Investment in Thailand*, a report to the National Planning Committee on the Third National Development Plan (Bangkok: 1971).

Blaug, M., *Education and the Employment Problem in Developing Countries* (Geneva: ILO, 1973).

Botswana, *A Social and Economic Survey of Three Peri-Urban Areas in Botswana* (Gaborone: Central Statistics Office, 1974).

Bourguignon, F., 'Pobreza y dualismo en el sector urbano de las economicas en desarrollo: el caso de Colombia', *Desarrollo y Sociedad*, No. 1 (January 1979).

Bowles, S., 'Unequal education and the reproduction of the social division of labour', *Review of Radical Political Economy*, Vol. 3, No. 4 (Fall/Winter 1971).

Bowles, S., and H. Gintis, *Schooling in Capitalist America: Educational Reform and the Contradictions of Economic Life* (London: Routledge & Kegan Paul, 1976).

Bowman, Mary Jean, 'Education and economic growth: an overview', in 'Education and income', World Bank Staff Working Paper No. 402 (July 1980, pp. 1–71).

Caldwell, J., *African Rural–Urban Migration: The Movement to Ghana's Towns* (Canberra: Australian National University, 1969).

Campbell, N. and J. Abbott, 'Botswana's primary school system: a spatial analysis', Institute of Development Management, Research Paper No. 1 (Gaborone: 1976).

Carnoy, M., 'Earnings and schooling in Mexico', *Economic Development and Cultural Change* (July 1967).

Cochrane, Susan, *Fertility and Education. What Do We Really Know?* (Baltimore: Johns Hopkins University Press (1979a).

Cochrane, Susan, 'Educational differentials in mortality of children' (Washington: World Bank, mimeo, 1979b).

Cochrane, Susan, 'The socio-economic determinants of mortality: the cross-national evidence' (Washington: World Bank, mimeo, 1980).

Colclough, C., 'Educational expansion or change? Some choices for Central and Southern Africa', *Journal of Modern African Studies*, Vol. 12, No. 3 (1974), pp. 459–470.

Colclough, C., 'Formal education systems and poverty-focused planning', *Journal of Modern African Studies*, Vol. 14, No. 4 (1977), pp. 569–589.

Colclough, C., 'Policies for educational reform', Chap. 7, in OECD, *op. cit.* (1978).

Cole, M., D. Sharp and C. Lave, 'The cognitive consequences of education: some empirical evidence and theoretical misgivings' (Rockefeller University, mimeo, 1978).

Coleman, J., *et al.*, *Equality of Educational Opportunity* (Washington: US Department of Health, Education and Welfare, 1966).

Dasgupta, A., 'Education and income distribution', (Washington: World Bank, mimeo, 1973).

de Moura Castro, C., 'Academic education versus technical education: which is more general?', in La Belle (ed.), *op. cit.* (1975).

Denison, E. F., *The Sources of Economic Growth in the United States* (New York: Committee for Economic Development, 1962).

Gintis, H., 'Education, technology and the characteristics of worker productivity', *The American Economic Review*, Vol. 61 (May 1971).

Heyneman, S., 'Influences on academic achievement: a comparison of results from Uganda and more industrialized societies', *Sociology of Education*, Vol. 49 (July 1976).

Heyneman, S., 'Differences between developed and developing countries: a comment on Simmons' and Alexander's determinants of school achievement', *Economic Development and Cultural Change*, Vol. 28, No. 2 (January 1979), pp. 403–406.

Heyneman, S. and W. Loxley, 'The impact of primary school quality on academic achievement across twenty-nine high and low income countries', paper presented to the annual meeting of the American Sociological Association (Toronto: August 1981).

Illich, I., *Deschooling Society* (New York: Harper & Row, 1972).

Inkeles, A. and D. Holsinger (eds), *Education and Individual Modernity in Developing Countries* (Leiden: E. J. Brill, 1974).

Inkeles, A. and D. Smith, *Becoming Modern* (Cambridge, Massachusetts: Harvard University Press, 1974).

Jallade, J., 'Basic education and income inequality in Brazil: the long-term view', World Bank Staff Working Paper No. 268 (June 1977).

Jencks, C., *et al.*, *Inequality* (New York: Basic Books, 1972).

Jencks, C., et al., Who Gets Ahead? (New York: Basic Books, 1979).

Jolly, R. and C. Colclough, 'African manpower plans: an evaluation', International Labour Review, Vol. 106. Nos 2–3 (1972), pp. 207–264.

Kann, Ulla, 'The relationship between socio-economic background and school achievement in Botswana', Institute of International Education Working Paper No. 2 (Stockholm: 1978).

Kugler, B., A. Reyes and Martha de Gomez, 'Educacion y mercado de trabajo urbano en Colombia: una comparacion entre sectores moderno y no moderno', Monografias de la Corporacion Centro Regional de Poblacion, No. 10 (Bogota: 1979).

La Belle, T. (ed.), Educational Alternatives in Latin America – Social Change and Social Stratification (Los Angeles: UCLA, 1975).

Layard, R. and G. Psacharopoulos, 'The screening hypothesis and the returns to education', Journal of Political Economy, Vol. 82, No. 5 (September/ October 1974).

Leslie, J. and S. Cochrane, 'Parental education and child health: malnutrition and morbidity', (Washington: World Bank, mimeo, 1979).

Lockheed, Marlaine, D. Jamison and L. Lau, 'Farmer education and farm efficiency: a survey', Economic Development and Cultural Change, Vol. 29 (October 1980), pp. 37–76.

OECD, Planning for Growing Populations [R. Cassen and M. Wolfson (eds)] (Paris: 1978).

O'Hara, D., 'Multivariate analysis of mortality' (Washington: World Bank, mimeo, 1979).

O'Hara, D., 'Toward a model of the effects of education on health' (Washington: World Bank, mimeo, 1980).

Postlethwaite, T., 'A selection of the overall findings of the IEA study in science, reading comprehension, literature, French as a foreign language, English as a foreign language, and civil education', Conference on Educational Achievement, Harvard University (November 1973).

Psacharopoulos, G., Returns to Education (Amsterdam: Elsevier, 1973).

Psacharopoulos, G., 'Returns to education: an updated international comparison', in 'Education and income', World Bank Staff Working Paper No. 402 (Washington: 1980, pp. 75–109).

Richards, P. and M. Leonor, Education and Income Distribution in Asia (London: ILO, Croom Helm, 1981).

Rutter, M., B. Mangham, P. Mortimore and J. Ouston, Fifteen Thousand Hours (London: Penguin, 1979).

Schiefelbein, E., 'The Jencks' impact on developing countries' (Washington, mimeo, 1973).

Shirk, S., 'Educational reform and political backlash: recent changes in Chinese educational policy', Comparative Education Review, Vol. 23, No. 2 (1979).

Shulaka, S., 'Achievement of Indian children in mother tongue (Hindi) and science', Comparative Education Review, Vol. 18 (June 1974).

Simmons, J., 'Education, poverty and development', World Bank Staff Working Paper No. 188 (Washington: February 1974).

Simmons, J., 'Retention of cognitive skills acquired in primary school', Comparative Education Review, Vol. 20 (February 1976), pp. 79–93).

Standing, G., Labour Force Participation and Development (Geneva: ILO, 1978).

Thias, H. and M. Carnoy, 'Cost–benefit analysis in education: a case study of Kenya', World Bank Staff Occasional Paper No. 14 (Washington, D.C.: 1972).

Turner, H., 'Wage trends, wage policies and collective bargaining: the problems for underdeveloped countries', Department of Applied Economics Occasional Paper No. 2 (Cambridge: 1965).

Turnham, D., The Employment Problem in Less Developed Countries: A Review of Evidence (Paris: OECD, 1970).

UNECA, 'Education and employment in Africa', in Survey of Economic and Social Conditions in Africa, 1976–1977 (Part 1) (New York: 1978), pp. 59–145.

UNESCO, Statistical Yearbook (Paris: 1977).

Wheeler, D., 'Human resource development and economic growth in the LDCs: a simultaneous model' (Washington: World Bank, mimeo, 1980).

Whitla, D., Value Added: Measuring the Outcomes of Undergraduate Education, a study conducted by the Office of Instructional Research and Evaluation, Harvard University (1977).

World Bank, Education Sector Policy, Report No. 2680 (Washington: 1979).

Higher Education 15: 283–297 (1986)
© *Martinus Nijhoff Publishers, Dordrecht – Printed in the Netherlands*

Financing public higher education in developing countries

The potential role of loan schemes

ALAIN MINGAT & JEE-PENG TAN
Research Division, Education and Training Department, The World Bank

Abstract. The financing of education has emerged as a major topic of discussion among policy makers in recent years. There is evidence that in many developing countries, governments can no longer continue to increase spending on education at the high rates characteristic in the 1960s and 1970s. The macroeconomic environment has worsened, and there is keen intersectoral competition for public funds. Thus unless educational development moves away from its present heavy dependence on public funds, the expansion of education would be frustrated. One policy option is to increase the private financing of education. In this paper, we evaluate the potential effectiveness of loans schemes as a cost recovery instrument in higher education. Essentially, loans permit students to finance the cost of their education from future income. So the effectiveness of loans would depend on the relation between costs and students' future income. It also depends on the incidence of repetition, dropout, and default, as well as on whether or not a grace period is incorporated in the loan scheme. Our simulations show that in Asia and Latin America, the potential rate of cost recovery is substantial under what appears to be bearable terms of repayment. In Francophone Africa and Anglophone Africa, however, loans schemes are unlikely to perform as well, but they would still permit a shift toward greater private financing of higher education

I. Introduction

In many developing countries, the government dominates in financing and providing education. School enrollments have expanded rapidly in the last two decades, reflecting the sustained increases in public spending on education. After the middle of the 1970s, however, this expansion began to level off. In many developing countries, the share of education in public spending had already become very large – reaching between one-tenth and one-third of the public budget – and it was increasingly difficult to compete for additional public resources. At the same time, poor macroeconomic conditions have constrained the growth of the public budget itself.

From a social perspective, additional investment in education remains profitable. Since there is limited scope for increased public spending on education, other policy options must be considered. Broadly, these options include policies to improve efficiency within the education system, leading to reduction in unit costs; and policies to increase the private financing of education.[1] In this paper, we shall assess the potential effectiveness of a specific instrument within the latter policy option: increased cost recovery in higher education implemented via student loans.[2]

284

The paper is organized as follows. In section II we review the arguments for increased cost recovery in higher education. The implementation of this policy through student loans is considered in section III. In section IV we compare the potential effectiveness of loans as a cost recovery instrument in four major developing country regions. Section V concludes the paper.

II. The case for increased cost recovery in higher education

An important reason for considering increased cost recovery in higher education is that it allows public spending to be reallocated toward the lower levels of education. Table 1 shows that although spending on education accounts for a large share of public spending, primary school enrollments remain low in some developing countries, particularly in Africa. Mingat and Tan (1985a) have shown in a study of ten African countries that if the cost of higher education could be fully recovered, the public funds thus freed would enable governments to expand primary school places by 20 to 40 percent, depending on country conditions. Alternatively, if the resources were channelled into secondary education, the result would be an increase of 35 to 75 percent in the supply of places. The sheer magnitude of these potential effects suggests that cost recovery in higher education would be an effective policy for sustaining the development of primary and secondary education at a time when the scope for increased public spending is constrained.

The argument for this policy is reinforced by efficiency and equity considerations. Estimates of the returns to education show that investing in primary education yields the highest social payoff, followed by secondary education,

Table 1. Public expenditure on education and enrollment ratios, by region, circa 1980.

Region	Public expenditure on education as % of		Gross Enrollment Ratio		
	Total Public budget	GNP	Primary	Secondary	Higher
Francophone Africa	22.6	4.9	46	14	2.4
Anglophone Africa	17.0	5.2	77	17	1.2
South East Asia & Pacific	15.0	4.2	87	43	9.1
South Asia	8.8	2.1	71	19	4.4
Latin America	16.9	4.5	90	44	12.0
Developing Countries	16.1	4.5	75	23	6.9
Developed Countries	9.0	4.9	107	80	21.0

Source: World Bank (1983) and UNESCO (1983).

then higher education (Psacharopoulos, 1985).[3] Thus the reallocation of public spending toward primary education would enhance efficiency in the allocation of resources. At the same time, greater cost recovery in higher education implies a narrowing of the gap between the social and private rates of return at this level of education. Thus private decisions to invest in higher education would be more closely linked to the social benefit of such investments. With increased private financing, students would be encouraged to behave more like "investors" than "consumers," and therefore to pay more attention to labor market signals in their choice, not only of course specialization, but also of whether or not to enroll.

Increased cost recovery in higher education would also improve equity in the distribution of public spending on education. In most developing countries, public expenditure per student in higher education far exceeds that at the lower levels of education, as Table 2 shows. Since enrollment in higher education is limited, and most of the students tend to come from relatively wealthy families, the high level of per student expenditure benefits a small privileged social group.

A longer term perspective of the inequities becomes apparent when it is recalled that students in higher education have already benefited from public spending at the previous two levels of education. Thus a more accurate picture is provided by the distribution of public spending among the adult out-of-school population. Those who grow up without entering primary school receive no share in the accumulated public spending on education. On the other hand, those who attain higher education appropriate a share comprising of

Table 2. Public expenditure per student on education and enrollment ratios, major world regions, around 1980.

Region	Public expenditure per student as percentage of per capita GNP			Number of Countries Reporting
	Primary	Secondary	Higher	
Anglophone Africa	18	50	920	16
Francophone Africa	29	143	804	18
South Asia	8	18	119	4
East Asia and Pacific	11	20	118	6
Latin America	9	26	88	19
Middle East and North Africa	2	28	150	11
Developing countries	14	41	370	74
Developed countries	22	24	49	20

Source: Mingat and Tan (1985b).

286

public subsidies in primary, secondary and higher education.

In many developing countries, the enrollment pyramid is steep and narrow, implying that the access to education is limited; and public spending tends to increase sharply with rising levels of education. The result is that a large share of the accumulated public spending is appropriated by the small group who attain higher education. Mingat and Tan (1985b) show that in the developing countries as a whole, this group represents only 6 percent of the adult population, but appropriates 39 percent of the total accumulated public spending on education. On the other hand, 71 percent of the population leave their school-age years with either no schooling or at most primary schooling. As a group, their share in public spending on education is only 22 percent.

The distribution of public spending would become more equitable if there is increased cost recovery in higher education, and public spending is reallocated toward lower levels of education. Under such a policy, the share of public spending received by the group with primary or less education would rise from 22 to 64 percent (Mingat and Tan, 1985b). The result would also benefit those from poor income groups since they are most widely represented at the lower levels of education.

III. Loans as a mechanism for cost recovery

In general, a policy of increased cost recovery can be implemented in two ways. The first is to require students to pay for their education at the time of enrollment. This arrangement is usually unsatisfactory because it limits the selection of students to those who have the funds at the time of enrollment. Because qualified students from poor families would be denied access to higher education, it is both inequitable and inefficient. An alternative arrangement is a student loan scheme. Essentially, such a scheme would allow students to mobilize their future earnings to finance present investment in their studies.

The effectiveness of loans as a cost recovery instrument can be analyzed as follows. Suppose the loan given to university students equals the public spending per student at this level of education. The question then is: To what extent would a loan of this size be recouped from the students?

a) Preliminary considerations

One important factor affecting the effectiveness of loan schemes is the relationship between the loan and graduates' future income. The larger the income relative to the loan, the more likely are borrowers to have the funds for full repayment, and the better the overall rate of cost recovery.

Table 3. Public spending per student in higher education and graduates salaries in major regions of the world, circa 1984[1].

Country/Region	Unit cost in higher education (1)	Graduates' salaries (2)	Salary-Cost ratio (2)/(1)
Anglophone Africa	9.2	10.0	1.09
Francophone Africa	8.0	19.4	2.43
Latin America	1.2	3.4	2.83
Asia	0.9	4.0	4.44

[1] The data in columns (1) and (2) are measured in terms of per capita GNP.
Source: Based on calculations from data in Unesco (1983), Tait and Heller (1984) and Wolff (1984).

A preliminary indication of the extent of cost recovery under a loan scheme can therefore be derived from the ratio of graduates' income to the public spending per student in higher education. The data for four major world regions appear in Table 3. In Asia, the relatively high ratio between graduates' earnings and public spending per student suggests that students could probably afford to repay the government for their education. In contrast, the same ratio for Anglophone Africa is quite low, pointing to the likelihood that students would have greater difficulty to repay all the subsidies they now receive from the government.

How fully the loans can be recovered also depend on the terms of repayment – the length of repayment and the percent of income that graduates allocate to repay the loans. It is in the government's interest to keep the repayment short so that the loan scheme can become self-financing more rapidly. The student, however, wants a longer repayment so as to spread out the debt burden. In some cases, it may be necessary for the government to incorporate a grace period in the terms, because some graduates may not find jobs immediately and will not have the funds to repay their loans. In general, the terms appropriate to a particular country depend strongly on the political and social acceptability of the debt burden they imply, and on the administrative feasibility of keeping track of borrowers over an extended repayment period. The latter factor is important because it affects the efficiency of debt collection, which in turn affects default rates in the scheme.

To illustrate how the performance of a loan scheme is affected by alternative terms of repayment, the incorporation of a grace period, and the incidence of default, we shall use data from Francophone Africa. Details of the calculations can be found in Mingat et al. (1986). Here we shall simply report the results.

288

b) Some simulations using data from Francophone Africa

To begin with, consider the outcome under the most favorable conditions. We assume that students enter university immediately after secondary school; follow a four year course without repeating or dropping out; start working immediately after graduation, earning the average salary of people of the same age and working experience and with similar academic qualification. Borrowers allocate (throughout the repayment period) a constant proportion of their current income to repay the loan. The calculations also assume that the flow of repayments is discounted at a real market interest rate of 5% p.a.[4]

The simulation results appear in Figure 1. This figure can be read in several ways: for example, it shows the number of years required for complete repayment of a loan if borrowers allocate a certain percentage of their income for repayment; alternatively, one can fix the length of repayment and look at the proportion of income that must be allocated to repay the loan fully. If, for administrative, social or political reasons, there are limits on these parameters, the figure can reveal the percentage of the loan recoverable under these constraints.[5]

If, for example, the repayment period is limited to ten years, and if the proportion of graduates' income allocated for loan repayment can be no more

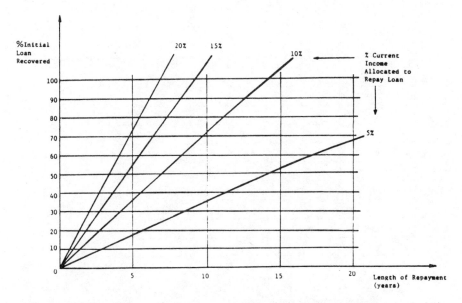

Fig. 1. % of Initial Loan Recoverable with Alternative Repayment Terms – *Simulations for Anglophone Africa under Optimistic Assumptions* (i.e., that there is no repetition, no dropout, no grace period and no default).

than ten percent, then the maximum recoverable proportion of the loan is about 72 percent. This rather favorable outcome has been obtained under optimistic assumptions. In particular, the calculations assume that borrowers neither repeat nor drop out; that they obtain jobs and start working immediately after graduation; and that there is no default. These problems are likely to lower the rate of cost recovery. The magnitude of their impact is analyzed below.

Repetition

The problem here is that a borrower will take five or six years to graduate instead of the normal four. As a result he will need a larger loan. Repayment of this loan will also be delayed. The impact of these implications can be measured in different ways: by how much would the proportion of income allocated to loan repayment have to increase in order to attain the same rate of cost recovery as before, given that the repayment period is limited to ten years; alternatively, by how many years would the repayment period have to be extended to achieve the same rate of cost recovery as before, given that the proportion of income allocated to discharge loan is fixed at 10 percent; or again, by how much would the rate of cost recovery be reduced if repeaters faced the same terms of repayment as non-repeaters?

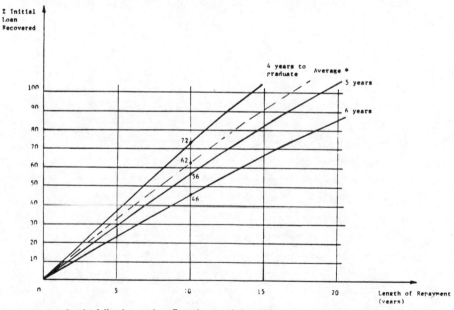

* Average for the following student flow characteristics: 50% graduate in 4 years; 30% repeat one year; and the remaining 20% repeat two years.

Fig. 2. % of Initial Loan Recoverable when there is repetition, given that borrowers allocate 10% of income to repay loan – *Francophone Africa.*

290

Figure 2 provides the simulation results to answer the last question. For clarity of presentation, it shows only the case where repeaters allocate ten percent of their current income to repay their loan.[6] Borrowers who finish in the normal four years repay 72 percent of their loans; those who repeat one year repay 56 percent; while those who repeat 2 years repay only 46 percent.

The overall performance of the loan scheme depends on the incidence of repetition among borrowers. To illustrate, if 30 percent of the graduates repeat one year, 20 percent repeat two years, while the rest finish on time, then the overall rate of cost recovery of the loan scheme would be 62 percent, as represented by the dotted line in Figure 2. Clearly, if better performance is desired, eligibility for loans should be restricted mainly to academically qualified students.

Dropout

Borrowers who drop out face a problem in that they have borrowed to finance one or two years of university education without obtaining any certification. To the extent they have acquired some additional knowledge during this time, and to the extent the labor market rewards such knowledge, they would earn more than people who just have secondary education. But to be conservative in our analysis, we shall assume that university drop-outs in fact earn the same income as secondary school graduates. Assume also that on average 20 percent of the borrowers drop out after one year, and ten percent after two years, while the rest of the students graduate on time. With these student flow characteristics, the overall rate of cost recovery would be 69 percent compared to 72 percent in the absence of dropouts, if all borrowers allocate ten percent of income to repay their loan over ten years. Thus, although the incidence of dropping out affects the performance of the loan scheme, its impact tends to be small.

Grace period

The incorporation of a grace period implies that loan schemes will take longer to become self-financing. But the impact on the overall rate of cost recovery of the scheme is quite limited. For example, with a grace period of two years, the average rate of cost recovery in Francophone African countries would, on average, be 65 percent, instead of 72 percent without the grace period, assuming that graduates allocate ten percent of their income for loan repayment over ten years.

Default on student loans

The actual importance of this problem obviously depends on the effectiveness of the existing arrangements for debt collection. For example, it is probably insignificant under an arrangement whereby employers are obliged to deduct repayment for education loans before paying out borrowers' wages. On the

Table 4. Rates of default on student loans in Latin America.

Country	Acronym of loan institution	% of loans in arrears
Brazil	APLUB	2
Colombia	ICETEX	11
Costa Rica	CONAPE	0.5
Ecuador	IECE	19
Honduras	Educredito	9
Jamaica	SLB	7
Mexico	BM	5
Peru	INABEC	22
Venezuela	Educredito	30
	SACUEDO	8
Average		11.4

Source: Woodhall (1984).

other hand, if no record is kept of borrowers, the default rate is likely to be high, since defaulters can more easily avoid detection.

Information about default rates on student loans is scarce, particularly for developing countries. Latin America is the only developing country region where loan schemes have existed for some time, and where there has been some experience with loan collection. Table 4 shows the rate of default on student loans in several countries in this region. It is of course not easy to generalize from these data the likely default rates that might apply to other countries or regions of the world. They do indicate, however, that it is feasible in the context of developing countries, to achieve relatively low rates of default on student loans.

To illustrate the impact of default, we assume that it is on average 15 percent. The rate of cost recovery in the loan scheme in Francophone Africa would be 61 percent instead of 72 percent, assuming that ten percent of borrowers' income is allocated for loan repayment over ten years. Thus the efficiency of loan schemes as a mechanism for cost recovery is not severely impaired by the incidence of default.

The cumulative effect of repetition, drop out, grace period, and default
Each of the problems exert a relatively small effect on the rate of cost recovery. But taken together, their impact can be significant. For example, suppose students repeat and drop out at the relatively high rates assumed above – 30 percent repeat one year, 20 percent repeat two years, 20 percent drop out after one year, 10 percent drop out after two years, while the remaining 20 percent graduate on time. Assume further that all borrowers are given a grace period of two years, and that, on average, the default rate is 15 percent. Figure 3 shows the

292

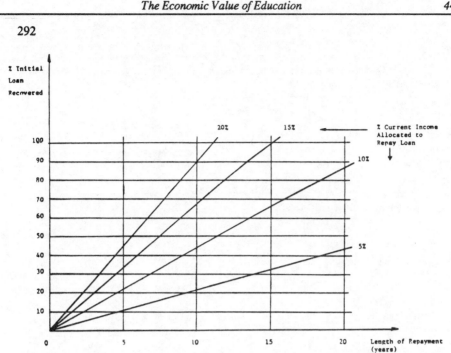

Fig. 3. % of Initial Loan Recoverable with Alternative Repayment Terms – *Simulations for Francophone Africa under Conservative Assumptions* (i.e., that 20% of the borrowers complete their studies on time; 30% repeat one year; 20% repeat two years; 20% drop out after one year; and 10% drop out after two years; that there is a grace period of two years for all borrowers; and that the default rate is 15%).

performance of the loan scheme in Francophone Africa under these conditions. If the same terms of repayment – ten percent of current income over ten years – as in the previous simulations apply, then only about 45 percent of their loans would be recovered. The large reduction in the rate of cost recovery (from 72 percent in the absence of these problems) is of course due to the extremely conservative assumptions for this simulation. The fact that even under these assumptions, the rate of cost recovery remains substantial indicates that loans can be an effective instrument for cost recovery in higher education.

IV. The potential effectiveness of loan schemes in four major world regions

The rate of cost recovery under a loan scheme is likely to differ between countries and regions because of differences in the cost of higher education, as well as in graduates' incomes. Table 5 shows the results for four major world regions.

Table 5. Cost recovery via loans under optimistic and conservative assumptions in four world regions.

Region	Length of repayment (years)	Share of graduates' annual income allocated to repay loan		
		Percentage of initial loan recovered[2]		
		5%	10%	15%
Anglophone Africa	10	16 (10)	32 (20)	49 (30)
	15	24 (15)	47 (30)	71 (44)
	20	30 (19)	60 (38)	90 (57)
Francophone Africa	10	36 (22)	72 (45)	108 (67)
	15	53 (33)	105 (66)	157 (99)
	20	67 (43)	134 (85)	201 (128)
Latin America	10	42 (26)	84 (52)	126 (78)
	15	61 (38)	122 (77)	183 (115)
	20	78 (50)	156 (99)	234 (149)
Asia	10	66 (41)	132 (82)	197 (123)
	15	96 (60)	191 (120)	287 (181)
	20	122 (78)	245 (156)	368 (233)

[1] *Optimistic assumptions:* all students complete their studies on time, that is, without repeating or dropping out. Also, they start repaying their loans immediately after graduation, without the benefit of a grace period. The simulations assume too that the default rate is zero.
Conservative assumptions (simulation results are in parenthesis): 20 percent of the intake complete their studies on time; 30 percent repeat one year; 20 percent repeat two years; 20 percent dropout after one year; and 10 percent dropout after two years. All borrowers enjoy a grace period of two years. The calculations also assume a default rate of 15 percent, that is, 15 percent of the borrowers fail to repay their loans.
[2] The calculations assume that a 5 percent real rate of interest is charged on the loans. Figures over 100 percent can be interpreted in any of the following ways: (i) a smaller proportion of income allocated for loan repayment would achieve full cost recovery; (ii) shorter repayment period would achieve full cost recovery; and (iii) graduates have the financial capacity to repay a larger loan.

Two sets of results are reported. The first set correspond to simulations under the optimistic assumptions of no repetition, no dropout, no grace period, and no default. They indicate the maximum possible rate of cost recovery for given terms of repayment. The second set of results, in parentheses in Table 5, are for simulations under conservative assumptions – only 20 percent of the intake complete their university course on time, while 30 percent repeat one year, 20 percent repeat two years, 20 percent drop out after one year, and 10 percent drop out after two years. Also, it is assumed that all borrowers enjoy

294

a grace period of two years. The default rate is assumed to be 15 percent.

In Anglophone and Francophone Africa, the loans would be large enough to cover all tuition and living expenses, since the public spending per student includes both items. But the simulations indicate that such a large loan would probably not be fully recouped, even under the optimistic assumptions. In Anglophone Africa, if graduates were to allocate 5 percent of their current incomes for loan repayment for 10 years, they would repay only 16 percent of what the government spends on their education. In Francophone Africa, the rate of recovery under the same terms would be 36 percent. The better performance is due largely to the higher incomes of graduates in Francophone Africa since the unit public spending on higher education is comparable between the two regions, as Table 1 above indicated.

Not surprisingly, the performance of the loan schemes worsens under the conservative assumptions. The rate of cost recovery — with the previous terms of five percent of current income allocated for repayment over ten years — drops to only 10 percent in Anglophone Africa, and to 22 percent in Francophone Africa.

These results clearly indicate that unless the loan amount is reduced drastically, cost recovery would be low with relatively easy repayment terms — say less than ten percent for less than ten years. If the current subsidies received by students were converted into loans, students are likely voluntarily to commit themselves to smaller loans, since the cost of wastage would be borne personally. In some African countries, living expenses are estimated to be less than 50 percent of the allowances currently given to university students (Eicher, 1984; Rasera, 1984; and Perrot, 1984). Thus the loan needed to finance higher education could be reduced by 25 percent, assuming that living expenses account for half the total cost, and that operating costs remain at current levels. Correspondingly, the rates of recovery for the two Africa regions would all increase by 33 percent. Given this possibility, student loan schemes look more promising as an instrument for cost recovery. Students' inability to repay an excessive living allowance argues not against the loan scheme itself, but rather for smaller loans. In Anglophone Africa, the potential rates of cost recovery would still remain low. So complementary policies to reduce the operating cost of higher education, and thereby the loan needed to cover tuition, would also be necessary.

In Latin American and Asian countries, student allowances account for a very small proportion of total public spending on higher education. Thus a loan equal in size to the current public spending per student would be large enough only to cover tuition. The results in Table 5 show that under optimistic assumptions — no repetition, no dropout, no grace period, and no default — a substantial part of such loans can be recovered with relatively easy repayment terms. In Asia, two-thirds of the initial loan can be recovered if graduates allocate five percent of their current income over ten years, while in Latin America, 40 percent would be recovered under the same repayment terms.

As before, however, these results represent upper-bound estimates of the potential cost recovery via loans. The incidence of repetition, dropout, default and incorporation of a grace period would predictably lower the rate of cost recovery. The simulations show that cost recovery would nevertheless remain substantial under reasonable terms of repayment. In Asia, if terms such as ten percent of income over 15 years are acceptable and feasible, graduates would be able to finance all tuition charges as well as living expenses amounting to 20 percent of the tuition charges.

V. Conclusion

In this paper, we have argued that a policy of cost recovery in higher education would be beneficial in many developing countries as it would improve economic efficiency and equity. Within higher education itself, however, such a policy could discourage enrollment among students from poor families. As a result, access to higher education could become socially more selective. For this and other reasons, a fee policy is likely to be unpopular among current and prospective students. However, once a decision has been taken to increase private financing in higher education, its social and political acceptability could be improved by implementing it through a loan scheme. As Woodhall (1984) has put it, such a scheme would give "students financial support today, when they need it, in return for a promise that they, in turn, will contribute directly... to support [future] students."

The introduction of student loans obviously raises new and difficult issues concerning the terms of repayment: would those required for full cost recovery be feasible to implement; would the implied debt burden, measured say, in terms of the duration of repayment, and proportion of a borrower's current income allocated to repayment, be "bearable?" An assessment of these issues requires political judgement as to the acceptability of different terms of repayment. Although this assessment is outside the scope of this paper, our analysis nevertheless provides important information about the potential effectiveness of loan schemes.

In Asia, and to a lesser extent, in Latin America, loans can be an effective mechanism for cost recovery because a substantial proportion of the public cost of higher education can be recovered under what appears to be reasonably bearable repayment terms. In Francophone and Anglophone Africa, loan schemes are unlikely to perform as well, because the terms of repayment required for a high rate of cost recovery are much more difficult to bear. The unit costs of higher education are too high and students would probably be

296

unable to finance them entirely from future income. However, if complementary policies to reduce the cost of higher education were also pursued, students would need a smaller loan to cover tuition and living expenses. Since the smaller loans can be financed more easily, the rate of cost recovery would be enhanced, and a greater shift toward the private financing of higher education would then be achievable.

Notes

1. These policy options complement each other, and can obviously be pursued simultaneously.
2. Our focus on higher education does not imply that increased cost recovery is irrelevant for other levels of education. See Mingat and Tan (1986) for an analysis of the potential impact of such a policy in secondary education.
3. The fact that these estimates neglect externalities is unlikely to invalidate the comparison. First, there is no reason to believe that the externalities are larger in higher education than primary education. Second, unit cost of higher education is much greater – among developing countries, it is on average 26 times that of primary education. Thus unless a higher education graduate generates, on average, more externalities than 26 primary school graduates, the conclusion based on the estimated returns – that primary education yields the highest social payoff – remains valid.
4. The market rate of interest is the appropriate rate for discounting the flow of repayments because we are evaluating loans as an instrument for cost recovery. It does not mean that all student loans should be charged at this rate. In fact, the government might be willing to subsidize the interest rate so as to reduce the debt burden on borrowers. The implicit assumption is that only partial cost recovery is envisaged from the outset. But if this is the desired outcome, it can equally be achieved by requiring borrowers to repay only part of the loan at the market interest rate.
5. It may, for example, be difficult to keep track of borrowers for a long period and the government might wish to restrict the repayment period to, say, ten years. Also, it might not be socially acceptable to borrowers if the loan repayment accounts for too high a proportion of their current income, or equivalently, reduces the private rate of return to university education too drastically.
6. Repeaters are therefore not penalized with stiffer repayment payments.

References

Eicher, J. C., "L'Enseignment Superieur en Afrique de l'Ouest Francophone: Synthese de Cinq Etudes de Case," Education and Training Department, The World Bank, August, 1984.

Mingat, A. and Tan, J. P. (1985a), "Subsidization of Higher Education Versus Expansion of Primary Enrollments: What Can A Shift of Resources Achieve in Sub-Saharan Africa?", in *International Journal of Educational Development*, vol. 5, No. 4, 1985.

Mingat, A. and Tan, J. P. (1985b), "On Equity in Education Again: An International Comparison." *Journal of Human Resources*, vol. XX, No. 2, Spring.

Mingat, A. and Tan, J. P. (1986), "Expanding Education Through User Charges in LDCs: What can be Achieved?", *Economics of Education Review* (forthcoming).

Mingat, A., Tan, J. P., and Hoque, M. (1986), "Recovering the Cost of Public Higher Education in LDCs. To what extent are Loan Schemes an Efficient Instrument?", Education and Training Department Discussion Series No. EDT14, The World Bank, Washington, D.C.

Perrot, J., 1984, "L'Enseignment Superieure au Benin," IREDU, Dijon, March.

Psacharopoulos, G. (1985), "Returns to Education: A Further International Update and Implications," in *Journal of Human Resources*, vol. XX, No. 3, Fall.

Rasera J. B. (1984), "Couts et Financement de l'Enseignement Superieure en Haute Volta," IREDU, Dijon, April (revised).

Tait, A. and Heller, P. (1983), *Government Employment and Pay: Some International Comparison*, Occasional Paper No. 24, International Monetary Fund, Washington, D.C.

Unesco (1983), Statistical Yearbook. Paris: Unesco.

Wolff, L. (1984), *Financing of Education in Eastern Africa*, Staff Working Paper No. 702, The World Bank, Washington, D.C.

Woodhall, M. (1983), *Student Loans as a Means of Financing Higher Education: Lessons from International Experience*, Staff Working Paper No. 599, The World Bank, Washington, D.C.

World Bank (1983), *Comparative Education Indicators*. Education and Training Department, The World Bank, Washington, D.C.

[24]

HIGHER EDUCATION AND INCOME DISTRIBUTION IN A LESS DEVELOPED COUNTRY

By GARY S. FIELDS*

THREE competing hypotheses have been advanced concerning the effect of government education spending and finance on income distribution. One hypothesis is that educational spending leads to income redistribution in favour of the poor. The alternative hypothesis is that educational spending results in an even wider gap between rich and poor. Finally, there is the null hypothesis, which holds that the aggregate distribution of income is determined by many things other than education which, by this hypothesis, has little or no effect. These hypotheses apply to the effects of education spending and finance on the size distribution of income within a generation and to the effects upon movement between (relative) income classes between generations.

The primary purpose of this paper is to empirically test among both the intra- and the inter-generational version of these three hypotheses for higher (i.e. post-secondary)[1] levels of education for one less developed country, Kenya.[2] A secondary purpose is to investigate other economic aspects of spending on higher education, most notably the question of horizontal equity in school finance.

Before proceeding, a methodological point is in order. There is no consensus in the public economics literature on what is a suitable criterion for assessing the equitability of a fiscal programme.[3] At least three criteria may be distinguished (the terminology is my own): (1) *The Equal*

* This paper was begun when the author was Visiting Research Associate, Institute for Development Studies, University of Nairobi; continued at the Chr. Michelsen Institute, Bergen, Norway; and completed at the Economic Growth Center, Yale University. Thanks are extended to the above institutions and to the Rockefeller Foundation, which provided the financial support for the author's stay in Kenya. John Akin, William Neenan, Svein-Erik Rastad, and David Stern provided helpful comments during the preparation of this paper. Finally, I wish to thank Julia Collins for her invaluable research assistance.

[1] Regrettably, no data exist to permit similar tests for lower levels of education.

[2] The Kenya data are particularly rich, especially for a less developed country. None the less, many assumptions and approximations have had to be made. The reader should bear the fragmentary nature of the underlying data in mind and interpret what follows with care.

[3] The methodology utilized here is similar in a number of respects (though different in many others) to that used in a study of California's higher education system by Hansen and Weisbrod [4]. An illuminating controversy on their work involving, among others, Joseph Pechman [8], has questioned the conceptual framework for evaluating the income distribution effects of a fiscal programme. The present paper borrows from both without taking either side, and in some ways is most similar to the treatment suggested by Robert Hartman [5].

246   HIGHER EDUCATION AND INCOME DISTRIBUTION

Opportunity Criterion. By this criterion, a fiscal programme is equitable if different groups in the population have access to the programme in proportion to their numbers in the population, irrespective of the costs paid by the different groups in relation to benefits received. (2) *The Cost–Benefit Criterion.* By this criterion, a fiscal programme is equitable if the costs paid by different groups in the population are proportional to the benefits they each receive, irrespective of access to the programme. (3) *The Ability to Pay Criterion.* By this criterion, due to diminishing marginal utility of income, a programme is equitable if the cost–benefit ratio of the programme rises as a function of income. Evidently, when confronted with a given set of facts, these criteria may yield very different qualitative judgements about the equitability of a fiscal programme.[1] We note that the cost–benefit and the equal opportunity criteria apply horizontally (i.e. between individuals in the same income class) as well as vertically (i.e. for comparisons across income classes). Note also that the equal opportunity criterion refers primarily to *inter*-generational distributional effects, whereas the other two are primarily *intra*-generational.

1. Students' socio-economic background

Kenya's educational system consists of seven primary grades (called standards), four years of secondary and two years of higher secondary schooling (called forms), and a post-secondary system comprised of teacher training colleges and a university.[2] The Kenya government has expressed a strong commitment to equalizing the distribution of income [12, pp. 2–3] and open recruitment to the educational system is seen as one of the main means of bringing this about. However, like many other less developed countries, Kenya has a very steep 'educational pyramid'. The reason this is important is that one cannot simply decide to continue his education

---

[1] Consider the following hypothetical example.

Income group	% of population	% of costs	% of benefits = % of beneficiaries
High-income people	25%	10%	10%
Low-income people	75%	90%	90%

By the cost–benefit criterion, the programme is *equitable*, because the percentage of costs equals the percentage of benefits for both high and low income people. By the equal opportunity criterion, the programme is inequitable and *favours low-income people*, who are 75 per cent of the population, yet 90 per cent of the beneficiaries. By the ability-to-pay criterion, the programme is inequitable and *favours high-income people*, who despite their higher incomes have the same cost-benefit ratio as low-income people. Although this lack of a single equity criterion does not affect the method of analysis, the choice of criterion does affect the interpretation of the results.

[2] Out of a total population of 10 million, in 1970 there were 1,300,000 children in primary school, 125,000 in secondary, and 10,000 in post-secondary, of whom 7,000 were in teacher training colleges and the remainder at the University of Nairobi. All these pupils, except for 50,000 secondary students, attended government-operated schools.

G. S. FIELDS 247

and do so. Rather, school admissions are highly competitive, the main criterion being performance on written examinations at the end of a course of study.[1] There is a great demand for education at all levels relative to the supply. This is because the educational system is almost entirely subsidized and the private benefits of education are very large. For instance, university education is free (except to non-citizens) and the starting salary of a university graduate in the civil service is four times that of a secondary graduate. Consequently, the private rates of return to investment in higher levels of education in Kenya are very high—of the order of 30 per cent per year (see Table II below).

These facts—a steep educational pyramid, express public policy in favour of greater income equality, and large private benefits to those few who receive higher education—raise the question of the socio-economic background of the children who receive the rewards. To answer this question, I was able to make use of unpublished data on the characteristics of the parents of university students which were already available,[2] and I supplemented these by personally gathering data from the teacher training colleges.[3] The basic findings are reported in Table I.

In general, as compared with all adult males in Kenya, the students' parents are more likely to be in a high-level occupation, to be better educated, to own land, and (if landowners) to have larger landholdings. If these are taken as measures of socio-economic status, we thus observe that Kenyan students come from families with higher-than-average socio-economic status. This is true for each type of higher education. Moreover, the parents of University of Nairobi students come from an even higher socio-economic background than students at the teacher training colleges. Thus, we find that the children of the relatively well-to-do tend to benefit more from Kenya's higher education system than the children of poorer families and that this tendency is most pronounced at the university level.

If all families contributed equally to the financing of the school system, these findings would in and of themselves indicate that the educational system is financed inequitably by all of the criteria discussed above.

---

[1] Both the examinations and the curriculum reflect the legacy of colonialism and are not very different from the British educational system of today.

[2] I wish to thank S. E. Rastad for making the University data available to me. These data were compiled from personal interviews with 188 students (out of a total graduating class of 220) at the University of Nairobi in 1970. Some of Rastad's results are reported in [9].

[3] During May and June of 1971 I visited six of the twenty-four primary teacher training colleges (these six were selected to include one school in each of the four major tribal areas plus two smaller but important tribes) and the two secondary teacher training colleges for the purposes of administering a 'Parents' Occupation Questionnaire'. In all, I received 1,732 usable responses from students in primary teacher training colleges and 449 from students in the secondary TTCs.

TABLE I

*Occupational distribution, educational attainment, and land
ownership of fathers of higher education students*

	Educational attainment			
	Primary TTCs	Secondary TTCs	University of Nairobi	Reference group
Occupational category				
High and middle level manpower[a]	23%	19%	35%	3%[d]
Entrepreneurs, traders, and businessmen[b]	9%	9%	20%	—[d]
Small-scale farmers	54%	60%	44%	66%[d]
Unskilled and traditional	14%	12%	1%	31%[d]
Educational attainment				
None	49%	48%	21%	80%[e]
At least some primary	44%	48%	56%	18%[e]
Secondary or beyond	7%	5%	22%	2%[e]
% Landowners	87%	87%	73%	72%[f]
Acreage if landowner				
0·1–4·9	34%	32%	15%	52%[g]
5·0–24·9	56%	56%	50%[c]	41%[g]
25·0 and over	10%	12%	38%[c]	7%[g]

[a] Includes professional, administrative, and managerial, teachers, armed forces and police, clerical, skilled and semi-skilled artisans, and large-scale farmers. As defined by the 1967 Manpower Survey, a large-scale farmer is one who employs fourteen or more labourers.

[b] This comprises a mixed group, ranging from high-level modern sector to low-level traditional sector and cannot be allocated to either category.

[c] Approximate.

[d] Reference group is all adult males in Kenya. Figures are calculated from data in [3] and [14, p. 176].

[e] Reference group is all African males in Kenya aged 40 and over. Data are taken from [14, pp. 16–17].

[f] These figures were obtained in the following manner. According to the 1969 Population Census, there were 2,172,000 African males aged 20 and over out of a total African population of 10,733,200. Thus, the proportion of potential landowners to the total population is just over 20 per cent. The fifteen districts for which size distribution of farms was available from the 1969 small farms census had a population in 1969 of 5,927,000. Applying the 20 per cent proportion, there would thus be 1,085,400 potential landholders. There were 777,000 landholdings in these districts, or 72 per cent of adult males.

[g] Reference group is percentage of landholdings. Data are taken from [14, p. 81].

However, one's taxes rise with one's income so it is not clear which income groups gain and which lose from educational spending. Our task in the remaining sections is to find out.

2. Magnitude of the costs and benefits

The magnitudes of the costs and benefits of different types of higher education and private rates of return to investment in each type are shown in Table II. Looking first at the costs, we see that the direct costs of

G. S. FIELDS 249

schooling are entirely subsidized.[1] Students receive tuition, books, room and board, a clothing allowance, and a very small cash living allowance. The government justifies these fee policies on the grounds that these people

TABLE II

Costs, benefits, and private returns to different types of educational investment in Kenya, 1971

(1 *Kenya shilling* = *U.S.* $0.14 *in* 1971)

	Educational attainment[a]		
	Primary TTCs	Secondary TTCs	University of Nairobi
Average annual cost			
(1) Social[b]	Shs. 3,140	Shs. 5,600	Shs. 17,740
(2) Direct private	0	0	0
(3) Forgone earnings (undiscounted)	18,160	27,600	47,100
(4) Total direct subsidy after Form 4[c]	6,280	16,800	55,600
(5) Starting public service salary (annual)[d]	8,940	14,040	24,240
Private benefits compared with Form 4[e]			
(6) $r = 0\%$	302,820	549,660	771,880
(7) $r = 5\%$	99,852	192,184	277,182
(8) $r = 10\%$	37,626	82,882	120,818
(9) Private internal rate of return over Form 4[f]	28%	33%	31%

[a] These educational attainments have the following meaning. The six years of secondary schooling are known as 'forms'. A student who completes Form 4 is recognized as having finished secondary school. The figures for primary school teachers are for the highest grade teacher (P1), one who completes two years of primary teacher training after Form 4. Likewise, the figures for secondary teachers are for the highest grade secondary teacher (S1), one who has completed three years of secondary teacher training after Form 4. The University course requires two years of higher secondary education plus three years of university.

[b] Average annual social cost = (recurrent expenditures + amortization of current development expenditures + depreciation on existing capital stock) divided by number of pupils. Source of Row (1): [2, Table 3].

[c] Total direct subsidy after Form 4 = (Average annual social cost less direct private cost) × number of years required to attain that education level.

[d] Source of Row (5): Ndegwa Commission.

[e] Constructed on the (unlikely) assumption that a Form 4 graduate would be fully employed at the government salary scale.

[f] Source of Row (9): [2, Table 4].

are the future leaders of the country and no able person should be discouraged on account of inability to meet the fees.

For the benefits of higher education, we take the public service salary schedule as our standard. The benefit streams shown in rows 6–8 are calculated on the assumptions that a person completes Form 4 at age 19 (the actual average completion age) and retires at age 55 (the compulsory

[1] There are two classes of exceptions to this generalization: foreign students at the University of Nairobi who are not subsidized by the Kenyan government (but who are usually fully subsidized by their own governments), and Kenya residents who are not citizens who receive only partial, not total, subsidies.

250   HIGHER EDUCATION AND INCOME DISTRIBUTION

civil service retirement age) and his earnings progress within his initial
civil service rank but he is not promoted.[1,2]

3. Incidence of the indirect costs

As we have seen, Kenya's higher education system is funded almost
entirely by the government. Consequently, in order to determine the
incidence of school costs, we must examine the sources of the government's
revenues. Duties and excises are the main sources of revenue, with
income taxes nearly as great. Graduated Personal Tax (GPT) is the only
other single item of any substantial magnitude. The specific revenue
sources are discussed briefly below.

A. Revenue sources

Income taxes

Kenya has both a personal and a corporate income tax which combined
account for 35 per cent of the government's revenues. The income tax is
administered by the East African Community.[3] The rate structure of the
personal income tax is highly progressive, with marginal rates from
12·5 to 77·5 per cent of chargeable income. The personal income tax
provides a single allowance of shs. 4,320, married allowance of shs. 9,600,
and children's allowance of shs. 2,400 per child up to a maximum of four.[4]
The allowances for a married man with four children are almost 20 times
the *per capita* income. Thus, most families pay no income tax. In 1967, the
last year for which data were available, fewer than 35,000 individuals
(compared with a population of 10 million) were subject to income tax.

The marginal company income tax rate is 40 per cent. The system of
deductions is less generous than in the U.S. and U.K. and other developing
countries.[5]

---

[1] Two objections to the use of the civil service salary scales might be voiced. First, the
private sector generally pays higher wages than the public sector. And second, since only
the best students (as measured by exams) are able to go on to the next level, only a portion
of the additional earnings is attributable to the education itself. To the first objection, we
note that nearly all Kenyans who have completed higher education are employed by the
government, so that the government salary scale is relevant. On the second point, two facts
are important: educational attainment determines the job for which an individual is hired,
and the salary is a function of the job. These facts mean that the entire civil service salary
differential *is* the private benefit an individual could expect to receive if he is able to
continue his education.

[2] No allowance is made for wastage (flunking out or dropping out) since both are rare.

[3] The East African Community includes the countries of Kenya, Tanzania, and Uganda.
Besides administering income tax collections, the Community operates such services as posts
and telecommunications, railways and harbours, and power in the three countries. The
Community also comprises a duty-free common market.

[4] In 1971 one Kenyan shilling equalled $0.14 U.S.

[5] See [1].

G. S. FIELDS 251

Graduated Personal Tax (GPT)

The GPT, accounting for 5 per cent of revenue, is a graduated lump sum tax, mildly regressive over low income ranges, mildly progressive over high income ranges, and strongly regressive within an income class. The bulk of the tax is collected from low income people. There are no personal allowances or deductions; gross income is the tax base.

Import duties and excise taxes

These sources together yield 40 per cent of government revenues. The rate structure of import duties is designed to protect local industries, encourage manufacturing by having low or zero rates on inputs, and place heavy taxes on luxuries. Imports from the other countries of the East African Community are exempted from duty. The most important revenue-producing items are fuels, textiles, transport equipment, and food, drink, and tobacco. The bulk of excise revenues were collected from beer, sugar, and cigarettes.

B. Incidence of personal taxes

Columns 2–5 of Table III present estimates of the incidence of taxation in Kenya. These data are derived largely from a recent study of Kenya's tax system by Westlake [10] [11], who analysed household budget survey data for 1,146 African[1] households in Kenya's three main urban areas. The most noteworthy feature of column 2 is the regressivity of indirect taxes over the lower brackets which include the vast percentage of the African population. In column 3, we see the regressivity of the over-all tax incidence in the lower brackets. Column 5 indicates that two-thirds of the personal tax burden falls on persons in the lowest income bracket.

C. Incidence of indirect education costs

From the information in Table III, we are able to estimate the incidence of the indirect costs of each type of higher education by making two simplifying assumptions: (1) Each person's contribution to the financing of the educational system is equal to his total tax bill multiplied by the fraction of the government budget which is spent on education. (2) His contribution to each type of higher education is proportional to the importance of that type of education in the over-all educational budget. The percentage of taxes paid to finance a particular type of higher education is then multiplied by the average tax bill within an income bracket to give an estimate of the tax contribution for each type of higher education

---

[1] 'African' is a racial term denoting blacks, as opposed to Asians (browns) and Europeans (whites).

TABLE III

Incidence of taxes and distribution by income of students' Parents[a]

| Income bracket (shs./yr.) (1) | % of income taken by indirect taxation alone (2) | % of income taken by all taxes (direct and indirect) (3) | % of taxpayers in that bracket (4) | % of taxes paid by taxpayers in that bracket (5) | Students' parents' income = % of benefits | | |
					Primary TTCs (6)	Secondary TTCs (7)	University of Nairobi (8)
0–2,400	8·7%	12·5%	90·5%	67·9%	70·7% (1,222)	74·7% (336)	60·2% (138)
2,400–3,600	7·3	10·9	5·4	8·8	3·8 (66)	4·0 (18)	2·2 (5)
3,600–4,800	5·4	8·1	1·3	2·2	6·2 (108)	4·9 (22)	2·2 (5)
4,800–6,000	4·6	7·6	0·7 } 8·4	1·4 } 16·3	5·6 (97) } 23·7	4·4 (20) } 19·8	11·8 (27) } 30·2
6,000–8,400	4·8	8·2	0·5	1·5	6·2 (107)	4·7 (21)	11·8 (27)
8,400–12,000	5·9	9·5	0·5	2·4	1·9 (33)	1·8 (8)	2·2 (5)
12,000–16,800	4·5	8·8 }			3·4 (58)	0·9 (4) }	
16,800–24,000	5·5	9·0 }	1·1	15·7	0·8 (14) } 5·6	2·2 (10) } 5·5	9·6 (22)
over 24,000	4·4	11·9 }			1·4 (24)	2·4 (11)	
Total			100·0%	100·0%	100·0% (1,729)	100·0% (450)	100·0% (229)

Sources of columns 2 and 3 [11, p. 10].

Columns (4) and (5) were calculated by the author. Details of the calculations of columns (4) and (5) have been omitted due to space limitations but are available from the author upon request.

[a] Number of students given in parentheses.

by income bracket.[1] These are found to range from a high of shs. 63 for the highest income bracket for the most costly (university) down to shs. 0 for a lowest income bracket individual's contribution to the primary TTCs.

Compared with the private benefits from higher education and the earnings forgone while in school (cf. Table II), these tax costs are trivial. Clearly, the families whose children receive higher education are subsidized by the other families whose children are not educated at this level. Thus, there is substantial horizontal inequity in the existing system of financing of higher education in Kenya.

4. Approximation of students' families' incomes

Having estimated the tax costs of Kenya's higher education system, we now seek to determine the number of students in each income category receiving each type of education, then calculate the costs of each type of higher education to families in each income bracket, and finally compare these with the present value of the benefits accruing to the educated individuals over their working lives. We will do this in Section 5, but first it is necessary to approximate the incomes of students' families based on the available socio-economic data.[2]

It should be noted at the outset that Kenya is mainly an agricultural country. Only 627,000 of its more than ten million people are employed in the 'modern sector'. Furthermore, few persons sever their ties with agriculture, and there is a constant flow of workers back and forth from the cities and towns to the farms. For this reason, we must approximate both farm and non-farm income in determining a student's family's total income.

A. Farm income

Farm income has two components: land income and cattle income. The land income of ith farm (L_i) is defined as:

$$L_i = \sum_j A_i f_{ij} V_{ij}, \tag{1}$$

---

[1] To give an example of how these figures were constructed consider the contribution of a person in the highest income bracket to the financing of the University of Nairobi. In 1969/70 the Kenya government spent 14 per cent of its budget on education. 15 per cent of the educational budget was spent on university education (6 per cent was spent on primary teacher training colleges and 3 per cent on secondary teacher training colleges). Thus, an estimated 2·1 per cent of a person's tax contribution went to financing the University. Persons in the highest income bracket paid an average of 12·5 per cent of their incomes in taxes (see column 3 of Table III). Evaluated at the midpoint of the income bracket, we estimate this person to have paid shs. 2,970 in taxes. 2·1 per cent of shs. 2,970 is shs. 63. The remaining figures were constructed in a similar manner.

[2] Additional details regarding the procedures by which these approximations were made are available from the author upon request.

where A_i = acreage of farm i, f_{ij} = fraction of i's acreage devoted to production of crop j, and V_{ij} = value added per acre of crop j on farm i. For empirical implementation, this definition of land income is modified by assuming (*a*) that the average fraction of land under cultivation on all Kenyan farms applied to each individual farm, and (*b*) that the land under cultivation was divided equally among the crops grown.[1] In addition, it was not possible to estimate farm-specific or region-specific value added per acre of crop. Rather, the value added per acre of crop j was the average figure for all farms in the country growing that crop. Thus, for empirical estimation, the land income of the ith farm is taken to be

$$L_i = c \sum_j \left(\frac{A_i}{J_i} V_j \right), \tag{2}$$

where c = average fraction of land under cultivation on all Kenyan farms, A_i = acreage of farm i, J_i = number of crops grown on the ith farm, and V_j = value added per acre of j for all Kenyan farms.

Farm-specific figures in (2) are derived from students' answers to the following survey questions: 'Does your father own any land? If "yes" how many acres does he own? Does your father (or your mother) grow any crops to sell for money? If "yes" which crops?' The crops listed as alternatives were coffee, tea, pyrethrum, cotton, and other. Figures for all Kenyan farms were derived from a small farm survey conducted by the Ministry of Agriculture covering 1,154 farms.[2]

The other component of farm income is the income attributable to cattle ownership. The cattle income of the ith farm is the number of grade cows multiplied by the value added per grade cow in the country as a whole plus the number of non-grade cows multiplied by the value added per non-grade cow. The annual value added per grade and non-grade cow were calculated from the Ministry of Agriculture's small farm survey and were found to be shs. 239 per year and shs. 34 per year respectively. Data on the ith farm's cattle ownership were taken from the student's response on the Parents' Occupation Questionnaire to the question: 'Does your

---

[1] The rationale for these assumptions is that it became apparent in a pretest of the survey questions that students did not know what fraction of their father's land was under cultivation or how many acres were allocated to each crop.

[2] Jerome Wolgin used these data for a doctoral dissertation at Yale; I am grateful to him for making the value added figures available to me. The average fraction of land under cultivation for crops to be sold for cash was 47 per cent. The average value added per acre planted was shs. 185 per year for both coffee and tea, 130 for pyrethrum, 162 for cotton, and 146 for other.

In addition, I used the data from the individual farms to test whether there were significant scale effects. Regressing value added per acre of crop j on the number of acres of that crop in both the linear and double-logarithmic form, I found that the regression coefficients and coefficient of determination were in all cases insignificantly different from zero. In light of this, the use of a single value added per acre figure regardless of farm size would appear justified.

father own any cattle ? If "yes" : how many non-grade (local) cattle does
he own ? If "yes" : how many grade (exotic) cattle does he own ?'

B. Non-farm income

To determine the non-farm income of parents, students were asked :
'What kinds of work does your father (or guardian) do and who does he
work for ? Write down all the kinds of work he does and describe them
as clearly as you can.' If more than one kind of work was reported, it was
assumed that the father's time was divided equally among the different
kinds. The responses were coded to conform with official government job
categories.

Data on monthly cash remuneration for each job category are collected
on a firm-by-firm basis by the Ministry of Finance and Economic Planning.[1]
Unpublished summary tabulations by one-digit industrial classification
were made available to me by the Ministry for purposes of this study. For
each job category, I took the average monthly cash remuneration in each
industry, weighted each by the number of employees in that job category
in that industry, and thereby constructed a weighted average of monthly
cash remuneration in each job category for the country as a whole. The
student's description of his parent's work was then matched with the
average earnings in the occupational category to determine a proxy non-
farm income.[2]

C. Total income

The total income of an individual student's family was estimated as the
sum of the farm and non-farm income derived in the manner described
above, and frequency distributions are presented in columns 6–8 of
Table III. These data reveal three outstanding features :

(1) The students in Kenya's higher education system come from families
with clearly higher incomes on average than Kenya's population as
a whole.
(2) University students come from higher income families than students
in the teacher training colleges.
(3) However, the majority of the students come from families which
could not by any standard be considered 'the élite' (cf. Table I).

5. Incidence of total costs paid and benefits received by income class

As noted earlier, the vast majority of students in higher education work
for government upon completion of their studies and are paid according

---

[1] For a description of the survey and some of the findings, see [13].

[2] This procedure, although the best possible, is far from ideal. Many things other than
occupation determine earnings (see [6]). However, national data on the correlates of
earnings are not available, so it was impossible to make any further refinements.

to a fixed government salary scale. It seems reasonable therefore to assume that each recipient of higher education receives the same monetary benefit as any other. Thus, the distribution of students by income class also is the distribution of the benefits of higher education.

We have also seen that Kenya's higher education system is funded almost entirely by government. On the assumption that a person's contribution to a given fiscal programme is equal to his total tax contribution multiplied by the ratio of spending on the fiscal programme in question to total government spending, the percentage of all taxes paid by persons in each income bracket also is the distribution of direct costs of higher education.

From the distributions of benefits, tax costs, and taxpayers by income class as shown in Table III, we find:

(1) Low and high income families each pay a larger share of the direct costs of the University of Nairobi than their respective fractions of the benefits; the reverse holds for middle income people.

(2) For the teacher training colleges, the lower and middle income people each receive a larger fraction of the benefits than their respective shares of the costs; as with the University, high income people receive a smaller fraction of the benefits than their share of the costs.

(3) Low income people pay a smaller percentage of the costs relative to their numbers in the population; middle and upper income people pay more.

(4) Relative to their numbers in the population, children of low income families are underrepresented in the higher education system, middle and high income children overrepresented.

Qualitatively, these results are not very different from studies of the higher education systems of California [4] [5] and Canada [7].

6. Conclusion

In this paper, we have examined Kenya's higher education system with the goal of testing among three alternative hypotheses: that the higher education system redistributes income from rich to poor, that it redistributes income from poor to rich, or that it has no important effect on the distribution of income.

In testing the inter-generational version of these hypotheses, we have adopted a so-called 'Equal Opportunity Criterion', whereby the educational system is equitable if different income groups have access to opportunities for higher education in proportion to their numbers in this population. By this criterion, Kenya's higher education system is found to be inequitable inter-generationally, since the few who are favoured are disproportionately the children of the well-to-do, whether measured by income class or various indices of socio-economic status.[1] For instance, 60 per cent of the students at the University of Nairobi are found to come from families in the lowest income brackets, but this bracket includes 90 per cent of the taxpayers.

The intra-generational version of these hypotheses may be tested by either of two criteria. According to the 'Cost–Benefit Criterion', by which a programme is held to be equitable if each group in the population pays a fraction of the costs equal to the fraction of the benefits they receive, we have found that there is something akin to vertical equity in the financing of Kenya's higher education system. The lowest income group pays a somewhat larger percentage of the direct costs of the University of Nairobi than it receives in benefits, but the reverse is true for the teacher training colleges. However, if alternatively we adopt the 'Ability to Pay Criterion', according to which a programme is equitable if the cost–benefit ratio rises as a function of income, the approximate vertical proportionality is inequitable and favours the well-off.

We should observe, though, that the main inequity in Kenya's higher education system, though this is by no means unique to that particular country, is horizontal. A select few receive a very large payoff and if they were not relatively rich when they started their higher education, they will be relatively rich when they complete it. In other words, the system is horizontally inequitable *ex post* though less so *ex ante*. While the amounts involved on a person-by-person basis are very small on the tax side, they are very substantial per person on the benefit side.

At first glance, it might appear that it is the higher education system which is responsible, but this does not seem to be the case. Rather, the cause seems to be adverse selection at the primary and secondary levels. Although the costs of schooling at these levels are heavily subsidized (about 80 per cent), pupils themselves must pay the remaining 20 per cent. This is a large and often overwhelming burden for many families, and as a result, many children are simply unable to attend. Even if they are able to get together the fees, poor families frequently find that they cannot forgo their children's labour during planting and harvest seasons. For such families, the quality of the education received undoubtedly suffers. And since admission to the higher education system is conditional on succeeding on examinations at earlier levels, there is a systematic process operating against the poor.

---

[1] The fact that the educational system is inequitable in this sense does not *necessarily* imply that the gap in opportunities could be lessened within the educational system. For in the absence of an educational system, the children of the well-to-do might have an even more exclusive hold on certain types of jobs. I thank the Editor for making this point to me.

258　　　HIGHER EDUCATION AND INCOME DISTRIBUTION

The policy conclusion which follows from these findings is straight-forward. In the absence of fundamental changes in the tax structure and/or wage structure, both the horizontal inequity at the higher education levels and the adverse selection at the lower levels could nevertheless be lessened by charging students the full costs of their education to be repaid over their working lives[1] and using the proceeds to provide selective subsidies for the primary and secondary education of the children of the poor. In [2], I have estimated that this would permit virtually universal primary education under present financial arrangements or permit the abolition of fees of all those now attending, while at the same time having little discouraging effect on the private attractiveness of investment in higher education, since private rates of return would remain very high (19 per cent for university, 23 per cent for secondary teacher training, and 21 per cent for primary teacher training). In this way, Kenya's higher educational system could contribute more to achieving 'a fundamental objective of the Government ... a just distribution of the national income'.

Yale University

REFERENCES

1. DIEJOMAOH, V. P., 'Tax mobilisation and government development financing in Kenya', Institute for Development Studies, University of Nairobi, Discussion Paper No. 86, Nov. 1969.
2. FIELDS, G. S., 'Private returns to investment in higher levels of education in Kenya', in Court, David, and Ghai, Dharam, ed., *Society, Education, and Development: Some Perspectives from Kenya*, Oxford University Press, forthcoming.
3. GHAI, D. P., 'Employment performance, prospects and policies in Kenya', to be published in proceedings of the 1970 Cambridge Conference on 'Employment Opportunities in the Seventies'.
4. HANSEN, W. L., and WEISBROD, B., *Benefits, Costs, and Finance of Public Higher Education*, Chicago, Markham Publishing Company, 1970.
5. HARTMAN, R., 'A comment on the Pechman–Hansen–Weisbrod controversy', *Journal of Human Resources*, Fall, 1970.
6. JOHNSON, G. E., 'An empirical model of the structure of wages in urban Kenya', Department of Economics, University of Michigan, June, 1972, mimeo.
7. JUDY, R. W., 'On the income redistributive effects of public aid to higher education in Canada', Institute for Policy Analysis, University of Toronto, Sept. 1969.
8. PECHMAN, J., 'The distribution effects of public higher education in California', *Journal of Human Resources*, Summer, 1970.
9. RASTAD, S. E., 'University students and the employment market—a profile of present graduates of University College, Nairobi', Institute for Development Studies, University of Nairobi, Staff Paper No. 74, June 1970.
10. WESTLAKE, M. J., 'Kenya's extraneous and irrational system of personal income taxation', Institute for Development Studies, University of Nairobi, Staff Paper No. 101, June 1971.
11. —— 'Kenya's indirect tax structure and the distribution of income', Institute for Development Studies, University of Nairobi, Staff Paper No. 102, June 1971.

[1] Details of such a scheme may be found in [2].

12. Republic of Kenya, *Development Plan : 1970–1974*, Nairobi, Government Printer.
13. Republic of Kenya, Ministry of Finance and Planning, *Employment and Earnings in the Modern Sector, 1968–1970*, Nairobi, Government Printer.
14. Republic of Kenya, *1970 Statistical Abstract*, Nairobi, Government Printer.

[25]

Excerpt from *International Comparisons of Productivity and Causes of the Slowdown*, 335–55

8 THE CONTRIBUTION OF EDUCATION TO ECONOMIC GROWTH: INTERNATIONAL COMPARISONS

George Psacharopoulos[1]

Since the concept of human capital was invented (or perhaps reinvented) in the late 1950s, we have been flooded with papers written about the contribution of education to economic growth. The most often cited early references are Schultz (1961) for the United States, Denison (1967) for the United States and other advanced countries, and Krueger (1968) and Nadiri (1972) for less advanced countries. After a rather long pause in the 1970s, triggered by lack of economic growth and ambivalence about the role of education in development, the topic has begun attracting renewed interest. Thus we have the less known recent works of Hicks (1980), Wheeler (1980), Easterlin (1981) and Marris (1982).

In this paper I first summarize past efforts to estimate the contribution of education to economic growth. Then I augment and reinforce this evidence by examining recent related analyses of the role of education in society that do not formally come under the popular heading of "the contribution of education to economic growth." The paper concludes with a response to recent attacks on the economic value of education, especially with reference to developing countries.

THE EXISTING EVIDENCE

Traditionally, estimates of the contribution of education to economic growth are arrived at by using one or another variant of the same basic accounting

335

336   INTERNATIONAL COMPARISONS OF PRODUCTIVITY

framework. Assuming there exists an aggregate production function linking output (Y) to various inputs such as physical capital (K) and labor (L),

$$Y = f(K,L) , \tag{8.1}$$

the observed average annual rate of growth (g_y) of the economy over a given time period can be disaggregated into capital and labor components (right-handed-side of equation (8.2), respectively),

$$g_y = \frac{I}{Y}r + g_L s_L , \tag{8.2}$$

where I/Y stands for the investment-output ratio, r is the rate of return to investment, g_L is the average annual rate of growth of the labor force, and s_L is the share of labor in national income.[2]

Early attempts to empirically balance the two sides of equation (8.2) have resulted in the well known sizeable "residual," and it has since become a scholarly sport to try to reduce it by introducing other variables, such as education.

Education can enter into equation (8.2) either per Denison:

$$\Sigma_i {}^g L_i {}^s L_i ,$$

where L_i refers to labor with educational level i, or per Schultz:

$$\sum_i \frac{(I_i)r_i}{Y} ,$$

where I_i is the level of investment in the i type of education and r_i the rate of return to this type of education. The two methods are logically equivalent since they use wage differentials by level of education either as weights to derive the share of different types of labor to national income (Denison) or as income ratios to derive the rate of return to particular levels of education (Schultz).[3] Computational differences may arise in using the two methods because of discrepancies in the counting of physical increments of labor with given educational attainments (Denison) and the value invested in a particular type of education (Schultz).

First-Generation Estimates

Table 8-1 gives a compilation of the various first-generation estimates of the contribution of education to economic growth using one or another of the above accounting frameworks, expressed as the percentage of the observed rate of economic growth "explained" by education. It will be immediately noted that no easy generalizations can be made on the basis of

THE CONTRIBUTIONS OF EDUCATION TO ECONOMIC GROWTH   337

Table 8-1. The Contribution of Education to Economic Growth (percentage).

Country	Growth Rate Explained
North America	
Canada	25.0
United States	15.0
Europe	
Belgium	14.0
Denmark	4.0
France	6.0
Germany	2.0
Italy	7.0
Greece	3.0
Israel	4.7
Netherlands	5.0
Norway	7.0
United Kingdom	12.0
USSR	6.7
Latin America	
Chile	4.5
Argentina	16.5
Colombia	4.1
Brazil	3.3
Equador	4.9
Honduras	6.5
Peru	2.5
Mexico	0.8
Venezuela	2.4
Asia	
Japan	3.3
Malaysia	14.7[a]
Philippines	10.5
South Korea	15.9[a]
Africa	
Ghana	23.2[a]
Kenya	12.4[a]
Nigeria	16.0[a]

[a]Estimates based on "Schultz-type" growth accounting.

Source: Psacharopoulos (1973: 116) and Nadiri (1972: 138).

Note: Unless otherwise noted, estimates are based on Denison-type growth accounting.

this table. Education seems to have contributed substantially to the growth rate of some highly advanced countries—such as the United States, Canada, and Belgium—as well as to the growth rate of African and Asian countries (with the exception of Japan). In Latin America, Argentina notably stands out from the rest with a much higher contribution of education to growth.

338   INTERNATIONAL COMPARISONS OF PRODUCTIVITY

Second-Generation Estimates

Characteristic of second-generation estimates is the use of econometric techniques relating inputs to output, rather than the growth accounting decomposition found in the work of Schultz and Denison. Such estimates cannot be easily summarized (as in Table 8-1), since each author followed a different estimating technique.

Hicks (1980) compared the growth rate of different countries in the 1960-77 period with each country's deviation from the 1960 expected literacy level. The latter was found by regressing the 1960 literacy level with the 1967 per capita income and its square in a sample of sixty-three developing countries. Table 8-2 shows that the top eight growth performers had clearly positive literacy deviations from the norm. In the case of the eight fastest growing countries, a 16 percent literacy advantage is associated with a higher growth rate of 3.3 percentage points. For all countries, Hicks found on the average that an increase in the literacy rate by 20 percentage points is associated with 0.5 percent higher growth rate.

Wheeler (1980) addressed the simultaneity problem inherent in previous analyses—namely, that the level of income might be influencing the level of education rather than the other way around. Pooling data from eighty-eight countries and working with differences in the variables (rather than levels) and simultaneous equation techniques, he found that education has an independent effect on income. For example, on the average, an increase of the literacy rate from 20 to 30 percent is the cause of an increase in real GDP by 8 to 16 percent. In the case of African countries the estimated elasticity of output with respect to literacy is double relative to the sample of all developing countries.

Table 8-2. Economic Growth and Literacy (percentage).

Top Eight Countries Ranked by Growth of GNP	Growth Rate of GNP Per Capita, 1960-77	Literacy Deviation from the Norm
South Korea	7.6	43.6
Hong Kong	6.3	6.4
Greece	6.1	7.5
Portugal	5.7	1.7
Spain	5.3	1.2
Yugoslavia	5.2	16.7
Brazil	4.9	8.6
Thailand	4.5	43.5
Average, top eight countries	5.7	16.2
Average, all LDC's	2.4	0.0

Source: Based on Hicks (1980), as cited in World Bank (1980: 38).

Marris's (1982) work is in effect an extension of Wheeler's. Using data from sixty-six developing countries in the 1965–79 period and a chain model of output determination, he confirmed previous results that the benefits of education in terms of economic growth are very high—and in particular that general investment plays a weak role when not supported by education. Costing the coefficients of the model, he estimated benefit/cost ratios for education (measured by the primary enrollment rate) ranging from 3.4 to 7.4. The benefit-cost ratios for education stood in a class of their own as compared, for example, with the corresponding ratios for investment in physical capital, which ranged from 0.4 to 1.0.

Finally, it should be noted that in a recent Denison-type growth accounting exercise by Kendrick (1981) splitting the 1960–79 period into two subperiods, it was found that in seven out of nine industrial countries, the contribution of education to economic growth was higher during the slowdown period of 1973–79 relative to 1960–73.

AN ENLARGEMENT

This section argues that the above evidence, especially the first-generation evidence, underestimates the true effect of education on economic growth and on social welfare in general. This point is made by raising a number of issues and by examining supplementary evidence that does not formally come under the heading of the contribution of education to economic growth.

To start with, let us abstract from the so-called interaction effects or complementarities between human and physical capital. The simply additive decomposition of the economic growth rate in the first-generation estimates has necessarily disregarded the interaction between education and other independent variables in promoting economic growth. For example, in an extremely macro exercise Krueger (1968) has shown that three variables normally associated with the concept of human capital (education, age, and sectoral distribution of the population) can explain more than half of the difference in income levels between the United States and a group of twenty-eight developing countries. Education alone was found to contribute one-quarter to one-third in explaining income differences, and its interaction with other variables was nearly equal to its direct effect. And it has repeatedly been found that human and physical capital complement each other in the process of economic growth. Griliches (1969), Psacharopoulos (1973), and Fallon and Layard (1975), among others, report results consistent with the hypothesis that a higher stock of human capital enhances the rental value of machines. Of course, the complementarity argument could be interpreted the other way around—namely, that an increasing stock of

340   INTERNATIONAL COMPARISONS OF PRODUCTIVITY

physical capital boosts the efficiency of educational investment, although Marris (1982), using a recursive path model, found that general investment plays a weak role in economic growth when not supported by education.

I want to abstract from interaction effects and complementarities because a correctly measured marginal product of labor used as a weight in growth accounting captures the mutually enhancing effect of an increased quantity of any input on other inputs. Also, if there exist nonlinearities in the sense of a mathematically more sophisticated growth decomposition than the one derived from Euler's theorem, one could, in fact, explain a greater part of the residual. However, it is not easy to attribute the extra-explanatory power of the nonlinear formulation to a particular factor of production like education (Nelson 1981). Instead, let us proceed on safer ground and make a distinction between the contribution of education to measured economic growth on the one hand and to a wider concept of social welfare on the other.

Contribution to Economic Growth

Typical growth accounting exercises underestimate the total effect of education for the following reasons:

The Maintenance Component.   Denison-type growth accounting, as commonly applied, underestimates the true contribution of education to economic growth because it neglects the educational maintenance component of a growing labor force. This is a fundamental distinction made by Bowman (1964) and Selowsky (1969) but that has not been followed up in the more recent literature. The distinction is important in the case of fast population growth developing countries where the educational system has a double burden: first, to maintain constant the level of educational attainment of the labor force and second, to augment its level of educational attainment. Denison-type accounting, as commonly applied, captures only the net increments of educated labor, neglecting the maintenance component. As shown in Table 8–3 the resulting underestimate errors of the contribution of education to economic growth are substantial, especially in developing countries.

The Educated Farmer.   The basic link between education and economic growth in typical growth accounting exercises is the classification of wages of labor by level of schooling. These wages are derived mainly from employment surveys in the modern sector of the economy. In developing countries, however, the majority of the economically engaged population does not work for wages but makes a living from agriculture or from self-employment in the informal sector of the economy.

THE CONTRIBUTIONS OF EDUCATION TO ECONOMIC GROWTH   341

Table 8-3. Downward Bias of the Estimated Contribution of
Education to Economic Growth Because of Omission of
the Maintenance Component (percentage).

Country	Downward Bias
Chile	58
Mexico	66
India	90
United States	38

Source: Selowsky (1969: 463).

Although the positive relationship between farmers' education and
agricultural productivity was one of the first and repeatedly documented
propositions in the empirical literature on human capital, such evidence has
failed to be integrated into growth models. Landmarks of past analyses in
this respect are the works of Griliches (1964) and Welch (1970) for U.S.
agriculture and Hayami and Ruttan (1970) on cross-country comparisons.
Thus, the output elasticities with respect to education in the United States
are of the order of 0.3 to 0.5, as compared to 0.1 to 0.2 for land, fertilizer,
and machinery. And nearly one-third of the difference in labor productivity
between developed and less developed countries has been accounted for by
differences in the human capital stock.

Of particular importance to this review is the recent work of Jamison
and Lau (1982). Mastering the results of thirty-one data sets that related
schooling to agricultural productivity, they concluded that, on the average,
the latter increases by 8.7 percent as a result of a farmer completing four
years of primary education. The importance of this finding stems from the
fact that (1) productivity measurements in agriculture are in real (physical)
output terms and (2) the usual objections raised when using wages as proxies for productivity in other studies have no relevance in a farm setting.
Jamison and Lau also report that in Thailand the marginal effect of education on output is greater in rural than in urban areas. To the extent this is
true in other countries, as one might reasonably suspect, past-growth accounting exercises using urban wage differentials must have underestimated
the contribution of education to economic growth, especially in developing
countries.

One of the prime indirect ways in which education contributes to
economic growth is that it enhances the adoption and efficient use of new
inputs. Whether the argument is cast in terms of the allocative efficiency of
farmers (Schultz 1964) or the more general ability to "deal with disequilibria" (Schultz 1975), the literature is full of evidence that schooling acts as a
catalyst in' behavioral change conducive to growth. For example, Jamison
and Lau (1982) report that in Thailand the probability of a farmer

342   INTERNATIONAL COMPARISONS OF PRODUCTIVITY

adopting a technology using chemical inputs is about 60 percent greater if the farmer has four years of education rather than none. In traditional Denison-type exercises this source of the contribution of education to growth is lumped into the unexplained residual.

The Use of Public Sector Weights. The wage differentials by level of schooling used in typical growth accounting are heavily influenced by salaries paid by the civil service, especially in developing countries. Although the salary level for some categories of labor might be higher than its marginal product in the noncompetitive sector of the economy, the salary *differential* by level of schooling is not. Comparisons of public-to-private sector wage differentials by educational level have shown that the earnings advantage of the more educated is higher in the private sector (see Table 8-4). To the extent earnings in the competitive sector are good proxies for the marginal product of labor, typical growth accounting studies, by using flatter differentials as weights, must have underestimated the true contribution of education to economic growth.

The Case of Women. For a variety of reasons, women earn substantially less than men. Thus it would appear that using male earnings—as the only data available in growth accounting—would overstate the contribution of education. However, the opposite is likely to be the case. For what matters in growth accounting is the within-sex earnings differential by level of education, or the rate of return to women's education. To the casual observer it comes as a surprise that the profitability of investing in education is higher for women than for men (see Table 8-5 for some examples).

There are two reasons for this apparently paradoxical finding. First, in the case of females the effect of education is not restricted to just raising their earnings; it also increases their chance of participating in the labor force. For example, Table 8-6 shows that in Puerto Rico the chances of a woman being formally engaged in economic activity is three times as much

Table 8-4.   The Earnings Differential by Economic Sector.

	Economic Sector	
Country	*Public*	*Private*
Portugal	0.99	1.12
Brazil	1.59	1.92
Colombia	1.07	1.48
Malaysia	0.62	1.13

Source: Psacharopoulos (1982: Table 3).

Note: Figures are ratios of mean earnings of employees with primary and less than primary educational qualifications.

Table 8-5. The Returns to Education by Sex (percentage).

Country	Educational Level/Type	Rate of Return	
		Males	*Females*
Colombia	Vocational	35.4	39.8
Puerto Rico	Secondary	26.3	44.9
New Zealand	Secondary	19.3	25.3
Germany	Vocational	9.0	11.3

Source: Woodhall (1973: Table 1).

as if she has received some college education rather than one to four years of primary schooling. Second, females tend to have lower foregone earnings, and this raises the rate of return. A third possibility is that discrimination against better educated women results in female wages that are lower than their true marginal product. This proposition could be documented by shadow pricing female labor by level of schooling. But perhaps the most persuasive evidence comes again from agriculture. Moock (1976) studied 152 maize farmers in Kenya and concluded that the impact of schooling on output, other factors remaining the same, is greater for the women than for the men. Considerations such as those listed above suggest that the use of male wages as weights in growth accounting understates the contribution of education to economic growth.

The Use of an Ability Adjustment.   The cornerstone of the contribution of education to economic growth is the earnings differential between well-educated and less well-educated labor. Such observed earnings differential has been typically discounted by as much as 40 percent before entering the growth accounting equation to allow for effects other than education, like differential ability. Although the so-called alpha coefficient adjustment has been both plausible and intuitive, recent econometric evidence does not support its use.

Table 8-6. Female Labor Force Participation by Level of Education (percentage).

Educational Level	Participation Rate
Elementary 1-4	16.3
Elementary 5-6	21.6
Elementary 7-8	23.5
High school 1-3	31.8
High school 4	38.6
College 1+	53.6

Source: Shields (1977: 65).

Earnings functions analysis using schooling and ability measures, such as IQ, point that the effects of education on earnings is substantial, even after controlling for ability (e.g., Griliches 1970). A review of the empirically derived alpha coefficient found that its value is more likely to be 0.90 rather than the originally assumed 0.67 used in typical growth accounting (Psacharopoulos 1975). Also, a recent study using nearly experimental data of farmers in Nepal found not only that education has a significant effect on increased efficiency in wheat production but also that its effect does not diminish when the farmers' family background and measures of ability were introduced as additional control factors (Jamison and Moock 1984).

On-the-Job Training (OJT). If "education" is given an all inclusive definition encompassing all forms of formal and informal learning, then OJT should be included in growth accounting. In spite of Mincer's (1962) early findings, however, that (1) in terms of costs, investment in on-the-job training in the United States is as important as formal education and that (2) the rate of return to on-the-job training investment is of the same order of magnitude as the return to investment in conventional schooling, no efforts have been made to incorporate OJT in formal growth models.

The observed wage level of a given type of labor certainly includes returns to OJT. To the extent a higher formal educational attainment facilitates investment in OJT, it reinforces the view that observed wage differentials between categories of labor classified by educational level should be attributed to one or another form of human capital.

Furthermore, the Beckerian distinction between general and specific training raises the question of second-round interaction effects between formal education and the trainability of the employee, and also brings to the surface the unrecorded benefits later reaped by the firm that has invested in specific employee training (Bowman 1980). A well-known proposition in the economics of education is that in the case of specific training, posttraining wages are less than the marginal product of the employee, the difference being the returns to the investment made by the employer. Since the latter appears in capital profits, failure to take OJT into account results to an underestimate of the contribution of education to economic growth.

Life Expectancy.   Once human capital is created via education or training it has to be preserved so that it yields a stream of benefits throughout its theoretical lifetime (which in this case is of the order of fifty years). Cochrane (1980) reports significant partial effects of literacy on life expectancy in a number of countries, after standardizing for the level of income. Also, Hicks (1980) reports positive deviations from norm life expectancy associated with a higher rate of growth of GNP per person. As shown in Table 8-7, a nine-year positive deviation of life expectancy from the income-

THE CONTRIBUTIONS OF EDUCATION TO ECONOMIC GROWTH   345

Table 8-7. Economic Growth and Life Expectancy.

Top Ten Countries Ranked by Life Expectancy in Relation to Income	Life Expectancy Deviation from the Norm, 1960	Growth Rate of GNP per Person, 1960–77
Sri Lanka	22.5	1.9
South Korea	11.1	7.6
Thailand	9.5	4.5
Malaysia	7.3	4.0
Paraguay	6.9	2.4
Philippines	6.8	2.1
Hong Kong	6.5	6.3
Panama	6.1	3.7
Burma	6.0	0.9
Greece	5.7	6.1
Average, Top ten countries	8.8	4.0
Average, eighty-three developing countries	0.0	2.4

Source: Hicks (1980) as reported in World Bank (1980: 38).

predicted value is associated with a 1.6 percent higher growth rate in per capita GNP. Typical growth accounting exercises neglect the indirect effect of education in lengthening the number of years during which individuals are productive; hence, they underestimate its real contribution to economic growth.

Migration.   Rural-urban and rural-rural migration is the process par excellence by which labor is reallocated to more productive uses. The migration literature is full of findings pointing at the positive relationship between education and the decision to move to another area (e.g., Greenwood 1975). This has been explained in terms of the "information hypothesis," which assumes that the economic attractiveness of a location is an increasing function of the level of education (Schwartz 1971). Growth accounting models do not take into account the effect of education on migration, hence they underestimate the indirect contribution mainly rural schools make to national output.

The Use of Literacy as Education Proxy.   Second-generation econometric estimates of the contribution of education to economic growth have typically used a basic education indicator, like the literacy rate of the population or the primary enrollment rate, as a proxy for the education variable. First-level education in developing countries carries a heavy weight in the construction of any educational quantity index (for an exception see Harbison and Myers 1964), and its benefits are more important relative to secondary and university education. On the other hand, the neglect of postprimary levels of schooling must underestimate the contribution of education to economic growth. Of course, second-generation econometric growth models have necessarily traded off the availability of more observations for the comprehensiveness of the education index.

Contribution to Social Welfare

The dependent variable in growth accounting exercises has typically been changes in the measured level of income (GNP or GDP). It is common knowledge, however, that part of the total income employed by households is not captured in the national accounts statistics and that there exist other welfare indicators, such as per capita income and distributive equity, that could be used as dependent variables in explaining well-being. Such considerations point to additional reasons why classic estimates, such as those presented above, are likely to underestimate the true contribution of education to economic growth and social welfare in general.

Fertility. This is one of a long series of demographic effects of schooling. Education affects fertility through different channels, such as the demand for children, contraception, and the child-bearing potential of women. Cochrane (1979) reports that the majority of case studies seem to conclude that education has a fertility reduction effect (see Table 8–8). Thus education has an important effect in *per capita* income increases in otherwise fast-growing population that goes unrecorded in ordinary growth accounting.

Table 8-8. The Relationship between Education and Fertility: Results of Case Studies.

Variable	Relation of Education to Variable	Probable Relation of Education through the Variable	Results (Number of Cases)	
			Supporting	Not Supporting
Age of marriage	Direct	–	59	12
Desired family size	Inverse	–	17	8
Perceived costs of children	Direct	–	2	0
Perceived costs to afford children	Direct	+	9	3
Contraceptive use	Direct	–	26	11
Knowledge of birth control	Direct	–	28	1

Source: Based on Cochrane (1979: 146).

Infant and Child Mortality.   Cochrane, Leslie, and O'Hara (1980) sum-marized evidence from a number of developing countries and reported par-tial effects of mother's literacy on infant and child mortality, as in Table 8-9. To the extent such considerations enter the social welfare function, they remain uncaptured in ordinary growth accounting.

Income Distribution.   If one is willing to accept a wider notion of develop-ment, the latter including not only the level of income but its distribution as well, education makes a further contribution to social welfare. Several studies in both advanced and developing countries have found that an in-creased level of educational attainment of the population or the labor force is associated with a more equal income distribution. For example, Marin and Psacharopoulos (1976) report that in the case of Mexico's giving primary education to 10 percent of those without would reduce the variance of the logarithm of earnings (a standard measure of income inequality) by nearly 5 percent. Also, Blaug, Dougherty, and Psacharopoulos (1982) found that the most recent (1972) raising of the minimum school-leaving age in England by one year, other things equal, is likely to reduce income in-equality in a future steady state by 12 to 15 percent.

Household Production.   What households consume and the goods and ser-vices actually enjoyed by its members is not totally captured in national ac-counts statistics. This proposition is more relevant in developing countries where a great part of household income is in kind.

There are many ways a higher level of educational attainment of the members of the household contributes to income, other than through the labor market or agricultural production. For example, education embodied in nonformally economically active females is likely to have a great payoff in terms of household production activities, such as better sanitation condi-tions, more nutritious meals for the family, better educated children, and more efficient consumption behavior. Also, of particular importance is the effect of a more educated mother imparting early abilities to preschool age children (Selowsky 1982). Although the beneficial effect of education in this respect has been mainly documented in advanced countries (Schultz 1974;

Table 8-9.   The Effect of Literacy on Mortality, Per 1,000 Population.

Population Reference	$\dfrac{\partial \,(Mortality)}{\partial \,(Literacy)}$
Infants	−0.55
Children	−0.25

Source: Cochrane, Leslie, and O'Hara (1980: 86).

Michael 1982), one might validly extrapolate that the corresponding effect of education in developing countries must be even greater given the relative scarcities of human capital in the two types of countries.

Corroborating Evidence

For the results of macro-growth accounting models to be credible they have to agree with other evidence on the economic effect of education, such as microstudies at the individual plant level, the returns to investment in education, and evidence drawn from the economic history of nations.

Evidence from Microstudies. Detailed microstudies on the effect of schooling on individual employees at the firm level are not as abundant in the literature as the more popular Denison-type aggregate exercises. However, several of them have documented the positive effect of education and training on productivity. Thus Aryee (1976) found a positive correlation between output and the educational level of industrial entrepreneurs in Ghana, net of capital inputs. Fuller (1972) studied millers and grinders in two Indian factories and reported positive correlations between time taken to complete a given task and the educational level of the worker.

The Returns to Education. Evidence on the returns to investment in education in many respects complements, corroborates, and also highlights the possible underestimates of Denison-type growth accounting calculations. Furthermore, it increases our understanding of the particular types of education that are more likely to contribute to economic growth, especially in developing countries. Table 8–10 presents a summary of the available evidence on the returns to education around the world. The rate of return (r) figures have been arrived at by solving the following equation for r:

$$\sum_{t=1}^{n} \frac{(Y_{st} - Y_{s-1,t} - C_{st})}{(1 + r)^t} = 0$$

where Y_{st} is the earnings of labor with s level of education in year t, $Y_{s-1,t}$ is the earnings of the control group (lower level of schooling), and C_{st} is the direct cost of educational level s in year t. The difference between the private and social rates of return is that the latter are calculated on gross of income tax earnings and the direct cost includes the full amount of resources committed to a given level of education. The returns to primary education, although conservatively estimated, are the highest among the three levels that point to the relative importance of this kind of education for economic development. The absolute size of the private returns in

THE CONTRIBUTIONS OF EDUCATION TO ECONOMIC GROWTH   349

Table 8-10. The Returns to Education by Region and Country Type (percentage).

Region or Country Type	N	Private			Social		
		Primary	Secondary	Higher	Primary	Secondary	Higher
Africa	(9)	29	22	32	29	17	12
Asia	(8)	32	17	19	16	12	11
Latin America	(5)	24	20	23	44	17	18
LDC average	(22)	29	19	24	27	16	13
Intermediate	(8)	20	17	17	16	14	10
Advanced	(14)	(a)	14	12	(a)	10	9

[a]Not computable because of lack of a control group of illiterates.

Source: Psacharopoulos (1981: 329).

Notes: N = number of countries in each group. Figures are not horizontally strictly comparable because in a given country the returns to education might not be available for all levels.

African countries: Ethiopia, Ghana, Kenya, Malawi, Morocoo, Nigeria, Rhodesia, Sierra Leone, and Uganda.

Asian countries: India, Indonesia, South Korea, Malaysia, Philippines, Singapore, Taiwan, and Thailand.

Latin America countries: Brazil, Chile, Colombia, Mexico, and Venezuela.

LDC countries are all listed above.

Intermediate countries: Cyprus, Greece, Spain, Turkey, Yugoslavia, Israel, Iran, and Puerto Rico.

Advanced countries: Australia, Belgium, Canada, Denmark, France, Germany, Italy, Japan, Netherlands, New Zealand, Norway, Sweden, United Kingdom, and United States.

general is consistent with the unsatisfied demand for school places, especially in poor countries. The declining pattern of the rate of return by educational level adds credibility to treating school expenditures and foregone student earnings as investment. And although the social returns are based mostly on observed market wages, shadow pricing and evidence from self-employment and agriculture lend support to the economic value of education, net of other influences.

Educational Quality. The education variable has been measured in a great variety of ways in growth models such as the level of educational attainment of the population, the number of years of schooling of the labor force, the percentage of literacy in a given country or the primary enrollment rate. Although it might appear that reference to the labor force is most relevant to growth accounting, the general population educational attainment measures are also pertinent in the sense of capturing economic effects of education other than through the labor market, as in the case of females and household production mentioned above.

350   INTERNATIONAL COMPARISONS OF PRODUCTIVITY

One dimension that is typically missing in quantitative measures of education used in growth accounting is its quality, although other studies have shown that not only the quantity of education is productive but its quality is, as well. Regardless of whether educational quality has been measured in terms of school buildings, laboratories, textbooks, teacher qualifications, nature of the curriculum, class size, composition of the student body, or per-pupil expenditures, the evidence shows that such measures have an impact on student achievement and later earnings (Solmon 1975; Wachtel 1975; Rizzuto and Wachtel 1980). With respect to the former, the impact is greater in low-income countries (Heyneman and Loxley 1983).

Consideration of school quality might help explain the widening gap in economic performance between developing and advanced countries or the alleged failure of some economies to grow in spite of the rising educational attainment of the population. Jamison, Searle, Galda, and Heyneman (1981) report that whereas in 1960 the average OECD country invested sixteen times more per pupil than did any of the thirty-six countries with per capita income below $265, by 1970 the difference grew to 22:1, and by 1975 to 31:1. According to unpublished estimates this ratio stood at 50:1 by 1977.

The View of Economic Historians.   Economic historians have often been intrigued by the relationship between education and economic development. Three pieces of evidence are worth citing. First, Landes and Solmon (1972) have found that minimum schooling legislation did not cause the observed increases in the level of schooling in late nineteenth and early twentieth century United States. This finding runs against the popular hypothesis that schooling follows economic development. Second, Saxonhouse (1977) in a study of the Japanese cotton spinning industry from 1891 to 1935 found that education, among other factors, had a large and significant impact on productivity growth. Third, Easterlin (1981) looked at the chicken-egg problem of the relationship between educational development and economic growth by examining historical data for twenty-five of the largest countries of the world. His conclusion was that the spread of technology in modern economic growth depended on the learning potentials and motivation that were linked to the development of formal schooling—or that the most likely causal link is from education to economic growth rather than the other way around.

CONCLUDING REMARKS

Without resorting to externalities, institution building, or other difficult-to-estimate but certainly positive effects of education in society, it is possible to substantially enlarge and reinforce the traditional evidence on the contribution of education to economic growth. This conclusion does not coincide with recent attacks on the role of education on productivity growth and income distribution. Screening for ability, job competition, labor market segmentation, nonclearing wages, nonprofit maximizing public sector pay scales, social class, and youth unemployment allegedly provide alternative explanations of the observed earnings advantage of the more educated or have been used to cast doubts on the social role of schooling. Such explanations are, at first sight, intuitively plausible and have often influenced the decision of policymakers and administrators against spending on schooling. Also, what might be partially true in the case of highly advanced industrial countries is often casually extrapolated to apply in developing countries.

To the careful reader of the literature, however, the challenges to the beneficial role of education in development are mostly superficial and in most cases have not been rigorously tested, especially in developing countries. Thus, the screening hypothesis (Taubman and Wales 1973) diminishes in importance when reference is made to the self-employed or the direct social product of education in agriculture (Jamison and Lau 1982). The job competition model (Thurow 1972) has never addressed or considered the possibility of a more educated person being more productive within a given occupational title.

The popular labor market segmentation or duality hypothesis (Gordon 1972) has faded away, following the critique by Cain (1976). When a distinction is made between nonclearing and competitive labor markets, as mentioned earlier, it is found that wage differentials in the public sector understate the true productive advantage of the more educated as the latter is measured by earnings differentials in the competitive private sector (Psacharopoulos 1982). In the sociological literature, social class is not the main determinant of earnings, net of the effect of education (Psacharopoulos and Tinbergen 1978). And unemployment does not permanently diminish the earnings advantage of the more educated because it is a sharply declining function of time since graduation, often measured in terms of weeks rather than years (Psacharopoulos and Sanyal 1981). When reference is made to developing countries, the argument for investment in schools and training becomes even stronger given the relative scarcity of human capital and the low score of such countries on any indicator of educational development.

NOTES

1.   The author is grateful to Mary Jean Bowman, Marcelo Selowsky, and Finis Welch for reading a first draft of this paper and offering suggestions for improvement. The views and interpretations are those of the author and should not be attributed to The World Bank.

352   INTERNATIONAL COMPARISONS OF PRODUCTIVITY

2.   For a proof of this and related growth accounting derivations, see Selowsky (1969), Robinson (1971), and Psacharopoulos (1972).
3.   For a proof of this proposition, see Psacharopoulos (1973: 113–14). For the most elaborate discussion of the differences between the two methods, see Bowman (1964).

REFERENCES

Aryee, G.A. 1976. "Effects of Formal Education and Training on the Intensity of Employment in the Informal Sector: A Case Study of Kumasi, Ghana." Geneva: International Labor Organization, World Employment Program, WP No. 14.

Blaug, M.; C.R.S. Dougherty; and G. Psacharopoulos. 1982. "The Distribution of Schooling and the Distribution of Earnings: Raising the School Leaving Age in 1972." *The Manchester School* 50 (March): 24–39.

Bowman, M.J. 1964. "Schultz, Denison and the Contribution of 'Eds' to Economic Growth." *Journal of Political Economy* 72, no. 9 (October): 450–64.

———. 1980. "Education and Economic Growth: An Overview." In *Education and Income*, edited by T. King, pp. 1–71. Washington, D.C.: World Bank, Staff Working Paper No. 402.

Cain, G. 1976. "The Challenge of Segmented Labor Market Theories to Orthodox Theory: A survey." *Journal of Economic Literature* 14 (December): 1215–17.

Cochrane, S.H. 1979. *Fertility and Education: What Do We Really Know?* Baltimore, Md.: Johns Hopkins University Press, for the World Bank.

———. 1980. "The Socioeconmic Determinants of Mortality: The Cross-National Evidence." In *The Effects of Education on Health,* by S.H. Cochrane, D.J. O'Hara, and J. Leslie, pp. 3–33. Washington, D.C.: World Bank, Staff Working Paper No. 405.

Cochrane, S.H.; J. Leslie; and D.J. O'Hara. 1980. "Parental Education and Child Health: Intra-Country Evidence." In *The Effects of Education on Health,* edited by pp. 56–95. Washington, D.C.: World Bank, Staff Working Paper No. 405.

Denison, E. 1967. *Why Growth Rates Differ: Post-War Experience in Nine Western Countries.* Washington, D.C.: The Brookings Institution.

Easterlin, R. 1981. "Why Isn't the Whole World Developed?" *The Journal of Economic History* 41, no. 1 (March): 1–19.

Fallon, R.P., and R. Layard. 1975. "Capital-Skill Complementarity, Income Distribution and Growth Accounting." *Journal of Political Economy* 83 (April): 279–302.

Fuller, W.P. 1972. "Evaluating Alternative Combinations of Education and Training for Job Preparation: An Example from Indian Industry." *Manpower Journal* 3: 7–38.

Gordon, E. 1972. *Theories of Poverty and Unemployment.* Lexington, Mass.: Lexington Books.

Greenwood, M.J. 1975. "Research on Internal Migration in the U.S.: A Survey." *Journal of Economic Literature* 3, no. 2 (June): 397–433.

Griliches, Z. 1964. "Research Expenditures, Education, and the Aggregate Agricultural Production Function." *American Economic Review* 54 (December): 961–74.

———. 1969. "Capital-Skill Complementarity." *Review of Economics and Statictics* 51: 465–68.

THE CONTRIBUTIONS OF EDUCATION TO ECONOMIC GROWTH   353

_____ . 1970. "Notes on the Role of Education in Production Functions and Growth Accounting." In *Education, Income and Human Capital,* edited by W. Lee Hansen. New York: National Bureau for Economic Research.

Harbison, F., and C.A. Myers. 1964. *Education, Manpower and Economic Growth.* New York: McGraw Hill.

Hayami, Y., and V.W. Ruttan. 1970. "Agricultural Productivity Differences among Countries." *American Economic Review* 60 (December): 985–11.

Heyneman, S., and W. Loxley. 1983. "The Effect of Primary-School Quality on Academic Achievement across Twenty-nine High and Low Income Countries." *American Journal of Sociology* 88, no. 6: 11–62.

Hicks, N. 1980. "Economic Growth and Human Resources." Washington, D.C.: World Bank, Staff Working Paper No. 408.

Jamison, D., and L. Lau. 1982. *Farmer Education and Farm Efficiency.* Baltimore, Md.: Johns Hopkins University Press.

Jamison, D., and P. Moock. 1984. "Farmer Education and Farm Efficiency in Nepal: The Role of Schooling, Extension Services and Cognitive Skills." *World Development* 12, no. 1: 67–86.

Jamison, D.T.; B. Searle; K. Galda; and S. Heyneman. 1981. "Improving Elementary Mathematics Education in Nicaragua: An Experimental Study of the Impact of Textbooks and Radio on Achievement." *Journal of Education Psychology* 73, no. 4 (August): 556–67.

Kendrick, J.W. 1981. "International Comparisons of Recent Productivity Trends." In *Essays in Contemporary Economic Problems: Demand, Productivity and Population,* edited by William Fellner, pp. 125–70. Washington, D.C.: American Enterprise Institute for Public Policy Research.

Krueger, A.O. 1968. "Factor Endowments and Per Capital Income Differences among Countries." *Economic Journal* 78 (September): 641–59.

Landes, W.M., and L.C. Solomon. 1972. "Compulsory Schooling Legislation: An Economic Analysis of Law and Social Change in the Nineteenth Century." *Journal of Economic History* 32, no. 1 (March): 54–91.

Marin, A., and G. Psacharopoulos. 1976. "Schooling and Income Distribution." *Review of Economics and Statistics* 58, no. 3 (August): 332–38.

Marris, R. 1982. "Economic Growth in Cross-Section." Department of Economics, Birbeck College. Mimeo.

Michael, R.T. 1982. "Measuring Non-Monetary Benefits of Education: A Survey." In *Financing Education,* edited by W.W. McMahon and T.G. Geske, pp. 119–49. Urbana: University of Illinois Press.

Mincer, J. 1962. "On-the-Job Training: Costs, Returns and Some Implications." *Journal of Political Economy* 70, no. 5, pt. 2 (October): 50–80.

Moock, P. 1976. "The Efficiency of Women as Farm Managers: Kenya." *American Journal of Agricultural Economics* (December): 831–35.

Nadiri, M.I. 1972. "International Studies of Total Factor Productivity: A Brief Survey." *Review of Income and Wealth* 18, no. 2 (June): 129–54.

Nelson, R. 1981. "Research on Productivity Growth and Productivity Differences: Dead Ends and New Departures." *Journal of Economic Literature* 19 (September): 1029–64.

Psacharopoulos, G. 1972. "Measuring the Marginal Contribution of Education to Economic Growth." *Economic Development and Cultural Change* 20, no. 4 (July): 641–58.

_____ . 1973. *Returns to Education: An International Comparison.* Amsterdam: Elsevier-Jossey Bass.

_____. 1975. *Earnings and Education in OECD Countries.* Paris: OECD.

_____. 1981. "Returns to Education: An Updated International Comparison." *Comparative Education* 17 (October): 321–41.

_____. 1982. "Education and Society: Old Myths versus New Facts." In *The Mixed Economy,* edited by Lord Roll of Ipsden, pp. 145–61. New York: MacMillan.

Psacharopoulos, G., and B. Sanyal. 1981. *Higher Education and Employment: The IIEP Experience in Five Less Developed Countries.* Paris: UNESCO, International Institute for Educational Planning.

Psacharopoulos, G., and J. Tinbergen. 1978. "On the Explanation of Schooling, Occupation and Earnings: Some Alternative Path Analyses." *De Economist* 126, no. 4 (December): 505–20.

Rizzuto, R., and P. Wachtel. 1980. "Further Evidence on the Returns to School Quality." *Journal of Human Resources* 15, no. 2 (winter): 240–54.

Robinson, S. 1971. "Sources of Growth in Less Developed Countries: A Cross-Section Study." *Quarterly Journal of Economics* 85 (August): 391–408.

Saxonhouse, G.R. 1977. "Productivity Change and Labor Absorption in Japanese Cotton Spinning, 1891–1935." *Quarterly Journal of Economics* 91, no. 2 (May): 195–200.

Schultz, R.W. 1961. "Education and Economic Growth." In *Social Forces Influencing American Education,* edited by N.B. Henry, National Society for the Study of Education, pp. 46–88. Chicago: University of Chicago Press.

Shultz, T.W. 1964. *Transforming Traditional Agriculture.* New Haven, Conn.: Yale University Press.

_____, ed. 1974. *The Economics of the Family.* New York: National Bureau of Economic Research.

_____. 1975. "The Value of the Ability to Deal with Disequilibria." *Journal of Economic Literature* 13, no. 3 (September): 827–46.

Schwartz, A. 1971. "On Efficiency of Migration." *Journal of Human Resources* 6, no. 2 (spring): 193–205.

Selowsky, M. 1969. "On the Measurement of Education's Contribution to Growth." *Quarterly Journal of Economics* (August): 449–63.

_____. 1982. "The Economic Effects of Investment in Children: A Survey of the Quantitative Evidence." In *Child Development Information and the Formation of Public Policy,* edited by T.E. Jordan, pp. 186–210. Springfield: Charles Thomas.

Shields, N. 1977. "Female Labor Force Participation and Fertility: Review of Empirical Evidence from LDC's." Washington, D.C.: World Bank, Population and Human Resources Division, February. Mimeo.

Solmon, L. 1975. "The Definition of College Quality and Its Impact on Earnings." *Explorations in Economic Research* 2, no. 4 (fall): 537–87.

Taubman, P.F., and T. Wales. 1973. "Higher Education, Mental Ability and Screening." *Journal of Political Economic* 81 (January/February): 28–55.

Thurow, L. 1972. *Generating Inequality.* New York: Basic Books.

Wachtel, P. 1975. "The Effect of School Quality on Achievement, Attainment Levels and Lifetime Earnings." *Explorations in Economic Research* 2, no. 4 (fall): 502–36.

Welch, F. 1970. "Education in Production." *Journal of Political Economy* 78 (January/February): 32–59.

Wheeler, D. 1980. "Human Resource Development and Economic Growth in Developing Countries: A simultaneous Model." Washington, D.C.: World Bank, Staff Working Paper No. 407.

THE CONTRIBUTIONS OF EDUCATION TO ECONOMIC GROWTH   355

Woodhall, M. 1973. "Investment in Women: A Reappraisal of the Concept of Human Capital." *International Review of Education* (spring): 9–29.

World Bank. 1980. *World Development Report 1980*. Washington, D.C.: World Bank.

Part V
Political Economy of Schooling

[26]

THE ROLE OF EDUCATION IN NINETEENTH-CENTURY DOCTRINES OF POLITICAL ECONOMY

by E. G. WEST, *Lecturer in Economics, University of Newcastle-upon-Tyne*

The classical economists are typically associated in the popular mind with the early nineteenth-century doctrine of *laissez faire*. Nevertheless, as has been frequently observed by historians of education, sometimes quizzically, but always with happy approval, these same writers were of all people among the most forceful advocates and pioneers of state education. It seems too, that with the present feverish emphasis on the idea of education for economic growth, reference to the 'respectable ancestry' of these early writers is enjoying something of a revival. It is interesting, for instance, that Lord Robbins, writing as a professional economist a few years ago, was anxious to settle the libel once for all that the classical economists objected to the principle of state intervention to provide for social services and to protect needy minorities, and he mentioned education as a typical case in point.[1]

In view of all this, an objective analysis of the precise nature of the educational contribution of these writers seems to be called for. It is necessary to add that such an investigation should be particularly careful to avoid the common and all too hasty tendency to take from out of his particular setting any nineteenth-century writer who spoke up for education and to present him as one of many characters who played an integral part in an unfolding plot of history, a plot which reached its triumphant climax in the 1944 Education Act. The purpose of this article is to question the appropriateness of this treatment as it is frequently applied to the classical economists. This will arise from an examination of the special form of their arguments and from an uncovering of serious conflicts of opinion on matters of policy, some of which lay beneath the surface of their main writings.

As a generalization it is fair to say that nearly all the economists looked upon education from a utilitarian point of view. Certainly it was Bentham who displayed this in its most rigid and mechanical form, a characteristic which in the matter of education was later reproduced more in his disciple, Edwin Chadwick, than in James Mill. But all the economists were strikingly united in one aspect at least of what can be called *negative* utilitarianism, that is, in the idea that education could

[1] The Robbins Report on *Higher Education* (October 1963) gives favourable mention to the classical economists, p. 204. See also John Vaizey, *The Economics of Education*, 1962, chapter 1.

NINETEENTH-CENTURY DOCTRINES OF POLITICAL ECONOMY

reduce crime. Adam Smith himself, the doyen of the classical economists, competed even with Jeremy Bentham for first place in persuasiveness and vigour on this matter. Referring to the education of the inferior ranks of the people, Smith asserted that

> 'The state however derives no inconsiderable advantage from their instruction. The more they are instructed, the less liable they are to the delusions of enthusiasm and superstition, which among ignorant nations, frequently occasion the most dreadful disorders.'[1]

Such views were by no means original. They had been expressed, for instance, although with less urgency, both by his own tutor Francis Hutcheson and by the seventeenth-century economist, William Petty. But there seems to be no doubt that Smith's attitude to them was considerably sharpened by the influence of the French physiocrats whom he visited on his continental tour in 1768. Whereas Petty and Hutcheson relied upon a religious education, the French writers were now urging scientific instruction. Turgot, for example, typified the current excitement of his confreres on this subject in the following memorandum addressed to his king:

> 'I venture to affirm that if this program [universal state education] be adopted, your subjects will have changed out of all recognition within a mere decade, and their intelligence, good behaviour, and enlightened zeal in your service and their country's will place them far above all other modern nations. For by that time children now ten years old will have grown up into young men trained to do their duty by the State; patriotic and law-abiding, not from fear but on rational grounds, understanding and respecting justice, and prompt to help their fellow citizens in time of need'.[2]

In the hands of the English Utilitarians such thinking became sharpened into cold calculations of social profit and loss. Bentham estimated that government funds spent on education would probably be more than offset by the reduction of expenditure on prisons, and that therefore state investment on education was socially profitable. This reasoning became common currency in the hands of such influential Parliamentarians as Henry Brougham, J. A. Roebuck and T. S. Macaulay. But several of the political economists also developed the argument to the same extent. Miss Martineau, the popularizer of the classical economists, seems to have faithfully represented many of her peers when she wrote:

> 'Nor can I see that political economy objects to the general rating for educational purposes. As a mere police-tax this rating would be a very cheap affair. It would cost us much less than we now pay for juvenile depravity.'[3]

[1] *The Wealth of Nations*, 1950, edited by Edwin Cannan, II, 272. Subsequent references are to this edition and will be referred to as *W.N.*

[2] Quoted in Alexis de Tocqueville, *The Old Régime and the French Revolution*, part III, ch. III. For an account of Smith's meetings with the Physiocrats in Paris, see I. Cumming, *Helvetius*, 1955.

[3] Quoted in Herbert Spencer, *Social Statics and Man Versus the State*, 1884.

NINETEENTH-CENTURY DOCTRINES OF POLITICAL ECONOMY

It is interesting that it was the Scottish members of the classical economists who appear to have been the most insistent in associating popular education with law and order. An observation they were continually fond of making was that the Scots were more law-abiding than others and that this was a consequence of their better education. Adam Smith having made the suggestion, his fellow Scottish economists, James Mill, J. R. McCulloch and Thomas Chalmers were quick to pursue it. Addressing the opponents of education James Mill stated that

> 'It is not necessary that they should compare a Turkish and a British population. Let them only reflect upon the state of the Irish as compared with the English population; then compare the population of Scotland with that of England.'[1]

T. R. Malthus seems to have been content to accept this opinion from his associates. He observed that

> 'The quiet and peaceful habits of the instructed Scotch peasant, compared with the turbulent disposition of the ignorant Irishman, ought not to be without effect upon every impartial reasoner.'[2]

Whitbread, who was avowedly influenced by Malthus, was one of the first to quote crude statistics in Parliament in support of such arguments. In the debate on his 'Bill for establishing a Plan for the Education of the Poor' in 1807, he said:

> 'Search the Newgate calendar. The great majority of the executed in London every year were Irish; the next in order were English, and the last Scots. This was in exact proportion with their respective systems of education among the lower orders.'[3]

Such triumphant reference to figures like these continued for half a century.[4] Apart from the general weaknesses in such simple statistical inferences it is difficult to see how Whitbread's particular argument could support a proposal for stage legislation on education, since Ireland was covered by legislative enactments for the compulsory provision of schools similar to those of Scotland.[5]

James Mill quoted figures to show that there were eleven times as many criminals in England as in Scotland in proportion to their

---

[1] *Westminster Review*, 1813, art. IX.

[2] *Essay on Population*, 7th edition, ch. IX.

[3] *Hansard*, IX, cols. 539–50.

[4] See, for instance, the more elaborate tables in *The Social Condition and Education of the People in England and France*, 1850 (Longman Brown) by Dr. J. Kay.

[5] 'An Act for the Erection of Free Schools' in 1570 had ordered the provision of free schools in every diocese. The equivalent legislation in Scotland was initiated in 1615. Bad administration hindered the implementation of the statutes in Ireland as compared with Scotland, but after a succession of Parliamentary commissions the system was strengthened by annual educational grants from the English Parliament to Irish voluntary education from 1816 onwards, that is seventeen years before the first Parliamentary grant to English education.

NINETEENTH-CENTURY DOCTRINES OF POLITICAL ECONOMY

respective populations.

> 'We desire our opponents to tell us in what respect the circumstances of the English population have not been more favourable than those of the Scottish except in the article of schooling alone?'[1]

There were several possible answers to this question, but one to which most of the economists themselves would have strongly subscribed is contained in the fact that Scotland did not have the English Poor Law.[2] All the classical economists, and not the least James Mill, were persuaded of the demoralizing effect of this legislation; and therefore it was not appropriate for them to neglect it in this particular context. Indeed, in an earlier article James Mill had advised that the reform of the Poor Law was far more urgent in England than provision of education.

Mill also partly answered himself later in his same article when he declared that schooling was rapidly growing in England. By 1826 he was convinced that literacy was typical among 'the lowest people'.[3] England had almost caught up with Scotland in school provision in 1835 without any compulsory provision.[4]

With regard to the general proposition that education reduces crime, the twentieth-century observer, with the benefit of hindsight, is much more sceptical. For one thing, even at the level of the classical economists' own statistical method of evidence, the growth of education in the subsequent one-and-a-half centuries has not been associated with a noticeable decline of delinquency; more and more modern authorities are pointing with bewilderment to the reverse. William Cobbett seems to have been quite alone in this observation in his own day. Cobbett opposed Roebuck's Bill on Education in 1833 on the ground that crime in England was even then increasing at the same time as education was spreading. 'If so, what reason was there to tax the people for the increase of education?'[5]

Apart from these difficulties, however, it is not at all clear that the very definitions of 'crime' that were used in the nineteenth century were always quite the same as those implied or accepted today. The Benthamites clearly separated 'crime' from 'sin'. Ethics were reduced by them to a science. In their view action which was 'bad' arose simply from ignorance of the best way of pursuing happiness. At this stage their philosophy was subtly transformed from *negative* to *positive* Utilitarianism, a much more elusive and metaphysical area of thought. For the

---

[1] *Westminster Review*, 1813, art. IX.

[2] The Scottish poor-relief system was based on the Acts of 1503 and 1579. Its outstanding feature was that no legal recognition was given to the right of able-bodied poor to support. Vagrancy and mendicity were therefore more prominent in Scotland.

[3] *Westminster Review*, VI, October 1826.

[4] See Brougham's speech in the Lords, 21 May 1835.

[5] *Hansard*, 1833, vol. XX. Cobbett continued: 'It was nothing but an attempt to force education—it was French—it was a Doctrinaire plan, and he should always be opposed to it.'

NINETEENTH-CENTURY DOCTRINES OF POLITICAL ECONOMY

Utilitarian, education programmes were aimed solely at removing a very special kind of ignorance. Their precise objective was to remove the ignorance of what they, the Utilitarians, thought to be the best happiness-seeking instruments. People, as J. Roebuck insisted in Parliament, could not be happy by themselves; they had to be taught how to be happy. Nobody could be truly liberated into a state of happiness unless his mind had previously been manipulated by Utilitarians. Only after state instruction would it be logical for the government to resort to punishment. Otherwise pleasure would be minimized and pain (crime) would be maximized. The narrowness of this view was no doubt best revealed in William Godwin's uncompromising attack upon it:

> 'It is not easy to say whether the remark, "that government cannot justly punish offenders, unless it have previously informed them what is virtue and what is offence", be entitled to a separate answer. It is to be hoped that mankind will never have to learn so important a lesson through so corrupt a channel. Government may reasonably and equitably presume that men who live in society, know that enormous crimes are injurious to the public weal, without its being necessary to announce them as such, by laws to be proclaimed by heralds, or expounded by curates. . . . All real crimes are capable of being discerned without the teaching of law. All supposed crimes, not capable of being so discerned, are truly and unalterably innocent.'[1]

Nevertheless, most of the classical economists ventured beyond the mere 'police argument' for education and shared some of the more paternalistic or *positive* Utilitarian thinking. Their reasoning at this level, however, was not always internally or externally consistent. The Malthusians, for instance, wanted to use state schools to instruct the people about the consequences of early marriages and large families, in the hope that the rate of population increase would be kept in check. Adam Smith, however, thought that an increasing population was normally a sign of increasing prosperity, and so could not have subscribed to this argument. For his part, Smith, too, had his own special and paternalistic prescriptions for happiness, prescriptions which derived from his individual system of philosophy and sociology, and which he also wished to administer through the semi-authoritarian instrument of state-assisted schools. Smith's argument was that the most serious contemporary cause of unhappiness was associated with the growing factory system and its division of labour. State education, he contended, was required mainly as an antidote to this new environment. This case is put forward in Book V of *The Wealth of Nations*, where he examined the several duties of government:

> 'In the progress of the division of labour, the employment of the far greater part of those who live by labour, that is, of the great body of the people comes to be confined to a few very simple operations, frequently to

[1] *Enquiry concerning Political Justice and its influence on Morals and Happiness*, London, 1796.

NINETEENTH-CENTURY DOCTRINES OF POLITICAL ECONOMY

one or two. But the understandings of the greater part of men are necessarily formed by their employments. The man whose life is spent in per-
forming a few simple operations, of which the effects are perhaps always
the same, or very nearly the same, has no occasion to exert his understanding or to exercise his invention in finding out expedients for removing
difficulties which never occur. He naturally loses, therefore, the habit of
such exertion and generally becomes as stupid and ignorant as it is possible
for a human creature to become. The torpor of his mind renders him not
only incapable of relishing or bearing a part in any rational conversation,
but of conceiving any generous, noble or tender sentiment, and consequently of forming any just judgement concerning many even of the ordinary duties of private life. . . .[1]

'His dexterity at his own particular trade seems, in this manner, to be
acquired at the expense of his intellectual, social and martial virtues. But
in every improved and civilized society this is the state into which the
labouring poor, that is, the great body of the people, must necessarily fall,
unless government takes some pains to prevent it.'[2]

This passage has often been referred to by historians of education, and
they are naturally more interested in this particular part of *The Wealth
of Nations* than in others. To economists, however, who are just as interested in many other sections of the work and especially in Book I, the
extract above comes as a strange surprise. For all the many other references to the division of labour elsewhere in the work are made with
abundant enthusiasm and optimism. Indeed a careful comparison with
certain phrases in Book I reveals an obvious inconsistency of treatment
of this subject. The very first sentence of the opening chapter of the book
sets the major theme subsequently developed:

'The *greatest* improvement in the productive powers of labour, and the
greater part of the skill, dexterity and judgment with which it is any
where directed, or applied, seem to have been the effects of the division of
labour.'[3] (Italics supplied.)

Later he claims:

'Men are much more likely to discover easier and readier methods of
attaining any object, when the whole attention of their minds is directed
towards that single object, than when it is dissipated among a great variety
of things. But in consequence of the division of labour, the whole of every
man's attention comes naturally to be directed towards some one very
simple object.'[4]

In the light of these conflicting views the quotation with which educa-
tionists are more familiar, and which seems disposed towards state
education, can hardly be accepted as completely representative or as a
final judgement on the matter.

It is sometimes suggested that the classical economists were anxious
to press arguments for state education based on presumed direct conse-

[1] *W.N.*, p. 267.
[2] *W.N.*, p. 268.
[3] *W.N.*, p. 5.
[4] *W.N.*, p. 11.

NINETEENTH-CENTURY DOCTRINES OF POLITICAL ECONOMY

quences for economic growth. This is not easy to substantiate. The reduction of crime and promotion of 'happiness' was easily their most overriding consideration. Anxiety for economic accumulation is indeed strongly disparaged in certain remarks of Adam Smith in the context of education, remarks which are very reminiscent of modern references to the 'affluent society'. In the Glasgow Lectures he argued that education was needed not to promote economic growth but to counter its undesirable consequences. The division of labour principle alone could be relied upon to foster sufficient production of goods and services and to open up job opportunities for old and young. It was because a boy could get a job easily that he

> '. . . begins to find that his father is obliged to him, and therefore throws off his authority. When he is grown up he has no ideas with which he can amuse himself. When he is away from work he must therefore betake himself to drunkenness and riot. Accordingly we find that in the commercial parts of England, the tradesmen are for the most part in this despicable condition; their work through half the week is sufficient to maintain them and through want of education they have no amusement for the other but riot and debauchery. So it may justly be said that the people who clothe the world are in rags themselves.'[1]

Criticisms based on Smith's dislike of 'mutual emulation' displayed by relatively opulent workers is to be found in *The Wealth of Nations*.[2] Again in his preceding book, *The Theory of Moral Sentiments*, he presented the case of the man who 'devotes himself for ever to the pursuit of wealth and greatness' who '. . . in the last dregs of life, his body washed with toil and disease . . . begins at last to find that wealth and greatness are mere trinkets of frivolous utility. . . .'[3] It is true that Smith advocated the modernization of school curricula to include such things as geometry and mechanics in order that the potential factory worker should be better acquainted with his environment. But the primary purpose of this does not seem to have been the pursuit of greater productivity or inventiveness for materialistic purposes. Such proposals should be read in reference to his philosophy and sociology, which contended that some basic knowledge of certain elements of a worker's surroundings would probably give rise to more reflection, and that this would probably develop into speculative and absorbing thought. This would produce a state of mind desirable in itself, and would ward off the mental boredom which so often encouraged restlessness, mischief and crime.

The later economist, J. R. McCulloch, was certainly exceptional in relating education with economic growth in statements which do have a twentieth-century ring about them. In attempting to explain the

---

[1] *Lectures*, p. 257. See my article, 'Adam Smith's Two Views on the Division of Labour,' *Economica*, February 1964.

[2] See p. 83.

[3] *The Theory of Moral Sentiments*, 6th ed., 1777, pp. 240–2.

NINETEENTH-CENTURY DOCTRINES OF POLITICAL ECONOMY

superior economic development of Britain over other countries which enjoyed similar *natural* advantages, McCulloch pointed to their relative failure to apply intelligence. They would not improve until 'the sun of science had shone upon them'. 'I do not know that it would be going too far to affirm that knowledge is really productive of all wealth in civilization'.[1]

But even here it is important to notice that such statements separate their author from those who were campaigning for a system of mainly government-supplied education. For McCulloch argued that the economic superiority of Britain over Prussia and France was precisely due to the relative failure of their education, and it was in these very countries that *centrally administered* school systems did exist. Britain, on the contrary, relied on a privately supplied education which McCulloch thought in 1825 to be 'now so generally diffused'.

Above all aspects of education this is one which clearly separates all the classical economists from those who have shaped our system as it now stands in Britain. While the early economists argued for *some* state education, they conceived it in very qualified terms indeed. If we were to select the most conspicuous of the main features which distinguish them from current practice, it would probably be their insistence that fees should not be abolished and should always cover a substantial part of the cost of education. Their main reason for this requirement has either been subsequently forgotten or carefully avoided by interested parties. Fee paying, according to most of the economists, was the one instrument with which parents could keep desirable competition alive between teachers and schools. Adam Smith's proposal for state provision for the education of the poor was limited to state subsidies to school *buildings*. He went to great lengths to insist that the teachers' salaries were to be derived largely from parental fees. It was the absence of such a principle in the case of endowed schools which caused him to write about them in his most condemnatory manner:

> 'The endowments of schools and colleges have necessarily diminished more or less the necessity of application in the teachers. Their subsistence, so far as it arises from their salaries, is evidently derived from a fund altogether independent of their success and reputation in their particular professions.'[2]

He spoke from personal experience on this matter. His years at Oxford University gave him a most unfavourable opinion of protected university teaching. ' . . . In the university of Oxford, the greater part of the public professors have, for these many years, given up altogether even the pretence of teaching.'[3] Very often the ultimate authority in this case

---

[1] *A Discourse, delivered at the Opening of the City of London Literary and Scientific Institution,* 30 May 1825.
[2] *W.N.,* p. 250.
[3] *W.N.,* p. 251.

NINETEENTH-CENTURY DOCTRINES OF POLITICAL ECONOMY

was one step beyond the corporate body which managed the endowment, 'as in the governor of the province; or, perhaps, in some minister of state'. But all that such remote control could do was to force the teacher to attend his pupils a certain number of hours or to give a certain number of lectures per week. The rest was left to the teacher's private diligence, upon which Smith from his own experience did not seem to have placed much value.

Adam Smith's own experience as a university teacher led him to favour a fee-paying system. His own salary at Glasgow may have been about £70 with a house, and his fees near £100.[1] He thought that this arrangement ensured at least some efficiency, since such a variable element of a teacher's reward was sensitive to the quality of the services rendered. Consequently, the greater proportion of the total reward made up in fees the greater the security against pedagogic inertia. The heavily endowed institutions, on the contrary, were usually arranged not in the interest of the students but for the ease of the masters. The most monotonous and uninspiring teaching, for instance, was protected against the normal sanction of derision.[2]

> 'The discipline of the college, at the same time, may enable him to force all his pupils to the most regular attendance upon this sham-lecture, and to maintain the most decent and respectful behaviour during the whole time of the performance.'[3]

Adam Smith contended that in such a situation it was not surprising that no innovations were made in the curriculum, and that dead languages prevailed while new sciences were neglected. The worst examples were the universities. These, according to Smith, had become sanctuaries of 'exploded systems' and 'obsolete prejudices'.

But although endowments thus blunted the ordinary forces of a free market in education, examples could be found where market forces were allowed to operate without such major restrictions and therefore with much better results. Those parts of education where there were no endowments were, according to Smith,

> '. . . generally the best taught. When a young man goes to a fencing or a dancing school, he does not indeed always learn to fence or to dance very well; but he seldom fails of learning to fence or to dance.'[4]

Complete failure presumably could only occur at public (i.e. endowed) institutions:

> 'The three most essential parts of literary education, to read, write and account, it still continues to be *more common to acquire in private than in public schools*; and it very seldom happens that any body fails of acquiring them to the degree in which it is necessary to acquire them.'[5] (Italics supplied.)

---

[1] Rae, *Life of Adam Smith*, 1895, p. 48.
[2] Lecturers often used to read from a book and sometimes in a foreign language.
[3] *W.N.*, p. 253.
[4] *W.N.*, p. 253.
[5] *W.N.*, p. 254.

NINETEENTH-CENTURY DOCTRINES OF POLITICAL ECONOMY

Most of the later economists upheld Adam Smith's principle. Thus Malthus argued that if each child had to pay a fixed sum, 'the school master would then have a stronger interest to increase the number of his pupils . . .'[1] Similarly, McCulloch thought that the maintenance of the fee system would

> ' . . . secure the constant attendance of a person who shall be able to instruct the young, and who shall have the strongest interest to perfect himself in his business, and to attract the greatest number of scholars to his school.'[2]

Otherwise, if the schoolmaster derived much of his income from his fixed salary, he would not have the same interest to exert himself,

> ' . . . and like all other functionaries, placed in similar situations, he would learn to neglect his business, and to consider it as a drudgery only to be avoided.'[3]

The most hesitant of the economists to accept this principle was John Stuart Mill. Education was one of those exceptional cases, in which, according to Mill, the *laissez faire* principle broke down because of the lack of adequate judgement on the part of the purchaser:

> 'Is the buyer always qualified to judge of the commodity? If not, the presumption in favour of the competition of the market does not apply to this case.'[4]

Medicine was an obvious example of this sort of market failure. Even if the patient could be relied upon to purchase some minimum amount at his own expense and from his own free will, we were not bound to admit 'that the patient will select the *right* medicine without assistance.[5] (Italics supplied.) Similarly with education: 'The uncultivated cannot be competent judges of cultivation.'[6] Long experience was necessary to appreciate education, and therefore the market could not adequately provide for it. Pecuniary speculation could not wait: 'it must succeed rapidly or not at all'.[7] Of the older classical economists, only Nassau Senior seems to have come out on the side of J. S. Mill in this serious difference of opinion. Senior, too, did not trust the average good sense of the parents, and for similar reasons. The fact was that neither Senior nor Mill liked the type of school that the free market was providing by the middle of the nineteenth century. This was undoubtedly due to their opinion that these schools were inferior to the large scale models which the poor law institutions were dutifully producing to the order of their

---

[1] Malthus, Letter to Whitbread, 1807.
[2] Note XXI, McCulloch edition of *The Wealth of Nations*, 1828.
[3] *Ibid.* James Mill also shared such reasoning—see *Westminster Review*, article 1813.
[4] J. S. Mill, *Principles of Political Economy*, p. 953.
[5] *Ibid.*, p. 954.
[6] *Ibid.*, p. 953.
[7] *Ibid.*, p. 954. Pushed to its extreme, this argument would preclude the possibility of *any* entirely new product gaining a threshold.

NINETEENTH-CENTURY DOCTRINES OF POLITICAL ECONOMY

Benthamite supervisors. With regard to the existing provision of education although Mill failed to quote the evidence, he believed that

'... even in quantity it is [1848] and is likely to remain, altogether insufficient, while in quality, though with some slight tendency to improvement, it is never good except by some rare accident, and generally so bad as to be little more than nominal.'[1]

This quotation stands in striking contrast to the belief of Adam Smith (quoted above) that private schools were superior in efficiency to those publicly provided. Whereas J. S. Mill thought that the competitive market principle broke down in education because the customer was not a competent judge of his interests, Adam Smith (and his later follower, Robert Lowe), argued that the competitive market principle had not been allowed to operate properly in the first place, owing to the hindrance of endowment. Smith quoted extensively from the literature of ancient Greece to show how well the free market worked in the absence of such obstacles.[2] He would probably have agreed with J. S. Mill that the *initial* competence of the customer to choose education was inadequate. But he would have opposed Mill's conclusion that education should be taken out of the market for this reason. For the day-to-day experience of this market was *itself a medium of instruction*, and one which Smith thought superior for the purpose to any government authority.

However, J. S. Mill presents another case where undue emphasis on partial quotations from his works can only too easily give a misleading impression of his over-all and final judgement. For despite his doubts about the efficiency of the market mechanism in education, Mill in the end, like Smith, came down in favour of private schools. His main reason for this was not, however, quite the same as Smith's. It was Mill's adherence to his principle of Liberty which was crucial to his final judgement on the subject. Liberty was required not only as an end in itself but because of certain consequences which Mill thought desirable, such as spontaneity, variety and experiment. A state school system would swamp these:

'A general state education is a mere contrivance for moulding people to be exactly like one another: and as the mould in which it casts them is that which pleases the predominant power in the government, whether this be a monarch, a priesthood, an aristocracy, or the majority of the existing generation; in proportion as it is efficient and successful, it establishes a

[1] *Ibid.*, p. 956.
[2] J. S. Mill's father, James Mill, was on the side of Adam Smith in this matter, supporting his opinion that 'all institutions for the education of those classes of people who are able to pay for it should be taken out of the hands of public bodies, and left to the natural operation of that free competition which the interests of the parties desiring to teach and to be taught would naturally create;—and it is easy to see that the same reasoning is applicable in a great degree even to the education of the poorest classes.' *Westminster Review*, 1813.

despotism over the mind, leading by natural tendency to one over the body.'[1]

J. S. Mill, therefore, despite his misgivings about the ability of ordinary people to buy education themselves, eventually confined his proposals for state intervention to a law rendering only education (not schooling) compulsory. 'The instrument for enforcing the law should be no other than public examinations, extending to all children.'[2] Thus the place or source of their education was immaterial after all. To see how radical such a provision would be today we have only to imagine children obtaining their knowledge by television, correspondence courses, dame schools or part-time academies or even by being taught by their parents at home in the same manner that J. S. Mill himself was educated. There would even be no official pressure to supply people with teachers previously instructed in government training colleges. In the words of Adam Smith: 'They would soon find better teachers than any whom the state could provide for them.'[3]

In view of this general investigation of the writings of the classical economists we are bound to conclude with the speculation that these authors would be acutely disappointed with the subsequent development of education in their own country in the succeeding century, and not least with the 1944 Education Act. They would probably have challenged nearly every piece of educational legislation after Lord Sandon's Act of 1876. This Act met J. S. Mill's desire for compulsory *education* as against compulsory *schooling*. At the same time such compulsion was reinforced by examinations, as Mill had also advocated, whilst another of his conditions had been satisfied in the provision against individual cases of poverty by the granting of special financial concessions. The legislation which followed the 1876 Act progressively undermined this position, and proceeded according to principles quite alien to the early writers. For there is indeed nothing in the evidence of their writings to suggest that any one of them would have supported the degree of state predominance in education that is experienced in our own times. Finally, their main case for any state intervention in the first place, the 'reduction of crime' thesis, would demand from them much rethinking in view of the apparent failure of this doctrine in the light of subsequent experience.

[1] *On Liberty*, Fontana edition, 1962, p. 239.
[2] *Ibid.*, p. 239.
[3] *W.N.*, p. 281.

[27]

WHY IS EDUCATION PUBLICLY PROVIDED? A CRITICAL SURVEY
John R. Lott, Jr.

Introduction

Schooling is publicly provided by every nation. Such a unique position is shared only by a very limited range of goods—national defense, courts, police, and roads. It is not immediately obvious, however, why education deserves such a special role. Nevertheless, in the United States educational outlays comprise more than 40 percent of the combined state and local budget expenditures. In countries such as Sweden, Israel, and the Netherlands, public non-capital expenditures on education account for more than 7 percent of the nation's gross domestic product.

What is especially perplexing about public provision of education is its cost. Per pupil expenditures are much higher in public schools than in private ones, but cognitive development has been found to be lower in public schools. Inefficiencies of public provision are not unique to education (Borcherding et al. 1982; Savas 1982)/ but the problem is to explain why all countries have adopted public provision even though it is less effective at teaching skills than private education).

A wide range of justifications and/or explanations of public provision of education can be found. This paper will argue that most of these hypotheses fail to explain why there is public provision instead of some other form of intervention. They also fail to explain why their reasoning is not equally applicable to other goods that are not publicly provided. Many of these explanations also share two additional problems: a paucity of empirical tests directly related to explaining public provision, and the lack of a general theory equally applicable to all countries.

Cato Journal, Vol. 7, No. 2 (Fall 1987). Copyright © Cato Institute. All rights reserved.

The author is Visiting Assistant Professor of Economics at Rice University. This paper was accepted while he was a National Fellow at the Hoover Institution. He wishes to thank Harold Demsetz, Gertrud Fremling, Finis Welch, and E. G. West for helpful discussions.

In the following sections, this paper reviews the costs of public provision and the conditions under which it arose in the United States and England, discusses the eight most frequently advanced explanations for public provision, and argues for a different hypothesis based on public choice theory.

The Cost of Public Provision

Per pupil costs are substantially higher in public schools than in private schools. Table 1 shows the case for the United States, where it costs about twice as much to educate public school pupils. About three-quarters of the private schools are church-affiliated, and services contributed by religious staff are valued at less than market value, thus lowering the cost figures for private schools. Yet, even relatively liberal assumptions of the implied subsidies do not significantly alter the case. If we assume that 11 percent of current expenses go to religious staff salaries and that religious teachers are paid one-half the rate of lay staff (Bredeweg 1982, pp. 38–56), public expenses are still at least 1.83 times greater than private costs. Savas (1982, p. 102) found similar public/private differentials in schooling for both the severely and nonseverely handicapped. Given the magnitude of public expenditures, the financial gains from contracting out for such services would be tremendous.

The evidence suggests that the organization of resources in public schools is also wanting. Hanushek (1972, 1986) presented empirical evidence that current hiring practices and salary scales in public schools do not encourage those skills in teachers that produce higher student achievement. Salary scales reward teachers based on expe-

TABLE 1

AVERAGE CURRENT EXPENDITURES PER PUPIL
IN PUBLIC AND PRIVATE SCHOOLS

School Year	Expenditures per Pupil ($)			Ratio: Public/ Private	Adjusted Private ($)	Ratio: Public/ Adjusted Private
	Average	Public	Private			
1976–77	1,353	1,544	760	2.03	844	1.83
1977–78	1,512	1,736	819	2.12	909	1.91

SOURCES: *NCES Bulletin*, U.S. Department of Health, Education, and Welfare, 23 October 1979; *United States Catholic Elementary and Secondary Schools 1981–1982: A statistical report on schools, enrollment, staffing, and finances*, 1982.

EDUCATION: A CRITICAL SURVEY

rience and level of graduate education, both of which were found unrelated to student achievement test scores. Instead, a teacher's intelligence, as measured by scores on verbal ability tests, was highly related to such gains. Staaf's (1977b, pp. 152–65) brief survey of the literature confirms these findings.[1]

Alchian (1965) explained such results by pointing out some general characteristics of public organizations and then, in a later paper, applied his reasoning specifically to education (1968).[2] Public organizations, according to Alchian, do not directly concentrate the costs and benefits on decision makers. Hence, they have an incentive to shirk. The market process, on the other hand, forces firms to compete for customers, and firms inept at providing services will lose their customers to other firms. The organization of public schools protects educators from such competition because payments are not made directly by the students receiving the services, nor do public employees bear the consequences of poor service.

Recent work on student cognitive achievement provides further support for this hypothesis. By contrasting private and public educational systems with data on 59,000 high school students, Coleman et al. (1982) found that, after controlling for family background variables that predict achievement, children attending private schools learn at a faster rate. Using standardized achievement test scores in two developing countries, Columbia and Tanzania, Cox and Jimenez (1987) provided evidence that private schooling is superior to public schooling.[3]

In sum, the evidence suggests that public provision is costly not only in terms of current expenditures but also in terms of forgone investment in human capital. Nor does the list of such costs end here. If we accept that some of the public benefits derived from education are related to the level of investment in human capital, then less efficient public provision may have other costs as well.

[1]See Lott (1984) for a further review of this literature. West (1970) also provides a useful survey of the history of economic thought on this subject.

[2]See Alchian and Kessel (1962) for a similar discussion.

[3]One difficulty with the Coleman et al. findings is that they fail to examine what differences in family characteristics cause certain children to be sent to private schools in the first place. For example, the decision to send a child to a private school may signal the presence of other parental investments in their children, which may be responsible for some portion of the differential rates. But since this last effect cannot explain all of the difference, the study does confirm Alchian's predictions. West (1983) provided a public opinion survey showing that consumers of these services also believe that private schooling is of a higher quality than public schooling. Cox and Jimenez attempted to control for why the child was sent to a private school. See also Lott (1987e).

The Introduction of Public Schools and the Level of Schooling

A brief survey of the history of education for the United States and Great Britain indicates that the introduction of public schools has produced only small gains in the general level of education. The 1860 U.S. Census shows that in states of the original 13 colonies, the white literacy rate in those states with public schooling was 99 percent compared with 93 percent in those states without it. This difference of only 6 percentage points may, however, be partly explained by the more rural nature of the states without public schools (Montgomery 1878, p. 6).[4]

In New York, the Free Schools Act abolishing fees for common (public) schools was not passed until 1867, and compulsory schooling was not instituted until 1874 (West 1967, p. 105). However, as early as 1812 a report commissioned by the state found: "In a free government, where political equality is established, and where the road to preferment is open to all, there is a natural stimulus to education; and accordingly *we find it generally resorted to unless some great local impediments* interfere" (quoted in West 1967, p. 103). In 1821 New York counted 352,479 students of all ages attending school out of a population of approximately 380,000 children aged 5 to 16 (p. 105). West (p. 127) concluded that, for New York, if "the term 'universal' is intended to mean, something like, 'most', 'nearly everybody', or 'over 90 percent' then we lack firm evidence to show that education was not already universal prior to the establishment of laws to provide a schooling which was both compulsory and free."

In his examination of the common school movement in New England, Fishlow (1966, pp. 40–67) argued that although the public system expanded both absolutely and in percentage terms, it did not add significantly to the percentage of children being educated. The primary effect of the public system was to shift children from private to public schools. Using data for Massachusetts, Field (1974, p. 22) found that "[Horace] Mann and his reformers were successful in the first one of their instrumental drives: curtailing the growth of private schooling." Field (p. 30) did not rule out the possibility that the entire increase in public attendance was at the expense of private attendance.

---

[4]Even if one argues that the states that first adopted public provision were the ones with the lowest initial literacy rates (and this does not seem to be the case), this does not affect my argument that in those states averaging a literacy rate of 93 percent, the potential gains from public provision were small.

478

EDUCATION: A CRITICAL SURVEY

State involvement in the public provision of education in England is usually dated from the Foster Act of 1870. Its objective was not universal free public schooling, but rather to "fill the gaps" in the private system; publicly provided schools received about one-third of their funds through fees from parents (West 1970, pp. xviii–xix). In fact, compulsory schooling was not established until 1880, and fees were not abolished until 1918. Yet ample evidence exists of widespread private schooling long before this act.

West discovered that in England "most people were already literate in 1870" and that "most parents bought education by modest fee-paying" (pp. 136, 131). Webb (1963) estimated that in the late 1830s between two-thirds and three-quarters of the working classes were literate. If anything, such figures may be underestimates, since those who performed the surveys usually were reformers anxious to establish the inadequacy of a purely private system (West 1970, p. 128).[5] Some have argued that if the government had any net effect on education during the first third of the 19th century, it was negative because of the imposition of taxes on schooling materials, the closing down of public reading rooms, and in certain cases the withdrawal of licenses from inns and coffee houses receiving particular newspapers (p. 127).

Table 2 provides convincing proof of West's claim that by 1858 most British children received some schooling. Out of a total population of 19.5 million in 1858, 2.5 million children were attending private schools. If there were 5.3 million children between the ages of 3 and 15, and if we accept the education commission's 1861 estimate that the average duration at school was 5.7 years, no apparent deficiency would have existed in the education of children (p. 142). West concluded that "what remains clearly to be shown [by the apologists of the 1870 Foster Act] is that the increase of school places in the government sector was not completely offset by the damage done to the growth of the private sector" (p. 156).

Using data from the *Michigan Income Dynamics Study* (1966–74), Lazear (1983) provided additional contemporary evidence that private incentives alone will yield investments in education relatively close to optimal levels. To the extent that parents cannot perfectly internalize the returns to investments in their child's education (that

[5]West (1970, pp. 129–30) presented evidence that in 1838, 87 percent of the workhouse children of Norfolk and Suffolk could read to some extent and 53 percent could write. In 1840, 79 percent of the miners of Northumberland and Durham could read, and about 92 percent of the adult population of Hull (population of 14,526) could read in 1839. West (pp. 132–35) provided additional evidence, such as the number of persons signing the marriage register, that confirms his earlier findings.

CATO JOURNAL

TABLE 2
GROWTH IN PRIVATE SCHOOLING, 1818–58

Year	Population	Population of 3 to 15 Year Olds	Number of Students in Day Schools	Ratio of Students to Number of 3 to 15 Year Olds
1818	11,642,683	3,504,448[a]	674,883	.193
1833	14,386,415	4,330,311[a]	1,276,947	.295
1851	17,927,609	5,295,780[b]	2,144,378	.405
1858	19,523,103	5,311,534	2,535,462	.477

[a]Derived in a similar manner as that for 1851, but I used the earliest estimates obtainable (1841) as a proxy for the percentage of population in this age group.
[b]Derived by assuming uniform distribution of population in the 0 to 4 and 15 to 19 age groups in 1851.
SOURCES: Mitchell (1980, p. 52); West (1970, p. 149).

is, intergenerational transfers cannot be enforced), their private return will lie below the social return on these investments. Lazear estimates an upper bound on this underinvestment of only 0.282 years for the mean individual.

A strong case can be made that, at least in some countries, public provision of schooling had a trivial (if any) effect on the proportion of children receiving education. In fact, as will be shown later, public provision was not necessarily the historical product of a belief that children would otherwise go uneducated, but rather of a belief that they were receiving the wrong type of education. It therefore seems difficult to argue that a universally applicable explanation for public provision can rest on the desire to end illiteracy.

Public Goods and Public Provision

Alleged inefficiencies resulting from private production of public goods are often assumed to be reduced by public intervention. Such reasoning has provided a positive theory of the state (see Kalt 1981 for a discussion of this literature).

Friedman (1955, pp. 124–25) provided what is perhaps the most influential argument for government support of schooling to secure external benefits. Because buyers of education confer external benefits on those not purchasing education, the result is too little education. By taxing those who receive these benefits and subsidizing those purchasing education, the welfare of both groups can be improved. Friedman's reasoning justifies rules that require minimum levels of education, and government financing may be the least expensive way of enforcing them.

EDUCATION: A CRITICAL SURVEY

More recently, however, Friedman (1976, p. 92) has stressed the differences between the existence of average and marginal net positive externalities:

> I have never found any plausible argument for net positive externalities from schooling that would not be satisfied if 90 percent, to take an arbitrary figure, received schooling—the three R's. I have yet to see a plausible argument for any net positive marginal externality from additional schooling. But if this be so, and if private interest alone could lead to at least this much schooling—as I believe it is overwhelmingly plausible that it would—then there is no case from externalities for either compulsory schooling or the governmental financing of schooling.

If we accept Friedman's arbitrary figure of 90 percent, then the historical evidence presented above strongly confirms his belief that private interest alone often was sufficient to assure this level even before the introduction of either free public provision or compulsory schooling.

Two questions remain: Do such benefits exist, and, if so, what would be the best means of obtaining them? The next section reviews what economists and educators believe with regard to these questions.

Democracy as a Public Good

The relationship between democracy and education has been assumed to take three different, though not mutually exclusive, forms, depending on whether the benefit is believed to be the product of an individual's cognitive skill level. There appears to be a consensus that cognitive skills are positively related to support for democracy.[6] Some even claim that education itself is used to instill democratic values and a common set of views.[7] Thus, the three views can be

---

[6]The relationship between cognitive skills and support for democracy requires few references. Cohn's (1979, p. 260) extensive survey of the literature on the economics of education concluded: "Education provides a broad understanding of various aspects of the sciences, literature, and arts that help in molding 'well-rounded' people who are more likely to strive for the survival of democracy. Government provision and/or support of education is therefore regarded as a means to perpetuate and strengthen democracy." Others, such as Stapleton (1978, p. 29), found that high school and college graduates are generally more likely to participate in political activities, although he warned this may not be equivalent to increased support of democracy. See also Weisbrod (1962, p. 119) and West (1968, pp. 35–38).

[7]The notion that education creates a common set of views is widely held. Friedman (1962, p. 86) wrote: "A stable and democratic society is impossible . . . without widespread acceptance of some common set of values." Tullock (1983, p. 139) claimed that history "indicate[s] very clearly that Americanization and improving the quality of the votes cast by citizens were major motives [for public education]." Gurwitz (1982, p. 22) wrote, "Education is one mechanism through which the shared norms and common experiences that contributed to social cohesion and stability are inculcated." And John Stuart Mill ([1848] 1973, p. 953) offered his famous statement that "the uncultivated cannot be competent judges of cultivation."

481

CATO JOURNAL

described as hinging on whether one believes (1) democracy is something innately valued; (2) the intrinsic value of democracy is somehow realized as one becomes more educated; or (3) support of democracy should be taught in schools. A further division can be made in the second view between those who regard education as a means of instilling specific views or as inculcating a willingness to accept disagreement of others.[8] These differing views are well summarized by Davis and North (1971, p. 237), who predict that those groups excluded from the political process will not have the cost of their education socialized.

Several observations conflict with these views. First, the existence of democracy did not necessarily follow public provision of education. In fact that was often not the case as witnessed by two rather pominent examples—the United States and Great Britain. Second, the homogenization-of-cultures argument does not appear to provide a universal explanation of public provision. For example, Sweden (Heidenheimer 1982, pp. 269–99; Huntford 1980), which is regarded as homogeneous by many different measures (religion, race, and language), instituted public schooling relatively early. An interesting implication of this homogenization is that if everyone agrees with each other, it may lower the returns to voting.

The view that parents are unable to judge what are the proper views to be taught in a democracy can be examined on two levels. First, how can individuals choose the representatives who will make this decision if they cannot adequately judge the education themselves (West 1970, p. 211)? Second, why do we allow people to make extremely complicated decisions involving other areas of life (for example, which doctor will operate on a child), but not which educator will teach their child? Ironically, the rationale for the First Amendment assumes the competition of ideas is a good (Coase 1974).

Rowley and Peacock (1975, p. 128) note that tolerance of others is not a difficult problem to solve. Vouchers can produce social mixing simply by attaching restrictions to their use. In any case, the present system, which vouchers would replace, often encourages social isolation by zoning children from highly homogeneous neighborhoods into a single school. Through an examination of American public, Catholic, and private schools, Coleman et al. (1982, pp. 28–71) found that while there are relatively few blacks (though not fewer Hispan-

---

[8]The third point of view focused on the use of public education to create "social mixing" that would foster tolerance of other views necessary to run a democracy. Levin (1980, p. 251) expressed this view: "What makes the voucher approach unique is that parents will be able to send their children to schools that will reinforce in the most restrictive fashion the family's political, ideological, and religious views."

EDUCATION: A CRITICAL SURVEY

ics) in private schools, minority groups are much less segregated in private schools than in public schools. Their report also supports the hypothesis that private schools are diverse with respect to family income. When one considers only the broad middle-income category (those families with annual income of $12,000 to $38,000 in 1978), the children in this group are similarly distributed across the three types of schools.

If one accepts the first argument—linking the level of human capital to external benefits from democracy—and if one believes private schooling produces more human capital, it follows that a private system with a subsidy is superior to the present public school system.

A strong argument against the first or third explanation for public provision of education is that using subsidies would be more effective. As will be shown in the next section, however, this does not apply to the indoctrination hypothesis for public education. The explanation that follows will be a variation on the indoctrination theme.

Crime Reduction as a Public Good

Historically, the link between crime and education played an important role in the adoption of public provision of schooling.[9] The literature has proposed two possible relationships between education and crime. The most prominent view among modern economists focuses on an individual's future income stream as the opportunity cost of committing crimes.[10] Others, particularly many classical economists, point out that inculcating certain beliefs (for example, religious views or respect for private property) makes committing a crime

---

[9]West (1967, p. 108) quoted proponents of a free public system as arguing that under such a system, "it will be found universally true that the *minimum* of crime exists, where the *maximum* of moral education is found." Field (1974, pp. 42–48) found similar evidence in his study of the roots of public education in Massachusetts.

[10]A few references illustrate the relationship between earnings and crime. Singer (1972, p. 291) explains: "By increasing labor productivity, education raises the opportunity cost of crime, the losses that the criminal suffers if he is caught and the income he might have earned as a member of the labor force." Weisbrod (1964, p. 101) notes: "Benefits of education may take the form of reduced social costs of other activities; inadequate education appears to contribute to low income, which is associated with delinquency and crime. Thus, education may provide social benefits by freeing some resources now devoted to law enforcement and allied activities." Finally, Cohn (1979) built on earlier work by Phillips et al. (1972) showing that labor market status is a sufficient factor to explain rising juvenile crime rates. Cohn conjectured that if education increases labor force participation rates, increased education could help reduce the crime rate. Other prominent contemporary economists, including Friedman (1976, p. 92), support these arguments.

more costly.[11] Presumably, this is mainly achieved through instilling guilt. Despite differing views on the causal relationship between education and crime, one observation is widely accepted: education lowers crime and therefore constitutes a public good.

Two policy implications can be derived from the two views. Accepting the first view that private schooling increases investment in human capital more (and/or at a sufficiently lower cost) than does public schooling implies the superiority of subsidies over public provision. Moreover, Lott (1987e) has found that, even after controlling for other factors, increases in the proportion of children attending public schools are associated with increased juvenile delinquency rates for both U.S. time series data and California cross-sectional data by county.

The second view, that public schools instill certain beliefs, has less clear implications for the relationship between crime and education. As Lott (1987a) has shown, even with subsidies limited to governmentally approved schools, competition between them under a voucher-type system could result in underproduction of the political and moral beliefs sought. However, this hypothesis also predicts that public schooling should be more effective than private schooling in lowering juvenile delinquency, and this is not the case.

Economic Growth

Some economists have justified past government intervention in education by pointing to divergences in the private and social rates of discount (Davis and North 1971, pp. 240–41). They claim the divergence results from "the poor state of development of the private capital markets and the relatively better state of the market for government funds, a situation that was probably characteristic of the

---

[11]In reviewing the opinions of classical economists, West (1970, p. 112) wrote: "But all the economists were strikingly united on one aspect at least of what can be called negative utilitarianism, that is, in the idea that education could reduce crime and disorder." Many believed the difficulty with private schooling was that it provided "the *wrong* sort of education," and they hoped to "lessen parental control over education" and obtain the "ultimate control of education" (West 1980, p. 5). Even Adam Smith (1776, vol. 2, p. 309) anticipated this later view: "The state however derives no inconsiderable advantage from their instruction. The more they are instructed, the less liable they are to the delusions of enthusiasm and supposition, which among ignorant nations, frequently occasion the most dreadful disorders." Sir William Petty, however, probably was the first to claim the link between education and crime; he argued in 1662 that by controlling religious views, government could reduce crime (High 1984, p. 4). Thus, the view of earlier economists differs from those of their intellectual descendants. Rather than using the pecuniary cost of crime explanation, they focused on indoctrination by the state. See High (1985, pp. 312–14) for a historical account of other economists who have believed that state education reduces crime.

EDUCATION: A CRITICAL SURVEY

United States in the early decades of the nineteenth century" (p. 240, see also pp. 105–66). For example, public provision of engineering classes at West Point in 1802 and the subsequent public employment of its graduates by the army were justified by virtue of their readiness to fill positions in private industry in the 1830s. Davis and North then explain the coinciding de-emphasis of engineering at West Point in the 1830s: "Once the potential demand for engineers had become a real demand, engineering education became profitable even at private rates of discount, and it was no longer necessary for the government to continue its subsidy."[12] The key word is "subsidy." As Cohn (1979, p. 262) pointed out, "[Government provision] does not require government control of schools; the same objective could be achieved via some form of subsidy."[13]

Finally, it is not clear that government intervention has achieved the desired results. From his analysis of data for Britain and the Netherlands, Chiswick (1969) concluded that if one also considers nonhuman capital assets, minimum schooling requirements actually lower the wealth of relatively poor people. This is presumably because their return to other activities is higher than that in education.

Public Provision as a Means of Creating Wealth Transfers to Educators

A hypothesis accepted by many economists (see Coase 1974, p. 390; High 1985, pp. 314–15; and Tullock 1983, p. 141) has been offered by West. West's (1967, 1968, 1970) studies of the history of public education in England and the United States have indicated that one primary force moving both countries toward free public

[12]Even if we accept the claim that the cost of government borrowing was less than for private groups during the early 1800s (and it is not evident that it was), the argument does not explain why public schooling was not introduced until the 1870s in many parts of the United States and in England. By itself the argument also explains too much. If the explanation were correct, the government should have subsidized the building of factories as well. Further, it is not clear why the differences in "potential" and "real" demand are important. While it is true that potential demand is associated with greater risk to the individual investor, it is also related to greater risk to the government. The cost to the government is forgone safer investments. See High (1985, pp. 315–36) for a discussion of the original debate over the economic growth arguments of Pigou, Smith and Sidgwick.

[13]After an extensive review of the literature, Cohn (1979, pp. 137–61) found that although the evidence for the United States suggests that more education increases income, some studies have shown only a very weak relationship between education and the growth of the real national product in a number of countries. This could possibly be caused by mandated increases in educational investment leading to less investment in sectors where the marginal product of capital is higher.

CATO JOURNAL

education and compulsory schooling was the desire to transfer wealth
to educators. By reducing competition from private schooling, as well
as the returns from alternative student activities such as work, the
efforts required by teachers to keep students in public schools were
diminished. Further, since state payments to schools and educators
varied according to the number of students in a school, the incentive
to further eliminate such alternatives was strengthened. Elimination
of private competition, however, did not always engender hostility
from private teachers, because private schools were at times incorporated into the public system through gradually increasing subsidies. An expanding public system should also provide employment
for displaced private-school teachers.[14]

Staaf (1977a) reasoned along similar lines, pointing to the relatively
recent consolidation of school districts as evidence of changes designed
to benefit members of the educational bureaucracy. Eugenia Toma
(1983) provided weak empirical evidence to explain why professionals support appointed rather than elected state school boards and
state superintendents. She found that educational professionals associated appointed boards with higher salaries, lighter teaching loads
(defined as pupils per teacher), and more administrators per pupil.[15]
Toma (p. 116) characterized the electoral process as a "monitoring
device [that] constrains the ability of bureaucrats to transfer surplus
to special interest coalitions or to themselves." But she failed to
investigate why politicians in certain states prefer adopting appointed
school boards and state superintendents for ensuring higher transfers. The fact that the transfers to educators vary systematically with
the type of bureaucracy (or institutional arrangement) implies that
such transfers are created purposely for educators.

While West is correct in claiming that public provision creates
wealth transfers to educators, such transfers cannot be a sufficient
motivation for public provision of education. Governments have been
able to create transfers to other occupations without resorting to
public provision. Given the costly nature of public education (both

---

[14]Public educators' desire to eliminate private competition is extensively documented
(Field 1974, pp. 17–18, 20; West 1967, pp. 114–15). In New York, West found the
agitation for compulsory schooling, which arose after the institution of free public
schools, consistent with the hypothesis that teachers seek to maximize their income
(1967, p. 124; 1968, p. 55). An examination of the history of English public schooling
favors the wealth-transfers-to-educators hypothesis (1968, pp. 53–55). Recently, public
school teachers in France demonstrated against President Mitterand's failure to keep
his campaign promise to abolish private schooling (Lepage 1983).

[15]Toma's control variables change across regressions; they are often insignificant and
sometimes of the wrong sign.

in terms of per pupil expenditures and forgone investment in human capital), why has some combination of licensing laws and subsidies not been used? If West's finding applied equally to all countries adopting public provision, why do they all choose this method of creating transfers? The answer is that transfers to educators must take this particular form because something else is being produced.

Public Provision as a Means of Creating Wealth Transfers to Capitalists

Recent Marxist literature links the rise of factory production to the introduction and expansion of public schooling in America. These studies argue that the growth in public schooling was the product of an increased demand for a properly socialized work force and citizenry (Field 1974, p. 43; Bowles and Gintis 1976, pp. 174–75). The gains obtained by capitalists range from less crime (Field 1974, pp. 42, 48–49) to a more docile work force (pp. 50–52). Schools are seen as a means of instilling certain values (pp. 40–42), but those who benefit from this indoctrination constitute only a subset of society.

According to Field, when business and the professions are broadly defined to include clergymen, educators, newspaper editors, and lawyers, 85 percent of the members of the Lowell, Massachusetts, school board in the mid-19th century were drawn from business and professional groups and fewer than 5 percent were workers (p. 54). Field also found that school boards attempted to expand education by lengthening school sessions when particularly unruly groups—in the Lowell case, the Irish—were present in the population. School attendance rates, however, show that they were unsuccessful in attracting the Irish to public schools. Thus, despite the school board's efforts, schools were relatively unsuccessful in instilling the "correct" beliefs (pp. 312–18).

Gintis (1971, p. 274) described the function of schooling in America as creating a reward system that supposedly produces students well-suited to the "authoritarian" structure of factory production. His evidence consists of the "arbitrary" nature of grading. The structure of grading is claimed to be only partially explained by a student's cognitive abilities and primarily is viewed as rewarding those students who conform to the behavioral demands of teachers.

Gintis used his findings to explain certain "outstanding anomalies." For example, he explained the numerous studies showing "very low monetary returns to the education of lower class people and blacks in the U.S., even with the level of cognitive development taken into account," as resulting from a "failure of schooling to inculcate the required noncognitive personality traits in the observed groups" (1971, p. 267). Bowles (1972), on the other hand, attempted to explain such differential returns by pointing to the direct effect of family background on earnings. He claims that the measurement error is greater for family background than for other variables. Therefore, not surprisingly, correcting for this error increases the relative importance of family background.

Both Bowles and Gintis ignore the findings of Becker and Chiswick (1966) and Chiswick (1969) that help explain differential returns to schooling. Chiswick (1969) found that minimum schooling legislation results in lower returns to schooling for poor people. Becker and Chiswick suggested that the differential returns to schooling may also result from not controlling for postschool investments. They point out that less well-educated people generally put more time into postschool investments than do better-educated people, and that since this investment takes place upon leaving school, the earnings of the less well-educated people will be particularly low at younger ages.

The primary difficulty with the claim that public education arose to subsidize businessmen is that it cannot explain the prevalence of public education across countries. It is not possible to limit the indoctrination aspect of education to capitalist systems. In fact, Lott (1986) has shown that it is actually the relatively more socialist countries that place a higher value on such indoctrination.

Wealth Transfers to the Middle Class: Director's Law

A public goods discussion of equality helps facilitate a comparison of goals and consequences. Although equality is deemed desirable, many argue that the reality of the transfers produced by public provision of education coincides much more closely with "Director's Law," which states that public expenditures are made primarily for the benefit of the middle class.

The public goods nature of equality in education is widely accepted. Guthrie (1980, p. 91) argued that "one of the primary goals of education is to bring about an equitable redistribution of income."[16] Levin (1980, p. 252) claimed public provision was necessary to ensure

---

[16]Weisbrod (1962, p. 119) concurred with this opinion: "Equality of opportunity seems to be a frequently expressed social goal. Education plays a prominent role in discussions of this goal, since the financial and other obstacles to education confronted by some people are important barriers to its achievement. If equality of opportunity is a social goal, then education pays social returns over and above the private returns to the recipients of education." Kohn (1969), Bowles (1973), and Bowles and Gintis (1976) also hold similar views.

EDUCATION: A CRITICAL SURVEY

equality, because a system of subsidies would not be as effective. Poor parents would send their children to schools that reinforce those values that caused the parents to be poor.

Does public provision really have the intended effect of lessening income disparities? Stigler (1970, pp. 1–2) takes a strong stand against the historical success of public schooling in producing equality.[17] Studies by Hansen and Weisbrod (1969a, 1969b) confirmed Stigler's hypothesis for higher education in California. They found that more affluent students typically attend more affluent schools, and a much larger fraction of the rich than the poor attend state-subsidized schools. Later, Peltzman (1973) found that the effect of subsidized higher education has been to shift students to public universities without greatly affecting total higher education enrollment. He concluded that the effect of such subsidies has been to transfer wealth to middle- and upper-income families who would have sent their children to college anyway.

Grubb (1971) found that supporting elementary and secondary schooling in Boston to be regressive. His findings also supported Stigler's argument that upper-income families receive a larger absolute benefit from education on average than lower-class families. Others have claimed that the quality of a public school is positively correlated with the neighborhood's level of income (West 1968, p. 29; Becker 1972, pp. 254–55).

Some have made the mistake of confusing income equality with equality of wealth. Gurwitz (1980, p. 92) proposed that one way of reducing inequality was to force people to purchase "more education than they would choose, or be able, to purchase in a perfectly free market." Chiswick (1969) suggested that minimum schooling legislation, which increases investments in schooling, lowers investments in assets that have higher returns than schooling. Compulsory schooling would therefore diminish the inequality of wage income but *increase* the inequality of wealth.

Stigler (1970), citing Director's Law, claimed that education redistributes wealth to middle-income families because income provides an easy way to discriminate between coalitions of voters. As with other forms of discrimination, redistribution only succeeds if those who are its beneficiaries are unable to resell the good to those who are being discriminated against. Education, like most services, is nontransferable.

The evidence supporting Director's Law—that publicly provided education redistributes wealth from the poorer to the richer—is con-

---

[17]See also Becker (1972, p. 254) and Demsetz (1982, p. 91).

CATO JOURNAL

vincing. But it ignores certain institutional considerations and therefore has missed the correct underlying explanation of public provision. For example, Peltzman's explanation that low prices reduce the cost of a college education to those who would have purchased it anyway, appears incompatible with evidence that subsidies are limited to only a restricted number of public colleges. Why would people not be allowed this subsidy at any college in the state? Assuming that increased competition between schools increases quality, the people already receiving the subsidy simply receive an even larger real subsidy under competition. Further, Director's Law does not explain why schools within any given school district are not forced to compete against each other. The assignment of students to schools closest to their residence seems unnecessarily restrictive. If one wanted to separate income groups, school districts could be drawn (as they are in fact often drawn anyway) to take this into account. Limiting competition to those schools within a particular school district would not be identical to a full-fledged voucher system, but it would be an improvement in efficiency and would retain the system's redistributive aspect.[18]

Possibly, this seemingly inefficient arrangement of forbidding competition can be explained by focusing on other outputs being produced, which are valued by politicians. One output could be the inculcation of views politicians value. If politicians have limited resources, but want as many children as possible to attend public schools, they must provide higher-quality schools to wealthier families because they have more elastic demands for public schooling with respect to quality. Creation of wealth transfers from the poor to the rich is only incidental and does not contradict the argument. However, questions of why other methods of indoctrination are not as effective must still be examined.

---

[18]The Marxist view also fails to explain geographical assignment of students. Bowles (1973, pp. 352–53) argued that "the social relations of schooling are a reflection of the social relations of production," and that the social relations of production are also reflected in the views of upper- and middle-income parents, who teach children to be self-directing and curious, and working-class parents, who want schools to emphasize "conformity to external authority." If this is true, a voucher or competitive public system would accomplish the same ends. To the extent it is not true, a competitive system must weaken the notion that the structure of production instills certain beliefs in parents. If geographical assignment is necessary because working-class parents value their children being taught to be imaginative, then the structure of the production must not be very effective in influencing the views of parents. The Marxian view also does not explain why school districts are not exclusive to either upper- or lower-class neighborhoods, with competition limited to a given school district.

EDUCATION: A CRITICAL SURVEY

Economies of Scale in Bureaucracy

Friedman (1962, p. 97) presented yet another explanation for providing public education rather than subsidizing private education to obtain any possible net marginal external benefits from education:

> Another factor that may have been important a century ago was ... the absence of an efficient administrative machinery to handle the distribution of vouchers and check their use. Such machinery is a phenomenon of modern times that has come to full flower with the enormous extension of personal taxation and of social security problems. In its absence, the administration of schools may have been regarded as the only possible way to finance education.

There are several problems with Friedman's reasoning. He does not explain why vouchers are now used for so many other goods (for example, Medicaid and food stamps) but not for education. An explanation based on inertia might help answer this: programs such as Medicaid and food stamps were adopted after vouchers became feasible, but public education was adopted before they became feasible. Once a certain method of provision is adopted, it may be too costly to change. Given the large gains apparently associated with such a change and assuming that inertia is the real explanation, the implied costs of changing the system must be very large. It appears unlikely, however, that the inertia would be of such a great magnitude.

The historical record provides a much more serious objection to Friedman's contention. Education was originally subsidized under voucher-type arrangements with private schools in such areas as New York. The government initially subsidized private schools "in proportion to the average number of pupils under instruction" (West 1967, p. 106; 1980, p. 5). Friedman does not explain why the voucher system preceded public education.

Monopsony Power for Educational Inputs

Bish and O'Donoghue (1970) and Borcherding (1971) claimed that the typical public goods analysis ignores instances in which the government faces upward-sloping supply curves for inputs. The implication is that in acting as a profit-maximizing monopsonist, the government underproduces public goods and pays inputs less than their marginal revenue product. The possibility of earning such monopsony rents created incentives for producers (that is, the government) to create monopsonies (Shibata 1973).

While no one has applied this argument explicitly to education, pay raises do attract additional public educators, and since higher salaries would also have to go to present educators, the marginal

491

CATO JOURNAL

outlay for additional teachers would be higher than the educators' salaries. In fact, educators state that higher wages are necessary to attract higher quality teachers.[19]

However, a simple test shows that public education was not introduced to create a monopsony for educational inputs. If such a hypothesis were true, we should observe both lower costs of education and lower teacher salaries. Since both are higher for public schools relative to private schools, this hypothesis must be rejected. Private schools would have an incentive to "chisel" on the monopsony arrangement by paying teachers higher prices and thus attracting those of higher quality. Public school teachers earn approximately 28 percent more than private teachers (see Table 3).

Any comparison of public and private teacher salaries will be objected to because the differences are not standardized for the amount of work required. Table 3 adjusts for this by showing the ratio of public to private teacher salaries divided by the ratio of pupils per teacher in public to private schools. This adjustment still leaves salaries of public school teachers 20 percent higher than their private school counterparts. Proponents of the monopsony explanation may

TABLE 3
EVIDENCE OF GOVERNMENT AS A MONOPSONIST

	Teachers' Salaries 1982–83		Pupils per Teacher 1981/82		Ratio of	Ratio of (1)/(2) to
	(1)	(2)	(3)	(4)	of	(3)/(4)
Region	Public	Private	Public	Private	(1)/(2)	
New England	18,812	15,536			1.211	
Mideast	23,083	16,188			1.426	
Southeast	17,715	14,519			1.220	
Great Lakes	21,755	17,056			1.276	
Plains	18,930	17,547			1.079	
Southwest	19,294	18,069			1.068	
Rocky Mountains	20,545	17,352			1.184	
Far West	23,612	17,660			1.337	
USA Average	20,531	16,103	18.89	17.87	1.275	1.206

SOURCES: *Statistical Abstract of the United States* (1984, p. 150); *United States Catholic Elementary and Secondary Schools, 1981–1982; USA Today* (17 March 1983): 2A.

[19]See *USA Today* (8 May 1984): 11A.

EDUCATION: A CRITICAL SURVEY

argue that this differential is caused by the higher quality of public school teachers. This contention is, however, contradicted by evidence presented above on the relative quality of the two systems.

Given that the teachers serve the same market and that the supply and demand for teachers in both the public and private sectors are in equilibrium, how can real wages differ? As already discussed, Hanushek (1972) noted that public teachers are required to invest in activities that do not improve their teaching skills. The imposition of more stringent requirements as a prerequisite to obtain the higher salaries associated with public schooling shifts back the supply curve in that sector. If these requirements do not raise the skill level of teachers in other activities (for example, teaching in private schools), the differences in public and private school salaries must be regarded as a rent public school teachers receive. But why do they receive such a rent?

Imperfect Capital Markets

Alfred Marshall was probably the first economist to point out that imperfect capital markets can lead to an underinvestment in a child's education: "Those who bear the expenses of rearing and educating him receive but very little of the price that is paid for his services in later years" (in Thompson and Ruhter 1981, p. 3).

Pigou (1920), Friedman (1962), and Nerlove (1975) also recognized that most types of loans require collateral provisions that provide lenders compensation in the event of a loan default. Antislavery laws, however, prevent repossession of investment in human capital, and this makes educational loans riskier. Hence, even where an investment in someone's education would yield a high rate of return (in the form of increased future earnings), loans may not be made because of the problems of enforcing repayment. The implication is that, if left to itself, society will underinvest in education. Though such underinvestment would not be a problem in a completely laissez-faire society, it does arise in the presence of certain laws.

Leffler and Lindsay (1982, p. 7), in their examination of the health care industry, pointed out that methods other than public provision of medical schools are available to solve this problem. Their list includes "offering tax deductions or direct subsidies to the purchase of care, by offering subsidies to medical schools which lower fees, subsidies (scholarships) to students, or interest subsidies to the lenders themselves." They found (pp. 18–20) that it is much less costly to subsidize training than to subsidize consumption. Their conclusion is based on the assumption that the government's social discount

493

rate is less than the medical applicants' subjective cost of delaying consumption, estimated to be about 10 percent for the period 1952–76. Their results seem equally applicable to other types of education.

Education as Indoctrination

The previous discussions relating crime and democracy to education have brought out the often explicit use of indoctrination by advocates of public schooling. The use of public education to instill certain religious views has long been widely accepted in many countries. Political indoctrination through schooling has an equally long history.

In many countries, public education often began at the instigation of churches (Tullock 1983, p. 140). In the United States, public education was for a long period openly religious. "In fact, the very growth of the Catholic school system was a result of the feeling that a majority view of religion and morality was being imposed through government schools that was in opposition to the minority beliefs of Catholics" (Spring 1982, p. 89). Field (1974, p. 52) cited school committee reports in Massachusetts requesting that teachers "impress some moral or religious instruction" on their students. Private religious schools in New York were subsidized during the early 19th century (West 1967, p. 106). Nasaw (1979, p. 40) stated, "The common school education would be a moral education."

The use of publicly provided education to instill political views seems no less explicit. Nasaw (1979, pp. 40–41) discussed how "Whig prejudices color[ed] the presentation of most issues" in early American public school history books. Even Thomas Jefferson "proposed to censor and control the political texts at the University of Virginia. His fear here was the possible teaching of his political enemy, federalism" (Spring 1982, p. 83).

In England the Utilitarians worried not so much that children were not receiving education, but that they were obtaining "the wrong sort of education" (West 1980, p. 5). West (1970, p. 127) examined why the desire to spread literacy was not always the guiding principle in British government actions. He noted:

> On this subject most modern specialists seem to be agreed and the documentary evidence is abundant. The frightened reactions of early 19th century English governments against the spread of political literature among the "lower orders" took the form of fiscal and legal action against the spread of newspapers especially those critical of government.

Marxist claims of indoctrination (Field, Bowles, and Gintis) have been examined above. Bethell (1983) and Lott (1986) provided con-

EDUCATION: A CRITICAL SURVEY

temporary evidence of inculcation of views. High (1985, pp. 309–11) provided a useful survey of the debate by economists concerning the use of state education to instill "values essential to a good society." Overall, the belief that public provision can be used to instill certain views is overwhelmingly accepted and is well-supported by the evidence.

A Possible Alternative View

Only the use of education to indoctrinate appears difficult to dismiss. It is still necessary, however, to specify the gains politicians receive from inculcating values. Virtually all government actions create wealth transfers, even when such actions solve free-riding problems. Moreover, when manipulating the size and distribution of such transfers, politicians act to maximize support. Utility-maximizing models of political behavior consistent with microeconomic theory have focused on the costs faced by the opposition and the benefits from the support these transfers create (Downs 1957; Buchanan and Tullock 1962; Stigler 1971; Peltzman 1976). What appears lacking in the literature is the analysis of specific investments governments make to enhance the support and/or mitigate the opposition arising from transfers.

Traditionally, political entrepreneurs are assumed to maximize a political support function consisting of the number of net gainers and net losers from government policy and the probability these respective groups will throw their support for or against the politicians. In turn, these probabilities depend on the size of the net transfers. This maximization procedure is performed subject to the costs of creating the transfers, such as organizing the groups that gain from the transfers. The politicians who gain the highest level of support win, given the technology of marshalling political constituencies. Innovations can also be made by the politicians in lowering the cost of making transfers.

One possible method of lowering the cost of transfer payments is to instill certain ideological beliefs—for example, the perceived legitimacy of the existing transfers. If individuals believe that the government is "fair" and "legitimate," the costs of undertaking government actions are reduced. Assuming that citizens have imperfect information and that additional information, including misinformation, will change behavior, then it does not matter whether this inculcation consists of changing tastes or holding them constant. The vigorous debate over ideology versus self-interest as an explanatory model aside (Stigler and Becker 1977; Kau and Rubin 1978, 1979;

Kalt and Zupan 1984; Lott 1987c, 1987d; Peltzman 1984), the outcome is the same. If people's views depend on the information they receive, it follows that changes in the relative costs of receiving information produce different views. Indoctrination, or "socialization," might serve as a substitute for expenditures on police in mitigating opposition. This sort of alternative investment does not need to arise from conscious plans to lower the costs of wealth redistributions by governments but can emerge as a "survival" characteristic. Governments making transfers at the lowest costs are challenged less frequently than others. Over time, governments exhibiting the characteristics associated with the lowest cost methods of action taking should grow larger and more numerous.

Government control over media and education changes the mix of information people receive. By raising the cost of antitransfer information and lowering the cost of protransfer information, views more sympathetic to transfers are produced. The level of opposition arising from a certain level of transfers can be mitigated by using force (totalitarianism) or indoctrination (education).[20] The higher the level of transfers, the greater the opposition and thus the greater the return to indoctrination. Likewise, if totalitarianism also makes people worse off by restricting their real opportunity set and raising the level of opposition, then, under certain conditions, the return to education will increase with the level of totalitarianism. In fact, Lott (1986) found both of these predictions to be true across 90 countries in 1975 and 41 in 1977. As noted above, the standard public goods explanation for democracy predicts the opposite relationship between totalitarianism and education. Leaders of totalitarian countries would avoid creating a more independent and critically reasoning constituency.

Lott (1984, 1987a) has shown that the returns to other investments used in producing this information can also vary predictably with the level of totalitarianism. One such investment can involve higher real salaries that public educators receive. Treating educators as any other interest group, however, will not explain why public provision is used for education. In terms of the indoctrination theory, the threatened loss of higher earnings can serve as a complement to exclusive territories in ensuring that the desired information is pro-

---

[20]Totalitarianism in the model is seen as having two essential characteristics: (1) the more costly it is for opposition groups to oppose government policy, the more totalitarian a country is defined to be; (2) totalitarianism is viewed as being similar to a tax in that it restricts people's real opportunity set. Higher levels of totalitarianism, like higher levels of taxes, make people worse off and generate more opposition to the ruling coalition.

EDUCATION: A CRITICAL SURVEY

duced. The loss of this income stream need not be explicitly linked to the information produced by educators in order to influence their behavior. Educators concerned about maintaining their earnings may produce information to defend their status.

Lott (1984, 1987b) found that the rents vary systematically among teachers in white and nonwhite school systems in South Africa. The wealth transfers to educators argument would seem to predict that since white teachers in South Africa have the greatest political power, they should be the most successful in lobbying for higher salaries. Instead, Lott's studies found that those with supposedly the least to gain from supporting the government—nonwhites teaching in the three nonwhite school systems—receive the larger rents. The hypothesis advanced here is consistent with precisely such a result since it predicts that the return to indoctrination is highest among nonwhite students.

Conclusion

The conventional explanations for publicly provided education are inadequate: they do not present a general theory of public provision; they do not explain why public provision is essential to their arguments; and they fail to consider the historical record. In their place, I have suggested that governments willingly bear the costs associated with public provision because it reduces the costs of other government actions—in particular, the costs of transferring wealth.

References

Alchian, Armen A., and Kessel, Reuben A. "Competition, Monopoly, and the Pursuit of Money." In *Aspects of Labor Economics*, pp. 157–75. Princeton, N.J.: Princeton University Press, 1962.

Alchian, Armen A. "Some Economics of Property Rights." *Il Politico* 31, no. 4 (1965): 816–29.

Alchian, Armen A. "The Economic and Social Impact of Free Tuition." *New Individualist Review* 5 (Winter 1968): 42–52.

Becker, Gary S. "Comment on Schooling and Inequality from Generation to Generation." *Journal of Political Economy* 80 (June 1972): S252–55.

Becker, Gary S., and Chiswick, Barry R. "Education and the Distribution of Earnings." *American Economic Review* 56 (May 1966): 358–69.

Bethell, Tom. "Liberation Literacy: But Can Juanito Really Read?" *National Review* (30 September 1983): 1196–99.

Bish, Robert L., and O'Donoghue, Patrick D. "A Neglected Issue in Public Goods Theory." *Journal of Political Economy* 78 (November/December 1970): 1367–71.

Borcherding, Thomas E. "A Neglected Social Cost of a Voluntary Military." *American Economic Review* 61 (March 1971): 195–96.

CATO JOURNAL

Borcherding, Thomas E.; Pommerehne, Werner W.; and Schneider, Friedrich. "Comparing the Efficiency of Private and Public Production: The Evidence from Five Countries." *Zeitschrift für Nationalökonomie* 42, suppl. 2 (1982): 127–56.

Bowles, Samuel. "Schooling and Inequality from Generation to Generation." *Journal of Political Economy* 80 (June 1972): S219–51.

Bowles, Samuel. "Understanding Unequal Economic Opportunity." *American Economic Review* 63 (May 1973): 346–56.

Bowles, Samuel, and Gintis, Herbert. *Schooling in Capitalist America: Educational Reform and the Contradictions of Economic Life*. New York: Basic Books, 1976.

Bredeweg, Frank H. *United States Catholic Elementary and Secondary Schools: 1981–1982*. Washington, D.C.: National Catholic Educational Association, 1982.

Buchanan, James M., and Tullock, Gordon. *The Calculus of Consent*. Ann Arbor, Mich.: University of Michigan Press, 1962.

Chiswick, Barry. "Minimum Schooling Legislation and the Cross-Sectional Distribution of Incomes." *Economic Journal* 79 (1969): 495–507.

Coase, Ronald. "The Market for Goods and the Market for Ideas." *American Economic Review* 64 (May 1974): 384–91.

Cohn, Elchanan. *The Economics of Education*. Cambridge, Mass.: Ballinger, 1979.

Coleman, James S.; Hoffer, Thomas; and Kilgore, Sally. *High School Achievement: Public, Catholic, and Private Schools Compared*. New York: Basic Books, 1982.

Cox, Donald, and Jimenez, Emmanuel. "Private-Public Differences in Secondary School Performance: The Role of Selection Effects in Columbia and Tanzania." Working Paper. Washington University, St. Louis, 1987.

Davis, Lance E., and North, Douglas C. *Institutional Change and American Economic Growth*. Cambridge, Mass.: Cambridge University Press, 1971.

Demsetz, Harold. *Economic, Legal, and Political Dimensions of Competition*. New York: North-Holland, 1982.

Downs, Anthony. *An Economic Theory of Democracy*. New York: Harper, 1957.

Field, Alexander James. "Educational Reform and Manufacturing Development in Mid-Nineteenth Century Massachusetts." Ph.D. diss., University of California, Berkeley, 1974.

Fishlow, Albert. "The American Common School Revival, Fact or Fancy?" In *Industrialization in Two Systems: Essays in Honor of Alexander Gerschenkron*, pp. 40–67. Edited by Henry Rosovsky. New York: John Wiley and Sons, 1966.

Friedman, Milton. "The Role of Government in Education." *Economics and the Public Interest*, pp. 123–53. Edited by Robert Solow. New Brunswick, N.J.: Rutgers University Press, 1955.

Friedman, Milton. *Capitalism and Freedom*. Chicago: University of Chicago Press, 1962.

Friedman, Milton. "Are Externalities Relevant?" In *Nonpublic School Aid*, pp. 92–93. Edited by E. G. West. Lexington, Mass.: Lexington Books, 1976.

EDUCATION: A CRITICAL SURVEY

Gintis, Herbert. "Education, Technology, and Characteristics of Worker Productivity." *American Economic Review* 61 (May 1971): 266–79.

Grubb, W. Norton. "The Distribution of Costs and Benefits in an Urban Public School System." *National Tax Journal* 24 (March 1971): 1–11.

Gurwitz, Aaron Samuel. "The Capitalization of School Finance Reform." *Journal of Educational Finance* 5 (Winter 1980); 297–319.

Gurwitz, Aaron Samuel. *The Economics of Public School Finance.* Cambridge, Mass.: Ballinger, 1982.

Guthrie, James W. "United States School Finance Policy 1955–1980." In *School Finance Policies and Practices, The 1980's: A Decade of Conflict.* Edited by James Guthrie. Cambridge, Mass.: Ballinger, 1980.

Hansen, Whittier Lee, and Weisbrod, Burton A. *Benefit Costs and Financing of Public Higher Education.* Chicago: Markham Publishing Co., 1969a.

Hansen, Whittier Lee, and Weisbrod, Burton A. "The Distribution of Costs and Direct Benefits of Public Higher Education: The Case of California." *Journal of Human Resources* 4 (1969b): 176–91.

Hanushek, Eric. *Education and Race: An Analysis of the Educational Production Process.* Lexington, Mass.: D. C. Heath, 1972.

Hanushek, Eric. "The Economics of Schooling." *Journal of Economic Literature* 24 (September 1986): 1141–77.

Heidenheimer, Arnold J. "Education and Social Security Entitlements in Europe and America." In *Development of Welfare States in Europe and America*, pp. 269–306. Edited by Peter Flora and Arnold Heidenheimer. New Brunswick, N.J.: Transaction Books, 1982.

High, Jack. "The Market, State, and Education," chap. 5. Manuscript, 1984.

High, Jack. "State Education: Have Economists Made a Case?" *Cato Journal* 5 (Spring/Summer 1985): 305–23.

Huntford, Roland. *The New Totalitarians.* New York: Stein and Day, 1980.

Kalt, Joseph P. "Public Goods and the Theory of Government." *Cato Journal* 1 (Fall 1981): 565–84.

Kalt, Joseph P., and Zupan, Mark A. "Capture and Ideology in the Economic Theory of Politics." *American Economic Review* 74 (June 1984): 279–300.

Kau, James B., and Rubin, Paul H. "Voting on Minimum Wages: A Time-Series Analysis." *Journal of Political Economy* 86 (April 1978): 337–46.

Kau, James B., and Rubin, Paul H. "Self-Interest, Ideology, and Logrolling in Congressional Voting." *Journal of Law and Economics* 22 (1979): 365–84.

Kohn, Melvin L. *Class and Conformity.* Homewood, Ill.: Dorsey Press, 1969.

Lazear, Edward. "Intergenerational Externalities." *Canadian Journal of Economics* 16 (1983): 212–28.

Levin, Henry M. "Educational Vouchers and Social Policy." In *School Finance Policies and Practices: The 1980's.* Edited by James Guthrie. Cambridge, Mass.: Ballinger, 1980.

Leffler, Keith B., and Lindsay, Cotton M. "Student Discount Rates, Consumption Loans and Subsidies to Professional Training." Working Paper no. 132. University of California, Los Angeles, November 1982.

Lepage, Henri. "Will Private Education Continue to Exist in France?" *Wall Street Journal*, 11 May 1983, p. 29.

CATO JOURNAL

Lott, John R. "Alternative Explanations for Public Provision of Education."
Ph.D. diss., University of California, Los Angeles, 1984.
Lott, John R. "Education, Democracy, and the Cost of Government Wealth
Transfers." Working Paper. Hoover Institution, Stanford, 1986.
Lott, John R. "The Institutional Arrangement of Public Education: The Puz-
zle of Exclusive Territories." *Public Choice* 54 (1987a): 89–96.
Lott, John R. "The Institutional Arrangement of Public Education: The Rents
to Public Educators." Working Paper. Hoover Institution, Stanford, 1987b.
Lott, John R. "The Effect of Nontransferable Property Rights on the Effi-
ciency of Political Markets: Some Evidence." *Journal of Public Economics*
32 (1987c): 231–46.
Lott, John R. "Political Cheating." *Public Choice* 52 (1987d): 169–86.
Lott, John R. "Juvenile Delinquency and Education: A Comparison of Public
and Private Provision." *International Review of Law and Economics* 7
(December 1987e): 163–75.
Mill, John Stuart. *Principles of Political Economy*. 1848. Reprint. Clifton,
N.J.: Augustus M. Kelley, 1973.
Mitchell, Brian R. *European Historical Statistics 1750–1970*. New York:
Columbia University Press, 1975.
Montgomery, Zack. *Anti-Parental Education*. San Francisco, 1878.
Nasaw, David. *Schooled to Order: A Social History of Public Schooling in
the United States*. New York: Oxford University Press, 1979.
Nerlove, Marc. "Some Problems in the Use of Income-Contingent Loans for
the Finance of Higher Education." *Journal of Political Economy* 83 (Feb-
ruary 1975): 157–83.
Peltzman, Sam. "The Effect of Government Subsidies-in-Kind on Private
Expenditures: The Case of Higher Education." *Journal of Political Econ-
omy* 81 (January/February 1973): 1–27.
Peltzman, Sam. "Toward a More General Theory of Regulation." *Journal of
Law and Economics* 19 (August 1976): 211–40.
Peltzman, Sam. "Constituent Interest and Congressional Voting." *Journal of
Law and Economics* 22 (April 1979): 181–210.
Philips, Llad; Votey, Harold L.; and Maxwell, Donald. "Crime, Youth, and
the Labor Market." *Journal of Political Economy* 80 (May/June 1972): 491–
504.
Pigou, Arthur C. *Economics of Welfare*. London: Macmillan, 1920.
Rowley, Charles K., and Peacock, Alan T. *Welfare Economics: A Liberal
Restatement*. New York: John Wiley and Sons, 1975.
Savas, Emanuel S. *Privatizing the Public Sector*. Chatham, N.J.: Chatham
House, 1982.
Shibata, Hirofumi. "Public Goods, Increasing Cost, and Monopsony: Com-
ment." *Journal of Political Economy* 81 (January/February 1973): 223–30.
Singer, Neil. "Criteria for Public Investment in Education." In Joint Eco-
nomic Committee Report, U.S. Congress, *The Economics and Financing
of Higher Education in the United States*. Washington, D.C.: Government
Printing Office, 1972.
Smith, Adam. *An Inquiry into the Nature and Causes of the Wealth of
Nations*. 1776. Reprint. Modern Library ed. New York: Random House,
1937.

EDUCATION: A CRITICAL SURVEY

Spring, Joel. "The Evolving Political Structure of American Public Schooling." In *The Public School Monopoly*. Edited by Robert B. Everhart. Cambridge, Mass.: Ballinger, 1982.

Staaf, Robert J. "The Public School System in Transition." *Budgets and Bureaucrats: The Sources of Government Growth*, pp. 130–47. Edited by Thomas E. Borcherding. Durham, N.C.: Duke University Press, 1977a.

Staaf, Robert J. "The Growth of the Educational Bureaucracy: Do Teachers Make a Difference?" In *Budgets and Bureaucrats: The Sources of Government Growth*, pp. 147–68. Edited by Thomas E. Borcherding. Durham, N.C.: Duke University Press, 1977b.

Stapleton, D. C. "External Benefits of Education: An Assessment of the Effect of Education on Political Participation." *Sociological Methodology*, 1978.

Stigler, George J. "Director's Law of Public Income Redistribution." *Journal of Law and Economics* 13 (April 1970): 1–12.

Stigler, George J. "The Theory of Economic Regulation." *Bell Journal of Economics and Management Science* 2 (Spring 1971): 3–21.

Stigler, George J., and Becker, Gary S. "De Gustibus Non Est Disputandum." *American Economic Review* 67 (March 1977): 79–90.

Thompson, Earl, and Ruhter, Wayne. "Parental Malincentives and Social Legislation." UCLA Working Paper No. 144, 1981.

Toma, Eugenia F. "Institutional Structures, Regulation, and Producer Gains in the Education Industry." *Journal of Law and Economics* 26 (April 1983): 103–16.

Tullock, Gordon. *Economics of Income Redistribution*. Boston: Kluwer-Nijhoff, 1983.

Webb, R. K. "The Victorian Reading Public." In *From Dickens to Hardy*. Edited by Borris Ford. Pelican, 1963.

Weisbrod, Burton A. "Education and Investment in Human Capital." *Journal of Political Economy* 70 (October 1962): 106–23.

Weisbrod, Burton. *External Benefits of Public Education*. Princeton: Princeton University Press, 1964.

West, E. G. "The Political Economy of American Public School Legislation." *Journal of Law and Economics* 10 (1967): 101–28.

West, E. G. *Economics, Education, and the Politician*. Norwich: Institute of Economic Affairs, Soman-Wherry Press, Ltd., 1968.

West, E. G. *Education and the State*. 2d ed. London: Institute of Economic Affairs, 1970.

West, E. G. "Education and Crime: A Political Economy of Interdependence." *Character* 1 (June 1980): 4–7.

West, E. G. "Are American Schools Working? Disturbing Cost and Quality Trends." *Policy Analysis* No. 26, Cato Institute, 9 August 1983.

Name Index

The International Library of Critical Writings in Economics